Presented to
BILL SIMPSON
on the occasion of the
COPYRIGHT LIBRARIANS' ASSEMBLY
Aberystwyth, July 1999

A NATION AND ITS BOOKS

A NATION AND ITS BOOKS
a history of the book in Wales

edited by Philip Henry Jones
and Eiluned Rees

The National Library of Wales
in association with
Aberystwyth Centre for the Book
1998

© Individual chapters — the contributors 1998
© The complete work —The National Library of Wales 1998

A catalogue record of this book is available from the British Library

ISBN: 1 86225 009 X

Printed by Cambrian Printers, Aberystwyth

CONTENTS

Foreword ix

Preface xi

Abbreviations xv

Chapters
1 The origins and the medieval period
  Huw Pryce 1

2 The medieval manuscript
  Daniel Huws 25

3 The Renaissance and Reformation
  Glanmor Williams 41

4 The first printed books, 1546—1604
  R. Geraint Gruffydd 55

5 Latin literature
  Ceri Davies 67

6 Early Welsh dictionaries
  M. T. Burdett-Jones 75

7 Scribes and patrons in the seventeenth century
  J. Gwynfor Jones 83

8 Printing and publishing in the seventeenth century
  Rheinallt Llwyd 93

9 The eighteenth century
  Geraint H. Jenkins 109

10 The Welsh book trade from 1718 to 1820
  Eiluned Rees 123

11 Country-house libraries of the eighteenth and nineteenth centuries
    Thomas Lloyd 135

12 The London-Welsh
    Glenda Carr 147

13 The nineteenth century
    Ieuan Gwynedd Jones 157

14 Two Welsh publishers of the golden age: Gee a'i Fab and Hughes a'i Fab
    Philip Henry Jones 173

15 Spurrell of Carmarthen
    Richard E. Huws 189

16 The periodical press to 1914
    Huw Walters 197

17 The newspaper press in Wales 1804—1945
    Aled Jones 209

18 Scholarly publishing 1820—1922
    B. F. Roberts 221

19 Music Publishing
    Rhidian Griffiths 237

20 Welsh Ballads
    Tegwyn Jones 245

21 Welsh publishing in the United States of America
    D. H. E. Roberts 253

22 The Welsh press in Patagonia
    Gareth Alban Davies 265

23 Welsh public libraries to 1914
    Philip Henry Jones 277

24 Welsh public libraries 1914 — 1994
    G. I. Evans 287

25 The Miners' Institute libraries of south Wales 1875 — 1939
    C. M. Baggs 297

26 Academic libraries in Wales to 1914
    Brian Ll. James 307

27 Women's writing in nineteenth-century Wales
    Kathryn Hughes 321

28 The mass media in twentieth-century Wales
    Jamie Medhurst 329

29 Welsh-language publishing 1919 to 1995
    Gwilym Huws 341

30 Anglo-Welsh literature
    John Harris 355

31 Private presses
    Dorothy A. Harrop 371

32 Children's literature in Welsh to 1950
    Menna Phillips 379

33 The National Library of Wales, the art of the book, and Welsh bibliography
    Gwyn Walters 387

34 The National Library of Wales and the future of the book
    Lionel Madden 399

Illustrations .... between pages 220 and 221

Index 407

FOREWORD

When William Salesbury, that distinguished Renaissance and Reformation Welshman and scholar — who was to acknowledge the extraordinary potential of the printing press — referred to Erasmus as 'the most learned, most eloquent and most recognized master in the whole of Christendom', he was expressing an opinion from which few could have demurred. For Erasmus, the merit of the book was clear, — 'When I get a little money, I buy books; and if any is left, I buy food and clothes'. It was eloquent testimony to the importance of the book in the history of our civilization. The first printed Welsh–language work to emanate from Wales, though printed in London in 1546, is known — significantly — by its opening words 'Yn y lhyvyr hwnn', 'In this book': it was to herald a stream of literature from presses outside and inside Wales, calculated to instruct, to inform, and to entertain. Books were to become one of the main sources of support for the language and culture of Wales.

The significance of the printed word, in its Welsh context, has been recognized and treated in various learned articles and dissertations — many of them in Welsh — presented over the years but there has never been a concise, comprehensive account of the history of the book in Wales as such until now.

This work is the brain-child of Philip Henry Jones and Eiluned Rees: in 1990, thirty-one scholars were invited to contribute chapters for this study, following in the main a chronological approach and doing so from the manuscript book right down to publications of our own day. It is a veritable storehouse of information together with perceptive evaluation and we are deeply indebted to all who have contributed.

It is singularly appropriate that the National Library of Wales, dedicated as it is to collecting and protecting the heritage of our people, should publish this account of our nation and its books.

R. Brinley Jones
President, National Library of Wales

July 1998

PREFACE

Although this volume, *A Nation and its Books,* takes its title from an overview of the book in Wales which appeared in 1916, the study of Welsh books can be traced back to the work of antiquaries of the late seventeenth and early eighteenth centuries. Printed contributions begin with the pioneering catalogue of manuscripts and their contents forming part of Edward Lhuyd's *Archaeologia Britannica* in 1707. This was followed in 1718 by the first retrospective bibliography of Welsh printed books, compiled by Moses Williams, *Cofrestr o'r holl lyfrau printjedig [...] yn yr Jaith Gymraeg [...] hyd y flwyddyn 1717* (A register of all the printed books [...] in the Welsh language [...] to the year 1717). A century and a half later, Williams's work was continued by the Wesleyan minister and enthusiastic book collector, William Rowlands, 'Gwilym Lleyn', whose *Llyfryddiaeth y Cymry* (Cambrian Bibliography), posthumously published in 1869, was the first attempt to provide a comprehensive retrospective bibliography of Welsh books to 1800. Towards the end of the nineteenth century Charles Ashton, a self-educated village policeman, prepared what still remains the fullest bibliography of Welsh nineteenth-century publications. Although only one volume, covering 1801-10, was posthumously published in 1908, Ashton's slips, now housed in the National Library of Wales, remain an important quarry for researchers.

Bibliographical activity was also promoted by the enthusiasm of Welsh book collectors and bibliophiles, several of whose libraries eventually passed into institutional hands. Two mid-nineteenth-century collectors are particularly important: Robert Jones, vicar of Rotherhithe, whose library was acquired by Swansea Public Library in 1879, and the lawyer and politician E. R. G. Salisbury, whose outstanding collection was purchased by the University College, Cardiff, in 1886. The ultimate disposal of the libraries of the two greatest bibliophiles of the late nineteenth and early twentieth centuries, Sir John Williams and J. H. Davies, played a vital part in determining the location of the National Library of Wales. Rivalry over the location of the National Library of Wales prompted Cardiff Free Library to amass an important Welsh collection in the 1890s. The Catalogue of its Welsh Department, published in 1898, remains a useful work of reference. Largely the work of Ifano Jones, it was the first of his contributions to Welsh bibliography which culminated in the invaluable *A history of printing and printers in Wales to 1810, and of successive and related printers to 1923,* published in 1925.

Yet another indication of a growing interest in historical bibliography in Wales is provided by the facsimiles of early printed books and manuscripts published from the later 1870s onwards by societies and institutions, and through the heroic efforts of J. Gwenogvryn Evans. The University of Wales (initially through its Guild of Graduates) came to play an increasingly important role in the publication of such scholarly editions. From the 1920s onwards research on Welsh subjects at the constituent colleges of the University of Wales tended increasingly to be presented in Welsh-language theses. Articles based on such research usually appeared in Welsh in periodicals such as Y *Llenor, Llên Cymru,* or *Journal of the Welsh Bibliographical Society,* or as Welsh-language monographs published by the University of Wales Press.

D. Rhys Phillips, Welsh Librarian at Swansea from 1905 onwards, was largely responsible for founding the Welsh Bibliographical Society in 1906. The first number of the society's periodical, *Journal of the Welsh Bibliographical Society,* was published in 1910. During its early years the society also published several valuable bibliographies, including a reprint of Moses Williams's *Cofrestr* (1912) and a substantial bibliography of eighteenth-century Welsh ballads (1908-11). Financial and other problems led to a decline in the Welsh Bibliographical Society's vigour from the later 1960s onwards and to its muted demise in the mid-1980s.

Paradoxically, the Society died at a time when Welsh interest in the history of the book was once again increasing. One striking manifestation of this is the publication from 1977 onwards of *Y Casglwr* (The Collector), the thrice-yearly Welsh-language periodical of *Cymdeithas Bob Owen*. The success of the society, named after a legendary Welsh bibliomaniac, testifies to widespread interest at a popular level in the printed and graphic heritage of Wales.

The presence of three institutions at Aberystwyth has made it the *de facto* centre for the study of the book in Wales. The National Library houses the most important collections in the field, collections which have formed the basis of large-scale bibliographical ventures such as Eiluned Rees's *Libri Walliae: a catalogue of Welsh-language Welsh books and books printed in Wales, 1546-1820* (1987), and the comprehensive bibliography of Welsh periodicals currently being compiled by Dr Huw Walters. The Welsh Books Council, established in 1962, has built up very considerable expertise in modern book production and distribution. Finally, from the early 1970s onwards the College of Librarianship Wales (now the Department of Information and Library Studies, University of Wales Aberystwyth) has offered courses in the historical bibliography of Wales. Following a measure of informal co-operation, these three bodies formally established the Aberystwyth Centre for the Book as a co-operative venture in 1997. One of its first activities has been to found a new bilingual journal Y *Llyfr yng Nghymru / Welsh Book Studies* devoted to publishing studies on all aspects, past, present, and future, of the book in Wales.

By 1990 the editors of this volume had, quite independently, come to believe that an English-language survey of work which had been carried out during the present century was necessary. Since so much material was either inaccessible to those who could not read Welsh or was concealed in theses, there was a danger that the history of the book in Wales might be regarded as no more than an appendix to the history of the book in Britain. Both editors believed that developments in Wales, despite links with the British book trade, were sufficiently distinctive to preclude the country from being considered merely as a region of Britain. The growing international interest in the history of the book and in publishing in minority languages also made the preparation of such a volume particularly timely. After gaining the enthusiastic support of the then Librarian of the National Library of Wales, Dr Brynley F. Roberts, we invited over thirty scholars in 1990 to contribute essays on aspects of the history of the book in Wales. Despite an academic climate which has become increasingly inimical to unfunded large-scale projects, all but one of the original contributors eventually submitted their chapters.

Despite its scale and its largely chronological arrangement, *A Nation and its Books* is not a comprehensive history of the book in Wales. Topics discussed elsewhere in English have had to be omitted to make room for those which are less accessible. In other areas—notably the history of reading and authorship—much of the basic research has yet to be undertaken. This volume is therefore of necessity biased towards discussions of the production and supply of books.

The spelling of Welsh place-names is based on the recommendations of the standard listing, the University of Wales Board of Celtic Studies *A gazetteer of Welsh place-names*. Where different English and Welsh names exist (e.g. Swansea, Abertawe), the English form has been employed. Where the English form is merely a garbled version of the Welsh (e.g. Aberdare, Aberdâr), the Welsh form is used. All references to counties are to the pre-1974 units. Welsh personal names generally follow the forms used in the *Dictionary of Welsh Biography* and its Welsh-language supplements.

One of the pleasures of editing a volume such as this is the ready assistance which scholars have provided. We particularly wish to thank Daniel Huws, Dr Ceridwen Lloyd-Morgan, Gareth Bevan, Gwilym Huws and, above all, Mary Burdett-Jones. William Howells compiled the index with his customary speed and accuracy. Huw

Ceiriog Jones of the National Library of Wales supervised all stages of the book's production with meticulous care.

The Library is indebted to the following for permission to reproduce illustrations: Royal Commission on the Ancient and Historical Monuments of Wales (National Monuments Record of Wales Collections) (1, 21, 22, 33); The Dean and Chapter of Lichfield Cathedral (2); The Syndics of Cambridge University Library (3); The British Library (13); a private collection (19); Mr Elvey MacDonald (55); The Founders' Library, University of Wales, Lampeter (56); Mrs Susan H. Llewellyn (60); The Trustees of the David Jones Estate (63).

The National Library is publishing this book in association with the Aberystwyth Centre for the Book and wishes to thank the University of Wales Aberystwyth, for sponsoring the production of the illustrations and the Welsh Book Council for sponsoring the design of the book jacket.

ABBREVIATIONS

AC	*Archaeologia Cambrensis*
Additional Morris Letters	*Additional Letters of the Morrises of Anglesey (1735-1786),* transcribed and ed. Hugh Owen, 2 vols (London, 1947-9)
BBCS	*Bulletin of the Board of Celtic Studies*
BLJ	*British Library Journal*
BLR	*Bodleian Library Record*
CA	*The Carmarthen[shire] Antiquary*
CCHMC	*Cylchgrawn Cymdeithas Hanes y Methodistiaid Calfinaidd*
CHST	*Caernarvonshire Historical Society Transactions*
CMCS	*Cambridge Medieval Celtic Studies / Cambrian Medieval Celtic Studies*
CROB	*Caernarvonshire Record Office Bulletin*
DWB	*The Dictionary of Welsh Biography* (London, 1959)
EA	*Efrydiau Athronyddol*
EcHR	*Economic History Review*
EfC	*Efrydiau Catholig*
EHR	*English Historical Review*
FHSP	*Flintshire Historical Society Publications*
JHSCW	*Journal of the Historical Society of the Church in Wales*
JLIS	*Journal of Librarianship and Information Science*
JMHRS	*Journal of the Merioneth Historical and Record Society*
JWBS	*Journal of the Welsh Bibliographical Society*
JWEH	*Journal of Welsh Ecclesiastical History*
LIC	*Llên Cymru*
LW	Eiluned Rees, *Libri Walliae: a Catalogue of Welsh Books and Books printed in Wales 1546-1820,* 2 vols (Aberystwyth, 1987)
MA	*The Monmouthshire Antiquary*
MC	*Montgomeryshire Collections*
MLR	*Modern Language Review*
Morris Letters	*The Letters of Lewis, Richard, William and John Morris of Anglesey (Morrisiaid Môn) 1728-1765,* ed. J. H. Davies, 2 vols (Aberystwyth, 1907-9)

NLW	National Library of Wales
NLWJ	*National Library of Wales Journal*
NWR	*The New Welsh Review*
PBA	*Proceedings of the British Academy*
PBSA	*Papers of the Bibliographical Society of America*
PH	*The Pembrokeshire Historian*
PRIA	*Proceedings of the Royal Irish Academy*
RMWL	Historical Manuscripts Commission, *Report on Manuscripts in the Welsh Language,* 2 vols (London, 1898-1910)
SC	*Studia Celtica*
STC²	A. W. Pollard and G. R. Redgrave, *A Short-title Catalogue of Books printed in England, Scotland and Ireland, and of English Books printed Abroad 1475-1640,* 2nd edn by W. A. Jackson, F. S. Ferguson, and K. F. Pantzer, 3 vols (London, 1986-91)
TCBS	*Transactions of the Cambridge Bibliographical Society*
TDHS	*Transactions of the Denbighshire Historical Society*
THSC	*Transactions of the Honourable Society of Cymmrodorion*
TNAS	*Transactions of the Neath Antiquarian Society*
TRHS	*Transactions of the Royal Historical Society*
UCNW	University College of North Wales, Bangor
WHR	*Welsh History Review*
YB	*Ysgrifau Beirniadol*

CHAPTER 1

THE ORIGINS AND THE MEDIEVAL PERIOD

Huw Pryce

BOOKS had been read, and very probably written, in what is now Wales for over a millennium before the publication of the first Welsh printed book in 1546. In Wales, as elsewhere in Europe, the manuscript book paved the way for the printed book, not only in its form and page layout but also in its content.[1] For the Middle Ages witnessed a diversification in the types of material written down in books, a diversification which has been described as a change 'from holy book to book-keeping'.[2] A central aim of this chapter is to trace the changing uses of books in Wales from the ending of Roman rule in Britain to the dissolution of the monasteries, and thereby to show how what was initially an ecclesiastical artefact produced to ensure the transmission of Latin Christian culture came to be used for the recording of a much greater variety of literary and other texts, in Welsh (and to a much lesser extent in English) as well as in Latin, and also for the keeping and compilation of administrative records. These developments were accompanied by an expansion in the numbers of people, amongst them lay men and (at least as readers) women, using and composing books. Of course, the scale of this increase should not be exaggerated: even in the early sixteenth century books will probably have been peripheral to the daily lives of the majority of the laity. Nevertheless, there can be no doubt that by then the value and utility of books, both religious and secular in content, were well established within limited sectors of Welsh society.

The value of books did not consist solely, however, of what was written in them. As physical objects whose production required considerable expenditure of time and energy, they were also a form of material wealth.[3] Thus the Lichfield Gospels were bought for a horse and then given, about the beginning of the ninth century, to the church of Llandeilo Fawr, while one of the medieval Welsh lawbooks lists books alongside gold, hauberks, and golden vessels as privileged commodities which could be pledged for a year and a day rather than the normal period of nine days.[4] Not surprisingly, books attracted thieves and also appear among the moveable goods bequeathed in wills surviving from the late thirteenth century onwards.[5] In addition, gospel-books believed to have been owned by saints were treasured as relics, whose sacredness derived from their association with their saintly owners rather than from the texts they contained; such books were used to inscribe churches' property rights, in the form of charters added as marginalia (such as those in the Lichfield Gospels), as well as for the swearing of oaths. This concept of books as relics originated in the early Middle Ages, but continued to the end of our period, serving as a reminder that the sacred qualities of books coexisted with later, more secular, uses of the written word.[6]

The study of books in medieval Wales cannot be undertaken without reference to other written artefacts: inscribed stones, seals, coins, or slates,[7] waxed tablets,[8] charters, letters, deeds and other documents on single sheets of parchment, or the rolls used for administrative purposes such as the keeping of court records. Some of these artefacts, especially administrative documents, were probably much more important than books in spreading familiarity with the written word, thereby helping to create a literate mentality. This had an impact on the contents of books, which became the repositories not only of religious, literary, legal, and historical texts but also of written records which had originated independently of books. For example, charters were copied in cartularies and, by the fifteenth century, both documents and literary texts were often found, sometimes side by side, in miscellanies and commonplace books.[9] In attempting to outline developments in the uses of books in medieval Wales it will be necessary, therefore, to touch on the broader issue of the changing uses of literacy.

The uses made of writing were part of, and need to be related to, wider changes in Wales from the fifth to the sixteenth centuries.[10] On the one hand, native concepts of ethnicity were transformed as post-Roman Britons became medieval Welsh, albeit still conscious of their British inheritance, a transformation accompanied by the emergence of Wales as a distinct territorial as well as cultural entity. Prose tales such as the *Four Branches of the Mabinogi*, chronicles, texts of Welsh law, and collections of Welsh poetry can all be seen as reflecting the promotion and preservation of a consciousness of Welsh identity. On the other hand, if the period marked a decisive stage in the construction of a Welsh Wales, this was not the only identity forged, nor was its hegemony unchallenged. Settlement by other peoples, often in the wake of conquest, meant that for much of this period sizeable regions of Wales contained multicultural societies, while areas still largely in British, and subsequently Welsh, hands did not remain immune to external cultural influences resulting from diplomatic and ecclesiastical contacts. Thus Irish settlers in fifth- and sixth-century Dyfed erected memorial stones with Irish inscriptions in the ogam alphabet; contacts with Anglo-Saxon England stimulated an interest in runes;[11] from the end of the eleventh century onwards Norman lords and religious orders of Continental origin brought with them new conventions of charter writing which superseded the 'Celtic' charter tradition; while the production of an unprecedented variety and number of fiscal, legal, and other administrative records, based largely on English models, followed hard on the heels of the Edwardian conquest of 1282-4.

Generalization about developments in the use of the written word and their historical contexts over such a long period is hazardous, if only because many aspects of the subject await detailed research. Perhaps the most fundamental difficulty arises from the fact that, owing to subsequent losses, the sources extant today constitute only a small proportion of those written in the Middle Ages, thereby raising the question of how far that proportion reflects the amount and, more importantly, the range of what was originally produced. In other words, it is not enough simply to survey the written materials which have happened to survive; we need to assess the significance of absences too. Nevertheless, despite the dangers of distortion posed by the incomplete and possibly unrepresentative nature of the surviving evidence, it is possible to identify three broad phases in the uses of the written word in Wales during this period: firstly, from 400 to 1100; secondly, from 1100 to 1282; and thirdly, from 1282 to 1546.

From 400 to 1100
The use of writing was part of the Britons' Roman inheritance, mediated through the Church. Between the beginning of the fifth century and the end of the eleventh it was

essentially an ecclesiastical instrument, although this does not mean that only churchmen read, composed, or commissioned written texts. According to Gildas, Maelgwn Gwynedd (d. 547) had been educated by a *magister elegans*, possibly meaning a teacher of Latin rhetoric, while a later king of Gwynedd, Merfyn Frych (d. 844) had scholars at his court and appears to have written a Latin letter to Cyngen, king of Powys (d. 854).[12] How many other British rulers in what is now Wales could read Latin in the pre-Norman period is unknown, but a number will at least have been familiar with Latin charters recording grants of land they made to churches as well as, especially between the fifth and mid-seventh centuries, with memorial stones bearing Latin inscriptions. In addition, it is possible that a few of those early Welsh poets who drew heavily on Latin learning were laymen. But the uses of literacy by kings or by native men of learning were essentially extensions of, and reliant on, the Church's uses of the written word, and therefore serve to underline the fundamentally ecclesiastical context of literacy in the early Middle Ages.

The origins of literacy in Wales are to be sought in the Romano-British Church which survived into the post-Roman period. Although pagan funerary and other inscriptions survive from certain Roman sites in Wales such as Caerleon[13] the Church was the institution which ensured that the written word, and the codex or book in particular, became a permanent, if for many a marginal, part of British and subsequently Welsh society. British clergy of the fifth and sixth centuries must have possessed biblical and liturgical texts. Moreover, to judge by Gildas (who, though he may not have written in Wales, knew about its early kingdoms and very probably reflects the kind of Latin culture obtaining in some of its churches), ecclesiastics in the early sixth century could still draw on the educational curriculum of the late Empire, with its emphasis on rhetoric and the works of pagan Latin authors such as Virgil, which may have been taught by private tutors.[14] In addition, it has been argued that the British Church of the late-Roman or post-Roman period invented the type of Latin charter distinctive to the Celtic world of the early Middle Ages. Although the earliest surviving original examples of such documents in Wales date from the ninth century, some of the heavily edited charters contained in the early-twelfth-century Book of Llandaf almost certainly derive from authentic charters of the seventh, and arguably even the sixth, century, and in any case the appearance of such documents in several Celtic areas strongly suggests a common origin in the fifth or sixth centuries when British Christianity was exercising a formative influence on the Irish and Breton churches.[15]

The earliest surviving original written artefacts from post-Roman Wales are neither books nor charters, however, but inscribed stones. There are about a hundred and forty Welsh examples of what Nash-Williams classified as Class I stones, datable to between the fifth and mid-seventh centuries; the great majority bear inscriptions in Latin, although twenty-six are bilingual, containing also Irish inscriptions in the ogam alphabet, and a further nine are in Irish only. The ogam inscriptions are concentrated in south-west Wales, reflecting considerable Irish settlement there at the end of the Roman period; Irish influence may also account for two features on some of the Latin stones, namely the inclusion of a filiation ('X son of Y') in the inscription and the cutting of the latter vertically along the stone.[16] It is possible that the ogam alphabet was invented in Ireland as early as the third century, before the advent of Christianity, and it may be that some of the earliest monolingual Irish inscriptions in Wales, datable to the mid-fifth century, were erected by pagans. However this is by no means certain, and the fact that the majority of ogam inscriptions in Wales are bilingual shows that they were part of a Latin, and therefore Christian, culture.[17] This was undeniably the case with those Latin inscriptions reflecting Gaulish influence in their use of formulae, notably *Hic iacet*, derived from fifth-century Christian tombstones in Gaul, especially in the Rhône valley and the Bordelais. These stones are important evidence for contact between the British and Gaulish churches in the post-Roman period and remind us that the use of the written word was related to wider ecclesiastical and cultural developments.[18]

At the same time it should be stressed that the early-Christian inscribed stones in Wales were adaptations of the Gaulish monuments rather than replicas. Whereas the latter's inscriptions were cut on marble plaques set flat in a horizontal tomb, those from northern and western Britain, including Wales, appear on upright monoliths, resembling, and perhaps influenced by, prehistoric standing stones, although Roman milestones have also been suggested as possible models.[19] That such adaptation occurred is not surprising in view of the inscribed stones' distribution overwhelmingly in the least Romanized areas of Wales, the south-west and north-west, areas in which writing had probably been rare before the mid-fifth century. The important point, however, is that those responsible for erecting the monuments — in all likelihood mostly members of the ecclesiastical and secular élite — valued the written word, probably because they regarded it as an integral element of the *romanitas* which they sought in certain respects to perpetuate or, perhaps more accurately, recreate, and which therefore provided a visible symbol of their status and power.[20]

The practice of erecting memorial stones seems to have largely died out towards the end of the seventh century; most cross-decorated stones conventionally dated to the seventh-to-ninth centuries (but very likely with a broader time-span) are uninscribed, and the inscriptions which appear on sculptured crosses from the ninth century onwards represent a different tradition.[21] However, the ending of the Class I series of monuments, while suggesting that the use of literacy for the purpose of public commemoration and display was no longer considered appropriate, does not necessarily indicate that the Britons in Wales were becoming less literate. After all, memorial stones are rare in the south-east (representing a secondary development from the more westerly areas) even though the south-east was the most Romanized region of Wales whose churches, such as Llanilltud Fawr (Llantwit Major) — referred to as a wealthy establishment under its learned abbot St Illtud in the sixth century in the possibly seventh-century Life of St Samson — may well have fostered high standards of Latin scholarship similar to those found in the work of Gildas.[22] Admittedly, apart from some charters in the Book of Llandaf and, very probably, a text of Pelagius's Commentary on the Pauline Epistles, little written evidence survives from Wales between the late seventh and late eighth centuries.[23] However, the archaic nature of a number of texts preserved in ninth- and tenth-century manuscripts points to the continuation of ecclesiastical learning from the fifth and sixth centuries, and it is likely that the impression of a dearth of writing is an illusion created by the loss of sources.[24] Yet the character of ecclesiastical culture probably did change, becoming increasingly isolated and backward-looking from the later seventh century as churches elsewhere in the British Isles abandoned certain traditional customs, notably their methods of calculating Easter, in favour of Roman orthodoxy. After 716, when Iona accepted the Roman Easter and tonsure, only the British Church in Wales clung to the old ways until in 768 Elfoddw, 'archbishop of Gwynedd' (d. 809), persuaded the Britons to fall into line with the rest of Britain and Ireland in the matter of paschal observance.[25]

It has been suggested, plausibly, that the acceptance of the Roman Easter in Wales gave an important impetus to the production of new kinds of texts. The need to compile new Easter tables may well have stimulated the writing of annals, which seem to have been kept at St David's from the late eighth century onwards. In addition, paschal orthodoxy smoothed the way for greater contacts between the clergy in Wales and those in neighbouring territories, especially the Anglo-Saxon kingdoms, with whom they had previously not been in communion, thereby providing channels for the transmission of books and ideas.[26] Political changes within Wales were important too. In 825 Merfyn Frych took power in Gwynedd, establishing a new dynasty. That his court was a centre of learning is indicated by an account of a visit to it by four Irish scholars, *en route* to the Continent, whose knowledge of Latin and elementary Greek was tested by a compatriot called Dubthach.[27] More important, it was in the fourth year of Merfyn's reign that an anonymous cleric composed, possibly at the king's court, the *Historia Brittonum*, a work attributed by the eleventh century to Nennius. The *Historia Brittonum* testifies not only to a strong interest in the past in early-ninth-century Wales but also to the limited amount and nature of Welsh written materials available to its author, who sought to harmonize a wide variety of sources, many originating from outside Wales in his attempt to construct a continuous history of the Britons down to the end of the Anglo-British wars in the late seventh century. These sources included Bede, Anglo-Saxon genealogies and king-lists, Irish and Welsh hagiographical texts, northern-British annals (possibly deriving from Strathclyde), a poem in Welsh cataloguing the battles of Arthur, and the story of the foundation of Gwynedd by Cunedda and his sons from Manaw Gododdin. This last item has all the appearances of an origin legend, and may even have been invented by genealogists to provide a pseudo-historical precedent for the seizure of power in Gwynedd by another outsider, Merfyn Frych.[28]

By the early ninth century, then, the written word was used in Wales to construct a picture of the past; moreover, that picture relied to a significant degree on sources originally composed outside Wales. Yet, though its synchronizing ambitions were probably something new, the *Historia Brittonum* also drew on native written sources, such as a Life of St Germanus of Powys, and needs to be set in a wider context of compiling annals and genealogies in Wales which continued into the later tenth century — as shown by the redaction at that time of both the A-text of the *Annales Cambriae* and the Harleian Genealogies — and indeed well beyond.[29] There were other continuities too. As elsewhere in Europe, the Latin literary culture of Wales remained firmly grounded in the Bible from the ninth to the eleventh centuries. Biblical, patristic, and liturgical texts were copied, for example in the *Liber Commonei* (817); Juvencus's fourth-century synoptic versification of the gospel narrative was copied in the latter half of the ninth century; while Ieuan ap Sulien of Llanbadarn Fawr copied, probably between

1085 and 1091, St Augustine's treatise *De Trinitate*. Welsh ecclesiastical culture of this period also embraced other branches of Latin learning, including grammar, philosophy, mathematics, and Latin poetry such as Ovid's *Ars amatoria*; indeed, two of Sulien's sons, Ieuan and Rhigyfarch, composed Latin poetry of their own.[30] Furthermore, this culture contributed to the revival of ecclesiastical learning in England in the late ninth and tenth centuries, as is shown by the career of Asser of St David's at King Alfred's court and the presence of Latin manuscripts from Wales in tenth-century Anglo-Saxon libraries.[31]

The Welsh origin of these Latin manuscripts is indicated by the appearance in them of glosses or other material in Welsh. The significance of this material for an understanding of the kinds of texts written down in Welsh in the pre-Norman period is disputed. The glosses suggest that students of the Latin texts in question had difficulty in construing the latter; the use of Welsh was thus prompted by practical necessity. It has, indeed, been argued on the basis of the glosses that standards of Latinity declined in ninth- and tenth-century Wales, although they were revived, at least at Llanbadarn Fawr, in the later eleventh century by Sulien and his sons, whose copies of Latin texts contain no Welsh glosses. Moreover, so the same argument goes, it was this decline in Latinity which provided the crucial stimulus to the development of written Welsh from the late eighth century onwards.[32]

There can be no doubt that the Latin learning of ecclesiastical schools was an important context for the writing of Welsh which, as the early-tenth-century Computus fragment reveals, extended from glossing to the composition of prose treatises on subjects dealt with in Latin texts.[33] In addition, it was the margins of Latin books which provided homes for the earliest surviving copies of Welsh poetry — the twelve *englynion* in the Juvencus manuscript have been assigned to the first half of the tenth century[34] — and for the 'Surexit' memorandum, recording the settlement of a dispute about land, copied in the early to mid-ninth century in the Lichfield Gospels.[35] It may be, then, that though an orthographical system for the writing of Welsh had been devised perhaps as early as the mid-sixth century, the range and amount of Welsh committed to writing was limited, presumably because the language lacked the prestige of Latin.[36]

On the other hand, it has to be accepted that Welsh poetry and prose could have been written down before the earliest surviving examples. It is, moreover, quite possible that books were written prior to *c.*1100 which contained texts in Welsh only, but that these have failed to survive. Certainly, their chances of survival would have been even slimmer than those of the Latin books from Wales extant, in whole or in part, from that period; the latter had all left Wales by 1600, some reaching England as early as the tenth century, and no doubt it was interest in their Latin, rather than their Welsh, contents which accounts for their survival.[37] After all, it is generally agreed that some of the Welsh poetry preserved in medieval manuscripts of the thirteenth century and later derives from exemplars written earlier than 1100 (although how much earlier is disputed): the poetry attributed to Aneirin and Taliesin, the Llywarch Hen poems, *Etmic Dinbych, Armes Prydein*, and various other poems in the Book of Taliesin are cases in point.[38] By contrast, no substantial medieval Welsh prose text (apart, perhaps, from *Culhwch ac Olwen*) is believed to derive from a manuscript copied earlier than the late eleventh century and, although narrative prose had been written before then, it is uncertain whether its variety and scale equalled those of vernacular prose writing in either early-medieval Ireland or Anglo-Saxon England.[39]

The nature of the evidence is such, therefore, that we simply do not know when Welsh literary and other texts were first written down, nor how wide a range of material was committed to writing in Welsh in the pre-Norman period. Nevertheless, two things are reasonably clear. First, the vernacular literary culture of Wales was largely oral: composition and performance, whether of poetry or traditional tales, did not require the creation of a written text. One important corollary of this is that the extant written texts are very unlikely to reflect the full range of 'literary' activity.[40] Yet, secondly, it does not follow that native poets or story-tellers were completely divorced from Latin ecclesiastical learning. Indeed, a significant proportion of the Welsh poetry datable to between the ninth and eleventh centuries is heavily indebted to that learning, indicating, together with other evidence, either that poets who were laymen drew on it to enhance their status as the custodians of orally transmitted traditional lore, or that some clerics were also practising poets. Either way, the notion of 'a wide rift between the Church and the native learned orders is scarcely tenable'.[41] This in turn serves to underline how the use of books and the development of Welsh as a written language occurred in an ecclesiastical context, suggesting that, as was generally the case in early medieval Europe, it was clerics who were responsible for producing texts in the vernacular, in large part probably for their own edification or amusement. Thus while the writing down of texts in Welsh entailed a diversification of the range of written material in pre-Norman Wales, it did not radically alter the restricted character of literacy as something belonging essentially to clerics and reflecting their needs and interests.

From 1100 to 1282
In the two centuries from the first Norman conquests and settlements to the Edwardian conquest of 1282-4 Wales experienced major political, ecclesiastical, social, and economic changes. At the same time, partly as a result of these changes, new uses for writing developed. Even allowing for the possible distortions created by the paucity of written sources surviving from the pre-Norman period, there can be little doubt that, as elsewhere in Europe, the range of material committed to writing in Wales was much greater in the twelfth and thirteenth centuries than it had ever been before.[42] Likewise there was a significant increase in the numbers of the laity brought into contact with the written word, a development related to the spread of a literate mentality from the Church to some sections of lay society. Although literacy remained above all an ecclesiastical attribute, books and other written artefacts were used for a wider variety of purposes, and impinged more extensively and deeply on people's lives, than in earlier centuries.

Latin ecclesiastical writing exhibited both continuity and change. Churches still produced and acquired gospel and service books.[43] By the thirteenth century some of the latter included musical notation: the Use of Salisbury was followed at St David's cathedral in the time of Bishop Iorwerth (1215-29), and an Office for St David may have been composed there as early as *c.*1224.[44] Annals continued to be kept at St David's down to the late thirteenth century; in addition, annals began to be compiled by the Cistercians of Margam, Strata Florida, and possibly some other houses.[45] The *vitae* of

Welsh saints composed in the late eleventh and twelfth centuries had antecedents in the pre-Norman period (as shown by the material concerning St Germanus in the *Historia Brittonum*),[46] although how far they drew on earlier Welsh Lives, and thus represent the continuation as opposed to the revival of a native hagiographical tradition, is far from clear. In many cases it is possible that the composition of the Lives was a reaction to the threat posed to Welsh churches by the Normans, although Lifris of Llancarfan's Life of St Cadog, datable to *c*.1100, may also have been aimed at aggressive native rulers.[47]

If the extent to which Welsh hagiography was stimulated by Norman conquest is in doubt, other kinds of Latin writing were closely connected with political and ecclesiastical changes from the late eleventh century onwards. New charter-writing conventions are one case in point. Another is the prolific literary output of Gerald of Wales (1146-1223), an author of European stature whose works included the first books on Wales, the *Itinerarium Kambriae* (1191) and *Descriptio Kambriae* (1194). Gerald was a product of the hybrid society created in the Marcher lordships of south Wales, and his writings provide the earliest literary articulation of a distinctive Marcher identity. Although brought up in Dyfed and subsequently active as archdeacon of Brecon in the diocese of St David's, Gerald had studied in the schools of Paris and been deeply influenced by a much wider variety of texts than those available in Welsh churches.[48] Other clerics likewise left Wales for the French and English schools in the twelfth and thirteenth centuries, following a pattern of study very different from that of Rhigyfarch ap Sulien (d. 1099) who 'had received instruction from no one save from his own father'.[49]

There were also important developments in native literary culture in the vernacular. This culture embraced the whole range of traditional lore known as *cyfarwyddyd*, whose existence as a single body of learning is attested, in Latin dress, as early as the ninth century in the *Historia Brittonum*, and included genealogy, origin legends, triads, and law as well as poetry and narrative tales.[50] Although some of this lore had been committed to writing in the pre-Norman period, much more of it was recorded thereafter. Thus the redaction of the Arthurian prose tale *Culhwch ac Olwen* has been dated to *c*.1100, and the *Four Branches of the Mabinogi* are unlikely to have been written down much earlier (and could be later). In both cases oral tales recited and transmitted by *cyfarwyddiaid* were transformed into written texts; other traditional tales were similarly given written shape in the twelfth and thirteenth centuries.[51] It has been argued that it was in the twelfth century, too, quite possibly in its second quarter, that the earliest written collection of Welsh triads was compiled.[52] By the mid-thirteenth century there are signs of a greater interest in collecting and recording Welsh poetry, both early and more recent. Thus two versions of the *Gododdin*, derived from earlier exemplars, were copied in the Book of Aneirin, while a compilation of religious and secular poetry of various dates was made in the Black Book of Carmarthen; in addition, there survives in NLW, Peniarth MS 3 a fragment of a manuscript datable to the second half of the thirteenth century containing poems by Cynddelw (*fl. c*.1155-95).[53]

The writing down of vernacular prose tales, triads, or poetry did not mean, of course, that oral composition and transmission became redundant and that native literary culture henceforth belonged predominantly to the written domain. This will have been particularly true of poetry: it has been suggested that 'vernacular poetic composition pre 1300 was normally oral' or at least 'closely modelled on orally composed poetry' and also that 'any transmission by writing was largely an incidental and peripheral feature.'[54] In contrast to the 'doctrinal/learned' poetry which constituted a notable element in the poetry of the early Middle Ages, moreover, the work of the twelfth- and thirteenth-century *Gogynfeirdd* or Poets of the Princes reveals little acquaintance with book learning.[55] True, Gerald of Wales observed that Welsh poets of his day possessed ancient books of princes' genealogies in Welsh, which they memorized, as well as a few written texts containing Merlin Silvester's prophecies. However, he also noted that most of the latter were transmitted orally, and there is no indication that the poets usually committed their own compositions to writing.[56] Indeed, it was not until the fifteenth century that Welsh poets began writing down their own work to any significant extent.

Traditional stories no doubt also continued to be recited orally in the twelfth and thirteenth centuries, without reference to written texts.[57] Nevertheless, the composition of prose tales in this period marked a decisive stage in the development of a written literature in a way in which the writing down of poetry did not. In essence, written texts of poetry simply recorded what was composed and performed orally. By contrast, the writing down of material from the repertoire of traditional story-tellers involved a reworking of that material, by individual authors, into literary compositions which, though indebted to oral narrative conventions and intended for oral performance, nevertheless possessed their own distinctive narrative structure and style. This narrative prose was the vehicle for a great variety of Welsh texts throughout the rest of the Middle Ages, including versions of Old French romances as well as translations of historical and religious works in Latin.[58] For example, Geoffrey of Monmouth's *Historia Regum Britanniae* was translated three times in the thirteenth century, and the resulting texts, known as *Brut y Brenhinedd*, furnished a remarkably durable framework for Welsh perceptions of the past.[59] Likewise the only surviving biography of a Welsh prince, the early- to mid-thirteenth-century *Historia Gruffud vab Kenan*, was translated from a Latin text commemorating Gruffudd ap Cynan (d. 1137) probably composed in the later twelfth century.[60] Furthermore, although these translations and also the composition of Welsh prose tales were probably the work of clerics,[61] the texts will also have been comprehensible to lay men and women; indeed, the translations of Geoffrey's *Historia* imply the existence of a potential lay audience which would have been unable to understand the original work in Latin.

Some laymen with special expertise in native Welsh law not only read books but also composed them in twelfth- and thirteenth-century Wales. When lawbooks were first written in Wales is unknown. The extant versions, all written in Welsh (apart from five in Latin), date from the thirteenth to the fifteenth centuries, and it cannot be demonstrated that any of them derive material from lawbooks composed before *c.*1100.[62] It may be, then, that the lawbooks were a new departure in the twelfth century, notwithstanding the assertion in their prologues that Welsh law had been reformed by Hywel Dda (d. *c.*950).[63] Irrespective of their origins, what needs to be stressed here is that the surviving lawbooks were the work of legal experts who drew on other lawbooks in making their compilations. Although some authors were clerics, many, and in thirteenth-century Gwynedd probably most, were laymen.[64] Why Welsh lawyers felt it necessary to equip themselves with books is unclear. Since there is no indication before the late thirteenth century of an expectation that legal judgements should be based on what was written in a lawbook, it is likely that until then lawbooks were used principally for the instruction of future lawyers.[65] Indeed, by the mid-thirteenth century lawyers in Gwynedd wishing to be invested as official judges were required to learn, and be tested on, the contents of the Test Book, a part of the Iorwerth Redaction of Welsh law earmarked for this purpose.[66] Yet in making books an integral element of legal training native lawyers may not originally have been prompted simply, or even mainly, by practical considerations. After all, as is assumed to have been the case with bardic composition, it would surely have been feasible to transmit and memorize legal knowledge without using books. A further possibility, therefore, is that lawyers appropriated what was still above all an ecclesiastical artefact in order to establish the credentials of native law as a learned tradition rather than mere custom, at a time when other secular customary laws were being written down in Europe and also, more importantly perhaps, some Welsh rulers and their subjects were starting to show an unwelcome preference for English legal procedures.[67]

Despite the importance of books to lawyers, writing played little or no part in the administration of native law before the Edwardian conquest: forms of proof were oral and visual, the use of written evidence and the making of court records exceptional.[68] Yet in other spheres there was a growing acceptance in twelfth- and thirteenth-century Wales of the need for legal rights to be based on written authority. The principal promoters of this reliance on documents were churchmen. This was not, of course, something entirely new. In the pre-Norman period grants of land to Welsh churches had been recorded in charters which, potentially at least, could serve as proof of title.[69] However, it is only from *c*.1100 onwards that clear indications are forthcoming of attempts by churches to compile collections of documents in support of their claims to lands and rights. The earliest example is the small collection of Llancarfan charters appended to Lifris's Life of St Cadog.[70] Much more ambitious in scope was the Book of Llandaf (*Liber Landavensis*). This was compiled in support of the ultimately unsuccessful attempt by Bishop Urban (1107-34) to obtain papal recognition of Llandaf's entitlement to extensive episcopal estates and diocesan boundaries, and contained, in addition to a text of the gospels, a variety of material relating to Urban's campaign — notably saints' Lives, papal privileges and, above all, over a hundred and fifty charters, edited in varying degrees from originals going back to at least the seventh century.[71] Likewise Bishop Bernard of St David's (1115-48) and, later (between 1198 and 1203), Gerald of Wales sought papal confirmation of the right of St David's to be an archbishopric, thereby generating a substantial body of documents, originating from both the Curia and Wales, which Gerald copied in his *De Invectionibus*, completed in 1216.[72]

The preservation by the churches of Llandaf and St David's of papal letters and privileges obtained in the twelfth century shows the value attached by some ecclesiastics in Wales to documentary evidence. In addition, written agreements were drawn up between churches,[73] and letters and charters were cited in disputes heard in Welsh ecclesiastical courts, although oral testimony was also admitted.[74] Indeed from the later twelfth century there seems, in Wales as in western Europe generally, to have been an increasing conviction, originating in some ecclesiastical circles, that written record was superior to memory as proof of title to land and rights; moreover, that record should be detailed and take particular forms. This is implied, for example, by the numerous charters issued in favour of the Cistercian abbey of Margam in the late twelfth and thirteenth centuries which include clauses whereby the grantor not only associates relatives in the grant but also warrants his (or occasionally her) donation against any challenges by kinsfolk.[75] The monks who drafted the charters clearly intended that these detailed stipulations would help to stave off such challenges in court — which indeed sometimes they did.[76] Also revealing is Gerald of Wales's account of his well-known clash with Bishop Adam of St Asaph in 1176 concerning the territory of Ceri. To support his contention that Ceri and its churches belonged to the diocese of St Asaph, Adam produced 'an ancient book' which allegedly set forth the diocesan boundaries he claimed. Gerald, however, was unimpressed: as far as he was concerned, only 'a charter or privilege with an authentic seal' would do, for Bishop Adam 'could have written what he wanted in his book'.[77] The dispute thus focused not on the merits of written as opposed to oral testimony but rather on differing views of what constituted authentic written proof.

How many churches possessed (or manufactured) written evidence of their rights in the twelfth and thirteenth centuries is admittedly hard to assess. In Gwynedd it was probably attempts to uphold the interests of native rulers which provided the most important stimulus. Thus the respective rights of Llywelyn ap Iorwerth (d. 1240) and the Cistercians of Aberconwy were specified in detail in the prince's two charters in favour of the abbey, while disputes between Llywelyn ap Gruffudd (d. 1282) and the episcopal churches of Bangor and St Asaph in the 1260s and 1270s prompted the holding of inquests whose results were committed to writing.[78] It may well be, indeed, that until the later thirteenth century most churches in Gwynedd (other than those of the Cistercians or other reformed religious orders) relied principally on memory rather than written record to preserve and uphold their rights. It is suggestive, for instance, that in 1275 Llywelyn ap Gruffudd conceded that if the bishop of St Asaph lacked princely charters setting forth the privileges he claimed for his church, those privileges would be the subject of an inquiry, implying that no such charters had been issued.[79]

The importance of charters in creating a literate mentality was not confined to their use as evidence. They also provided the principal point of contact between many lay landholders and the written word. This had already been true in pre-Norman Wales, but both the volume of charters produced and the numbers of grantors almost certainly increased considerably after 1100. Moreover, the form of charters changed: although 'Celtic' charter writing is still attested in the second quarter of the twelfth century, the Norman settlers in Wales had introduced their own forms of charter writing, ultimately derived from Carolingian models, which native Welsh rulers and their subjects were swift to imitate.[80] One major difference between the new kind of charter which rapidly gained ground from the early twelfth century and the earlier 'Celtic' one was the authentication of the former by a seal bearing the name of the grantor. As we have seen, this was regarded as the distinguishing characteristic of genuine charters, as also of papal privileges, by Gerald of Wales. The need to append a wax impression of a seal meant that its possessor was directly involved in the process of charter production and this must have contributed significantly to making some of the laity familiar with the use of documents.[81] Moreover, the possessors of seals extended beyond the ranks of great Marcher lords or native princes to encompass such lesser landholders as the freemen of Morgannwg who endowed Margam abbey. On the other hand, freemen at Llangollen in 1234 turned to their lord, Madog ap Gruffudd, to seal a document in favour of Valle Crucis abbey because they lacked seals of their own.[82]

If the charter was probably the most common form of writing with which the laity came into contact in twelfth- and thirteenth-century Wales, the most novel lay uses of literacy occurred in secular government. Some pre-Norman Welsh kings issued charters and almost certainly also letters, but it is unlikely that even in the eleventh century they made any extensive use of writing in administration comparable, say, to that of Carolingian or late-Anglo-Saxon rulers.[83] The main reason for this view is that it was Marcher lords and English kings who took the lead in promoting administrative uses of literacy from the twelfth century onwards, native Welsh rulers following suit belatedly and to a limited extent only. For example, as early as 1126 Bishop Urban of Llandaf and Robert of Gloucester, Norman lord of Glamorgan, each drew up lists of their Welsh tenants which were submitted to the other for approval,[84] while in the thirteenth century Marcher lords borrowed the procedures of the English common law, including the use of writs and final concords; by the end of the century, indeed, the great lordships of the March possessed chanceries issuing writs in the lord's name as well as exchequers which kept written accounts. These features were of course indebted to seignorial and especially royal example in England.[85] At the same time, John (1199-1216) and Henry III (1216-72) exploited the potential of the written word as an instrument of lordship over native Welsh rulers by means of documents which spelled out the latter's obligations far more precisely than had ever been done before.[86]

Native Welsh rulers in turn emulated the practical uses of literacy of the Marchers and English crown. This can be seen most clearly in respect of the thirteenth-century princes of Gwynedd. Llywelyn ap Iorwerth employed notaries and possessed both a great and a privy seal;[87] in 1244 his son and successor, Dafydd ap Llywelyn (1240-6), 'sent messengers and letters to summon to him all the princes of Wales';[88] while the clerks of Llywelyn ap Gruffudd wrote financial accounts, sent mandates in the prince's name to his officials, and drafted agreements between Llywelyn and other Welsh princes detailing their mutual obligations.[89] Nevertheless, although the numbers of documents issued on behalf of native Welsh rulers were no doubt much greater than the surviving examples might lead us to conclude, the diplomatic of princely *acta* is arguably insufficiently uniform to indicate that even Llywelyn ap Gruffudd's administration was bureaucratic, producing — let alone referring to — documents in a routine and systematic way.[90]

From 1282 to 1546
From the end of the eleventh century to the Edwardian conquest Welsh society had witnessed an increasing use of the written word not only by ecclesiastics but also by native men of learning and, above all, by secular rulers. In the later Middle Ages the uses of literacy expanded much further. This is particularly true of administration. Whereas before 1282 the bureaucratic structures and procedures of the English state

had impinged on Wales only fitfully and indirectly, thereafter they were transplanted, albeit with some adaptations, more or less wholesale into the royal counties of the north and south and were also borrowed extensively in the March.[91] On the whole, the language of records continued to be Latin, but French was also used as was English and, much less commonly, Welsh.[92] The intensification of bureaucratic forms of governance was crucial in engendering a greater familiarity with, and recourse to, the written word on the part of the governed, if only because they were compelled to make use of documents, particularly in certain legal transactions and processes, to an extent unprecedented in the period of native rule. At the same time there was a very substantial increase in the amount and variety of literary, religious, historical, and other texts written in Welsh, some of which were commissioned by members of the native gentry who were also highly conversant with practical uses of literacy in their capacity as administrators on behalf of the post-conquest regime.[93]

The extension of bureaucratic administration and of lay uses of literacy were major developments, then, in later medieval Wales. Before examining these in greater detail, however, it is important not to overlook the continuing role of the Church in the production of texts. In several respects ecclesiastical uses of literacy matched, or indeed served, those of the secular world. That ecclesiastical administration became more document-minded than previously is shown by the recording of a survey of the episcopal estates of St David's in the Black Book of St David's (1326) as well as by the compilation, probably a little earlier in the fourteenth century, of the Red Book of Asaph (Llyfr Coch Asaph), a collection of documents pertaining to the church of St Asaph. There survive also a fourteenth-century extent of the lands of the bishop of Bangor, a fifteenth-century collection of St Asaph documents, *Liber Antiquus*, which includes a detailed rental of St Asaph, and the Statute Book of St David's, a compilation of capitular statutes and other material made in the time of Edward Vaughan, bishop of St David's (1509-22).[94]

Turning from pragmatic literacy to that of professional (that is, ecclesiastical or scholarly) and cultivated readers,[95] it was clerics in the main who translated and adapted Latin religious writings into Welsh between the late thirteenth and mid-fourteenth centuries, texts brought together in the White Book of Rhydderch and the Book of the Anchorite.[96] The Church played a crucial part in historiography, too, for it was almost certainly the Cistercians of Strata Florida who, after the Edwardian conquest, drew on their annals to compile the Latin chronicle which formed the basis of the Welsh chronicles generically known as *Brut y Tywysogyon*, and the surviving versions of the latter were monastic, and therefore quite possibly Cistercian, products as well.[97] This historical writing can be compared with the production of the Hendregadredd manuscript, a major collection of the poetry of the *Gogynfeirdd* almost certainly begun at Strata Florida *c*.1300: in both instances the written word was used to commemorate the passing of a political order.[98] At about the same time Marcher perceptions of the past were committed to writing at Neath in a short Latin history of the abbey's benefactors, the lords of Gower.[99]

In addition, Welsh ecclesiastics continued to acquire and contribute to Latin learning. Over a hundred students from Wales have been identified at Oxford, by far the most popular university among the Welsh, in the period from the conquest to 1400, and a further 260 or so in the fifteenth century.[100] Some Welsh clerics had successful university careers in England before returning to Wales. For example, John of Monmouth (d. 1323) had been vice-chancellor, and Henry Gower (d. 1347) chancellor, of the University of Oxford before becoming, respectively, bishops of Llandaf and St David's.[101] Other graduates returned to ecclesiastical benefices, especially in the diocese of St David's.[102] Probably it was men of this kind, familiar with studying texts of canon law, whom the later medieval native law-texts of south Wales had in mind when they enjoined that 'canons versed in truth' should adjudicate between two contradictory statements of written law.[103] But the most advanced readers and authors, in the first half of the fourteenth century at least, were members of the mendicant orders. A number of Welsh friars composed (albeit outside Wales) important theological works during that period which added fuel to the fire of contemporary debates: the Dominican Thomas Waleys (d. ?1350), a prolific writer imprisoned at Avignon for attacking papal views on the Beatific Vision, is a notable case in point.[104]

Nevertheless, important though it continued to be as an institution which valued the written word, from about the middle of the fourteenth century onwards the Church occupied a much less central place in the development and diffusion of literacy in Wales than it had done before. In part this was the result of a decline in ecclesiastical scholarship and literary activity, reflecting the general decline of monasteries. Very few new Welsh translations and adaptations of Latin religious works were made after *c*.1350, while the achievements of the earlier fourteenth century in historiography and theology were unmatched thereafter.[105] True, the libraries of major churches almost certainly still dwarfed the largest collections of books amassed in the later Middle Ages by laymen such as Hopcyn ap Tomas. Nevertheless, some, perhaps many, ecclesiastical libraries — including those of the abbeys of Aberconwy and Llantarnam and the priories of Carmarthen and Llanthony Prima — suffered severe losses, especially in the fifteenth century, as a result of fire, poverty, and the rebellion of Owain Glyndŵr.[106] The ecclesiastical contribution to book production also declined after the early fourteenth century; the only professional scribes identified at the end of the century were laymen.[107]

The activity of lay scribes attested from *c*.1400 onwards serves as a reminder that the diminishing role of the Church in providing an institutional context for literacy was as much to do with greater lay participation in the production and reading of texts as with any ecclesiastical failings. From the late thirteenth century lay men and women from amongst the native gentry were the recipients of translations into Welsh, and it was members of the same class who commissioned the important anthologies of Welsh texts, the White Book of Rhydderch (*c*.1350) and the Red Book of Hergest (*c*.1400). Books began to feature among the possessions of the upper echelons of Welsh society: Cynwrig Sais of Northop, Flintshire (d. 1311) left a book in his will, while Llywelyn Bren of Glamorgan (d. 1317) possessed eight books, including a copy of *Le Roman de la Rose*.[108] How many of the Welsh gentry owned, let alone read, books in the fourteenth century, we can only guess. Few though they may have been, their interest in books marks a significant step in the development of lay literacy. Further steps were taken in the following century. A grammar school was founded at Oswestry *c*.1420 and at Caernarfon before 1500; there appears to have been a school open to the laity at Basingwerk abbey in the 1480s; while, also in the 1480s, John Edwards of Chirk compiled

— and indeed almost certainly wrote — a Latin grammar, in English, possibly for his son.[109] (Increasing educational provision for the laity in turn helps to explain the tendency for laymen to replace clerics as administrators responsible for writing royal and seignorial documents from about the middle of the fifteenth century.)[110]

Another development associated with the increase of lay persons reading and, in some instances, writing books in later medieval Wales is the growing textualization of native literary culture. This textualization is evidenced, for example, in the colophon to the prose tale *Breuddwyd Rhonabwy* (a work possibly written towards the end of the thirteenth century) which claims that no one could recite the tale without referring to the book.[111] From the mid-fifteenth century poets, too, not only read widely, mainly in Welsh though in some cases also in Latin, but began to commit their own work to writing as well as to make compilations of other authors' poetry and prose. Indeed some poets, notably Lewys Glyn Cothi (*fl.* 1447-86) and Gutun Owain (*fl.* 1455-1500), hired out their services as scribes, copying a wide variety of manuscripts.[112] Of course, not all poets wrote down their own work — none of the poetry of Gwerful Mechain (d. *c.*1500) was written down in her lifetime any more than was that of most of her male contemporaries — and even when copies were made poems continued to be transmitted orally.[113] Nevertheless, there was a clear shift towards regarding Welsh literature as something to be read, quite possibly silently by individuals, rather than merely listened to.[114] At the same time the range of material written in Welsh continued to expand. In the legal sphere new lawbooks were compiled and texts of frontier agreements, known as *cydfodau*, drawn up;[115] bardic grammars and medical writings were composed (albeit possibly dependent on thirteenth-century precursors);[116] and translators turned their hands not only to literary and religious works but also to Walter de Henley's treatise on estate management.[117]

The most significant developments in lay literacy in later medieval Wales occurred, however, not in the sphere of learning and literature but in government. The Edwardian conquest resulted in, and was indeed partly consolidated by, an explosion of documentation. Not surprisingly, much of this derived its form and content from England. Thus the Statute of Wales (1284) included a selection of common-law writs applicable in the royal counties of north Wales, while by 1301-2 the administrators of the Principality of south Wales at Carmarthen were provided with not only a register of writs but also with a book of English statutes, a treatise on the common law, and a variety of formularies, including one on the making of extents of land.[118] Moreover, because the post-conquest princes of Wales were normally resident in England, as also often were the greater Marcher lords, the need for written communication between rulers and administrators became all the greater, while dissatisfied subjects were compelled to present petitions in writing partly for the same reasons.[119]

Much of this bureaucratic elaboration and intensification served a simple purpose: the extraction of surplus.[120] Obligations to pay rents and taxes were listed in territorial extents or surveys (such as that of the lordship of Denbigh in 1334) and in lay subsidy rolls; income from royal lands and Marcher lordships was recorded in account rolls and estimated in valors; while judicial profits were noted in court rolls — which began to be kept regularly for the first time in Wales — as well as in lists of fines and amercements.[121] A desire to maximize profits and assert seignorial authority was also a crucial factor in encouraging recourse to writs, issued at a price to litigants in certain legal actions under English or Marcher law,[122] and in the production of the hundreds of deeds recording the leasing of land for a term of years as *tir prid* which survive from the Principality and the Marcher lordships of later-medieval north Wales.[123] (More generally, deeds — of which the *prid* documents are but a small proportion — constitute important evidence for the practical use of literacy by lay landholders, not least by highlighting, in common with other sources, the widespread possession of seals; already by 1295 we find over a hundred individuals with seals in the two north-eastern *cantrefi* of Rhos and Rhufoniog alone.)[124] Since leases of land in *prid* provided a means of overcoming seignorial restrictions on the alienation of land, they required the lord's consent, often (if not always) obtainable on payment of a fee. In the lordship of Dyffryn Clwyd, indeed, it became mandatory from 1345 for all *prid* transactions, once licensed, to be enrolled in the lord's court, thereby providing the lord with a written record in the event of any dispute.[125] This was symptomatic of the literate mentality of Wales's later medieval rulers who clearly perceived the advantages of written record over memory in upholding their rights. Sometimes documents were referred to generations after they had originally been made. Thus Henry VII's administrators scrutinized fourteenth- and fifteenth-century documents concerning the governance of the Principality of north Wales and had them transcribed in the *Record of Caernarvon* as part of their efforts to increase the Crown's revenues from the territory.[126] That accounts and court rolls were occasionally forged likewise implies that records were regarded as authorities to which reference might be made.[127]

How far the example of governmental and seignorial uses of literacy influenced the rest of society in later-medieval Wales is hard to assess. It is quite possible, however, that the sharp increase in the production of documents for practical ends by the secular authorities in Wales after the Edwardian conquest provided a major impetus to the spread of pragmatic literacy in the fourteenth and fifteenth centuries, just as in England 'the proliferation of royal documents disseminated literate modes' during the previous two centuries.[128] (If so, the time-lag between the two countries is significant, arguably serving to underline the central importance of a strong bureaucratic state in promoting a shift towards wider social uses of literacy.)[129] Certainly, landholders, the upper echelons of Welsh society, some of whom served as royal officials in Wales, increasingly made use of the written word for their own private needs: for example, by recording their children's births in missals or psalters, making wills, assembling deeds relating to their estates, or compiling their own books of letters and legal documents. What is difficult to determine, though, is the extent to which, even by the early sixteenth century, the written word impinged on the lives of those belonging to less powerful and wealthy social strata.[130] Obviously Wales in the reign of Henry VIII was still very far removed from the emergence of modern mass literacy. Nevertheless, there can be no doubt that the proliferation and diversification of written materials over the preceding millennium constituted a profound transformation in the uses of literacy in Wales, with the result that writing had come to occupy a much more central place in society than it had in the pre-Norman era of the holy book.

NOTES TO CHAPTER 1

I am very grateful to Daniel Huws and Nancy Edwards for their valuable comments on a draft of this chapter, and also to Rees Davies for clarifying my ideas on important aspects of the subject in his observations on a different, but related, paper.

1. Cf. M. T. Clanchy, 'Looking back from the invention of printing', in *Literacy in historical perspective*, ed. Daniel P. Resnick (Washington, DC, 1983), pp. 7-22.
2. Hagen Keller, 'Vom "heiligen Buch" zur "Buchführung": Lebensfunktionen der Schrift im Mittelalter', *Frühmittelalterliche Studien*, 26 (1992), 1-31. For general background and orientation see also his 'Die Entwicklung der europäischen Schriftkultur im Spiegel der mittelalterlichen Überlieferung: Beobachtungen und Überlegungen', in *Geschichte und Geschichtsbewusstsein: Festschrift Karl-Ernst Jeismann*, ed. Paul Leidinger and Dieter Metzler (Münster, 1990), pp. 171-204; M. T. Clanchy, *From memory to written record: England 1066-1307*, 2nd edn (Oxford, 1993) (includes a useful bibliography); *The uses of literacy in early mediaeval Europe*, ed. Rosamond McKitterick (Cambridge, 1990); Harvey J. Graff, *The legacies of literacy* (Bloomington and Indianapolis, 1987); and Brian V. Street, *Literacy in theory and practice* (Cambridge, 1984). Since this chapter was written much of relevance to it has been discussed in *Literacy in medieval Celtic societies*, ed. Huw Pryce (Cambridge, 1998).
3. Cf. Rosamond McKitterick, *The Carolingians and the written word* (Cambridge, 1989), Chapter 4.
4. Dafydd Jenkins and Morfydd E. Owen, 'The Welsh marginalia in the Lichfield Gospels: Part I', *CMCS*, 5 (1983), 37-66 (p. 48); *Ancient laws and institutes of Wales*, ed. Aneurin Owen (London, 1841), I, 726-7.
5. *Vitae Sanctorum Britanniae et Genealogiae*, ed. A. W. Wade-Evans (Cardiff, 1944), p. 306; Rhys W. Hays, *The history of the abbey of Aberconway 1186-1537* (Cardiff, 1963), p. 47; R. R. Davies, 'The administration of law in medieval Wales: the role of the *Ynad Cwmwd (Judex Patrie)*', in *Lawyers and laymen*, ed. T. M. Charles-Edwards, Morfydd E. Owen, and D. B. Walters (Cardiff, 1986), pp. 258-73 (p. 267); J. Fisher, 'Three Welsh wills', *AC*, 6th ser. 19 (1919), 181-92 (p. 186).
6. Jenkins and Owen, 'Welsh marginalia [...] Part I', 50-66; Huw Pryce, *Native law and the Church in medieval Wales* (Oxford, 1993), pp. 41-3; Edward Owen, 'An episode in the history of Clynnog Church', *Y Cymmrodor*, 19 (1906), 66-88 (pp. 77-9, 83).
7. For inscribed slates at late fifteenth-century Strata Florida, see E. D. Jones, 'Ysgriflechi Cymraeg Ystrad Fflur', *LlC*, 1 (1950-1), 1-6; and his 'Inscribed slates from Strata Florida', *Ceredigion*, 1 (1950-1), 103-5. I am very grateful to Ceridwen Lloyd-Morgan for bringing this material to my attention.
8. *Vitae Sanctorum Britanniae*, p. 50; *Llyfr Du Caerfyrddin*, ed. A. O. H. Jarman (Cardiff, 1982), no. 10, line 39; *The Book of Taliesin*, ed. J. Gwenogvryn Evans (Llanbedrog, 1910), p. 25, line 11 (I owe the last two references to Marged Haycock). Cf. Clanchy, *From memory*, pp. 118-19.
9. Llinos Beverley Smith, 'The grammar and commonplace books of John Edwards of Chirk', *BBCS*, 34 (1987), 174-84.
10. Recent surveys include: Wendy Davies, *Wales in the early Middle Ages* (Leicester, 1982); R. R. Davies, *Conquest, coexistence, and change: Wales 1063-1415* (Oxford, 1987); and Glanmor Williams, *Recovery, reorientation, and Reformation: Wales c.1415-1642* (Oxford, 1987).
11. Nora K. Chadwick, 'Early culture and learning in north Wales', in *Studies in the early British Church*, ed. N. K. Chadwick (Cambridge, 1958), pp. 29-120 (pp. 45-6, 98-100); Rosamund Moon, 'Viking runic inscriptions in Wales', *AC*, 127 (1978), 124-6.
12. Michael Lapidge, 'Gildas's education and the Latin culture of sub-Roman Britain', in *Gildas: new approaches*, ed. Michael Lapidge and David Dumville (Woodbridge, 1984), pp. 27-50 (p. 50); Chadwick, 'Early culture', pp. 95-6. For a full discussion of literacy in the pre-Norman period, see now Patrick Sims-Williams, 'The uses of writing in early medieval Wales', in *Literacy in medieval Celtic societies*, pp. 15-38.

[13] Jeremy K. Knight, 'Glamorgan A.D. 400-1100: archaeology and history', in *Early Glamorgan: prehistory and early history*, ed. H. N. Savory, Glamorgan County History, III (Cardiff, 1984), pp. 315-64 (p. 334).

[14] Lapidge, 'Gildas's education'. See also K. R. Dark, *From civitas to kingdom: British political continuity 300-800* (Leicester, 1994), pp. 184-91.

[15] Wendy Davies, *The Llandaff charters* (Aberystwyth, 1979); Wendy Davies, 'The Latin charter-tradition in Western Britain, Brittany and Ireland in the early mediaeval period', in *Ireland in early mediaeval Europe*, ed. Dorothy Whitelock, Rosamond McKitterick, and David Dumville (Cambridge, 1982), pp. 258-80; Patrick Sims-Williams, review in *JEH*, 33 (1982), 124-9; Patrick Sims-Williams, 'The emergence of Old Welsh, Cornish and Breton orthography, 600-800: the evidence of archaic Old Welsh', *BBCS*, 38 (1991), 20-86 (pp. 28-30). For a different view, see Dark, *Civitas to kingdom*, pp. 140-8. Cf. also Dauvit Broun, *The charters of Gaelic Scotland and Ireland in the early and central Middle Ages* (Cambridge, 1995), esp. pp. 38-42.

[16] V. E. Nash-Williams, *Early Christian monuments of Wales* (Cardiff, 1950), pp. 3-8. See also Ken Dark, 'Epigraphic, art-historical, and historical approaches to the chronology of Class I inscribed stones', in *The early Church in Wales and the west*, ed. Nancy Edwards and Alan Lane (Oxford, 1992), pp. 51-61; Dark, *Civitas to kingdom*, pp. 267-9; Charles Thomas, *And shall these mute stones speak? Post-Roman inscriptions in western Britain* (Cardiff, 1994).

[17] Anthony Harvey, 'Early literacy in Ireland: the evidence from ogam', *CMCS*, 14 (1987), 1-15; Jane Stevenson, 'The beginnings of literacy in Ireland', *PRIA*, 89 C (1989), 127-65 (pp. 143-5); Damian McManus, *A guide to ogam* (Maynooth, 1991), pp. 40-1, 55-61; T. M. Charles-Edwards, 'The context and uses of literacy in early Christian Ireland', in *Literacy in medieval Celtic societies*, pp. 62-82 (pp. 62-4, 77-8).

[18] Nash-Williams, *Early Christian monuments*, pp. 4, 8-10; Kenneth Jackson, *Language and history in early Britain* (Edinburgh, 1953), pp. 163-5; Jeremy K. Knight, '*In tempore Iustini Consulis*: contacts between the British and Gaulish churches before Augustine', in *Collectanea historica: essays in memory of Stuart Rigold*, ed. A. Detsicas (Maidstone, 1981), pp. 54-62; Jeremy K. Knight, 'The early Christian Latin inscriptions of Britain and Gaul: chronology and context', in *Early Church in Wales and the west*, pp. 45-50.

[19] Knight, 'Early Christian Latin inscriptions', p. 45.

[20] Cf. Nash-Williams, *Early Christian monuments*, p. 14; Huw Pryce, 'Pastoral care in early Medieval Wales', in *Pastoral care before the parish*, ed. John Blair and Richard Sharpe (Leicester, 1992), pp. 41-62 (pp. 47-8); and also Stephen T. Driscoll, 'Power and authority in early historic Scotland: Pictish symbol stones and other documents', in *State and society: the emergence and development of social hierarchy and political centralization*, ed. John Gledhill, Barbara Bender, and Mogens Trolle Larsen (London, 1988), pp. 215-36.

[21] Nash-Williams, *Early Christian monuments*, pp. 17-47.

[22] Knight, 'Glamorgan A.D. 400-1100', pp. 335-9; *La Vie de Saint Samson*, ed. Robert Fawtier (Paris, 1912), pp. 105-6, 108-10, 113, 119-20; Ian N. Wood, 'Forgery in Merovingian hagiography', in *Fälschungen im Mittelalter* (MGH Schriften, 33; Hannover, 1988), V, 380-4.

[23] See above, n. 15; David N. Dumville, 'Late seventh- or eighth-century evidence for the British transmission of Pelagius', *CMCS*, 10 (1985), 39-52.

[24] Michael Lapidge, 'Latin learning in Dark Age Wales', in *Proceedings of the seventh international congress of Celtic studies, Oxford 1983*, ed. D. Ellis Evans, John G. Griffith, and E. M. Jope (Oxford, 1986), pp. 91-107.

[25] *Nennius: British History and the Welsh Annals*, ed. John Morris (Chichester, 1980), p. 88.

[26] Kathleen Hughes, *Celtic Britain in the early Middle Ages* (Woodbridge, 1980), pp. 68-9; David N. Dumville, 'The historical value of the *Historia Brittonum*', *Arthurian Literature*, 6 (1986), 1-26 (p. 24).

[27] Chadwick, 'Early culture', pp. 79-110.

[28] Dumville, 'Historical value'. See also his '*Historia Brittonum*: an Insular history from the Carolingian age', in *Historiographie im frühen Mittelalter*, ed. Anton Scharer and Georg Scheibelreiter (Munich and Vienna, 1994), pp. 406-34.

29   Dumville, 'Historical value', pp. 5-22; Kathryn Grabowski and David Dumville, *Chronicles and annals of mediaeval Ireland and Wales* (Woodbridge, 1984), pp. 223-4; *Early Welsh genealogical tracts*, ed. P. C. Bartrum (Cardiff, 1966), p. 9.
30   W. M. Lindsay, *Early Welsh script* (Oxford, 1912); Lapidge, 'Latin learning in Dark Age Wales'; *Saint Dunstan's classbook from Glastonbury*, ed. R. W. Hunt (Amsterdam, 1961), pp. vii-xiii; Ifor Williams, 'The Juvencus poems', in *The beginnings of Welsh poetry*, ed. Rachel Bromwich, 2nd edn (Cardiff, 1980), pp. 89-121; T. A. M. Bishop, 'The Corpus Martianus Capella', *TCBS*, 4 (1964-8), 257-75; Michael Lapidge, 'The Welsh-Latin poetry of Sulien's family', *SC*, 8-9 (1973-4), 68-106; Alison Peden, 'Science and philosophy in Wales at the time of the Norman Conquest: a Macrobius manuscript from Llanbadarn', *CMCS*, 2 (1981), 21-45.
31   *Alfred the Great: Asser's Life of King Alfred and other contemporary sources*, trans. Simon Keynes and Michael Lapidge (Harmondsworth, 1983), pp. 48-53; Bishop, 'Corpus Martianus Capella', p. 258; David N. Dumville, 'English square minuscule script: the background and earliest phases', *Anglo-Saxon England*, 16 (1987), 147-79 (pp. 159-61).
32   D. Simon Evans, *Llafar a llyfr yn yr Hen Gyfnod* (Cardiff, 1982); cf. Peden, pp. 22-3.
33   Ifor Williams, 'The Computus fragment', *BBCS*, 3 (1926-7), 245-72.
34   On these glosses see Anthony Harvey, 'The Cambridge Juvencus glosses — evidence of Hiberno-Welsh literary interaction?', in *Language contact in the British Isles*, ed. P. Sture Ureland and George Broderick (Tübingen, 1991), pp. 181-98; and for their date compare Williams, 'Juvencus poems', pp. 89, 100 and n. 7 with David N. Dumville, 'Palaeographical considerations in the dating of Early Welsh verse', *BBCS*, 27 (1976-8), 246-51 (p. 248, n. 6), and Patrick Sims-Williams, 'The Early Welsh Arthurian poems', in *The Arthur of the Welsh: the Arthurian legend in medieval Welsh literature*, ed. Rachel Bromwich, A. O. H. Jarman, and Brynley F. Roberts (Cardiff, 1991), pp. 33-71 (p. 35).
35   Jenkins and Owen, 'Welsh marginalia [...] Part I', pp. 57-61.
36   Sims-Williams, 'Emergence of Old Welsh, Cornish and Breton orthography'; Anthony Harvey, 'Latin, literacy and the Celtic vernaculars around the year AD 500', in *Celtic languages and Celtic peoples: proceedings of the second North American congress of Celtic studies*, ed. Cyril J. Byrne, Margaret Harry, and Pádraig O Siadhail (Halifax, Nova Scotia, 1992), pp. 11-26 (p. 22). See now also T. M. Charles-Edwards, 'Language and society among the Insular Celts AD 400-1000', in *The Celtic World*, ed. Miranda Green (London, 1995), pp. 703-36.
37   Kenneth Jackson, 'Some questions in dispute about early Welsh literature and language', *SC*, 8-9 (1973-4), 1-32 (pp. 9-13); Davies, *Wales in the early Middle Ages*, p. 199; Sims-Williams, 'Early Welsh Arthurian poems', p. 35; Daniel Huws, 'Llyfrau Cymraeg 1250-1400', *NLWJ*, 28 (1993-4), 1-21 (p. 3).
38   See e.g. *Beginnings of Welsh poetry*; John T. Koch, 'When was Welsh literature first written down?', *SC*, 20-21 (1985-6), 43-66; *Early Welsh poetry: studies in the Book of Aneirin*, ed. Brynley F. Roberts (Aberystwyth, 1988); *The Gododdin of Aneirin*, ed. John T. Koch (Cardiff, 1997).
39   Proinsias Mac Cana, *The Mabinogi*, 2nd edn (Cardiff, 1992), pp. 19-20, 22-3, 125; Dafydd Jenkins and Morfydd E. Owen, 'The Welsh marginalia in the Lichfield Gospels, Part II: the 'Surexit' memorandum', *CMCS*, 7 (1984), 91-120 (pp.112-14); Brynley F. Roberts, 'Oral tradition and Welsh literature: a description and survey', *Oral Tradition*, 3 (1988), 61-87 (pp. 75-6); *Gododdin*, ed. Koch, p.civ. Cf. C. P. Wormald, 'The uses of literacy in Anglo-Saxon England and its neighbours', *TRHS*, 5th ser. 27 (1977), 95-114; Richard Sharpe, *Medieval Irish saints' lives: an introduction to Vitae Sanctorum Hiberniae* (Oxford, 1991), pp. 20-4.
40   Roberts, 'Oral tradition', pp. 65-6; Sims-Williams, 'Early Welsh Arthurian poems', p. 36.
41   Marged Haycock, '"Preiddieu Annwn" and the figure of Taliesin', *SC*, 18-19 (1983-4), 52-78 (p. 57). See also her '"Some talk of Alexander and some of Hercules": three early medieval poems from the Book of Taliesin', *CMCS* 13 (1987), 7-38 (pp.17-22), and her *Blodeugerdd Barddas o ganu crefyddol cynnar* (Llandybïe, 1994); Jenny Rowland, 'Genres', in *Early Welsh poetry*, pp. 179-208 (p. 181); Sims-Williams, 'Early Welsh Arthurian poems', pp. 33-5.
42   Cf. Keller, 'Die Entwicklung der europäischen Schriftkultur', pp. 173-80.
43   Daniel Huws, 'The making of Liber Landavensis', *NLWJ*, 25 (1987-8), 133-66; *Calendar of [...] papal*

letters, I, 1198-1304, ed. W. H. Bliss (London, 1893), 151. Also note the biblical, liturgical, and theological texts listed in *Medieval libraries of Great Britain*, ed. N. R. Ker, 2nd edn (London, 1964), 5, 12, 23, 119-20, 170, 191; and see Daniel Huws, 'The Tintern Abbey Bible', *MA*, 6 (1990), 47-54.

[44] Owain Tudor Edwards, *Matins, Lauds and Vespers for St David's day* (Cambridge, 1990), pp. 151-2, 163-4.

[45] Hughes, *Celtic Britain in the early Middle Ages*, pp. 74-85; David N. Dumville, review in *SC*, 12-13 (1977-8), 461-7; F. G. Cowley, *The monastic order in south Wales 1066-1349* (Cardiff, 1977), pp. 148-50.

[46] Dumville, 'Historical value', p. 22.

[47] Kathleen Hughes, 'British Museum MS. Cotton Vespasian A. XIV ('Vitae Sanctorum Wallensium'): its purpose and provenance', in *Studies in the early British Church*, pp. 183-200 (reprinted in Hughes, *Celtic Britain in the early Middle Ages*, pp. 53-66); Wendy Davies, 'Property rights and property claims in Welsh *Vitae* of the eleventh century', in *Hagiographie, cultures et sociétés, IVe-XIIe siècles*, ed. Evelyne Patlagean and Pierre Riché (Paris, 1981), pp. 515-33.

[48] Robert Bartlett, *Gerald of Wales 1146-1223* (Oxford, 1982); I. W. Rowlands, 'The making of the March: aspects of the Norman settlement in Dyfed', in *Proceedings of the Battle conference on Anglo-Norman studies, III, 1980*, ed. R. Allen Brown (Woodbridge, 1981), pp. 142-57 (pp. 155-6). See also Cowley, *Monastic order*, pp. 150, 152-3.

[49] Pryce, *Native law and the Church*, p. 76 and n. 21; C. H. Talbot, 'Cadogan of Bangor', *Cîteaux in de Nederlanden*, 9 (1958), 18-40. Quotation from *Brut y Tywysogyon or the Chronicle of the Princes, Red Book of Hergest version*, ed. Thomas Jones, 2nd edn (Cardiff, 1973), pp. 38-9.

[50] P. P. Sims-Williams, 'Some functions of origin stories in early medieval Wales', in *History and heroic tale: a symposium*, ed. Tore Nyberg et al. (Odense, 1985), pp. 97-131 (pp. 100-2); Sims-Williams 'Early Welsh Arthurian poems', pp. 34-6.

[51] Roberts, 'Oral tradition', pp. 69-73. Koch (*Gododdin*, p.civ) tentatively dates the redaction of *Culhwch ac Olwen* to c. 1000, however.

[52] *Trioedd Ynys Prydein*, ed. Rachel Bromwich, 2nd edn (Cardiff, 1978), pp. cxi-cxii, cxx-cxxi.

[53] A. O. H. Jarman, *Y Gododdin* (Llandysul, 1988), pp. xiii-xvii; *Llyfr Aneirin: ffacsimile / Llyfr Aneirin: a facsimile*, ed. Daniel Huws (Aberystwyth, 1989); A. O. H. Jarman, 'Llyfr Du Caerfyrddin / The Black Book of Carmarthen', *PBA*, 71 (1985), 333-56; *Gwaith Cynddelw Brydydd Mawr, I*, ed. Nerys Ann Jones and Ann Parry Owen (Cardiff, 1991), pp. xxx-xxxi, xlvii.

[54] Marged Haycock, 'Early Welsh poetry', in *Memory and poetic structure*, ed. Peter Ryan (London, 1981), pp. 91-135 (p. 99). Cf. Roberts, 'Oral tradition', pp. 65-6.

[55] Rowland, 'Genres', p. 181; *Gramadegau'r Penceirddiaid*, ed. G. J. Williams and E. J. Jones (Cardiff, 1934), pp. xcv-xcvii.

[56] *Giraldi Cambrensis opera*, ed. J. S. Brewer, J. F. Dimock, and G. F. Warner (Rolls Series, London, 1861-91), VI, 167-8 (*Descriptio Kambriae*, I, 3); *Expugnatio Hibernica / The conquest of Ireland, by Giraldus Cambrensis*, ed. A. B. Scott and F. X. Martin (Dublin, 1978), pp. 254-5.

[57] Cf. Rachel Bromwich, 'Cyfeiriadau traddodiadol a chwedlonol y Gogynfeirdd', in *Beirdd a thywysogion: barddoniaeth llys yng Nghymru, Iwerddon a'r Alban*, ed. Morfydd E. Owen and Brynley F. Roberts ([Cardiff and Aberystwyth] 1996), pp. 202-18 (esp. p. 205).

[58] Roberts, 'Oral tradition', pp. 73-7. See also Sioned Davies, 'Storytelling in medieval Wales', *Oral Tradition*, 7(2) (1992), 231-57, as well as her *Crefft y cyfarwydd: astudiaeth o dechnegau naratif yn y Mabinogion* (Cardiff, 1995) and her 'Written text as performance: the implications for Middle Welsh prose narratives', in *Literacy in medieval Celtic societies*, pp. 133-48.

[59] *Brut y Brenhinedd, Peniarth MS. 1 version*, ed. Brynley F. Roberts (Dublin, 1971), pp. xxiv-xxix, 55-74.

[60] *Historia Gruffud vab Kenan*, ed. D. Simon Evans (Cardiff, 1977), pp. ccxxvii, ccli-cclix; for a different view, see K. L. Maund, *Ireland, Wales, and England in the eleventh century* (Woodbridge, 1991), pp. 172-74.

[61] Roberts, 'Oral tradition', p. 75; *Culhwch and Olwen: an edition and study of the oldest Arthurian tale*, ed. Rachel Bromwich and D. Simon Evans (Cardiff, 1992), p. lxxxii; Mac Cana, *Mabinogi*, p. 49.

[62] T. M. Charles-Edwards, *The Welsh laws* (Cardiff, 1989), esp. pp. 68-86.

[63] Huw Pryce, 'The prologues to the Welsh lawbooks', *BBCS*, 33 (1986), 151-87.
[64] Dafydd Jenkins, 'A family of medieval Welsh lawyers', in *Celtic law papers*, ed. Dafydd Jenkins (Brussels, 1973), pp. 121-33; Pryce, *Native law and the Church*, pp. 23-36.
[65] Charles-Edwards, *Welsh laws*, pp. 15-16, but cf. Dafydd Jenkins, 'The medieval Welsh idea of law', *Tijdschrift voor Rechtsgeschiedenis*, 49 (1981), 323-48 (pp. 330-1).
[66] *Ancient laws and institutes of Wales*, I, 216-18; cf. Paul Russell, 'Orthography as a key to codicology: innovation in the work of a thirteenth-century Welsh scribe', *CMCS*, 25 (1993), 77-85.
[67] Cf. Pryce, *Native law and the Church*, pp. 78-81. I hope to discuss the issues raised here in detail elsewhere.
[68] Davies, 'Administration of law in Medieval Wales', pp. 258-9; Davies, *Conquest, coexistence, and change*, pp. 131-5.
[69] Davies, 'Latin charter-tradition', pp. 267-8.
[70] *Vitae Sanctorum Britanniae*, pp. 124-36; Christopher N. L. Brooke, *The Church and the Welsh border in the central Middle Ages* (Woodbridge, 1986), pp. 90-2.
[71] Wendy Davies, '*Liber Landavensis*: its construction and credibility', *EHR*, 88 (1973), 335-51 (pp. 336-9); Huws, 'Making of Liber Landavensis'; David Crouch, 'Urban: first bishop of Llandaff', *JWEH*, 6 (1989), 9-15; and see above, n. 15. On the compilation of *Liber Landavensis* see now also John Reuben Davies, 'The Book of Llandaf in its early twelfth-century Cambro-Norman context' (unpublished doctoral dissertation, Cambridge, 1997).
[72] Michael Richter, *Giraldus Cambrensis: the growth of the Welsh nation*, 2nd edn (Aberystwyth, 1976), pp. 38-52, 94-126.
[73] See e.g. *Cartae et alia munimenta quae ad dominium de Glamorgancia pertinent*, ed. G. T. Clark, 2nd edn (Cardiff, 1910), II, 289, 330-2; *The cartulary of Haughmond Abbey*, ed. Una Rees (Cardiff, 1985), no. 800; and *Registrum vulgariter nuncupatum 'The Record of Caernarvon' e codice MS. Harleiano 696 descriptum*, ed. Henry Ellis (London, 1838), p. 252.
[74] See e.g. *Llandaff episcopal acta 1140-1287*, ed. David Crouch (Cardiff, 1989), nos. 26, 77.
[75] See e.g. *Cartae*, ed. Clark, II, 232, 238-9, 372, 403-4, 417-18, 490-1; VI, 2299-2300.
[76] *Llandaff episcopal acta*, no. 77; cf. Matthew Griffiths, 'Native society on the Anglo-Norman frontier: the evidence of the Margam charters', *WHR*, 14 (1988-9), 179-216 (pp. 199-201).
[77] *Giraldi Cambrensis opera*, I, 35.
[78] William Dugdale, *Monasticon Anglicanum*, ed. John Caley, Henry Ellis, and Bulkeley Bandinel (London, 1817-30), V, 673-4; *Record of Caernarvon*, p. 148; *Councils and ecclesiastical documents relating to Great Britain and Ireland*, ed. A. W. Haddan and W. Stubbs (Oxford, 1869-78), I, 489-91, 502-3.
[79] *Councils and ecclesiastical documents*, p. 504; Pryce, *Native law and the Church*, pp. 196-8.
[80] Huw Pryce, 'The church of Trefeglwys and the end of the "Celtic" charter tradition in twelfth-century Wales', *CMCS*, 25 (1993), 15-54; Robert Bartlett, *The making of Europe: conquest, colonization and cultural change 950-1350* (Harmondsworth, 1993), pp. 283-8; David Crouch, 'The earliest original charter of a Welsh king', *BBCS*, 36 (1989), 125-31. Since this chapter was written a re-examination of the Aberconwy charters by Charles Insley has raised doubts, so far unresolved, as to how far the texts in their extant form represent documents issued on behalf of Llywelyn ap Iorwerth.
[81] Cf. Clanchy, *From memory*, pp. 51, 308-12, 317; David H. Williams, *Catalogue of seals in the National Museum of Wales, Vol. 1: Seal dies, Welsh seals, papal bullae* (Cardiff, 1993).
[82] Morris C. Jones, 'Valle Crucis abbey: its origin and foundation charter', *AC*, 3rd ser. 12 (1866), 400-17 (p. 415). For another example see *The charters of the abbey of Ystrad Marchell*, ed. Graham C. G. Thomas (Aberystwyth, 1997), 179 (no. 37).
[83] Cf. Janet L. Nelson, 'Literacy in Carolingian government', in *Uses of literacy*, ed. McKitterick, pp. 258-96; Simon Keynes, 'Royal government and the written word in late Anglo-Saxon England', in *Uses of literacy*, pp. 226-57.
[84] *The text of the Book of Llan Dâv*, ed. J. Gwenogvryn Evans and John Rhys (Oxford, 1893; repr. Aberystwyth, 1979), p. 29.
[85] Davies, *Conquest, coexistence, and change*, pp. 282-3, 285-6, 293-4, 297, 304-5.
[86] R. R. Davies, *Domination and conquest: the experience of Ireland, Scotland and Wales 1100-1300*

(Cambridge, 1990), pp. 94-6; J. Beverley Smith, 'Magna Carta and the charters of the Welsh princes', *EHR*, 99 (1984), 344-62.

[87] *Calendar of the Charter Rolls, II, 1257-1300* (London, 1906), 459-60; *Calendar of Ancient Correspondence concerning Wales*, ed. J. Goronwy Edwards (Cardiff, 1935), p. 51; Williams, *Catalogue of seals*, pp. 34, 77.

[88] *Brut y Tywysogyon, Red Book of Hergest version*, pp. 238-9.

[89] Davies, *Conquest, coexistence, and change*, p. 264; *Calendar of Ancient Correspondence*, p. 53; J. Beverley Smith, *Llywelyn ap Gruffudd: Tywysog Cymru* (Cardiff, 1986), pp. 136-7, 204-8.

[90] Cf. David Stephenson, *The governance of Gwynedd* (Cardiff, 1984), pp. xxxvi, 27-8; K. L. Maund, *Handlist of the acts of native Welsh rulers, 1132-1283* (Cardiff, 1996); Clanchy, *From memory*, pp. 31-2.

[91] W. H. Waters, *The Edwardian settlement of north Wales in its administrative and legal aspects (1284-1343)* (Cardiff, 1935); Ralph A. Griffiths, *The principality of Wales in the later Middle Ages: the structure and personnel of government, I, South Wales, 1277-1536* (Cardiff, 1972); William Rees, *South Wales and the March, 1284-1415* (Oxford, 1924), pp. 68-109; R. R. Davies, *Lordship and society in the March of Wales, 1282-1400* (Oxford, 1978), Ch. 9.

[92] Llinos Beverley Smith, 'Pwnc yr iaith yng Nghymru, 1282-1536', in *Cof cenedl [1]*, ed. Geraint H. Jenkins (Llandysul, 1986), pp. 1-33 (pp. 11-17, 27-31). D. A. Trotter, 'L'anglo-français au Pays de Galles: une enquête préliminaire', *Revue de linguistique romane*, 58 (1994), 461-87. See now also Llinos Beverley Smith, 'The Welsh language before 1536', in *The Welsh language before the Industrial Revolution*, ed. Geraint H. Jenkins (Cardiff 1997), pp.15-44.

[93] Daniel Huws, 'Llyfr Gwyn Rhydderch', *CMCS*, 21 (1991), 1-37 (pp. 2, 17, 19-24). See now also Llinos Beverley Smith, 'Inkhorn and spectacles: the impact of literacy in late medieval Wales', in *Literacy in medieval Celtic societies*, pp. 202-22.

[94] R. Ian Jack, *Medieval Wales* (London, 1972), Ch. 5 and references given there.

[95] For these distinctions, see Malcolm Parkes, 'The literacy of the laity', in *Literature and civilization: the medieval world*, ed. David Daiches and Anthony Thorlby (London, 1973), pp. 555-77.

[96] Glanmor Williams, *The Welsh Church from conquest to Reformation*, revised edn (Cardiff, 1976), pp. 84-104; D. Simon Evans, *Medieval religious literature* (Cardiff, 1986).

[97] *Brut y Tywysogyon or the Chronicle of the Princes, Peniarth MS. 20 version*, trans. Thomas Jones (Cardiff, 1952), pp. xxxix, lxi-lxiii; *Brut y Tywysogyon, Red Book of Hergest version*, pp. lii-liii.

[98] Daniel Huws, 'Llawysgrif Hendregadredd', *NLWJ*, 22 (1981-2), 1-26 (pp. 4-6, 13-15).

[99] F. R. Lewis, 'A history of the lordship of Gower from the missing cartulary of Neath abbey', *BBCS*, 9 (1937-9), 149-54.

[100] Rhys W. Hays, 'Welsh students at Oxford and Cambridge universities in the Middle Ages', *WHR*, 4 (1968-9), 325-61.

[101] Williams, *Welsh Church*, pp. 70-1, 81.

[102] Hays, 'Welsh students', pp. 336-9.

[103] Pryce, *Native law and the Church*, pp. 31-2.

[104] Williams, *Welsh Church*, pp. 82-4; *DWB*, p. 1010.

[105] Williams, *Welsh Church*, pp. 178-84.

[106] Cowley, *Monastic order in south Wales*, pp. 145-6; Hays, *History of the abbey of Aberconway*, pp. 134, 142.

[107] Huws, 'Llyfrau Cymraeg', pp. 13-14.

[108] *The history of Flintshire, I*, ed. C. R. Williams (Denbigh, 1961), p.99; Huws, 'Llyfrau Cymraeg', p. 14. For some English comparisons, see Joel T. Rosenthal, 'Aristocratic cultural patronage and book bequests, 1350-1500', *Bulletin of the John Rylands University Library of Manchester*, 64 (1981-2), 522-48 (pp. 532, 535-48).

[109] *DWB*, pp. 359-60; Ralph A. Griffiths, 'Public and private bureaucracies in England and Wales in the fifteenth century', *TRHS*, 5th ser. 30 (1980), 109-30 (p. 116); David Thomson, 'Cistercians and schools in late medieval Wales', *CMCS*, 3 (1982), 76-80; Smith, 'Grammar and commonplace books of John Edwards', pp. 179-82.

[110] Griffiths, 'Public and private bureaucracies', pp. 117-18. Cf. Davies, *Lordship and society*, p. 209.

[111] Roberts, 'Oral tradition', pp. 69-71; Ceridwen Lloyd-Morgan, '*Breuddwyd Rhonabwy* and later Arthurian literature', in *Arthur of the Welsh*, pp. 183-93.

[112] G. J. Williams, 'Hanes y llawysgrifau Cymraeg', in *Agweddau ar hanes dysg Gymraeg*, ed. Aneurin Lewis (Cardiff, 1969), pp. 1-30 (pp. 7-9); Gilbert E. Ruddock, *Dafydd Nanmor* (Caernarfon, 1992), pp. 22-5.

[113] Ceridwen Lloyd-Morgan, 'Women and their poetry in medieval Wales', in *Women and literature in Britain, 1150-1500*, ed. Carol M. Meale (Cambridge, 1993), pp. 183-201. See also Daniel Huws, 'The transmission of a Welsh classic: Dafydd ap Gwilym', in *Recognitions: essays presented to Edmund Fryde*, ed. Colin Richmond and Isobel Harvey (Aberystwyth, 1996), pp. 182-92. On the literacy of women, see Ceridwen Lloyd-Morgan, 'More written about than writing? Welsh women and the written word', in *Literacy in medieval Celtic societies*, pp. 149-65.

[114] Cf. Paul Saenger, 'Silent reading: its impact on late medieval script and society', *Viator*, 13 (1982), 367-414.

[115] Charles-Edwards, *Welsh laws*, pp. 90-3; J. Beverley Smith, 'Cydfodau o'r bymthegfed ganrif', *BBCS*, 21 (1964-6), 309-24; J. Beverley Smith, 'Cydfodau o'r bymthegfed ganrif: testunau ychwanegol', *BBCS*, 25 (1972-4), 128-34.

[116] *Gramadegau'r Penceirddiaid*, ed. G. J. Williams and E. J. Jones (Cardiff, 1934); Iestyn Daniel, 'Awduriaeth y gramadeg a briodolir i Einion Offeiriad a Dafydd Ddu Hiraddug', *YB*, 13 (1985), 178-208; Morfydd E. Owen, 'Meddygon Myddfai: a preliminary survey of some medieval medical writing in Welsh', *SC*, 10-11 (1975-6), 210-33.

[117] Stephen J. Williams, 'Rhai cyfieithiadau', in *Y traddodiad rhyddiaith yn yr Oesau Canol*, ed. Geraint Bowen (Llandysul, 1974), pp. 303-11.

[118] Llinos Beverley Smith, 'The Statute of Wales, 1284', *WHR*, 10 (1980-1), 127-54 (pp. 135-7, 141-6); Rees, *South Wales and the March*, pp. 87-8, n. 5; and cf. Davies, *Lordship and society*, pp. 163, 200.

[119] See e.g. J. Beverley Smith, 'Crown and community in the principality of North Wales in the reign of Henry Tudor', *WHR*, 3 (1966-7), 145-71 (pp. 146-7); Davies, *Lordship and society*, p. 215.

[120] Cf. James Given, 'The economic consequences of the English conquest of Gwynedd', *Speculum*, 64 (1989), 11-45; Davies, *Lordship and society*, Chs. 5-8.

[121] Jack, *Medieval Wales*, Chs. 3-4 and references given there; *The Merioneth Lay Subsidy Roll, 1292-3*, ed. Keith Williams-Jones (Cardiff, 1976); *The Marcher lordships of South Wales, 1415-1536: select documents*, ed. T. B. Pugh (Cardiff, 1963); Davies, *Lordship and society*, pp. 149-50, n. 3; Waters, *Edwardian settlement*, p. 132.

[122] Waters, *Edwardian settlement*, pp. 160-5; Davies, *Lordship and society*, pp. 159-60, 163.

[123] Llinos Beverley Smith, 'The gage and the land market in late medieval Wales', *EcHR*, 2nd ser., 29 (1976), 537-50.

[124] Llinos Beverley Smith, '*Tir Prid*: deeds of gage of land in late medieval Wales', *BBCS*, 27 (1976-8), 263-77; Francis Jones, 'Welsh bonds for keeping the peace, 1283 and 1295', *BBCS*, 13 (1948-50), 142-4. See now also A. D. Carr, ' "This is my act and deed": the writing of private deeds in late medieval north Wales', *Literacy in medieval Celtic societies*, pp. 223-37.

[125] Smith, 'Gage and the land market', pp. 544-5.

[126] Smith, 'Crown and community', pp. 158, 163-6, 168-9.

[127] Rees, *South Wales and the March*, p. 109; Davies, *Lordship and society*, p. 171.

[128] Clanchy, *From memory*, Ch. 2; quotation at p. 77.

[129] Cf. R. R. Davies, review of first edition of Clanchy, *From memory* in *History*, 68 (1983), 312.

[130] Smith, 'Gage and the land market', p. 546; Smith, 'Grammar and commonplace books of John Edwards'; Smith, 'Proofs of age in medieval Wales', *BBCS*, 38 (1991), 134-44; Williams, *Recovery, reorientation, and Reformation*, p. 145.

CHAPTER 2

THE MEDIEVAL MANUSCRIPT

Daniel Huws

PART of the Roman inheritance of the Britons, later the Welsh, together with Christianity and the use of letters, was the form of an artefact which had been adopted by the Christianized Romans for the preservation of literature: the codex. The codex, loosely speaking *liber,* a word still recognizable both in Romance (*livre, libro*) and Celtic languages (*llyfr, leabhar*), had been adopted by Christians for biblical texts before becoming the vehicle for literature in general. The roll, the traditional format of the literature of Roman antiquity in its papyrus form, and also of Hebrew sacred texts in its parchment or leather form, made a prominent reappearance in medieval Britain, but this later use was mostly restricted to legal and administrative records.

For want of evidence one cannot begin to speak of the history of the book in Wales before the eighth century. While the history of the book does not depend solely on surviving specimens, they are the prime witnesses and it has to be remembered how few they are. From the eighth to the twelfth century the number of surviving books or fragments of books from Wales does not exceed twenty. For the whole medieval period the number of books of Welsh origin, while well over two hundred, may not exceed two hundred and fifty (excluding fragments of post-1200 date). About one hundred and sixty of these are in Welsh. The main reason for the considerable uncertainty as to number is the difficulty of proving the Welsh origin of Latin books of later Welsh provenance, not to mention the absence of clues to the provenance, let alone the origin, of most medieval Latin books. Nor can the possibility of books being written in medieval Wales in French and English be dismissed, though no certain examples have been identified other than books where these languages occur beside Latin or Welsh.[1]

There are good grounds for maintaining that in Wales fewer than one in a hundred medieval manuscripts in Latin has survived; certainly a lower percentage than in England. On the other hand, an informed guess might be that one in five medieval manuscripts in Welsh has survived, perhaps more. In Wales, as elsewhere, the parchment of books was recycled as their content became outmoded, often as a consequence of legal or liturgical changes. But the main reasons for the scarcity in Wales of surviving books in Latin must have been the destruction of liturgical works during the Reformation — not a dozen books survive — and the apathy and wanton destructiveness which led to the loss of the Welsh monastic and cathedral libraries (perhaps already badly neglected) at the time of the Dissolution. Whereas fifteen medieval libraries in England are each represented by over a hundred surviving books, only one Welsh library, that of Llanthony Prima, is represented by more than four, and the books of this Augustinian priory had found shelter well before the Dissolution in Gloucestershire at Lanthony Secunda.[2] Of 242 titles listed at the rich Cistercian abbey of Margam in the early fourteenth century not one book is known to survive.[3]

Serious losses must have occurred even before the Dissolution. None of the few surviving pre-Norman books from Wales is likely to have been in its original home at the Dissolution, unless possibly at St David's. Few even of the post-Norman religious houses in Wales escaped damage in war, particularly in the rising of Owain Glyndŵr during the first decade of the fifteenth century when many monasteries were devastated.

A church would treasure above all its relics. These might include a gospel-book associated, as in many a saint's *vita*, with its founder. The covers of the gospel-book, like a reliquary, would often be adorned with precious metals and gems. Aptly enough, the earliest Welsh book is a magnificent eighth-century gospel-book, though one which is neither complete nor in its original covers. The gospel-book of St Chad has been at Lichfield cathedral for over a thousand years, but marginal entries reveal that an earlier home was in a church of St Teilo in Wales, evidently at Llandeilo Fawr. The St Chad Gospels belong to the most illustrious of all families of early Insular books: the group of gospel-books which includes the Book of Durrow, the Lindisfarne Gospels, and the Book of Kells. The places of origin of many of these remain undetermined. Close affinities of the St Chad Gospels with some others of this family have led to the suggestion of an English origin. The absence of other Welsh books for comparison will ensure that scholarly debate continues.[4] The only other possibly Welsh gospel-book of the eighth century, more modest in execution and perhaps half a century later in date, is Hereford Cathedral MS P. l. ii, probably at Hereford since the eleventh century.[5]

The famous gospel-book of St Asaph, which was to be exhibited in four Welsh and two English dioceses in 1277 and 1284 to raise money for the rebuilding of the cathedral, must have been of venerable age.[6] Two books, doubtless gospel-books, which reached the sixteenth century in their precious bindings before disappearing were the 'worm-eaten book covered over with silver plate' with which the feast of St David was solemnized at St David's in 1538, to the dismay of the reforming bishop, William Barlow, and the 'Tiboeth', its cover decorated with a black stone, at Clynnog Fawr.[7] The Book of Llandaf, a gospel-book and cartulary, is a late, twelfth-century, representative of the tradition, still retaining an original board which was once covered in metal.[8]

When King Alfred began to restore learning to his kingdom he sought help from many quarters. From Wales he drew his bishop and biographer, Asser. Welsh books were to be found at a number of tenth-century English religious houses. It was by finding an early haven in English churches that some of the oldest Welsh books survived. A fine example is Oxford, Bodleian Library, MS Auct. F.4.32, a composite book. Among its component parts, used by St Dunstan, are the *Liber Commonei* (The Book of Commoneus), written in 817 x 835, the earliest datable Welsh book, and a copy of Book 1 of Ovid's *Ars amatoria*, probably written in the late ninth or early tenth century.[9] *Liber Commonei* includes various short computistical tracts together with an archaic form of the Easter Vigil lessons and canticles in Greek and Latin. Glosses in Old Welsh confirm the Welsh provenance of these two books.

The script of the St Chad Gospels is, like that of its kindred gospel-books, Insular half-uncial, the rounded near-majuscule script used in Britain and Ireland for writing of the highest grade. Its companion script, used for ordinary purposes, was the related minuscule now known as Insular.[10] As early as the ninth century, Welsh Insular minuscule occurs in several forms: a 'pointed', which does not appear to have survived beyond about 900; a more rounded script which has come to be called 'Welsh Reformed minuscule', in use in the later ninth and early tenth centuries; and a 'flat-topped' form which in its last phase is met in Llanbadarn Fawr books at the end of the eleventh century. The diversity of script-form found in the small surviving sample of Welsh books, and even sometimes within a single book, is notable.

Insular script represented a tradition common to the Celtic West (including Brittany), to England, where it was introduced by Irish influence, and to some centres on the Continent to which it had been introduced by Irish or English missionaries. The tradition was not simply a matter of script: most aspects of book production differed from continental practice. Insular parchment was suede-like, matt rather than smooth (thus offering a better surface for paint); the number of bifolia in quires might be five (or irregular) rather than the four normal on the Continent; bifolia were arranged with hair sides all outermost rather than with like side facing like; pricking and ruling were done after rather than before folding the bifolia; the ink, probably containing more carbon, tended to be blacker; punctuation, syntax marks (to aid construing), and abbreviations differed widely. More noticeable than any of these distinctions, more striking even than the difference in script, is the difference in style of decoration, seen at its most elaborate in the great gospel-books.

Surviving books of known Welsh origin earlier than 1100 belong in all respects to the Insular tradition. Indeed, they belong so firmly to a common tradition that confident assertion of their Welsh origin can usually be made only on the strength of the presence of Welsh glosses or other explicit evidence. Distinctive features of Welsh script are only now beginning to receive recognition.[11] Other possibly Welsh symptoms, be they of abbreviation or syntax marks, have not proved decisive.

The earliest writing in Welsh is on stone monuments, the earliest example, the 'Cadfan Stone' in Tywyn church, Meirionnydd, being probably of eighth-century date. The earliest Welsh in a book, other than isolated words, is probably the memorandum known (from its opening word) as 'Surexit', added perhaps about the year 800 on a page of the St Chad Gospels.[12] A number of ninth- and tenth-century books embracing a range of texts are glossed in Welsh. Two in particular deserve mention. A manuscript of Juvencus (Cambridge UL, Ff.iv. 42) is not only extensively glossed in Welsh and Irish, but also contains in its margin the earliest recording of poetry in Welsh, the 'Juvencus englynion', added in the late ninth or early tenth century. Cambridge UL, Add. 4543 includes a two-leaf fragment containing on one page a text in Welsh on computation, probably of the first half of the tenth century, the earliest example of a treatise in Welsh.[13] The sample is so small that it would be rash to attach great significance to the high proportion of scientific texts among the surviving early Welsh books.

Whatever their content, whether scientific, liturgical, exegetical, or literary, Welsh books were likely to have been made at a *clas*, at one of the major religious communities and centres of learning. No Welsh book can, however, be associated with an identifiable *clas* before the closing years of the eleventh century. At that time the *clas* of Llanbadarn Fawr was dominated by the family of Sulien (d. 1091), an outstanding Irish-trained cleric, who twice served as bishop of St David's. Ieuan, one of Sulien's sons, provided the fine decoration in a psalter written about 1080 for his brother, the scholar Rhigyfarch (the 'Ricemarch Psalter', Dublin, Trinity College MS 50). About 1090 Ieuan beautifully wrote, and probably also decorated, Cambridge, Corpus Christi College, MS 199, containing Augustine's *De Trinitate*. These two splendid Llanbadarn Fawr books are the earliest which can be attributed to an identifiable Welsh scriptorium.[14] The breadth of scientific learning at Llanbadarn Fawr at this time has been demonstrated by analysis of the commentary in another of its books, the early-twelfth-century Macrobius, *In somnium Scipionis*, BL, Cotton Faustina C.I, fols 66-93, while the Latin poetry of Sulien's family reflects a high level of familiarity with Latin literature.[15] Sulien's Irish education, however, poses unanswerable questions: how representative of contemporary Welsh *clasau* was Llanbadarn Fawr? Do Ieuan ap Sulien's decorated initials, closely akin to contemporary Irish work, represent a style then prevalent in Wales or merely a local one? The evidence which would permit a helpful comparison has not survived.

The conquest of extensive areas of Wales by the Normans brought new modes of government and a new ecclesiastical structure. Under the patronage of Norman lords and, later, of native rulers, religious houses of the regular monastic orders were introduced. During the thirteenth century the friars were also welcomed by both Marcher lords and native rulers. Only vestiges remained of the pattern of *clasau* which until the twelfth century had, at least in some centres, sustained the learning and produced the books of Wales. The new order brought about changes in the appearance of books as striking as those it brought to architecture.

A new minuscule script, now called Caroline or Carolingian minuscule, was developed in the Frankish kingdom towards the close of the eighth century. The script, a triumph of design (and the basis of modern roman type), slowly came to prevail in most of Western Europe, supplanting Insular script in Brittany in the mid-ninth century and in England (for most purposes) in the second half of the tenth. It may perhaps have penetrated parts of Wales at about the same time: it makes a fleeting appearance in one tenth-century Welsh book.[16] But, in general, Insular script seems to have held its own in Wales until the twelfth century. The latest Welsh books wholly in the Insular tradition are Ieuan ap Sulien's two books from Llanbadarn Fawr.

With the Caroline script came continental fashion in the making-up of quires, in decoration of initials, and abbreviation. Three of the few surviving twelfth-century Welsh books exemplify the transition: the Book of Llandaf (NLW, MS 17110E), BL, Cotton Faustina C.I, fols 66-93 (from Llanbadarn Fawr), and NLW, Peniarth MS 540 (Bede, *De natura rerum*). Although Caroline script has prevailed, each of these shows residual traits of Insular practice.[17]

Twelfth-century Europe produced books of unsurpassed quality, in great numbers, largely to meet the needs of the burgeoning monastic orders. Books, particularly patristic texts, were required for their libraries, and most were produced by monasteries themselves in their own scriptoria. The libraries of many continental religious houses, and a few in England, have survived substantially intact. In Wales, the best evidence is that for the Cistercian abbey of Margam, where an early-fourteenth-century catalogue, which aimed to include theological works only, listed 242 titles. Although the Margam library is almost totally lost, the archive of the abbey is perhaps the fullest monastic archive to have survived in Britain. A recent analysis of this archive has detected the activity of at least fifteen 'secretarial scribes' in the early thirteenth century, one of whom is also identifiable as the scribe of a manuscript of the 'Margam Annals'.[18] How many of these scribes also worked on books must remain an unanswered question.

During the thirteenth century the activity of monastic and cathedral scriptoria declined as the primary needs for books became satisfied. Universities emerged as new centres of learning, and an increasingly commercialized book trade, employing lay scribes, was developed by the stationers in university towns. Since Wales possessed no university, most learned Latin texts and many liturgical ones to be found in Wales from now on were probably written elsewhere, even if their scribes were Welsh.

There were, however, a number of Latin texts which were of particular interest to the Welsh: Welsh law, Welsh historical texts, and the *vitae* of Welsh saints. It is a fair presumption that all Latin texts of Welsh law were written in Wales.[19] Of the four surviving Latin versions of Welsh chronicles, generically known as *Annales Cambriae*, three were evidently written in Wales (at St David's, Neath abbey, and Whitland abbey), but the earliest is from England or the Continent.[20] The Cistercian order, even in the period of its pristine strictness, encouraged the keeping of annals; later, Cistercian houses seem to have been largely responsible for propagating the Welsh versions of these chronicles which came to be known as *Brut y Tywysogyon*.[21] Geoffrey of Monmouth's *Historia Regum Britanniae* was linked with the Welsh chronicles to provide the Welsh with a legendary past. Some manuscripts of the *Historia* seem to be of Welsh provenance.[22] In its Welsh translations (there were several), the *Historia,* under the title *Brut y Brenhinedd*, became the most widely copied of all Welsh medieval narrative texts.[23]

The earliest surviving books written in Welsh appear, a flurry of them, around the middle of the thirteenth century. They include texts of the Law of Hywel Dda, *Brut y Brenhinedd*, and the earliest collection of Welsh poetry, that in the Black Book of Carmarthen. Their Welsh is already a developed literary medium, almost free of the colouring of local dialect. It is known that Welsh was in literary use by the ninth century, and there is evidence (including mention by Giraldus Cambrensis of 'old' books of genealogies kept by the poets) that books in Welsh existed in the twelfth century. Yet not one example survives from before the mid-thirteenth century. One can speculate on reasons for this total loss: the lack of continuity in the histories of Welsh ecclesiastical libraries, and the fact that the Insular script of the earliest Welsh books would have become difficult for later readers. But even allowing that a body of Welsh literature was to be found in books by the twelfth century, the pattern of development of compilations of Welsh literature after about 1250 suggests that Wales lagged far behind Ireland in the recording of vernacular literature. Compilations comparable in scope and size to the Irish *Lebor na hUidre*, written not later than about 1100, are not encountered in Wales until the fourteenth century.

The century from about 1250 onwards is outstandingly the most important in the conservation of Welsh literature. It generated not only the most important lawbooks, the best texts of *Brut y Brenhinedd* and *Brut y Tywysogyon*, the Welsh version of the Roland cycle, and the best of the religious prose, but also the White Book of Rhydderch, which more or less established the canon of what came to be known as the 'Mabinogion', and four of the five great collections of pre-1300 Welsh poetry: the Black Book of Carmarthen, the Book of Aneirin, the Book of Taliesin, and the Hendregadredd Manuscript. In all, over fifty books in Welsh survive from this period.[24]

With few exceptions, Welsh vernacular books of the period 1250 to 1350, while their parchment and pigments may not be of the best nor the skills of the highest, conform to the regular practices of good contemporary book production in layout, ruling, and decoration. The script is now the international book hand of the day, Textura or 'Gothic', the angular child of Caroline minuscule. The merest traces of Insular tradition survive. Any strangeness seen by outsiders in a page of written Welsh is likely to be the result of letter-frequency rather than script: a prevalence of diagonal hair-strokes in the letters *h* and *y* often give the page a diagonal grain. The only peculiar letter-form is a development of *v* (commonly with the value of modern Welsh *w*) which resembles the figure 6, in vogue during the fourteenth century. At the beginnings of sections, scribes tried to observe the convention (more or less standard in Western Europe from the thirteenth to the fifteenth century) of alternating red and blue initials. But blue, expensive and hard to obtain, is often represented by outmoded green in Welsh books (even in some from the fourteenth century), or by a blue-green which may be a particularly Welsh feature; sometimes red alone had to suffice. Apart from the general occurrence of coloured initials, decoration in Welsh vernacular books is scarce. There seem to have been few hands capable of good decorative penwork. Miniatures are almost wholly absent.

Colophons are rare in the medieval books of Wales, as indeed in the books of all countries until the late Middle Ages. The circumstances of the making of a book — where, when, by whom, for whom — are seldom known. Two pre-1400 books in Welsh bear dated colophons. Ieuan Ysgolhaig ('Ieuan the Scholar' or 'Ieuan the Cleric') wrote NLW, Peniarth MS 9, containing the Welsh Roland cycle, in 1336; and in 1346 a good scribe who identifies himself as 'the Anchorite of Llanddewibrefi' compiled 'Llyfr yr Ancr' (The Book of the Anchorite), Oxford, Jesus College, MS 119, a collection of religious texts made for a named, layman, friend. Although neither of these scribes was necessarily working in a scriptorium, even the Anchorite did not work in complete isolation. His hand appears, with other collaborating hands, in the White Book of Rhydderch, and in NLW, Peniarth MSS 46 and 47, alongside a hand capable of excellent flourished penwork initials.[25] During this period, the regularity of scribal practice, an expectation that more expert hands would follow to add the coloured initials, and other small indications such as the word *correctus*, written by a corrector at the end of quires in NLW, Llanstephan MS 1, all suggest collaboration centred on scriptoria rather than private piece-work, even when the patron is a layman.

The association of the skills of a scriptorium with a sympathy for Welsh literature points towards the houses of the one monastic order which had enjoyed extensive patronage from the Welsh princes, the Cistercian. Although Whitland and Strata Florida were initially Norman foundations, they soon came under Welsh control and their daughter houses and grand-daughters were Welsh foundations.[26] Several became, at an early stage, the burial places of native princely families. By the mid-fourteenth century some Cistercian abbots were patrons of Welsh bards. A surprising degree of worldliness co-existed with the austere Cistercian ideals, providing native learning and culture with patronage of a sort hardly enjoyed since the waning of the *clasau*. The Hendregadredd Manuscript, probably put together at Strata Florida, is a striking example of a collaborative work, suggestive of an active scriptorium: during the first quarter of the fourteenth century, nineteen good scribes, near-contemporaries, made systematic additions to this carefully planned anthology of court poetry.[27]

Lawbooks, comprising a quarter of the survivors, are the most numerous Welsh medieval books to survive. Although Welsh law lost much of its force following the Statute of Wales (1284), it retained some validity as customary law. Books of Welsh law were still required by Welsh officials who helped their English superiors administer law in the Principality and in the Marcher lordships: indeed, all but a handful of the forty surviving lawbooks date from after 1284.[28] Some of the less elegant lawbooks may have been written by lawyers but most of the evidence points to production of lawbooks by the same, probably clerical, hands responsible for other vernacular books. The scribe who wrote the two earliest texts of *Brut y Brenhinedd*, the scribe of the Book of Taliesin, the chief scribe of the Red Book of Hergest, and other scribes associated with literary texts, all also copied lawbooks. An apparent specialist, scribe of three lawbooks, identified himself in a colophon as Gwilym Wasta (Was Da) of Y Drenewydd. Gwilym Wasta is named as a burgess of Newtown, Dinefwr, in 1302/3.[29]

Even allowing for reduction in size after cropping by later binders, the early Welsh books were mostly small; few are now more than 20 cm tall. As the producers of books in the vernacular acquired confidence, both size and scope became more ambitious. Although the fragmentary condition of many early books makes it difficult to establish their original extent, the first century and a half of production seems to show an increase from an average of some sixty leaves to one of about double this length. These larger compilations reflect greater editorial enterprise, exemplified by comprehensive anthologies of poetry such as the Book of Taliesin and the Hendregadredd Manuscript, and by the collections of secular and religious prose in the White Book of Rhydderch and the Book of the Anchorite. These developments reach their climax in the Red Book of Hergest, physically by far the largest (34 x 21 cm) and conceptually by far the most ambitious of medieval books in Welsh. The Red Book, probably written shortly before 1400 for Hopcyn ap Tomas of Ynysforgan, near Swansea, a leading Welsh patron, has been described as a library of Welsh literature in one volume.[30] It embraces a comprehensive and well-edited collection of narrative prose, both native stories (including the Mabinogion) and translations, poetry, historical texts, medicine, and grammar. Of known pre-1400 Welsh literature it lacks only religious prose and law (presumably because Hopcyn ap Tomas possessed these texts in other books), some early poetry (notably that in the Books of Aneirin and Taliesin, probably not available for copying), and the poetry of the previous two generations in the *cywydd* metre (probably regarded as too newfangled for inclusion in a collection of Welsh classics). The chief scribe of the Red Book, who identifies both himself and his master in a colophon to another book, was Hywel Fychan ap Hywel Goch of Buellt. He and the two other scribes who assisted in writing the Red Book, and eight other manuscripts, represent a last flourish of communal book production. But their one known employer was a layman. Book production had largely receded from the milieu of the monastic scriptoria.

Although the Red Book marked a peak in its grandeur of conception, the quality of its execution already marked a decline. In penmanship, clarity of script, regularity of procedure, and quality of decoration, many of the vernacular books written between 1250 and 1350 are superior. After the Red Book, a general decline in standards is even more noticeable; examples of fine book production become rare. The contrast in quality between vernacular books in Welsh and English, not remarkable before 1400, becomes an arresting one as the commercial production of vernacular books made rapid advances in England while Wales entered a lengthy depression after the devastating rising of Owain Glyndŵr. Book production in Wales between 1400 and 1550 appears to have become largely a do-it-yourself activity. Standards were maintained here and there: there is the excellent scribe who wrote NLW, Peniarth MS 263 and NLW, Wynnstay MS 36, but whose books waited in vain for the limner he had anticipated; there is the bard Lewys Glyn Cothi who, although no calligrapher, left a reputation as one of the best text scribes of his day; and there is another bard, Gutun Owain, notable more for his learning and productivity as a scribe than for the refinement of his script.[31] Probably more significant than these is Gwilym ap John ap Gwilym, a clumsy scribe who around 1500 copied in large format for Sir Rhys ap Thomas (1449-1525) the Welsh version of the legend of the Holy Grail (NLW, Mostyn MS 184): telling evidence that not even the most powerful Welshman of the day could command good scribal skills.

The use of paper as a substitute for parchment spread from Spain, where it had been introduced by the Arabs, through France and into England. Books on paper began to appear in France in the thirteenth century and in England in the fourteenth. The earliest use of paper in a surviving book in Welsh may be in NLW, Peniarth MS 50, part parchment and part paper, datable to about 1445; no other examples appear to be earlier. Paper was known in Wales considerably earlier: there are references to it in fourteenth-century Welsh literature but its use was probably restricted to records. During the second half of the fifteenth century paper gained respectability; about a third of the surviving Welsh books of this period are on paper. As elsewhere in Europe, a few conservatives despised or distrusted the new material; Lewys Glyn Cothi, for instance, was said never to have written on paper.[32] Beyond 1500 the parchment manuscript book becomes a rarity except in those classes of records where its use continued by force of tradition (as in court records) or legal requirement (as in parish registers).

The provincial old-fashionedness evident in the tardy acceptance in Wales of paper can also been seen in Welsh handwriting. Textura, the universal high-grade script of the later Middle Ages, is the script of almost all Welsh literature until 1400, contaminated here and there by cursive influence. A variety of cursive scripts, used for business purposes, had developed in western Europe since the twelfth century. The form of cursive which had come into common use in England in the thirteenth century, sometimes called court hand or documentary hand, is today generally referred to as Anglicana.[33] By the late thirteenth century Anglicana found occasional use among men of letters; by 1350 it was being used for English vernacular books. Its use in Wales for business and administrative documents must have paralleled that in England, but its appearance in books in Welsh came much later. Except in added entries, notably in the Hendregadredd Manuscript, Anglicana cannot be said to have gained recognition as a script worthy of literature until after 1400. Subsequently, written in varying degrees of formality it came into common use for books in Welsh, particularly those on paper.

Secretary script, a new cursive, came to England, evidently from France, towards the end of the fourteenth century. During the fifteenth century the two cursives were in concurrent use; cross-fertilization produced many hybrids. In the later fifteenth century Secretary comes into literary use in Wales, in a pure form or as an ingredient in a modified Anglicana. In its later form as 'Tudor Secretary' it became the common everyday script of Tudor times. In Wales, however, Anglicana survived in some quarters after it had vanished from literary use in England, notably in bardic circles. It is, for instance, the hand of Gruffudd Hiraethog (d. 1564), bard and teacher of bards. Tudor Secretary itself was rendered somewhat old-fashioned by the humanistic cursive script, the italic. While italic was already favoured in refined English Court and university circles in the first half of the sixteenth century, no significant use was made of it in Welsh manuscripts before 1550. The first Welsh literary figure to adopt italic was the pioneering humanist, William Salesbury (?1520-?99).

Illumination, the most eye-catching feature of many of the best-known medieval books, has only the most modest place in Welsh books. The few books of the Insular period show good initials of types common to that tradition but, given the doubts about the origin of the St Chad Gospels, the most notable undeniably Welsh achievement is that of the Llanbadarn Fawr books. During the great age of monastic book production there are many Welsh examples of the fine coloured 'arabesque' initials characteristic of the period, but no examples of illumination, or indeed of any miniatures or drawings. Official disapproval of illumination by the Cistercian order, the dominant order in Wales, could be one reason for this. The earliest example of an illustrated Welsh text is NLW, Peniarth MS 28, a mid-thirteenth-century Latin text of Welsh law, which includes drawings integrated into the text of the king and officials of his court, and of things of legal value.[34]

In thirteenth-century England, illumination, like book production in general, moved to a more commercial, predominantly urban milieu. There is no evidence that the patronage to support illuminators of high skills existed in Wales in the thirteenth or later centuries.[35] Books in Welsh or of Welsh interest were probably conceived with only modest decorative ambition; they must be appreciated on their own terms. An indication of the limitations is the use of gold in the decoration of only two vernacular manuscripts, BL, Cotton Cleopatra B.V, pt ii, and the first part of NLW, MS 7006D.

The only known illuminated book containing full-page miniatures which are apparently of Welsh origin is the Llanbeblig Hours (NLW, MS 17520A). The book was probably written in England in the late fourteenth century. It came to Caernarfon (in the parish of Llanbeblig) and an appropriate calendar was added, together with seven full-page miniatures which were grouped at the beginning of the book rather than being integrated into the text. The poor quality of the parchment used for these and the bold roughness of style are evidence in favour of local work. There seems to have been an artist and illuminator at work in Caernarfon shortly before 1400 who was also perhaps employed by the officials of the exchequer which was located in the town. The obit of Isabella Godynogh, dated 1413, which is entered in the calendar, connects the Llanbeblig Hours with a family in the neighbouring borough of Conwy.[36] The most remarkable drawings in fifteenth-century Welsh books accompany medical texts by Gutun Owain in NLW, Peniarth MS 27 i and NLW, Mostyn MS 88. These include figures of a 'zodiac man' and a 'blood-letting man', both good examples of internationally recognized types.[37]

The abiding creativity of Welsh medieval literature lay in its poetry. In essence the tradition was oral. Until the fifteenth century the writing of poetry in books belonged more to the realm of the antiquarian enthusiast than to that of the practising poet. Four of the great pre-1400 collections — the Black Book of Carmarthen, the Book of Aneirin, the Hendregadredd Manuscript, and the Red Book of Hergest — were original retrospective compilations and the fifth, the Book of Taliesin, was a fair copy of such a compilation. An exception is the third stratum of the Hendregadredd Manuscript which in its *ad hoc* additions constitutes, in rudimentary form, the first example of a 'house-book', a collection of poems associated with one man or family. The Hendregadredd poems associated with Ieuan Llwyd ab Ieuan were added contemporaneously in the second quarter of the fourteenth century, some conceivably being autograph. Such house-books became a feature of later Welsh manuscript tradition.

The golden age of Welsh poetry, the age of the *cywyddwyr*, extended from the mid-fourteenth to the mid-sixteenth century. Yet, excluding casual additions on blank pages or margins of other books, there is no collection of the poems of the *cywyddwyr* earlier in date than the mid-fifteenth century, a hundred years after the death of the greatest if not also the first of the tradition, Dafydd ap Gwilym. Possibly when the poetry was in its full vigour few, if any, bards or patrons felt the need to write down what the bards and *datgeiniaid* (professional declaimers) had by heart as part of their repertoire. There may also have been an element of deliberate restrictiveness amongst bards and *datgeiniaid* (who relied for their living on *clera,* touring the houses of their patrons) which inhibited the writing down of texts. On the other hand, the poetry was too recent to engage antiquarian interest.

It was in the second half of the fifteenth century that books of Welsh poetry became numerous: the earliest attempts to collect the poems of Dafydd ap Gwilym, and the earliest unquestionably autograph manuscripts of contemporary poets, including Lewys Glyn Cothi, Gwilym Tew, Dafydd Nanmor (perhaps), Hywel Dafi, Hywel Swrdwal, Huw Cae Llwyd, Dafydd Epynt, and, probably, Rhys Fardd. When the great age of the *cywyddwyr* began to wane in the sixteenth century, the collections of poetry become larger and more comprehensive as antiquarian zeal recovered yet more of the works of the early *cywyddwyr* and as anthologies became more commonly prized by cultured *uchelwyr* (gentry).

The book whose covers must have been most familiar to the medieval Welsh — to the medieval inhabitants of western Europe — was the missal in the parish church. A handful of books in the care of the parish priest must have been the only 'library' in many parishes. The stark scarcity of surviving liturgical books from Wales is testimony to the effectiveness of the destruction of service books ordered after the Reformation and subsequent losses under Elizabeth and during the Civil War. Only two manuscript missals (from the parishes of Crucadarn and Tre'r-gaer) and two printed missals (from Conwy and Llanbadarn Fawr) are known to survive.[38] Had manuscript missals or other service books survived in greater numbers, it might be easier to determine whether such books were produced locally or acquired from major centres of production such as Oxford or London. The one surviving monument of medieval Welsh liturgical music, the sung office of the feast of St David, is in the fourteenth-century 'Penpont Antiphonal' (NLW, MS 20541E) which was probably in use in the eastern part of the diocese of St David's, around Brecon; but its production is likely to have been English.[39] Further evidence of the great destruction of service books is provided by the fragments of these books which have survived through re-use as covers or in the bindings of later books. It is a fair presumption that fragments found in association with books in Welsh and with archives of Welsh origin were acquired locally. In a sample of sixty fragments of likely Welsh provenance found in such associations, over half are from liturgical books (twenty of them derived from missals).[40]

The book of private devotion in the late Middle Ages, and by far the most popular of all privately owned books, was the Book of Hours, often a finely illuminated article de luxe. The scant survival of specimens from Wales and the relative paucity of Welsh medieval probate records make it hard to generalize about the extent of ownership of Books of Hours. There seems to be no survivor which belonged to an unambiguously Welsh owner, as distinct from Welsh owners with English affiliations, such as the owners of the Llanbeblig Hours. The cheaper Books of Hours were mass-produced. Those encountered in Wales would mostly have come from England, or, like many of those in England, from Flanders. A vernacular version of part of the Book of Hours, the Hours of Our Lady, known as *Gwassanaeth Meir*, was produced in Wales. Probably of Dominican origin, it corresponds roughly to the English *Primer*. *Gwassanaeth Meir* probably did not enjoy wide currency; only two medieval manuscripts of the text survive.[41]

Very few medieval Welsh books would today be recognizable from the outside to their first owners. Only a single oak board and a few reported observations testify to metalled and jewelled covers. Only some half-dozen medieval bindings of any sort survive intact, together with a few bindings where medieval boards appear to survive under new covers. Most medieval Welsh books come from the period in which oak boards and whittawed leather covers were usual. Such, indeed, are the materials of the few surviving bindings, none of which are earlier than the fourteenth century. The names of some of the best-known Welsh books (although attested only from the sixteenth century) are consistent with the presumption that their covers were also of whittawed leather. Its off-white colour would explain the appellation 'Llyfr Gwyn' (White Book); a book with covers stained pinkish-red with kermes, as was popular in the thirteenth and fourteenth centuries, could become 'Llyfr Coch'; 'Llyfr Du' might be a book in black-stained leather, or a name bestowed when centuries of use had blackened a book's covers. Many of the smaller and thinner books were probably never, in the strict sense, bound. For some it is demonstrable, and for others likely, that their quires were originally tacked to limp parchment wrappers, or stabbed and tacked between wrappers. Some books may have survived even to modern times as loose quires.

The only institutional libraries in medieval Wales were ecclesiastical; the scale of losses from these has already been noted. Information about private libraries depends on evidence of ownership in surviving books, and on contemporary literature and documentation, particularly inventories. More often than not, relevant inventories relate to the clergy, professional users of books. There is, for instance, a list of over thirty titles (a considerable library for the time) belonging to John Trevor, bishop of St Asaph from 1346 to 1357.[42] There were also book owners amongst the laity. As early as the thirteenth century lay patrons of literature and learning in Wales (both men and women) commissioned Welsh translations of religious and secular texts. However, it is not until the fourteenth century that laymen can be associated with surviving books, on the basis of colophons and inscriptions and circumstantial evidence. The two most notable of these owners, both also outstanding patrons of the bards, are Rhydderch ab Ieuan of Parcrhydderch, near Llangeitho, associated with the White Book of Rhydderch, and Hopcyn ap Tomas, for whom the Red Book of Hergest was written.

Books in Welsh of the latter part of the fifteenth century show a sudden new interest in historical and antiquarian matters, one which was to flourish in the sixteenth century. Surviving books suggest that this interest was particularly alive in north-east Wales. Genealogical tracts and collections become numerous; heraldic treatises and armorials appear; pedigree-chronicles in roll form, fashionable in fifteenth-century England, developed in the sixteenth century into the pedigree-rolls so much favoured by the Welsh gentry;[43] *Brut y Brenhinedd* was re-edited in a shorter version known as 'Brut Tysilio'.[44] Two scribes involved in copying and editing genealogical and heraldic texts were Gutun Owain and Thomas ap Ieuan ap Deicws (*fl.* 1500-23), both of whom had connections with Valle Crucis Abbey. The same area and milieu produced two books of Latin grammatical tracts which reflect contemporary schooling at Valle Crucis and, perhaps, at Basingwerk: NLW, Peniarth MS 356, a composite book probably begun in the 1460s by Thomas Pennant, later abbot of Basingwerk, and NLW, MS 423, written by John Edwards of Chirk in the 1480s.[45] Hugh Pennant, brother of the abbot, made his own collection of Welsh poetry and antiquarian matter in NLW, Peniarth MS 182.

The dissolution of the greater monasteries in 1539 marked the end of an era. In Wales there was no large-scale rescue of the contents of their libraries, though a new interest in the past and a new critical regard for evidence were already beginning to appear in the 1540s in the writings of Sir John Prise (?1502-55) and in the antiquarian notes of Gruffudd Hiraethog. A more significant development of the 1540s was the appearance of the earliest printed books in Welsh, the first edited by Prise himself, others by the humanist scholar and reformer, William Salesbury. Yet the advent of the printed book did little to check the vigour of the manuscript tradition which began to abate only following the publication of editions of medieval Welsh literature in the eighteenth century: of Welsh law in William Wotton and Moses Williams's *Cyfreithieu Hywel Dda ac eraill, seu Leges Wallicae* (1730), of the poetry, notably of the *cywyddwyr*, in Rhys Jones's *Gorchestion Beirdd Cymru* (1773) and Owen Jones's and William Owen's *Barddoniaeth Dafydd ab Gwilym* (1789), and of the main body of early Welsh poetry and the *Brutiau* in the monumental *The Myvyrian Archaiology of Wales* (1801-7). This last publication, more than any other, could be said to symbolize the end of a manuscript tradition unbroken since the thirteenth century, but even well into the nineteenth century it remained far from extinct.

THE MEDIEVAL MANUSCRIPT

NOTES TO CHAPTER 2

Incomparably the best general guide to all aspects of medieval book-production in western Europe is Bernhard Bischoff, *Paläographie des römischen Altertums und das abenländischen Mittelalters*, 2nd edn (Berlin, 1986), published in English (with a careless index which, unlike the original German text, omits all references to Wales, see pp. 89 and 198-200) as *Latin palaeography: Antiquity and the Middle Ages*, trans. D. Ó Cróinín and D. Ganz (Cambridge, 1990). The only handbook for Insular Welsh manuscripts is W. M. Lindsay, *Early Welsh script* (Oxford, 1912). The only general treatment of later Welsh script is in N. Denholm-Young, *Handwriting in England and Wales* (Cardiff, 1954). J. J. G. Alexander, *A survey of manuscripts illuminated in the British Isles: Insular manuscripts 6th to 9th century* (London, 1978) is an admirable guide to the few Welsh and possibly Welsh illuminated books up to AD 1100.

The indispensable guide to vernacular Welsh manuscripts is the Royal Commission on Historical Manuscripts *Report on manuscripts in the Welsh language*, compiled by J. Gwenogvryn Evans, 2 vols (London, 1898-1910). To Gwenogvryn Evans we also owe publication of facsimiles of a number of the most important Welsh manuscripts: *Facsimile of the Black Book of Carmarthen* (Oxford, 1888); *Facsimile and text of the Book of Aneirin* (Pwllheli, 1908); *Facsimile and text of the Book of Taliesin* (Llanbedrog, 1910); and *Facsimile of the Chirk codex of the Welsh laws* (Llanbedrog, 1909). *Llyfr Aneirin: ffacsimile / Llyfr Aneirin: a facsimile*, ed. Daniel Huws (Aberystwyth, 1988), supersedes Gwenogvryn Evans's edition.

[1] For example, memoranda in French were added to the Book of Llandaf (NLW, MS 17110E) about 1350. NLW, Peniarth MS 7 was bound in thirteenth-century fragments of the French metrical romance *Berinus*, of Welsh provenance but probably not of Welsh origin (see *NLWJ*, 1 (1939-40), 103-5). English and Welsh occur side-by-side not infrequently after about 1450, for example, in miscellanies such as NLW, Peniarth MSS 50 and 53, and in two Latin school-books, NLW, Peniarth MS 356 and NLW, MS 423.

[2] N. R. Ker, *Medieval libraries of Great Britain*, 2nd edn (London, 1964); *Supplement to the second edition*, ed. A. G. Watson (London, 1987).

[3] *Registrum Anglie de libris doctorum ed auctorum veterum*, ed. R. A. B. Mynors, R. H. Rouse, and M. A. Rouse (London, 1991), pp. 289-91.

[4] J. J. G. Alexander, *A survey of manuscripts illuminated in the British Isles: Insular manuscripts 6th to 9th century* (London, 1978), no. 21; D. Brown, *The Lichfield Gospels* (London, 1982); G. Henderson, *From Durrow to Kells: the Insular Gospel-books 650-800* (London, 1987), pp. 122-9, P. McGurk, *Latin gospel books* (Amsterdam, [etc.], 1961), no. 16.

[5] W. M. Lindsay, *Early Welsh script* (Oxford, 1912), pp. 41-3; E. A. Lowe, *Codices Latini antiquiores*, II, 2nd edn (Oxford, 1972), no. 157; Alexander, no. 38; McGurk, no. 15; D. N. Dumville, *Liturgy and ecclesiastical history of late Anglo-Saxon England* (Woodbridge, 1992), p. 118; P. Sims-Williams, *Religion and literature in western England 600-800* (Cambridge, 1990), p. 181.

[6] *Registrum epistolarum fratris Johannis Peckham*, ed. C. T. Martin, Rolls Series 77, 3 vols (London, 1882-5), II, 725.

[7] *CSPD 1538*, 31 March 1538; D. Rhys Phillips, 'The Twrog MS', *JWBS*, 1 (1910-15), 183-7.

[8] D. Huws, 'The making of *Liber Landavensis*', *NLWJ*, 25 (1987-8), 133-60 (pp. 133-4, 146-7).

[9] *Saint Dunstan's classbook from Glastonbury*, ed. R. W. Hunt (Amsterdam, 1961); Michael Lapidge, 'Latin learning in Dark Age Wales', *Proceedings of the seventh International Congress of Celtic Studies, Oxford, 1983*, ed. D. Ellis Evans, John G. Griffith, and E. M. Jope (Oxford, 1986), pp. 91-107.

[10] On Insular script in general see B. Bischoff, *Latin palaeography: antiquity and the Middle Ages*, trans. D. Ó Cróinín and D. Ganz (Cambridge, 1990); *A palaeographer's view: the selected writings of Julian Brown*, ed. Janet Bately, Michelle P. Brown, and Jane Roberts (London, 1993). On Welsh Insular script, W. M. Lindsay remains the main guide. I am grateful to Dr David Dumville for sight of the draft introduction of his *Manuscripts of Wales and Cornwall, A.D. 800-1150*, a work which should meet a long-felt need; meanwhile, see his remarks in 'English square minuscule script: the background and earliest phases', *Anglo-Saxon England*, 16 (1987), 147-79 (pp. 159-61).

[11] Dumville, *Manuscripts*.

[12] Dafydd Jenkins and Morfydd E. Owen, 'The Welsh marginalia in the Lichfield Gospels', *CMCS*, 5 (1983), 37-66; 7 (1984), 91-120.

[13] Michael Lapidge, 'The study of Latin texts in late Anglo-Saxon England: the evidence of Latin glosses', in *Latin and the vernacular languages in early medieval Britain*, ed. N. Brooks (Leicester, 1982), pp. 99-140 (pp. 111-13); also his 'Latin learning'; Ifor Williams, 'Tri englyn y Juvencus', *BBCS*, 6 (1931-3), 101-10; his 'Naw englyn y Juvencus', *BBCS*, 6 (1931-3), 205-24, and his 'The computus fragment', *BBCS*, 3 (1926-7), 245-72. Both Williams articles are available in English translation in his, *The beginnings of Welsh poetry*, ed. R. Bromwich (Cardiff, 1972), pp. 89-121.

[14] H. J. Lawlor, *The psalter and martyrology of Ricemarch*, Henry Bradshaw Society, Vols 47-48 (1914); Michael Lapidge, 'The Welsh-Latin poetry of Sulien's family', *SC*, 8/9 (1973-4), 68-106; Alexander, no. 75. Gillian Conway, 'Towards a cultural context for the eleventh-century Llanbadarn manuscripts', *Ceredigion*, (13(1) (1997), 9-28. Nancy Edwards, '11th-century Welsh illuminated manuscripts: the nature of the Irish connection', in *From the Isles of the North: early medieval art in Ireland and Britain*, ed. Cormac Bourke (Belfast, 1995), pp. 147-55; Timothy Graham, 'The poetic, scribal and artistic work of Ieuan ap Sulien in Corpus Christi College, Cambridge, MS 199: addenda and assessment', *NLWJ*, 29 (1995-6), 241-56.

[15] Alison Peden, 'Science and philosophy in Wales at the time of the Norman conquest: a Macrobius manuscript from Llanbadarn', *CMCS*, 2 (1981), 21-45 and plates I to VI; Lapidge, 'Welsh-Latin poetry'.

[16] Cambridge, Corpus Christi College, MS 153 (Martianus Capella), fol. 17[r]. See W. M. Lindsay, plate IX and pp. 19-21; T. A. M. Bishop, 'The Corpus Martianus Capella', *TCBS*, 4 (1964-8), 257-75; Dumville, *Liturgy*, pp. 116-17.

[17] Both A and B, the main scribes of *Liber Landavensis*, make occasional use of Insular forms of letters: on these scribes see J. Gwenogvryn Evans, *The text of the Book of Llan Dâv* (Oxford, 1893, reprinted Aberystwyth, 1979) and Huws, 'The making of *Liber Landavensis*'. On Cotton Faustina C.I, see Peden, and on Peniarth 540 see D. Huws, 'A Welsh manuscript of Bede's *De natura rerum*', *BBCS*, 27 (1976-8), 491-504.

[18] R. B. Patterson, 'The author of the "Margam Annals": early thirteenth-century Margam Abbey's Compleat Scribe', *Anglo-Norman Studies*, 14 (1992), 197-210 (pp. 203, 209).

[19] H. D. Emanuel, *The Latin texts of the Welsh laws* (Cardiff, 1967); T. M. Charles-Edwards, *The Welsh laws* (Cardiff, 1989).

[20] Kathleen Hughes, 'The Welsh Latin chronicles: *Annales Cambriae* and related texts', *PBA*, 59 (1973), 233-58, reprinted in her *Celtic Britain in the early Middle Ages* (Woodbridge, 1980).

[21] The earliest manuscripts of the two versions of *Brut y Tywysogion* come, respectively, from Valle Crucis and, probably, Strata Florida, while the earliest manuscript of the more distantly related chronicle, *Brenhinedd y Saesson*, also comes from Valle Crucis. For the texts, all edited and translated by Thomas Jones, see *Brut y Tywysogyon: Peniarth MS 20 version* (Cardiff, 1941, 1952); *Brut y Tywysogyon: Red Book of Hergest version* (Cardiff, 1955), and *Brenhinedd y Saesson* (Cardiff, 1971).

[22] Notably, a high proportion of manuscripts of the 'First Variant version' have Welsh associations. See Julia C. Crick, *The Historia Regum Britannie of Geoffrey of Monmouth: III: a summary catalogue of the manuscripts* (Cambridge, 1989); Neil Wright, *The Historia Regum Britannie of Geoffrey of Monmouth: II: the First Variant version* (Cambridge, 1988).

[23] B. F. Roberts, *Brut y Brenhinedd: Llanstephan MS. 1 version* (Dublin, 1971); also his 'Geoffrey of Monmouth, *Historia Regum Britanniae* and *Brut y Brenhinedd*', in *The Arthur of the Welsh: the Arthurian legend in medieval Welsh literature*, ed. R. Bromwich, A. O. H. Jarman, and B. F. Roberts (Cardiff, 1991), pp. 97-116.

[24] D. Huws, *Llyfrau Cymraeg 1250-1400*, Darlith Syr John Williams 1992 (Aberystwyth, 1993). Also published in *NLWJ*, 28 (1993-4), 1-21. See now also his *Five ancient books of Wales*, H. M. Chadwick Memorial Lecture 6 (Cambridge, 1996).

[25] D. Huws, 'Llyfr Gwyn Rhydderch', *CMCS*, 21 (1991), 1-37 and plates I to IV (pp. 9, 12-13).

[26] On the Welsh Cistercians see Glanmor Williams, *The Welsh church from Conquest to Reformation*, revised edn (Cardiff, 1976); F. G. Cowley, *The monastic order in south Wales, 1066-1349* (Cardiff,

27 D. Huws, 'Llawysgrif Hendregadredd', *NLWJ*, 22 (1981-2), 1-26; T. M. Charles-Edwards and P. Russell, 'The Hendregadredd Manuscript and the orthography and phonology of Welsh in the early fourteenth century', *NLWJ*, 28 (1993-4), 419-62.

28 The manuscripts are conveniently listed in T. M. Charles-Edwards, *The Welsh laws*, pp. 100-2.

29 Morfydd E. Owen and Dafydd Jenkins, 'Gwilym Was Da', *NLWJ*, 21 (1979-80), 429-30. On the Book of Taliesin scribe, see Marged Haycock, 'Llyfr Taliesin', *NLWJ*, 25 (1987-8), 357-86.

30 On the Red Book and its patron and scribes see G. J. Williams, *Traddodiad llenyddol Morgannwg* (Cardiff, 1948), pp. 11-14, 147-8; B. F. Roberts, 'Un o lawysgrifau Hopcyn ap Tomas o Ynys Dawy', *BBCS*, 22 (1966-8), 223-8; Prys Morgan, 'Glamorgan and the Red Book', *Morgannwg*, 22 (1978), 42-60; G. Charles-Edwards, 'The scribes of the Red Book', *NLWJ*, 20 (1979-80), 246-56; Christine James, '"Llwyr wybodau, llên a llyfrau": Hopcyn ap Tomas a'r traddodiad llenyddol Cymraeg', in *Cwm Tawe*, ed. Hywel Teifi Edwards (Llandysul, 1993), pp. 4-44.

31 On Lewis Glyn Cothi as scribe, see E. D. Jones, 'A Welsh *pencerdd's* manuscripts', *Celtica*, 5 (1960), 17-27; on Gutun Owain's manuscripts see Thomas Roberts, 'Llawysgrifau Gutun Owain a thymor ei oes', *BBCS*, 15 (1952-4), 99-109.

32 E. D. Jones, p. 17.

33 The term 'Anglicana' has been in general use since the appearance of M. B. Parkes, *English cursive book hands 1250-1500* (Oxford, 1969).

34 D. Huws, *Peniarth 28: darluniau o lyfr cyfraith Hywel Dda / Illustrations from a Welsh lawbook* (Aberystwyth, 1988).

35 The Bangor Cathedral pontifical, written, it seems, for Bishop Anian II (1309-28) includes one fine full-page miniature, but it has been recognised as the work of an artist active in London and East Anglia. On the pontifical see N. R. Ker, *Medieval manuscripts in British libraries* (Oxford, 1969+), II, 48-53; L. F. Sandler, *A survey of manuscripts illuminated in the British Isles: Gothic manuscripts 1285-1385* (London, 1986), II, 77-8, and illustrations 177-8 and 181; Sally Harper, 'The Bangor Pontifical: a pontifical of the use of Salisbury', *Welsh Music History/Hanes Cerddoriaeth Cymru*, 2 (1997), 65-99.

36 The Llanbeblig Hours is described in G. F. Warner, *A descriptive catalogue of illuminated manuscripts in the library of C. W. Dyson Perrins* (Oxford, 1920), pp. 59-61. Isabella wife of William Godynogh is referred to in Bangor, University College of North Wales, Baron Hill documents 2111-12 (dated 1373 and 1387); see also documents 2118 and 2125-7. All these documents relate to Conwy.

37 Reproduced in *Drych yr oesoedd canol*, ed. Nesta Lloyd and Morfydd E. Owen (Cardiff, 1986), pp. 143, 145. For medical illustration see P. M. Jones, *Medieval medical miniatures* (London, 1984).

38 The manuscript missals are Oxford, All Souls, MS 11, and Hereford Cathedral, MS P.3, iv. On the printed missals see S. M. Harris, 'A Llanbadarn Fawr calendar', *Ceredigion*, 2 (1952-5), 19-26, and D. Huws, 'The earliest Bangor missal', *NLWJ*, 27 (1991-2), 113-30.

39 O. T. Edwards, *Matins, Lauds and Vespers for St David's Day* (Cambridge, 1990); also his *National Library of Wales MS. 20541E: the Penpont Antiphonal*. Institute of Medieval Music; Facsimile No. 22 (Ottawa, 1997).

40 Based on an inchoate list of fragments, to which the Peniarth MSS are the main contributors.

41 B. F. Roberts, *Gwassanaeth Meir* (Cardiff, 1961).

42 The inventory of John Trevor's books is reproduced from BL, Add. MS 23459 in S. H. Cavanaugh, 'A study of books privately owned in England 1300-1450' (unpublished doctoral thesis, University of Pennsylvania, 1980), pp. 879-81.

43 P. C. Bartrum, 'Notes on the Welsh genealogical manuscripts', *THSC*, (1968), pp. 63-98, his 'Further notes on the Welsh genealogical manuscripts', *THSC*, (1976), pp. 102-18, and his 'Notes on the Welsh genealogical manuscripts (Part III)', *THSC* (1988), pp. 37-46. M. P. Siddons, *The development of Welsh heraldry*, 3 vols (Aberystwyth, 1989-93), I.

44 B. F. Roberts, *Brut Tysilio* (Swansea, 1980).

45 David Thomson, *A descriptive catalogue of Middle English grammatical texts* (New York and London, 1979), pp.103-31; and his 'Cistercians and schools in late medieval Wales', *CMCS*, 3 (1982), 76-80.

CHAPTER 3

THE RENAISSANCE AND REFORMATION

Glanmor Williams

WALES, like other European countries during the fifteenth century, was profoundly affected by changes which modified many of the distinctive features of earlier medieval society and culture. Institutions and ideals which had dominated the medieval scene, like the feudal aristocracy, chivalry, the crusades, the Empire, the Papacy, the religious orders, the clerical monopoly of education and learning, and scholastic philosophy, underwent marked decline or drastic change. Their former supremacy was being called into question by a rise in the power of the lay state, an increase in trade, the spread of a money economy, the growth of towns and cities, the enhanced importance of merchants and lawyers, the growing awareness of nationality, and the greater significance of vernacular tongues.[1] Particularly far-reaching in its effects had been the wider dispersion of formal education among the laity, to such an extent that by 1500 something like half the urban population of Europe is estimated to have been literate. To meet the growing demand for instruction, a large number of schools had been opened. Thirty-three new universities were added between 1400 and 1500 to the forty-five already in existence, and between 1500 and 1550 nearly half as many more.[2] Another consequence of the extended diffusion of literacy was the vastly enlarged demand for reading material which made the fifteenth century a golden age for scribes and copyists.

Between c.1470 and 1520 there occurred four major developments whose repercussions could with truth have been said to be revolutionary: the emergence of 'new' monarchies; the appearance of the printing-press; the spread of the Renaissance from Italy; and the outbreak of the Reformation. All four were to be closely linked in a number of respects.

A number of European countries, most notably perhaps Spain, Portugal, France, Sweden, Denmark, and England, were now ruled by monarchies which, if not strictly new, were at least rejuvenated. Furthermore, within many of the individual polities of much-fragmented Germany and Italy the same kind of centralization of power could be observed. Everywhere, the ruler was becoming the focus of loyalty, authority, and jurisdiction among his subjects, creaming off the growth in trade and wealth to increase his revenue from tolls and taxation, harnessing the talents and allegiance of emergent social classes, exploiting the advent of wider education and training, making use of the new techniques of communication and propaganda provided by printing, and alert to the opportunities of extending secular authority over the Church.

To meet the huge demand for all kinds of reading material to which the spread of literacy had given rise, a new technology was created which enabled documents to be reproduced far more quickly, cheaply, and accurately.[3] By 1450, Johann Gutenberg, a goldsmith of Mainz, had become the first European to devise an effective method for printing books from moveable type, on a commercial scale, for profit. Printing replaced the age-old, laborious, and now inadequate handicraft of one-off transcription. Whereas it took about eighteen months for a scribe to prepare a single manuscript copy of the Bible, it was now possible to print hundreds, even thousands, of copies in the same time and at much less expense per copy. The new invention spread rapidly from Germany to other countries: Italy (1465), Switzerland (1467), France (1470), the Low Countries (1470), Spain (1473), Poland (1474), and England (1476). Since the object of printers was to sell commodities and offer services, nearly all their workshops were set up in populous cities along the major trade routes. By 1500, eighty presses had been set up in Italy, sixty-four in Germany, and forty-five in France. Estimates of their total output depend on assumptions concerning edition sizes:[4] at least eight million and perhaps as many as twenty million books were produced during the first half-century of printing — far more than had been copied by hand since the time of the Roman Empire. Printing revolutionized the communication of ideas and stimulated contemporary trends: it markedly extended literacy, the demand for reading materials, and the practice of private silent reading. It encouraged the production of books in the vernacular tongues as well as the classical languages; seventy-four of the ninety books published by Caxton in England were in English. The governments of the day, too, were quick to enhance their authority by printing proclamations and laws, thereby ensuring their speedier circulation. Of even greater significance was the extraordinary assistance the printing press rendered the Renaissance and the Reformation; without it, neither would have been broadcast as extensively or as speedily, or have achieved such a lasting impact.

The origins of the Renaissance were, admittedly, at least a century older than the invention of printing; but its rapid progression outside Italy not only coincided with the emergence of the printing presses but was also dramatically reinforced by them. Renaissance scholarship brought to Europe north of the Alps the revival and diffusion of texts in the classical languages of Latin, Greek, and Hebrew and a vastly extended and improved knowledge of those languages. Nor did the process end with the classics; from them the same emphasis on a more correct and elegant use of language spread to the vernaculars. From the Italian *volgare*, it soon percolated to the other major European languages, each of which aspired to attain the same elevated status as the classics. As the Welsh scholar, William Thomas (d. 1554), observed: 'To triumph in civil knowledge the means must be that each man first covet to flourish in his own natural tongue'[5] (by which he meant English). Thomas was only one of thousands to participate in a brisk exchange of scholars between Italy and other countries; one of the main reasons for enticing the Italians elsewhere being to promote the adoption of humanist skills and knowledge in government and polite society. But perhaps the outstanding benefit conferred by the Renaissance on northern Europe was to install the New Learning there as the handmaiden of religion. Pre-eminent among northern humanists in the first two decades of the sixteenth century was the incomparable Erasmus, described by William Salesbury as 'the most learned, eloquent, and recognized teacher in all Christendom of our age and many ages before'.[6] Erasmus seized upon the priceless advantage of the printing press to scholarship and made unprecedentedly effective use of it. He insisted on returning to the sources of Christian knowledge, supreme among which, of course, were the Scriptures. His Greek New Testament of 1516 and Latin translation of it constituted one of the great pinnacles of the golden years between

1480 and 1520, which may justly be regarded as the era of the *preparatio evangelica*, when scholars in many parts of Europe applied themselves with optimistic zeal to study and edit the Scriptures in their original languages.[7]

Such an emphasis was perfectly compatible with outspoken demands for the reform of the Church from within. Erasmus and men like him cherished a burning desire to put Scripture at the heart of religious life and strip the Church of the superstition, ignorance, and corruption which sullied it; in Spain, for instance, Cardinal Ximenes purified the Church in a thoroughgoing but unswervingly conservative campaign for reform. Such attitudes continued to inspire the Catholic Reformation throughout the sixteenth century.[8] Nevertheless, the impact of the Renaissance might equally well prepare the way for a more root-and-branch programme of reform which it would prove impossible to contain within the framework of the existing Church. It could herald the advent of the arch-rebel Martin Luther, or of Ulrich Zwingli, who arrived at his equally explosive conclusions independently of the Wittenberg reformer. Their core doctrines of justification by faith, the priesthood of all believers, and the irrelevance of good works in achieving salvation, threw down a challenge to the Church which awakened sympathetic chords in many countries. What gave their heretical clarion-calls such widely echoing resonance was the ready availability of the printing press and the general incidence of literacy. Whereas before Luther's protest in 1517 an average of forty books had been published in Germany each year, as a result mainly of his challenge that number had increased twelve-fold to 495 in 1525. Luther justified his teachings on the basis of scriptural authority and hastened to translate the Bible into German in order to reach the widest audience. By the time of his death in 1546, 377 editions of his Bible had been published, and before the end of the sixteenth century a printed Bible was available in many European languages. Without it the Reformation would never have succeeded so quickly or lasted so long; though it is as well to remember also that it would not have sparked off a conflagration that was allowed to sweep like fire through stubble without the backing of a number of secular authorities — kings, electors, princelings, or city-states. These rulers and the élites who allied with them saw in the Reformation an opportunity to realize their religious ambitions and also to extend their political and economic power. Conversely, some particularly powerful monarchs, like those of Spain or France, already exercised such control over religion within their kingdoms as to have every incentive to preserve the status quo in the Church.

One of the kingdoms in which the major tendencies of the age could clearly be discerned in ferment was England. Ever since the Yorkist Edward IV had secured the throne in 1471, the monarchy had been seeking to intensify its authority, a process which continued just as vigorously under the Tudors. Tudor monarchs exploited the same instruments and personnel to achieve power as other contemporary rulers: tightening their control over the king's council, courts, Parliament, and the Church; domesticating the aristocracy and encouraging the 'middling men' — gentry, lawyers, merchants, and clerics. They fostered new cultural and intellectual trends at court and university; and it was no accident that Erasmus should have been so warm an admirer of Henry VIII's patronage of the Renaissance. Royal government tightened its hold over the press and employed its own authors and publicists, especially when Henry and his ministers dismantled papal jurisdiction and replaced it with the royal supremacy. To safeguard the augmented royal authority and protect the infant Anglican Church, the king's government aimed to project itself more widely — to the neighbouring kingdom of Scotland, to Ireland where royal authority was hardly more than nominal, to the Channel Islands and Calais (part of the kingdom until 1557), and also to those parts of his domain where the king's jurisdiction was less complete than a centralizing monarch might have wished — the north of England, the west country, and Wales.

Wales lay on the periphery not only of the English kingdom but also of Europe.[9] Its communities, like those of the rest of the 'Celtic Fringe', were rural, kin-based, and mainly self-sufficient. An upland country, divided by hills and moorland, with difficult communications between one part and another, and a largely empty centre, its economy was that of a poor, mixed and mainly pastoral farming, sustaining only a sparse and dispersed population. Towns were small, their population ranging from about two hundred and fifty to the largest, Carmarthen, at 2,000. Commerce depended on small-scale, seaborne foreign and coastal exchanges, and on a growing cattle and wool trade overland with England. There were few influential resident aristocrats, successful merchants, or wealthy households. Having no capital, court, or university of their own, Welshmen who aspired to make their careers in such milieux were obliged to migrate to England, and did so in considerable numbers.[10] Welsh literature and culture remained primarily a public and social affair, rather than a private and individual experience as in more urbanized countries. In so far as literary and intellectual activities were not conducted by word of mouth, they were transmitted by manuscript. There was no printing press in Wales, nor likely to be one for centuries, as long as printing was a relatively capital-intensive industry, requiring funds to purchase plant and materials and to await a return on investment, not to mention its dependence for patrons, authors, markets, and forward planning on powerful courts, large towns, centres of scholarship, and flourishing trade routes. The first Welsh printed book, *Yny lhyvyr hwnn*, would not appear until 1546,[11] though it is worth noting that a number of Welsh authors had ventured into print long before then in languages other than their own and would continue to do so.[12]

Although Wales had finally lost its political independence in 1282-3, it had not been fully integrated into the English kingdom and still remained divided between the Principality shires of the north and west and the Marcher lordships of the south and east. From 1471 onwards, however, it was brought more completely within the orbit of the English monarchy. Psychologically, that process went on apace from 1485, when Henry VII, though only one-quarter Welsh, was regarded by the Welsh by virtue of his Welsh birth as the vindicator of ancient prophecies that a British (Welsh) king would rule the island again. But the major transformation was brought about by Henry VIII's Acts of Union, 1536-43,[13] which unified Wales within its own borders and incorporated it fully within the realm by giving it representation in Parliament. The Acts established throughout Wales the contemporary English systems of law, lawcourts, shire administration, and local government personnel such as sheriffs and justices of the peace. They also made English the language of law and government and insisted that every person holding office in Wales should be able to speak English. At much the same time as these political and legal changes were being implemented, the Reformation was being imposed in Wales by statute; and an English Bible, and later in Edward VI's reign an English Prayer Book, were being introduced into Welsh parish churches.

It would be a grievous misinterpretation, nonetheless, to conceive of early-Tudor Wales as no more than a moribund political and cultural entity being drawn into the modernity and enlightenment of a progressive kingdom. On the contrary, it possessed its own autonomous and lively culture. Its vital literary tradition, dating back for many centuries, was the object of intense and universal pride on the part of a professional order of littérateurs and their patrons among a ruling élite who regarded their language and its literature as the distinctive tokens of their nationhood and the guarantees of its continued existence. It was the classic verse of the poets which had kept these historic values evergreen among the gentry — the *uchelwyr* — of Wales. This heritage was transmitted from one generation to another through the agency of the bardic schools whose tutors not only educated intending poets but also many clerics and sons of the gentry. In addition to the main body of *cynghanedd* poetry there probably existed a considerable body of verse composed in what were known as the 'free metres' by poets of inferior rank, whose effusions were not considered worthy of preservation in writing until the sixteenth century.

The large and varied corpus of literary compositions noted in Chapters 1 and 2 was increasingly committed to writing between c.1450 and 1600, when manuscripts proliferated to keep pace with growing demand and a manuscript was as valid a literary medium for an author as a printed book. The treasures contained in these manuscripts were as enthusiastically snapped up by laymen with literary tastes and inclinations as by leading monasteries such as Neath, Strata Florida, or Aberconwy. Nonetheless, when the monasteries were dissolved in 1536-40 it was a serious blow to the copying and preservation of manuscripts no less than to the patronage of poets, even though leading Welsh families like the Prises of Brecon, the Stradlings of St Donat's, the Owens of Henllys, the Wynns of Gwedir, or the Salusburys of Llweni, were eager to safeguard many monastic manuscripts. To most Welsh literati of the age, the traditional oral and manuscript methods of preservation and circulation of literature may perhaps have appeared perfectly adequate. Even when some anonymous translator rendered parts of William Tyndale's New Testament into Welsh, it had to remain, for the time being at least, in manuscript form, though whether that was because of limited demand or financial constraints, or both, it is now impossible to tell.[14] The translator was one of many in Wales for whom publication would proceed no further; even the most assiduous publisher of Welsh books, William Salesbury, does not seem to have been unwilling to leave two major works, 'Llysieulyfr Meddyginiaethol' (a herbal) and 'Llyfr Rhetoreg' (a study of rhetoric), in manuscript.[15] Similarly, circles of upper-class connoisseurs, active in places like Dyffryn Clwyd, the Vale of Glamorgan, or north Pembrokeshire, were happy to exchange literary and antiquarian manuscripts with one another. Elegant manuscripts might, indeed, seem to sixteenth-century eyes to be the equivalent of designer-goods while printed books bore the stigma of plebeian mass-production.[16]

In addition to their enthusiasm for indigenous culture, a number of Welshmen were attracted to educational institutions and opportunities in England: at Court, in London and other English cities; and at the universities, grammar schools, and the Inns of Court.[17] No fewer than 3,000 Welsh students entered Oxford, Cambridge, and the Inns of Court between *c*.1545 and 1642.[18] The ablest among them avidly imbibed the cultural mores of the period: those of the printed book, the Renaissance, and the Reformation. Some were keen to publish books on their own account, like Richard Whitford (*c*.1470-1541), originally from Flintshire, a graduate, monk of Syon, and close friend of Erasmus and Thomas More, who wrote a number of English books in defence of the old faith. Two other Welsh authors, also strongly attracted to Renaissance ideals but equally firm in their attachment to the papal church, were Edward Powell (?1478-1540) and John Gwynedd (?1490-?1562).[19] By contrast, two young Welshmen early drawn into the Protestant camp via the Renaissance were George Constantine (*c*.1500-?60), dealer in Protestant books in the 1520s, and William Salesbury, the ablest scholar of all among early-Tudor Welshmen.

Salesbury was also the most percipient of that small group of Welshmen who, having been brought up to appreciate keenly the intrinsic merits of their own cultural patrimony and then learning to savour to the full the criteria of the new age, became all too vividly aware of the latter's perils and possibilities for the former. On the one hand, they readily sensed the dangers. There was a risk of Welshmen abandoning their own language in favour of English: as Gruffudd Hiraethog observed, '*And all those who tarry any time away from home abhor and forget the language of their native land and mother tongue.*'[20] English was indeed a language easily acquired by Welshmen. It was the medium of law and government, and of church services after 1549. It was regularly heard in the market towns of Wales; going to England was easy and attractive; many books were published in English; and it was the language of grammar school, university, and Inn of Court. Additionally, it was the passport to polite and polished society and was becoming one of the recognized European languages of learning, extending its scope with astonishing speed and diversity. The temptation for a Welshman to write and publish in English, and thereby to create a reputation for himself, must have been very difficult to resist, especially in view of the printing presses in England, its many wealthy patrons, and its much more numerous and prosperous book-buying public. Personal and professional opportunities drew some of the most talented Welshmen there to seek a career, notably lawyers and clerics, the ones most likely to embark upon a career of authorship. Finally, there was a persistent and deeply worrying tendency, commented on by a number of sixteenth-century Welsh writers, for their compatriots to be deficient in appreciating the great antiquity and distinctiveness of their language and its potential as a literary and intellectual medium. Salesbury sometimes despaired that his fellow-Welshmen would ever '*make natural provision for the protection of the patriotic good of the same language. Oh! to what end did I speak of patriotism, since a Welshman today does not know what patriotism consists of.*'[21] Ifan Llwyd ap Dafydd was equally scathing on the unmistakable temptation for many Welshmen to learn English: '*we all neglect the British language and apply ourselves to learn a foreign tongue, for Welsh is the strangest thing under heaven in its own country.*'[22]

On the other hand, this group was intensely conscious of the opportunities for revival and renewal which the New Learning offered. Welsh was, in their view, potentially better placed than almost any European language to rank with the languages of the classical world. Its champions believed, and were encouraged to do so by leading English scholars like John Leland or John Bale, that since the origins of Welsh went back to the Tower of Babel and its literature to the Druids, it was as worthy of admiration as Latin, Greek, or Hebrew.[23] The anonymous author of *Y Drych Cristianogawl* (1585) was one of those who had no doubt that '*comparing languages together I do not see any one of the other common languages of which Welsh is not the equal of the best of them [...] and indeed excelling many other languages in a number of respects that I could name.*'[24] They believed that its astonishing preservation under divine Providence through so many vicissitudes down the centuries clearly indicated that God had some unique mission in store for it. Moreover, they knew that among their countrymen many were literate in their own tongue only and constituted a potentially influential public for printed books if appropriate provision were made for them. In the introduction to *Yny llyvyr hwnn*, Sir John Prise, deploring the absence of printed books in Welsh, urged the '*many Welshmen who could read Welsh but not a word in English or Latin*'[25] to take advantage of God's great gift of printing as other nations had done.

Of course, it was not lost on these enthusiasts that if Welsh were to capitalize on its opportunities it must measure up to the desiderata of the new age. Printed books would have to replace manuscripts as soon as practicable. Cherished possessions though manuscripts might be, they were far too few in number and too restricted in circulation to cope with current needs. Manuscripts that were jealously guarded by their owners during their lifetime might subsequently suffer neglect and abuse: children making dolls of them, shopwives wrapping spices in them, or tailors using them to make patterns.[26] Another writer observed in the mid-1560s how liable manuscripts were to damage as a result of carelessness, snivelling noses, dirty hands, candle-grease, damp, or smoke.[27] Only an abundance of printed volumes would adequately serve the purposes of communication in a rapidly changing world. They would certainly be needed to introduce to the mother tongue the immensely improved knowledge of language resources and structures associated with Renaissance scholarship, which was being given to the world in the shape of dictionaries, grammars, works of literary criticism, and the like. Finally, and probably most urgently of all, pride of place had to be given to the indispensable role in the reformed religion which a Welsh Bible and service book were required to fill. The vernacular Bible, which Welsh humanists (mistakenly) believed to have been the foundation of the beliefs of the Ancient Britons, must once more be made freely available in a 'second flowering'.[28] This was the ultimate test: unless Welsh could successfully respond to the call for a printed Bible, then most of those who spoke it would find the reformed services unintelligible and the language inadequate to swim with the fast-flowing tides of the Renaissance and the Reformation. Among the minority who were alert to these issues, none set them forth more clearly or starkly than Salesbury. For him the religion, language, and literature of Wales were standing at a fateful cross-roads. One route pointed to a bright and progressive future with all that was most dynamic and forward-looking in Renaissance and Reformation Europe. The other, along which an unchanged Wales was doomed to stagger, encumbered by the dead weight of an outmoded religious and cultural lifestyle, led only to stagnation and sterility. As early as 1547 he passionately exhorted his countrymen to appeal to the king for permission to obtain the Scriptures in their own language:

> *unless you wish to abandon completely the faith of Christ, unless you wish to have nothing at all to do with Him, and unless you wish entirely to forget and neglect His*

will, obtain the scripture in your own tongue as once it existed among your happy ancestors, the ancient Britons.[29]

Nor was it Protestants alone who were aware of the crisis. Roman Catholic scholars too, like Gruffydd Robert (pre-1532 - post-1598) or Morus Clynnog (1525-81), were no less captivated by the prospect of the gains which the Renaissance stood to confer upon the language.[30] True, they adhered staunchly to the old Church and its Latin rites and could not therefore place the same emphasis on the need for a vernacular Bible and service, but they fully appreciated how vital it was to indoctrinate the faithful by means of their mother tongue and stressed the importance of printed catechisms and other works of instruction in Welsh. Nor were they less insistent that the Welsh language should be brought in line with the linguistic evolution common to Renaissance Europe. However much each group might differ in its interpretation of doctrine, both set to work with a will to provide, as far as they could, a new-style printed literature in Welsh.

Those who prescribed such a task for themselves were confronted by formidable obstacles.[31] The absence of a printing press in Wales obliged Welsh authors to look to presses outside their native land. For Protestants, publishing with the consent and goodwill of the established regime in State and Church, that ordinarily meant arriving at an agreement with London printers. But having to employ compositors who knew little or no Welsh, and being obliged to spend long spells in London to see their books through to publication, 'owing to the Welsh language being so hard and unusual a language to set for the press',[32] added hugely to the cost of printing and to the number of printer's errors.[33] Roman Catholic authors, who had to contend with the fearsomely strict controls imposed by a rigorous press censorship,[34] found conditions even more daunting. They had no choice but to make use of the few short-lived, illicit, clandestine, Catholic-owned presses set up in the teeth of savage persecution.[35] Or else they were compelled to use Continental presses, which were themselves not at all easy of access, and then to smuggle in their books and distribute them in secret. Small wonder that only two Roman Catholic books printed in Welsh are known to have survived from the sixteenth century, as compared with about a hundred and fifty English titles.[36]

Furthermore, customers able and willing to buy books in any language were none too plentiful. As late as 1643 the Stationers' Company complained that:

> books (except the Sacred Bible) are not of such general use and necessity as some staple commodities are, which feed and clothe us, nor are they so perishable or require change in keeping [...] few men bestow more in books than what they can spare out of their superfluities.[37]

If that was true of England, in Wales the potential book-buyers were much fewer again. Only some 250,000 to 400,000 people spoke Welsh in the sixteenth century,[38] though more of them might have been able to read it than might have been supposed. Even so, in a poor and largely rural population not many would be able to buy books or have access to them. It was exceptional for authors to have anything like a captive public in the shape of parishes being required by law to buy a copy of a Welsh Bible and Prayer Book and making them available to be read publicly by literate and well-disposed parishioners to those who could not read. Visions of pious heads of households using books to instruct their families and servants remained a distant dream.[39] So the financial risks entailed in printing, publishing, and selling Welsh books had to be carefully calculated. Even though an individual author like William Salesbury or William Morgan might impoverish himself by publishing a book,[40] in most instances it needed a well-to-do patron to ensure a book's appearance. He might be an influential cleric like Archbishop Whitgift or Cardinal Sirleto, a wealthy landowner like the Earl of Pembroke or Sir Edward Stradling, or a successful merchant like Humphrey Toy or Rowland Heylyn.[41]

At the end of the day, the number of Welsh books of all kinds printed during the sixteenth century was only thirty, with a further 150 in the seventeenth century. That was a depressingly small number, compared not only with the output in the larger and more productive European countries,[42] but probably also with what Welsh authors and scholars had themselves hoped for. Particularly disappointing, perhaps, was the almost complete failure to reproduce in print any part of the principal achievement of Welsh literature — the *cynghanedd* verse. This was in spite of the importunate efforts by literary critics on both sides of the religious divide — Gruffydd Robert or Siôn Dafydd Rhys among the Catholics, and Protestants like William Salesbury or Edmwnd Prys (1544-1623).[43] Despite eloquent pleas for a new kind of poet of Christian learning and the challenge of the printed book, Welsh poets almost without exception continued along the customary paths of oral declamation and manuscript recording. That outspoken advocate of a new style, Edmwnd Prys, ventured into fresh pastures only at the end of his life with his publication of the metrical Psalms — in free metres — as late as 1621. The appeal for printed poetry of the novel kind could only have been responded to had there existed in Wales patrons liberal in purse and attitude, and a reading and book-buying public of a kind not seen until the eighteenth century. The sad truth appears to have been that the ambitions of the scholars and littérateurs of Wales outstripped its economic and social development. They aspired to produce the courtly and urban literature of the Renaissance in a country that remained mostly impoverished and pastoral; the gap was too wide to be completely bridged. The only way in which it could be partly closed was by means of the Reformation. The success of Protestant humanists in obtaining a Welsh translation of the Scriptures and getting it used in public worship wherever Welsh was normally spoken, enabled the Welsh, alone among the Celtic-speaking peoples, to move on — to some degree at least — from the oral and manuscript tradition of the Middle Ages to the printed-book culture of the sixteenth and seventeenth centuries. Although they had not attained all they had dreamed of, their achievement was substantial and was to prove enduring.[44]

The range of Welsh books published basically comprised two kinds: the one sort related to religion and the other to language and literature. There was no significant popular demand for religious reformation in early-sixteenth-century Wales. Only a tiny minority, even among the better educated, desired change and its influence was distinctly limited. Moves away from the papal church in the direction of a reformed regime were in the main dictated to the Welsh from above by royal command; furthermore, until 1567 they were introduced very largely in the English language, which was unintelligible to most of the Welsh, and were seemingly in blatant contradiction to the age-old conviction of the Welsh that as a people they were unswervingly loyal to the religion they had inherited.[45]

Welsh reformers saw in such measures a critically dangerous threat. They profoundly believed that even if their countrymen knew little or nothing about reformed doctrine they had a hunger for religious truth which could be assuaged only in their own language by the widespread publication of appropriate printed books. Sir John Prise argued,

> *Now that God has placed print in our midst to multiply knowledge of his blessed words, it is proper for us, as all Christendom has already done, to participate in that goodness with them, so that so excellent a gift should be no less fruitful to us than to others.*[46]

And Salesbury besought them,

> *Go on pilgrimage barefoot to the King's grace and his Council to seek permission to obtain Holy Scripture in your own language, for the sake of those among you who are not able nor likely to be able to learn English.*[47]

Publishing the Bible in Welsh took three-quarters of a century to complete, from 1551 to 1620,[48] and was fraught with difficulties. Formal permission had to be obtained in the Act of Parliament of 1563 for the translation to be made; and allowing the use of Welsh in public worship meant a major change in government policy. Discerning use of the Hebrew, Greek, and Latin texts of the Bible called for a high degree of scholarship and judgement. There also had to be a sensitive deployment of the Welsh language itself; freed from archaic and medieval expressions, not over-dependent on a single dialect, flexible and intelligible, yet preserving the classic qualities of purity and strength associated with the literary language. Dealing with London printers necessitated skill and patience, and paying for the venture entailed considerable financial sacrifice. The long and arduous enterprise required of the men principally involved clear vision, unremitting dedication, and a willingness to devote themselves unflaggingly to what they conceived to be the service of God and the highest good of their countrymen.

Nearly as notable an achievement was the translation of the Book of Common Prayer, which either accompanied or soon followed the translation of the New Testament of 1567 and the Bible in 1588. Welsh versions of the Catechism, and later the Primer, which were indispensable if the clergy were to perform their primary duty of instructing their parishioners in Christian doctrine, figured as prominently as any early printed books.[49] Two notable translations of classic English works which appeared in the mid-1590s pointed the way forward to many future translations of the same kind. The one was a rendering of Bishop John Jewel's *Apologia* by Maurice Kyffin (c.1555-98), the other, *Perl mewn Adfyd*, a free translation by Huw Lewys (1562-1634) of a text by Miles Coverdale, was the first Welsh book to be printed in Oxford.[50]

A handful of Catholic authors was just as committed to bringing out Catholic literature in Welsh for the edification of those who remained steadfast to the old faith. Most of their works were circulated in manuscript and only two managed to find their way into print during the sixteenth century: *Athravaeth Gristnogavl* by Morus Clynnog

(1568) and the anonymous *Y Drych Cristianogawl* (1585), part of which was printed in a cave at Rhiwledin.[51] Another work which seems to have been printed in 1600, but no copy of which has survived to the twentieth century, was a volume of Catholic verse by the martyr Richard Gwyn (*fl.* 1557-84).[52]

The other small group of Welsh books to be printed related to the Welsh language and its literature — dictionaries, grammars, discussions of literary form, and the like.[53] Works of this kind sprang from the irrepressible ambition of Welsh scholars to make their language and literature worthy of the improved knowledge and raised aspirations of the age, by giving Welsh what Renaissance culture insisted upon in terms of copiousness, accuracy, and elegance. They wanted to put it on a par with the culture emerging on all sides in Europe; an ambition which sought to elevate the vernacular tongues to the upper slopes of Parnassus along with the classical languages. That would happen only when learned works had revealed in detail their inherent scope, wealth, and comeliness.

Less than satisfied though these pioneer authors of Welsh printed books may have been with the number of titles which they were able to publish, and reproachfully though they chided their countrymen with the latter's lack of concern, they can, nevertheless, now be seen to have accomplished more than they themselves may have realized. Their urge to ensure that Welsh became the language of worship did more than anything else to keep it in a flourishing state in all parts of Wales, whereas if English had continued to be the medium of the Established Church, that would have made every parish church, in even the remotest areas of Wales, into a centre for the dissemination of English. Moreover, the Christian ministry, the one educated section of the community which, as a result of the Act of 1563 and the translations which followed, had a vital interest in making use of Welsh for professional purposes, would have had virtually no incentive to do so. An Anglicized clergy would have deprived Wales in subsequent centuries of most of its poets, prose-writers, and educational pioneers. Without them it is difficult to see how Welsh literature could have survived as buoyantly as it did. But for this merging of reformed religion with pride in the language, literature, history, and antiquities of Wales in the persons of its mainly clerical intelligentsia, its awareness of nationhood might well have dwindled to near-extinction.[54]

NOTES TO CHAPTER 3

1. A selection of the most useful general guides to the huge volume of literature on fifteenth-century Europe is listed in *The Celts and the Renaissance: tradition and innovation*, ed. Glanmor Williams and Robert Owen Jones (Cardiff, 1990), pp. 14-15.
2. Glanmor Williams, 'Cefndir Ewropeaidd y cyfieithiadau beiblaidd', in *Y gair ar waith*, ed. R. Geraint Gruffydd (Cardiff, 1988), pp. 1-26 (p. 5).
3. S. H. Steinberg, *Five hundred years of printing*, new edn, revised by John Trevitt (London, 1996); Elizabeth L. Eisenstein, *The printing press as an agent of change*, 2 vols (Cambridge, 1979).
4. Lucien Febvre and Henri-Jean Martin, *The coming of the book: the impact of printing 1450-1800*, trans. David Gerard, ed. Geoffrey Nowell-Smith and David Wootton (London, 1976), pp. 216-19.
5. Williams, 'Cefndir', p. 19.
6. 'Erasmus Roterodamus yr athro dyscedickaf, huotlaf, ac awdurusaf yn Cred oll or a vu in oes ni ac ys llawer oes or blayn' (*Oll Synnwyr pen Kembero ygyd*, reproduced in *Rhagymadroddion 1547-1659*, ed. Garfield H. Hughes (Cardiff, 1951), p. 14).
7. Williams, 'Cefndir', pp. 21-2.
8. H. Daniel-Rops, *The Catholic Reformation* (London, 1962); H. O. Evennett, *The spirit of the Counter-Reformation* (Cambridge, 1968); H. Jedin, *Katholische Reformation oder Gegenreformation* (Lucerne, 1946).
9. Geraint H. Jenkins, *Hanes Cymru yn y cyfnod modern cynnar 1536-1760* (Cardiff, 1983); J. D. H. Thomas, *A history of Wales, 1485-1660* (Cardiff, 1972); W. S. K. Thomas, *Tudor Wales* (Llandysul, 1983); Glanmor Williams, *Recovery, reorientation, and Reformation: Wales c.1415-1642* (Oxford, 1987).
10. Glanmor Williams, 'The Welsh in Tudor England', in his *Religion, language and nationality in Wales* (Cardiff, 1979), pp. 171-99.
11. R. Geraint Gruffydd, '*Yny lhyvyr hwnn* (1546); the earliest Welsh printed book', *BBCS*, 23 (1968-70), 105-16.
12. Glanmor Williams, 'Welsh authors and their books, c.1500-1642', in *The world of books and information: essays in honour of Lord Dainton*, ed. Maurice B. Line (London, 1987), pp. 187-96.
13. P. R. Roberts, 'The Acts of Union and Wales', *THSC*, 1972-73, pp. 49-72, and his 'The union with England and the identity of "Anglican" Wales', *TRHS*, 5th ser. 22 (1972), 49-70.
14. Henry Lewis, 'Darnau o'r efengylau', *Y Cymmrodor*, 31 (1921), 193-216; R. Geraint Gruffydd, 'Dau destun Protestannaidd cynnar o Lsgr. Hafod 22', *Trivium*, 1 (1966), 56-66.
15. W. A. Mathias, 'Astudiaeth o weithgarwch llenyddol William Salesbury' (unpublished master's thesis, University of Wales, Cardiff, 1949); Glanmor Williams, 'The achievement of William Salesbury', in his *Welsh Reformation essays* (Cardiff, 1967), pp. 191-205.
16. J. W. Saunders, 'The stigma of print', *Essays in Criticism*, 1 (1951), 139-64.
17. Williams, 'Welsh in Tudor England'.
18. W. P. Griffith, *Learning, law and religion: higher education and Welsh society, c.1540-1640* (Cardiff, 1996).
19. Glanmor Williams, 'Two neglected London-Welsh clerics: Richard Whitford and Richard Gwent', in his *Welsh Reformation essays*, pp. 67-89; Williams, 'Welsh authors', pp. 187-8.
20. 'A phob vn o'r rhai a dariont nemor oddi kartref yn kashav ac yn gillwng dros gof iaith i ganedic wlad a thavodiad i vam gnawdawl' (*Rhyddiaith Gymraeg [...] 1488-1609*, ed. T. H. Parry-Williams (Cardiff, 1954), p. 60).
21. '[...] yn darbod yn natural tros ymgeledd gwladwrieth yr vnryw iaith. Oh y pa peth ydd yngeneis i am wladwriaeth, can na ys gwyr Kymbro heddyo o pa han yw gwladwriaeth' (*Oll Synnwyr pen*, reproduced in *Rhagymadroddion*, p. 10).
22. '[...] am fod pawb o honom yn yskyluso yn iaith Fruttanaeg, ag ymroi i arfer ag i ddysgu tafodiaith estronawl, o blygid dieithra iaith dan y ffurfafen yn i gwlad i hun yw Camberaeg' ('Ystorie Kymru', reproduced in *Rhagymadroddion*, p. 103).
23. R. Brinley Jones, *The old British tongue: the vernacular in Wales, 1540-1640* (Cardiff, 1970); G. J. Williams, *Agweddau ar hanes dysg Gymraeg*, ed. Aneirin Lewis (Cardiff, 1969); Glanmor Williams, 'Dadeni,

Diwygiad, a diwylliant Cymru', in his *Grym tafodau tân: ysgrifau hanesyddol ar grefydd a diwylliant* (Llandysul, 1984), pp. 63-86; R. Geraint Gruffydd, 'The Renaissance and Welsh literature', in *Celts and the Renaissance*, pp. 17-39.

[24] '[...] wrth gymharu ieithoedd ynghyd ny wela fi yr un or ieithoedd cyphredin eraill, nad yw r Gymraeg yn gystal ar oreu o honynt oll [...] ie ag yn blaenori ar lawer o ieithoedd ereill mywn aml foddau a fedrwn eu henwi' (reproduced in *Rhagymadroddion*, p. 53).

[25] '[...] llawer o gymry a vedair darllein kymraeg, heb vedru darllein vn gair saesnec na lladin' (reproduced in *Rhagymadroddion*, p. 3).

[26] Introduction to John Davies (Siôn Dafydd Rhys), *Cambrobrytannicae Cymraecaeve Linguae Institutiones et Rudimenta* (London, 1592), reproduced in *Rhagymadroddion*, p. 67.

[27] '[...] chwilod o blant o'i ddylofi ne bawenne bvdron ne drwyn ysnitwedd ne dropiad kanwyll Baris ne drwyn kanwyll frwyn ne ffenesdr ddyfrllyd ne gilfach fyglyd' (introduction to 'Llyfr Bicar Woking' reproduced in *Rhagymadroddion*, p. 68).

[28] 'Ail vlodeuat' was the phrase used by Bishop Richard Davies for the publication of the Welsh New Testament of 1567 in his prefatory 'Epistol at y Cembru'.

[29] '[...] a ny vynwch ymado yndalgrwn dec a ffydd Christ, a ny vynnwch yn lan syth na bo ywch ddim a wneloch ac efe, ac any vynnwch tros gofi ac ebryfygy i ewyllys ef y gyd achlan, mynwch yr yscrythur lan yn ych iaith, mal ac y bu hi y gan ych dedwydd henafieit yr hen Uryttanneit' (introduction to *Oll Synnwyr pen*, reproduced in *Rhagymadroddion*, p. 11).

[30] *Gramadeg Cymraeg gan Gruffydd Robert*, ed. G. J. Williams (Cardiff, 1939), pp. v-cliv.

[31] Glanmor Williams, 'Religion and Welsh literature in the age of the Reformation', in his *The Welsh and their religion* (Cardiff, 1991), pp. 138-72.

[32] Rowland Vaughan, *Yr ymarfer o dduwioldeb [...] 1630*, ed. J. Ballinger (Cardiff, 1930), Rhagymadrodd, p. xiv.

[33] Most authors of early Welsh printed books refer with deep dismay to the frequency of printers' errors. Although Bishop Morgan claimed that there were twice as many errors in other Bibles as in his, 209 errors have been traced in his Bible of 1588 (Wyn Thomas, 'The Trinity College Carmarthen copy of William Morgan's Bible', *CA*, 24 (1988), 110-13).

[34] D. M. Loades, 'The theory and practice of censorship in sixteenth-century England', *TRHS*, 5th series, 24 (1974), 141-58.

[35] R. Geraint Gruffydd, *Argraffwyr cyntaf Cymru* (Cardiff, 1972) and Chapter 4 of this volume.

[36] H. W. Lloyd, 'Welsh books printed abroad in the sixteenth and seventeenth centuries', *Y Cymmrodor*, 4 (1881), 25-69; A. C. Southern, *English Recusant prose, 1559-1582* (London, 1950).

[37] Quoted in E. H. Miller, *The professional writer in Elizabethan England* (Cambridge, MA, 1959), p. 152.

[38] For the population of Wales at this time see Williams, *Recovery, reorientation, and Reformation*, pp. 406-9.

[39] Williams, *Welsh and their religion*, pp. 160-1.

[40] Williams, *Welsh Reformation essays*, pp. 200-1; Williams, *Welsh and their religion*, pp. 210-11, 216.

[41] R. Geraint Gruffydd, 'Dau lythyr gan Owen Lewis', *LlC*, 2 (1952-3), 36-45; Williams, *Welsh and their religion*, pp. 136-7, 151, 192.

[42] STC^2 for example lists some 26,000 titles.

[43] Williams, *Welsh and their religion*, pp. 162-4.

[44] See Chapters 1 and 2 of *Celts and the Renaissance*.

[45] Williams, *Welsh and their religion*, pp. 37-8.

[46] 'Ac yr awr y rhoes duw y prynt yn mysk ni er amylhau gwybodaeth y eireu bendigedic ef, iawn yni, val y gwnaeth holl gristionogaeth heb law, gymryt rhann or daeoni hwnnw gyda yn hwy, val na bai ddiffrwyth rhodd kystal a hon yni mwy noc y eraill' (*Yny llyvyr hwnn*, reproduced in *Rhagymadroddion*, p. 3).

[47] 'Pererindotwch yn droednoeth, at ras y Brenhin ae Gyncor y ddeisyf cael cennat y cael yr yscrythur lan yn ych iaith, er mwyn y cyniver ohanoch or nyd yw n abyl, nac mewn kyfflypwriaeth y ddyscy Sasnaec' (*Oll Synnwyr pen*, reproduced in *Rhagymadroddion*, p. 12).

[48] *Y gair ar waith*; R. Geraint Gruffydd, 'Y Beibl a droes i'w bobl draw' (Cardiff, 1988); P. T. J. Morgan,

Beibl i Gymru: a Bible for Wales ([s.l.], 1988); Isaac Thomas, *Y Testament Newydd Cymraeg, 1551-1620* (Cardiff, 1976); Isaac Thomas, *Yr Hen Destament Cymraeg, 1551-1620* (Aberystwyth, 1988); Glanmor Williams, 'Bishop William Morgan and the first Welsh Bible', in his *Welsh and their religion,* pp. 173-229.

[49] *LW*, I, 131-3,141-2. See also R. Geraint Gruffydd, 'Religious prose in Welsh from the beginning of the reign of Elizabeth to the Restoration' (unpublished doctoral thesis, Oxford, 1952).

[50] *Deffynniad Ffydd Eglwys Loegr [...]*, ed. W. P. Williams (Bangor, 1908); *Perl mewn Adfyd [...]*, ed. W. J. Gruffydd (Cardiff, 1929).

[51] R. Geraint Gruffydd, 'Gwasg ddirgel yr ogof yn Rhiwledyn', *JWBS*, 9 (1958-65), 1-23 and his *Argraffwyr cyntaf Cymru*.

[52] *Carolau Richard White [...]*, ed. T. H. Parry-Williams (Cardiff, 1931).

[53] Thomas Parry, *A history of Welsh literature,* trans. H. Idris Bell (Oxford, 1955), pp. 201-13.

[54] Glanmor Williams, *Wales and the Reformation* (Cardiff, 1997).

CHAPTER 4

THE FIRST PRINTED BOOKS, 1546—1604

R. Geraint Gruffydd

AS was shown in Chapter 3, Welshmen who were making their careers in England or on the Continent had broken through into print from the early sixteenth century, although not in Welsh. Of more immediate Welsh interest is the Strata Marcella indulgence of 1528, printed in London by Richard Pynson, although that naturally is in Latin.[1] About the same time 'Sir' Lewis Gethin, rector of Llandegla-yn-Iâl and Llanferres in 1529,[2] expressed with striking clarity the anxiety of Welsh men of letters lest the printing press should bypass Wales altogether, to the great detriment of the language:

> *Every country, by the grace and favour of the Triune God,*
> *Has begun to print in towns:*
> *Through the exercise of virtue it would be no harder*
> *If the same work were done in our language.*
>
> *Let us all set our minds on uplifting our language,*
> *Goodness will come at once [from that];*
> *Although we might lose our land and our towns*
> *Let us keep our language in our possession [lit. with us].*[3]

So lucidly did Gethin express the aspirations of the intellectual élite in Wales at that time that its leader, William Salesbury, saw fit to include the first of the two *englynion* as a kind of coda to his *A briefe and a playne introduction* of 1550.

The man responsible for the breakthrough into print in Welsh, however, was not William Salesbury but Sir John Prise, Secretary of the King's Council in Wales and the Marches. In 1546 he published *Yny lhyvyr hwnn y traethir. Gwyddor kymraeg. Kalandyr. Y gredo [...] Y pader [...] Y deng air deddyf. Saith Rinwedd yr egglwys. Y kampey arveradwy ar Gwyddieu [sic] gochladwy ae keingeu* (In this book are set out the Welsh alphabet, a calendar, the Creed, the Paternoster, the Ten Commandments, the Seven Sacraments of the Church, the virtues to be practised and the vices to be avoided and their ramifications).[4] This is not only a late-Henrican attempt to disseminate elementary religious knowledge in the vernacular, but also a humanist endeavour to put into print part of the ancient literary heritage of Wales. Prise specifically appeals in his introduction for proper use to be made of the printing press. These two motives dominate Welsh printing for the rest of the century and it will be convenient to treat them apart, although few of the authors or translators who achieved print were untouched by a combination of reforming zeal (whether for Protestantism or Catholicism) and a humanistic desire to see the language flourish.[5] In what follows, little mention will be made of Latin works or of dictionaries, since these are treated at length in other chapters, and hardly any reference will be made to English works by Welsh authors unless they refer primarily to Wales.

Humanism

Following the appearance of *Yny lhyvyr hwnn*, the torch was quickly taken up by William Salesbury, the most important figure in the history of early printing in Wales.[6] Salesbury, a Denbighshire country gentleman and lawyer, was educated at Oxford and (probably) one of the Inns of Court. At Oxford, it seems, he underwent a double conversion to humanism and Protestantism, and also became vastly learned, especially in languages. His humanistic activities began in early 1547 with *A Dictionary in Englyshe and Welshe*,[7] the chief object of which was to help Welsh people to learn English. It appears to have been followed later in the same year by *Oll Synnwyr pen Kembero ygyd*[8] (*All the wisdom in a Welshman's head gathered together*), a slim collection of Welsh proverbs compiled by the important professional poet Gruffudd Hiraethog which had been copied by Salesbury while the two were travelling together to London some three years previously. Salesbury's introduction is at once an impassioned plea that both learning and true (i.e. biblical) religion should be made available in Welsh, and a fine example of Welsh humanistic prose. A second, much-enlarged, edition of *Oll Synnwyr pen* appeared in 1567, probably under the title of 'Crynodab or Diarebion sathredig' (A collection of the proverbs in common use).[9] After a three-year gap, 1550 saw the publication by Salesbury of four titles including *A briefe and a playne introduction teaching how to pronounce the letters in the British tong*, written for the benefit of English speakers who wished to learn Welsh,[10] and an English translation of Thomas Linacre's Latin version of an astronomical treatise by Proclus. An enlarged second edition of *A briefe and a playne introduction* appeared in 1567 under the title *A playne and a familiar Introduction*. The remaining two titles of 1550 are religious rather than humanistic, as were all Salesbury's later publications, with one exception: he almost certainly had a hand in the appearance in 1571 of a broadside containing Martial's epigram on the Happy Life (X, 47) with an anonymous English version and a Welsh translation by the professional poet Simwnt Fychan (aided by his patron Simon Thelwall).[11] Two further humanistic texts by Salesbury, a handbook of rhetoric based on Petrus Mosellanus and a medicinal herbal based on Leonhard Fuchs and William Turner, unfortunately remained unpublished.[12]

In 1567 a work equalling Salesbury's in brilliance appeared in Milan, the Roman Catholic humanist Gruffydd Robert's *Dosparth byrr ar y rhan gyntaf i ramadeg Cymraeg* (*A short treatise on the first part of Welsh grammar*); a further five parts followed between *c*.1584 and *c*.1594.[13] Robert was heavily influenced by contemporary Italian linguistic and literary theory[14] and his book offers not only a humanistic grammar of the Welsh language but also an analysis of Welsh versecraft (coupled with some penetrating literary criticism), an anthology of Welsh strict-metre verse, and a remarkable example of polished Ciceronian prose in Welsh. Because of the circumstances of its publication it had regrettably little influence in Wales.

Humphrey Lhwyd's posthumous historical publications of 1572-3 are discussed in Chapter 5, as is Sir John Prise's posthumous *Historiae Brytannicae Defensio* of 1573. In 1584 David Powel, vicar of Rhiwabon, edited Lhwyd's translation of the important medieval Welsh 'Chronicle of the Princes' and published it, with wood-engravings borrowed from Holinshed's *Chronicles*,[15] as *The Historie of Cambria now called Wales*; further editions of historical texts by Powel, together with his contribution to the historiographical debate concerning Geoffrey of Monmouth, were in Latin.

In spite of the example set by Gruffydd Robert, all the remaining humanist grammars of Welsh which achieved publication were written in Latin: within our period fall the compendious *Cambrobrytannicae Cymraecaeve Linguae Institutiones* (1592) by John Davies of Brecon, 'Siôn Dafydd Rhys', and Henry Salesbury's slighter *Grammatica Britannica* of 1593. The same year, however (or possibly 1594), saw the publication of *Bardhoniaeth neu brydydhiaeth, y llyfr kyntaf*[16] (*Poetry or verse, the first book*), an introduction to Welsh versecraft by Wiliam Midleton, a friend of Siôn Dafydd Rhys, an amateur poet of some distinction, and captain of a privateer: no further 'book', alas, ever appeared. Two years later, a more substantial and significant humanist publication was Henry Perri's *Eglvryn Phraethineb*[17] (*The elucidator of eloquence*), a handbook of rhetoric based on Salesbury's earlier effort but also displaying the influence of both Pierre de la Ramée and Henry Peacham. Two further publications which may broadly be classed as humanist deserve mention. Robert Holland's (fragmentary) Welsh translation of James I's *Basilikon Doron*, which appeared in 1604, could be regarded as a contribution to the art of statecraft,[18] while George Owen Harry's companion *Genealogy of the High and Mighty Monarch, James* attempted to press Welsh humanist historiography into the service of the incoming House of Stuart.[19]

Religion

Yny lhyvyr hwnn is a religious as well as a humanistic text: it is, however, reforming Catholic rather than Protestant.[20] The first overtly Protestant text is William Salesbury's bilingual pamphlet of 1550, *Ban wedy i dynny air yngair allan o hen gyfreith Howel dda / A certaine case extracte out of the aunciente Law of Hoel da*,[21] a misjudged attempt to appeal to Welsh medieval law in support of clerical marriage, then a matter of much controversy. Salesbury's vehement *Baterie of the Popes Botereulx* (1550) has no particular reference to Wales.[22] It was the following year that saw the beginning of what was to become Salesbury's life-work, the translation of the Scriptures into Welsh: he had already pleaded in 1547 that the task be undertaken as a matter of urgency. In 1551 appeared his *Kynniver llith a ban or yscrythur lan ac a ddarlleir yr Eccleis pryd Commun y Sulieu a'r Gwilieu trwy'r vlwyddyn*[23] (*As many lections and excerpts from Holy Scripture as are read in Church at Communion time on Sundays and Feast Days throughout the year*), a Welsh version of the biblical passages (excluding the Psalms) that are included in the Book of Common Prayer, some 184 of them in all. Already the twin hallmarks of Salesbury's biblical translations are apparent: full exploitation of the latest scholarship in the field, and an exaggerated reverence for the humanistic ideals of *copia* and *antiquitas* in his use of language.[24]

During Mary's brief reign Salesbury's reforming zeal had to be subdued somewhat, but when Elizabeth I succeeded to the throne in 1558 he was once again free to prosecute his cause. Some use may have been made of *Kynniver llith a ban* in the early Elizabethan church, as also of a Welsh catechism, possibly a translation of that found in the Book of Common Prayer.[25] The passing of 5 Eliz. I c. 28 on 10 April 1563 laid upon the four Welsh bishops and the bishop of Hereford the obligation to have both Bible and Book of Common Prayer translated into Welsh by 1 March 1567. In the meantime, use was to be made not only of *Kynniver llith a ban* but also of Welsh versions of the Lord's Prayer, the Apostle's Creed, the Ten Commandments, and the Litany; the Stationers' Registers in 1562-3 and again in 1566-7 and 1567-8 bear witness to an intention to make available such elementary teaching aids (the Litany in 1562-3, a catechism in 1566-7, the Ten Commandments in 1567-8).[26] On 6 May 1567 *Lliver Gweddi Gyffredin* (Book of Common Prayer), translated by Salesbury, was published: this included the Psalms in full.[27] It was followed on 7 October 1567 by the New Testament, *Testament Newydd ein Arglwydd Jesv Christ*, also largely translated by Salesbury: his collaborators were Richard Davies, bishop of St David's, who supplied translations of five epistles (1 Timothy, Hebrews, James, 1 & 2 Peter) and Thomas Huet, precentor of St David's Cathedral, who translated the Book of Revelation.[28] Davies also contributed an important introduction, arguing that Protestantism had ancient roots in Wales. Salesbury's translations received a mixed reception because of his relentless application of the principles of *copia* and *antiquitas* to all aspects of his use of language, particularly orthography, but their extraordinary brilliance is indisputable. While in London overseeing the printing of the *Lliver Gweddi Gyffredin* and *Testament Newydd*, Salesbury appears to have made arrangements for the publication of second editions of two of his humanistic works and also for the printing of a broadside, now lost, bearing the text of an anti-Catholic poem by Siôn ap Robert ap Rhys ap Hywel, 'Be da fai y byd a fu' (Even if the world that is now gone were good).[29]

Salesbury recedes from view at this point: it is not known whether a second edition of *Lliver Gweddi Gyffredin* in 1586 was his work. For a time his place at the side of bishop Richard Davies may have been taken by Siôn Dafydd Rhys, but Rhys succeeded in producing no more than Welsh translations of Alexander Nowell's *Catechismus parvus* (1578) and of a similar catechism by Gervase Babington (c.1583): the latter is now lost and may indeed never have been published.[30] Richard Davies's last publication was a *Funerall sermon* for Walter Devereux, Earl of Essex, in 1577, which illuminates his pastoral ideals and problems.[31] William Salesbury's torch was eventually handed on to William Morgan (1545-1604), a Cambridge graduate who was to become successively bishop of Llandaf (1595-1601) and St Asaph (1601-4).[32] In September 1588 Morgan published his *Beibl Cyssegr-lan*, a new translation of the whole of the Old Testament (except the Psalter) and Apocrypha, and a revision of Salesbury's translation of the Psalter and New Testament; Morgan's Psalter was also published separately as *Psalmau Dafydd*.[33] No less learned than Salesbury, Morgan had a far surer sense of what was acceptable linguistically and his Bible became the foundation classic of modern Welsh prose. Like Salesbury before him, he took advantage of his sojourn in London to publish additional material, in his case a funeral sermon for an influential neighbour, Sir Evan Lloyd of Bodidris: it is deeply regrettable that no copy of this has survived.[34] Somewhat earlier, according to the Stationers' Registers, a London Welshman called Hugh Griffith composed an English epitaph for Lloyd, but this too, as well as Griffith's 'a Sonett or synners solace [...] bothe in Welshe and Englishe', has disappeared.[35] Morgan, helped by John Davies, later rector of Mallwyd, also brought out an important revision of Salesbury's Welsh Book of Common Prayer in 1599.

After a few years' delay, the appearance of the Welsh Bible stimulated the publication of a considerable number of Protestant religious texts, of which several are to be connected with the London-Welsh stationer Thomas Salisbury.[36] A translation by Henry Salisbury of Thomas Becon's *Sick Man's Salve* (1594) has not survived,[37] but several copies remain of Maurice Kyffin's translation of John Jewel's *Apologia Ecclesiae Anglicanae*[38] and of *Perl mewn Adfyd*,[39] a rendering by Huw Lewys of Miles Coverdale's English translation of Otto Werdmüller's *Ein Kleinot von Trost und Hilfe in allerlei Trübsale* (*A pearl of consolation and succour in various troubles*) (both 1595). Robert Holland's brilliant little pamphlet on witchcraft, 'Ymddiddan Tudur a Gronw' (A dialogue between Tudur and Gronw) (also 1595), survives in a second edition of 1681, as well as in an earlier manuscript copy.[40] In 1597 Thomas Salisbury registered for publication an anonymous Welsh translation of Queen Elizabeth's version of Margaret of Angoulême's *Le Miroir de l'âme pecheresse* but this has disappeared without trace,[41] as has David Powel's Welsh primer of a.1598 and a second edition of the same work registered for publication in 1599.[42] Another work registered for publication in the same year, Holland's translation of William Perkins's *Exposition of the Lord's Prayer*, 'Agoriad byrr ar Weddi'r Arglwydd', survives (although, alas, in somewhat amplified form) in a second edition of 1677;[43] a third book by Holland, 'Darmerth neu arlwy i weddi' (A preparation and provision for prayer) (1600), was known to the bibliographer Moses Williams in 1717 but is now lost.[44] Finally Wiliam Midleton published part of a metrical psalter at an indeterminate date between 1595 and 1603,[45] the complete work appearing posthumously in 1603; in the same year Maurice Kyffin's brother Edward also published part of a metrical psalter, but because of his death by plague this remained uncompleted.[46]

All these were Protestant books. The Welsh Roman Catholics also embarked on a modest literary effort, although, because Roman Catholic printing was prohibited, they had to rely far more on the production and distribution of manuscript copies than did the Protestants. In 1568 Gruffydd Robert saw through the press in Milan his friend Morus Clynnog's *Athravaeth Gristnogavl* (*Christian doctrine*), said some eleven years later to be a translation of a catechism by Fr Juan Alfonso de Polanco SJ.[47] After that, until Welsh Roman Catholic printing resumed in Paris in 1609, the only Welsh Catholic works to achieve print came from secret presses. The first part of *Y Drych Cristianogawl*[48] (*The Christian Mirror*), possibly by the missionary priest Robert Gwyn, was printed by Roger Thackwell in Rhiwledin cave in the Little Orme's Head near Llandudno early in 1587 (although the imprint says Rouen 1585); an attempt, apparently later in the same year, to print the remaining two parts of the *Drych* in the house of Siôn Dafydd Rhys in Brecon, was foiled because of government intervention.[49] About the same time devotional verses by Gruffydd Robert, entitled *Ynglynion*, also achieved print, but the circumstances of their production are obscure.[50] Some time between 1717 and 1742 Moses Williams saw a copy of five religious poems or 'Carolau' composed by St Richard Gwyn, which Williams says was printed in 1600 :[51] he does not say where, but it was almost certainly on a secret press; unfortunately no copy is now extant.

Ephemera

All the books mentioned so far have fallen fairly neatly into the twin categories of humanism or religion. A Welsh broadside of 1591, licensing John Salisbury of Gwyddelwern to beg for alms after having been wounded while serving on land and sea, can be placed in neither category, but deserves to be mentioned here because it is the only one of its kind to have survived.[52]

Patrons, publishers, and printer
The dedications of many of these books and the introductions written for the benefit of their readers form an extraordinarily interesting and imposing body of prose-writing from the point of view of both style and content.[53] Sometimes, however, books are left undedicated or are given dedications which convey little. For example, it has been suggested that *Yny lhyvyr hwnn*, and indeed early Welsh printing in general, owed much to the encouragement of William Herbert, first Earl of Pembroke of the second creation,[54] but the only dedications to him are of Gruffydd Robert's *Dosparth byrr* and (posthumously) Sir John Prise's *Defensio*. The Protestant reformer Robert Crowley was clearly highly supportive of William Salesbury during the productive years 1550 and 1551, yet none of Salesbury's books is dedicated to him.[55] In Salesbury's *annus mirabilis* of 1567 the London-Welsh stationer Humphrey Toy obviously played a key role, but only *A playne and a familiar Introduction* is dedicated to him. Sir Edward Stradling's munificent support of Siôn Dafydd Rhys's *Institutiones* was, however, properly acknowledged. Most intriguing of all is the shadowy role played by Richard Vaughan, bishop successively of Bangor, Chester, and London, in the output of the period 1594-1604 (and possibly beyond), although he emerges from the shadows only in 1595 as the probable author of a commendatory verse for Perri's *Eglvryn* and as the dedicatee of Lewys's *Perl mewn Adfyd*.[56]

Before printing in England and Wales was restricted in 1557 to London (although Oxford and Cambridge were later granted special concessions), the Worcester stationer John Oswen appears to have had his eye on the Welsh market, but apparently to no avail. Welsh authors soon made compacts with London publishers and printers. At the strikingly early date of 13 December 1545 William Salesbury and John Walley obtained a royal privilege to publish Salesbury's *Dictionary* and various translations, and in 1563 — the date of 5 Eliz. I c. 28 — they apparently made an unsuccessful attempt to have the privilege renewed: Walley's entry of 'the lateny in Welshe' in the Stationers' Registers for 1562-3 was presumably part of the same campaign.[57] It was natural that Edward Whitchurch, as patent-holder for Prayer Books with Richard Grafton, should have printed *Yny lhyvyr hwnn*. Robert Crowley's support of Salesbury in 1550-1 and Humfrey Toy's in 1567 have already been mentioned. The London-Welsh stationer William Griffith is associated with only one item, 'the x commandments in Welshe' entered in the Stationers' Registers for 1567-8, but his putative compatriot Richard Jones promoted at least five, ranging from the Lhwyd / Twyne *Breuiary* of 1573 to Morgan's 'Sermon [...] at the death of Sir Ieuan Lloyd' in 1588: the other items are the Rhys / Nowell catechism of 1578 — by assignation from the patent-holder John Day — and the twin effusions of Hugh Griffith in 1587.[58] Christopher Barker, as Queen's Printer, was privileged to publish the Morgan Bible and Psalter of 1588 and also the Morgan Book of Common Prayer of 1599, all of which tasks devolved upon his Deputies George Bishop and Ralph Newbery (and, by 1599, Christopher's son, Robert). Similarly we may assume that Thomas Chard published by privilege the two early primers (*a*.1598, 1599) as well as — possibly as a legatee of Humphrey Toy — the second edition of Salesbury's Book of Common Prayer in 1586. Although Thomas Salisbury's notable career was largely abortive in the sense that many of the publications he planned never appeared, and that several of those that did appear are now lost or survive only in fragmentary form, between 1593 and 1604 he appears to have published at least seven items in Welsh or relating to Wales, starting with Henry Salesbury's *Grammatica* (1593) and including the Salesbury / Becon 'Sick Man's Salve' (1594), the anonymous translation of Margaret of Augoulême's *Miroir* (1597), the Midleton *Psalmae* and Kyffin's *Rhann o Psalmae* of 1603, and the Holland / James I *Basilikon Doron* and Harry *Genealogy* of 1604.[59]

Those stationers who did not print for themselves employed master printers to print for them. Such arrangements are not always fully explained in the imprints of books, and it is sometimes unwise to take statements such as 'printed by' at face value. Edward Whitchurch was both a printer and a publisher, and *Yny lhyvyr hwnn* was almost certainly printed on his press. John Walley, on the other hand, was probably not a printer, and it is likely that Salesbury's *Dictionary* and *Oll Synnwyr pen* were printed for him by the Dutch exile Nicholas Hill: intriguingly the imprint of the *Dictionary* names only Walley and that of *Oll Synnwyr pen* only Hill. The *Dictionary* also includes a delightful letter to the reader signed by Walley but clearly written by Salesbury. Robert Crowley, who published Salesbury's four works of 1550-51, was almost certainly not a printer, all four items being probably printed by Richard Grafton who is nowhere mentioned in the imprints; incidentally, the imprint 'by Roberte Crowley for Wiliam Salesbury' in *Kynniver llith a ban* implies that Salesbury bore at least part of the expense of production. Humphrey Toy, who did not print, employed Henry Denham to produce Salesbury's four books of 1567 but Henry Bynneman for Prise's *Defensio* of 1573; Toy may also have been the intended publisher of Davies's *Funerall sermon* of 1577 but he died that year and the book appeared under Denham's name alone. Denham also printed Powel's *Historie* for Ralph Newbery in 1583 and the same author's digest of historical texts for Newbery and Edmund Bollifant the following year. Denham may indeed be the most likely candidate for the supreme honour of printing Morgan's Bible and Psalter of 1588, since neither George Bishop nor Ralph Newbery, Christopher Barker's Deputies, were printers: the matter clearly demands further investigation. By 1599 Robert Barker, who did print, had joined Bishop and Newbery as one of his father's Deputies, and he therefore could have undertaken the production of Morgan's Book of Common Prayer in that year. John Windet apparently printed in Welsh only Thomas Chard's problematic publication of the second edition of Salesbury's Book of Common Prayer in 1586, although he may of course have also been responsible for printing Chard's lost primers of *a*.1598 and 1599. Finally, Thomas Salisbury began his publishing career by employing the Eliot's Court press to print Salesbury's *Grammatica* in 1593, but by 1603-4 was making exclusive use of Simon Stafford.

When Joseph Barnes was permitted to set up a press at Oxford in 1585, one of his objectives, as it had been one of Oswen's, was to supply the Welsh market.[60] Ten years later he did indeed print and publish *Perl mewn Adfyd* and possibly Midleton's *Rhann o Psalmae Davydd* and Holland's 'Ymddiddan'.[61] Around 1600 the Holland 'Darmerth' appeared from his press.

Welsh Roman Catholic authors who wished to have their books printed had to resort either to Continental printers or to secret presses. Both Robert's *Dosparth byrr* (1567) and Clynnog's *Athravaeth* (1568) were printed in Milan, probably by Vincenzo Giradoni; the remaining five parts of Robert's grammar may also have been printed in Milan, although Paris has been proposed as an alternative.[62] Judging by the evidence both of the books themselves and of documents, at least five secret presses were set up in Wales. The first part of *Y Drych Cristianogawl* was printed in a cave on the Little Orme in 1587, but the attempt to have the second and third parts printed at Brecon apparently failed, as did William Hamner's endeavour to set up a press in a cave on the Shropshire / Flintshire border three years later. We have yet to find a provenance for Gruffydd Robert's *Ynglynion* and St Richard White's 'Carolau'.[63]

Between 1546 and 1604 there appeared some sixty printed items in Welsh or relating to Wales, although it must be added that of this total five were in Latin and a further six in English; also as many as fifteen of the sixty are now lost. This is a risibly small total for a country which can claim one of the finest medieval literatures in Europe. On the other hand it could be argued that this total, small as it is, represented a decisive breakthrough into modernity, a breakthrough best exemplified by Gruffydd Robert's remarkably innovative grammar and William Morgan's epoch-making Bible.

NOTES TO CHAPTER 4

This chapter is based on the distilled wisdom of two major works of scholarship: W. A. Jackson, F. S. Ferguson, and K. F. Pantzer, *A short-title catalogue of books printed in England, Scotland, & Ireland [...] 1475-1640*, 2nd edn, 3 vols (London, 1986-91) and E. Rees, *Libri Walliae [...] 1546-1820*, 2 vols (Aberystwyth, 1987). A third essential aid has been A. F. Allison and D. M. Rogers, *A catalogue of Catholic books in English printed abroad or secretly in England 1558-1640*, 2nd edn (London, 1968) and their *The contemporary printed literature of the English Counter-reformation between 1558 and 1640* (Aldershot, 1994). Annotation is therefore limited to those points where it is necessary to supplement the information in these works. Since this chapter was written, *A guide to Welsh literature c. 1530-1700,* ed. R. Geraint Gruffydd (Cardiff, 1997) has appeared.

1. E. D. Jones, 'A form of indulgence issued by the abbey of Strata Marcella, 1528', *NLWJ*, 14 (1965-6), 246-7.
2. On Gethin see D. R. Thomas, *History of the diocese of St. Asaph,* new edn, 3 vols (Oswestry, 1908-13), II, 91.
3. Pob gwlad aeth, o rad Un a Thri — a'u braint,
   I brintio mewn trefi:
   Nid anos, mewn daioni,
   Fod yr un gwaith i'n hiaith ni.

   Rhown ein bryd i gyd ar godi — ein hiaith,
   Daw unwaith daioni;
   Er colli ein lle a'n trefi
   Cadwn ein hiaith cyda ni! (NLW, Mostyn MS 131B, 190, 749).
4. Reprint: *Yny lhyvyr hwnn a Ban o gyfreith Howel,* ed. J. H. Davies (Bangor & London, 1902). See also R. Geraint Gruffydd, '*Yny lhyvyr hwnn* (1546): the earliest Welsh printed book', *BBCS*, 23 (1968-70), 105-16, and his 'Y print yn dwyn ffrwyth i'r Cymro: *Yny lhyvyr hwnn,* 1546', *Y Llyfr yng Nghymru / Welsh Book Studies,* 1 (1998), 1-20.
5. For a general introduction see R. Geraint Gruffydd, 'The Renaissance and Welsh literature', in *The Celts and the Renaissance: tradition and innovation,* ed. Glanmor Williams and Robert Owen Jones (Cardiff, 1990), pp. 17-39.
6. Glanmor Williams, 'The achievement of William Salesbury', in his *Welsh Reformation essays* (Cardiff, 1967), pp. 191-205; W. Alun Mathias, 'William Salesbury — ei fywyd a'i weithiau' and 'William Salesbury — ei ryddiaith', in *Y traddodiad rhyddiaith (Darlithiau Rhydychen),* ed. G. Bowen (Llandysul, 1970), pp. 27-53, 54-78.
7. Reproduced by the Honourable Society of Cymmrodorion (London, 1877) and by the Scolar Press (Menston, 1969).
8. Reprint: *Oll Synnwyr pen Kembero ygyd,* ed. J. Gwenogvryn Evans (Bangor & London, 1902).
9. W. Alun Mathias, 'Gweithiau William Salesbury', *JWBS*, 7 (1950-3), 125-34.
10. Reproduced by the Scolar Press (Menston, 1969).
11. E. J. Jones, 'Martial's epigram on the happy life', *BBCS*, 3 (1925-7), 286-97; the device discussed on pp. 293-7 (and further in E. J. Jones, '"Tra vo lleuad"', *NLWJ,* 5 (1947-8), 76-8) seems to me to belong to Salesbury himself rather than to the printer John Awdley.
12. For the handbook of rhetoric, see W. Alun Mathias, 'Llyfr Rhetoreg William Salesbury', *LlC*, 1 (1950-1), 259-68; 2 (1952-3), 71-81. For the herbal see *Llysieulyfr Salesbury,* ed. Iwan Rhys Edgar (Cardiff, 1997).
13. Reprint: *Gramadeg Cymraeg gan Gruffydd Robert,* ed. G. J. Williams (Cardiff, 1939). Text reproduced by the Scolar Press (Menston, 1971-2).
14. T. Gwynfor Griffiths, 'A borrowing from the *Cortegiano*', in *Homenaje a Robert A. Hall, Jr.,* ed. D. Feldman (Madrid, 1977), 149-52; H. Hayes, 'Claudio Tolomei: a major influence on Gruffydd Robert', *MLR*, 83 (1988), 56-66.

[15] V. Scholderer, 'Powel's *Historie* (1584)', *NLWJ*, 3 (1943-4), 17-18; R. S. Luborsky, 'Woodcuts in Tudor books; clarifying their documentation', *PBSA*, 86 (1992), 67-81 (p. 79).

[16] Reprint: *Barddoniaeth neu brydyddiaeth gan Wiliam Midleton*, ed. G. J. Williams (Cardiff, 1930). See also G. A. Williams, 'Wiliam Midleton, bonheddwr, anturiwr a bardd', *TDHS*, 24 (1975), 74-116.

[17] Reproduced: *Egluryn ffraethineb [...] gan Henri Perri*, ed. G. J. Williams (Cardiff, 1930); B. L. Jones, 'Testunau rhethreg Cymraeg y Dadeni' (unpublished master's thesis, University of Wales, Bangor, 1961), pp. 119-75.

[18] Reproduced: *Basilikon Doron [...] fragment of a Welsh translation by Robert Holland*, ed. John Ballinger (Cardiff, 1931).

[19] E. D. Jones, 'George Owen Harry c.1553-1614', *PH*, 6 (1979), 58-75.

[20] Glanmor Williams, *Wales and the Reformation* (Cardiff, 1997), provides an authoritative introduction.

[21] Reprinted in *Yny lhyvyr hwnn a Ban o gyfreith Howel*. See also C. James, '*Ban wedi i dynny*: medieval Welsh law and early Protestant propaganda', *CMCS*, 27 (Summer 1994), 61-86.

[22] Glanmor Williams, 'William Salesbury's *Baterie of the Popes Botereulx*', *BBCS*, 13 (1948-50), 146-50.

[23] Reprinted: *Kynniver Llith a Ban*, ed. J. Fisher (Cardiff, 1931).

[24] Authoritative accounts of the Welsh biblical translations are provided by I. Thomas, *Yr Hen Destament Cymraeg 1551-1620* (Aberystwyth, 1988) and his *Y Testament Newydd Cymraeg 1551-1620* (Cardiff, 1976). A more summary treatment will be found in *Y gair ar waith*, ed. R. Geraint Gruffydd (Cardiff, 1988).

[25] D. R. Thomas, I, 89.

[26] W. Ll. Davies, 'Welsh books entered in the Stationers' registers', *JWBS*, 2 (1916-23), 167-74, 204-9 (pp. 168-9).

[27] Reproduced: *Llyfr Gweddi Gyffredin 1567*, ed. M. Richards and Glanmor Williams (Cardiff, 1967).

[28] There is, unfortunately, no twentieth-century reprint of the 1567 New Testament, although one was published in Caernarfon in 1850. For Davies see Glanmor Williams, 'Bishop Richard Davies (?1501-1581)', in his *Welsh Reformation essays*, pp. 155-90.

[29] NLW, MS 727D, pp. 236-8; NLW, Peniarth MS 112D, pp. 845-9, 870-1. I hope to discuss this broadside and the rejoinder to it at greater length elsewhere.

[30] R. Geraint Gruffydd, 'The life of Dr John Davies of Brecon (Siôn Dafydd Rhys)', *THSC*, (1971), pp. 175-90.

[31] E. J. Jones, 'The death and burial of Walter Devereux, Earl of Essex', *CA*, 2 (1945-57), 184-201.

[32] Glanmor Williams, 'Bishop William Morgan and the first Welsh Bible', in his *The Welsh and their religion* (Cardiff, 1991), pp. 173-229.

[33] The Bible was reproduced as: *Y Beibl Cyssegr-lan 1588* (Aberystwyth, 1988), the Psalms as: *Psalmau Dafydd*, ed. T. Powel (London, 1896).

[34] W. Ll. Davies, p. 169.

[35] *Ibid.*

[36] R. Geraint Gruffydd, 'Thomas Salisbury o Lundain a Chlocaenog: ysgolhaig-argraffydd y Dadeni Cymreig', *NLWJ*, 27 (1991-2), 1-19.

[37] E. D. Jones, 'Thomas Salisbury [...]', *NLWJ*, 1 (1939-40), 53 (but correcting 'salice' to 'salve').

[38] Reprint: *Deffynniad Ffydd Eglwys Loegr [...] gan Maurice Kyffin*, ed. W. P. Williams (Bangor, 1908).

[39] Reprint: *Perl mewn Adfyd gan Huw Lewis*, ed. W. J. Gruffydd (Cardiff, 1929).

[40] S. Clark and P. T. J. Morgan, 'Religion and magic in Elizabethan Wales: Robert Holland's dialogue on witchcraft', *JEH*, 27 (1976), 31-46. The manuscript copy is at NLW, Cwrtmawr MS 114B, pp. 243-65.

[41] W. Ll. Davies, pp. 169-70.

[42] *Ibid.*, p. 170; see also the 'Bibliographical note' by J. Ballinger in *Y Llyfr Plygain 1612*, ed. J. Fisher (Cardiff, 1931), pp. 241-50, and the review by G. J. Williams in *Y Llenor*, 11 (1932), 61-2.

[43] W. Ll. Davies, p. 170.

[44] Moses Williams, *Cofrestr o'r holl Lyfrau Printjedig* (London, 1717), sig. A6^r.

[45] W. Williams, 'Three fragments', *JWBS*, 4 (1932-6), 257-61.

46 Reproduced: *Rhan o Salmau Dafydd Broffwyd [...] gan Edward Kyffin 1603*, ed. J. Ballinger (Cardiff, 1930).
47 Reproduced by the Honourable Society of Cymmrodorion (London, 1880) and the Scolar Press (Menston, 1972). See also R. Geraint Gruffydd, 'Dau lythyr gan Owen Lewis', *LlC*, 2 (1952-3), 36-45, and G. Bowen, '*Dottrina Christiana*, Polanco ac *Athravaeth Gristnogavl*, Clynnog', *NLWJ*, 13 (1963-4), 88-91.
48 Reproduced by the Scolar Press (Menston, 1972). See also G. Bowen, *Y Drych Cristianogawl: astudiaeth* (Cardiff, 1988) (published as a supplement to *JWEH*, 5 (1988)), and *Y Drych Kristnogawl*, ed. W. Alun Mathias and G. Bowen (Cardiff, 1996).
49 R. Geraint Gruffydd, 'The life of Dr John Davies of Brecon', pp. 184-6. For a general study see R. Geraint Gruffydd, *Argraffwyr cyntaf Cymru* (Cardiff, 1972).
50 Reproduced by the Scolar Press (Menston, 1970).
51 See Williams's interleaved copy of his *Cofrestr* at the Bodleian Library, Oxford (press mark BS 8°. Art. Z.59); the reference to the 'Carolau' is opposite sig. A7^v.
52 Reproduced in *An Elizabethan broadside in the Welsh language*, ed. R. Ellis (Oxford, 1904). A similar broadside in English, printed by O. Rogers in 1560, is *STC²*, no. 7922.
53 See *Hen gyflwyniadau*, ed. H. Lewis (Cardiff, 1948); *Rhagymadroddion 1547-1659*, ed. Garfield H. Hughes (Cardiff, 1951); C. Davies, *Rhagymadroddion a chyflwyniadau Lladin 1551-1632* (Cardiff, 1980).
54 See Gruffydd, '*Yny Llyvyr hwnn*'.
55 O. E. Illston, 'A literary and bibliographical study of the work of Robert Crowley' (unpublished master's thesis, University of London, King's College, 1952-3).
56 See Gruffydd, 'Thomas Salisbury'.
57 See *LW*, p. xiii for a discussion; but the patent drafted in favour of Salesbury and Walley was apparently not enrolled since it does not appear in the *Calendar of Patent Rolls [...] 1560-63* (London, 1948). For Walley's entry of the 'latenye' see Davies, pp. 168-9.
58 W. Ll. Davies, p. 169. On the catechism see R. Geraint Gruffydd, 'Catecism y Deon Nowell yn Gymraeg', *JWBS*, 7 (1950-3), 114-15, 203-7. That it was published by 1583 is shown by J. Roberts and A. G. Watson, *John Dee's library catalogue* (London, 1990), p. 93 (no. 1647).
59 Gruffydd, 'Thomas Salisbury'.
60 S. Gibson and D. M. Rogers, 'The Earl of Leicester and printing at Oxford', *BLR*, 2 (1941-9), 240-5 (p. 245).
61 See Williams, 'Three fragments'. *LW*, no. 465, says 'London or Oxford, *c.*1600' but *STC²*, no. 2742.5, says 'London, *c.*1595'; without resorting to typographical analysis (which may, indeed, have been done for *STC²*), 'Oxford, *c.*1595' would appear to be the safest guess.
62 See *LW*, nos 1262, 4378-81.
63 Gruffydd, *Argraffwyr cyntaf Cymru*.

CHAPTER 5

LATIN LITERATURE

Ceri Davies

GREAT is the solemn mystery of the Latin language, truly great its divine majesty [...] Wherever the Roman tongue has dominion, there too is the Roman Empire.' So wrote the fifteenth-century humanist and scholar, Lorenzo Valla,[1] in praise of the Latin language and the cultural sway which it had held in Europe for a millennium and a half. Not only did Latin forge a link for the men of the Renaissance with Rome's classical past and with the literary and ecclesiastical learning of the Middle Ages, but it also provided them with an 'antidote to the divisions of Babel'.[2] In the world of Renaissance humanism Latin remained a European lingua franca which transcended the claims of individual vernaculars. Meanwhile the advent of printing gave Latin its special status as the universal 'typographic language'[3] and increased the opportunities for scholars to cross national or linguistic boundaries and communicate with one another in the ancient tongue.

It has been estimated that 'about one in ten of the items printed in England between *c*.1550-1640 is in Latin'.[4] The authors of such works were, in the main, the products of the two English universities and the Inns of Court, and among them were not a few scholars from Wales. One such Welshman, Siôn Dafydd Rhys, speaks for them all when he says that he wrote in Latin so that the information which he wished to impart '*might the more easily spread to other nations too*',[5] and so that the glory of the Welsh language might be revealed '*to the whole of Europe in a language common to all*'.[6] Latin was assuredly the means whereby to achieve such an end. For, as Thomas Wiliems of Trefriw epigrammatically put it, '*Latin is the most universal language in the whole of Europe*'.[7]

As might be expected, not all Latin writers who had Welsh connections wrote within a Welsh, or even a British, context. Their command of Latin provided some of them with a passport which took them far beyond local boundaries. One of the most notable of Wales's wandering humanists is Leonard Cox (fl. *c*.1512-*c*.1547), originally from Monmouth, who early in the sixteenth century went to the universities of Paris and Tübingen, possibly to Wittenberg and Prague, and then to Kraków in Poland where he was for a time Professor of Rhetoric.[8] In Kraków he appears to have published a number of Latin works, especially a short but important treatise on education and the study of classical languages, *Libellus de Erudienda Iuventute* (Kraków, 1526).[9] Cox is best remembered for a work written in English after his return to Britain, *The art or crafte of rhetoryke* (London, 1532), based on Melanchthon's *Institutiones rhetoricae*.

Not many Welsh writers were as widely travelled as Leonard Cox. However, that blend of scientist and wizard, Dr John Dee (1527-1609), the Cambridge-educated 'Arch Conjuror' of England, as a young man took the University of Louvain and the College of Reims in Paris by storm, and in later life went on a rather disastrous journey to spread his Hermetic ideas in central Europe. Dee was born in London, the son of a minor official in the Tudor court, and claimed descent on his father's side from Rhodri Mawr. He also claimed to be related to the contemporary historians, John Lewis of

Llynwene and John Prise of Brecon, and like his kinsmen became engaged in the defence of Geoffrey of Monmouth's account of the 'British History'. Dee's earliest major publication, *Propaedeumata Aphoristica* (London, 1558), explaining how the physical universe is governed by magical principles, is written in Latin. He also maintained his Welsh connection by, for example, supplying a liminary Latin epigram to Henry Perri's *Eglvryn Phraethineb* (London, 1595).[10]

Other Latin writers of Welsh descent made their mark in an English context. Hugh Lloyd of Denbigh (1546-1601) became headmaster of Winchester and composed for his wards a Latin phrase book which was posthumously published, *Phrases elegantiores ex Caesaris Commentariis, Cicerone, aliisque, in usum Scholae Winton* (Oxford, 1654).[11] Griffith Powell of Llansawel in Carmarthenshire (1561-1620), a Fellow (and later Principal) of Jesus College, Oxford, was renowned for his works on Aristotle. His Latin commentaries on the *Posterior Analytics* (1594) and the *Sophistici Elenchi* (1598), both printed in Oxford by Joseph Barnes, played a vital part in the neo-scholastic revival of interest in Aristotle in the sixteenth century.[12] Meanwhile, Powell's Oxford contemporary Matthew Gwinne (c.1558-1627), son of a London-Welsh grocer, composed a Latin play published as *Nero: Tragaedia Nova* (London, 1603).[13]

Among neo-Latin poets of the age, the young William Vaughan (1577-1641) of Golden Grove, later of Llangyndeyrn near Carmarthen, promoter of colonization in Newfoundland, produced at the end of the sixteenth century four volumes of Latin verse, the most notable being his *Poematum Libellus* (London, 1598). In a later work, *Cambrensium Caroleia* (London, 1625), Vaughan includes some spirited writing on his Welsh origins and versifies his wish that a colony named 'Cambriola' be established in the New World.[14] Another high-ranking figure, Sir John Stradling of St Donat's (1563-1637), heir to the childless Sir Edward Stradling, published a delightful collection of Latin epigrams, *Epigrammatum Libri Quatuor* (London, 1607).[15] The best known British writer of Latin epigrams was John Stradling's Oxford contemporary, the immensely popular John Owen (c.1564-c.1628) of Plas Du, Llanarmon. Owen appears to have given up his career as a teacher to live on what patronage he could enjoy as a Latin poet. Between 1606 and 1612 he produced fifteen hundred or so Latin epigrams in four volumes (arranged as ten 'books'), all first published in London by Simon Waterson and printed by either John Windet or Nicholas Okes. Owen's wit and satiric comment on human foibles won him immense popularity in Britain and throughout Europe. His work ran to many editions and countless translations. It has been accurately said of him that 'on the Continent he was much better known than Shakespeare his contemporary; he was probably the best known British man of letters'.[16] Precisely so. The Latin poems of William Vaughan, John Stradling, and John Owen, while they do contain a number of Welsh references and echoes, primarily belong to the cultural world of late-Renaissance Britain as a whole.

Of greater significance, within the framework of the present study, are the works of Latin writers who wrote within a Welsh context or whose subject-matter was specifically Welsh. Three areas may be singled out for special mention.[17]

Firstly, there are the works of those Welshmen who came to the defence of Geoffrey of Monmouth's *Historia Regum Britanniae* against its detractors. John Dee's concern with the 'matter of Britain' has already been mentioned, but the standing of the British

History had exercised the minds of certain Welsh Renaissance scholars long before it engaged his attention. Chief among them was one of the earliest of Welsh humanists, Sir John Prise of Brecon.[18] Prise wrote, in Latin, the fullest of all defences of Geoffrey's work against the calumnies, as he saw them, contained in the *Anglica Historia* (1534) of the Italian diplomat and historian Polydore Vergil. That Prise's trust in the truth of Geoffrey's writing was misplaced in no way detracts from the significance of what he says, and his *Historiae Brytannicae Defensio* remains one of the most important of the early writings of the Renaissance in Wales. The *Defensio* was not published until almost twenty years after his death, his son Richard having it printed in London by Henry Bynneman and Humphrey Toy in 1573. In a prefatory letter addressed to William Herbert, Earl of Pembroke, Prise explains that he writes in Latin because he has to draw on so many classical historians, authorities whose works had to be reconciled with the matter of the British History. Furthermore, Polydore Vergil had written his book in Latin, and the ancient tongue was clearly the right medium for discussing an issue which had now been given international circulation. In the same preface Prise also confesses to a sense of inadequacy for scaling the heights of eloquence, and thereby alludes to contemporary concern about writing elegant Latin and the debate whether Cicero's style should be slavishly imitated.

Two other notable Welsh humanists, both from Clwyd, both educated at Oxford, concerned themselves with the controversy which surrounded the British History and also made important contributions in Latin to historical and chorographical studies. Humphrey Lhwyd of Denbigh (1527-68), described by William Salesbury as 'the most famous *Antiquarius* of all our countrey',[19] enjoyed the patronage of Henry Fitzalan, twelfth Earl of Arundel, and his son-in-law John, Baron Lumley. Both were noted antiquarians and book-collectors, and under their inspiration Lhwyd supplemented and produced an English version of *Brut y Tywysogyon*. Thanks to Arundel he also met the Dutch cartographer Abraham Ortelius, for whom he wrote a Latin essay on Anglesey, *De Mona*, printed by Ortelius in his atlas, *Theatrum Orbis Terrarum* (first edition, Antwerp, 1570), and also by Richard Prise as an appendix to his father's *Historiae Brytannicae Defensio*. Lhwyd's other Latin work, sent from his death-bed to Ortelius, was his *Commentarioli Britannicae Descriptionis Fragmentum,* on British historical geography and place-names. First published in Cologne in 1572, this became particularly well known through Thomas Twyne's English translation, *The Breuiary of Britayne* (1573).

David Powel of Rhiwabon (*c.*1540-98) was for nearly thirty years domestic chaplain to Sir Henry Sidney, at whose request he published his renowned *Historie of Cambria* (1584), an expanded version of Lhwyd's rendering of *Brut y Tywysogyon*. In 1585 Powel made a further contribution to British antiquarian studies by editing and publishing the works of two Latin authors: first, a summary by the Italian Virunnius Ponticus of Geoffrey's *Historia*, and, second, the Latin writings about Wales, *Itinerarium Cambriae* and *Descriptio Cambriae,* of Gerald of Wales, with Powel's own comments on each chapter. In dedicatory letters addressed to Henry Sidney and to his son, the poet Philip Sidney, Powel presents himself as a defender of Geoffrey's British History, and is at great pains to cite classical authorities who appear to support and corroborate it. The same issue, the interrelationship of native and classical material, is the subject of a Latin essay, *De Britannica Historia Recte Intelligenda, et cum Romanis Scriptoribus*

Reconcilianda, which Powel published at the end of his edition of Ponticus and Gerald. Brief though it is, Powel's essay is one of the most measured statements on a matter which was of paramount importance for Welsh Renaissance scholars.[20]

The second area of study which was of particular importance to Welsh humanists, and which they discussed in Latin, was the study of the Welsh language, its grammar and poetics, its vocabulary and lexicography. The compilation of dictionaries is discussed in Chapter 6, but it is worth noting here that Latin is the language placed alongside Welsh in the dictionaries produced by Thomas Wiliems, Henry Salesbury, and Dr John Davies of Mallwyd. The study of grammar, based on the works of Priscian and Donatus, had a position of honour within the bardic tradition of medieval Wales. Now Renaissance concerns with the study of language led to a spate of humanist grammars of the Welsh language. The earliest such grammar was written, in Welsh, by the Catholic exile Dr Gruffydd Robert and published in parts from 1567 onwards, initially — and perhaps wholly — in Milan.[21] Gruffydd Robert saw the art of translation as vital for extending the capabilities of a language in the modern world, and in the sixth part of his Grammar he put his ideas into practice: he transposed Ciceronian style into a Welsh medium by translating the beginning of Cicero's *De Senectute*. Another Welsh humanist who went to Italy for a time was the Anglesey-born Siôn Dafydd Rhys, also known as Dr John Davies (of Brecon).[22] He graduated as Doctor of Medicine from Siena in 1567, but also made a distinctive contribution to classical teaching. Three books came from his pen during his stay in Italy: a Latin work, now lost, on Greek grammar and syntax; an Italian treatise on Latin grammar and syntax, *Della costruttione latina* (Venice, 1567); and a guide, in Latin, to the pronunciation of Italian, *Perutilis Exteris Nationibus De Italica Pronunciatione et Orthographia Libellus* (Padua, 1569).[23] Siôn Dafydd Rhys had returned to Wales by the early 1570s and eventually moved, after periods in Bangor and Carmarthen, to the Cardiff area. There he came in contact with the Herbert family (of Cardiff Castle and Wilton), and with Sir Edward Stradling and his family at St Donat's. Siôn Dafydd Rhys found in Stradling a matchless patron for his humanistic aspirations. He was encouraged by Sir Edward to translate from Latin and Italian into Welsh, and promised to prepare a Welsh version of a compendium of Aristotelian metaphysics.[24] The most important of the scholarly works which Rhys produced thanks to Edward Stradling's support was a grammar of the Welsh language, written in Latin, *Cambrobrytannicae Cymraecaeve Linguae Institutiones*. This was the work of Rhys's mature years, composed after his removal to his final home in Brecon. Its 1,250 copies were printed in London by Thomas Orwin, at Stradling's expense, in 1592.[25] Much of the grammar is in a more traditional mould than that of Gruffydd Robert, its most perceptive section being that on the phonology of Welsh. What is beyond doubt is that both Edward Stradling and Siôn Dafydd Rhys viewed it as incumbent upon them to use the resources of the Latin tongue for the purpose of presenting the language of Wales to the community of scholars throughout Europe. A similar motive lay behind the publication of Henry Salesbury's slighter *Grammatica Britannica* (London, 1593).[26]

The crowning glory of such Renaissance grammars of Welsh is the *Antiquae Linguae Britannicae [...] Rudimenta* (London, 1621)[27] of Dr John Davies (*c*.1567-1644) of Mallwyd.[28] This Latin work, the result of a lifetime's study of the language of Welsh poets down to Davies's own day, has been said to reveal 'a grammarian of genius at work, systematically analysing and describing the language used by the professional poets, some eighty of whom are referred to'.[29] Of equal brilliance is the work's preface, addressed in Latin to Edmwnd Prys, archdeacon of Merioneth. Together with the Latin preface to Davies's *Dictionarium Duplex* (London, 1632) it presents the reader with an outstanding statement of the distinction (as Davies saw it) of the Welsh language — its antiquity, its place among the major tongues of the world, its claim to special attention. Like John Prise, Humphrey Lhwyd, and David Powel, he lays great emphasis on the traditions of Geoffrey's *Historia*, and in presenting his picture of the antiquity of the Welsh tongue he adduces the standard passages from classical authors to support his thesis. He also displays considerable familiarity with the works of some of the main humanistic scholars who had written in England and on the Continent, men like John Caius, William Camden and Edward Brerewood, Juan Luis Vives and Justus Lipsius, Joseph Justus Scaliger and Paulus Merula. As was befitting for a biblical scholar and translator (he had assisted both William Morgan and Richard Parry in the task of translating the Bible into Welsh), he knew about the writers on the biblical languages and their expository works: Franciscus Junius, Sebastian Münster, and David Parraeus are among the authorities to whom he alludes. He is steeped in classical literature and in the Church Fathers, and regularly quotes the works of Erasmus, especially the *Adagia*. John Davies's approach is throughout that of the humanist, the man of the Renaissance. It is no wonder that he was hailed by his contemporary Rowland Vaughan as *'the one outstanding Plato of our language'*.[30]

The third significant area in which Latin is used in books produced in the second half of the sixteenth century and the early seventeenth is that of prefatory and dedicatory writing, both prose and verse.[31] In some instances the preface becomes an important essay in its own right: this is especially true of John Davies's introductory material, and also of Humphrey Prichard's *Praefatio* at the beginning of Siôn Dafydd Rhys's Grammar. Furthermore, in dedicating the work to an aristocrat or notable churchman, possibly even the sovereign, an author is given a chance not only to explain the purpose of his work but also to enhance the status of his book through its association with a grand dedicatee. John Prise had prepared two prefaces for his *Historiae Brytannicae Defensio*, one addressed to William Herbert, Earl of Pembroke, and the other to King Edward VI, while his son Richard Prise added in 1573 yet a further epistle to William Cecil, Lord Burghley. In the same way we have seen David Powel addressing his patrons Henry and Philip Sidney, and Siôn Dafydd Rhys dedicating his work to Edward Stradling. Such Latin addresses and dedications are not confined to works whose main text is written entirely, or mainly, in Latin: William Salesbury, in *Kynniver llith a ban* (London, 1551), has a Latin dedication to the bishops of St David's, Llandaf, Bangor, St Asaph, and Hereford, and Henri Perri, in *Eglvryn Phraethineb*, addresses a Latin *Epistola Dedicatoria* to the younger John Salusbury of Lleweni. The most notable examples of Latin preliminary material of this kind are William Morgan's dedication of his translation of the Bible (London, 1588) to Queen Elizabeth I and Bishop Richard Parry's dedication of its 1620 revision to the Holy Trinity and to King James I.

As popular with the humanists as preliminary material in prose was the adorning of their books with short Latin poems which were usually expressions of good wishes and compliments from friends and fellow-scholars.[32] Sir John Prise's *Historiae*

Brytannicae Defensio contains prefatory verses from, among others, the notable English classicists Bartholomew Clerke and Edward Grant. Siôn Dafydd Rhys's Grammar is preceded by epigrams written by William Camden and John Stradling. (Stradling, it is interesting to note, was one of many who wrote Latin poems to greet the 1607 edition of Camden's *Britannia*.) John Dee supplied liminary verses for Henri Perri's *Eglvryn Phraethineb*, as did Huw Lewys, translator of *Perl mewn Adfyd*. John Davies's Preface to his Grammar, formally addressed to Edmwnd Prys, is followed by a delightful *Rescriptum* by Prys himself, written in hexameters. Some of the most engaging of Latin liminary verses were written for Maurice Kyffin's English translation of Terence's *Andria* (London, 1588). Among the poems to greet Kyffin's work there is a pleasing eight-line epigram by William Morgan, probably written in London during the year which Morgan spent there to oversee the printing of the 1588 Bible.[33] In a different strain, the sermon preached in November 1576 by Bishop Richard Davies at the funeral in Carmarthen of Walter Devereux, Earl of Essex, and printed in London in 1577, is prefaced with elegies in Greek, Latin, and Hebrew by Hugh Broughton. The work also contains a series of Latin epigrams, probably written by scholars of the Queen Elizabeth Grammar School, founded in Carmarthen in 1576 by the Earl of Essex and Bishop Davies.[34]

Humanism in a Welsh context, coupled with a devotion to writing and publishing in Latin, did not flourish long. The ever-increasing anglicization of the gentry, and their looking towards the schools and universities of England, meant that few of the natural heirs of Renaissance classicism thought in Welsh terms. The twin brothers Henry and Thomas Vaughan did, to some extent, see themselves in a Welsh light. '*Wales gave me birth*' is the boast of Henry, 'The Silurist', in one of his many Latin poems,[35] but in essence his work belongs to the world of seventeenth-century English poetry.[36] A few writings of the eighteenth-century 'Welsh Augustans' — six poems, mainly juvenilia, by Goronwy Owen, and Evan Evans's thirty-page essay 'De Bardis Dissertatio' — were to provide the last faint flowering of Latin composition by writers who were consciously Welsh.[37]

NOTES TO CHAPTER 5

I am grateful to Emeritus Professor R. Geraint Gruffydd for reading an earlier draft of this chapter, and for his very helpful comments.

1. *Elegantiae linguae Latinae* (1471), Praefatio (Laurentius Valla, *Opera omnia* i, reprint, (Turin, 1962), p. 4).
2. John Hale, *The civilization of Europe in the Renaissance* (London, 1993), p. 152.
3. W. J. Ong, *The barbarian within, and other fugitive essays and studies* (New York, 1962), p. 208.
4. J. W. Binns, *Intellectual culture in Elizabethan and Jacobean England: the Latin writings of the age* (Leeds, 1990), p. 1.
5. 'quo facilius ad exteras quoque gentes illius linguae cognitio dimanaret' (*Cambrobrytannicae [...] Institutiones* (1592), sig *2ᵛ).
6. 'i olwc holl Ewrôpa mywn Iaith gyphrêdin i bawb' (*Cambrobrytannicae [...] Institutiones*, sig ***1ʳ, reprinted in *Rhagymadroddion 1547-1659*, ed. Garfield H. Hughes (Cardiff, 1951), p. 70).
7. 'Llatin sydd gyphredinaf iaith yn holl Europa' (NLW, Peniarth MS 228, printed in *Rhagymadroddion*, p. 112).
8. A. Breeze, 'Leonard Cox, a Welsh humanist in Poland and Hungary', *NLWJ*, 25 (1987-8), 399-410; Henryk Zins, 'A British humanist and the University of Kraków at the beginning of the sixteenth century: a chapter in Anglo-Polish relations in the age of the Renaissance', *Renaissance Studies*, 8 (1994), 13-39.
9. Modern edition, with introduction, translation and notes, ed. A. Breeze and J. Glomski, *Humanistica Lovaniensia*, 40 (1991), 112-67.
10. Sig. B2ᵛ. Reproduced: *Egluryn Ffraethineb [...] gan Henri Perri*, ed. G. J. Williams (Cardiff, 1930). On Dee's Welsh connections, see G. A. Williams, *Madoc, the making of a myth* (London, 1979), pp. 31-67, and his *Welsh wizard and British empire: Dr John Dee and a Welsh identity* (Cardiff, 1980); R. J. Roberts, 'John Dee and the Matter of Britain', *THSC*, (1991), pp. 129-43.
11. F. Madan, *Oxford books [...]*, 3 vols (Oxford, 1895-1931), III, 38-9.
12. Madan, I, 36-7, 44-5. See also J. K. McConica, 'Humanism and Aristotle in Tudor Oxford', *EHR*, 94 (1979), 291-317 (p. 297).
13. Facsimile reprint, with an introduction by Heinz-Dieter Leidig, Renaissance Latin drama in England, First series, 13 (Hildesheim, 1983).
14. L. Bradner, *Musae Anglicanae: a history of Anglo-Latin poetry 1500-1925*, MLA General Series, 10 (New York & London, 1940), pp. 51-2; W. K. D. Davies, 'The Welsh in Canada: a geographical overview', in *The Welsh in Canada*, ed. M. E. Chamberlain ([s.l.], 1986), pp. 1-45 (pp. 16-18).
15. Glanmor Williams, 'Sir John Stradling of St Donat's', *Glamorgan Historian*, 9 ([1973]), 11-28.
16. J. Henry Jones, 'John Owen, the epigrammatist', *Greece and Rome*, 10 (1941), 65-73 (p. 73). Owen's work has been re-edited by J. R. C. Martyn, 2 vols (Leiden, 1976-8).
17. For a fuller discussion of some of these areas and also of the poetry of John Stradling and John Owen, see Ceri Davies, *Latin writers of the Renaissance* (Cardiff, 1981) and his *Welsh literature and the classical tradition* (Cardiff, 1995), Chapter 3.
18. N. R. Ker, 'Sir John Prise', *The Library*, 5th ser. 10 (1955), 1-24.
19. Salesbury's letter to Archbishop Matthew Parker, 19 March 1565 (Cambridge, Corpus Christi College, MS 114, p. 491) is printed in R. Flower, 'William Salesbury, Richard Davies, and Archbishop Parker', *NLWJ*, 2 (1941-2), 7-14 (pp. 9-10). On Lhwyd, see R. Geraint Gruffydd, 'Humphrey Llwyd of Denbigh: some documents and a catalogue', *TDHS*, 17 (1968), 54-107 (and errata in *TDHS*, 18 (1969), 178-9) and his 'Humphrey Llwyd: dyneiddiwr', *EA*, 33 (1970), 57-74.
20. Lhwyd and Powel are discussed in the context of Welsh sixteenth-century historiography in I. M. Williams, 'Ysgolheictod hanesyddol yr unfed ganrif ar bymtheg [...]', *LlC*, 2 (1952-3), 111-24, 209-23.
21. Reprint: *Gramadeg Cymraeg gan Gruffydd Robert*, ed. G. J. Williams (Cardiff, 1939).
22. R. Geraint Gruffydd, 'The life of Dr John Davies of Brecon', *THSC*, (1971), pp. 175-90, and his 'Dr

John Davies, "the old man of Brecknock"', *AC*, 141 (1992), 1-13.
23. Facsimile reprint in *Trattati di fonetica del cinquecento*, ed. Nicoletta Maraschio (Florence, 1992), pp. 93-193, followed by an Italian translation and discussion, pp. 195-264. Siôn Dafydd Rhys and Gruffydd Robert are discussed in their Italian context in T. G. Griffith, *Avventure linguistiche del cinquecento* (Florence, 1961).
24. *Cambrobrytannicae [...] Institutiones*, sig *3ᵛ.
25. Davies, *Latin writers*, p. 3.
26. Reproduced by the Scolar Press (Menston, 1969).
27. Reproduced by the Scolar Press (Menston, 1968).
28. Rhiannon F. Roberts, 'Dr John Davies o Fallwyd', *LlC*, 2 (1952-3), 19-35, 97-110.
29. R. Geraint Gruffydd, 'The Renaissance and Welsh literature', in *The Celts and the Renaissance: tradition and innovation*, ed. Glanmor Williams and Robert O. Jones (Cardiff, 1990), pp. 17-39 (p. 26).
30. 'yr hwn yw'r vnig Plato ardderchawg o'n hiaith ni' (reprint of *Yr Ymarfer o Dduwioldeb*, ed. J. Ballinger (Cardiff, 1930), p. xxi); *Rhagymadroddion*, p. 120).
31. For a collection of Latin prefaces and dedications translated into Welsh, see Ceri Davies, *Rhagymadroddion a chyflwyniadau Lladin, 1551-1632* (Cardiff, 1980).
32. In the British context, see Franklin B. Williams, jun., *Index of dedications and commendatory verses in English books before 1641* (London, 1962).
33. Ceri Davies, 'Dysg ddyneiddiol cyfieithwyr y Beibl', *LlC*, 16 (1989-91), 7-22 (pp. 17-18).
34. E. J. Jones, 'The death and burial of Walter Devereux, Earl of Essex', *CA*, (1945-57), 184-201.
35. CAMBRIA *me genuit*, patulis *ubi* vallibus *errans / Subjacet* aeriis montibus ISCA pater ('Ad Posteros' from *Olor Iscanus* (1651)).
36. Roland Mathias, 'In search of The Silurist', *Poetry Wales*, 11(2) (1975), 6-35. But see also M. Wynn Thomas, *Morgan Llwyd: ei gyfeillion a'i gyfnod* (Cardiff, 1991), pp. 34-50 and his inaugural lecture ' "No Englishman": Wales's Henry Vaughan', *Swansea Review* 15 (1995), 1-19.
37. Davies, *Welsh literature and the classical tradition*, pp. 95, 107-8.

CHAPTER 6

EARLY WELSH DICTIONARIES

M. T. Burdett-Jones

WHEN William Salesbury talked of 'what a bonde and knotte of loue and frendshyppe the communion of one tonge is' in his dedication to Henry VIII of *A Dictionary in Englyshe and Welshe* of 1547,[1] it was to the English language that he was referring, his aim being to aid his fellow Welshmen to learn English. Given that he showed evidence of the Renaissance delight in the copiousness of language in his *Kynniver llith a ban* of 1551 and even more so in his *Testament Newydd* of 1567 where different sizes of type and brackets and numerous variants in the margin show different forms and ways of expressing things, what is striking is how incomplete and unfinished is his dictionary.[2] To give one example: though Salesbury later compiled a herbal,[3] in what was in fact a Welsh-English dictionary where he often gives Welsh synonyms or explanations as well as English synonyms, under *penllwyd* he gives only *llysieuyn*, 'a plant', though *Geiriadur Prifysgol Cymru*, the University of Wales historical dictionary of Welsh, gives three botanological meanings to this word in addition to other meanings. There are words noted but left without any explanation, and other signs of haste to get 'the boke [...] entreating of a matter byfore towchede of no man & therefore rude' through the press. Salesbury drew on the vocabularies in John Palsgrave's *Lesclarcissment de la langue Francoyse* of 1530,[4] a book written in English which aimed to teach French, but Salesbury did not work on anything like the same scale, nor did he follow Palsgrave's layout of separate sections for nouns, adjectives, and other parts of speech.[5] In his introductory material Salesbury gives the Welsh alphabet as: *a b c ch d dd e f ff g gh* (= modern Welsh *ng*) *h i k l ll m n o p r s t th v u w y*. Oddly, since he says all the words beginning in *b, c, ch,* and *d* are to be found together, he lists both *c* and *k*, but in the dictionary itself repeats under *k* the few words which occur under *c*.[6] He deals with the problem of initial mutation of consonants in Welsh by telling readers to look under the unmutated form, for as he says, *'only an idiot going to the woods to gather twigs would expect them to grow in the same shape as if they were woven through the rods of a wattle wall.'*[7]

Salesbury was the first Renaissance scholar in Wales to compile a dictionary.[8] Previous activity in this field had taken the form of glossaries of specialist terms such as plant names, which were of practical use for physicians as herbs were commonly used ingredients in medical recipes, and bardic vocabularies for the use of practising poets. Poets, like the later Renaissance scholars, delighted in variety of vocabulary and committed vocabularies to writing from the fifteenth century onwards as well as thesauri listing epithets for, e.g. a king, to equip them with the terms in which to praise their patrons in the manner prescribed in the bardic grammars. As was shown in Chapter 2, the fifteenth century was a period of bardic scribal activity when a number of *cywyddwyr* committed their own work to paper, including Lewys Glyn Cothi, Gutun Owain, and, most interestingly in this context, Gwilym Tew who compiled a vocabulary of archaic words which he had found in the Book of Aneurin.[9]

Thomas Wiliems of Trefriw,[10] who was among other things a physician, copied many manuscripts (including Wiliam Llŷn's bardic vocabulary)[11] and drew on a wide range of sources when he was collecting material for his dictionary in an age when one man could write a whole dictionary. He clearly intended it for publication and when he finished it in 1607 he gave it the title *'The treasure of the Latin language and Welsh, or the richest and most extensive dictionary of the true pure British'*.[12] In his preface he addressed the lords, scholars, and *'the dear common people of all Wales'* with full command of rhetoric in Welsh rather than in Latin, the language of scholarship, presenting his work as fulfilling his duty to his country and his mother tongue by writing a dictionary such as most countries in Christendom possessed. Having waited in vain for others to produce dictionaries which would have lightened his burden, he took Thomas Thomas's Latin-English dictionary, the first edition of which was published in 1587, as the framework to organize the store of material which he had spent many years amassing. To the Latin headwords Wiliems supplied Welsh translations of the definitions and added illustrative quotations from poetry and prose. His work remains a storehouse for modern lexicographers. He saw his dictionary as being of use to rhetoricians, preachers, and translators of every art from Latin into Welsh, and here we remember that men such as Gruffydd Robert considered translation a way of extending the Welsh language. The common people were thus to benefit from his work indirectly through translations. He thanked people who had helped him but also took the opportunity to describe in unflattering terms those who had kept manuscripts from him and referred derisively to Welshmen who simper a foreign language, English, to each other rather than speak their sweet mother tongue. One of those who lent him manuscripts was John Edwards III of Chirk who copied out a substantial part of Thomas Wiliems's dictionary in NLW, Brogyntyn MSS 9 and 10,[13] and it was probably his offer of financial support to publish which spurred Thomas Wiliems to set about editing his material. John Edwards was a fellow Catholic (Thomas Wiliems had reverted to Catholicism) and as a recusant lost the greater part of his possessions in 1613, doubtless the reason why nothing came of the plan to publish the dictionary. Thomas Wiliems received patronage from Sir John Wynn of Gwedir during the four years when he devoted himself exclusively to composing his dictionary.[14] They corresponded in 1620 about publishing it but nothing had come of these plans either by the time Thomas Wiliems died, and the manuscript came into Sir John Wynn's hands in 1623. The scholar and cleric Dr John Davies of Mallwyd wrote to Sir John in August 1623 asking to see the dictionary which he understood the latter wished to have printed. If the dictionary met with his approval, Davies would prepare it for the press and any gain would go to whoever Sir John would appoint. If Wiliems had dedicated it to Sir John Wynn, the dedication would stand, and if not, the printing of it at his cost would be a sufficient dedication. John Davies would not expect to bear any of the costs, giving freely of his labour.[15] He emphasized the cost a few months later in another letter to Sir John Wynn:

> you knowe so greate a volume cannot be printed without verie greate charge, which I know no printer will, by any meanes vndergo, being that the printers conceive so smalle hope of gaine by our Welshe bookes [...] the booke had neede be first corrected in diverse places, & being of the authors handwriting, must all

[be] transcribed before any printer (of an other Language especially) can reade it.[16]

In March 1624 John Davies wrote:

> I beleeve the charge of the printing, besides the tending of the presse, will be no lesse than 120 li. The gayne will be uncertayne, because of the uncertenty of the sale of the bookes. And the charge will be more or lesse according to the smalleness or bignesse of the letter it shall be printed in, for a greate letter will have the more paper. If I might be worthie to give advise about it, the wholle book should be reviewed, & made lesse then it is by a fourthe parte at leaste [...] & so the charge of the printing would be lesse [...] I have 3 or 4 good writers about me. But I will doe nothing till I heare from you.[17]

Although Davies was authorized to proceed he did not obtain the promise of money. He explained in August that progress with the transcription was slow as 'the hand is so harde to rede that I canne gette no bodie to write it but I must be at his elbowe'[18] and discontinued his practice of abbreviation and correction as Sir John Wyn had wanted the manuscript copied verbatim. In May 1625 Davies sent Wynn a poor transcription of part of the dictionary which, apart from errors, preserved Thomas Wiliems' orthography, e.g. the use of *lh* for *ll*, *dh* for *dd*, as used by other Renaissance scholars. Had Wiliems's orthography been retained, the two parts of the *Dictionarium Duplex* would have been inconsistent since John Davies, one of the editors of the 1620 Bible, in his Welsh-Latin dictionary, which was to form the other half, used the orthography which had been to a considerable extent standardized, to the great gain of the Welsh language, in the Bibles of 1588 and 1620. As Davies had hoped, Sir John Wynn realized that an unedited transcription of the dictionary would not do, and work on editing and transcribing continued, a further delay being caused by Davies making a fair copy of the Welsh-Latin dictionary which he had started in 1593 and which follows the modern Welsh alphabetical order (*a, b, c, ch, &c*).

On 1 March 1627 Sir John Wynn died and John Davies wrote to his son Owen Wynn in January 1628 saying that he had told Sir John that the costs of printing would be some £140. Although Sir John had disbursed only £10, Davies understood that Sir Richard Wynn intended to pay a greater proportion. The charge of the 'corrector, to attend the printing' would come to £60 or £70 more. He hoped that Sir Richard would 'make tryal of friends, and to see what may be had towards that charge'.[19] Owen Wynn sent John Davies a list of printers in London and he replied in May 1629 saying that some of them were poor men, not able to deal with the book themselves. He had been told, rather oddly given the legal restrictions on printing, that 'Mr Jones, of Whitecrosse-streete'[20] wished to move his press to the Marches. Were he to do so 'shortly', Davies would prefer to deal with him since he would be nearer, otherwise he would be glad to deal with:

> such of them as would beare half the charge, and take half the book. The same l're will serve as Rider is printed in, by Adam Islip, 1617;[21] and the same volume, but that this will not be so bigge. The l'res must be Romane and Italique, and

now and then among some Hebrewe and Greeke l'res, and a fewe English l'res. Yf none will beare half the charge, the way to treate with them will be, to agree with them by the sheete, for 500 or 600 copies, they bearing all the charge; and so I hope they may take xii[s] a sheete or somewhat more, if paper be deerer than ordinarie. I would have the paper to be good pott paper and not the paper that Rider is in, of a° 1617.[22]

In September 1629 Davies wrote to Owen Wynn:

> I know Mr Beale and have bene at his house. Yf he will adventure 100[l], I knowe he would expecte but his share of the printed copies according to that charge: but it is to no purpose for us to make him beleeve that every p'ishe in Wales will buy a booke; for I, for my parte, doe not like that course: but let them be bought as they deserve, without compulsion. As for the estimate of the printing, I have sent you the printed leafe enclosed; whereby I have cast over the wholle booke and do guesse it will amount to 245 sheets a booke, of the letter that this leafe is printed in [...] let me heare from you [...] whether he will undertake a share of the worke; and if he will undertake the halfe, or the 1-4th part.[23]

Despite further correspondence, the *Dictionarium Duplex* was not published until 1632, being then printed at the house of R. Young at John Davies's own expense, despite the dedication to Sir Richard Wynn.[24]

Henry Salesbury was a minor figure of the Renaissance in Wales and one of several who, doubtless spurred to experimentation in orthography by the printing press where the different frequencies of use of type for the Welsh language caused problems, devised symbols, some of which found their way into print in his *Grammatica Britannica* (1593/4). He also experimented in his dictionaries with the order of the alphabet by grouping letters according to their phonetic characteristics. He clearly hoped to publish one of his dictionaries together with a revised edition of his grammar,[25] dedicating the bilingual one (a copy of which survives in NLW, MS 13215E) to King Charles I, but was no more successful in this than Thomas Wiliems was in his lifetime. This was the fate of the dictionaries of other lexicographers, such as Siôn Dafydd Rhys, Henri Perri, and David Powel, even though some of their other work found its way into print.

John Davies's dictionary, still valuable to scholars today, set the pattern for what a dictionary should be in that it included a list of plant names and additional material (notably a list of proverbs) such as we see in Thomas Richards's dictionary of 1753 which was virtually a translation of the Welsh-Latin section of the *Dictionarium Duplex*, with the addition of material from other sources.[26] In the 1670s the religious reformer Stephen Hughes was concerned that readers in south Wales did not understand many north-Wales words in books published by the Welsh Trust. As 'Corrector of the Press' for the Trust he attempted to alleviate the problem by adding brief vocabularies explaining the less common terms in colloquial Welsh. Since *'a Welsh dictionary could not be obtained in London',*[27] he believed that the Welsh gentry ought to be persuaded to finance an enlarged reprint of the *Dictionarium Duplex*.[28] Although this project proved abortive, the idea of a dictionary which provided modern Welsh words and their English equivalents was realized in 1688 with the appearance of *Y Gymraeg yn ei Disgleirdeb [...] The British Language in its Lustre* a small book, relatively cheap (selling at 1s. 6d.) and suitable for carrying around in the pocket.[29] Published by Thomas Jones the almanacer in order to preserve the Welsh language from the encroachments of English, it was based on the Welsh-Latin section of the *Dictionarium Duplex* (omitting much material) and included a list of plant names. Jones, who was himself to become a printer following his move to Shrewsbury, was clearly unhappy about the extensive errata, claiming that the London printers 'being unacquainted with the British Tongue' had even bungled 'where I had Writ and truly Corrected'. He explained further (in Welsh only) that he had paid these conscienceless printers as much for the worst as for the best parts, and vented his indignation in a denunciatory *englyn*.[30] Siôn Rhydderch's English-Welsh dictionary of 1725 (the first such) was of a similar size to that of Thomas Jones, again intended for everyday rather than scholarly use, badly printed, and strewn with errors.

The status of the *Dictionarium Duplex* as the standard work of reference[31] prompted several Welsh scholars to compile lists of omissions.[32] Although Edward Lhuyd resisted persuasion to bring out a new edition of the *Dictionarium Duplex*,[33] he included a section entitled 'Some Welch words omitted in Dr. Davies's Dictionary' in his *Archaeologia Britannica* of 1707. As well as making use of Henry Salesbury's manuscript dictionary, Lhuyd was given access through the Revd Humphrey Foulkes (1673-1737) to John Davies's own copy of the *Dictionarium* with additions. Foulkes was one of those to whom G. J. Williams referred when he spoke of a sort of 'lexicographical passion'[34] amongst clerics in north-east Wales, and his correspondence refers to a list of words compiled by them which unfortunately arrived too late to be included in Thomas Jones's dictionary. An industrious Denbighshire cleric, Thomas Lloyd of Plas Power (?1673-1734), inserted many thousands of detailed references to printed books and manuscripts into an interleaved copy of the *Dictionarium Duplex* over a period of years up to his death in 1734. As Lloyd indexed many of the poetry manuscripts he saw, his collection of materials for a dictionary, which he did not, as far as we know, attempt to prepare for publication, is today of great value to the staff of *Geiriadur Prifysgol Cymru*. William Gambold (1672-1728), a Pembrokeshire cleric and friend of Lhuyd, produced a substantial and valuable English-Welsh dictionary which he was unable to publish when he finished it in 1722, though it was extensively drawn upon by the Revd John Walters of Cowbridge (1721-97) in compiling an English-Welsh dictionary on a Johnsonian scale which was published by subscription in parts between 1770 and 1794.[35] Unfortunately the next Welsh-English dictionary to be accepted as a standard work was that of William Owen Pughe, published between 1793 and 1803.[36] Pughe's eccentric ideas on word derivation and bizarre orthography were to have dire consequences during the nineteenth century (not least for compositors and owners of printing offices) which were not fully exorcised until the establishment of a standard orthography in 1928.

NOTES TO CHAPTER 6

I am grateful to Gareth Bevan for his comments on a version of this chapter.

1. *STC²*, no. 21616. Reproduced by the Honourable Society of Cymmrodorion (London, 1877) and by the Scolar Press (Menston, 1969).
2. R. Brinley Jones, *William Salesbury* (Cardiff, 1994), pp. 12-16.
3. NLW, MS 4581B. Now published as *Llysieulyfr Salesbury*, ed. Iwan Rhys Edgar (Cardiff, 1997).
4. *STC²* no. 19166.
5. W. Alun Mathias, 'William Salesbury a'r Testament Newydd'', *LlC*, 16 (1989-91), 40-68 (pp. 40-1). See also his 'Cyd-ddigwyddiad geiriadurol', *Taliesin*, 95 (Oct. 1996), 97-102.
6. The order *a b ch ... k l m* can be seen in a series of *englynion* by the fifteenth-century poet Lewys Glyn Cothi (*RMWL*, I, 473-4), edited by Dafydd Johnston, *Gwaith Lewys Glyn Cothi* (Cardiff, 1995), pp. 1-14. Much work remains to be done on alphabetization in Welsh.
7. ' [...] na ddysgwyl neb onid ynfyd pan el i wiala ir koet gaffael gwiail yn tyfy yn vn ystym y byddant wedy r eilio am gledyr y plait' (*Rhagymadroddion 1547-1659*, ed. Garfield H. Hughes (Cardiff, 1967), p. 7).
8. J. E. Caerwyn Williams, *Geiriadurwyr y Gymraeg yng nghyfnod y Dadeni* ([s.l.] 1983), on which, together with his article on Thomas Wiliems (see note 10), I have drawn heavily for this chapter.
9. Williams, *Geiriadurwyr*, p. 14; Daniel Huws, *Llyfr Aneirin* (Aberystwyth, 1989), p. 42.
10. On Thomas Wiliems see J. E. Caerwyn Williams, 'Thomas Wiliems, y geiriadurwr', *SC*, 16/17 (1981-2), 280-316.
11. Roy Stephens, 'Geirfâu Wiliam Llŷn', *LlC*, 15 (1987-8), 303-19 (p. 308).
12. 'Trysawr yr iaith Latin ar Gymraec, ne'r Geiriadur cywoethocaf a helaethaf o wir dhiletiaith Vrytanaec'; '[y]r hygar gyphredin yn holh Gymru Benbaladr,' *Rhyddiaith Gymraeg, [...] 1488-1609*, ed. T. H. Parry-Williams (Cardiff, 1954), pp. 137-44 (p. 137).
13. E. D. Jones, ''The Brogyntyn Welsh Manuscripts', *NLWJ*, 6 (1949-50), 309-28 (pp. 323-5).
14. For the history of the printing of the *Dictionarium Duplex* see Williams, 'Thomas Wiliems', pp. 314-16.
15. *Cambrian Register*, 2 (1796), 470-1.
16. E. D. Jones, p. 318.
17. *Ibid*.
18. *Ibid*.
19. *Cambrian Register*, 2 (1796), 473.
20. This is the William Jones identified in *STC²* as William Jones 3 who had operated a clandestine puritan press between 1604 and 1608.
21. F. Holyoke's edition of the Latin-English section of John Rider's dictionary (*STC²* no. 21034), a quarto volume.
22. *Cambrian Register*, 2 (1796), 473.
23. *Gentleman's Magazine*, 60 (1790), 23-4.
24. *LW*, nos 1551-2 (*STC²*, no. 6347).
25. Ceri Davies, 'Y berthynas rhwng Geirfa Tafod Cymraeg Henry Salesbury a'r *Dictionarium Duplex*', *BBCS*, 18 (1979), 399-400; M. T. Burdett-Jones, 'Dau eiriadur Henry Salesbury', *NLWJ*, 26 (1989-90), 241-50.
26. I am grateful to Richard Crowe for sight of a draft of a forthcoming article on Thomas Richards; see also T. J. Morgan, 'Geiriadurwyr y ddeunawfed ganrif', *LlC*, 9 (1966-7), 3-18.
27. '[nid] oes *Dictionary cymraeg* iw gael yn *Llundain* am arian' (quoted in G. J. Williams, 'Stephen Hughes a'i gyfnod', in *Agweddau ar hanes dysg Gymraeg: detholiad o ddarlithiau G. J. Williams*, ed. Aneirin Lewis (Cardiff, 1969), pp. 171-205 (p. 192)).
28. G. J Williams, pp. 191-3.
29. Wing J 997.
30. Thomas Jones, *Y Gymraeg yn ei Disgleirdeb* (London, 1688), sigs X3ᵛ, X8ʳ. See also p. 95 of this work.

[31] A status which was not confined to British scholars: the Dutch scholar M. Z. Boxhorn included in his posthumously published *Originum Gallicarum liber* (Amsterdam, 1654) the Welsh-Latin portion of the *Dictionarium Duplex,* the list of plant-names, and a fancifully druidized Latin translation of the proverbs (Prys Morgan, 'Boxhorn, Leibniz, and the Welsh', *SC,* 8/9 (1973-4), 220-8).

[32] Several examples of such unpublished lists can be found in the indexes to RWML.

[33] G. J. Williams, 'Edward Lhuyd', in *Agweddau ar hanes dysg Gymraeg,* pp. 207-31 (pp. 211, 222-3).

[34] G. J. Williams, 'Edward Lhuyd a thraddodiad ysgolheigaidd Sir Ddinbych', *TDHS,* 11 (1962), 37-59 (pp. 54-5).

[35] T. J. Morgan, pp. 9-12 stresses the value of Walters's work; T. C. Evans, 'John Walters and the first printing press in Glamorganshire', *JWBS,* 1 (1910-15), 83-9 outlines its lengthy publishing history.

[36] For a detailed discussion of this work see Chapter 12.

CHAPTER 7

SCRIBES AND PATRONS IN THE SEVENTEENTH CENTURY

J. Gwynfor Jones

THE century following the 1530s revealed the permanent effects of the Tudor settlement on Welsh administrative and social life. The Acts of Union which assimilated Wales into England accelerated rather than initiated trends that were to have a significant impact on Welsh social development. In particular, they contributed to a gradual change of attitude among the most privileged members of society towards the native culture of Wales, a change which became increasingly apparent in the course of the seventeenth century. Social and economic developments favoured the creation of large landed estates and enabled the more successful families to strengthen their hold over their localities, exercise authority in regional government and enjoy the fruits of public office, establish cadet families, and extend their influence over their dependants. They also led to the forging of closer social and economic links with England. Cultural life must thus be viewed in the context of gradual transition and the adoption of new attitudes in politics, administration, and social relationships based on Renaissance principles. Amongst the *uchelwr* families who had benefited so greatly from the Acts of Union more traditional concepts of *uchelwriaeth* (gentility) gradually yielded to new codes of conduct. The *'prosperous and perfect [regional] statesman'*[1] described by Morus Dwyfech and his contemporaries matched Sir Thomas Elyot's 'perfect governor'; a man who possessed all the attributes — learning, loyalty, and authority — of the ideal Tudor gentleman devoted to public duties.[2] Even so, reputable ancestry continued to be an essential feature for those claiming gentle status, for the 'credit' so highly valued by the head of the household depended on his success in linking his lineage with illustrious forbears. Sir John Wynn of Gwedir (1553-1627), for example, expressed the pride felt by families of his rank in pedigree and their scorn for 'upstarts'. 'A great temporal blessing it is, and a great heart's ease', he maintained, 'to a man to find that he is well descended.'[3]

Difficult economic conditions, combined with a growing estrangement among the gentry, caused the poets much anxiety. This coincided with a crisis within the bardic order itself. As shown in Chapter 3, sixteenth-century Welsh humanist scholars concerned at the decline of the bardic order had advocated its reform so that it might conform to the literary ideals of the Renaissance. In his *ymryson* (poetic debate) with Wiliam Cynwal during the 1580s, Edmwnd Prys denounced the conservatism of the bards, and, like Siôn Tudur, reprimanded them for exploiting their art by awarding false pedigrees to unworthy patrons for gain.[4] Prys further accused the poets of inferior learning and craftsmanship, total disregard for rhetoric, and an unwillingness to make public the secrets of their art. Much of the criticism was levelled at the inability or reluctance (or both) of bards to comply with the requirements of the New Learning, but social and economic problems were also responsible for the decline of the profession as some of the major families began gradually to withdraw their patronage in the rural areas, and the minor gentry, diminished by the economic impact of inflation and subsequently by the Civil Wars, declined into the ranks of small freeholders and leaseholders. They had been badly hit by the practice of *cyfran*, their inheritance being morcellated by gavelkind, 'the destruction of Wales' as Sir John Wynn described it.[5] As a result, bardic practitioners were increasingly drawn from those whom John Jones of Gellilyfdy described as 'meane menn of byrth havinge good qualities [...] admitted to studdy the doctrine of the Bards & to proceed in their profession to there graduacione, but under the title and vocatione of *Prydyd[d]ion*'.[6] Despite their contribution to the economic development of Wales, the *nouveaux riches* who had settled in the urban centres of Wales and the Marches and had prospered through their commercial, legal, and administrative activities were not regarded by the more traditional gentry families as being worthy of bardic acclamation. It is this criticism that is expressed by Siôn Tudur and Edmwnd Prys. Transition in society had led to social mobility which threatened the concept of a rigid and divinely ordained hierarchical structure upheld by successive generations of bards as fundamental to the social order.

Although some of Gruffudd Hiraethog's disciples, most notably Wiliam Llŷn (d. 1580), Siôn Tudur (d. 1602), and Simwnt Fychan (d. 1606), were major poets and the grandiose panegyric or elegy still retained its high status, the quality of strict-metre poetry declined considerably from the first quarter of the seventeenth century onwards and technical weaknesses became increasingly obvious despite efforts to maintain the tradition. Poets such as Siôn Mawddwy (d. 1613), Gruffudd Hafren (c.1590-?1630), Rhisiart Cynwal (d. 1634), Huw Machno (c.1560-1637), and Watcyn Clywedog (fl. 1630-50), continued to compose in different parts of Wales but, although Siôn Mawddwy sang to families throughout Wales, the *teithiau clera* (bardic itineraries) became increasingly restricted. The most important family of traditional poets was the Phylipiaid of Ardudwy in Meirionnydd, whose activities spanned the period from the early 1540s to 1678. The prolific Siôn Phylip (c.1543-1620) was one of the most perceptive of early-seventeenth-century poets, his compositions reflecting the social malaise that had seriously undermined the traditional cult of *uchelwriaeth*. A number of minor poets were also active, especially in the early part of the seventeenth century, men such as Dafydd Llwyd Mathau (fl. 1601-29), Thomas ab Ifan of Hendreforfudd near Corwen (fl. 1596-1633), a scribe and collector of manuscripts, and Edward Dafydd (c.1600-?1678), the last professional poet of any importance in Glamorgan.

To some extent the place of the professional itinerant poets was filled by poets of independent means: poets *'singing on their own food'* (beirdd yn canu ar eu bwyd eu hun). Huw Llwyd of Cynfal (?1568-1630),[7] for example, was a man of considerable standing whose impressive library was praised by Huw Machno: *'What a fine sight it is to see his books all together on shelves'*.[8]

The failure of the bards to devise new methods of addressing a gradually decreasing number of *uchelwyr* in a social environment that saw the withdrawal of active patronage intensified their difficulties. Although traditional concepts of gentility were still widely cherished down to the Civil Wars, the gentry were increasingly identified by their role as officeholders and beneficiaries of material progress. Greater emphasis was placed on 'civilizing' (and Anglicizing) trends such as education and learning, bonds of matrimony, and the cultivation of social graces. The privileges of knighthood, parliamentary representation, and service in local government were the chief indicators of a new direction in public life.

Civil war and the Puritan interregnum led to a further decline in patronage. Wiliam Bodwrda (1593-1660), Fellow of St John's College, Cambridge, and rector of Aberdaron, a diligent copyist of poetry manuscripts,[9] struck a discordant note in 1647 when, in a Welsh letter to Siôn Cain, he rightly referred to his correspondent as the last of the herald poets in a period which *'saw the demise of this laudable art'*.[10] A few years later Rowland Vaughan of Cae'r-gai (a house destroyed in the Civil War) received a *cywydd* *'lamenting the death of all Welsh poets'*.[11]

As the bardic tradition declined, free-metre verse emerged as a strong competitor by appealing to a less privileged order and by offering critical social comment. Huw Morys (1622-1709), 'Eos Ceiriog', for example, composed inferior examples of traditional *cywyddau* but gained far greater popularity through his alliterative carols, a more popular type of poetry which could more easily be disseminated by singing. Other examples of important free-metre compositions are discussed in Chapter 8.

Many families, such as those of Dolau Gwyn, Bodwrda, Glynllifon, Gogerddan, Penrhyn, Melai, Plas Iolyn, Botryddan, and Rhiwedog, had withdrawn their patronage in the mid-seventeenth century, a decline which coincided with the demise of the last generation of itinerant poets like Edwart Urien (d. 1614), Huw Pennant (*fl.* 1565-1619), Edward Maelor (*fl.* 1586-1620), and the long-lived Siams Dwnn (*c.*1570-*c.*1660). Even so, not all the gentry forsook their traditional responsibilities. In Gwynedd several families such as the Cefnllanfair family of Llŷn,[12] the Corbets of Ynysymaengwyn,[13] and Vaughans of Corsygedol[14] continued to support the bardic tradition into the eighteenth century. Notable seventeenth-century patrons included Siôn Llwyd of Ceiswyn (d. 1634), a lawyer, antiquarian and expert in languages, whose two prime concerns according to his elegist, Siôn Cain, were to practise piety and *perchentyaeth* (maintaining a hospitable household).[15] Siôn ap Hywel ab Owain of Cefn Treflaeth, Llanystumdwy, who rendered part of the *Rhetorica ad Herennium* into Welsh, was praised by Huw Machno following his death as a learned and impartial administrator of the law and provider of hospitality to poets.[16] Robert Vaughan of Hengwrt (*c.*1592-1667) was eulogized by John Griffith of Llanddyfnan, Anglesey, for preserving Welsh manuscripts and maintaining standards of learning in the vernacular,[17] and Robert Wyn of Maesyneuadd, Llandecwyn, known for his historical and heraldic interests, was the subject of an elegy by Siôn Dafydd La(e)s of Penllyn (*c.*1660-95), one of the last poets to receive patronage.[18]

Awareness of the Welsh past continued among those Welsh gentry eager to preserve their national and often regional identity. In the early years of the century, for example, Sir William Maurice (1542-1622) of Clenennau censured a kinsman for underrating native poets.[19] His interest in the 'Cambro-British' and vaticinatory themes of the Middle Ages inspired him to interpret the union of the English and Scottish crowns as being symbolic of the ancient unity of the 'Isle of Britain'. James I was the fulfilment of the prophecy of the 'coronog vaban' (*crowned child*), and a legitimate claimant to the title 'Emperor of Great Britain'.[20] Similar sentiments were expressed by Robert Holland in the dedicatory epistle to his translation of James I's *Basilikon Doron* (1604) where he maintained that the Welsh were 'the very remnant of the ancient *Bryttaines*'.[21] Maurice's kinsman, Sir John Wynn of Gwedir, compiled a family history and, in his letter to Sir William Jones of Castellmarch, Lord Chief Justice of the King's Bench in Ireland, declared that a study of bardic composition was essential to preserve lineage.[22] Traditional bardic eulogy and elegy had made great use of genealogical material; in the mid-sixteenth century Gruffudd Hiraethog had continued the genealogical tradition established by Gutun Owain, bequeathing his craft to the last generation of prominent bardic genealogists, notably Wiliam Cynwal, Dafydd Benwyn, Wiliam Llŷn, Hopcyn ab Einion, Robin Achwr, and Rhys Cain (d. 1614).[23] Another noted poet-genealogist of this generation was Lewys Dwnn (c.1550-c.1616) of Betws Cedewain who, in 1585, obtained the office of Deputy-Herald to Robert Cooke, Clarenceux King-of-Arms and William Flower, Norroy King-of-Arms.[24] As this tradition died out, genealogy and heraldry became a popular pursuit among individual members of the gentry who thus gave this feature of native culture a new lease of life. An early example was George Owen of Henllys, Pembrokeshire (c.1552-1613), who investigated the privileges of marcher lords and established the antiquity of Pembrokeshire families.[25] Together with George Owen Harry, rector of Dinas and Whitchurch, he complied an armorial for his native shire. Owen extended the sources of the professional bards by using title-deeds and official records, and was in contact with the College of Arms and other institutions where records were kept.

Scribal activity and the collecting of manuscripts often went hand-in-hand with antiquarian interests and genealogical research. In the early years of the seventeenth century, Jaspar Gryffyth (d. 1614) of Cegidfa, Welshpool, vicar of Hinckley, Leicestershire, was active as a copyist, possessed many important Welsh and Latin manuscripts (particularly Welsh law texts), and corresponded with Sir Robert Cotton.[26] The foremost Welsh copyist of the early seventeenth century doubtless was Thomas Wiliems (c.1545/6-1622), who was educated at Gwedir and, possibly, at Brasenose College, Oxford. Wiliems, curate of Trefriw, who turned recusant and became a country physician, is remembered for his copy of a Latin text of the Welsh laws (NLW, Peniarth MS 225), for compiling the best Renaissance collection of Welsh proverbs (NLW, 3064B), and for his main work, 'Thesaurus Linguae Latinae et Cambrobrytannicae' (NLW, Peniarth MS 228), which became the basis of the Latin-Welsh section of Dr John Davies's *Antiquae Linguae Britannicae Dictionarium Duplex* (1632).[27] He also compiled 'Prif Achau Holl Gymru Benbaladr', a collection of Welsh genealogies (NLW, Llangibby MSS 1 and 2). Wiliems's near-contemporary, John Jones (c.1578-1658) of Gellilyfdy, in the parish of Ysgeifiog, Flintshire,[28] a lawyer by training, was a prolific copyist of manuscripts, often under difficult circumstances: much of his work was done during lengthy terms of imprisonment for debt in London. Over a hundred manuscripts of his have survived, mostly in the Peniarth collection in the National Library of Wales. His skill as a calligrapher is impressive and may reveal the influence of Italian and German manuals of penmanship. On a smaller scale were scribes such as the gentleman bard and patron of poets, Richard ap John (*fl.* 1578-1611) of Ysgorlegan, Llangynhafal, an expert copyist who transcribed parts of a bardic grammar and *Brut y Tywysogyon* as well as poetry.

The greatest squire-antiquary of the century, Robert Vaughan of Hengwrt, claimed descent from noble stock and was educated at Oriel College, Oxford. He learned the art of genealogy from Rhys and Siôn Cain, whose manuscripts he subsequently acquired.

An untiring collector, he made the Hengwrt library the richest repository of Welsh manuscripts before the founding of the National Library. Vaughan corresponded with a wide circle of Welsh antiquaries, notably Dr John Davies of Mallwyd, John Jones, Gellilyfdy, William Maurice of Cefn-y-braich, and the poet Ieuan Llwyd Sieffre, and also with English and Irish scholars such as Sir Simonds d'Ewes, John Selden, and James Ussher.[29] As well as being an assiduous copyist he translated *Brut y Tywysogyon* into English, and published in 1662 *British Antiquities Revived*, his only printed work, in which he claimed superiority amongst medieval Welsh rulers for the house of Gwynedd.

William Maurice (d. 1680) of Cefn-y-braich, Llansilin, was the first scholar to attempt to classify the Welsh law-texts, compiled the first catalogue of Hengwrt manuscripts, and diligently collected manuscripts such as *Llyfr Gwyn Hergest*, a collection of religious and other prose texts which was destroyed by fire (probably) in 1810. Like Dr John Davies, Mallwyd, and Robert Vaughan, Maurice could afford to employ amanuenses and even went to the expense of erecting a building to house his collection. Many of his manuscripts eventually passed to the Wynne family and were destroyed in the Wynnstay fire of 1858.[30] Meredydd Lloyd of Welshpool (*c*.1620-95), who acquired some of Thomas Wiliems's manuscripts and was on close terms with both Vaughan and John Jones, Gellilyfdy, formed an important link between them and later antiquaries.[31] Humphrey Humphreys (1648-1712), bishop of Bangor between 1689 and 1701, was an antiquary and enthusiastic genealogist who was frequently consulted by the College of Arms. His friend, Edward Lhuyd, thought him 'incomparably the best skill'd in our Antiquities of any person in Wales'[32] and Thomas Hearne believed he was 'next to Mr Edw. Lhuyd for knowledge in the British language'.[33] As well as supporting poets — such as his elegist, the weaver Owen Gruffydd of Llanystumdwy (*c*.1643-1730) — Humphreys also encouraged Welsh prose-writers such as Ellis Wynne of Y Lasynys (1671-1734), and Samuel Williams of Llandyfriog (*c*.1660-1722), himself an important copyist and collector of manuscripts. William Lloyd (1627-1717), bishop of St Asaph from 1680 to 1692, was also a patron of bards and an avid collector of Welsh genealogical manuscripts.[34] Lloyd was a friend of Sir Thomas Mostyn (1651-92), second baronet, an enthusiastic collector of Welsh and other manuscripts who commissioned copies of a number of texts from the poet Siôn Dafydd La(e)s.[35] Another late-seventeenth-century collector of books and manuscripts in north-east Wales was Robert Davies of Gwysaney and Llannerch (*c*.1658-1710), a noted naturalist and antiquarian.[36]

Glamorgan scribes and collectors of manuscripts also made a notable, if lesser, contribution in this period.[37] While at Llandaf (*c*.1595-1601), Dr John Davies of Mallwyd acquired a collection of Dafydd ap Gwilym's *cywyddau* transcribed 'from the book of Mr Wm Mathew' of Llandaf. In 1631 he copied 'Gwassanaeth Meir' (a Middle-Welsh translation of the *Officium Parvum Beatae Mariae Virginis*) from a now lost manuscript compiled at Llanhari *c*.1537,[38] and in 1634 borrowed the *Red Book of Hergest* from Sir Lewis Mansel.[39] One of the most prolific scribes of his day, the recusant poet Llywelyn Siôn of Llangewydd (1540-?1615), was paid to copy texts by local gentlemen.[40] Thirteen complete manuscripts of his have survived, containing strict and free-metre poetry, pedigrees, and prose works including all three parts of the Catholic tract, *Y Drych Cristianogawl*, a variant version of *Chwedleu Seith Doethon Rufein*, and the unique copy of a Welsh version of the *Gesta Romanorum*.[41] His most distinguished products, copied late in life in a distinctive tall oblong format, were three collections of poetry, *Llyfr Hir Amwythig* (NLW, Llanstephan MS 134), *Llyfr Hir Llanharan* (Cardiff MS 5.44), and *Llyfr Hir Llywarch Reynolds* (NLW, MS 970E). John Jones of Gellilyfdy copied a collection of odes in the possession of Llywelyn Siôn as well as texts owned by Hopcyn ap Hywel of Pen-y-fai, his brother, Antoni Powel of Llwydarth, and several other Glamorgan gentlemen. Antoni Powel (*c*.1560-1618/19), a gentleman genealogist, collected a variety of manuscripts and Lewys Dwnn referred to him as being one among others who had shown him *'old records and books of religious houses'*.[42]

Despite a decline in the art of compiling pedigrees and copying manuscripts in Glamorgan in the latter part of the seventeenth century, it was then that the assiduous Thomas Wilkins (1625/6-99), rector of St Mary Church, amassed a notable collection of Welsh manuscripts. This included *Llyvyr Agkyr Llandewivrevi* and the *Red Book of Hergest*, both of which were given to Jesus College, Oxford, in 1701 by his eldest son. Other Wilkins manuscripts included 'The Book of Llywelyn the Priest' (Oxford, Jesus College, MS 3), a copy of *Brut y Tywysogyon, Brut y Saesson* (NLW, Peniarth MS 253), a version of the laws of Hywel Dda (NLW, Peniarth MS 258), and *Llyfr Baglan* (Cardiff, MS 2. 278), a collection of south Wales genealogies. Wilkins also prepared and copied *Analectica Glamorganica* or *Analectica Morganica Archaeographia, Fragments of ye Antiquityes of Glamorganshire* (Cardiff MS 3. 464), the best collection of documents relating to Glamorgan that had yet been compiled by an individual scholar in that county.

One of the scholars permitted to make use of Wilkins's library was Edward Lhuyd (*c*.1660-1709). Lhuyd, Keeper of the Ashmolean Museum from 1691 to 1707, was a many-sided scholar, his interests including chemistry, botany, geology, palaeontology, and archaeology. From about 1693 onwards, however, he concentrated on antiquities and philology. In 1695 he contributed material on the Welsh counties for Edmund Gibson's new edition of Camden's *Britannia*[43] and in the same year published *A Design of a British Dictionary, Historical and Geographical* which contained a section entitled 'Archaeologia Britannica'. In 1701, after returning to Oxford following his lengthy tour of the Celtic countries, he amassed many transcripts of manuscripts and other antiquarian material and, in 1707, published the first (and only) volume of his *Archaeologia Britannica* (entitled *Glossography*), a major contribution to Celtic philology.[44] The *Archaeologia* also contained, amongst other things, the first printed list of the contents and locations of Welsh manuscripts which, despite its inevitable omissions, was to prove of great value to later scholars.

The seventeenth century was of great significance in the social development of Wales. The impact of the Civil Wars and the Puritan interregnum brought about fundamental changes leading eventually to the widening gap between the more affluent and Anglicized squirearchy and the less opulent homekeeping gentry. While modest gentry families were adversely affected by the redistribution of property, the exorbitant land-tax, high mortgage rates, and economic depression, the more substantial families tapped the mineral resources of their lands, established commercial ventures, arranged advantageous marriage-alliances, paraded their social grandeur, exhibited their political domination, and exploited their good fortune to the full.[45] Literary scholars, aware of the decline of patronage and the Anglicization of the more substantial families, have tended to view the seventeenth century as a bleak period in the history of Welsh literature and scholarship. Yet, although the bardic tradition declined, an interest in Welsh literature and antiquities survived in some country houses. Despite political and social upheavals, the copying and preservation of manuscripts undertaken during the Stuart century played a vital part in maintaining the Welsh literary and historical tradition. Nor were the worst fears of Tudor humanist scholars realized since the century produced several notable Welsh prose classics, as well as lexicographers, genealogists, scribes, and antiquaries. Despite its instability it was an era which made possible the remarkable eighteenth-century revival in Welsh literature, scholarship, and book-publication.

NOTES TO CHAPTER 7

For background see Glanmor Williams, *Recovery, reorientation, and Reformation: Wales c.1415-1642* (Oxford, 1987), pp. 253-78; T. Parry, *A history of Welsh literature*, trans. H. I. Bell (Oxford, 1955), pp. 203-24; G. H. Jenkins, *The foundations of modern Wales, 1642-1780* (Oxford, 1987), pp. 213-53; Nesta Lloyd (ed.), *Blodeugerdd Barddas o'r ail ganrif ar bymtheg, Cyfrol 1* (Llandybïe, 1993), pp. xiii-xxiv. See now also Graham C. G. Thomas, 'From manuscript to print: 1: manuscript', in *A guide to Welsh literature c. 1530-1700*, ed. R. Geraint Gruffydd (Cardiff, 1997), pp. 241-62.

[1] 'Gwladwr perffaith goludawg' (NLW, Llanstephan MS 124, 312).
[2] F. Caspari, *Humanism and the social order in Tudor England* (Chicago, 1954), pp. 80-5, 121-3.
[3] John Wynn, *The history of the Gwydir family and memoirs*, ed. J. Gwynfor Jones (Llandysul, 1990), p. 35.
[4] *Cywydd* 26, quoted in *Ymryson Edmwnd Prys a Wiliam Cynwal: fersiwn llawysgrif Llanstephan 43*, ed. Gruffydd Aled Williams (Cardiff, 1986), pp. 116-18; 'Cywydd i'r beirdd', no. 151 in *Gwaith Siôn Tudur*, ed. Enid Roberts, 2 vols (Cardiff, 1980), I, 606-12; English translation, 'Warning to the poets' in *The Penguin book of Welsh verse,* trans. Anthony Conran (Harmondsworth, 1967), pp. 197-9.
[5] Wynn, p. 15.
[6] NLW, Llanstephan MS 144, 18, quoted in *RMWL*, II, 721.
[7] Glenys Davies, *Noddwyr beirdd ym Meirion* (Dolgellau, 1974), p. 56.
[8] 'I lyfrau ar silffiau sydd / Deg olwg gidai gilydd' (*Gweithiau Morgan Llwyd o Wynedd*, Vol II, ed. J. H. Davies (Bangor, 1908), p. 311).
[9] R. Geraint Gruffydd, 'Llawysgrifau Wiliam Bodwrda o Aberdaron', *NLWJ*, 8 (1953-4), 349-50.
[10] '[...] yn awr pallv a myned ar goll a wnaeth y Gelfyddyd ganmoladwy hon' (NLW, Peniarth MS 327E, ii, p. 35, printed in Dafydd Ifans, 'Wiliam Bodwrda (1593-1660)', *NLWJ*, 19 (1975-6), 88-102, 300-10 (p. 97)).
[11] 'Kowydd [...] yn kwyno marfolaeth holl brydyddion kymrv' (NLW, Peniarth MS 114, 142-3, printed in D. J. Bowen, 'Ail Eistedd Caerwys a chais 1594', *LlC*, 3 (1954-5), 139-61 (p. 161)).
[12] J. E. Griffith, *Pedigrees of Anglesey and Caernarvonshire families* (Horncastle, 1914), p. 224; NLW, Add. MS 18, p. 10.
[13] A. Lloyd Hughes, 'Rhai o noddwyr y beirdd yn Sir Feirionnydd', *LlC*, 10 (1968-9), 137-206 (pp. 198-9).
[14] Here patronage survived until the death in 1775 of William Vaughan, first President of the Cymmrodorion Society (Hughes, pp. 149-51).
[15] G. Davies, pp. 30-5.
[16] Bedwyr L. Jones, 'Siôn ap Hywel ab Owain a'r *Rhetorica ad Herennium* yn Gymraeg', *LlC*, 6 (1960-1), 208-18 (p. 209).
[17] G. Davies, p. 122; BL, MS 14898, 83b.
[18] G. Davies, pp. 150-1; NLW, MS 12731E, 68.
[19] NLW, Brogyntyn MS 474.
[20] J. Gwynfor Jones, 'The Welsh poets and their patrons, c.1550-1640', *WHR*, 9 (1978-9), 245-77 (pp. 250-1).
[21] *Basilikon Doron [...] fragment of a Welsh translation by Robert Holland*, ed. John Ballinger (Cardiff, 1931), sig. B3^v.
[22] NLW, MS 9058E, 1005.
[23] *Gwaith Gruffudd Hiraethog*, ed. D. J. Bowen (Cardiff, 1990), pp. xix-xliv; D. J. Bowen, *Gruffudd Hiraethog a'i oes* (Cardiff, 1958); Francis Jones, 'An approach to Welsh genealogy', *THSC*, (1948), pp. 303-466 (pp. 365-78).
[24] F. Jones, pp. 375-8, and *DWB*.
[25] B. G. Charles, *George Owen of Henllys* (Aberystwyth, 1973), pp. 179-82; F. Jones, pp. 407-10.
[26] E. D. Jones, 'Jaspar Griffith (Gryffyth), Warden of Ruthin (*d.* 1614)', *NLWJ*, 1 (1939-40), 168-70; Richard Ovenden, 'Jaspar Gryffyth and his books', *BLJ*, 20 (1994), 107-39.

[27] J. E. Caerwyn Williams, 'Thomas Wiliems, y geiriadurwr', *SC,* 16/17 (1981-2), 280-316.

[28] Nesta Lloyd, 'John Jones, Gellilyfdy', *FHSP,* 24 (1969-70), 5-18, which draws upon her 'Bywyd John Jones, Gellilyfdy' (unpublished master's thesis, University of Wales, Bangor, 1964), and her 'Welsh scholarship in the seventeenth century, with special reference to the writings of John Jones, Gellilyfdy' (unpublished D.Phil. dissertation, Oxford, 1968).

[29] T. Emrys Parry, 'Llythyrau Robert Vaughan, Hengwrt (1592-1667)' (unpublished master's thesis, University of Wales, Bangor, 1961).

[30] *DWB.* G. J. Williams, *Agweddau ar hanes dysg Gymraeg; detholiad o ddarlithiau G. J. Williams,* ed. Aneirin Lewis (Cardiff, 1969), p. 85.

[31] Nesta Lloyd, 'Meredith Lloyd', *JWBS,* 11 (1973-6), 133-92.

[32] E. G. Wright, 'Humphrey Humphreys, Bishop of Bangor and Hereford', *JHSCW,* 2 (1950), 72-86 (p. 81).

[33] Wright, p. 78.

[34] R. Alun Charles, 'Teulu Mostyn fel noddwyr y beirdd', *LlC,* 9 (1966-7), 74-110 (pp. 92-8); Lord Mostyn and T. A. Glenn, *History of the family of Mostyn of Mostyn* (London, 1925), pp. 155-68.

[35] Daniel Huws, 'Sir Thomas Mostyn and the Mostyn Manuscripts', in *Books and collectors 1200-1700: essays presented to Andrew Watson,* ed. James P. Carley and Colin C. G. Tite (London, 1997), pp. 451-72.

[36] Hywel D. Emanuel, 'The Gwysaney manuscripts', *NLWJ,* 7 (1951-2), 326-43.

[37] I am indebted to the detailed study by Ceri W. Lewis, 'The literary history of Glamorgan from 1550 to 1770', in *Early modern Glamorgan, from the Act of Union to the Industrial Revolution,* ed. Glanmor Williams, Glamorgan County History iv (Cardiff, 1974), pp. 535-639 (pp. 577-608).

[38] *Gwassanaeth Meir, sef cyfieithiad Cymraeg Canol o'r Officium Parvum Beatae Mariae Virginis,* ed. Brynley F. Roberts (Cardiff, 1961), pp. lviii-lix.

[39] Lewis, pp. 578-9.

[40] G. J. Williams, *Traddodiad llenyddol Morgannwg* (Cardiff, 1948), pp. 79-80.

[41] Lewis, pp. 582-3.

[42] 'Hen Regords a llyfrau y tai o grefydd' (*RMWL,* II, 397-8).

[43] Gwyn Walters and Frank Emery, 'Edward Lhuyd, Edmund Gibson, and the printing of Camden's *Britannia* 1695', *The Library,* 5th ser., 32 (1977), 109-37.

[44] G. J. Williams, 'Edward Lhuyd', *LlC,* 6 (1960-1), 122-37 (reprinted in his *Agweddau ar hanes dysg Gymraeg,* pp. 207-31); Brynley F. Roberts, *Edward Lhuyd: the making of a scientist* (Cardiff, 1980); his 'Edward Llwyd's collection of printed books', *BLR,* 10 (1979), 112-27, and now his 'Cyhoeddiadau Edward Lhwyd', *Y Llyfr yng Nghymru/Welsh Book Studies,* 1 (1998), 21-58.

[45] E. D. Evans, *A history of Wales, 1660-1815* (Cardiff, 1976), pp. 175-95; Jenkins, pp. 87-103.

CHAPTER 8

PRINTING AND PUBLISHING
IN THE SEVENTEENTH CENTURY

Rheinallt Llwyd

THE fifty to sixty Welsh books and books relating to Wales that appeared during the second half of the sixteenth century represented a considerable triumph for an intellectual élite which wished, for religious and humanist reasons, to ensure that Wales took advantage of the printing press. The number of titles published during the seventeenth century was low, probably amounting to no more than about a hundred and fifty works.[1] Growth during the first half of the century was at best slow, and during the 1660s the number of titles published had actually fallen to a level which might have suggested that Welsh-language book production was entering upon terminal decline. Fortunately, large-scale philanthropic activity from the early 1670s onwards revitalized Welsh-language publishing and further expansion followed from the 1680s with the beginnings of a commercial trade in cheap Welsh books.

As in the previous century, seventeenth-century Welsh authors faced very considerable difficulties. To the long-standing problems of relative underdevelopment and poor communications were added the economic, social, political, and religious upheavals discussed in Chapter 7. Despite considerable educational progress amongst the gentry following the establishment of grammar and town schools from the mid-sixteenth century onwards, probably the factor which most limited the market for Welsh books was widespread illiteracy. Because of inadequate and frequently conflicting evidence, estimates of literacy in seventeenth-century Wales differ considerably and the picture is further complicated by whether one is discussing the ability to read Welsh, English, or Latin. The safest conclusion would appear to be that by the 1640s some fifteen to twenty per cent of the population could read.[2] There would, of course, be considerable variations between different parts of the country, between different social groups, and between men and women.

The structure of the book trade itself adversely affected the growth of printed literature in Welsh. Until the Printing Act lapsed in 1695, publishing was necessarily dominated by London. Of the 232 seventeenth-century items listed in *Libri Walliae* over three-quarters (75.8% or 176) bear London imprints. Of the remainder, 10.8% (25) bear Oxford imprints and the remaining 31 titles (13.4%) bear a wide range of imprints (some spurious), including Cambridge, Paris, Dublin, St Omer, Amsterdam, Shrewsbury, and Chester. As well as providing valuable information about several London-printed Welsh books which are no longer extant,[3] the archives of the Stationers' Company also enable us to trace the participation of Welshmen in the London book trade.[4] Between 1601 and 1700 121 youths from Wales (mainly from counties bordering England) were apprenticed to members of the Company. The majority of those apprenticed to masters active in the book trade were apprenticed to booksellers, but from 1660 onwards there was a marked increase in the number apprenticed to printers. A few of the sixty-two apprentices who gained their freedom subsequently made their mark in the London book trade, men such as Augustine Mathewes, Luke Meredith, and John Salisbury. Others, such as Peter Bodfel and Lewis Thomas, served at offices which printed Welsh texts.

Despite the presence of Welshmen in the London book trade, London was not a satisfactory centre from which to supply the needs of book buyers in Wales. The obvious problems of distribution to the remoter parts of the country was not tackled in earnest until the establishment of the Welsh Trust in 1674. The limited market for Welsh books also meant that for much of the century sales would be so low or so slow that publishing Welsh books could not be a commercial activity. In 1670 Stephen Hughes maintained that:

> *It will be a long time before the Welsh Bible is printed, unless wealthy men lay out a thousand pounds towards its printing; because, claim the London booksellers, we will not lay out our money on this work, since a printing or an impression of six thousand Welsh bibles will take twenty years, or fourteen years to sell (whereas we sell about thirty thousand English Bibles every year) and we who live by our crafts cannot afford to wait so long to recoup our money.*[5]

Welsh books, therefore, as in the sixteenth century, had to be subsidized by wealthy patrons. The prefaces to many seventeenth-century books pay tribute to members of major Welsh gentry families and the higher clergy who had sponsored the production of books in Welsh.[6] Without their support and that of philanthropic businessmen in London who maintained their Welsh connections, very few books could have been produced in the first half of the century.

From the earliest days of Welsh printing the peculiarities of Welsh orthography had posed problems for authors and printers alike.[7] The most pressing problem, however, was that London printers were unacquainted with the Welsh language and were apparently disinclined to familiarize themselves with such a barbarous tongue. Time and again apologies for the disproportionate number of mistakes and misprints appear in prefaces to books.[8] Thus a long list of errata in *Allwydd neu Agoriad Paradwys i'r Cymru* is headed by the note:

> *Although the conscientious Editor took infinite pains in trying to correct the countless errors the alien Printer had made (on account of his ignorance of the language) on every page of this work; even so, many escaped his scrutiny.*[9]

Proof correcting was the key to producing accurate texts but because most authors and editors were so distant from the printers it would remain a major problem for most of the seventeenth century. Dr John Davies spent time in London supervising some of his works through the press in the early 1620s (and probably also in the early 1630s), and in the latter half of the seventeenth century Stephen Hughes, Charles Edwards, and Thomas Jones would similarly be closely involved in supervision. Few authors could afford this expense, and in any case residence in London did not guarantee reliable texts since, as Thomas Jones complained in 1688, there were so many '*conscienceless printers*' (digydwybod argraphyddion):

> *I am very sorry that some parts of this book, and my almanac for the year, 1688, have been printed so poorly; I paid as much for the worst parts as the best parts: And indeed it is not my fault, but that of conscienceless printers. If we are to wait for faultless books, until the printers are of good conscience, we might have to wait for ever before we get them.*[10]

To placate aggrieved purchasers, Jones explained in greater detail how some of the mistakes had arisen:

> As there is no Book whatsoever printed without faults, neither is this; Altho I have taken all the care I could to perform it perfect, yet some faults have passed the Press, and those faults that are in it are not all mine, for the Printers (being unacquainted with the British Tongue), have committed some errours herein (after my corecting of it) by taking out Letters, and some words with their Balls, and not putting them in aright again.[11]

The importance of having someone at hand to read proofs becomes apparent when Welsh books printed in London are compared with those printed in Oxford. The standard of accuracy in the latter is considerably higher, possibly because Welsh students could be called upon to serve as proof-readers.

Despite all these obstacles, printed books in Welsh were produced. By far the majority of them were religious in nature as Anglican, Catholic, and Puritan writers all attempted to present their tenets to Welsh readers. Although Anglicans produced the largest number of printed books, relatively few of these were original works. Their first concern was to ensure that the Scriptures were available in the vernacular. Six editions of the Welsh Bible were published during the seventeenth century, the most important being the revision of Morgan's 1588 Bible by Bishop Richard Parry of St Asaph and Dr John Davies, Mallwyd, which appeared in 1620.[12] Both men had worked closely with Morgan for many years and their revision was to remain the 'authorized' version of the Welsh Bible until an entirely new translation appeared in 1988. In 1630, through the generosity of two wealthy London Welshmen, Sir Thomas Myddelton (1550-1631) and Rowland Heylyn (?1562-1631), who contributed a thousand pounds towards its costs, what has been called the 'first people's edition' was made available for five shillings.[13] At last, ordinary people could hope to acquire their own Bibles and, to mark the occasion, Rhys Prichard, vicar of Llanymddyfri, exhorted his fellow-countrymen :

> *The little Bible is now accurately*
> *To be had in your mother's tongue for a crown,*
> *Sell your shirt rather than be without it,*
> *It will keep you better than your father's inheritance.*[14]

Other texts required by the clergy for church services and by heads of households for private worship and religious instruction were also published. Several editions of *Llyfr Gweddi Gyffredin* (*Book of Common Prayer*) were produced during the course of the century, as were catechisms and primers.[15] Here Dr John Davies made an important contribution.[16] He probably had a hand in the revised version of *Llyfr Gweddi Gyffredin* of 1621 and edited a new version of *Llyfr Plygain* (the Primer) in 1633.[17] He was also responsible for a Welsh version of another essential Anglican text, *Articulau neu Byngciau*

(*The Thirty-nine Articles*)[18], although this was not published until the mid-1660s, some twenty years after his death. Yet another important contribution was the appearance in 1632 of *Llyfr y Resolusion*,[19] Davies's translation of Edmund Bunney's Protestant version of *The First Book of the Christian Exercise, Appertayning to Resolution* by the Jesuit Robert Parsons.[20] Although these religious texts display John Davies's mastery of Welsh prose, his greatest achievement was the publication of two remarkable works of scholarship, his grammar of the Welsh language, *Antiquae Linguae Britannicae [...] Rudimenta* (1621), and his Welsh-Latin Dictionary *Antiquae Linguae Britannicae [...] Dictionarium Duplex* (1632), which is discussed in Chapter 6. Yet, despite their scholarly excellence and enduring influence, these works represented the end of a tradition since the death of Davies in 1644 marked the close of Renaissance humanism in Wales.

No other Anglican writer could hope to match the scholarship of John Davies but several produced important prose works, albeit mainly translations. In 1606 *Pregethau a osodwyd allan trwy awdurdod i'w darllein ymhob Eglwys blwyf a phob capel er adeiladaeth i'r bobl annyscedig*[21] was published, an excellent translation of the Book of Homilies by Edward James (?1569-?1610), chancellor of Llandaf.[22] After a gap of over twenty years, translations of a number of standard texts appeared from the end of the 1620s. Robert Llwyd (1565-1655), vicar of Chirk, published translations of two works by Arthur Dent, *Pregeth Dduwiol* (*A Sermon of Repentance*) in 1629/30, and *Llwybr Hyffordd yn cyfarwyddo yr anghyfarwydd i'r Nefoedd* (*The Plaine man's Pathway to Heaven*) in 1630.[23] In his introduction to *Llwybr hyffordd* Llwyd appealed to the monoglot Welsh reader to ensure the spiritual well-being of his family. He explained that the book (which is in dialogue form) avoided infrequently used words, preferring to '*use such common words that the ordinary people know and are familiar with*'.[24] He also emphasized the importance of '*buying the few little books of your own language and understanding to console your soul when the whole world can offer no benefit to you*'.[25]

Llwyd's introduction stated that another Welsh book was in the press ('tan y Printwasc') and before the end of 1629 *Yr Ymarfer o Dduwioldeb*, a translation by Rowland Vaughan (*c*.1587-1667) of Bishop Lewis Bayly's popular devotional handbook, *The Practice of Piety*, had appeared.[26] Vaughan was a member of the minor gentry in Merioneth and an accomplished poet who, as a staunch Anglican and fervent Royalist suffered considerably during the Civil War. The Civil War years were difficult times for Welsh Anglican authors but from 1650 onwards several translations of works of proven popularity appeared including *Madruddyn y Difinyddiaeth Diweddaraf*, a translation by John Edwards, the deprived incumbent of Tredynog, of *The Marrow of Modern Divinity* (1651).[27] Rowland Vaughan resumed work during the 1650s, six more of his translations, mainly of devotional works, appearing by the end of 1658.[28] Other Anglican translations included *Ystyriaethau Drexelius ar Dragwyddoldeb*,[29] a rendering by Elis Lewis of *Drexelius's Considerations on Eternity* (1661), *Holl Ddled-swydd Dyn*,[30] a translation of *The Whole Duty of Man*, by John Langford, rector of Derwen (1672), and *Ymadroddion Bucheddol ynghylch Marwolaeth*,[31] a translation by Thomas Williams, vicar of Llanrwst, of William Sherlock's *A Practical Discourse concerning Death* (1691). Original works by Anglican writers became increasingly rare as the century progressed, an interesting exception being *Profiad yr Ysprydion* (1675) by Rondl Davies, vicar of Meifod, a robust attack on Catholics, Presbyterians, Independents, and Quakers.[32]

Despite the importance of these Anglican prose writings, it has been maintained that it was printed verse in the free metres that made the common people of Wales Protestants and Anglicans.[33] The role of free-metre verse in formal religious worship was emphasized by the inclusion of the metrical psalms of Edmwnd Prys in the 1621 edition of *Llyfr Gweddi Gyffredin*.[34] Prys, archdeacon of Merioneth, a humanist scholar and competent strict-metre poet, was aware of the need to present the Scriptures and Christian doctrine in a memorable format to the ordinary, 'unlearned' members of his congregations. He became convinced that this could be done best through the medium of free-metre verse, claiming that *'all children, servants, and every unlearned person will learn a verse of carol whereas only a scholar could learn a cywydd or some skilful song'*.[35] His *Salmau Cân* proved immensely successful, almost a hundred editions being published between 1621 and 1885.

Even more successful were the popular didactic verses composed by another Anglican clergyman, Rhys Prichard (1579-1644), vicar of Llandovery.[36] Although none of them appeared in print during his own lifetime, once published they became bestsellers. This was because Prichard (unlike Prys, who retained literary diction in his metrical psalms) unashamedly used colloquial words and phrases in order to communicate effectively with ordinary illiterate people. Since they preferred simple poems to complicated sermons, Prichard set about paraphrasing sections of the Bible, and even succeeded in presenting difficult theological concepts in a simplified and highly memorable form. Precisely when a selection of Prichard's verses first appeared in print has been the subject of prolonged controversy.[37] The only sure conclusion is that the first part had appeared before the end of 1658, since a second edition published in 1659 as *Rhan o waith Mr. Rees Prichard [...] Some part of the works of Mr. Rees Prichard* states that this was the second time the work was printed.[38] Other parts were to appear in 1659 and 1671, and in 1672 four parts were brought together to form the first fairly complete edition. *Canwyll y Cymru*, published in 1681, consisted of the 1672 edition with some additional verses. These editions were all prepared by Stephen Hughes (c.1622-1688), a Carmarthenshire-born Puritan whose role in the development of Welsh publishing will be examined below.[39]

Although Roman Catholicism remained outlawed until the 1689 Act of Toleration, a sufficient number of the Welsh remained faithful to '*Yr Hen Ffydd*' (The Old Faith) for the practice of sending missionaries to Wales and the circulation of recusant texts in manuscript continued throughout the seventeenth century. A handful of Catholic printed books were also produced. During the first two decades of the century, Dr Roger Smyth (1541-1625), a native of St Asaph who became a priest on the Continent, published at least four titles, each bearing a Paris imprint. Two were Welsh versions of Petrus Canisius's *Summa Doctrinae Christianae,* an abridged version, *Crinnodeb o adysc Cristnogaul,* appearing in 1609,[40] and a complete version, *Opus Catechisticum,* in 1611.[41] His *Coppi o lythyr crefydhvvr a merthyr dedhfol discedig at i dad,* a translation of Robert Southwell's *An epistle of a religious priest to his father,* appeared in 1612, but remained unknown until a copy was discovered at the Bibliothèque Mazarine, Paris, in 1992. The fourth work by Smyth, *Theater du mond sef ivv Gorsedd y byd* (1615?), is also a translation, this time from a French text, *Théâtre du monde,* by Pierre Boaistuau.[42] Although this work bears a Paris imprint, the present consensus is that it was surreptitiously printed in London.

Three years later, in 1618, the clandestine press at the English College at St Omer printed Richard Vaughan's *Eglvrhad Helaeth-lawn o'r Athrawaeth Gristnogavvl*, a translation of Bellarmino's *Dottrina Christiana*.[43] In 1661, following a gap of over forty years, *Drych Cydwybod* (*The mirror of conscience*), a translation of Francisco Toledo's *Summa Casuum Conscientiae*, was published. Moses Williams saw a copy of the book some time before 1717, but no copy seems to have survived.[44] Before the end of the century, two other Catholic texts of considerable interest appeared. The first, *Allwydd neu Agoriad Paradwys i'r Cymru* (1670),[45] a translation by John Hughes (1615-86) drawn from various sources, bore the imprint 'Yn Lvyck', but is now thought to have been produced in London, not Liège. It was followed in 1684 by *Dilyniad Christ*, a translation by Hughes's father, Hugh Owen of Gwenynog (?1575-1642), of Thomas à Kempis's *De Imitatione Christi*.[46] Hughes claimed in *Allwydd Paradwys* that his aim was to produce a book for all Welshmen irrespective of their religious allegiance, but its publication caused a great deal of disquiet to Anglicans and Puritans alike and reinforced the fear of a reversion to Catholicism by the monoglot Welsh which underlay much of their publishing activity.

Although early Puritanism seemed foreign to most parts of Wales and did not flourish until the Civil War, the Puritans were to became increasingly prominent in Welsh-language publishing as the century progressed. Indeed it was some of the Puritan writers who, with their emphasis on a more personal and evangelical religion, were to be the most creative and original of the century's authors. A group of early Puritans produced works of particular interest.[47] Foremost amongst them was Oliver Thomas (*c*.1598-1652) who later became one of the Approvers under the 1650 Act for the Better Propagation and Preaching of the Gospel in Wales. In 1630 and 1631 he produced two books, both bearing the title *Car-wr y Cymru* (*A Lover of the Welsh*). The first, *Car-wr y Cymru, yn anfon ychydig gymorth i bôb Tad, a mam sy'n ewyllysio bod eu plant yn blant i Dduw hefyd*, was a twelve-page catechism intended, according to its full title, to help parents ensure their children became children of God. The 1631 volume, *Car-wr y Cymru, yn annog ei genedl anwyl, a'i gydwlad-wyr er mwyn Crist ai heneidiau i chwilio, yr Scrythyrau yn ol gorchymyn Crist*, is a much longer work designed to convince adults of the need to search the Scriptures.[48]

The two books by Oliver Thomas, the Welsh Bible of 1630, the publication of Rowland Vaughan's *Yr Ymarfer o Dduwioldeb* and of Robert Llwyd's *Llwybr Hyffordd* all reflected the aspirations of a group of Welsh scholars and of London-Welsh businessmen — Sir Thomas Myddelton and Rowland Heylyn in particular — to ensure that not only was the Bible itself published in an accessible and affordable format but that other edifying literature was also made available. On the title page of the 1631 *Car-wr y Cymru* the author acknowledges the assistance provided to produce the pocket-sized version of the Welsh Bible:

> these, recently printed anew in Welsh are available and on sale as a book, small in size and price, and brought about through much industry and cost by religious famous and willing men who wish to do good for Wales.[49]

During the Civil War and Interregnum there were no Welsh-language newsbooks: Welsh publishing remained dominated by religious publications. Foremost during the

1640s and 1650s were those produced by Welsh Puritans and, in particular, those of Morgan Llwyd (1619-59). Llwyd holds a unique position in the history of Wales and Welsh literature on account of his originality, his intellectual power, and the quality of his prose.[50] Brought up in a famous Merionethshire household (Cynfal Fawr, Maentwrog) and steeped in the culture of the Welsh bards, he was a competent poet but is chiefly remembered for his prose works. Llwyd was very aware of the importance of books. He opens his *Llythur ir Cymru Cariadus* (*A Letter to the beloved Welsh people*) by proclaiming that *'books are like wells'* (Mae llyfrau fel ffynnonnau)[51] and complains in the most famous of all his works, *Arwydd i Annerch y Cymru*, usually referred to as *Llyfr y Tri Aderyn* (*The book of the Three Birds*), that *'there are not many Welsh books in Wales'* (Nid oes chwaith fawr lyfrau cymreig ynghymru).[52] Llwyd attempted to fill the gap by writing and publishing eleven books between 1653 and 1657, eight in Welsh and three in English. Six of the Welsh texts were original works and one of them, *Gwaedd Ynghymru yn Wyneb pob Cydwybod* (*A cry in Wales in the face of every conscience*), is of particular bibliographical interest as the first Welsh book printed in Dublin in 1653.[53]

In addition to the production of some notable Puritan publications, the years of the Interregnum witnessed another development that had implications for the book trade. Following the Act for the Better Propagation and Preaching of the Gospel in Wales (1650), sixty-three schools were established in the larger towns of Wales to provide free education to boys and girls alike. It represented a first attempt at providing subsidized education in Wales although the effectiveness of these schools, like their successors, was limited by the fact that instruction was entirely in English, the Welsh language being regarded as an anachronism and an obstacle to enlightenment.

The first decade after the Restoration saw a marked reduction in Welsh publishing output, only sixteen titles, ten of which were in Welsh, being recorded between 1660 and 1669. Amongst the authors of the handful of books published during the 1660s there appears the name of Charles Edwards (1628-?1691), one of the many ministers ejected after 1662 and a highly talented writer.[54] The first edition of his *Y Ffydd Ddi-ffuant* (*The unfeigned faith*) was published at Oxford in 1667,[55] and from then until his death he worked ceaselessly to produce and edit Welsh books. From the beginning of the 1670s he and Stephen Hughes began a fruitful partnership that would further develop the Welsh book trade. Despite differences in background, education, and temperament, Hughes and Edwards had much in common. Both had suffered persecution for their Puritan convictions and were dedicated to the task of preaching the gospel in a simple forthright manner. They were both convinced of the need for a constant supply of books especially written and adapted for ordinary people in their own language. Stephen Hughes explained his position in his introduction to *Rhan o waith Mr Rees Prichard* (1658):

> *Another consideration which impelled me to print these things is the great likelihood that this will stir many who are illiterate to learn to read Welsh. People are eager for new things, and these printed are new to our country, and possibly many (influenced alas by the aim of amusement rather than improving their souls) will set about learning to read the work of the Vicar of Llanymddyfri. And after learning to read this, what hindrance will there be to reading other Welsh books, through which (if not through this one) great*

goodness can be gained; therefore if the book is likely in some way (even if only by chance) to do good, it is to be hoped we have a strong reason for printing it.[56]

Capital was required if books were to be printed and this was supplied through the agency of another 'ejected' minister, Thomas Gouge (?1605-81), formerly incumbent of St Sepulchre, London. Gouge managed to solicit substantial sums of money from Anglicans and Dissenters alike to promote the education and spiritual well-being of the poor. He took a particular interest in the plight of the ordinary people of Wales and, with the financial support of prosperous London businessmen, formally established in 1674 the Welsh Trust to evangelize and to promote literacy amongst them:

> in regard that a few poor Children there are brought up to Reading, it is another good work of Charity, to raise and maintain several Schools, for teaching the poorest of the Welsh Children to read English, and the Boys to learn to Write and cast Accounts.[57]

Within a few years the Trust could claim that it had established 'some scores of Schools in which many hundreds of Poor Welsh Children have been taught to read, and write'.[58]

In addition to setting up schools, the Trust developed a publishing policy and a strategy for distributing books throughout Wales. Although the language of instruction in the Trust's schools was English (a policy of which Stephen Hughes disapproved), the books sponsored by the Trust were, of necessity, in Welsh. Many of these were to be 'freely given away to such poor people as can read them, and are not able to buy Books'.[59] In order to develop its publishing strategy the Trust set about discovering what Welsh books were available. Its 1675 Report claimed that 'there are few Divinity Books in the Welsh Language', according to evidence supplied by the mercers of the main towns in Wales who were 'the only Traders in Books there'. The Trust set about buying up what stock they possessed and also 'did forthwith buy up all the Divinity Books in the British Language that could be found in London'.[60]

Both Hughes and Edwards became active participants in the work of the Trust,[61] Hughes providing his organizational abilities and intimate knowledge of the spiritual needs of ordinary folk and their levels of literacy, and Edwards his scholarship and editorial skills. Both would devote the rest of their lives, even after the demise of the Welsh Trust, to the production of moral, devotional, and didactic books. Several of these were reprints of works of proven popularity such as Vaughan's *Yr Ymarfer o Dduwioldeb*, Oliver Thomas's *Car-wr y Cymru* and *Drych i dri math o bobl* (*A mirror for three kinds of people*), Robert Llwyd's *Llwybr hyffordd*, and Dr John Davies's *Llyfr y Resolusion*. One indication of the scale of the scale of the Trust's activity is that 2,500 copies of Vaughan's *Ymarfer* (revised by Charles Edwards) were printed and 'freely given to Poor people in Wales'.[62]

The Trust also published new translations, including works by Gouge himself such as Charles Edwards's version of *The Principles of Christian Religion* published as *Gwyddorion y Grefydd Gristianogol* in 1679.[63] But of all the newer translations, the one that would eventually become a perennial best-seller was the Welsh version of John Bunyan's *Pilgrim's Progress*, *Taith neu Siwrnai y Pererin*, which appeared in 1688.[64] The translation was undertaken by Hughes with the assistance of three other unnamed persons, one of whom, 'Gwr bonheddig o Wynedd' (A Gentleman from Gwynedd) would certainly have been Charles Edwards.[65]

In addition to reprinting old favourites and publishing new translations, the Welsh Trust brought about the publication of a new edition of the Welsh Bible. Stephen Hughes secured sufficient subscriptions from members of the nobility, Anglican clergymen, and leaders of other religious denominations in Wales to permit the printing of eight thousand 'Welsh Bibles in Octavo with a fair Letter, on good Paper', seven thousand of which were:

> to be sold in Wales at the Printing price, viz. 4s. 2d. And the other thousand remaining are to be freely given to such Poor Families and Persons as are not able to buy a Bible, and yet can read, and are like to make good use therof.[66]

Despite its undoubted successes, the Trust was not without its problems. The motives of Stephen Hughes, in particular, came to be increasingly questioned by leading Anglicans in Wales. In 1684, three years after the death of Thomas Gouge, the Welsh Trust was dissolved and its schools in Wales closed. Stephen Hughes and Charles Edwards, however, attempted to continued with the task of producing and distributing Welsh books. Hughes, in particular, entertained ambitious publishing plans up to the time of his death which were frustrated by lack of money. As he explained in his introductory letter to the Welsh which precedes the 1688 *Taith y Pererin*, '*The money was lacking to print it all*' (Yr oedd arian yn niffyg i brintio'r cwbl).

By that time another enterprising Welshman had arrived on the scene and had begun to expand the frontiers of Welsh publishing in a remarkable manner. Thomas Jones (1648-1713), from Tre'r-ddol, near Corwen, arrived in London in 1666 to work as a tailor. Within a few years, he had abandoned that trade and was to devote the rest of his life to the book trade as author, printer, publisher, bookseller, and distributor.[67] His business acumen and boundless energy would, despite considerable impediments (not least his wretched health and rampant paranoia), bring about fundamental changes in the Welsh book trade. By the mid-1670s he had set up as a bookseller and published his first title, *The Character of a Quack-doctor*, in 1676. Welsh books soon followed. Although Jones had received little formal education, he was involved in publishing standard religious texts such as his edition of *Yr Hên Lyfr Plygain* (1683),[68] a version of the Book of Common Prayer (1687),[69] and in 1688 his translation of the Thirty-nine Articles, *Y Namynun-deugain Erthyglau Crefydd Eglwys Loegr*.[70] In the same year Jones published possibly the most enterprising of all his publications, *Y Gymraeg yn ei Disgleirdeb, Neu helaeth Eir-lyfr Cymraeg a Saesnaeg [...] The British Language in its Lustre, Or a Copious Dictionary of Welsh and English*.[71] Like his other publications this dictionary (discussed in Chapter 6) was not intended for the educated minority but rather the ordinary people. Jones wished to enhance their ability to write and spell both Welsh and English. Its publication is indicative of the change that had taken place in Welsh publishing during the half-century following the appearance of the *Dictionarium Duplex* in 1632. John Davies's dictionary represented the pinnacle of humanist scholarship in Wales whilst that of Thomas Jones attempted to come to terms with an entirely different world.

Thomas Jones realized that as the common people became literate in Welsh, they would require reading material that would entertain as well as educate and edify. He knew that poetry had a particular appeal to his fellow-countrymen and he published a number of anthologies which included both strict-metre and free-metre verse such as *Carolau, a Dyriau Duwiol*, 1696.[72] Jones is, however, best known for his almanacs. In January 1679 he secured a privilege granting him a monopoly of almanac publishing in the 'British Language' which was soon confirmed by the Stationers' Company. He proceeded to publish an almanac for each year from 1680 until his death in 1713, a development which would prove to be one of the most far reaching in the whole history of Welsh publishing since these twopenny almanacs reached (and created) an extensive readership. His almanacs have been characterized as 'a curious amalgam of miscellaneous information'[73] which 'served as a diary, a calendar, a reference-book, an astrologer's guide, a periodical, a newspaper, a song-book and a primer'.[74] Some of the information such as the dates of fairs and markets was factual but much of it — such as the astrological information and the prognostications — derived from Jones's fertile imagination. The almanacs reflected many of Jones's own views and prejudices, not least his violent hostility to Roman Catholicism and Louis XIV. By providing an outlet for the work of contemporary poets the almanacs also played a crucial role in preserving *cerdd dafod* (Welsh prosody), particularly following the inauguration of *eisteddfodau'r almanaciau* (the almanac eisteddfods) from 1701 onwards.[75] Unfortunately for Jones, others soon realized that publishing Welsh almanacs was a profitable business and his paranoia was exacerbated by pirates who infringed his monopoly.[76]

Throughout the 1680s Thomas Jones managed to produce an impressive number of Welsh titles but he was becoming increasingly disenchanted with life in London and with the roguery of many of the printers he had to deal with. When the Printing Act lapsed in 1695 he promptly took advantage of the new freedom to print outside London by moving to the strategic border town of Shrewsbury where he remained for the remaining eighteen years of his life.[77] From 1696 onwards a constant flow of publications bearing Thomas Jones's imprint at Shrewsbury appear such as *Yr A.B.C. neu'r llyfr cyntaf i ddechrau dysgu darllain Cymraeg wrtho* (*The A.B.C. or the first book to start to learn reading Welsh*),[78] and in 1699 his own translation of the *Pilgrim's Progress*.[79] His almanac for 1699 advertised an important new publication, *Pedwar math o faledau Cymraeg* (*Four kinds of Welsh ballads*), which marked the true beginning of an immensely popular type of publication examined in Chapter 20. These ballads were aimed at ordinary people who wanted cheap literature of a stimulating, entertaining, and sometimes improving nature. By pioneering the production of such popular material Thomas Jones made an invaluable contribution to the growth of literacy in Welsh and the expansion of the Welsh reading public.

His abilities as a shrewd businessman were also of great importance in fostering this expansion. The Welsh Trust had already shown the importance of developing a distribution network and Thomas Jones set about securing representatives who would act as wholesalers in a number of important market towns and villages throughout Wales. He also employed pedlars to sell his publications at fairs. Another technique which he gradually adopted was publishing by subscription, although he was initially rather suspicious of the practice. From the beginning of the eighteenth century this became a common method of publishing and Thomas Jones employed it most effectively.

Thomas Jones's move to Shrewsbury and that town's development as the printing centre for Wales was not the only factor promoting Welsh publishing towards the end of the seventeenth century. The Toleration Act of 1689 gave greater freedom to Dissenters and encouraged them to make greater use of the printing press, and the consequent increase in Nonconformist literature would be one of the most important developments of the next hundred years. At the end of the century, however, it was the founding of The Society for Promoting Christian Knowledge (SPCK) in 1698 which would prove to be most immediately beneficial in the fight against illiteracy. Like the Welsh Trust, the SPCK made the establishment of charity schools in Wales one of its principal objectives but similarly limited their effectiveness by offering monoglot Welsh children an English-language education. Like the Welsh Trust, the SPCK would also be involved in the large-scale distribution of cheap or free devotional literature, and would undertake the preparation of new editions of the Welsh Bible. The rapid expansion of Welsh publishing which would take place during the eighteenth century owed much to those who had struggled against great odds during the previous century.

NOTES TO CHAPTER 8

The background to this period is covered by Glanmor Williams, *Recovery, reorientation, and Reformation: Wales, c.1415-1642* (Oxford, 1987); Geraint H. Jenkins, *The foundations of modern Wales: Wales 1642-1780* (Oxford, 1987); T. Parry, *History of Welsh literature to 1900*, trans. H. I. Bell (Oxford, 1955). For the book trade in Wales the following are indispensable: E. Rees, *Libri Walliae: a catalogue of Welsh books and books printed in Wales 1546-1820* (Aberystwyth, 1987); also her 'Welsh Publishing before 1719', in *Essays in honour of Victor Scholderer*, ed. D. E. Rhodes (Mainz, 1970), pp. 323-36; her *The Welsh book-trade before 1820* (Aberystwyth, 1988); and her 'Wales and the London book trade before 1820', in *Spreading the word: the distribution networks of print 1550-1850*, ed. Robin Myers and Michael Harris (Winchester, 1990), pp. 1-20. A comprehensive analysis of the Welsh book trade in the later seventeenth century is provided by G. H. Jenkins, *Literature, religion and society in Wales 1660-1730* (Cardiff, 1978). See now also Charles Parry, 'From manuscript to print: II: printed books', in *A guide to Welsh literature c.1530-1700*, ed. R. Geraint Gruffydd (Cardiff, 1997), pp. 263-76.

[1] LW contains 232 entries for the period 1600 to 1699, 170 (82%) of which are in Welsh, 27 (12%) in English, and the remaining 15 (6%) in Latin. A number of these entries, however, refer to variant issues of the same work, e.g. LW, 3437-40 are all issues of *Y Llyfr Plygain* of 1633.

[2] Williams, *Recovery, reorientation, and Reformation*, p. 437.

[3] W. Ll. Davies, 'Welsh books entered in the Stationers' Company's Registers', *JWBS* 2 (1916-23), 167-74, 204-9.

[4] The following is based on Philip Henry Jones, 'Wales and the Stationers' Company', in *The Stationers' Company and the book trade 1550-1990*, ed. Robin Myers and Michael Harris (Winchester, 1997), pp. 185-202. I am grateful to him for allowing me to see this paper prior to publication.

[5] 'Ac am y bibl cymraeg, hi fydd hir cyn printier ef, on i fydd i wyr arianog osod allan fil o bynne tuag at ei brintio; canys, medd gwerthwyr llyfrau yn Llyndain, ni ddodwn ni mo'n harian i maes i'r gwaith hwn, o herwydd fe fydd printiad neu impressiwn o chwech mîl o fiblau cymraeg ugain mlynedd, neu bedair blynedd ar ddeg yn eu gwerthu (ble'r ydym ni'n gwerthu ynghylch deng mil ar hugain o Fiblau saesneg bob blwyddyn) ac ni allwn ni sy'n byw wrth ein crefftau aros cyd, i gael ein harian i mewn'. Quoted in Rees, *The Welsh book-trade before 1820*, p. xiv.

[6] For examples in Welsh see *Hen gyflwyniadau*, ed. Henry Lewis (Cardiff, 1948) and *Rhagymadroddion, 1547-1649*, ed. Garfield H. Hughes (Cardiff, 1953); for Welsh translations of Latin examples see Ceri Davies, *Rhagymadroddion a chyflwyniadau Lladin 1551-1632* (Cardiff, 1980).

[7] Rees, *The Welsh book-trade*, pp. ix-xiii; also her 'Wales and the London book trade before 1820', p. 4; A. Crawford and A. P. Jones, 'The early typography of printed Welsh', *The Library*, 6th ser., 3 (1981), 217-31.

[8] Rees, *The Welsh book-trade*, pp. ix-xiii; *Rhagymadroddion*, p. 130.

[9] 'Er maint y fu gofal a dyfalwch y Golygwr astud yn ceisio diwygio y beiau aneirif yr oedd y Printiwr dieithr yn eu gwneuthur (o ran ei anwybodaeth o'r jaith) ym-mhob dalen o'r gwaith ymma; etto fe a ddiengodd llawer ohonynt ei olwg ef.' Quoted in Rees, *The Welsh book-trade*, p. xiii.

[10] 'Y mae yn ddrwg iawn ganif fôd rhai mannau o'r llyfr hwn, ac om halmanac am y flwyddyn, 1688, gwedi eu hargraphu cyn ddrygced; mi a delais gymmaint am y mannau gwaetha, ag am y mannau goreu: Ac yn wîr nid arna i y mae'r bai, ond ar y digydwybod argraphyddion. Os arhoswn am lyfrau difai, hydoni bô'r Argraphyddion yn ddâ eu cydwybod, gallwn fôd fyth heb eu cael.' Thomas Jones, *Y Gymraeg yn ei Disgleirdeb [...]* (London, 1688), sig. X8r.

[11] Jones, *Y Gymraeg yn ei Disgleirdeb*, sig. X3v.

[12] R. Geraint Gruffydd, 'Richard Parry a John Davies', in *Y traddodiad rhyddiaith*, ed. Geraint Bowen (Llandysul, 1970), pp. 175-93.

[13] 1,500 copies may have been printed according to *The Bible in Wales* (London, 1906), p. 10.

[14] Mae'r bibl bach yn awr yn gysson,
Yn iaith dy fam iw gael er coron,
Gwerth dy grys cyn bod heb hwnnw,

Mae'n well nâ thre dy dâd i'th gadw.
Quoted in *The Bible in Wales*, under entry no. 11.
15 Although earlier editions of *Llyfr Plygain* are noted in the Stationers' registers from 1599 onwards, the earliest extant copy is an edition by Daniel Powel published in 1612 (*LW*, 3435). The modern reprint, *Y Llyfr Plygain 1612* (Cardiff, 1931), includes a bibliographical note, a note on the origin and content of *Y Llyfr Plygain*, and a comparative table of the contents of various editions of *Y Llyfr Plygain* from 1612 to 1791. See also *Hen gyflwyniadau*, pp. 12-14.
16 Rhiannon F. Roberts, 'Y Dr. John Davies o Fallwyd', *LlC*, 2 (1952-3), 19-35, 97-110.
17 *LW*, 3437-40.
18 *LW*, 4767.
19 *LW*, 3869.
20 Saunders Lewis, 'Llyfr y Resolusion', *Ysgrifau Catholig*, 3 (1964), 1-6, reprinted in his *Meistri'r canrifoedd: ysgrifau ar hanes llenyddiaeth Gymraeg*, ed. R. Geraint Gruffydd (Cardiff, 1973), pp. 147-52.
21 *LW*, 1162.
22 Glanmor Williams, 'Edward James a *Llyfr yr Homilïau*', *Morgannwg*, 25 (1981), 79-99, reprinted in his *Grym tafodau tân: ysgrifau hanesyddol ar grefydd a diwylliant*, (Llandysul, 1984), pp. 180-98.
23 *LW*, 1684, 1682.
24 ' [...] geiriau an-arferedig a ochelais yn oreu ac y medrais, gan ymfodloni a r cyfryw eiriau sathredig, ac y mae cyffredin y wlâd yn gydnabyddus â hwynt, ac yn yspys ynddynt.' Robert Llwyd, *Llwybr hyffordd yn cyfarwyddo yr angyfarwydd i'r nefoedd*, (Llundain, 1630), sig. A10^v, reproduced in *Rhagymadroddion*, p. 130.
25 ' [...] prynu y chydig lyfrau bychain o'th iaith a'th ddeall dy hûn i gyssuro dy enaid pan na allo yr holl fyd ddim llesâd i ti.' *Rhagymadroddion*, p. 129.
26 *LW*, 320-21; Reprinted as Lewis Bayly, *Yr Ymarfer o Dduwioldeb* (Cardiff, 1930); Gwyn Thomas, 'Rowland Vaughan' in *Y traddodiad rhyddiaith*, pp. 231-46.
27 *LW*, 2032.
28 *LW*, 708-9, 1874, 3526, 4150, 4988; Thomas, 'Rowland Vaughan', p. 236.
29 *LW*, 1712.
30 *LW*, 2448.
31 *LW*, 4637.
32 *LW*, 1611-12; *Hen gyflwyniadau*, pp. 48-51.
33 A claim made by Nesta Lloyd in the valuable introduction to her *Blodeugerdd Barddas o'r ail ganrif ar bymtheg*, *Cyfrol 1* (Llandybïe, 1993), p. xxii.
34 *LW*, 587.
35 ' [...] pob plant, gweinidogion, a phobl annyscedic a ddyscant bennill o garol, lle ni allai ond ysgolhaig ddyscù Cywydd neu gerdd gyfarwydd arall.' Quoted in *Canu rhydd cynnar*, ed. T. H. Parry Williams (Cardiff, 1932), p. xxxvii; Glanmor Williams, *The Welsh and their religion* (Cardiff, 1991), pp. 164-5.
36 *Cerddi'r Ficer: detholiad o gerddi Rhys Prichard*, ed. Nesta Lloyd (Llandybïe, 1994) is the latest and most authoritative selection of Prichard's works.
37 Eiluned Rees, 'A bibliographical note on early editions of *Canwyll y Cymry*', *JWBS*, 10(2) (1966-71), 36-41.
38 *LW*, 3955, 3956. One publication by Rees Prichard, a Catechism entitled *Cyngor Episcob y bob enaid oddi vewn y Episcobeth*, had been published in 1617.
39 How Hughes attempted to purge Prichard's verses of what he considered to be undesirable or debased words is examined in Nesta Lloyd, 'Sylwadau ar iaith rhai o gerddi Rhys Prichard', *NLWJ*, 29 (1995-6), 257-80.
40 *LW*, 3955.
41 *LW*, 3966. A. F. Allison and D. M. Rogers, *The contemporary printed literature of the English Counter-Reformation between 1558 and 1640*, 2 vols (Aldershot, 1989-94), II, 144 (no. 725.5); J. Ryan, 'The sources of the Welsh translation of the Catechism of St Peter Canisius', *JWBS*, 11 (1973-6), 225-32.

[42] LW, 579; Rhosier Smyth, *Theatr du Mond (Gorsedd y Byd)*, ed. T. Parry (Cardiff, 130); facsimile published as Pierre Boaistuau, *Gorsedd y Byd 1615* (Menston, 1970).

[43] LW, 332; Geraint Bowen, 'Richard Vaughan, Bodeiliog, ac *Eglvrhad Helaeth-lawn*, 1618', *NLWJ*, 12 (1961-2), 83-4.

[44] LW, 1718; Geraint Bowen, 'Fersiwn Cymraeg o *Summa Casuum Conscientiae*, Francisco Toledo', *JWBS*, 10(2) (1966-71), 5-35.

[45] LW, 2501; Reprinted as John Hughes, *Allwydd neu Agoriad Paradwys i'r Cymru, 1670*, ed. John Fisher (Cardiff, 1929); Geraint Bowen, 'Allwydd neu Agoriad Paradwys i'r Cymru 1670', *THSC* (1961), 88-160.

[46] LW, 3190; Saunders Lewis, 'Thomas à Kempis yn Gymraeg', *EfC*, 4 (1949), 28-44, reprinted in his *Meistri'r canrifoedd*, pp. 183-205.

[47] N. A. Gibbard, *Elusen i'r enaid: arweiniad i weithiau'r Piwritaniaid Cymreig, 1630-1689* (Bridgend, 1979); R. G. Gruffydd, 'In that gentile country ...': the beginnings of Puritan Nonconformity in Wales (Bridgend, 1977).

[48] LW, 4887, 4885-6; *Gweithiau Oliver Thomas ac Evan Roberts, dau Biwritan cynnar*, ed. Merfyn Morgan (Cardiff, 1981) reproduces five texts: *Car-wr y Cymru* (1630), *Car-wr y Cymru* (1631), and *Drych i Dri Math o Bobl* (1647) by Oliver Thomas; *Sail Crefydd Ghristnogol* (1640) which Oliver Thomas and Evan Roberts co-authored and *Sail Crefydd Gristnogawl* (1649) by Evan Roberts.

[49] 'Y rhai, yr awr' hon yn ddiweddar â brintiwyd o newydd yn Gymraec; ac a geir ar werth yn llyfran cynnwys, a bychain eu maintioli a'i prîs, drwy fawr ddiwydrwydd, a thraul swrn o wyr Duwyol, enwog ac ewyllys-gar i wneuthur daioni i'r Cymru.' Title-page, *Car-wr y Cymru* (1631); *Gweithiau Oliver Thomas*, p. [21].

[50] Excellent introductions to the life and work of Morgan Llwyd are M. Wynn Thomas, *Morgan Llwyd* (Cardiff, 1984); his *Morgan Llwyd: ei gyfeillion a'i gyfnod* (Cardiff, 1991); Goronwy Wyn Owen, *Morgan Llwyd* (Caernarfon, 1992).

[51] Morgan Llwyd, *Gweithiau Morgan Llwyd o Wynedd*, Vol. 1, ed. Thomas E. Ellis (Bangor, 1899), p. 115.

[52] M. Llwyd, *Gweithiau*, p. 261.

[53] LW, 3408; W. Ll. Davies, 'A argraffwyd llyfr Cymraeg yn Iwerddon cyn 1700?', *JWBS*, 5 (1938), 114-19; *Gweithiau Morgan Llwyd o Wynedd, Cyfrol III*, ed. J. Graham Jones and Goronwy Wyn Owen (Caerdydd, 1994), p. 139n. suggests that two of Llwyd's works were printed in Dublin in 1653.

[54] Derec Llwyd Morgan, 'Charles Edwards (1628-1691?): awdur *Y Ffydd Ddi-ffuant*', in *Y traddodiad rhyddiaith*, pp. 213-30; also his *Charles Edwards* (Caernarfon, 1994).

[55] LW, 1761

[56] 'Peth arall am hannogodd i brintio'r pethau ymma, yw, y tybygoliaeth mawr, y cynhyrfir wrth hyn laweroedd ni fedrant ddarllain, i ddyscu darllain cymraeg. Awyddys yw bobl at bethau newyddion, a'r rhain yn printiedig ydynt newydd i'n gwlad: ag odid, na bydd llawer (er ys-catfydd nid ag amcan i gael lleshad i heneidiau, etto o ran ei dyfyrwch) yn ymdynnu, i ddyscu darllain gwaith *Vickar Llanddyfri*. Ag ar ol dyscu darllain hwn, pa rwystir fydd i ddarllain llyfrau cymraeg eraill, trwy ba rai (oni chesglyr trwy hwn) y gellir casglu daioni mawr; ag felly os yw'r llyfyr mewn rhyw fodd (pe bae ond trwy ddigwyddiad) dybygol i wneuthur lles, gobeithio fod genym resswm cryf am ei brintio.' Quoted in G. J. Williams, 'Stephen Hughes a'i gyfnod', in *Agweddau ar hanes dysg Gymraeg: detholiad o ddarlithiau G. J. Williams*, ed. A. Lewis (Cardiff, 1969), pp. 171-206 (p. 176).

[57] M. G. Jones, 'Two accounts of the Welsh Trust, 1675 and 1678(?)', *BBCS*, 9 (1937-9), 71-80 (p. 72). For a detailed history of the Welsh Trust see M. G. Jones, *The charity school movement, a study of eighteenth century Puritanism in action* (Cambridge, 1938).

[58] Jones, 'Two accounts', p. 77.

[59] *Ibid.*, p. 72.

[60] *Ibid.*, p. 77.

[61] Jenkins, *Literature, religion and society*, p. 43; also his 'Apostol Sir Gaerfyrddin: Stephen Hughes 1622-1688', in his *Cadw tŷmewn cwmwl tystion: ysgrifau hanesyddol ar grefydd a diwylliant* (Llandysul,

1990), pp. 1-28; and his '"A lleufer dyn yw llyfr da": Stephen Hughes a'i hoff awduron', in *Agweddau ar dwf Piwritaniaeth yng Nghymru yn yr ail ganrif ar bymtheg*, ed. J. Gwynfor Jones (Lampeter, 1992), pp. 203-27.
62 Jones, 'Two accounts', p. 77.
63 *LW*, 2175.
64 *LW*, 781.
65 *Taith neu Siwrnai y Pererin* (London, 1688), sig. A2^v.
66 Jones, 'Two accounts', pp. 77-8.
67 The fullest account of his life and career is provided by Geraint H. Jenkins, *Thomas Jones yr Almanaciwr 1648-1713* (Cardiff, 1980). See also his '"The sweating astrologer"; Thomas Jones the Almanacer', in *Welsh society and nationhood: historical essays presented to Glanmor Williams*, ed. R. R. Davies *et al*. (Cardiff, 1984), pp. 161-77.
68 *LW*, 3443.
69 *LW*, 593.
70 *LW*, 4768.
71 *LW*, 3099.
72 *LW*, 3104.
73 Jenkins, '"The sweating astrologer"', p. 164;
74 *Ibid*., pp. 175-6.
75 *Ibid*., p. 171.
76 E. Rees and Gerald Morgan, 'Welsh almanacks, 1680-1835: problems of piracy', *The Library*, 6th ser. 1 (1979), 142-63.
77 The importance of Shrewsbury as a centre of Welsh printing is discussed in Rees, *The Welsh book-trade*, pp. xvii-xxii.
78 *LW*, 6. Another work seen by Moses Williams before 1717 which is no longer extant.
79 *LW*, 782.

CHAPTER 9

THE EIGHTEENTH CENTURY

Geraint H. Jenkins

WILLIAM Williams of Llandygái, the self-taught son of a marble mason from Trefdraeth in Anglesey, was a gifted antiquary, steeped in the traditions, folk-lore, and legends of the Welsh people. Literature — both Welsh and English — was very dear to him and in his youth in the 1750s he spent every spare penny on books and candles so that he might read into the small hours.[1] His reading was extensive and omnivorous, and his thirst for knowledge was characteristic of the patriotic middling sorts whose drive, determination, and ingenuity were to a large degree responsible for 'the remaking of Wales in the eighteenth century'.[2] Whenever slights and injustices inflicted upon the Welsh were topics of conversation, Williams could be stirred to speak his mind with uncompromising bluntness. He particularly disliked and mistrusted the new 'Leviathans' who had displaced the traditional landowning families and who, by the end of the eighteenth century, exercised untroubled economic and political sway in Wales. Although there are undoubtedly elements of misinformation and exaggeration in the following passage (written in 1805), it vividly conveys how patterns of landownership had been transformed during the eighteenth century:

> How melancholy is it to observe, the immense number of withered mansions we meet with in these countries, where in past and better times, opulency, hospitality and good neighbourhood, dwelt and cheered the drooping spirit of the indigent, when Charity's benevolent countenance smiled in every door. Now, these adored residences have disappeared: harassed and oppressed annual Lodgers are the present inmates, bending their heads to the heavy Yoke of rack rents, poor rates and many other ponderous impositions, and charity long ago has been kicked out of doors, and scarcely considered any more as a virtue. All those venerable habitations have sunk by marriages, purchases & etc., into one irrecoverable gulph; their possessors strangers, and those of opulency gone to enjoy themselves in the town, spending their time in all kind of dissipation, neglecting and forgetting their duty as men and Christians.[3]

Those factors which conspired in favour of the accumulation of great estates by a tiny group of wealthy and powerful landowners have received a good deal of scholarly attention of late.[4] The demise of traditional gentry families — nostalgically described by Edmund Hyde Hall as 'a very useful order of society'[5] — had been hastened in most cases by crippling debts, mortgages and encumbrances, administrative ineptitude, sheer improvidence, a self-destructive fondness for lethal doses of alcohol, and curious failures in the male line. Massive shifts in the balance of wealth and power led to a proliferation of deserted mansions. In the 1770s Thomas Pennant, the bookish gentleman-traveller who was one of the most thoughtful and intelligent observers of his time, noted the names of thirty-five deserted seats in Merioneth, 'most of these now swallowed by our Welch Leviathans'.[6] Throughout Wales estate after estate had fallen victim to a new ruling class, many of whose members had kept a watchful eye open for eligible, well-dowered, and vulnerable heiresses as well as for financially ruined estates. With dewy-eyed nostalgia, many writers like William Williams, Llandygái, mourned the passing of what they considered a more equitable, paternalistic order.[7] Old patriarchs had been elbowed aside by new parasites. The direct beneficiaries of the decline of the Welsh squirearchy were generally absentee landlords, bearing un-Welsh names like Bute, Douglas-Pennant, Plymouth, Talbot, and Wynne-Finch, whose socio-cultural interests differed sharply from those whom they had replaced. Such a profound economic transformation clearly had far-reaching implications for the world of books.

As the traditional county community was undermined, it soon became clear that the new ruling clique could scarcely be considered an organic part of the fabric of Welsh rural society. Estates were governed by agents or stewards whose dynamic, innovative entrepreneurship, as well as their unscrupulous and sometimes oppressive conduct, proved a further threat to communal solidarity. The landed behemoths displayed little enthusiasm for the culture of the 'mountain Welsh great or small'[8] and consciously distanced themselves from the history, language, and literature of Wales. The smaller gentry were simply 'bumpkins', 'rabble', and 'ragamuffins', while plebeian culture was rowdy, unsophisticated, and abhorrent. Some of their derisive comments betrayed a profound racial antipathy towards the Welsh. William Jones, the 'rural Voltaire' from Llangadfan in mid-Wales, deplored the malign influence of the new Leviathans and the class divisions which their presence had created: 'the [...] notion the Englishman and our own Anglified gentry have of our capacity, vizt., that we can scarcely be distinguished from brutes [...] and that our language was but an incoherent jargon'.[9] Evan Evans, 'Ieuan Fardd', writing in similar vein, fulminated against Welsh gentry families who sought to emulate the 'new' giants by 'adopting the language of their conquerors, which is the mark of the most despicable meanness of spirit, and of a mind lost to all that is noble and generous'.[10] A barrage of hostile verse penned by balladmongers, almanackers and minstrels confirmed this widely held view.[11] It was left to the smaller squires in the sheltered parts of north-west and west Wales to sustain the native language, poetry, and literature. As late as the end of the eighteenth century, as many as twenty gentry families in Merioneth continued to welcome scholars and poets to their country homes,[12] but it could hardly be claimed that many of them were well versed in the subtle intricacies of *cynghanedd*.

In most counties, particularly in progressive Glamorgan, the reconstitution of the gentry class meant that the most influential sections of society now cherished different literary and recreational pursuits. Savouring the pleasures of London life was considerably more attractive to them than the humdrum tempo of rural Wales. By frequenting theatres, coffee houses, salons, taverns, and clubs, the gentry kept themselves in close touch with the world of English letters and polite society in general. Their reading habits were cosmopolitan and, since they had money in their pockets and time on their hands, they stocked their libraries with books on antiquarianism, classics, geography, history, philosophy, theology, and travel. London newspapers and periodicals like the *Tatler, Spectator, Guardian, Craftsman*, and *Gentleman's Magazine* were avidly read and helped to create interest in the affairs of the realm as well as to widen literary horizons.[13] When the Margam estate fell into the hands of the Talbot family in 1750, its library contained over 2,500 volumes.[14] Sir John Philipps of Picton Castle whiled away his leisure hours reading evangelical discourses and English novels, and Thomas Johnes of Hafod instructed his servants to protect his books and priceless French manuscripts from the effects of rising damp and leaking roofs by keeping fires alight night and day.[15] But they were exceptions to the rule. Most of the gentry derived pleasure from heavy drinking, gambling, fox-hunting, horse-racing, hare-coursing, and whoring, diversions which were loudly denounced by earnest Dissenters and Methodists. It is true, of course, that Welsh authors continued to dedicate their volumes to those whom they believed were well-disposed gentry patrons and that many kinds of pressures might induce an affluent man to donate a few shillings to add lustre to a devotional tract or an antiquarian treatise. But there must have been many authors like Iolo Morganwg who 'shivered at the doors of great and opulent names waiting [in vain] for the paltry sum of four shillings'.[16] The names of well-born gentlemen figure prominently in many subscription lists,[17] but there is no guarantee that they ever read these books. As Colonel James sharply exclaimed in Fielding's *Amelia*: 'Heaven forbid I should be obliged to read half the nonsense I have subscribed to!'

The decline of the small gentry families and the antipathy which the new landowners exhibited towards things Welsh had profound social repercussions and in some sense was a pre-requisite for cultural change. It compelled the increasingly numerous, articulate, and assertive middling ranks to re-examine the nature of Welshness, to open up new avenues in the socio-cultural life of Wales, and in particular to appreciate the vital importance of print as a means of shaping a new identity.[18] More than enough time and energy has been expended in studying the lives of the tiny gentry élite, and the time is surely ripe to pose Bill Speck's question — 'Will the Real Eighteenth Century stand up?'[19] — in a Welsh context. More attention needs to be focused on the manner in which the middling sorts gained sufficient courage and confidence to transform traditional ways of life in a country which lacked institutions of statehood and a tangible cultural infrastructure. The middle station, as Defoe liked to describe the middling sorts who filled the yawning gap between the privileged world of the gentry and plebeian society, was still numerically small in Wales and was by no means as affluent or influential as what Paul Langford has characterized as the 'polite and commercial people' of England.[20] But from the 1740s onwards the pace of life in Wales was changing — in some industrial and urban communities very swiftly — and there are good grounds for arguing that the ability and readiness of the middling sorts to respond creatively at a time of socio-economic change had a decisive impact on the demand for books and patterns of readership.

The Welsh middling sorts, made up largely of tradesmen, merchants, professional people, shopkeepers, farmers, and craftsmen, may loosely be described as those below the gentry class but above labourers, servants, and wage-earners. Demographic growth, urban development, the expansion of trading centres, new patterns of ownership, and the commercialization of leisure contributed to an up-turn in their fortunes. Their lifestyle, needs, and aspirations were clearly different from those of the propertied élite and the toiling masses. Although they could boast of a modicum of capital and often found themselves embroiled in the world of enterprise, trade, and property, they were conscious of the barriers of rank and birth and knew full well that they could never emulate the living standards of the upper classes. Nevertheless, many of them diligently accumulated material objects and luxury items, including books, clocks, china, and looking-glasses, which satisfied their cultural needs as much as their material requirements.[21] Their desire to earn a relatively comfortable living, combined with their hunger for knowledge and self-improvement, meant that they became a significant influence in the campaign to promote education and literacy, revivalism and godly reformation, scholarship and civility, and a new and enhanced sense of nationhood. To a substantial degree, the success of this ambitious programme owed much to the contribution of the printing presses, subscription ventures, book clubs and circulating libraries. *Libri Walliae* reveals that around 2,500 books (excluding ephemera) were published in Wales during the eighteenth century, four-fifths of them after 1740, precisely the years when the lower middling sorts became pace-setters in the spiritual and literary life of Wales.

The opportunities afforded by literacy and its role as a force for change were much more widely appreciated in mid-eighteenth century Wales than ever before. Pressure to acquire reading skills was most effectively exerted by Griffith Jones, rector of Llanddowror in Carmarthenshire from 1716 to 1761, who launched a remarkably durable and successful educational scheme in 1731.[22] In many ways Jones epitomized the earnest, puritanical, middling-sort 'improver' in mid-eighteenth century Wales. A melancholy, fastidious, frugal man (he subjected himself to a strict dietary regime), Jones sought to compensate for the 'misfortune' of his own 'mean education' by advancing the practical and spiritual utility of literacy as a means of preventing the souls of 'poor perishing wretches' from dropping into 'the dreadful abyss of eternity'.[23] The extraordinary increase in book production, the emergence of a substantial, pious, book-reading public, and much wider access to printed literature were clearly related to Jones's success in establishing a network of Welsh-medium circulating schools in town and countryside from the 1730s onwards. By the time of his death in 1761, some 3,325 schools had been established in nearly 1,600 different places in Wales. In view of the absence of a national educational system funded by the government, Griffith Jones was obliged to seek financial support from well-disposed patrons beyond Offa's Dyke in order to augment generous subventions provided by Madam Bridget Bevan, his principal sponsor. Like many religious reformers of his day, Jones believed that the pursuit of wealth for its own sake was 'the nurse of lust and luxury' and he drew on all his powers of rhetoric, as well as biblical knowledge, to berate the gluttonous few who 'live rich and idle on the Fat of the Land'.[24] He regularly visited Bath, the most attractive place of resort for lovers of pleasure as well as the sick, in order to establish contacts with philanthropists and plead for funds. 'Every soul you help to save', he reminded bankers, baronets, divines, and physicians in the spa's assembly rooms, thermal baths, and bowling greens, 'may be as so many shining pearls, to your never-fading crowns of glory.'[25] Jones's deep-seated fear of Popery, coupled with his melancholic and sometimes cantankerous nature, often prompted him to speak gloomily of 'the last days' and of the need to defend the Protestant religion and constitutional liberties. One of his primary aims was clearly to instil into pupils a proper awareness of their political and civil obligations. None of his protégés was encouraged to acquire ambitions or ideas above his station or to succumb to the temptation to seek new adventures in America. He had no wish to see the reading habit lead either to economic advancement or political emancipation. Similarly, he made it clear that the use of the Welsh language as the principal and often sole medium of education in his schools would protect the 'vulgar sorts' from the pernicious influence of 'Atheism, Deism, Infidelity, Arianism, Popery, lewd Plays, immodest Romances, and Love Intrigues'.[26] No effort was made to supply pupils with up-to-date knowledge of current affairs or digests of the various branches of learning. Yet Griffith Jones's plan of action was based on such carefully defined methods and was so well suited to the needs of the people that it was almost universally well received.

Even though he was a powerful and often moving preacher, Griffith Jones believed that printed books could exert a much more lasting influence on people than sermons delivered in cold and draughty churches. Feeling and understanding, he argued, went hand in hand, and in order to impose his own imperatives on the culture of common people he supplied them with Welsh Bibles, catechisms, and works on practical divinity. Although he publicly distanced himself from the official policy of the SPCK of imparting a knowledge of English to pupils in its charity schools, he gladly availed himself of the Society's offer to support his scheme by distributing thousands of Welsh Bibles, primers, and catechisms in every county in Wales. The circulating schools flourished mightily and it was a matter of considerable pride to Jones that the brightest pupils became fluent readers within a six-week period of tuition and that even illiterate septuagenarians were able to acquire rudimentary reading skills within three months. Some degree of rote learning in the reading programme — mastering relatively undemanding portions of the catechism and learning scriptural passages by heart — was employed by teachers, but the use of the Welsh language as the chief medium of instruction provided the dynamic which created by the end of the century a substantial reading public in Wales. The surge in literacy rates, particularly among craftsmen, artisans, and tenant farmers, significantly enhanced people's knowledge and understanding of the cardinal doctrines of the Protestant Reformation. Small wonder that this 'old and much honoured soldier'[27] was widely revered by Churchmen and Dissenters alike and that his contribution as an educational pioneer is now widely recognized and acclaimed by historians.[28]

Advances in schooling and literacy coincided with the arrival of the religion of enthusiasm, a movement which was part of a much larger international phenomenon of revival and renewal stretching from eastern Europe to the American colonies.[29] The causes of the so-called Methodist Revival are still the subject of dispute, but even those who detect the Lord's hand on the mission now grudgingly concede that it was a much more complex and many-sided movement than has been traditionally assumed. No longer can it be claimed, as did William Williams, Pantycelyn, that 'the Sun of righteousness'[30] cast its bounteous rays over a dark and benighted Wales from 1735 onwards. For Methodism was an amalgam of the old and the new, of 'head knowledge' as well as 'heart knowledge', of coteries of Dissenters as well as Churchmen, of the printed word as well as extravagant preaching. Long before the dawn of revivalism, increasing numbers of godly books which emphasized the need for subjective faith, inward scrutiny, personal devotion, and a reformation of manners had predisposed devout and literate men and women to respond favourably to the language of enthusiasm. Methodist leaders freely confessed their debt to 'the good old orthodox Reformers and Puritans'[31] and to the homiletic and didactic literature which had enhanced the quality of their spiritual experiences.

The 'spiritual father of the movement' (as he liked to be called) was Howel Harris, a carpenter's son from Trefeca in Breconshire and a soul-stirring enthusiast who ranks among the most dynamic and influential Welshmen of modern times.[32] Like his mentor and confidant Griffith Jones, Harris exemplified many traits associated with the active middling ranks. He was an inveterate social climber. Following a profound personal conversion, at the age of twenty-one, in 1735 (an experience which he dubbed 'the great struggle'),[33] Harris sneered at his modestly endowed parents but greatly admired his prosperous brothers. Thomas Harris was an accomplished, well-to-do tailor in London, and Joseph Harris, a scientist of no mean ability, became chief assay-master of the King's Mint. Acutely conscious of his relatively humble background and his elementary grasp of theology, Howel Harris longed to get on in the world. 'I Thirst for Improvement', he declared in May 1735,[34] and once he had established his position as commander-in-chief of the Methodist movement he mixed freely with 'the polite sort' in London and spent long hours in the company of the likes of Marmaduke Gwynne, the pious esquire of Garth in Breconshire, the redoubtable Lady Huntingdon, and the handsome Madam Bridget Bevan. He seldom wrote in Welsh and often complained to his English friends that his countrymen were 'so poor and so Welchy'.[35] Nevertheless, what Harris lacked in learning he made up for in robust zeal. As a preacher — 'striking bright and fiery sparks' according to Williams Pantycelyn,[36] he laboured with impressive energy and success in the 1740s. He thought nothing of preaching five times a day, often for several hours at a time, and left little respite for meals or sleep. This Welsh Zinzendorf drove his body to the point of exhaustion and his fellow enthusiasts, at least until Harris's expulsion from the movement in 1750, could only marvel at his stamina and commitment. A censorious, arrogant, and stubborn man, he was eventually undone by his own private weaknesses. Even so, on the occasion of his funeral in July 1773 it was claimed that 20,000 people assembled to pay homage to him.

As Harris constantly stressed, spiritual conversion lay at the heart of Methodism. In *Ffarwel Weledig* (1766), Williams Pantycelyn spoke of the 'spirit, zeal, enjoyment of God, and experience' which characterized the revivalist movement.[37] Fervent evangelical preaching was reckoned to be the most effective means of promoting 'true' religion, and exhorters deliberately excited the passions and affections of hearers. At Llangeitho in particular, Daniel Rowland's spirit-filled ministry often provoked extraordinary scenes: men and women cried, groaned, sang, danced, jumped, clapped their hands, hugged one another, and collapsed in cataleptic trances. Rowland's riveting sermons prompted Harris to refer admiringly to him as 'a second Paul',[38] but scenes of ecstasy and gnashing of teeth in Welsh Jumper territory were not universally applauded, even within Methodist circles. Clerics loathed the 'enthusiastical Rants'[39] of the young revivalists, and common people were not easily intimidated by hell-fire preaching. Internal divisions and factionalism dogged the movement and its growth was relatively slow and uneven. Much of north Wales, where the Established Church was strong and popular, remained barren territory until the 1780s, and preachers who ventured northward invariably suffered a host of indignities at the hands of parish mobs. The landed gentry regarded them with the utmost contempt and Evan Evans spoke for most parish clergymen when he denounced them as 'the most arrant rogues under the sun'.[40] Nevertheless, Methodist exhorters seldom refused an invitation to spread the Gospel and convert hardened sinners, and by 1750 the best part of 8,500 people had joined society meetings in which prayer, meditation, scriptural study, and inward reflection were encouraged.[41] Those who assembled in remote farmhouses, cottages, and chapels of ease were modestly well-to-do men and women — 'the better sort', as Howel Harris liked to call them.[42] Lower middling ranks, with some stake in property and a certain pride in their independence, were consistently attracted to the 'vital religion' of Methodism. Skilful, literate, self-improving blacksmiths, maltsters, millers, shoemakers, tailors, weavers, and yeomen farmers gained an enhanced sense of personal worth as well as profound spiritual satisfaction within the four walls of a Methodist society.[43] Young people, especially unmarried females, often formed a majority, and could be found within the godliest cells behaving 'like drunkards from the wineshop, deliriously happy having imbibed the wine of heaven'.[44] Backsliders, persistent sinners, and apostates were summarily expelled and so the tide of membership tended to ebb and flow. But Methodism gained its true strength from the close bonds of friendship, mutual support, and spiritual conviction which characterized the exclusive brethren who assembled regularly in the love of God.

Methodism clearly unleashed powerful spiritual forces which, in turn, created a desire for book-reading. From the 1740s onwards revivalist literature began to dominate the output of printing presses, especially in south Wales, and itinerant preachers went to great pains to ensure that bookshops were heavily stocked with religious literature. Although Howel Harris was wary of 'head knowledge' and instinctively shied away from the powers of human reason, he described works of practical divinity as 'God's property'.[45] A slack rein enable him to read as he travelled on horseback, and books were passed around in his society meetings. Saving literature could enrich sermons as well as nourish personal piety. On one occasion William Romaine, the English evangelist, playfully mocked Daniel Rowland for venturing as far as Bristol to buy books: 'I thought you had the Spirit of God to study his word, and to compose your sermons?'[46] In fact, as Howel Harris admitted, Rowland gave 'as much time as possible to reading'[47] and never tired of encouraging society members to read for edification rather than pleasure. Judging by the content of *Templum Experientiae apertum, neu Ddrws y Society Profiad* (1777), none had a better rapport with *pobl y seiat* (society members) than Williams Pantycelyn. Williams was an uncommonly gifted and widely read man whose sonorous prose works and memorable hymns not only dominated popular reading and singing in Methodist societies but also captured the imagination of worshippers over a wide spectrum.[48] More than anyone else, the 'Sweet Singer' succeeded in conveying the joyous passion of eighteenth-century enthusiasm and many of his works have retained their freshness and vitality to this day.

Revivalism clearly played a vital role in stimulating and satisfying the demand for printed books. Intense spiritual experiences were transmitted in a wide range of prose epics, sermons, hymns, elegies, and books of practical divinity and inward scrutiny. Methodist leaders were acutely aware that books were an essential weapon in the war against ignorance and sin. The printed word could coax, cajole, and hector readers into wrestling with their consciences and convince them of the awfulness of sin. By reinforcing sermons preached in churches and in the open air, saving literature helped to sustain the appeal of Methodism, promote literacy, and expand the book trade in general.

Just as evangelists were driven by a sense of mission to win souls, so were cultural patriots impelled by a passionate desire to revive Welsh scholarship and learning.[49] A quest of this nature involved rediscovering rich literary treasures preserved in old and dusty manuscripts locked up in private libraries and making them accessible to mainly middle-class readers. Such a daunting task faced seemingly insurmountable barriers. Wales had no national library or museum, no university or conservatory. Its bishops were drawn from outside Wales and spoke little or no Welsh. Jesus College, Oxford — a traditional magnet for talented young Welsh students — woefully neglected Welsh studies following Edward Lhuyd's untimely death in 1709. Even more critically, Wales could not boast a thriving cultural capital like Dublin or Edinburgh. Although towns like Carmarthen, Swansea, and Wrexham were enjoying greater prosperity than ever before and were responding admirably to the growing demand for consumer services, the growing trend was for London to cream off gifted and ambitious Welshmen.[50] By 1801 London's population of close on a million was nearly twice that of Wales. An enormously affluent city, it dominated the economic life of England and Wales. London life offered a challenging and often irresistible variety of opportunities for Welsh migrants in search of enhanced social status, prosperous businesses, and civilized or convivial social life. No urban community in England, let alone Wales, could match London in terms of wealth, consumer goods, sociability, and the pursuit of pleasure. It became, almost inevitably, the surrogate capital of Wales.

It is not surprising, therefore, that London was the home of the Honourable Society of Cymmrodorion, founded in 1751, the first serious society established outside Wales to promote the language, literature, and history of Wales.[51] The presiding influence over the Cymmrodorion was Lewis Morris, a remarkably gifted, busy, and energetic representative of the Welsh middling sorts. The son of a farmer-cum-cooper from Llanfihangel Tre'r-Beirdd in Anglesey, Morris was the eldest of three extraordinarily talented brothers, each of whom promoted projects 'for the glory and honour of our language'.[52] He inherited his father's skills as a craftsman and could turn his hand to making microscopes, harps, watches, sash windows, and sailing boats. An inventory of his goods, drawn up at the time of his death in 1765, included 'A Cabinet of Curiosities a Pair of Old Globes a Parcel of Books Mathematical & Musical Instruments'.[53] Morris bought a printing press in Dublin, published the first Welsh periodical in 1735, and later showed that even a specialist work like *Plans of Harbours, Bars, Bays and Roads in St. George's Channel* (1748) could attract 1,368 subscribers. Although he spent most of his adult life in north Cardiganshire, he enjoyed hobnobbing with aristocrats in the metropolis and revelled in urban sociability. He abused his belly, lusted after maidservants, tumbled with whores, and pitted his wits against hack-writers, journalists, and poets in the taverns, gin-shops, and garrets of London. A self-styled 'proud hot

Welshman',[54] Morris could be selfish, arrogant, and litigious. According to his nephew John Owen: 'He causes more trouble and requires more pampering than half a dozen people.'[55]

Lewis Morris's manuscripts are brim full of satirical verse, literary criticism, pieces of fiction, and political comment. But scholarship was his main preoccupation. He revered the works of Edward Lhuyd above all others and was determined to revive his ambitious plans. He deliberately distanced himself from plebeian culture and the oral-based *mentalité* of 'common unanimated clay',[56] and set about assembling a literary circle of like-minded scholars, antiquaries, and poets, notably the poet Goronwy Owen, the cleric Evan Evans, and the schoolteacher Edward Richard. Morris enlisted them as corresponding members of the Cymmrodorion Society and urged them to grasp what he liked to call 'the Labouring oar'.[57] This entailed implementing the grandiose *Gosodedigaethau* (Constitutions), drafted by Morris himself, which committed members to an ambitious programme of collecting, transcribing, and publishing Welsh poetry and literature. Morris hoped to persuade aristocrats and gentlemen that supporting literary causes would 'preserve your Names to Eternity',[58] but swiftly discovered that prosperous London-Welshmen preferred wine, women, and song to serving their native land. Although the taverns and drinking-rooms frequented by the Cymmrodorion proved a valuable focus for conversation and gossip, it was left to poets, scholars, and patriots within the Morris Circle in Wales to devote themselves to Welsh studies. Evan Evans clearly cherished widening opportunities to correspond with men of learning and confessed that reading scholarly books was his 'chief delight and entertainment'.[59] His *magnum opus*, *Some Specimens of the Poetry of the Antient Welsh Bards* (1764), is a seminal work in the history of Celtic literature. His own personal collection of books was so voluminous that two men and horses were required to move it in 1767. Goronwy Owen stocked his shelves with an impressive array of anthologies of poetry by the English Augustans, while Edward Richard's wonderful library at Ystradmeurig school in Cardiganshire drew gasps of admiration from visiting scholars. Even the casual reader of the celebrated *Morris Letters* cannot fail to be impressed by the sheer delight which members of the Morris Circle derived from the printed word.[60]

It should not be presumed that the influential reformers and scholars referred to earlier were unfamiliar with religious, literary, and intellectual trends beyond the British Isles. Far from it. Religious reformers were well acquainted with spiritual influences at work in America, Germany, and Holland. Griffith Jones, Llanddowror, was receptive to continental influences and his annual publication, *The Welch Piety*, was based on the Hallesian model in Saxony. Moravianism heavily influenced the thinking of Howel Harris and he established fruitful contacts with Count von Zinzendorf and Anton Wilhelm Böhme,[61] while Rousseau's emphasis on feelings, affections, and human psychology in general informed much of William Williams's writings.[62] Lewis Morris's prolonged labours covered a wide field of Celtic literature and the Cymmrodorion Society which he founded was not, at least in its ideals, unlike the literary societies and clubs which were emerging in America, France, and Spain.[63]

It was chiefly from the 1770s onwards, however, that writers in Wales derived inspiration from Europe. The diverse, complex, and often contradictory concept known as Romanticism redrew the cultural map of western Europe and by its very nature encouraged spontaneity, creativity, and self-expression. Poets, philosophers, and scholars increasingly adopted words such as 'genius' and 'sensibility' as they responded to the passions and pleasures of the age. But Romanticism did more than simply cultivate an obsession with images of man and nature; it encouraged new and interesting modes of writing, a taste for myth-making and exotic fantasies, liberating ideas about politics, and a heightened sense of nationhood. The finest exemplar of late-eighteenth-century Romanticism in Wales was unquestionably Edward Williams (better know by his bardic name 'Iolo Morganwg'), a Glamorgan stonemason of such brilliant accomplishments that, following the death of Evan Evans in 1788, he towered above all others as the most learned and knowledgeable Welsh scholar of his day.[64] Even within his own lifetime Iolo Morganwg was a legendary figure who aroused a curious variety of emotions. Discomfited by his uncertain moods, boastfulness, and waspish tongue, his enemies detected a strain of madness in him and dubbed him 'mad Ned'. To English romanticists he was 'poor Iolo', the original Welsh Bard who found solace in laudanum and eccentricity. But his admirers in south Wales and in London were legion and they viewed him as an exceptionally intelligent polymath. Iolo was an object of wonder and curiosity to the illiterate and erudite alike, and although a wide range of influences, including druidism, Freemasonry, Quakerism, pacifism, and republicanism bore heavily upon him,[65] he remained in many ways a singular creature, 'so much a being *sui generis*', as his friend Elijah Waring described him.[66] 'I have always', Iolo declared with no hint of false modesty, 'with an *Ancient Briton's warm pride*, preserved the freedom of my thoughts, and the independence of my mind.'[67]

Iolo repudiated the smug complacency displayed by champions of the Hanoverian cause and deplored the growing dominance of English culture on powerful landowners in Wales. He revelled in the company of lively political radicals and democrats who were a growing force in the London-based Gwyneddigion Society during the 1790s. In particular, he set himself the task of conflating history and myth and transforming them into a creative force. A common theme within the world of Romanticism was 'the forging of historical myths to bolster indigenous national cultures',[68] and Iolo was so well versed in lost cultural traditions and so outrageously fond of bold and innovative fantasies that he was able to use the past and the present to create a new concept of Welshness. He epitomized what historians like to call 'the invention of tradition'[69] by passing off his marvellous forgeries as the work of Dafydd ap Gwilym, creating a bizarre Gorsedd of the Bards of the Island of Britain based on allegedly druidic lore, offering a new vision of Welsh history in his introductory essay to *The Myvyrian Archaiology of Wales* (1801-7), and discovering and copying thousands of manuscripts which cluttered his tiny cottage at Flemingston in the Vale of Glamorgan. He saw himself as an agent of change, an intuitive genius who could alter the course of history.

Keenly conscious that he was living in a time of rapid social and political change, Iolo Morganwg responded enthusiastically to the challenges evoked by the French Revolution by railing against the arrogance of the new Leviathans and the evangelical seriousness and conservatism of the Methodists. He was not alone, for *fin de siècle* Wales had produced a new intelligentsia of politically active middling sorts who warmly embraced the ideals of the American and French Revolutions.[70] Welsh Jacobins and *sans-culottes* like John Jones, 'Jac Glan-y-gors', Morgan John Rhys, William Jones, and

Thomas Evans, 'Tomos Glyn Cothi', were voracious readers who appreciated the revolutionary powers of the printed word. Pressure for radical change increased appreciably among this vociferous minority during the 1790s and support was forthcoming among Unitarians, Baptists, and Deists within academies and Dissenting chapels as well as irate freeholders and ironworkers in communities in and around Merthyr Tudful. As these disaffected and articulate democrats gave vent to increasingly sophisticated political ideas and class feelings, the ironmaster Richard Crawshay was moved to condemn the 'evil Spirit [which] prevails Strongly amongst our Dissenters from the Damnable Doctrines of Dr Priestley and Payne'.[71] The best part of six hundred Welsh books (excluding almanacs and ballads) were published in the 1790s,[72] many of them political pamphlets and journals which deplored the damaging effects of power and privilege, tithes and rack-rents, evangelical religion, and creeping Anglicization. Prior to the French Revolution most Welsh books had been unambiguously conservative and deferential in their aims and assumptions, but the fall of the Bastille ushered in a period when new and thought-provoking questions were asked and when the ruling élite could no longer automatically expect that deference and obedience which had characterized the behaviour of their dependants since time immemorial.

Thus the proliferation of print in the eighteenth century was closely associated with vigorous social and economic change. Books are not written, produced, or read in a vacuum; they reflect underlying changes in society which, in turn, shape and govern the needs and aspirations of people. It may be true that normal, day-to-day social functions remained predominantly oral, but literate middling sorts now expected people to do rather more than listen and hear. A plethora of circulating and charity schools, Methodist societies, book clubs, academies, and literary societies clearly encouraged the reading habit. By the end of the century, virtually every town of any consequence in Wales possessed at least one printing press.[73] The volume of publication had increased appreciably, subscription methods had emboldened printers to increase the size of editions, and specialist booksellers as well as itinerant hawkers and chapmen had developed effective means of marketing their products. By 1800 books were cheaper, more wide-ranging in content, more widely available, more intelligently read, and more deeply pondered by larger numbers of readers than was the case a hundred years earlier. In view of the originality of his mind, his delight in poring over manuscripts and books, and the fact that his pen hardly ever dropped from his hand until his death in 1826, Iolo Morganwg deserves the last word on the eighteenth century: 'If the new world is an infant in Learning and Science, the Old one is truly Old, grey, and quite worn out to the stump with wickedness.'[74]

NOTES TO CHAPTER 9

1. *Y Gwyliedydd*, 6 (1828), 97-101; *Y Gwladgarwr*, 8 (1840), 193-9; William Williams, *Prydnawngwaith y Cymry* (Trefriw, 1822), pp. 172-80.
2. Trevor Herbert and Gareth E. Jones (eds), *The remaking of Wales in the eighteenth century* (Cardiff, 1988).
3. NLW, MS 821C, fols 121^v-122^v.
4. Peter R. Roberts, 'The decline of the Welsh squires in the eighteenth century', *NLWJ*, 13 (1963-4), 157-73; J. Glyn Parry, 'Stability and change in mid-eighteenth century Caernarfonshire' (unpublished master's thesis, University of Wales, Bangor, 1978); T. M. Humphreys, 'Rural society in eighteenth-century Montgomeryshire' (unpublished doctoral thesis, University of Wales, Swansea, 1982); J. Philip Jenkins, 'The demographic decline of the landed gentry in the eighteenth century: a south Wales study', *WHR*, 11 (1982-3), 31-49; J. Philip Jenkins, *The making of a ruling class: the Glamorgan gentry 1640-1790* (Cambridge, 1983); J. V. Beckett, 'The pattern of landownership in England and Wales, 1660-1880', *EcHR*, 37 (1984), 1-22; D. W. Howell, *Patriarchs and parasites: the gentry of south-west Wales in the eighteenth century* (Cardiff, 1986).
5. Edmund Hyde Hall, *A description of Caernarvonshire (1809-11)*, ed. Emyr Gwynne Jones (Caernarfon, 1952), p. 43.
6. NLW, MS 2532B, fol. 27^v.
7. Geraint H. Jenkins, *The foundations of modern Wales: Wales 1642-1780* (Oxford, 1987), p. 265.
8. A. H. Dodd, *A history of Wrexham* (Wrexham, 1957), p. 237.
9. NLW, MS 13221E, fol. 377.
10. Evan Evans, *Casgliad o bregethau*, 2 vols (Shrewsbury, 1776), I, sig. B2^v.
11. J. H. Davies, *A bibliography of Welsh ballads printed in the 18th century* (London, 1908-11).
12. Martin Davis, 'Hanes cymdeithasol Meirionnydd 1750-1859' (unpublished master's thesis, University of Wales, Aberystwyth, 1987), pp. 181-2.
13. Cecil Price, 'Polite life in eighteenth-century Wales', *Welsh Anvil*, 5 (1953), 89-98; John Feather, *The provincial book trade in eighteenth-century England* (Cambridge, 1985); Jeremy Black, *The English press in the eighteenth century* (London, 1987).
14. Jenkins, *The making of a ruling class*, p. 230.
15. Howell, pp. 205-6; Dafydd Jenkins, *Thomas Johnes o'r Hafod 1748-1816* (Cardiff, 1948), pp. 53-60.
16. NLW, Iolo Morganwg Letters 1025.
17. Eiluned Rees, 'Pre-1820 Welsh subscription lists', *JWBS*, 11 (1973-6), 85-119; Geraint H. Jenkins, *Literature, religion and society in Wales 1660-1730* (Cardiff, 1978), Chapter 10.
18. Jenkins, *The foundations of modern Wales*, Chapters 6 and 10.
19. W. A. Speck, 'Will the real 18th century stand up?', *Historical Journal*, 34 (1991), 203-6.
20. Paul Langford, *A polite and commercial people: England 1727-1783* (Oxford, 1989).
21. For the general background see *Consumption and the world of goods*, ed. John Brewer and Roy Porter (London, 1993), and Jenkins, *The foundations of modern Wales*, Chapter 7.
22. Thomas Kelly, *Griffith Jones Llanddowror: pioneer in adult education* (Cardiff, 1950); Glanmor Williams, 'Griffith Jones Llanddowror', in *Pioneers of Welsh education*, ed. C. E. Gittins (Swansea, [1964], pp. 11-30; Geraint H. Jenkins, *Hen filwr dros Grist: Griffith Jones Llanddowror* (Llandysul, 1983) and his '"An old and much honoured soldier" Griffith Jones, Llanddowror', *WHR*, 11 (1982-3), 449-68.
23. NLW, Ottley MS 100; *The Welch Piety* (London, 1740), p. 32.
24. *The Welch Piety* (London, 1749-50), p. 38.
25. *Selections from the Welch Piety*, ed. W. Moses Williams (Cardiff, 1938), p. 36.
26. *The Welch Piety* (London, 1739), p. 38.
27. Jenkins, '"An old and much honoured soldier"', p. 453.
28. Regrettably, however, his scheme is not even mentioned in the otherwise splendid work by R. A. Houston, *Literacy in early modern Europe: culture and education 1500-1800* (London, 1988).
29. Michael Watts, *The Dissenters* (Oxford, 1978), pp. 394-406; W. R. Ward, *The Protestant evangelical awakening* (Cambridge, 1992).

30 Geraint H. Jenkins, 'Llenyddiaeth, crefydd a'r gymdeithas yng Nghymru, 1660-1730', *EA*, 41 (1978), 36-52 (p. 36).
31 *Selected Trevecka letters (1742-1747)*, ed. Gomer M. Roberts (Caernarfon, 1956), p. 166.
32 G. F. Nuttall, *Howel Harris 1714-1773: the last enthusiast* (Cardiff, 1965); Gomer M. Roberts, *Portread o ddiwygiwr* (Caernarfon, 1969).
33 Richard Bennett, *The early life of Howell Harris* (London, 1962), p. 24.
34 Bennett, p. 37.
35 NLW, CM Archives, Trevecka Letter 1220.
36 Gomer M. Roberts, 'Y deffroad yn Nhrefeca a'i ledaeniad, 1735-1742', in *Y deffroad mawr: hanes Methodistiaeth Galfinaidd Cymru 1*, ed. Gomer Morgan Roberts, (Caernarfon, 1973), pp. 95-118.
37 Glyn Tegai Hughes, *Williams Pantycelyn* (Cardiff, 1983), p. 85.
38 *Selected Trevecka letters*, I, 64.
39 Theophilus Evans, *A history of modern enthusiasm* (London, 1752), Chapter 8.
40 *Additional Morris letters*, II, 688.
41 Derec Llwyd Morgan, *The great awakening in Wales* (London, 1988), p. 17.
42 Eryn M. White, *Praidd Bach y Bugail Mawr. Seiadau Methodistaidd de-orllewin Cymru* (Llandysul, 1995), pp. 79-116.
43 W. G. Hughes-Edwards, 'The development and organization of the Methodist society in Wales 1735-1750' (unpublished master's thesis, University of Wales, Bangor, 1966), pp. 170-1.
44 *Gweithiau William Williams Pantycelyn. Cyfrol 2 Rhyddiaith*, ed. Garfield H. Hughes (Cardiff, 1967), p. 185.
45 Bennett, p. 146.
46 *Ministerial records; or brief accounts of the great progress of religion*, ed. Edward Morgan (London, 1840), pp. 90-1.
47 Eifion Evans, *Daniel Rowland and the great evangelical awakening in Wales* (London, 1985), p. 144.
48 Gomer M. Roberts, *Y Pêr Ganiedydd*, 2 vols (Aberystwyth, 1949-58).
49 The best introduction is Prys Morgan, *The eighteenth century renaissance* (Llandybïe, 1981). See also Jenkins, *The foundations of modern Wales*, Chapter 10.
50 Emrys Jones, 'The Welsh in London in the seventeenth and eighteenth centuries', *WHR*, 10 (1980-1), 461-79.
51 R. T. Jenkins and Helen M. Ramage, *A history of the Honourable Society of Cymmrodorion and of the Gwyneddigion and Cymreigyddion Societies 1751-1951* (London, 1951).
52 Morgan, *The eighteenth century renaissance*, Chapter 3.
53 Hugh Owen, *The life and works of Lewis Morris [...] 1701-65* ([s.l.], 1951), p. xcix. See also Tegwyn Jones, *Y Llew a'i deulu* (Tal-y-bont, 1982).
54 *Morris letters*, I, 346.
55 *Additional Morris letters*, II, 928.
56 *Morris letters*, I, 238.
57 *Morris letters*, II, 192.
58 *Tlysau yr Hen Oesoedd* (Holyhead, 1735), p. 3.
59 *The correspondence of Thomas Percy & Evan Evans*, ed. Aneirin Lewis ([Baton Rouge], 1957), p. 107.
60 Jenkins, *The foundations of modern Wales*, p. 406.
61 Ward, p. 322.
62 *Meddwl a dychymyg Williams Pantycelyn*, ed. Derec Llwyd Morgan (Llandysul, 1991).
63 Gwyn A. Williams, *The Welsh in their history* (London, 1982), p. 49.
64 G. J. Williams, *Iolo Morganwg* (Cardiff, 1956); Prys Morgan, *Iolo Morganwg* (Cardiff, 1975); Gwyn A. Williams, 'Iolo Morganwg: bardd rhamantaidd ar gyfer cenedl nad oedd yn cyfrif', in *Cof Cenedl V*, ed. Geraint H. Jenkins (Llandysul, 1990), pp. 58-84; Ceri W. Lewis, *Iolo Morganwg* (Caernarfon, 1995).
65 Geraint H. Jenkins, 'Cyffesion Bwytawr Opiwm: Iolo Morganwg a Gorsedd Beirdd Ynys Prydain', *Taliesin*, 81 (April 1993), 45-57.
66 Elijah Waring, *Recollections and anecdotes of Edward Williams* (London, 1850), p. 34.

[67] Edward Williams, *Poems, lyric and pastoral*, 2 vols (London, 1794), I, xix.
[68] *Romanticism in national context*, ed. Roy Porter and Mikuláš Teich (Cambridge, 1988), p. 5.
[69] *The invention of tradition*, ed. E. J. Hobsbawm and T. Ranger (Cambridge, 1983).
[70] Gwyn A. Williams, *The search for Beulah Land* (London, 1980), Chapter 1.
[71] Chris Evans, *The labyrinth of flames: work and social conflict in early industrial Merthyr Tydfil* (Cardiff, 1993), p. 186.
[72] *LW*, II, 833-9.
[73] Eiluned Rees, 'Developments in the book trade in eighteenth-century Wales', *The Library*, 5th ser., 24 (1969), 33-43 (p. 33).
[74] NLW, Iolo Morganwg Letters, 1023.

CHAPTER 10

THE WELSH BOOK TRADE FROM 1718 TO 1820

Eiluned Rees

THE first catalogue of Welsh printed books, *Cofrestr o'r holl Lyfrau Printjedig [...] yn y Jaith Gymraeg [...] hyd y flwyddyn 1717*, compiled by Moses Williams, appeared one year too soon to include any items legitimately printed in Wales. In 1718, Isaac Carter printed two unprepossessing little ballads in the Cardiganshire village of Trefhedyn and Wales was never again to be bereft of a printing house within its bounds.

There was no drastic, overnight revolution; no avalanche of books descended from Welsh presses. For fifty years, books printed in Wales were outnumbered by Welsh books printed elsewhere and a century elapsed before a printing house became an integral part of a Welsh townscape.

Trefhedyn, a tiny settlement across the river Teifi from Newcastle Emlyn, seems an unlikely place for a pioneering printing venture. There was, however, a remarkable coterie of clerics and littérateurs in that area, of which Isaac Carter was one. Patriotic idealism inspired him to set up his press, aptly reflected in the title of an English work he printed in 1726: *Choice collections, collected out of large and valuable volumns [sic] for the benefit of all that have not the opportunity of reading them; but especially for those who have not the wherewith to purchase the same*. Although commercial gain was not uppermost in his thoughts, practical considerations prompted him to move in 1725 to Carmarthen, then the largest town in Wales. Books with a Carmarthen imprint were already in circulation, for one of Carter's circle, Nicholas Thomas (who had reputedly learned the rudiments of printing in Shrewsbury), had set up a press there by 1721.

Shrewsbury was rapidly rivalling London in output of Welsh material. There was no fierce competition because Welsh publishing was diverging into two distinct streams: scholarly and subsidized philanthropic works flowed from London and Oxford, popular works from Shrewsbury and Chester. The Society for Promoting Christian Knowledge used its regular printers for the production of Welsh Bibles, Books of Common Prayer, and 'small books in the Welch Language, together with the addition of the Catechisme of the Church of England and private prayers for the use of Servants [...] and also at the end of the said books [...] the Welch alphabet, whereby Servants and others may the more easily learn to read.'[1] For specialized antiquarian works, Edward Lhuyd, Moses Williams, and fellow-scholars naturally favoured leading English printers such as the University Press at Oxford or Bowyer in London.

The educational programme of the Society for Promoting Christian Knowledge and its predecessor, the Welsh Trust, bore fruit to such a degree that the demand for books outgrew the supply. Thomas Jones and his successors in Shrewsbury were shrewd enough to diagnose the needs of an expanding reading-public. More books at affordable prices were required and not merely those prescribed by Anglican clerics and gentry, however well-meaning. Nonconformists hankered after their own sectarian publications and, generally, people who had discovered the joys of literacy now wanted to read for pleasure as well as edification. Consequently, from Shrewsbury presses came ballads, chap-books and almanacs, cheap editions of well-loved religious classics, the works of Bunyan and Rees Prichard; Thomas Durston even risked printing an unauthorized Welsh Common Prayer.

The book-buying public in Wales, although steadily increasing, was still limited. Thomas Jones took some financial risks in publishing Welsh books, but his more circumspect successors in Shrewsbury were reluctant to follow suit. They laid the onus for publication on the author (who was often the translator or editor of the work in hand). He in turn made use of the safe option of subscription publishing, testing the market by issuing proposals and requiring some payment in advance. The final payment would be gathered on delivery of the book. An embryo network of booksellers in Wales was duly utilized and expanded, and full advantage was taken of important fairs; Shrewsbury printers attended the Wrexham Fair in person whenever possible and often designated it a date of publication for major works.

Early book-production in Wales was barely distinguishable from that of Shrewsbury. The books were similar in content; they were published and distributed in the same manner to the same customers. They displayed the same preoccupation with cutting costs, being printed on poor-quality paper with scant regard for aesthetics. The standard of presswork in Wales compared unfavourably even with that of Shrewsbury. Not only did the amateur Welsh pioneers lack technical experience, but initially they also lacked the wherewithal to purchase anything other than second-hand type and worn ornaments. In any case, their main concern was with the content of their publications. They ran little risk of complaint from purchasers, who would greet any reasonably legible text with undiscriminating satisfaction.

Carter was the first printer in Wales, but it was Nicholas Thomas whose business practices pointed to future developments in the Welsh book trade. He adopted subscription publishing and the fact that booksellers are listed in his first known subscription list (1723) demonstrates that he was developing a trade distribution system rather than relying on the good will of friends and relatives of the author or publisher. Thomas could arrange for books to be bound for his customers by calling on the services of a local bookbinder and bookseller, Crispianus Jones, whose advertisements he carried on spare pages of certain of his publications. The success of his business was such that Carmarthen was assured of an unbroken tradition of printing.

Elsewhere in Wales, during the next forty years, printing ventures proved short-lived. Lewis Morris bought a press in Dublin, but the sole surviving product of his ambitious project was the pioneering periodical, *Tlysau yr Hen Oesoedd*, printed in Holyhead in 1735. Another Anglesey man, a schoolmaster, John Rowland, set up a press in Bodedern in 1759, moving to Y Bala a couple of years later.

In 1740, Samuel and Felix Farley, printers from Bristol, and Samuel Mason, a bookseller from London, were summoned to Pontypool by leading Nonconformist gentlemen. During the ensuing two years, they printed Welsh translations of George Whitefield's sermons, a Baptist catechism, and some Welsh hymnals. The Farley family continued to print Welsh books after 1742, but from their Bristol base.

The Trefeca Press was a unique phenomenon, as indeed was the Methodist 'Family' (an early commune) where it was originally based. Howell Harris's concept of a press was both visionary and practical. Two men, Evan Roberts and James Prichard, were despatched to London to learn all they could about printing and the results (dating from 1770 onwards), while far from elegant, compared favourably with the products of earlier Welsh printers.

The man who unwittingly changed the course of Welsh printing was a Scotsman, John Ross. He came in 1762 to Carmarthen as a partner to Rhys Thomas. The partnership lasted a year; in 1764 Thomas moved to Llandovery but Ross stayed in Carmarthen and flourished. He had been formally apprenticed to the trade and had served seven years as overseer of a London printing-house. Here was a printer who was capable of competing with his counterparts in England, the first of a generation of professionals, whose advent would eclipse the amateur.

Meanwhile, in north Wales, the virtual monopoly of the Shrewsbury printers was being eroded by printing establishments which survived their founders. Richard Marsh, bookseller in Wrexham since 1753, who had often acted as agent for the most prolific of Shrewsbury printers, Thomas Durston, in 1772 himself became a printer. Dafydd Jones, author and bookseller, bought Lewis Morris's old press and set up a printing-house in his native Trefriw in 1776. His grandson, the experienced and innovative printer, John Jones (1786-1865), moved the business to Llanrwst in 1825. John Rowland's old Blaeu press was put to good use when Robert Saunderson was lured from Chester to Y Bala in 1803, initially as compositor for Thomas Charles and, after 1814, as proprietor in his own right. In 1807, the Broster family of Chester opened a branch in Bangor.

The Chester printers' contribution to the Welsh book trade, while not as extensive as that of the Shrewsbury printers during this period, was by no means negligible. Two notable Chester printers were Welsh by birth, Thomas Huxley and William Collister Jones. At least four men who became master-printers in Wales served an apprenticeship with William Collister Jones: Robert Saunderson, Y Bala; John Broster, Bangor; Thomas Gee, Rhuthun and later Denbigh; and Jonathan Harris, Carmarthen. W. C. Jones's own business was to receive a mortal blow when he lost customers to the Bala press.

By the end of the eighteenth century, professional printers could expect to make a decent living from the book trade. They could bequeath flourishing concerns to their families and found dynasties of printers. Titus Evans of Machynlleth was the father of John Evans, the Carmarthen printer, whose four sons in due course became printers. Printers' widows showed commendable business acumen, two of the most successful being Mary, widow of Thomas Roberts of Caernarfon, and Esther, widow of Samuel Williams of Aberystwyth. The market for Welsh books was still expanding, while better standards of book-production and a greater variety in type-faces attracted non-Welsh-language customers. Carmarthen printers stocked Greek and Hebrew type for the benefit of their clerical patrons, many of whom were associated with the Society for Promoting Christian Knowledge in the Diocese of St David's. In north Wales, the Bangor Religious Tract Society provided work for Caernarfon and Dolgellau printers. Local Auxiliary Bible Societies sprung up in the wake of the London-based British and Foreign Bible Society. The Cambrian Tract Society and the Unitarians of south Wales gave a further impetus to the book trade. Another London-based society, the Religious Tract Society, perpetuated the tradition of philanthropic Welsh-language publishing exemplified by the SPCK.

The gentry could now consider having fine works printed locally. John Painter of Wrexham produced quite a handsome volume in Philip Yorke's *The Royal Tribes of Wales* in 1799; William Wilmot of Pembroke did justice to the *Catalogue of Books belonging to the Pembroke Society* in 1791.

Copper-plate printing had reached Wales by 1810 and was rapidly adopted in the more enterprising establishments. It proved a particular asset for the jobbing printing which guaranteed the printer his daily bread since the twirls and swirls on bill-heads and labels so beloved by tradesmen could now be produced to order locally. Jobbing printing benefited the neighbourhood probably to a greater degree than did book-production. Societies were mushrooming, not only religious societies but also the secular agricultural societies, friendly societies, associations for the prosecution of felons, and savings banks. They generated a steady demand for notices, registers, and reports, as did churches, chapels, and schools, including Sunday schools. Solicitors, magistrates, overseers of the poor, surveyors of the highways, turnpike trusts, and auctioneers placed regular orders for the plethora of papers required for legal transactions. Landowners commissioned all kinds of notices, from announcements of rent days to injunctions against poachers. Book-collectors ordered personal book-plates. Farmers advertised the services of their prize bulls; couples contemplating wedlock sent out printed bidding letters; people with unbridled tongues were forced to issue recantations. Elections were a lucrative bonus, especially if the contest was acrimonious, when the customary posters and election papers would be supplemented by propaganda broadsides and scurrilous ballads. Printers in maritime towns were kept busy with demands for bonds for licensed vessels, notices of sailing, and all the ephemera associated with shipping and customs. Towns patronized by polite society generated a demand for theatre posters and tickets, notices of balls and ball-cards. Special occasions could be honoured by printing on silk: in 1801, Charles Heath of Monmouth printed the Freedom of the Borough for Lord Nelson on white satin.

In 1817, Edward Williams, 'Iolo Morganwg', tried to persuade his son, Taliesin Williams, to set up a printing office:

> You could set up well for two hundred pounds, half of which to be promptly paid and the other half in three years, which is the usual thing in this line of business [...] The fair and legal profits of printing are very great, without embezzling the Authors profits: if you could set up an honest Printing office, you would soon have all the business of Wales: at least of South Wales. You would also keep a good Book binder, you would sell Books and Stationery, Patent medicines, perfumery &c.[2]

The advice was based on Iolo's extensive dealings with the book trade, though care must be taken not to pay too much heed to the aspersions he casts on the probity of Welsh printers.

Very little information has survived relating to the actual costs involved in setting up a business. There is a Memorandum of an agreement between John Rasbrook of Bangor and John Broster concerning premises Broster was renting from Rasbrook at a rent of £27 6s. a year.[3] Broster was erecting a printing office and counting house in the yard belonging to the premises at a cost of £135, for which he would pay an additional nine guineas a year rent. With regard to equipment, John Bird of Cardiff admitted that he was fortunate in purchasing the press and types of Henry Walters of Cowbridge for 'the trifling sum of Seventeen Guineas' payable over six months.[4] There are several instances of printers buying the press and stock of a retiring printer, a considerable boon, as normally presses and other materials had to be transported by sea from London to the nearest port, thence by carrier. The purchase of new type was invariably announced with pride. Paper was expensive, especially as the government repeatedly increased paper duty from the early 1780s onwards; John Painter of Wrexham informed Walter Davies, 'Gwallter Mechain', in 1801 that the duty on printing and writing papers was about to be doubled, which would bring the price to 30s. a ream.[5] By 1800 there were at least ten paper-mills in Wales, a few of which produced paper of good quality, possibly too superior and too expensive for general use.[6]

'You would sell books', advocated Iolo Morganwg, and indeed all Welsh printers sold books, their own publications and those bought through the trade. According to John Painter, the trade discount was twenty-five per cent.[7] Sometimes the nature of a printer's involvement with a work would be manifest in the imprint, with his (or her) name prefixed by 'and sold by'. Subscription lists reveal that printers subscribed to one another's publications, often ordering multiple copies. Wales being a comparatively small country, members of the book trade were frequently either personally acquainted or linked by blood ties. One gets a strong impression of co-operation rather than rivalry.

There was nothing insular about the Welsh book trade. Printers and booksellers had contact with their counterparts in Shrewsbury, Chester, Oswestry, Liverpool, Bristol, and Dublin. The Eddowes family of Shrewsbury, for example, was a powerful force in the Welsh book-scene; its trade in Welsh material extended throughout Wales and in London. The long-established London-Welsh trade acquired a new dimension; as Welsh printing outgrew its amateurism, reputable London firms were prepared to sell books printed in Wales. Lackington, Allen & Co. is named in certain Carmarthen, Merthyr Tudful, Chepstow, and Swansea imprints. The most impressive involvement of the firm with Wales, however, was when it published William Turton of Swansea's multi-volume translation of Linnaeus, using three Swansea printers: Zechariah Bevan Morris, John Voss, and David Williams.[8] Lackington, Allen & Co. found it worthwhile advertising its catalogues in the Swansea newspaper, *The Cambrian*, and, from a letter written by Lewis Weston Dillwyn in 1804, was clearly also providing a binding service for the newly established proprietary library, the Glamorgan Library.[9]

Influential Welshmen operating in the London book trade strengthened its links with their native land. William Davies, son of a Welshpool clergyman, was a partner in Cadell and Davies. Owen Rees, scion of a well-respected Unitarian family from Glamorgan, became partner in the firm of Longman, doubtless accounting for its incidence in so many south-Walian imprints. Two Cardiganshire brothers, Evan and Thomas Williams, were London booksellers specializing in Welsh books. Thomas Williams returned in 1801 to pursue a career in banking in Aberystwyth but Evan remained in London until his death in 1835, making No. 11 Strand a focal point for the London-Welsh book trade. He published several works of antiquarian interest and used his contacts in London, Wales, and Shrewsbury to build up an impressive stock of new and second-hand books, a ready source of supply to individual customers and bookshops.

Books were sold by mercers, chemists, ministers of religion, and by the full-time booksellers who kept shops in towns and often a stall at the market. These retailers acquired their stock by the same means as the printer/booksellers and supplemented their incomes in comparable manner by selling stationery, fancy goods, and patent medicines.

The second-hand book trade flourished on an unprecedented scale. 'Money for any Library or Parcel of Books or Books exchanged' was a common form of advertisement. Sales of the contents of country houses and the collections of bibliophiles were well publicized, as were sales of the stock of a printer or bookseller. The goods of the bankrupt George North of Brecon, auctioned by Wise of Bath in 1816, included 'about five thousand volumes, in various languages and branches of literature; many rare and curious old books; some valuable modern books; several copies of Jones's History of Brecknockshire [a work North had printed]; near one thousand choice engravings, ancient and modern; four hundred reams of paper; a select Circulating Library, in one lot'.[10] The Brosters of Chester and Bangor issued catalogues of 'rare and curious antient books', which they also advertised in their weekly newspaper, *The North Wales Gazette*. Being accustomed to cataloguing the contents of libraries in preparation for auction, they extended the service, informing nobility and gentry that 'they regulate libraries alphabetically, and according to subjects, upon an entire new plan, which has been universally approved of'.[11]

Printers had always utilized spare, blank pages at the end of a publication for advertising forthcoming books, books they had printed, or works associated with the author, but at the end of the eighteenth century such lists evolved into full catalogues. A prototype catalogue was the eight-page list appended by John Daniel of Carmarthen to John Harris's almanacs for 1797 and 1800. English and Welsh books were listed separately, the English ones being the archetypal components of a gentleman's library. In 1801, Thomas Williams, one-time drover turned printer in Dolgellau, issued *Cofrestr o Lyfrau Cymraeg* (*A Register of Welsh books*), priced 2*d*. deductible from the price of a purchase if the catalogue was returned in a fit state. Sizeable catalogues were subsequently issued by Ann Scott (John Ross's daughter), Richard Jones of Dolgellau, and Jonathan Harris of Carmarthen. The catalogues of John Evans of Carmarthen are of especial interest. That of 1812 is unusual in that its title describes it as a *Register of valuable books published by subscription, in parts*. Details are given of each publication, with an assurance that whoever subscribed to any of them was guaranteed delivery of the part issues at his house regularly, at stipulated times. The latter part of the catalogue is given over to advertising current Welsh books in stock. Two major catalogues were published in 1822 and 1825, the former containing 346 Welsh items and the latter 244.[12]

Listed among the distribution agents for the 1822 catalogue are fifteen itinerant booksellers. Although books were sold from the premises of printers, booksellers, bookbinders, and general shopkeepers, the livelihood of the itinerant bookseller was seemingly unaffected. Without this category of bookseller, subscription publishing could not have survived, for they were often the vital link between publisher, printer, and customer. Their remuneration usually took the form of a free copy with every order of a specified number, which they could sell on their travels from fair to fair, from market to market. The Sales Book of Samuel Williams discloses the somewhat unexpected information that women took to the road as booksellers: one of them appears under the vague appellation 'a ballad songstress', but Gwenni Ellis and Sarah Thomas are named.

Booksellers were not the only itinerant members of the book trade; bookbinders were also prepared to bind books on site. Hugh Stodart of St Asaph advertised in the *Chester Chronicle* in 1799 'Gentleman's Libraries repaired at home or abroad'. Since books were normally issued unbound, in wrappers, in theory there was ample work for bookbinders. In fact, of course, bound books were a luxury which all save the affluent were compelled to forego. This meant that bookbinding tended to be combined with other trades, almost invariably bookselling but sometimes cobbling, watch-making, or school-teaching; the craft also attracted sextons and ministers of religion. Many binders had arrangements with local printers for contract work. A manuscript ledger of David Morris, a Carmarthen bookbinder, records work done for at least fourteen identifiable members of the Carmarthen book trade.[13] Occasionally, binders 'lived in', as did John Jones, whose agreement with Samuel Williams is noted in the latter's Sales Book.[14] The work done by most Welsh binders of this period is of little artistic value. The only fine bindings would be those commissioned for gentry libraries; Thomas Pennant found 'a most admirable binder' in Thomas Roden of Denbigh.[15]

Bookbinders could buy their materials from printers or booksellers. The diary of John Davies, a cobbler and bookbinder from Llanfihangel Ystrad, Cardiganshire,[16] records the purchase of pasteboard in Carmarthen. Samuel Williams supplied millboards, pasteboards, marbled paper, parchment, various kinds of skins, and large quantities of paper for blank books. Binders found the demand for blank books and registers by business and professional people a steadier source of income than binding books.

The bookbinding materials would have been found in the stationery department. As early as 1718, a Wrexham bookseller, Edward Wicksteed, included an impressive array of stationery amongst his wares. In addition to 'all sorts of books in all faculties, [viz.] Divinity, History, Law, Phisick, Poetry &c, in English, Latin & other Languages' he sold:

> Musick Books, fine Table-Books with Silver, work or plain, Gilt & plain Writing Paper of all sorts, Shop books, gilt and Plain Pocket-books; The most Correct Globes and Maps; all sorts of Copper Prints, English and French Meszo Tintos, in Crown Glass and Japan'd Frames, neat Japan'd and plain Wall paper for hanging Rooms, Marble and German Gilt Paper, Stamp paper and Parchment, Holman's London Ink powder, Japan Ink, Ink horns, Wood, Lead and Glass Standishes, Pen-knives, superfine Sealing wax and Wafers, Seals, Sandboxes and Tompsons fine shining Sand, Reading Glasses, Spectacles of all sorts, with Shagareen and gilt Cases, Canes, black Lead and Camils hair, Pencels, best Snuff and neat boxes, with several sorts of Goods, at reasonable rates.[17]

If one adds painting materials and fancy goods, this list becomes fairly representative of what was available in a profitable branch of the book trade. Broster opened a 'wholesale stationary warehouse for shopkeepers, at the Port of Bangor' in 1808.[18]

Iolo Morganwg showed commercial acumen in recommending the stocking of stationery and perfumery, together with patent medicines. Shrewsbury printers had already introduced Welsh readers to the wonders of Bateman's pectoral drops and Daffy's Cordial Elixir. Ann Scott of Carmarthen devoted a page and a half of her 1808 catalogue to 'Genuine medicines, &c'. John Daniel's range of patent medicines occupied as much advertising space in the *Carmarthen Journal* as did his books. John Evans of Carmarthen subsequently bought Daniel's stock, added it to his own and advertised his medicinal wares from 'Evans's Patent Warehouse'.[19] Mark Willett of Chepstow went a stage further and became a chemist and druggist, finally a surgeon.

There is no better testimony to the book trade's ability to respond to public demand than its promotion of libraries. Book-clubs, circulating libraries, and newspaper reading-rooms were set up in every town at the turn of the century. Advertisements and catalogues indicate that they were designed for 'polite' society and the tourist trade. Welsh books are conspicuous by their absence.

Proprietary libraries, the preserve of gentry and clergy, could build up a formidable collection for their exclusive use through annual subscriptions. They became popular from the first decade of the nineteenth century onwards, though there were two earlier ones: the Cowbridge Book Society (which evolved in 1736 from the Cowbridge Diocesan Library) and the Pembroke Society (established before 1741).[20] Significantly, no works of fiction appear in the printed catalogues of the Pembroke Society,[21] while the rules of the Swansea-based Glamorgan Library (founded in 1804) require that 'novels shall be excluded'.[22]

Book clubs were slightly different. They too had subscribing members but at the end of a stipulated period, to quote annual notices placed in *The Cambrian* by the Cardiff Book Society, 'The Books returned from circulation will be sold by auction.'[23] The role of the bookseller with regard to proprietary libraries and book clubs was usually marginal, but there are exceptions. The key figure of the Wrexham Book Society (commenced 1810) was John Painter. The Annual Meeting was held in his house, members returned their books to him, and no book 'was to be transferred from one Member to another but through the medium of the bookseller'.[24] Members could either order books to the amount of 10s. 6d. a year or 'forfeit that sum for the use of the Society'. They were not allowed to order 'any Elementary Professional Books, nor more than one Novel in the year' and 'books of Prints and Maps' were excluded.

One suspects that the nature of reading societies varied from place to place. Thomas Morgan paid 2s. 6d. annually to what appears to be an informal reading society in Carmarthen in the mid-eighteenth century.[25] Beaumaris Home Reading Society (1813) allowed three weeks for reading a book.[26] The Welshpool Reading Society was evidently in a different league: in 1820 the printer, Robert Owen, begged 'to inform his Friends and the Public, that in consequence of his engagement as Book-seller and Librarian to the Welsh-pool Reading Society, he forwards his Orders for New Books, New Music, Musical Instruments, Magazines, Reviews [...] to London about the 26th of every month'.[27] In this instance again, the involvement of the bookseller is marginal.

Circulating libraries, however, were inextricably linked to the book trade. Both John Ross and John Daniel were operating circulating libraries in Carmarthen by the 1780s. Most libraries set terms for yearly, half-yearly, quarterly, and monthly subscribers. They range through twelve shillings a year (William Cox, Aberystwyth), a guinea (Joseph Potter, Haverfordwest), £1 4s. (Filmer Fagg, Swansea), to £1 6s. (J. Pearson, Caernarfon). In seaside towns, special terms were offered to visitors. John Bates took advantage of Holyhead being the ferry-port for Ireland by filling his circulating library with 'a variety of new and entertaining books, which prove a very agreeable resource to passengers when detained by contrary winds'.[28] John Hughes of Wrexham and J. Pearson of Holyhead opened their circulating libraries with a modest 600 and 800 volumes respectively, but Mr Griffiths's library in Tenby boasted 2,000 volumes.[29] Unlike book clubs, circulating libraries were only too eager to stock novels. Thomas Ridd's library in Cardiff consisted 'of an entire new Collection of Novels, of the most esteemed merit'.[30] Such libraries were catering for the fair sex in a way that the book clubs, at this period still a male preserve, failed to do — a situation soon to change.

Complementing the circulating library was the subscription reading-room, the forerunner of the newspaper room subsequently found in public libraries. The reading-rooms of David Jenkin in Swansea and William Cox in Aberystwyth were stocked with current London and provincial newspapers, magazines, army and navy lists, and court calendars. A contemporary guide-book pays tribute to 'the library kept by Mr. W. Cox' as 'a pleasing addition to the amusements of the place; the news and reading rooms are a great acquisition, and a means of easy communication to strangers'.[31] Subscribers paid a guinea a year for using his Subscription Reading Room, which remained open from 8 a.m. to 8 p.m.; visitors could take out monthly or three-monthly subscriptions and 'Piano Fortes could be hired for any specified time.'[32] As additional bait, the book-label of Cox's circulating library lists wares the dilettante visitor would find irresistible: 'perfumery, stationary, jewellery, cutlery, writing desks, ladies fashionable work boxes, walking sticks, umbrellas, parasols [...] an assortment of gloves.'

The range of activities undertaken by members of the book trade was by now formidable. In common with their English counterparts, certain Welsh printers ran Stamp Offices, served as auctioneers, or acted as insurance agents. Richard Jones of Dolgellau took advantage of the tourist trade by offering visitors lodgings as well guide-books.

As printing houses expanded, more workmen had to be employed. Newspaper advertisements were a useful means of recruiting staff. For non-Welsh-speaking printers, it was vital to have a Welsh corrector of the press such as Daniel Jones of Wrexham who assisted William Collister Jones and, subsequently, John Painter. There was a general demand for journeymen printers of the calibre sought by William Williams of Brecon in 1820: 'a steady, sober man, who understands both the English and Welsh languages, and can work at Case and Press. None need apply but such as can produce undeniable character for honesty and sobriety.'[33] The latter quality was sadly wanting in a Bristol printer who had come to Brecon a few years earlier to expedite production of Theophilus Jones's *History of Brecknockshire*, 'one of the most rascally imps that ever issued from Pandemonium; he drinks on one or two days in the week, and not only sins himself, but like his brother or his uncle Beelzebub seduces the other black boys'.[34] The average age required of apprentices seems to have been around fourteen. Thomas Ridd of Cardiff set his sights high in an advertisement for three apprentices in 1811: 'Young men who have had a classical education, and understand the Welsh language would be preferred.'[35] John Daniel of Carmarthen was prepared to waive a premium if he got an 'active lad'.[36] John Davies of Llandeilo stressed 'respectable connexions' when advertising for an apprentice aged 14 to 16.[37]

Apprentices did occasionally abscond, though a notice such as the one which appeared in *The Carmarthen Journal* on 30 January 1813 is rare:

> To Master Printers, &c. Whereas David Jones, an Indentured Apprentice of J. Daniel, Carmarthen, having absconded and left his master's employ, without any cause or provocation whatsoever: now this is to caution all Master Printers, and others, from harbouring or employing [...] the said David Jones, after this public notice, as legal proceedings will be had recourse to, for recovery of his salary, &c. against such person or persons who may offend against the Statute in that case made and provided.

It is interesting to note that for printing purposes, Welsh was regarded as a foreign language even in Wales itself, John Painter charging two shillings per sheet extra.[38] The more enterprising printers offered a translation service; accounts show both John Ross and Samuel Williams charging for Welsh translations of legal documents. Titus Evans of Machynlleth advertised that anything could be translated from English into Welsh at a reasonable price.[39]

In 1718 there was one printer in Wales and a scattering of booksellers; in 1820 there were over fifty printers, supported by a vigorous fraternity of booksellers, bookbinders, and stationers. The size of editions had already grown from a maximum of 500 to a minimum of 500 copies, and editions of thousands were not uncommon. The printer, as master of his craft and a businessman, was a respected member of society, worthy to be immortalized in portraits such as those of John Evans and his family and of Hannah White painted by Hugh Hughes in 1822-3.[40] Even so, Wales was lagging twenty years behind its neighbours. Whereas 1800 is regarded as a watershed in the development of the book trade elsewhere in Britain, in Wales investment in up-to-date equipment, mechanization, and the adoption of modern trade practices were post-1820 developments. By 1820, the book trade had matured, ironically by tempering Carter's idealism with due regard for the 'filthy lucre' he denigrated, in preparation for a Golden Age of book publishing in Wales.

NOTES TO CHAPTER 10

With reluctance and diffidence, I refer readers to two more detailed studies of mine on this subject, in order to reduce the number of footnotes: *The Welsh book-trade before 1820* (Aberystwyth, 1988) and 'The Welsh printing house from 1718 to 1818', in *Six centuries of the provincial book-trade in Britain*, ed. Peter Isaac (Winchester, 1990), pp. 101-24.

1. Letter from John Vaughan of Derllys, 8 July 1717, quoted in *Correspondence and minutes of the S.P.C.K. relating to Wales, 1699-1740*, ed. Mary Clement (Cardiff, 1952), p. 94.
2. NLW, MS 21286E (956), Edward Williams to Taliesin Williams, 28 July 1817.
3. NLW, Arthur Ivor Pryce, 806 (dated 1808).
4. *The diaries of John Bird of Cardiff [...] 1790-1803*, ed. Hilary M. Thomas, (Cardiff, 1987), p. 66.
5. NLW, MS 1807E, fols 1029-44 are letters from John Painter to Walter Davies concerning printing the latter's works.
6. Alun Eirug Davies, 'Paper-mills and paper-makers in Wales 1700 - 1900', *NLWJ*, 15 (1967-8), 1-30.
7. NLW, MS 21286E (956), Edward Williams to Taliesin Williams, 28 July 1817.
8. C. Linnaeus, *A general system of nature*, 7 vols (Swansea, 1800-6).
9. Swansea University Library, L. W. Dillwyn Letters, 250.
10. *The Cambrian*, 24 August 1816.
11. *A walk round the walls and city of Chester* (Chester, [1810?]).
12. Both catalogues are entitled *Cofrestr o lyfrau Cymraeg, ar werth gan J. Evans [...] Caerfyrddin*.
13. Carmarthen County Record Office, Museum 363.
14. NLW, MS 2844E.
15. Manuscript version of Thomas Pennant's *Literary Life*, NLW, MS 12706E, 56.
16. NLW, MS 12350A.
17. Advertisement at the end of *Holl ddyledswydd dyn* (Shrewsbury, 1718).
18. *North Wales Gazette*, 25 Feb. 1808.
19. *Carmarthen Journal*, 12 Feb. 1819.
20. Ewart Lewis, 'Cowbridge Diocesan Library, 1711-1845', *JHSCW*, 4 (1954), 36-44; 7 (1957), 80-91.
21. Gwyn Walters, 'The eighteenth-century "Pembroke Society"', *WHR*, 3 (1966-7), 291-8.
22. *Rules and regulations of the Glamorgan Library* (Swansea, 1808).
23. For example, 5 Nov. 1816.
24. Details found affixed to upper cover of *Anonymiana* (London, 1809).
25. NLW, MS 5437A.
26. Note on flyleaf of British Library copy of Sir George Staunton, *An authentic account of an embassy* (1798).
27. Advertisement in *Appointment and charge for surveyors of the highways* (Welsh-pool, 1820).
28. *Universal British Directory, 3 (1791-5)*, p. 386.
29. *Chester Chronicle*, 21 Aug. 1789; *North Wales Gazette*, 21 January 1808; *The Tenby guide* (Swansea, 1810), p. 27.
30. *The Cambrian*, 26 Jan. 1811.
31. J. Feltham, *A Guide to all the watering and sea-bathing places*, new edn (London, 1815), p. 3.
32. *The Aberystwyth guide* (Aberystwyth, 1816), p. 79.
33. *The Cambrian*, 4 November 1820.
34. Theophilus Jones to Edward Davies, 10 March 1809, quoted in Edwin Davies, *Theophilus Jones, F.S.A.* (Brecon, 1905), p. 96.
35. Advertisements in *The Cambrian* throughout October 1811.
36. Advertisements in *The Cambrian* throughout June 1806.
37. *The Cambrian*, 11 March 1820.
38. NLW, MS 1807E, fol. 1034.
39. Note in the imprint to T. Collier, *Enwaediad a bedydd* (Machynlleth, 1790).
40. Peter Lord, *Hugh Hughes, arlunydd gwlad 1790-1863* (Llandysul, 1995), pp. 111-12.

CHAPTER 11

COUNTRY-HOUSE LIBRARIES OF THE EIGHTEENTH AND NINETEENTH CENTURIES

Thomas Lloyd

THERE is that beguiling image of a country-house library, steeped in waxed autumnal shades: a writing-desk, deep armchairs, a glowing fire, tall polished bookcases, and those old, inviting books, among which 'no one has felt or can feel solitary'.[1] It evokes a golden age of book collecting and of peace and time to read. George Borrow had such a room in mind when passing Dolaucothi in Carmarthenshire in 1854: 'With what gravity could I sign a warrant in its library and with what dreamy comfort translate an ode of Lewis Glyn Cothi, my tankard of rich ale beside me.'[2]

Too few such libraries survive in Wales today. Perhaps not fifty retain a family collection going back half a dozen generations. Disasters like the Wynnstay fire of 1858 have removed a few; some were just abandoned, burned, or thrown away as valueless when old country seats were vacated earlier this century; but most, such as that of Stackpole Court, Pembrokeshire, in 1962, have been sold. Even the great libraries at Powis Castle, Chirk Castle, and Mostyn Hall, formed well before the eighteenth century, have been thinned, while more recent sales of complete libraries at Penpont near Brecon in 1991, Court Colman near Bridgend in 1993, and Coedrhiglan near Cardiff in 1997, indicate that the trend continues. This may seem dispiriting, although the cycle of collection and dispersal is part and parcel of the world of books: some of the greatest treasures of the National Library of Wales have passed through several fine collections.

Although every rural parish had its scholars — notably the parson, minister, and schoolmaster — their collections, lacking the security of an entailed country house, have generally been scattered, though fleeting glimpses can occasionally be gained from inscriptions in odd volumes in antiquarian bookshops.[3] Here, therefore, we must confine ourselves to gentleman book collectors, not because they alone were privileged to own libraries, but rather because the evidence comes overwhelmingly from there. A gentleman was expected to be well-read and new books were a focus of polite conversation: in the 1870s the Revd R. J. Lloyd of Troedyraur (Cardiganshire) 'used to read and insist on discussing all the latest books'.[4] Local book-clubs, such as the Cardigan Book Society,[5] proprietary libraries, and the better commercial subscription libraries were widely patronized by the gentry. Many members of the gentry had literary and scholarly interests and their wealth and continuity encouraged them to build fine library rooms to house their burgeoning collections. The 1891 obituary of Charles Kemeys-Tynte of Cefn Mabli (Glamorgan) recalls 'a most cultured man who spent a great portion of his time in the splendid library he had gathered, and published for private circulation two or three volumes of verse'. Less usually, he was also 'very keen on the Welsh language'.[6]

Although subscription lists indicate that the upper ranks of Welsh society supported scholarly works in the English language relating to Wales, they showed little enthusiasm for acquiring books in the Welsh language save when displaying patronage to local authors. Unlike Welsh manuscripts, which were obviously rare, valuable, and attractive to antiquarians, printed books in the Welsh language normally comprised an insignificant element in gentry libraries. A recent scholarly study claims that even before 1720 the gentlemen of Glamorgan, despite the county's strong Welsh culture, were not in the habit of buying Welsh books.[7] The religious works which constituted the typical product of Welsh presses were scarcely calculated to appeal to polite society, and knowledge of the language itself became increasingly uncommon. It has also been suggested that cheaply made Welsh books looked less attractive on the library shelf.[8] Of the four hundred books listed in the 1830 catalogue of Lancych near Newcastle Emlyn, only four are Welsh and one of these is given the dismissive but illuminating entry: 'One old Welsh religious book'. The only Welsh book in the far more splendid collection at Fonmon Castle (Glamorgan) is a seventeenth-century book of Common Prayer.[9]

Reliable references to sixteenth-century libraries are rare, but it is known that the Renaissance scholar Sir Edward Stradling assembled a notable collection of manuscripts and printed books at St Donat's. This may have been augmented by his successor Sir John Stradling (1563-1637), but had been sadly depleted before the end of the seventeenth century and is impossible to trace after 1738.[10] Edward, first Baron Herbert of Cherbury (1583-1648), amassed a large and valuable library 'abundantly replenished with books of his own purchasing and choice' at his house at Montgomery Castle.[11] Over nine hundred scholarly volumes from his library were bequeathed to Jesus College, Oxford, and much of the remainder eventually passed to Powis Castle. Those treasures from the Powis Castle library, including incunables, Renaissance printed books, and early Welsh printed books, which were sold in 1923,[12] were however probably largely accumulated by the bibliophile second and third Earls of Powis during the nineteenth century.[13] Although references to collecting printed books in early-seventeenth-century Wales can be found in, for instance, the papers of the Wynn family of Gwedir, listings of library contents are rare.[14] About 1659 Robert Vaughan of Hengwrt compiled a catalogue which still survives of his priceless manuscripts and printed books.[15] Unfortunately some of his descriptions, even of manuscripts, are unhelpful, notably '*A tattered and incomplete book of cywyddau and another far worse than the first*'.[16]

From the end of the seventeenth century onwards, however, an increasing body of evidence accumulates in inventories, sale catalogues, and advertisements, and through bookplates, subscription lists, private letters, descriptions, and tours. Surprisingly unhelpful among the latter is Dr Johnson's *Diary of a Journey into North Wales in the year 1774*. Only at Maesmynan near Caerwys was his appetite for study assuaged, and he acclaimed John Myddleton of Gwaenynog as 'the only man who in Wales has talked to me of literature'.[17] Johnson unfortunately missed what was probably the best library on his route by failing to visit Llannerch. A 1778 catalogue of its library, a collection largely built up by the naturalist and antiquarian Robert Davies, listed over 1,700 printed books, more than 800 pamphlets and 93 manuscripts.[18] A far more satisfactory contemporary source is Thomas Pennant's account of the treasures in the Mostyn library,[19] chief, perhaps, among those formed in the generation after the Civil War along with those at Chirk Castle, Wynnstay, Gregynog, and Margam Abbey.[20]

Nothing brings us closer to collectors than the books themselves. Lists tell us what owners possessed — had often inherited — not what they read. Annotations, shelf marks, bindings, and repairs reveal what was cared for, while damaged books or uncut presentation volumes indicate the opposite. Books from the unrecorded, scattered library of J. J. Holford (b. 1765) of Cilgwyn (Carmarthenshire) are prominently marked with the bookcase and shelf numbers of a well-planned library. At Picton Castle near Haverfordwest the fine library formed in the eighteenth century gives valuable insights on its cultured owners, Sir Erasmus Philipps (d. 1743), his brother Sir John Philipps (d. 1764), and the latter's son, Lord Milford (d. 1823). Each brother bought fine folios for the beautiful library room constructed in the 1730s and Lord Milford subsequently purchased second-hand folios (a size then going out of fashion) to complete the lower shelves. Their acquisitions can be traced since Sir Erasmus Philipps signed his books, Sir John had a bookplate, and Lord Milford used a stamp and left in the prices that he paid. All the classics of their day are here and much more across the widest range. Fine plate books stand out, notably on the arts and literature. Interesting too are runs of London newspapers from 1748 to 1753, the prime source of information for books published, subscriptions sought, and library auctions. Although the library contains books in half a dozen European languages, the only books in Welsh are a well-bound 1744 prayer book and Bible. It is telling that only the first instalment (1793) of William Owen Pughe's controversial Welsh dictionary appears, still in printer's boards. Two subscription copies of *The Primitive History* (1789) by a learned neighbour, William Williams of Ivy Tower, similarly languish unbound, the author's compendious scheme for dating the events of prehistory clearly failing to inspire Lord Milford.

Such libraries have always given extra pleasure through their ephemera, accretions, inscriptions, and unexpected rarities. Inside a book from Sir John's student days are his Oxford lectures for a term. At Nanhoron near Pwllheli a copy of the second edition of Thomas Richards's Welsh-English dictionary (1815) is inscribed: 'The paper of this book was manufactured at Trefriew, the book was printed at Trefriew and bound at Llanrwst.' Another volume contains its owner's sorrowful account of how it was damaged by water in its careless transport by boat from Caernarfon. Miller's *Gardening Dictionary* (1763) was used to record plantings in the garden, and there is a Gaelic Bible from the 1820s. Herbert Vaughan, writing of south Wales libraries earlier this century 'seldom visited a country house that did not own a literary treasure'[21] and cites examples ranging from a chained book at Stradey Castle near Llanelli to Georgian pornography concealed behind a secret panel in a house that he forbore to name.

Ten miles from Picton, the library of the Allens at Cresselly (Pembrokeshire) shows a very different character. Their fortunes had risen in the eighteenth century and the generation born between 1764 and 1781 shared an intellect and energy that took them far.[22] The heir became a politician, his brother Master of Dulwich College; two sisters married sons of Josiah Wedgwood; one married Sir James Mackintosh, political philosopher; another married J. C. L. de Sismondi, the Swiss historian; one had the Governor of the Bank of England for brother-in-law; yet another was connected to the great judge, Lord Eldon. The library at Cresselly, much of it gathered by the two unmarried, fiercely opinionated daughters (owners of first editions of Jane Austen), is full of works, many with association inscriptions, which form a biographical collection for the early nineteenth century of great depth. The elegant but now overlooked literary scholarship of their neighbour the Revd Charles Symmons of Narberth is also well represented. Here too is an earlier survival. Two generations earlier a learned younger brother, the Revd Joshua Allen (d. 1765), became chaplain to Sir Thomas Robinson, ambassador in Vienna in the 1740s. On his travels, Allen collected a small library, mostly second-hand classical and religious texts printed in France, Holland, Austria, and Italy, writing in each the date of purchase and sometimes the city where it was bought. In 1751 he published two volumes of sermons containing an extensive list of subscribers which includes many Pembrokeshire names.[23] Such a survival (about sixty books, not all bought abroad) is an all-too-small reminder of learned eighteenth-century Welsh clergy.

A few libraries, housing no more than what it was correct to have, yield little indication of personality. The author C. E. Vulliamy vividly recalled such a library at Stouthall in Gower in the 1890s: 'the taste of [its] collectors, though invariably sound, was always discreet and orthodox: it was not the taste of litterateurs or of unhampered bachelors: one had to think of the wives and daughters and the awful risk of contamination.'[24] Sporting squires have been cast as an unliterary crew, though an old sporting library (as recently sold from Ynysfor, Merioneth) is itself of interest. Nonetheless, the few books at Llanerchaeron (Cardiganshire), a temple to the chase, offer little to the general reader. Where special interests can be found, the range is wide. Local history is common, as at Nanhoron, Treberfydd (Breconshire), and Court Colman (sold in 1993). Abercamlais near Brecon is packed with Bibles from a line of parson owners. The library at Blaenpant near Cardigan, which was sold in 1920, was noted for Restoration drama and travels; the libraries formerly at Holyland (Pembroke) and of the Dillwyns in Swansea stood out for botany and natural history.[25] Foreign postings brought back Persian manuscripts to Llangoedmor near Cardigan in 1797 and to Boultibrook near Presteigne in 1811.[26] Library sales at Rhiwlas near Y Bala in 1927 and at Nerquis Hall near Mold yielded groups of Regency three-decker novels, and an even finer collection of three-deckers amassed by three generations of Powells at Nanteos near Aberystwyth has also been dispersed.[27] The Welshman's love of law and genealogy are united at Erddig near Wrexham. Although the Bosanquets of Dingestow Court near Monmouth were newly settled in Wales, their splendid library includes a group of early-nineteenth-century Welsh poetry books, usually subscription copies, which no doubt reveals the influence of Lady Llanover on her learned neighbour Samuel Bosanquet.

For some, collecting was a passion. Prince of pure bibliophiles in Victorian Wales was John Cole Nicholl of Merthyr Mawr (Glamorgan), who at his death in 1894 left well over twenty thousand books. His collection, its progress recorded in his diary, would have been even larger had not marriage in 1860 and declining rental income checked his collecting career and forced the sale of his large collection of early works of Dante. As he confessed to his less than enthusiastic wife, 'he could not live without buying books.'[28] An earlier zealous but discriminating collector was the polymath John Lloyd of Wigfair (Flintshire), whose library of 'near ten thousand volumes, comprising the most rare productions of early typography and some unique specimens of Welsh M.S., books of prints and maps' was sold in 1816.[29] Thomas Johnes of Hafod lost one marvellous collection to fire in 1807 but restocked his shelves so quickly that he could soon tell friends that he was richer in books than ever before.[30] Among later large-scale collectors, Gladstone amassed a huge collection at Hawarden Castle in a purpose-built wing ('The Temple of Peace') before putting thirty thousand books into the trust for public benefit that became in 1902 the splendid St Deiniol's Library.[31] The Pembrokeshire antiquary, Dr Henry Owen of Poyston Hall, filled a large, galleried, two-storey library (built in 1899) with the fruit of his life's collecting.

Few eighteenth-century women bibliophiles can be traced but one name must belatedly be put on record. When the greater part of the combined Leeswood and Tower libraries near Mold was sold in the 1980s, it was noticed that hundreds of books bore the signature of Catherine Davies, sister of the noted collector Robert Davies of Llannerch and later the second wife of Sir William Williams of Llanforda (d. 1740). Her early-eighteenth-century collection of several thousand books places her amongst the first of all Welsh women collectors.[32] The evidence provided by bookplates gives her a few counterparts. Some, such as Anna Maria Owen (c.1720) of the Owen of Henllys (Pembrokeshire) family, Frances Brigstocke of Blaenpant (her label dated 1769), and Miss Williams of Penpont (c.1790), were from literary or library-owning families. Others, such as Lady Lloyd (d. 1734) of Garth, near Welshpool were ladies of title, and yet others, such as Emilia Gwinnett of Penllyn Castle (Glamorgan), one of the select band of Welsh ladies to build a country house (c.1790),[33] Lady Bulkeley of Baron Hill (Anglesey) (c.1750), and Eliza Gulston of Derwydd near Llandeilo (c. 1780), who had three bookplates which she probably engraved herself, were of notably independent spirit. By the later eighteenth century, women's names are common in subscription lists and during the nineteenth century figures such as Angharad Llwyd (possessor of a notable collection),[34] Lady Llanover, and Lady Charlotte Guest all made an important contribution to Welsh literature and antiquarianism.

Bookplates can reveal long-forgotten book collectors. Their popularity increased when the commercially minded William Jackson, based near the Inns of Court in London, solicited business from 1696 onwards from the Universities and nearby lawyers. Jackson offered attractively engraved and dated armorials in two sizes for large and small books.[35] His first Welsh customers were from Glamorgan, Sir John Aubrey of Llantrithyd and Francis Gwyn of Llansannor (both plates dated 1698), and Sir Humphrey Mackworth of Gnoll. North Walians soon followed, among them Sir Thomas Trevor of Trefalun in 1702; Robert Price of Giler in 1703, and Sir Thomas Hanmer, MP, in 1707. The opportunity for elegant armorial display made bookplates popular. Beautiful examples appeared increasingly in Wales; in mid-century in the highly ornamental rococo style, and later more heroically, in the hands of notable engravers like Bartolozzi, who set the shield of Sir Foster Cunliffe of Acton Park (Wrexham), amongst the heavens. Other shields, as for Griffiths of Brynodol (Anglesey), rest in landscapes of classical ruins, or are held up by a druid, as for Sir Robert Howell Vaughan of Hengwrt and Nannau, Merioneth houses famous for bardic patronage. Nearly all these plates were engraved in London, Bath, or Bristol. The very few made locally are conspicuously crude, such that for Philip Puleston of Esclusham (Denbighshire) (c.1770) signed by an otherwise unknown E. Evans.

For some owners, a love of heraldry may have exceeded their love of books. The Jones-Parrys of Madryn (Caernarfonshire) were forever changing designs during the

Victorian era, and Edward Abadam of Middleton Hall (Carmarthenshire) ordered bookplates for each of his six children in turn in the 1860s. Conversely, some major library owners never had a bookplate, conspicuously Thomas Johnes, even though his father possessed one. So the evidence of bookplates, especially when they are removed from books (as in the extensive collections acquired by the National Library),[36] is not an automatic guide, unless plates are seen *in situ*, like those in books once owned by Richard Fenton, Paul Panton, and Thomas Pennant. In surviving libraries, plates will identify a mixed inheritance. At Bryngwyn (Montgomeryshire) the books of William Madocks of Tremadoc fame can be discerned; at Nanhoron the bequest from a cousin, the Revd Howell Holland Edwards of Pennant (Denbighshire), can be traced, and at Hartsheath near Mold bookplates and signatures attest to several legacies.

Despite the vogue for bookplates, the use of armorial stamps on spines and covers is rare. Two splendid books from Brogyntyn bear the monogram and crest of Sir Robert Owen, MP, of Clenennau and Brogyntyn (d. 1698) on the central of ten silver mounts,[37] but the fashion was mainly confined to the more showy of the aristocracy, of whom Wales had few. Books from Plas Power (Denbighshire), now in the National Library of Wales, have large crests, and handsome late-eighteenth-century gilded spines incorporating the crest of the Thomas family are found in their library at Cefndyrys near Builth Wells. But pride of place goes to a quarto volume, Settle's *Heroic Poem on the Protestant Succession* (1709), at Derwydd which has the coat of arms of Sir Thomas Stepney (d. 1745) resplendent upon both covers.

Subscription lists also reveal keen collectors. A select band of gentry subscribed to general works up to 1750, sometimes ordering multiple copies. From north Wales various Wynns and Wynnes, Mostyns, Hanmers (though mostly non-resident), Myddletons of Chirk, and the influential William Vaughan of Corsygedol; from south Wales, the Philippses of Picton predominated. Lists for the period *c*.1720 to *c*.1750 show the latter to be the most consistent of Welsh subscribers, followed by John Campbell of nearby Stackpole Court; from Glamorgan, the Mansels of Margam, and from Gwent, Horace Walpole's friend, Sir Charles Hanbury Williams of Coldbrook Park. Some lists show unexpected support from certain areas. Mary Jones's *Miscellanies in Prose and Verse* (Oxford, 1750) includes a crowd of ladies from Gwent and Glamorgan, no doubt her home, but why John Collinsons's *Beauties of British Antiquity* (London, 1779) drew 39 of its 174 subscribers from Carmarthenshire and Swansea is unclear.

Inventories of libraries reveal their state at one fixed point in time. The listing of possessions was natural for disciplined collectors, and death required a valuation (often a rounded figure to be approached perhaps with scepticism). Some lists, as of the Plas Nantglyn (Denbighshire) collection, note purchase prices;[38] others list books by size and shelf. That for Margam Abbey (*c*.1755) systematically sets out in fifty-two neat folio sheets the enormous library of the Mansels, working upwards from the heavy folios each with its author, title, place, and date of publication noted.[39] It also clearly shows that the death of Edward Lhuyd's patron Sir Thomas Mansel in 1723 signalled a tailing-off of purchasing. The inventory of 1718 for the old Wynn house, Cesail Gyfarch near Tremadoc, shows old theology, probably acquired by the scholarly Bishop Humphrey Humphreys.[40] That for Garthewin (Denbighshire) of 1722 lists chiefly the legal books of lawyer Richard Wynne, many marked 'in my study'.[41] The Chirk Castle inventory of 1736 covers 'History Ancient and Modern, Divinity, Classicks, English Poetry, Philosophy, Physick, Miscellanies and Law, Rang'd under their different Subjects and in their respective Classes and marked with Alphabetical Letters and Numbers, as they are refer'd to in the Following Catalogue'.[42] Gregynog (Montgomeryshire) has a huge list of books up to 1741 which reveals massive acquisition in the 1680s.[43] At Trawsgoed (Cardiganshire) in 1784 there were only fifty folios 'on the lowest shelf in the Hall press' and 250 other volumes, mostly sermons and law books, the latter undoubtedly those of Chief Justice Sir John Vaughan (d. 1674) who had been bequeathed some of Selden's books.[44] An updated inventory of 1824 shows very few additions.[45] One thing these lists emphasize is that the accumulations of centuries were all regarded as comprising a single collection, both new and old books being equally valued.

Sale catalogues give a different perspective. Multiple lotting diminishes detail but expert descriptions highlight choice rarities. Sotheby's catalogue of the 1893 sale of Lewis Llewelyn Dillwyn's historical and botanical books from Hendrefoilan, Swansea, highlights fine bindings, private printings, and black-letter pamphlets but does not reveal whether any volumes in the sale came from the library of Theophilus Jones, the Breconshire historian, which we know were there.[46] Many libraries, however, were sold at small country auctions and the listings are consequently sketchy. Newspaper advertisements from the early nineteenth century onwards cover hundreds of book sales for which no catalogues survive. Details are usually tantalizingly basic, but one exception is the advertisement for the auction sale in 1836 of the collection of the Revd John Bowen of Bath, a neglected member of Iolo Morganwg's coterie.[47] As well as Roman gold coins, a famous old watch, and musical instruments, the advertisement noted twelve hundred books, including works by Camden, Stowe, Hearne, and the Welsh authors Thomas Pennant and Edward Pugh. Such auctions were a magnet for buyers. Mrs Allen of Freestone Hall (Pembrokeshire) said of a nearby auction (probably at Orielton) in 1825: 'I very much wished for the books and Mr A. bid for most of them till he got three or four shillings beyond their original value, therefore we have only bought Hume and Smollett for half a crown more than a new one. He is gone today commissioned to bring home Rollins "Ancient History" cost what it may.'[48] More specialized collectors attended London sales; thus Lewis Weston Dillwyn wrote to Lord Cawdor in 1829: 'I write in haste for I am going to bring a part of the botanical library which I bought yesterday in King Street and I want to get back in time for Hibbert's sale this afternoon.'[49]

The survival of accounts from a much earlier auction of the contents of Peterwell, Lampeter, held in Carmarthen in 1781, lists the buyers and prices.[50] Most of the books were bought by members of the local gentry (including three ladies), but the chief purchaser, paying £30 of the total of £69, was John Ross, Carmarthen's leading printer. This emphasizes what is known from advertisements and other sources, that local printers conducted a flourishing trade in second-hand books.[51] Major figures like John Ross could supply most local needs for both new and second-hand books, but major orders inevitably went to London. When setting up the Glamorgan Library, a proprietary library for the upper ranks of Swansea society, in 1804, Lewis Weston Dillwyn turned to the London booksellers Lackington, Allen & Co., a firm with established Welsh contacts. After receiving the first batch with satisfaction (except for a binder's error), he requested their new catalogue to be sent down by coach together with the *London Catalogue*.[52] Carriage of heavy parcels to Wales was often by boat, by which means the purchases of Richard Vaughan of Golden Grove came home via Carmarthen.[53]

As collections grew, thought was needed how to keep them. At first this had meant storage out of sight, stacked flat in cupboards, probably in the owner's private closet.[54] Serious scholars retreated into studies separate from the house. William Maurice of Cefn-y-Braich, Llansilin (Denbighshire), 'erected close to his house a lofty pile of three stories high for his library; where he immured himself the greater part of his time'.[55] Richard Fenton noted the small square building at Plas Gwyn (Anglesey), 'in which old Rowlands who wrote the *Mona Antiqua* used to study'.[56]

The library came, literally, out of the closet in the early eighteenth century. Extensive house rebuilding in the Georgian style provided space for rooms to display books which were themselves increasingly decorative. That this was a major innovation was pinpointed by Mrs Morgan in 1791 when viewing Picton Castle: 'There is a gloom in this library which seems perfectly suited to study; and has not the appearance that most modern ones have of being more for show than use.'[57] Small, but exquisitely designed in the 1730s inside a castle tower, the library has curved bookcases in a continuous run, divided by pilasters which reveal themselves as fronts to hidden shelves. Likewise we learn that in July 1722: 'Mr Skelton came from Mr Middleton of Chirk Castle today, desiring to be instructed as to the manner and disposition of my lord's presses there; Mr Middleton designing to build himself a library soon.'[58] The Chirk Castle library fell victim to later changes but a panelled 1720s library still survives at nearby Erddig.

Later the library turned into a reception room designed to display the fine taste of its owner. Exceptionally, it became a great artistic statement; at Hafod (1794), there was an octagonal Pantheon under a wonderful dome (initially with a gallery), by John Nash,[59] below which plaster tableaux stood over the bookcases and on the floor, great works of sculpture. At Stackpole Court, John Campbell intended his new library to house a large cast of the Apollo of Belvedere.[60] More usually the books became a backdrop to a second drawing room, as at Fonmon Castle where a long room with superb plasterwork was inserted into the Norman keep in the 1750s to hold Robert Jones's collection of fine books in cases placed at intervals along the walls. A similar grand long room had been created a little earlier at Iscoyd Park, close to the Cheshire border, since 1843 housing the library of the Godsal family. This less intense approach is evident later in the century at Slebech Park (Pembrokeshire), built *c*.1775-80, where the original plans show only a single elegant, pedimented bookcase against one wall of a spacious room.[61] In the two biggest houses of the 1830s, Penrhyn Castle and Margam Castle, the huge library rooms are by no means dominated by the several bookcases around the walls. Such houses of course also possessed studies. Finally, the astonishingly grand Painted Library at Trawsgoed created for the Earl of Lisburne *c*.1900 with its brilliantly decorated ceiling and Roman columns, placed its books behind brass-latticed doors, as if golden caged to discourage touch.

Other libraries, particularly those in smaller houses not so given to grand entertaining, remained the realm of books. At Stouthall there is a lovely oval room of 1790 designed by a leading local architect, William Jernegan of Swansea. At Boultibrook, an elongated, top-lit octagon of 1812-15 by Robert Smirke, architect of the British Museum, was built to house Sir Harford Jones Brydges's Persian manuscripts. In 1814, David Pennant added a library extension to Downing to house his late father's collection. Lancych, probably designed by P. F. Robinson (1820), has a small square library fitted out with shelves. Much grander and more detailed are two early-Victorian creations; Dingestow Court, by Lewis Vulliamy (1845-6) in classical dress, and Ambrose Poynter's new library at Mostyn (1848-9) in an appropriate Elizabethan style. In Breconshire, J. L. Pearson's new Treberfydd (1848-52) includes a library intense and snug in dark and deeply moulded oak, while at Coedmor near Cardigan the library was at the top of a broad octagonal tower c.1880, as if a throwback to the 'lofty pile' of William Maurice. Dr Henry Owen's library at Poyston, by D. E. Thomas of Haverfordwest (1899), would have done justice to a college.

Reshelving existing rooms could have been influenced by new theories of librarianship. Thus Broster and Son of Chester advertised that they regulated libraries 'alphabetically, and according to Subjects, upon an entire new plan which has been universally approved of'.[62] The Stackpole library was reshelved in 1823 by the noted cabinet-maker William Owen of Haverfordwest, who had the chilling foresight to pin a letter to the back addressed 'To the Demolisher of these Libraries'.[63] At Bodrhyddan (Flintshire) flamboyantly carved shelving was installed c.1840 and at Vaynor Park (Montgomeryshire) shelving with Jacobean arcading was carved to match Thomas Penson's mid-nineteenth-century external remodelling.

At some ancient houses libraries were never remodelled. At Abercamlais books run along the first floor landing. At Bodysgallen (Caernarfonshire), Fenton was shown old manuscripts in a basket[64] and at nearby Gloddaith the 'vast number of the best stock books, several Classics of the best editions, and large paper copies of almost every book'[65] were in a small narrow room, which Pennant thought quite unworthy.[66] Rather strangely, a few grand Georgian houses, where a library room might be confidently expected, never had one. Thus Brynbella (Flintshire), built for Dr Johnson's friend, Hester Piozzi in 1792-5, had a music-room especially designed for her second husband but lacked a library.

Perhaps the last word amid so much variety should be left to one who was himself a contradiction; a sociable reactionary, legendary hunting man, and fine man of letters too, 'Nimrod' or C. J. Apperley, of Plas Gronow, Wrexham:

> Every upstarting three-windowed house we now see advertised, has its 'drawing room' and its 'library', whereas Plasgronow, although suitable to the accommodation of a family of twenty with rooms to spare, had neither one nor the other. There was the 'tea-room' and the 'anti-tea-room' and there was the 'breakfast-parlour', which might well have been called the library inasmuch as it contained a most valuable collection of books. That which my father called his own room was likewise nearly choked up with books, but it was not even dignified by the modest appellation study.[67]

For some, perhaps, this may be an even more beguiling image than that with which this chapter opened.

NOTES TO CHAPTER 11

The writer wishes to thank Eiluned Rees for notes on the library inventories and other references at the National Library of Wales. Her two essays 'An introductory survey of 18th century Welsh libraries', *JWBS*, 10 (1966-71), 197-258, and *The Welsh book-trade before 1820* (Aberystwyth, 1988) contain a wealth of documentary evidence relating to these libraries.

1. W. E. Gladstone, quoted in 'Gladstone's "Temple of Peace"', *Y Ddolen*, (Spring 1992), pp. [1]-[4] (p. [3]).
2. George Borrow, *Wild Wales*, Chapter 96.
3. Thus a book recently purchased by the author contains the following note, dated 16 December 1859: 'N. B. I do hereby give you intelligence that I, Evan Davies Jones, have received these books, viz about 62 books in all, which were the property of my grandfather, the Rev Morgan Jones, Minister of Roscwm [Ruscombe] near Stroud, Gloucestershire [...] these books were distributed among his brothers and sisters and these became to my father's share David Parry Jones, who gave and presented them to me [...] his youngest son.' The Carmarthen museum possesses the books of Jonathan Jones, the schoolmaster of Tre-lech, *c.*1840, a miscellaneous collection of about thirty second-hand books from the eighteenth century.
4. Herbert M. Vaughan, *The south Wales squires* (London, 1926), p. 123.
5. *Cardigan & Tivy-Side Advertiser*, 27 June 1902.
6. *Tenby Observer*, 15 Jan. 1891.
7. Philip Jenkins, *The making of a ruling class: the Glamorgan gentry 1640-1790* (Cambridge, 1983), p. 231.
8. Herbert M. Vaughan, 'Old country-house libraries in south Wales', *Wales*, 7 (1947-8), 290-6 (p. 290).
9. Margaret Evans, *A catalogue of the library at Fonmon Castle, Glamorgan* (Cardiff, 1969), p.3.
10. Graham C. G. Thomas, 'The Stradling library at St. Donat's, Glamorgan', *NLWJ*, 24 (1985-6), 402-19.
11. J. D. K. Lloyd, 'Montgomery castle and the Herberts', *AC*, 104 (1955), 52-64 (p. 62).
12. Sotheby's *Catalogue of a selected portion of the valuable library from Powis Castle* (London, 1923) includes *inter alia* a copy of William Salesbury's *Dictionary* (1547), two copies of his *A playne and a familiar Introduction* (1567), and two copies of the 1567 Welsh New Testament.
13. Gwyn Walters, 'The Herbert libraries of Montgomery and Powis', *NWR*, 3(4) (1990-1), 10-13.
14. The *Calendar of Wynn (of Gwydir) papers 1515-1690 in the National Library of Wales and elsewhere* (Aberystwyth, 1926) includes, *inter alia*, references to a 1648 list of 21 'books on physic' owned by Owen Wynn (1852) and to a 1655 catalogue of books at Mostyn (2092).
15. NLW, MS 9059B (Panton Papers 45).
16. 'Llyfr cowyddae cerpyn drylliog ac un arall gwaeth o lawer na'r cyntaf' (quoted in E. D. Jones, 'Old catalogues of the Hengwrt Manuscripts', *Handlist of manuscripts in the National Library of Wales Part 1* (Aberystwyth, 1940), p. xviii).
17. *Boswell's life of Johnson [...] together with [...] Johnson's diary of a journey into north Wales*, ed. George Birkbeck Hill, revised and enlarged by L. F. Powell, 6 vols (Oxford, 1935-50), V, 443.
18. Hywel D. Emanuel, 'The Gwysaney Manuscripts', *NLWJ*, 7 (1951-2), 326-43 (p. 329).
19. Thomas Pennant, *The history of the parishes of Whiteford and Holywell* (London, 1796), pp. 71-85.
20. Margam contained over 2,500 volumes by the mid-eighteenth century (Jenkins, p. 230).
21. Vaughan, 'Old country-house libraries', p. 293.
22. E. Inglis-Jones, 'A Pembrokeshire county family in the eighteenth century', *NLWJ*, 17 (1971-2), 136-60, 217-37, 321-42.
23. J. Allen, *Twenty-six sermons on the most important subjects of the Christian religion* (London, 1751).
24. Quoted in Robert Lucas, *A Gower family* (Lewes, 1986), p. 123.
25. Blaenpant and Holyland: Vaughan, 'Old country-house libraries', pp. 292-3.; Dillwyn: Sotheby's *Sale catalogue of select portion of the library of Lewis Llewelyn Dillwyn, 30 October 1893*.

[26] *DWB* articles on Benjamin Millingchamp of Llangoedmor and Sir Harford Jones Brydges of Boultibrook.
[27] Information provided by David Hughes, antiquarian bookseller, Llandudno. For the Nanteos three-deckers, see Robert Lee Wolff, *Strange stories and other explorations in Victorian fiction* (Boston, 1971), pp. 36-7.
[28] M. McLaggan, 'The library of a bibliomaniac great-grandfather', in *Bibliophily*, ed. Robin Myers and Michael Harris, Publishing History Occasional Series 2 (Cambridge, 1986), pp. 121-37.
[29] *New Monthly Magazine*, (January 1816), p. 523. For a detailed analysis see Gwyn Walters, 'Bibliotheca Llwydiana: notes on the sale catalogue (1816) of John Lloyd's library', *NLWJ*, 10 (1957-8), 185-204.
[30] R. J. Moore-Colyer, 'Thomas Johnes of Hafod (1748-1816): translator and bibliophile', *WHR*, 15 (1990-1), 399-415 (p. 403).
[31] 'Gladstone's "Temple of Peace"'.
[32] Information supplied by T. Lloyd Roberts, antiquarian bookdealer, Caerwys, who acquired a portion of the collection. The earliest date he noted was 1699, but he ascertained that only about half of her books had come to Tower.
[33] C. Shephard, jun., 'A tour through Wales and the central parts of England', *Gentleman's Magazine*, 69 (1799), p. 932.
[34] Mary Ellis, 'Angharad Llwyd, (1780-1866)', *FHSP*, 26 (1973-4), 52-95; 27 (1975-6), 43-84.
[35] B. N. Lee, *British bookplates* (Newton Abbott, 1979).
[36] Briefly noted in W. Ll. Davies, *The National Library of Wales: a survey of its history, its contents, and its activities* (Aberystwyth, 1937), p. 167.
[37] On deposit from Lord Harlech at the National Library of Wales.
[38] NLW, Plas Nantglyn 6. The book bears the autograph of William Lloyd of Llangwm (1766-1835).
[39] West Glamorgan Archive Service, Margam D/DP885.
[40] NLW, Sotheby 13.
[41] NLW, MS 889E.
[42] NLW, Chirk Castle A31.
[43] NLW, MS 903C.
[44] Vaughan, 'Old country-house libraries', p. 295.
[45] NLW, Crosswood (Trawsgoed) 1672B (both inventories).
[46] Gwenllian E. F. Morgan, 'Theophilus Jones, F.S.A.', in Edwin Davies, *Theophilus Jones [...]* (Brecon, 1905), pp. 1-35 (p. 32).
[47] *Carmarthen Journal*, 4 March 1836.
[48] Unpublished letter in a collection of Allen family letters at Cresselly, Pembrokeshire.
[49] Carmarthen Record Office, Cawdor Box 140.
[50] 'An account of silver plate, books, china, pewter [...] late the property of John Adams of Peterwell esq. Sold at auction at Carmarthen [...] 1781' (NLW, Gogerddan Papers). Herbert J. Lloyd Johnes, 'A Cardiganshire library', *NLWJ*, 6 (1949-50), 304-5, discusses the contents of the library.
[51] Eiluned Rees, *The Welsh book-trade before 1820* (Aberystwyth, 1988), pp. XXXVIII, XL.
[52] For Lackington, Allen & Co., see Rees, *Welsh book-trade*, p. XLVI. The letter is in the writer's possession.
[53] Francis Jones, 'The Vaughans of Golden Grove', *THSC*, 1966 (1), 149-237 (p. 162).
[54] G. Jackson Stops, 'Most learned decoration', *Country Life*, 24 March 1988, p. 120.
[55] *Gwaith y Parch. Walter Davies [...]*, ed. D. Silvan Evans, 3 vols (Carmarthen, 1866-8), III, 45.
[56] Richard Fenton, *Tours in Wales (1804-13)*, ed. John Fisher (London, 1917), p. 261.
[57] M. Morgan, *A tour to Milford Haven in the year 1791* (London, 1795), p. 294.
[58] *The diary of Humphrey Wanley 1715-26*, ed. C. E. Wright and Ruth C. Wright, 2 vols (London, 1966), I, 152.
[59] Richard Suggett, *John Nash: architect in Wales* (Aberystwyth, 1995), pp. 77-80.
[60] Morgan, p. 353.
[61] Architect's drawings in the possession of the present owners. Although undated and unsigned they are attributed to Anthony Keck.

[62] Eiluned Rees, 'An introductory survey of 18th century Welsh libraries', *JWBS*, 10 (1966-71), 197-258 (p. 222).
[63] A photograph of this letter, found when the house was demolished in 1962, is in the National Monument Record, Aberystwyth.
[64] Fenton, p. 200.
[65] *Ibid.*, p. 244.
[66] Thomas Pennant, *Tours in Wales [...]*, ed. John Rhys, 3 vols (Caernarfon, 1883), III, 136.
[67] C. J. Apperley, *My life and times* (Edinburgh and London, 1927), p. 6.

CHAPTER 12

THE LONDON-WELSH

Glenda Carr

LONDON has always drawn Welshmen seeking their fortune. The attitude of the lexicographer William Owen Pughe (1759-1835) is typical; he left his home in Ardudwy for the city at the age of seventeen, 'familiar with the name of London from its being, in our rustic conversations, the primary point in the geography of the world'.[1] R. T. Jenkins refers to the 'inordinately large number of young Welshmen at the Inns of Court' as early as the sixteenth century,[2] and the law does seem to have attracted many bright young Welshmen; William Owen Pughe himself was a solicitor's clerk and so was Robert Hughes, 'Robin Ddu yr Ail o Fôn' (1744-85), who introduced him to the Gwyneddigion Society. Pughe's elder brother, John, had also gone to London and become a publisher and bookseller with a business in 168 Piccadilly. The various branches of the book trade seem to have been popular with London Welshmen from an early date; Bob Owen, Croesor, claims to have identified no fewer than 345 Welsh members of the trade in the city between 1500 and 1700.[3] Not only did London provide these ambitious young men with work but it was also a lively and convivial place with a strong Welsh atmosphere to many of its taverns and coffee houses. It was natural that the Welsh should forgather in such places, thereby making new friends and acquaintances from back home. It was natural, too, that these informal gatherings should lead to more organized meetings and that societies of London Welshmen should spring up at different periods.

Not all those who came to the city prospered. The plight of the children of such families touched the hearts of their wealthier compatriots and prompted them to found the 'Honourable and Loyal Society of Antient Britons' in 1715. The Society originally paid for two Welsh boys from needy families to be apprenticed to trades, but its charitable activities later extended to founding a school in Clerkenwell for the sons of Welsh parents. Girls were admitted in 1768, and after 1882 boys were excluded and the school became 'The Welsh Girls' School' which moved to Ashford in Middlesex. The Antient Britons met only once a year, to celebrate St David's Day, when a sermon was preached and a collection made for the upkeep of the School. However, this proved inadequate either to strengthen the bond of the exiled Welshmen or to support the Charity School. The desire to remedy this lack was one of the main incentives for the founding of the first society to bear the name of the Honourable Society of Cymmrodorion.

The history of the Cymmrodorion can be divided into three periods: from its inception in 1751 to 1787, a second spurt between 1820 and 1843, and the modern period from 1873 to the present day. Before embarking on a discussion of the aims and achievements of the first Society, however, its founders, the versatile Morris brothers of Anglesey, must be introduced. Lewis, Richard, and William Morris were the sons of a cooper, carpenter, and small-time farmer from Llanfihangel Tre'r-beirdd, Anglesey. Lewis and his brothers learned their father's craft, but Lewis (1701-65) was considered to be especially dextrous; he was said to be able 'to build a boat and sail it and construct a harp and play it'. Originally a land surveyor, then a 'waiter and searcher' at the customs houses in Beaumaris and Holyhead, by 1742 he had mining interests in Cardiganshire, and by 1744 he was collector of customs at Aberdyfi. He set up a printing press in Holyhead, and in 1735 produced *Tlysau yr Hen Oesoedd*, an unsuccessful attempt to publish a periodical reproducing early texts which is discussed in Chapter 16. In 1746 Lewis became Deputy Steward of the Crown Manors in Cardiganshire, a post which involved him in much litigation with the local gentry over grants of lead mining rights. During the last fifteen years of his life he was engaged on an ambitious work with a self-explanatory title: *Celtic Remains: or the Ancient Celtic Empire described in the English Tongue. Being a Biographical, Critical, Historical, Etymological, Chronological and Geographical Collection of Celtic Materials towards a British History of Ancient Times*. Unfortunately this was not published until 1878 and then only in part and poorly edited.

Richard (1702/3-79), seems to have been a sunnier character, although we know less about him as fewer of his letters have survived and these are mainly confined to the years 1759 to 1763. On arriving in London around 1721 or 1722 he found work as a book-keeper and accountant and seems to have lived fairly comfortably until about 1734 or 1735 when he was imprisoned in the Fleet for standing surety for a defaulting debtor. By 1742 he seems to have recovered, having been given the task of correcting the proofs of Welsh pamphlets published in London and in 1744 the responsibility of correcting the new SPCK edition of the Bible and Book of Common Prayer. This, together with auditing, accounting, and translating in the courts, seems to have been his means of livelihood. Eventually he found more steady employment as a clerk in the Navy Office, and by 1757 had become 'Chief Clerk for Foreign Accounts to the Controller of the Navy', a responsible post which carried the impressive salary of £100 a year. Despite his own frequent bouts of poverty, Richard was said to be generous to a fault, especially to fellow Welshmen who fell on hard times. Of the Morris brothers, Richard can be called the true father of the Cymmrodorion.

William Morris (1705-63), Collector of Customs in Holyhead by 1736/7 and Comptroller of Customs in 1759, was the most settled of the brothers. An enthusiastic gardener, he also shared his brothers' intellectual interests and was the most prolific letter-writer of the three. It is through his letters that we learn most of what is known of these remarkable men.[4]

These, then were the men who felt the need for a more vigorous society to represent the Welsh in London. The convivial element was still a strong incentive in forming the new society; 'at eight they meet and seldom part till twelve or two in the morning — all boozy,'[5] says Lewis Morris in a letter to William, describing the activities of the Cymmrodorion in 1757. However, the Morris brothers felt that they had also been called to higher things and that they had a duty to open the eyes of their compatriots to the glory of their own language and literature.

Wales at that time had no focal point for its intellectual activities; no university, no national library, not even a national eisteddfod. With the migration of so many of its natural leaders to London it was, perhaps, not surprising that these men should assume the responsibility of enlightening the Welsh, not only in the city but at home, and that their leadership should be accepted. The Cymmrodorion Society is said to have come into existence in September 1751, and its Constitutions were set out in 1755, with Richard Morris as its first President. Members were admitted by proposal and a ballot. At first the entrance fee was a once-and-for-all payment of 10s. 6d., but after 1777 this sum was charged annually 'for the support of Welsh publications'. This must have been inadequate for the ambitions of the Society as its aim was to buy *every* printed book, old and new, in Welsh for its library as well as any manuscript it could afford.[6]

The rank and file of the Society included many tradesmen and craftsmen, a fact which the snobbish Morris brothers tried their best to disguise so 'that every English fool may not have room to laugh in his sleeve and say "such a society indeed"',[7] but there was a nucleus of talented men such as Richard Morris, Lewis when he was in London, and many clergymen and lawyers. Among the 'corresponding members' were William Morris and the hard-drinking poets Goronwy Owen (1723-69) and Evan Evans, 'Ieuan Fardd' (1731-88).

The first Cymmrodorion Society came to an end in 1787. The death of its founder and guiding light, Richard Morris, in 1779 had been a blow from which it did not fully recover. Its achievements had hardly fulfilled the high hopes and expectations of its founders. Although individual members made a valuable contribution to Welsh culture, the corporate achievement of the Society is more difficult to evaluate. One thing that is certain, however, is that the Society won the respect of Welshmen everywhere; it established a precedent so that Welshmen even in the remoter parts of Gwynedd hereafter automatically turned to London for guidance on literary matters. This trend was to continue with the societies that sprang up as the original Cymmrodorion Society declined.

Two members of the Cymmrodorion became the founders of a new society which came into being in 1770. This was the Gwyneddigion Society, and the two men were Robert Hughes, 'Robin Ddu yr Ail o Fôn', and Owen Jones, 'Owain Myfyr' (1741-1814). In 1764 Hughes left his native Anglesey for London where he worked as a barrister's clerk. About the same time Owen Jones left Llanfihangel Glyn Myfyr to be apprenticed to a London furrier and before very long he had his own flourishing business. The Gwyneddigion shared many of the aims and aspirations of the Cymmrodorion but they were probably less snobbish. Although the buying of Welsh books for their library was one of the society's aims, only a few of the members were truly committed to the cause of Welsh literature; for most the society was an excuse for a jovial night out. The Gwyneddigion did, however, do much to foster the early eisteddfod, thereby giving much encouragement to poets in Wales.

The Morris brothers had collected and copied many Welsh manuscripts, in particular the work of Dafydd ap Gwilym. These manuscripts later came to the library of the Gwyneddigion. Owain Myfyr's ambition was to publish a volume of Dafydd's work using the Morris collection as its basis. He hoped, however, to find additional poems lying neglected in private hands in Wales, and advertised in newspapers circulating in the Principality in an attempt to discover them. He also appealed to scholars and collectors and it was in this way that the poems forged by Edward Williams, 'Iolo Morganwg', found their way into the collection. Since the volume was ready before the bulk of Iolo's contribution arrived, they had to be included in the now notorious appendix to the volume. *Barddoniaeth Dafydd ab Gwilym* was published in March 1789.[8]

Most of the groundwork had been done by Owain Myfyr and the manuscript of the book, now in the library of the University of Wales, Bangor, is in his hand. A great deal of the editing had been done by William Owen Pughe. The Gwyneddigion were among the first to realise that an eisteddfod could be a good opportunity to sell books, and they hoped that the eisteddfod which they were sponsoring in Y Bala in September 1789 would provide them with an opportunity for selling many copies of *Barddoniaeth Dafydd ab Gwilym*. Their expectations were disappointed. Since Owain Myfyr had paid £180 for the printing out of his own pocket he was naturally peeved at the apathy which greeted his efforts. There were suggestions that this was the Welsh poets' way of avenging themselves on the Gwyneddigion whom they suspected, with reason, of being less than honest in their eisteddfodic adjudications but Owain Myfyr preferred to blame the ignorance and lack of taste of his compatriots. Another reason why the book did not sell well was the lackadaisical way in which the enterprise was handled. Copies dispatched to Wales vanished without trace since no-one seems to have made much effort to keep any check on their distribution or their sales. By 1802 David Thomas, 'Dafydd Ddu Eryri' (1759-1822), was given permission to give copies away to his friends. It seems strange that Owain Myfyr, who was so successful in his own business, allowed himself to lose a great deal of money in this venture through sheer incompetence.

The comparative lack of success of *Barddoniaeth Dafydd ab Gwilym* did not deter the Gwyneddigion from pressing ahead with other publishing enterprises. In particular, William Owen Pughe, who had seen the wealth of early manuscripts in the Society's collection and in the private libraries in Wales while he was researching into Dafydd ap Gwilym's poetry, was now determined that these texts should be rescued and published while there was yet time. Ieuan Fardd had already studied and copied the Llywarch Hen *englynion*, and so had two brothers from Eifionydd, John and Richard Thomas, whose copies had come into the hands of Owain Myfyr after their early deaths. Pughe's edition, *The Heroic Elegies and Other Pieces of Llywarç Hen*, was published ostensibly in 1792, although 1793 may possibly be the actual year of publication.[9] The volume was not a success for several reasons. Pughe, in an attempt to rid the Welsh language of its digraphs (such as 'll' and 'dd'), had experimented disastrously with the orthography; his translation of the *englynion*, too, was rather a hit-and-miss attempt as the copies from which he worked were often inaccurate, and it was a slow and difficult business to gain access to the private libraries in order to check the original manuscripts. Although Pughe cannot be blamed unduly for failing to recognise that Llywarch Hen was the subject of the poetry rather than its author, the volume was marred by his unprofessional editing and translation. However, as Robert Southey said,

> It is a serious evil that no man of adequate talents will take the Welsh antiquities in hand, and that no encouragement is given those who do. Owen [Pughe] has translated 'Llywarch Hen' badly, that is evident, yet his version is better than none, and eminently useful to all those who want information either in old history or our old manners. I wish that the Literary Society, as they call themselves, would employ their fund better.[10]

The 'literary society' referred to in this letter may have been the *Ofyddion* (Ovates) founded in 1794. Although the influence of Iolo Morganwg and his *Gorsedd Beirdd Ynys*

Prydain (the Gorsedd of Bards of the Isle of Britain) can be seen in its name, its aims were unimpeachable. It intended to publish a journal which would contain transcripts and translations of Welsh texts, not just the early poetry, but works with rather more popular appeal such as the laws of Hywel Dda and the Mabinogi. The first number of the *Cambrian Register*, that for 1795, was edited by William Owen Pughe and appeared in 1796. Its topics seem to have been varied enough to attract a wide range of readers, dealing as they did with history and antiquities, topography, music and poetry and including letters and reviews. But only three volumes were published: one in 1796, one (for 1796) in 1799, and a final volume in 1818 before it was abandoned for lack of support.

While assisting Owain Myfyr in the task of collecting and publishing the early Welsh texts, William Owen Pughe was also involved in an enterprise of his own. The Morris brothers had often complained that the Welsh had no comprehensive dictionary to serve both the scholar and the poet. The early Cymmrodorion had dreamed of producing such a dictionary and Pughe had inherited their ambition. Patriotism was undoubtedly a strong incentive, but was hardly enough to support him through the years of thankless labour. He persevered in order to prove wrong his London friends who deplored the valuable time he devoted to 'what they called so unprofitable a sacrifice of time as the collecting together the words of a nearly expiring language'.[11] He was fortunate in his supporters; Iolo Morganwg, despite his whims and duplicity, was unequalled in his knowledge of Welsh manuscripts and was energetic enough to visit private libraries the length and breadth of Wales in order to transcribe them. Many library owners, men such as Paul Panton of Plas Gwyn in Anglesey and Thomas Johnes of Hafod in Cardiganshire, were interested in the work carried out by the London scholars and proved more than ready to open their collections to them and even lend them manuscripts. Friends in Wales sent Pughe their own lists of specialist words.

Pughe's *Geiriadur Cymraeg a Saesoneg: A Welsh and English Dictionary* was originally published in instalments, the first appearing in June 1793, price six shillings. This, like *The Heroic Elegies*, was marred by orthographic experiments which he now developed even further. The second part appeared in June 1794, but the high price and bizarre orthography had already frightened off many potential customers. The third part, published in December 1795, marked the end of the first volume. It took five years for the fourth part to appear, and it was not until 1803 that the *Dictionary*, which Pughe boasted contained over a hundred thousand words, was published in its entirety. At the same time, Pughe's idiosyncratic *A Grammar of the Welsh Language* was published, both as part of the *Dictionary* and separately. As the *Dictionary* was obviously too large and too expensive for the ordinary reader, it was decided to publish an abridged edition in 1806. Since Pughe's publisher, Evan Williams, a native of Cardiganshire who had a bookselling business in the Strand, had lost a considerable sum of money on the dictionary, he insisted that this time a more standard orthography was used. A second edition of the abridged version appeared in 1836, and a second edition of the original version in a more standard orthography was published in Denbigh by Thomas Gee senior between 1828 and 1832. In 1866 Gee's son published a much-revised third edition, edited by Robert John Pryse, 'Gweirydd ap Rhys'.

The main thrust of the Gwyneddigion's work in the final years of the eighteenth century was directed at collecting and publishing Welsh texts. Lewis Morris had set the ball rolling in 1735 with *Tlysau yr Hen Oesoedd*. Ieuan Fardd, a zealous researcher despite his wayward life, had published in 1764 *Some Specimens of the Poetry of the Antient Welsh Bards*, a selection of poetry from Aneirin onwards. William Owen Pughe had been interested in the early poetry since he read Rhys Jones's important anthology, *Gorchestion Beirdd Cymru neu Flodau Godidowgrwydd Awen* (Shrewsbury, 1773), when he was a lad of fourteen. Such tantalizing glimpses made Welsh scholars all the more eager to see these hidden treasures. The activities of forgers such as MacPherson and Chatterton did no good to the cause of publishing the texts as they cast doubt upon their provenance. The English scholar Sharon Turner realised this, so in 1803 he published *A Vindication of the Genuineness of the Antient British Poems*, in which he attempted to prove the authenticity of the ancient texts. He claimed that the very fact that the Welsh had neglected them for so long proved that they were not fakes:

> They do not owe their discovery to any individual. No friendly chest — no ruinous turret — no auspicious accident — has given them to us. No man's interest or reputation is connected with their discovery. Their supporters are therefore at least disinterested.[12]

Owain Myfyr and William Owen Pughe certainly did not profit in any material way from their efforts. The former had lost money on *Barddoniaeth Dafydd ab Gwilym*, and *The Heroic Elegies* had done little to enhance Pughe's reputation. So it must have been patriotism and love of literature that spurred them on to embark on a yet more ambitious enterprise. Originally they had intended to publish a separate volume for each major poet's work, but by about 1797 the plan began to take a different shape, more like the eventual plan of the *Myvyrian Archaiology*. Subscribers were sought in an attempt to make the work pay its way. At the beginning Pughe had enrolled the help of several scholars in Wales but as time went by he himself and Owain Myfyr shouldered the whole burden, with the help of Iolo Morganwg, which was later revealed to be more in the nature of a hindrance.[13]

The work was originally called *The Welsh Archaiology* (a spelling adopted by the editors at the request of Paul Panton, a patron whose wishes they could not afford to ignore), but his fellow workers wanted to honour Owain Myfyr, by naming it after him. His modesty made him hesitate for so long that *The Welsh Archaiology* is the title inside the first volume of 1801. At the last moment his friends managed to persuade him, and the title page and cover were changed to *The Myvyrian Archaiology of Wales*. Although both Pughe and Owain Myfyr were prominent members of the Gwyneddigion, the work was more a private venture on the part of these two men and Iolo Morganwg than a concerted effort by the society. Many members paid lip service to the cause of Welsh literature, but few went so far as to buy the book. Owain Myfyr, Pughe, and Iolo each had his own part to play. Iolo, who was a great walker, once again trudged the length and breadth of Wales in search of manuscripts, often disappearing for weeks on end to the consternation of his fellow editors. Pughe's task was to sift through the material which Iolo collected and prepare it for the press. Owain Myfyr's role, as usual, was to finance the enterprise. He is said to have spent a thousand pounds on publishing costs alone, in addition to supporting Pughe and Iolo. Altogether the

Myvyrian Archaiology is estimated to have cost him the enormous sum of between four and five thousand pounds. Robert Southey acknowledged the scale of his contribution when he said:

> When a foreigner asks us the names of the nobility and gentry of the Principality who published the *Myvyrian Archaiology* at their own expense, we must answer that it was none of them but *Owen Jones, the Thames-Street furrier*.[14]

Unfortunately, despite all the money and labour devoted to it, the work was not entirely a success: many valuable and significant texts had been omitted at the expense of less interesting ones. The Mabinogi, for example, were not included, though in all fairness it must be said that Pughe was working on these texts and had hoped to publish them later. There were faults in transcription and misinterpretations, but the greatest drawback of all was the inclusion of Iolo Morganwg's forgeries comprising many of the Triads and some of the *Brutiau*. William Owen Pughe, an honest but notoriously gullible man, would never have dreamt that such treachery was possible; Owain Myfyr, although cultured in his own way, had not the depth of scholarship necessary to pick up the clues which eventually gave the game away. A few contemporaries had their suspicions, but it was not until this century that the true extent of Iolo's forgeries was revealed by G. J. Williams. Three volumes of the *Archaiology* were published between 1801 and 1807 before the whole enterprise collapsed in quarrelling and recriminations as Iolo and Owain Myfyr parted company, mainly because of arguments over money.

The Gwyneddigion did not lack perseverance; although most of their ventures ended in comparative failure they always proved resilient. In 1805, when they must have known that the future of the *Archaiology* was rather precarious, the minutes of their March meeting recorded that Owain Myfyr had proposed that the Society publish a 'book called "Greal y Gwyneddigion" in London every quarter'. The first number of *Y Greal* appeared on 24 June 1805. The printed advertisement sent to Wales listed the topics that the journal hoped to discuss: antiquities, customs, genealogy, agriculture, horticulture — prospective readers must have felt a sense of *déjà vu*. The Gwyneddigion was not the only London society to support *Y Greal*; it was also backed by the Cymreigyddion, a more plebeian and jolly sort of society which had been founded in 1794, mainly as a forum for radical political debates. No fewer than four editors were appointed, the indefatigable William Owen Pughe and Thomas Jones, 'Y Bardd Cloff' (1768-1828), for the Gwyneddigion, and the radical inn-keeper John Jones, Glan-y-gors (1766-1821), and John Humphreys Parry (1786-1825) for the Cymreigyddion. When the first number appeared in June 1805 Iolo Morganwg was quick to criticize it: the language and style was stiff and unnatural — 'nothing but rank *Hottentotic*' — and the poetry was faulty, demonstrating the editors' ignorance of *cynghanedd* and the metres. But it was squabbling over the orthography that sounded the death-knell for *Y Greal*. Pughe had seized the chance to try out his whims once again, and the Gwyneddigion (at least the members that counted, such as Owain Myfyr) supported him. Owain Myfyr reacted characteristically to the opposition by offering to pay for the whole venture out of his own pocket but this time his offer was in vain: cracks were appearing in the solidarity of the Gwyneddigion themselves. David Thomas, 'Dafydd Ddu Eryri', dared to cross Owain Myfyr and was expelled from the society. The Cymreigyddion, too, had had enough, and *Y Greal* fell victim to the quarrelling, only nine issues appearing before its termination in June 1807.

It was quarrelling, as we have seen, that brought an end to the activities of the trio who had done so much to foster Welsh literature: Owain Myfyr, Pughe, and Iolo Morganwg. There were other factors. Pughe had been beguiled by the teachings of the strange prophetess, Joanna Southcott. Iolo had gone his own way, sinking (with the aid of heavy doses of laudanum) ever more deeply into his world of private fantasy. Owain Myfyr had got married in his old age, a step which seems to have unhinged him, according to Evan Williams, who told Iolo in 1813:

> Your once old friend Owen Jones is become one of the greatest misers in London — he Rolls himself up in fur & curses all Welsh literature — & is turned pagan, he has married his maid servant — & no Venus, and she has brought him several young Bratts! & he is grown poor, pure & virtuous.[15]

William Owen Pughe, though lacking Iolo's genius, persevered, and, in his own way, did much to preserve the ancient texts. As well as the material printed in the *Archaiology*, he had also copied and translated the Mabinogi and the Romances. The text of *Pwyll Pendefig Dyfed*, with Pughe's translation, was published in the first volume of *The Cambrian Register* in 1795, with more appearing in the second volume in 1799. A manuscript volume preserved in the National Library of Wales contains Pughe's revised text of *Geraint fab Erbin* copied from the Red Book of Hergest.[16] This volume can be dated around 1801, the year when he informed Iolo Morganwg that he had also completed his translation of *Peredur*. As his own enthusiasm for the medieval tales increased he managed to fire the interest of his fellow literati; in January 1802 he delivered a paper on the Welsh manuscripts to the Society of Antiquaries. Walter Scott wrote to him about his own efforts in the same field: 'I am a labourer in a different enclosure of the same vineyard which Mr Owen [Pughe] cultivates with so much success.'[17] Southey and Coleridge both expressed an interest in learning Welsh in order to enjoy the texts in their original form, and Sharon Turner claimed to have mastered the language.

The text of *Breuddwyd Macsen* from the Red Book of Hergest was published in *Y Greal* in 1806, but after that no more is heard of Pughe's work on the Mabinogi for several years. His diary shows that he had taken up the work once more by 1816-17 and was seeking a way of publishing it. An opportunity came in the form of the *Cambro-Briton*, yet another attempt by the London-Welsh to find a means of discussing their antiquarian interests. The editor this time was John Humphreys Parry, a clever but hot-headed man who was to die in a tavern brawl. The *Cambro-Briton* was published monthly from September 1819 to June 1822, with a lapse between July and October 1821, Pughe's translation of *Pwyll* appearing in the February 1821 number. His translation of *Math* appeared in 1829 in the *Cambrian Quarterly Magazine*, yet another London periodical aimed at Welsh readers. This fragmentary way of publishing the texts was not satisfactory, and Pughe's ambition was to have them all included in a single volume. Unfortunately, two leading London publishers, Murray and Longman, both refused the work because they did not feel that it was a viable proposition. Pughe then offered his material to T. Crofton Croker, who published a few pieces in the third volume of his *Fairy Legends and Traditions of the South of Ireland* in 1828. Pughe, meanwhile, was desperately seeking subscribers with little success.[18] The *Cambrian Quarterly Magazine* claimed that the public was 'on the very tiptoe of expectation' so imminent was the appearance of the long-promised volume. But the public remained in suspense; Pughe's plans were thwarted yet again. By now his health was failing, and he died in 1835, three years before Lady Charlotte Guest's translation of the Mabinogi began to appear. Pughe's laborious efforts still lie in neat manuscript bundles in the National Library of Wales.

With the passing of the stalwarts of the early Gwyneddigion, the golden age of the London-Welsh societies came to an end. It is true that the Cymmrodorion Society was revived in 1820 and continued until 1843 but (as is shown in Chapter 18) the role of the second Society was very different. It still possessed the library founded by its predecessors, augmented in 1814 by Owen Jones's valuable collection of books and manuscripts, which it attempted to extend by appealing for assistance to buy Welsh books and manuscripts to create the foundation of a 'national library'. However, the world had changed: the old London-Welsh who used to meet to drink, smoke, and socialize to the sound of the harp had been superseded by an earnest and sober generation who were more concerned with the educational and social problems of Wales than discovering Welsh manuscripts, men who were more at home in church, chapel, and committee-room than in the tavern.

NOTES TO CHAPTER 12

1. William Owen, *A dictionary of the Welsh language* (London, 1803), Introduction, sig. b3^r.
2. R. T. Jenkins and Helen M. Ramage, *A history of the Honourable Society of Cymmrodorion and of the Gwyneddigion and Cymreigyddion Societies 1751-1951* (London, 1951), p. 8.
3. Jenkins and Ramage, p. 9.
4. These were printed in *The letters of Lewis, Richard, William, and John Morris of Anglesey*, ed. J. H. Davies, 2 vols (Aberystwyth, 1907-9), and *Additional letters of the Morrises of Anglesey (1735-1786)*, transcribed and ed. Hugh Owen, 2 vols (London, 1947-9).
5. *Letters of Lewis, Richard, William, and John Morris*, II, 2.
6. Article XVI of the Society's 'Constitutions' (1755) was extraordinarily ambitious and anticipated by over a century and a half the charter of the National Library of Wales:

    The Librarian [...] shall purchase at the Society's Expence one copy (if to be had) of every Book that hath ever been printed in the antient *British* Language; and of every one that shall be printed hereafter: also as many antient *British* Manuscripts as can be procured at a reasonable price: Likewise such Books in any other Language, treating of the History and Antiquities of *Britain* [...] (Jenkins and Ramage, p. 236).

7. Lewis Morris to Richard Morris, 21 Sept. 1761 (*Letters of Lewis, Richard, William, and John Morris*, II, 386).
8. T. Parry, 'Barddoniaeth Dafydd ab Gwilym 1789', *JWBS*, 8 (1954-7), 189-99.
9. Glenda Carr, *William Owen Pughe* (Cardiff, 1983), p. 54.
10. *Selections from the letters of Robert Southey*, ed. J. Wood Warter (London, 1856), p. 166.
11. William Owen, sig. b1^r.
12. Sharon Turner, *A vindication of the genuineness of the antient British poems* (London, 1803), pp. 5-6.
13. G. J. Williams, 'Hanes cyhoeddi'r *Myvyrian Archaiology*', *JWBS*, 10(1) (1966-71), 2-12.
14. *The Cambrian Quarterly Magazine*, 1 (1829), 248.
15. NLW, MS 21283E.
16. NLW, MS 13245B (Mysevin 25).
17. NLW, MS 13223C (Mysevin 3), p. 439.
18. Arthur Johnston, 'William Owen-Pughe and the Mabinogion', *NLWJ*, 10 (1957-8), 323-8.

CHAPTER 13

THE NINETEENTH CENTURY

Ieuan Gwynedd Jones

THE history of the book in Wales in the nineteenth century is the history of society and of the changing mental and spiritual culture of the people of Wales in that century. It is therefore about people, their numbers and distribution, and it is about the economies that sustained them: it is about the rise and decay of societies and communities, both rural and urban; it is about the creation of wealth and its distribution among the various grades and classes in those societies, and it is about communication, by road, canal, sea, rail, and telegraph; about technologies and inventions, and about the art of printing and the making and distribution of books, and therefore about the rise of business concerns designed to exploit new technologies. But it is also about things of the mind, about the changing relativities of the Welsh and English languages, about literacy and patterns of education, formal and informal, about religion and belief; about politics and ideologies and about the spread of ideas and the means available at any particular time for their dissemination. As such it is about social change at the profoundest levels. It was well appreciated by contemporaries that the creation of a mass reading public by the invention of printing presses harnessed to steam power — that 'Elixir of Life' as one observer put it[1] — was the profoundest change of all in a century which had experienced changes more fundamental and rapid than any experienced by previous generations. This was the combination which had changed their world and which would further transform it in the future. It was, as one historian put it, 'the most pregnant emblem of their achievement and aspirations [...] and the most potent instrument of social improvement ever conceived'.[2] For, as the jury for the Paper, Stationery, Printing and Bookbinding Section of the Great Exhibition of 1851 declared, 'In every age, and in all countries, printing denotes the state of civilization of which books are the reflex, and the history of the human mind is written in the progress of bibliography.'[3]

With that judgement, and with the pride in the immense achievements in science and technology which inspired it, and faith in the unending progress which it implied, Welshmen unhesitatingly agreed. Writing in 1846, the year of the visitations of the Education Commissioners whose Reports (published in 1847)[4] were to have such dramatic effects on Welsh intellectual developments, Thomas Thomas of the Pontypool Baptist Academy observed that:

> Literary and scientific works of great value, published in cheap form, are now placed within the reach of the common people, and many other means of mental improvement are furnished to the masses in the reading societies and mechanic institutions [...] The sciences are much cultivated and new discoveries are brought to light; and the arts which adorn life and multiply its elegances and conveniences are greatly promoted. We witness the stupendous results in machinery, navigation, railroads, telegraphs, steam-presses, and a thousand other things of

which our forefathers knew nothing, but all of which will conduce to the elevation and happiness of the human race.[5]

A few years later, *Yr Haul*, a Church of England monthly not noted for its support for radical causes or faith in the beneficent effects of progress, sang the praises of printing: *'This art is the most precious ever to have come to our world: if it is not the mother, it is certainly the nurse, of every other art.'*[6] *Y Drysorfa*, the Calvinistic Methodist monthly, rejoiced to point out how, *'as the desire for knowledge increases so too the demand for printing presses grows'*.[7] It rejoiced too in the efficient way in which this demand was satisfied by London makers of printing machines; in this way, mental cultivation determined technical inventiveness and market efficiency.

Such sentiments, typical of commentators in the first half of the century, were, over-optimistic, for the market was not free, books were very expensive, and nowhere in Wales were there publishers on a scale big enough to exploit mass-production techniques. The demand for reading matter was still relatively low. Newspapers were few and often as transient as butterflies, and periodicals, with few exceptions, found it difficult to survive except within the not always comfortable embrace of the religious denominations. The Education Commission Reports of 1847 and the contemporary reports of HM Inspectors revealed the deplorably low standards of formal education available in most places:[8] realistically, the demand for books was not such as to point to a mass readership developing in the first half of the century. The turning point came in the 1850s and 60s. The expansion of the economy and the slow beginnings of a rise in the standard of living coincided with the repeal of the so-called 'taxes on knowledge', the consolidation of the religious expansion of the first half of the century, the coming of universal elementary and secondary education, public libraries, and enhanced adult educational provision, and the politicization of the common people. Hence, by the end of the century the possibility existed that the hopes and dreams of men such as Thomas might be realized, and the mass of the Welsh people be as well, if not better, provided with reading matter as the inhabitants of any other part of Great Britain.

Of the many and complex forces bringing about this great transformation in the lives of the people, two were of fundamental importance. Firstly, were the changes in the size, distribution, and structure of the population,[9] and secondly, the concurrent changes taking place in economic life which determined the nature of those population movements. From just over half a million in 1801, the population of Wales had doubled by 1851 (1,163,139), and almost doubled again by the turn of the century (2,012,876). The rate of growth was markedly different in the first and second halves of the century. In the first half it ranged between 18% (in the decade 1811 to 1821) and 12% (in the decade 1841-51). Such high rates did not occur again until the last decade of the century and the opening decades of our own, when it was in excess of 20% for nearly thirty years. In numerical terms, 575,804 people were added to the total population in the first half of the century, and 849,697 in the second half. In this way the market potential for a mass readership was being continuously and massively increased, especially from the middle of the century onwards.

But this pattern of growth varied from county to county. Each had its own population history, and consequently a different potential for the creation of a reading public. In the first half of the century rates of growth varied enormously, Merionethshire's 32% rise during this period contrasting strikingly with Monmouthshire's massive 225% and Glamorgan's 227%. Only the industrializing counties of Caernarfonshire, Monmouthshire, and Glamorgan doubled their populations during that half century. Where industrial growth on any significant scale was absent or, as in Anglesey, industry was in decline, population numbers stagnated. Growth could be stupendous in individual parts of otherwise deeply rural counties, as in the mountainous parishes on the northern rim of Monmouthshire and the eastern extremity of Breconshire which experienced a population explosion greater than in any other part of Great Britain.[10]

In the second half of the century this pattern was transformed. Rural counties which lacked significant industrialization went into relative population decline. Those counties whose industrial economies had earlier taken off into sustained growth experienced spectacular population explosions. By the end of the century Glamorgan had a population of more than three-quarters of a million (859,931), and was on the verge of another tremendous expansion, as was its neighbour, Monmouthshire (298,076). Caernarfonshire (125,649) and Denbighshire (131,582) were likewise expanding in a similar, though less spectacular fashion in response to the growth in quarrying and mining and their associated industries.

These divergent patterns of population change corresponded to, and were determined by, the course of economic change in different parts of the country. In the industrializing south-east, the economy was dominated during the first half of the century by the iron industry. New towns and villages appeared on the northern rim of the coalfield where both raw materials and water power were to be found in close conjunction. By the 1840s the lineaments of an industrial conurbation had already appeared, stretching from Hirwaun in the west to Bryn-mawr in the east. By the end of the 1850s canals and railways bound these places together and linked them with the expanding markets for their products in England and abroad.

The pattern of industrialization was different in the second half of the century. Iron lost its supremacy as a new and expanding export market developed for steam coal deep-mined in the south Wales valleys. In the north-west during those same years the slate industry grew massively to feed an insatiable home and overseas market, while on the Denbighshire and Flintshire coalfields more diversified industries, including lead, chemicals, and paper manufacture were established. As in south Wales, new towns, like Bethesda, were planted near the quarries, and ancient boroughs, like the ports of Caernarfon, Bangor, and Flint, and market towns like Denbigh, were transformed into populous and modern places. Entirely new seaside resorts grew up along the coasts, strung out along the railways, while older middle-class resorts were adapted to provide entertainment for the masses.[11] The railways which, during the second half of the century, expanded to cover the whole of the country, played a crucial role in the transformation of society by linking the rural to the industrial regions, facilitating commerce, and encouraging the rapid movement of people and transmission of ideas and information.

Thus, the population of Wales was being redistributed. North Wales, which had about one-third of the total population in 1851, had only a quarter in 1891. Glamorgan, which had always been the most populous county, increased its share of the total population from one-fifth in 1841 to nearly one-third in 1871. By 1901 no less than 57.5% of the total population of Wales lived in the two counties of Glamorgan and Monmouthshire. Wales attracted labour from outside, it is true, but until the last decades of the century (and much later in the western anthracite coalfield), it was not migration from outside Wales that accounted for population growth. Wales was being colonized by its own people, and the inhabitants of the new, densely populated mining and manufacturing regions consisted predominantly either of Welsh people newly arrived or the descendants of earlier migrants.[12]

Clearly this redistribution of population and the consequent distinction between rural and urban populations were major factors in the development of a reading public. The reservoir of people was deepest and most ample in the industrial areas, and it consisted mainly of people who spoke the same language, or languages, and shared the same cultural background. The Registrar General observed in 1861 that 'the English nation' had 'assumed the character of a preponderating city population'.[13] If we take this to mean a predominantly urban population (not necessarily the same thing) then clearly a fundamental shift along those lines was beginning to occur in Wales also, though at a much slower pace than in England where industry was much more diversified and complex. In 1801 only about one-tenth of the total population of Wales lived in towns of any size or description. This proportion had risen to over a fifth by 1851, and to more than a half in 1901. In 1841 only Merthyr Tudful, with a population of 35,000, ranked as a 'large town' (i.e. having 20,000 or more inhabitants), but ten years later Swansea (31,461) had joined the list and Newport (19,323) and Cardiff (18,351) were approaching that scale of magnitude. Many more places on the coalfields were growing almost as rapidly. By the beginning of the twentieth century three-quarters of the total population was reckoned to be urban.

The scale and nature of urbanization differed from county to county and from place to place. By 1901 eighteen towns or urban areas accounted for 81% of the population of Glamorgan and sixteen accounted for 72% of that of Monmouthshire. No other counties were as urbanized as these: generally speaking, about a quarter of the inhabitants of the other industrialized counties, including Caernarfonshire and Carmarthenshire, lived in towns or industrial villages and under urban local authorities: but in all the counties there were towns and industrial villages which were large in comparison with their rural hinterlands. Blaenau Ffestiniog, for example, contained roughly a quarter of the total population of Merioneth, and Llanelli and Carmarthen between them about the same proportion of Carmarthenshire's population. This process of urbanization and its uneven incidence throughout the country was a major factor in the development of Welsh culture, and especially in the growth of a mass reading public.

The largest of the new towns were the creation of industry, called into being by the imperative needs of manufacturing and of transport. The combination of industrial change and population growth led also to the expansion of pre-industrial towns (especially seaports), in some of which a wider diversity of manufacturing industries existed than in the industrial south and north where extractive industries predominated.[14] But not all towns were dependent on industry. Many remained what they had always been, market towns serving the needs of purely agricultural communities. Virtually all the county towns became centres of local government, and as central government imposed new responsibilities upon local administration in the fields of poor law, public health, and education, so their status was enhanced and new occupational elements appeared in their populations. Slowly at first, but by the last quarter of the century spectacularly, their size, wealth, and relative commercial importance came to be expressed visually in civic buildings, and their town halls and assembly rooms became centres not only for administration and politics but also for new and exciting cultural developments. Together these constituted the material expressions of civic pride.

Publishing and printing were urban industries, located where the market was strongest, communications easiest, and finance and skilled labour most readily available. Hence the movement of printer-publishers in the middle years of the century away from small rural towns and villages to the burgeoning centres of industry and population, and the concentration in a relatively few places of the largest, most advanced and technologically efficient printing and publishing firms.[15] Caernarfon, Blaenau Ffestiniog, Wrexham, and Denbigh in the north and Carmarthen, Aberdare, Merthyr Tudful, Swansea, Cardiff, Newport, and Monmouth in the south all had thriving printing firms and publishing houses. By the early twentieth century the concentration of printing in even fewer places was well advanced. For example, over 62% of the total of 818 printers and lithographers in north Wales were employed in Caernarfonshire and Denbighshire. None of these firms, however, could bear comparison with the large publishing houses in London or Scotland. Nor were they able to satisfy fully the extraordinary growth in demand for reading matter in Welsh which characterized the third quarter of the century and created a market which large English and Scottish firms were quick to exploit. Yet places of lesser size, wealth, and importance were not denuded of their own printing businesses. Well before the end of the century virtually every county town in Wales, whatever its size or commercial importance, boasted a newspaper, or what passed for a newspaper, whose owners commonly undertook the printing of pamphlets and such like intended for a local readership. But these were small firms, even more dependent on jobbing printing for a local market than their larger competitors.

Concurrently, the structure of the population was changing as it became more diversified occupationally and socially. The new extractive and manufacturing industries, which everywhere were the main engines of change, created a vastly more complicated occupational structure than that of the rural countryside. It would be a great error to imagine that rural communities were uncomplicated, but their occupational structures were far simpler. Farmers had to turn their hands to meet most of the daily needs of their farms, calling upon craftsmen only for specialized skills, like those of the carpenter and the blacksmith.[16] Technical innovations were notoriously slow to be adopted, especially in the remoter counties.

By contrast, the demand of industry for specialized skills was insatiable, the development of new technologies creating new classes of artisans and workmen. Behind the ranks of the unskilled labourers, who constituted the majority of workers, were the production workers without whose skills quarries and collieries, ironworks and non-ferrous industries could not prosper. Behind these again were the engineers and master-craftsmen who operated, repaired, and sometimes manufactured the increasingly complex machinery upon which production depended. The railways, which were everywhere the visible symbols of the progress of the age, employed great numbers of skilled and semi-skilled men in the direct operation of the trains and railroads, in the maintenance and repair shops, and in the regiments of station staff. And everywhere, but especially in the growing urban areas, the building trades flourished as never before. Craftsmen and skilled workmen, provided that they were in more-or-less regular employment, were considerably better off financially than the bulk of the unskilled labour force and potentially, at least, enjoyed higher standards of living. Their appearance in industrial towns and villages, especially during the second half of the century, was an important, if not the key element in the growth of the reading public.

Of great significance, also, was the expansion in the numbers of professional men and the appearance of new professions. Between 1851 and 1881, for example, their numbers doubled as the demand grew for lawyers, medical men, architects, local government officers, and the employees of central government. The largest single profession in this overwhelmingly religious country was that of minister of religion. There were 2,243 in 1851 and 4,025 in 1891.[17] Bankers and commercial men, works managers and agents, substantial tradesmen, and specialized shopkeepers like chemists and druggists, were ever more prominent in the new industrial towns and villages. At a lower social level, the number of shopkeepers and small tradesmen, tailors, shoemakers, cobblers, clerks, and people employed in the provision and distribution of household goods and food, grew enormously. Few published sources are more revealing of the transformation in the structure of society that this entailed than the trade directories which found it necessary to publish new editions at increasingly shorter intervals. Shopkeepers, especially drapers and ironmongers, were often in effect heads of households which would normally include not only their own family but also apprentices and servants. Commonly all of these might live in the same premises, and all be in varying states of legal and moral subjection to the head of the household. Such structures resembled those of farming households which customarily consisted of the parents and their children together with the male and female servants.

The growth of the servant class, male and female, was the most spectacular change of all. Small shopkeepers and clerks invariably kept one or more servants, while prosperous middle-class people sometimes employed almost as many servants as the country gentry whose life-style they sought to emulate. Large households such as these were organized hierarchically, authority flowing downwards through closely defined channels of deference. In such socially diverse and deferential societies, moral, educational, cultural, and literary standards were determined by a small élite in town and country.

The growth of the book trade during the century reflected these changes in the structure of society. Growth, measured by the total number of men and women employed, was greatest in the second half of the century as aggregate numbers almost quadrupled from 1,239 in 1851 to 5,532 in 1901, the twenty years after 1871 seeing the highest growth.[18] As it grew, the industry became increasingly concentrated in the populous mining and manufacturing parts of the country; by 1891, for example, three-quarters of the total number of people employed in printing in Wales were located in Glamorgan and Monmouthshire — 1,544 out of a total of 2,053. There were 222 printers in Caernarfonshire and 183 in Denbighshire. Nevertheless, this urban concentration was not at the expense of rural populations, nor did it mark a socio-cultural split between urban and rural Wales. On the contrary, the printing and publishing industry was one of the factors, along with religion and language, which delayed such a cultural rift.

It is highly significant that the decades of highest growth were a time of rising prosperity and of relative peace in the coalfields of the south and the north-east and in the quarries of Gwynedd. The social unrest which had been so characteristic of the first half of the century in both urban and rural Wales had given way to something like the harmonious coexistence of capital and labour. Not without cause did contemporaries see a relation between the advance of intelligence, as embodied in the growth of publishing, and the growing political and moral maturity of the people. But this was already changing by the mid-1890s, and the opening decades of this century were memorable for the bitterness of the industrial unrest both on the coalfields and in the quarry towns of north Wales.

Two great developments, related both in their origins and their aims, accounted for this. Firstly, the religious character of the culture of the age, and secondly, the nature of educational provision.

The two outstanding characteristics of religion in Wales as it developed in the course of the nineteenth century were its immense numerical strength and the apparently irresistible influence it exerted over the whole of Welsh life. To people accustomed to think of religion and industry as incompatible and contradictory forces, and of urbanism as synonymous with ignorance and immorality, the success of the various denominations was astonishing. Wherever they looked, in town or country alike, they found a superfluity of places of worship, and marvelled at their size, the chaste uniformity of their appearance, and their wide distribution. Clearly, Welsh religious leaders had been extraordinarily successful in their endeavours to bring religion to the people.

From the middle of the century there was ample statistical evidence to support the oft-repeated claim that Wales was the most religious part of Great Britain. Since Wales lacked any other distinctive institutions of a national kind, it is not surprising that this specific and peculiar difference should have been an object of pride and that institutionalized religion should have been regarded, consciously and unconsciously, as a kind of surrogate for those legal, political, and other social institutions around which patriotism and nationalism cohere. Even the Welsh language could not entirely fulfil such functions, for language was considered to be no more than a means of communication and, unlike religion, a wasting asset and irretrievable when lost.

The foundations of this achievement had been laid early in the first half of the century: the second half saw its consolidation. With increasing prosperity, rising standards of living, shorter hours of work and greater leisure time, even more of the resources of the common people were lavished on chapels and churches and schoolrooms. Nowadays, it is fashionable to point to the 'over-building', with its inevitable consequence of chapel debts, which was so characteristic of the last quarter of the century. But contemporaries understood and accepted this long-recognized and deplored phenomenon as the only way in which individual religious causes could give visible and concrete expression to their existence as real, identifiable communities, and also to their legitimate, natural desire for public recognition of their contribution to the image Wales was presenting to the world.

For this miracle of growth of what Henry Richard called 'these marvellous organizations'[19] had been the achievement of the ordinary Welsh people themselves, most of them monoglot Welsh-speakers. That organized religion could be exploited as a means of social control was as obvious to industrialists and landed proprietors as it was to governments and magistrates. It was also well understood by the worshippers themselves. Hence, this phenomenal expansion in Wales had not been directed from above: neither aristocratic landowner nor bourgeois industrialist, nor any other wealthy commercial interest, had determined what chapel members believed, nor, except marginally, had they influenced emergent congregations in their choice of denomination. Many such 'secular' interests had been involved in the great advance of religion: some had released land, others had contributed to building costs. They were honoured for their philanthropy and occasionally they left their mark on the architectural styles of chapels. But the expansion of the denominations in the first half century — that 'silver age' in the history of Nonconformity — had never been a product of paternalism, nor had philanthropy shaped the beliefs or fashioned the social behaviour of the beneficiaries.

Belief and morality had been instilled by the preachers and teachers who perambulated the country from end to end, knitting the complex nexus of chapels into a self-conscious whole, proclaiming the basic truths of evangelical Protestantism, disciplining the wayward, maintaining the faith, and keeping alive the tradition of revivalism. The greatest among them, men of penetrating intelligence and extraordinary eloquence, like the Calvinistic Methodist John Elias, the Baptist Christmas Evans, and the Independent William Williams, Y Wern, were the Dominicans of Victorian Wales. In the key periods of growth, especially during the first half of the century, the majority of them were men (very rarely women) of little learning outside the strict boundaries of orthodox, Bible theology, within which, however, they were uncommonly learned. For the most part they had received little formal, collegiate training for their vocation; most of them entered school or academy, if at all, as mature men, from 'behind the plough', or out of the pit or quarry. Scholarship was not an option at a time of missionary zeal. Their appeal lay precisely in the fact that they were ordinary men gifted in extraordinary ways, especially with the gift of words, and it was their skill as preachers, honed in chapels and in denominational gatherings, that was the secret of their success. It was as the handmaiden of religion that the Welsh press came to maturity, for it depended to an unique extent upon that same ministerial class for its authors, editors, and readers and, in some instances, its publishers also. It was the greater diffusion of elementary and higher education in the second half of the century, the founding of the University of Wales, and a concurrent rise in the standard of living which made it possible for the press to begin to diversify into more secular modes of publishing.

The popularity of the religious press in the nineteenth century was thus not a mere reflection of the strength of organized religion but rather an essential, organic, constituent element within it, part of the indispensable structure of a dominating culture. By its means ideas were formed, propagated, and transmitted far and wide, but equally, it was an instrument for restricting or preventing the spread of ideas which those who controlled it judged to be antipathetic to the dominating culture. Most of the periodicals which constituted the staple source of reading matter — for many people, the only source — had been founded by ministers of religion and depended to a large extent on denominational support for their survival. Many were short-lived, but some survived into a ripe old age, a few even into our own days. It is impossible to exaggerate the formative importance of this reading-matter in the shaping of Welsh religion and culture in the course of the century. The combination of preaching and publishing, of Pulpit and Press, the existence of a network of outlets in the chapels and of perambulating ministers as authors, agents and, sometimes, as carriers, gave to Welsh publishing a unique character, and to the nation at large a sense of its own cultural distinctiveness and unity.

Nevertheless, the pulpit was more effective than the press in the dissemination of religion and the conversion of the people. For three-quarters of the century at least, literacy was seen as consequential upon religious adherence rather than as a precondition of membership. The emphasis placed upon acquiring the ability to read was as old as the Reformation, and the success of various philanthropic societies in the eighteenth century, especially of Griffith Jones's circulating schools, established a tradition which was taken over by the Sunday schools, both Anglican and Nonconformist. Sunday schools existed primarily to teach people to read the Bible and religious material, like Bible commentaries, exegetical works and sermons and, that most popular genre of all, biographies of famous (and not so famous) preachers. In this, judged by the explosion in publishing as the century advanced, they were amazingly successful. Virtually the only favourable observation that the Education Commissioners of 1846 had to make about Welsh religion was to note the extraordinary success of the Sunday schools which were 'real fields of mental activity'. 'Almost every child', the Report continued, 'possesses his own Bible. The elementary books used are little stitched pamphlets of the commonest kinds.'[20]

It is as well to realize, however, that there were severe limits to this success. Religious bodies were always in a minority in the total population: their appeal was by no means universal. The proportion of the population attending Sunday schools according to the Education Census of 1851, was one-third (32.9%) in north Wales, and less than a quarter (22.4%) in south Wales.[21] Although this was the highest proportion of all the counties of England and Wales, and hence a statistic to be treasured and used to justify the Welsh claims to a superior religiosity, the same kind of proportions relating to attendances at day schools placed north and south Wales at the bottom of the list.[22] So, Welsh pride in the success of religious education was balanced by the disgrace of the failure to provide adequate secular education.

Religion was not the only motivation at work among the people. Self-improvement, or a desire for 'rational' amusement like choral singing, could sometimes be a more effective spur to literacy. But the appalling social conditions in the mining and manufacturing areas in the first half of the century and the terrible poverty of the farming communities were not conducive to educational progress. In many places it required an enormous effort to overcome the apathy of the masses and the hostility of the masters. For many men and boys — perhaps a majority — physical and technical skills were more to be desired than the ability to read, and informal modes of education, often group activities like listening to books or newspapers being read, were felt to be both effective and sufficient. Early capitalism, like the deep Toryism of the landed gentry, was antipathetic to any system of education which might enable the people to think for themselves and perhaps nourish a spirit of insubordination, and attitudes such as these survived for many years. Nevertheless, official and unofficial reports, as well as the opinions of religious leaders, do support the presumption that high levels of literacy could, and often were, achieved in Wales despite these obstacles.

In urban Wales, standards of literacy may have fallen as one of the consequences of industrialization and of the dreadful social conditions in the new towns, and it is possible that some such places did not recover the levels of reading ability achieved in the eighteenth century until after the coming of free and universal education in the last quarter of the century. Official reports by government inspectors in the 1840s would certainly seem to support this view.[23] The very process of industrialization was creating a wide range of jobs which could be performed by illiterate or sub-literate labourers. It is also likely that only the élite among the workers and craftsmen and the clerks, traders, and shopkeepers for whom reading and writing were necessary were fully literate. The reports of HMIs strongly indicate that literacy of both kinds was also patchy geographically and was nearly always dependent upon accidental conditions, like the paternalism of some industrialists and landed proprietors, superior standards of living, better school accommodation, and the presence of highly motivated teachers and organizers. In 1846 it was estimated that two-thirds to three-quarters of the population of England and Wales could read, with a higher proportion in Wales.[24] This undoubtedly reflected the greater relative success of the Sunday school movement in Wales, which in turn was testimony to the popularity of religion among the people.

Though the role of religion as an educative force in society was therefore very significant, it was not the only inspiration. The drive for education, a consuming passion in Victorian Britain, gathered force in Wales after the publication of the 1847 Education Reports and was furthered by many organizations whose links with religion were more or less tenuous. Self-help societies, especially the many friendly societies, flourished in rural as well as industrial Wales, and though they existed primarily to assist their members in times of sickness and bereavement, they also sought to inculcate ideals of thrift, sobriety, and respectability, and they actively encouraged literacy. By the third quarter of the century most of the friendly societies active in Wales had become affiliated to the great English provincial Orders, like the Manchester Order of Odd Fellows. The friendly societies together had almost as many members as the churches; in 1876, for example, there were 2,386 registered societies with an aggregate membership of 214,740, as well as 86 female societies with 7,740 members.[25] Wales even possessed its own unique Order, *Y Gwir Iforiaid* (The Philanthropic Order of True Ivorites), which had been founded in 1836 with the aim (in addition to the statutory objectives) of fostering Welsh language and culture. This it did by organizing eisteddfodau and publishing its own periodical and numerous pamphlets and books. Ideally, there could not be an illiterate Ivorite.

Other institutions were purely cultural and educative. By the middle of the century some industrial towns and a number of county towns possessed reading rooms where members could read the leading London and provincial newspapers. Bookseller-stationers sometimes offered reading facilities on their premises. Literary societies, many of them offshoots of the old Welsh patriotic societies of London, encouraged the study of antiquities and literature. The Society for the Diffusion of Useful Knowledge in Wales maintained that since 60,000 copies of Welsh publications were printed each month and were read by 200,000 people out of a monoglot population of about half a million,[26] the prime cultural deficiency in Wales at the end of the 1840s was an ignorance of English. If popular, secular works could be made available in Welsh, the appetite of Welsh readers for English works would be aroused. More directly, and to greater effect, the revival of the eisteddfod, both as a 'national' institution and in its manifold local and provincial manifestations, played an incalculable part in the growth of a reading public. This was because of the high esteem accorded to prize-winners in literary competitions, and because it was the aim of all eisteddfod organizers to publish prize essays and poetry, either in the form of pamphlets or in the local newspapers or magazines. Indeed, for many aspiring authors this was probably the only way they were likely to see their work in print. In this way authors were brought into contact with each other, with the press, with critics, and with readers, and since the scale of this activity was so great its cumulative effect on the publishing scene cannot be exaggerated. It produced a serious, 'quality' press which aspired to print and to circulate only what was uplifting and which shied away from any material or any ideas which might open their authors and editors to the charge of irreligion, scepticism, or even levity. Welsh cultural leaders liked to boast that there were no 'Penny Dreadfuls' in Welsh and no indigenous cheap press intended for a semi-literate audience, as in England.

Public libraries were largely ineffective because the Acts which enabled local authorities to set them up were permissive.[27] Their adoption depended upon the political complexion of elected town councils and the effectiveness of political pressure groups. The few towns such as Cardiff and Swansea where public libraries were relatively effective were those which were already best provided with subscription and institutional libraries. Rural Wales remained virtually untouched by public libraries until the 1920s.

Libraries attached to literary and scientific societies were scarcely more flourishing. The 1849 Select Committee on Public Libraries claimed that there were only two, or possibly four, Mechanics' Institutes in Wales;[28] the Monmouth Reading Society had only seventeen members and a library of sixty volumes, Newport Athenaeum was more flourishing with 256 members and a library of 800 volumes, and there was less 'authentic information' about Aberystwyth and Cardiff. A far more reliable source, the 1851 Education Census, could find only a very few places with flourishing Literary and Scientific Institutions. Swansea's Royal Institution was the outstanding exception. With its 4,500 books it was by far the best 'public' library in Wales. Of the others — a total of thirty-three in the whole of Wales — only six possessed a thousand or more books and a few had no books at all. Fortunately, these were not the only facilities available. Booksellers and newsagents often operated lending libraries and reading rooms, but these, like the public and institutional libraries, were most commonly to be found in large industrial towns and in county towns where an educated élite could support them. Some chapels (probably a growing number by the end of the century) set up libraries for their members, and a Dolgellau club combined cricket and reading.

It was thus from a pretty low base that the advocates of adult education and self-improvement were obliged to work. It is as if the bulk of the respectable classes were content with the contribution the chapels were making to general culture, suspecting that as libraries multiplied so too would other, less elevating forms of entertainment grow. This deep-seated, conservative attitude delayed the advent of a wider and more secular culture until the end of the century, by which time the trade unions and the Labour movement were beginning to fashion an alternative culture to that of organized religion and official Liberalism.

This, the greatest and profoundest transformation in the cultural life of Wales in the course of the century, did not come of its own accord, but was brought about by a prolonged and intensive effort on the part of individuals, pressure groups, and political parties, religious and secular alike, all of which had in common the desire for more democratic forms of government, without which none could hope to attain its political goals.[29] To flourish, democratic institutions required an informed electorate, alive to the issues confronting both the local community and the nation, and also individuals prepared to agitate, to organize, to stand for election, and, if called upon, to participate in the processes of government. Since an ignorant democracy was thus a contradiction in terms, throughout the century numerous voluntary societies, political organizations, and pressure groups became, in effect, agencies for the creation of a literate people. This had been the case with Chartism, the Anti-Corn Law League, and the Liberation Society, all of which dated from the 1840s, and it remained true of the many societies and associations founded later in the century. By the third quarter of the century education and literacy were at the heart of Welsh radicalism: the power of argument and of rational persuasion had taken the place of force, and their contribution to the creation of a mass reading public was very considerable.

This was particularly true of the Liberation Society.[30] No political movement or pressure group exerted a profounder influence on the shaping of the Welsh political consciousness than this society. The secret of its success was the way it harnessed the radical political goals of universal male suffrage to the old Dissenting determination to sever the link between the Anglican Church and government. That the establishment was the source of the injustices and inequalities from which the Nonconformist majority of Wales had suffered over the years was taken as axiomatic, for this was the *raison d'être* of Dissent. What was not sufficiently understood in Wales, it was claimed, was that this great political evil could be broken if only the people knew how to think and to act politically. The politicization of the people, which the Society's electoral programme envisaged, could be achieved only by means of education. William Rees, 'Gwilym Hiraethog', founder-editor of the first truly successful newspaper in Welsh, *Yr Amserau* (1843-59), was concurrently opening the eyes of Welshmen to the inequalities in society and to levels of ignorance which permitted them to flourish. The Liberation Society brought an expertise to the task which Wales had never before experienced to the same degree. It published books, had its own magazine, *The Liberator* (1855), was the major institutional supporter of the radical newspaper, *The Nonconformist* (1841), and published pamphlets and tracts by the hundreds of thousands in both languages. These were distributed through its agents and its hundreds of branches and, more efficiently yet, through the chapels which thus became, in effect, cells for the inculcation of ideas and centres of political activity. In the chapels were to be found the readers of the Welsh radical periodicals in which translations of leading articles and reports of meetings and conferences were to be found in generous profusion. In the chapels, too, were the potential voters on whose fidelity in times of elections the success of its campaigns depended. By the late 1860s town and country equally felt the power of its appeal and learned the same political lessons from its example.

Ecclesiastical politics in general, and the disestablishment campaign in particular, thus enormously stimulated the creation of a reading public. Thus, the Church Defence Institution[31] founded, or more correctly, revived out of the moribund Church Institution in 1871, sought to emulate the success of the Liberation Society by concentrating on reaching the public by means of its newspaper, *The National Church* (1870), the publication of pamphlets, and the circulation of tracts. The propaganda methods of the old Anti-Corn Law League, which had assumed the existence of a reading public, still invited imitation. Contemporaneously, other political movements were in formation. Trade unionism grew as industry developed, though more spasmodically, and by the end of the century even agricultural workers were being organized. Workers in the mining and manufacturing regions of north and south Wales supported radical newspapers in both languages which they could claim as their own, in which they had confidence, and which could represent their ideals and their political aims truly and faithfully.[32] By then elementary education was compulsory, gaps in the geography of literacy were being filled, the English language was being taught systematically, the University of Wales had been founded, and intermediate and secondary schools established to feed it. The old ideal of universal literacy was no longer an idle dream, and a mass reading public had been created.

NOTES TO CHAPTER 13

1. Quoted in T. H. Lewis, 'Y wasg Gymraeg a bywyd Cymru, 1850-1901', *THSC*, (1964), pp. 93-127, 222-36 (p. 103).
2. Richard D. Altick, *The English common reader: a social history of the mass reading public 1800-1900* (London 1957), p. 64.
3. *Reports by the Judges on the thirty classes into which the Exhibition (of 1851) was divided* (London, 1852), c. 397b.
4. *Report of the Commission of Inquiry into the state of education in Wales*, 3 vols (London, 1847).
5. Thomas Thomas, *A course of lectures on the present duties devolving on Christian professors* (London [etc.], 1847), pp. 17-18.
6. '[Y] gelfyddyd hon ydyw yr un werthfawrocaf a ddaeth i'r byd erioed; os nad hi ydyw mam, mae yn sicr o fod yn famaeth pob celfyddyd arall' (*Yr Haul*, cyfres Caerfyrddin 1 (1857), 44-5 (p. 44)). Contemporary journals published numerous articles on this theme; e.g. *Taliesin*, 2 (1860-1), 168-82 and *Yr Eurgrawn Wesleyaidd*, 54 (1862), 243-5.
7. 'Fel y mae yr awyddfryd am wybodaeth yn mwyhau, y mae'r alwad hefyd am beiriannau argraffyddol yn cynnyddu' (*Drysorfa*, 12 (1842), 202-5, 270-1, 333-7 (p. 336)).
8. See, in addition to the Education Commission *Report* (note 4 above), Sir Thomas Phillips, *Wales: the language, social condition, moral character, and religious opinions of the people, considered in their relation to education* (London, 1849).
9. Unless otherwise indicated all population statistics are taken from John Williams, *Digest of Welsh historical statistics*, Vol. 1 ([Cardiff],1985).
10. For the population of individual sub-districts and parishes consult the relevant decennial Census Reports. Sian Rhiannon Williams, *Oes y byd i'r iaith Gymraeg: y Gymraeg yn ardal ddiwydiannol Sir Fynwy yn y bedwaredd ganrif ar bymtheg* (Cardiff, 1992), Appendix 1, pp. 126-7, prints a table of statistics relating to population change in Monmouthshire, 1801 to 1891.
11. For the growth of towns see 'Population of Towns 1801-1971', Population Table 13 in Williams, *Digest*, I, 62-7.
12. This paragraph is based on the Census Reports of 1851, 1891, and 1901.
13. Census of 1861, Report, p. 9.
14. See Population Table 13 in Williams, *Digest*, where these towns are listed by county.
15. This and the next paragraph are based on the Occupations and Industries Tables, Census of 1861, and on Ifano Jones, *A history of printing and printers in Wales to 1810 and of successive and related printers to 1923, also a history of printing and printers in Monmouthshire to 1923* (Cardiff, 1925).
16. J. Geraint Jenkins, *Life and tradition in rural Wales* (London, 1976) and David Jenkins, *The agricultural community in south west Wales* (Cardiff, 1971), pp. 93 and 103.
17. Figures based on Occupation Tables in the Census Reports of 1851 and 1891. The 1891 totals were made up of 1,585 Anglican clergy, 101 Roman Catholic priests, 2,053 Nonconformist ministers, and 439 missioners, of whom 153 were women.
18. See the Occupations Tables in Williams, *Digest*, pp. 95-131. My calculations are based on the Occupations Tables in the decennial censuses of 1851 to 1901 counting numbers of persons employed in the Paper, Print, Books and Stationery trades.
19. In an election speech at Merthyr Tudful in 1868 reported in the *Aberdare Times*, 29 August and 14 November 1868. See also his *Letters and essays on Wales* (London, 1884), p. 123.
20. *Report of the Committee of Inquiry into the State of Education in Wales*. Part l (London, 1847), pp. 3 ff.
21. Census of Great Britain, 1851. *Education. England and Wales. Report and Tables*. (London, 1854), Table 23, showing the proportion per cent of Sunday Scholars to population, p. lxxvi. These statistics correspond fairly closely to those collected by Seymour Tremenheere and published in *Minutes of the Committee of Council on Education, 1839-40*, and subsequent reports of the HMIs. Compare also the results of an investigation by the Nant-y-glo ironmaster, George S. Kendrick, *The population of Pontypool and the parish of Trevethin* (London, 1840). For full references and a

discussion of the evidence see Ieuan Gwynedd Jones, *Mid-Victorian Wales, the observers and the observed* (Cardiff, 1992), pp. 113-49. Kendrick carried out a similar survey of Merthyr Tudful published under the title 'Statistics of Merthyr Tydfil' in *Journal of the Royal Statistical Society*, March 1846, pp. 14-21.

[22] Census of Great Britain. Education 1851, Table 6, showing proportion per cent of day scholars to population, p. xxxviii.

[23] The Reports of HMIs are discussed in *Mid-Victorian Wales*, pp. 109-22.

[24] Robert K. Webb, 'Working class readers in early Victorian England', *EHR*, 65 (1950), 333-51 (pp. 343-4).

[25] Based on official returns, Parliamentary Papers 1877 LXXV11.

[26] *Yr Haul*, n.s. 2 (1851), 157.

[27] Based on official returns under the Free Library Acts, especially PP 1890-91 LXI (5).

[28] Based on Select Committee on Public Libraries, PP 1849.

[29] For this theme see Ryland Wallace, *Organise! Organise! Organise! A study of reform agitations in Wales, 1840-1886* (Cardiff, 1991).

[30] For the Liberation Society see 'The Liberation Society and Welsh Politics, 1844 to 1868' in Ieuan Gwynedd Jones, *Explorations and explanations: essays in the social history of Victorian Wales* (Llandysul, 1981), pp. 236-68.

[31] For this institution see Adrian John Parry, 'The Church Defence Institution 1859-1896, with special reference to Wales' (unpublished master's thesis, University of Wales, Aberystwyth, 1982).

[32] See Aled Gruffydd Jones, *Press, politics and society: a history of journalism in Wales* (Cardiff, 1993).

CHAPTER 14

TWO WELSH PUBLISHERS OF THE GOLDEN AGE: GEE A'I FAB AND HUGHES A'I FAB

Philip Henry Jones

THE second half of the nineteenth century, particularly the period from the later 1850s to the 1890s, is generally regarded as the golden age of the Welsh-language press — the only time, it has been claimed, that publishing Welsh books was truly profitable.[1] Reliable figures are hard to come by, but the publisher Charles Hughes calculated that £100,000 was spent on 'Welsh literature of all kinds' in 1875.[2] As demographic, economic, and educational developments expanded the market for reading material in Welsh, a few Welsh printing houses became increasingly involved in publishing, grew in size, and increased in organizational complexity. Even so, most firms remained small, continued to rely on printing, and tended to produce books for a local or at most a regional readership.[3]

Amongst the largest and most important Welsh-language publishers were two Denbighshire firms, Gee a'i Fab of Denbigh and Hughes a'i Fab of Wrexham, each of which employed some fifty hands and had about two hundred Welsh titles in print by the later nineteenth century. Many of their publications enjoyed extensive sales. Gee's twice-weekly newspaper, *Baner ac Amserau Cymru* (*Banner and Times of Wales*), sold about 13,000 copies a week from the 1880s to 1914.[4] Hughes published a penny almanac, *Almanac y Miloedd* (*The almanac of the thousands*), which, despite considerable competition, had a print order of some 60,000 copies a year during the 1870s.[5] Sales of shilling volumes of verse could be high: between 1866 and 1914 over 17,500 copies were printed of the first volume of verse by Richard Davies, 'Mynyddog', at least 13,500 copies of the second volume, and 19,500 of the third.[6] Cheap popular handbooks also sold well: Hughes printed almost 36,000 copies of a shilling English-Welsh letter-writer between 1870 and 1912.[7]

Both firms built on foundations securely laid in the first half of the century. Gee's firm had its origin in 1808 when the wealthy Calvinistic Methodist leader, Thomas Jones (1756-1820), established his own press in order to expedite the publication of his voluminous writings and avoid a repetition of the mortifying experience of having a drink-bribed compositor show the proofs of one of his controversial works to its intended victim.[8] He appointed Thomas Gee (1780-1845), who had gained experience of setting Welsh while an apprentice at Chester, to take charge of the office. In October 1813, on completion of his anti-Catholic *magnum opus*, *Diwygwyr, Merthyron a Chyffeswyr Eglwys Loegr* (*Reformers, martyrs and confessors of the Church of England*), Jones sold the office to Gee.[9]

Richard Hughes (1794-1871) was not brought up as a printer: after working in a Wrexham bank he was employed as an accountant at the Esless paper mill, Bersham. Following the death of his employer in 1814, Hughes operated the mill with a partner. In 1820 he opened a paper warehouse in Wrexham and, abandoning paper making, built up a stationery business which, by 1823, was also retailing books and periodicals. By 1827 he had set up his own press.[10]

Both firms were initially typical members of the provincial book trade. As well as selling books, periodicals, stationery, and wallpaper, they engaged in a variety of ancillary activities such as acting as local agents for insurance companies. In the 1820s and 1830s Gee sold tea and dubious patent medicines, and ran a circulating library, while Richard Hughes supplemented his income by occupying official positions, serving as the first Registrar of Marriages for the Wrexham District under the 1836 Act and as the town's Postmaster from 1840 to the late 1850s.

Gee's office was far more active than that of Hughes during the first half of the century, probably because it enjoyed a monopoly of printing in the Denbigh area whereas Hughes had to compete against several long-established concerns. Hughes was a bookseller and stationer with a subsidiary printing business, but Gee was primarily a printer. Between 1813 and 1845 Gee produced about 130 books and pamphlets, some three times as many as Hughes. While Hughes was slow to venture into publishing at his own risk rather than printing for others, Gee did so from as early as 1814.[11] His books covered a far wider range of topics, about a third of them dealing with secular matters, while Hughes concentrated almost entirely on religious books. Several of the most ambitious works produced by Gee were in English but Hughes printed virtually no books in that language. By the early 1830s Gee's office, now calling itself 'Clwyd Wasg' or the 'Clwydian Press', had gained a reputation for producing scholarly works relating to Wales, largely, perhaps, because of its links with William Owen Pughe who became a close friend of Gee.[12] The press consequently catered for two distinct readerships until the early 1850s, its books in English for the gentry and clergy being well-printed on good paper, while most of its Welsh books were produced as cheaply as possible for impecunious purchasers. The growing demand for Welsh books might well have crowded out English works eventually, but Thomas Gee the younger had the decision forced upon him following a boycott of his firm by county society in reprisal for his prominence as an anti-Tory campaigner in the 1852 election.[13]

Since it took two or three generations of capable printers to establish a truly successful concern,[14] both Gee and Hughes were exceptionally fortunate in their sons. Thomas Gee the younger (1815-98) received a good education locally before being apprenticed to his father from 1829 to 1836. He spent much of 1837 in London, initially with Eyre and Spottiswoode (a 'rat house' which he hastened to leave)[15] and then with the large firm of Gilbert & Co., in order to improve his knowledge of fine printing and of technical developments such as roller-making and lettering the cloth cases of books.[16] On his return to Denbigh in January 1838 he took over supervision of the office and, although not made a partner until February 1845, soon became responsible for long-term planning as his father, widowed in the autumn of 1838, gradually lost interest in the business. The firm was sufficiently profitable for him to have paid the £1,050 the partnership had cost him by May 1853.[17]

Gee was a man of wide interests and inexhaustible energy: a prominent radical politician, an ordained minister who was both a leader and a thorn in the side of the Calvinistic Methodists, and a relentless enemy of the drink trade. A strong believer in setting 'slumbering surplus capital' to work, he was also a farmer, the owner of a haematite mine, slate quarry, and water-mill, a founder of the North Denbighshire Building Society, one of main promoters of the Vale of Clwyd Railway, and a director of the Ruthin Soda Water Company. All these concerns, as well as public bodies with which he was connected such as the North Wales Counties Lunatic Asylum and Denbighshire County Council, were valuable sources of jobbing printing.[18]

Charles Hughes (1823-86) was very similar in his upbringing and interests.[19] After attending Bridgnorth Grammar School and (possibly) serving his apprenticeship at his father's office he spent the years between 1844 and 1848 in London with the leading firm of publishers and wholesalers, Simpkin Marshall. At the end of December 1848 he became a partner in his father's firm. Like Gee, he was an active Liberal politician, a prominent Calvinistic Methodist (but belonged to the English branch), a temperance activist, a supporter of the peace movement and of non-denominational education, and a significant local capitalist whose interests in finance and industry included the extremely successful Provincial Insurance Company (of which he was a founder and director), the Wrexham, Ruabon and North Wales Benefit Building Society, local lead mines, and the Wrexham, Mold & Connah's Quay Railway.

During the 1850s both Gee and Hughes transformed their firms from small-scale, craft-based concerns dependent on human power to sizeable industrial enterprises employing the latest steam-powered machinery to supply a national market. Although the firms were direct competitors in certain areas, most notably in the provision of biblical expositions, sermons, material for Sunday schools, and popular handbooks, their activities were largely complementary since each specialized quite markedly. Thus Gee published a twice-weekly Welsh newspaper: Hughes avoided this potentially lucrative field. Gee published little music (apart from hymn tunes) from the early 1860s, while Hughes proceeded to publish popular music on a very large scale from that time onwards. Gee published several substantial works of reference and scholarship, including a ten-volume encyclopaedia, *Y Gwyddoniadur Cymreig* (1854-79), the largest Welsh book ever published, scholarly dictionaries, and a reprint of the *Myvyrian Archaiology* (completed in 1870): Hughes concentrated on popular reference books such as the famous *Llyfr Pawb ar Bob-peth* (*Everybody's book on everything*) (1874) which provided 1,500 snippets of information for 3s. 6d. Gee published hardly any contemporary verse: Hughes brought out an extremely successful series of shilling volumes by the popular poets of the day. The difference in output reflected a fundamental difference in outlook. Gee, like the Welsh humanists of the sixteenth century, realized that if the Welsh language was to survive it had to be capable of discussing the latest advances in knowledge. In order to expand its range and enhance its status he initiated a number of bold projects from the mid-1840s onwards such as *Y Traethodydd* (*The Essayist*), the first Welsh quarterly review, *Y Geiniogwerth* (*The Pennyworth*) (1847-51), the first Welsh-language mass-market monthly, a series of books on useful knowledge, and above all, *Y Gwyddoniadur Cymreig*. As early as the mid-1850s his contemporaries recognized Gee's unique status as a patriotic innovator.[20]

Charles Hughes was far more limited in his objectives: as he told the Aberdare Committee, 'we only publish what we think will pay for publishing', pointing out that since publishing books in Welsh was 'entirely dependent on private enterprise, it is difficult to get persons to risk the laying out of their capital on scientific and literary books [...] on the chance of whether they would take'.[21] In keeping with his cautious outlook, Hughes specialized in exploiting the successful innovations of others, notably Isaac Clarke of Rhuthun (1824-75), who had pioneered the publication of cheap music (especially solo songs) and shilling volumes of verse in the late 1850s and early 1860s but lacked the capital, drive, and business skills to exploit them fully.[22]

By the 1880s Gee's reading of the market began to falter, several of his later ventures such as a non-denominational hymn-book, *Emynau y Cyssegr* (*Hymns of the sanctuary*), published in various versions from 1885 onwards, and a 400-page collection of family prayers, *Yr Allor Deuluaidd* (*The family altar*) (1892), being costly failures.[23] His son J. Howel Gee (1854-1903), although able and well-trained, was overshadowed by his autocratic father and, after the latter's death, his failing health prevented him from giving the firm the new orientation it required.[24] After Howel Gee's early death, the firm remained in family hands until 1914 but did little more than mark time. Hughes, however, moved into new areas from 1886 onwards under the guidance of the third generation of the family, Charles Tudor Hughes (1859-1932) and Albert Llewelyn Hughes (1864-1944), by publishing the works of Daniel Owen (1836-95), the most popular Welsh novelist of the day, and by supplying Welsh reading material for the day-school market during the 1890s. Charles Tudor Hughes saw the firm through the First World War, amalgamating it at the beginning of the 1920s with the Oswestry concern, Woodall, Minshall, Thomas & Co.[25]

Although most of the nineteenth-century records of both firms were pulped during the First World War, sufficient material has survived to indicate how they set about the task of producing and selling Welsh books on an unprecedented scale. The most notable difference was that Gee carried out as much work as possible itself while Hughes, because of the restricted working and storage space at its premises in the centre of Wrexham, had to contract out a great deal of work to specialist firms in England and Scotland. The arrangements for producing books in this way were often complex: *Llyfr Emynau* (1869), a hymn-book compiled by E. Stephen and J. D. Jones, was set and stereotyped in Wrexham. The plates were sent to Ballantyne in Edinburgh, who printed 10,000 copies on paper ordered by Hughes from McCorquodale of Liverpool. The printed sheets were cased in London by Straker in five different styles and the finished books sent to Wrexham for distribution.[26] Although Hughes, unlike Gee, followed the trend towards increasing specialization and consequent integration into a Britain-wide book trade set by the leading London publishers of the day, it had no intention of abandoning printing. It always executed as much as it could of its own printing and invested heavily in the mid-1890s in purpose-built premises and new plant in order to expand its printing operations. Welsh publishers thus followed the Scottish pattern of combining publishing with the physical production of books rather than the London pattern of becoming purely publishing houses.

Although both firms occasionally purchased unsolicited manuscripts, most of their publications were commissioned as part of a systematic programme of developing their lists. Despite pursuing such long-term plans, they could respond rapidly to public demand. Thus both brought out translations of Pae's apocalyptic *Armageddon* in 1853, and were keenly aware of the demand amongst monoglot Welsh readers for prompt translations of English-language best-sellers. Translations and adaptations formed an important part of the output of both firms, comprising between ten and twenty per cent of the items published by Gee between 1845 and 1898.[27] Books published in the United States were a favoured source since, in the absence of an international copyright agreement, no payment had to be made for the translation rights. It is no accident that the second-largest work published by Gee (over 3,650 pages) was a six-volume translation of a commentary on the New Testament by Albert Barnes of Philadelphia. The translation rights of books published in Britain were often acquired cheaply, either because their authors were unaware of the profitability of the Welsh market[28] or because the authors of religious works were more anxious to propagate their message than make a profit.[29]

From time to time both publishers took advantage of the reverses that tended to overtake their smaller and less well-capitalized competitors by purchasing, often at distress-sale prices, books that had proved successful. Hughes acquired several works in this way from the hard-pressed Bala printer, Griffith Jones, in the 1860s.[30] In 1872 the firm took advantage of the tribulations of Isaac Clarke and Isaac Foulkes, purchasing the copyrights of volumes of verse by 'Ceiriog' and the *Gems of Welsh Melody* from the former and several works, including a very popular collection of Welsh folklore, *Cymru Fu* (*Old Wales*), from the latter.[31] Gee specialized in snapping up promising books which their authors had prepared for publication but had been unable to put through the press because of financial problems, acquiring in this way for £90 one of his best-sellers (at least 10,000 copies were printed), a collection of the sermons of John Jones, Talsarn, complete with an introduction and list of subscribers.[32] When purchasing the copyright of previously published books Gee usually required the author to add extra material so that his new edition might tempt even those who had purchased the original work.[33] As well as acquiring the copyrights and sometimes the stereotype plates of books printed by others, Hughes frequently bought works in sheets, issuing them in its own cases, often with a new title-page and catalogue of its publications added to mislead potential purchasers.

The firms differed considerably in the way that they paid authors. Gee invariably adhered to the old system of outright purchase of copyright whereby the author assigned all his rights in the work to the publisher in exchange for a stipulated payment. If the book proved to be unexpectedly successful the publisher alone profited since he was under no legal obligation to make any further payment to the author. Authors understandably resented the system and its prevalence may be one reason why so many nineteenth-century Welsh writers attempted to publish their own works.[34]

There was a gradual trend in Victorian England towards new and apparently fairer methods of paying authors, notably an increasing use of the royalty system which linked payment directly to the commercial success of a book. In following this path Hughes explored a wide range of possibilities in its agreements with authors. One common arrangement was to grant authors an additional sum should a book sell more than a specified number of copies. When offering W. T. Thomas £5 for the copyright of a Welsh book on wills in 1862, Hughes agreed to make a second and final payment of £5 should more than 3,000 copies be printed.[35] Hughes sometimes leased copyrights from authors. Such agreements could be quite complex: in 1865 Hughes undertook to publish the collected works of Lewis Edwards, paying £25 for the right to publish

5,000 copies of each part and a further £7 for each additional 1,000 copies printed of any part. Edwards retained the copyright and at the end of five years, if the agreement were not renewed, he could buy the stereotype plates at cost.[36] By the end of the century Hughes viewed the royalty system as the norm but would still purchase certain copyrights, such as the later novels of Daniel Owen, for each of which it paid £100.[37]

Payment could take several forms. Authors might be given copies of their books in exchange for the copyright: thus Gee agreed in November 1864 to purchase the copyright of the second part of the turgid religious epic, *Emmanuel*, from William Rees, 'Gwilym Hiraethog', for 500 copies.[38] This primitive arrangement, reminiscent of the earliest days of printing, was favoured by many ministers since they could sell their books while on preaching or lecturing tours but became less popular as the practice of selling books in chapels came under increasing attack. Again, payment sometimes took the form of crediting the author's account with the publisher for the supply of other goods such as *Baner* subscriptions. Publishers found this most advantageous since the value of the goods was calculated at their retail price rather than the cost of production. When cash was paid, unless the sum was less than some ten to fifteen pounds it would be paid in instalments, which were generally linked to the supply of copy or to the progress of the book through the press.[39]

The rewards offered by publishers did little to promote the growth of professional authorship in Wales. Apart from a few journalists and one or two writers employed by publishers as office hacks (as R. J. Pryse, 'Gweirydd ap Rhys', was by Gee), authorship in nineteenth-century Wales remained a part-time activity, largely undertaken by the ever-growing band of Nonconformist ministers, educated men who enjoyed a modicum of leisure, who believed they had a duty to inform and enlighten their compatriots, and whose stipends generally failed to keep pace with the expenditure required by status. It was the values of these preacher-authors, bound by ties of friendship to the surprising number of preacher-publishers, that Welsh-language publications expressed. Contemporary observers rejoiced at this hegemony,[40] but the absence of 'infidel or immoral' works represented a narrowing of the scope of printed Welsh, and the exclusion of some potential authors. Not that publishers had any cause for concern: although works submitted to them might not always fully meet their requirements, they never experienced any general shortage of copy.

All type for books was set by hand at both offices throughout the nineteenth century. Gee acquired two Linotype machines in the mid-1890s but, as elsewhere in Britain, these were restricted to newspaper work. Both firms therefore required a considerable number of compositors, Gee employing ten to twelve on book- and jobbing-work in the 1860s, and a further eight or nine who concentrated on setting the *Baner*.[41] Hughes had many books set elsewhere. For much of the nineteenth century major London printers employed sufficient Welsh compositors to allow even manuscript copy to be set there satisfactorily.[42] Although setting Welsh was charged for at a higher rate as a 'foreign language' by London compositors, Hughes may have found this to be less of a drawback than did other Welsh publishers since, as it was unionized from the early 1860s (unlike Gee which was a non-union office as late as 1918),[43] its wages were comparatively high, 20 to 25% higher than in Rhuthun, for example.[44] Even so, as London prices rose, Hughes transferred work to low-wage Scottish printers, some of whom had come to employ Welsh compositors as a result of their forays into Welsh-language publishing from the 1850s onwards.[45]

Both offices used concurrent production to ensure a regular flow of work and maximize flexibility. Books which were not urgently required might be held back: setting a 206-page book, *Hanesiaeth a Gwyddoniaeth y Beibl yn Wir a Chywir* (*The historiography and science of the Bible true and accurate*), took over eighteen months, during five of which it was put aside to expedite more urgent work. On the other hand, Gee ensured that a 279-page biography of H. M. Stanley was ready in time to profit from the public enthusiasm inspired by the mendacious hero's wedding; by putting six compositors to work on it, the whole book was set between 19 February and 27 May 1890.[46] Most compositors in Gee's office were on individual piece rates rather than paid by time but there was some flexibility. This tended to favour the employer; when trade was dull in 1860, Hughes imposed piece rates on its compositors rather than the time rates hitherto in force, so that the hands, rather than their employers, experienced the full rigour of the recession.[47]

Two problems arose when setting Welsh material. Firstly, since Welsh letter-frequencies are very different from those of English, offices specializing in Welsh books had to order the correct proportions of each sort: thus when ordering 260 lbs of nonpareil type for *Almanac y Miloedd* from Miller and Richard in 1869, Hughes explained that the sorts were for a Welsh fount.[48] A second, far graver problem was that Welsh orthography was not officially standardized until 1928. Throughout the nineteenth century every author and each printing office used a different system of spelling. The problem was particularly acute when setting dictionaries and works of multiple authorship such as periodicals or encyclopaedias. As early as 1844 Gee's office employed a printed list of the approved spellings of 489 words which was revised and enlarged in 1853.[49] Gee supported attempts to establish an agreed orthography by publishing *Orgraph yr Iaith Gymraeg* (*Orthography of the Welsh language*) in 1859 and adopting many of its recommendations. Even so, the firm's orthography did not meet with the approval of all its authors: in 1881 Robert Ambrose Jones, 'Emrys ap Iwan', pointed out in his Welsh grammar that the orthography used was that of Gee's office rather than the one he himself favoured.[50]

Both offices made extensive use of stereotyping. Since type was expensive until the advent of the mechanical type-caster from mid-century onwards greatly reduced its price,[51] even large offices such as these attempted to minimize the amount of capital tied up in their stock of type. Work on the *Traethodydd* in the later 1840s was delayed because of a shortage of type[52] and Gee ran short of some sorts as late as 1858 because of the amount of type locked up in standing formes.[53] Stereotyping was of vital importance when books were published in parts since the earlier parts of a successful book had to be reprinted (perhaps repeatedly) for new subscribers and it would have been far too costly and inconvenient to keep so much material in standing type. Stereotyping also made possible the cheap and prompt reissue of successful books and facilitated the ambitious programme of reprints, in shilling parts, of popular works which Gee advertised in 1871.[54]

Gee set up a stereotype foundry using the plaster-of-Paris method in 1853-4, the plates (cast from the metal linings of old tea-chests) being stored in an isolated stone building at the rear of his premises where they would be safe from fire.[55] This was a vital precaution since his business could scarcely have survived the destruction of the plates. Hughes had also set up a foundry by the early 1860s, stereotype plates of books set in Wrexham being frequently sent elsewhere for printing. Stereotyping was also carried out for Hughes in London, Bungay, and Edinburgh. As early as 1865 Hughes was interested in having text electrotyped by Ballantyne, presumably because the process produced more durable plates.[56]

Although both firms initially made some use of locally produced paper, by mid-century both relied on English suppliers. Gee's sources are poorly documented but watermarks show that he obtained newsprint from James Wrigley of Bury in the late 1850s and early 1860s. Hughes made extensive use of the same firm for book-printing papers during the later 1860s and early 1870s but by the late 1880s tended to favour John Dickinson and Samuel Evans of Derby. Hughes was sufficiently large to deal directly with paper manufacturers rather than with wholesale stationers, normally ordering paper to be made to its own specifications.[57] It would usually make its own arrangements for the supply of paper when other firms printed books on its behalf, ordering, for instance, paper to be sent from Evans of Derby to Childs of Bungay.[58]

The wooden hand-press could, in theory, turn out in an hour about 250 sheets printed on one side. In practice its productivity was considerably lower.[59] Iron presses, used in a few Welsh offices before 1820 and increasingly common during the 1830s, did not increase productivity since make-ready took longer and the presses were more fatiguing to use.[60] Since Richard Hughes possessed an Albion in the early 1830s his office probably used an iron press from the start.[61] He later added another Albion and at least one Columbian press,[62] possibly reflecting contemporary printers' belief that each press had its own peculiar virtues.

As the demand for Welsh-language material increased, the larger printer-publishers found it necessary to invest in machinery. Since Thomas Gee had experienced considerable difficulty in producing 15,000 or more copies each month of *Y Geiniogwerth* in the late 1840s[63] and was planning an ambitious programme of publications, it is not surprising that he was the first Welsh printer to acquire steam-powered plant; two machines were in operation by March or April 1853, a few weeks before the first generally recognized use of machines in Wales by the Swansea newspaper, *The Cambrian*.[64] Hughes mechanized a few years later: by 1857 one steam-powered machine was in use to supplement three hand-presses.[65] Both offices then added to and upgraded their plant so that by 1860 Gee possessed four steam-powered printing machines and a folding machine, the latter being restricted to newspaper work because of its technical shortcomings.[66] Hughes disposed of its first double demy machine for £90 in 1863, probably installing a cylinder machine in its place.[67] A new demy platen machine costing £280 was added in 1869, but Hughes anticipated this would need to be supplemented almost immediately by a cylinder machine of the Wharfedale pattern.[68] Cylinder machines of this type proved to be sufficiently productive to meet the needs of Welsh printers for the remainder of the century.

Steam-powered machinery made possible considerable economies of scale as the unit-cost per copy decreased sharply for the first 10,000 copies printed.[69] Gee took full advantage of this by printing impressions of 10,000 to 12,000 copies of many titles so that, as insurance records reveal, printed sheets worth several thousand pounds were stored in various premises in Denbigh from the 1860s onwards.[70] The firm's attempt in 1903 to dispose of thousands of remainders, some dating from the late 1860s, suggests that the prospect of decreasing unit costs had frequently tempted Gee to print more copies than the market could absorb.[71] Because of storage problems, Hughes could not take full advantage of mechanization for Wrexham-printed books, its machine-room books indicating that it normally printed impressions of two or three thousand copies with frequent reprints from stereotype plates.[72] This is probably one reason why so few of the works it published between the early 1850s and the 1890s bear the date of publication on their title-pages.

Hughes contracted out much of its printing. In the early 1860s it used London firms, normally Clay Sons and Taylor, with a little work going to Clowes and to Eyre and Spottiswoode. Some sol-fa printing was entrusted to Childs of Bungay but, as metropolitan prices rose, Hughes turned to the Edinburgh firm of Ballantyne Hanson from April 1868 onwards, forming a link which was to last until 1916.[73] Hughes went to considerable lengths to conceal from purchasers the fact that non-Welsh printers were responsible for producing, for instance, the novels of Daniel Owen.

Since most Welsh-language books were intended for readers of limited means, many titles were offered for sale both in paper covers and cased. The difference in price was substantial: typically 1/- in wrappers, 1s. 6d. cased, or 2s. 6d. in wrappers, 3s. 6d. cased. Gee carried out its own edition binding at Denbigh, probably using cases purchased from specialist suppliers. Since all work was done by hand a substantial labour-force was required: in 1860 some fifteen women and girls were employed in the bindery.[74] The long history of Gee's firm provides a sequence of bindings which illustrate the various stages in the development of edition binding; from paper boards in the late 1820s to cloth with paper labels in the 1830s, cloth with gold-blocked spines in the 1840s, and subsequently an increasingly lavish use of gilt (and later ink) blocking on covers.

Although Hughes possessed its own busy bindery, its letter-books show that most of its London-printed books were cased by the leading trade binders of the capital such as James Burn and Straker and Son, and that Ballantyne normally cased those printed in Edinburgh. London firms also supplied cases for the books bound at Wrexham, often at very short notice, and by 1887 in response to orders placed by telegram.[75] No more than a few hundred copies at a time would usually be cased in order to minimize capital unproductively tied up in stocks of bound books. This practice generated very many minor binding variants and it is worth noting that Hughes would often order small batches of 100 to 250 cases in assorted (but unspecified) 'bright' colours.[76]

Charles Hughes maintained that the 'one great difficulty' of the Welsh book trade was 'the machinery of circulation', claiming that until the 1860s there was 'no machinery to bring the books within the reach of the people', so that his firm had had to 'create a class of people to sell our books'.[77] His experience of the English book trade may have induced him to exaggerate, but retail bookselling in Victorian Wales retained several primitive features. It was carried on by a variety of outlets, many of which still sold books as a sideline, although specialist booksellers' shops were becoming increasingly important. Despite the granting of 'long' (six months') credit, accounts were rarely settled when due. 'There is so much hanging back when the time of payment comes' complained Charles Hughes in 1863, observing on another occasion that 'the great difficulty [...] is not so much to sell the stock as get the money'.[78] Since — as the lengthy list of Welsh publishers' bankruptcies shows — success in publishing was based on balancing debt and credit, credit control was vitally important. Hughes systematically weeded out the worst risks during the later 1860s[79] and subsequently restricted credit to retailers who could provide satisfactory trade or bank references.[80]

By the 1860s booksellers were regularly visited by the travellers of the leading Welsh publishers. Joseph Roberts, for example, called twice a year on Hughes's behalf on every significant bookseller in Wales and in those English towns with large Welsh communities in order to publicize new books, receive orders, and attempt to collect debts.[81] An indication of the scale of his task is that in the 1860s Hughes sent parcels every three or four months to upwards of three hundred trade customers.[82] Robert Williams, Gee's clerk, similarly acted as traveller for that firm for over half a century.[83] The role of the traveller was so important that Charles Tudor Hughes himself attempted to undertake it in the early 1880s before his increasing deafness made it impossible for him to continue.[84]

Itinerant booksellers, typically picking up parcels of books at the nearest railway station, played an important part in the Welsh book trade to 1914.[85] Although many were honest and reliable, others displayed a marked aversion to settling their accounts with publishers and tended to vanish when threatened with legal action. Even when they paid their debts, they tended to demand exceptionally long credit. A further problem was their general reluctance to handle cheap books.[86]

Expensive books were sold in parts, largely through a network of *dosbarthwyr* (distributors), most of whom sold books as an ancillary occupation. As late as 1887 Charles Tudor Hughes claimed that seven out of ten copies of a biblical dictionary had been sold by *dosbarthwyr* rather than by booksellers.[87] Concessionary postal rates for printed matter and cheap clerical labour enabled publishers to maintain small accounts with men such as Evan Lloyd, a Corwen smith, who acted as a local distributor for Gee's publications during the 1860s, handling some four or five pounds' worth of books a year.[88]

By the mid-1880s the lack of a centralized wholesaling service for Welsh books was beginning to be regarded as a serious problem.[89] It was claimed that booksellers (particularly those in south Wales) found it so expensive and inconvenient to deal directly with individual publishers and were often so poorly informed about which titles were available that many had concluded that Welsh books were more trouble than they were worth.[90]

Both firms were keenly aware of the importance of publicity. As well as placing paid advertisements in periodicals, Gee could advertise twice-weekly in the *Baner* at no expense and Hughes made effective use of its music periodicals and of *Almanac y Miloedd*. New titles and special offers were also promoted by handbills and posters. Both firms regularly produced substantial catalogues of their publications from mid-century onwards in impressions of 5,000 or 10,000[91] to supplement press advertisements and catalogues bound into books. They also issued prospectuses, even for shilling and two-shilling books.[92] Some of these were intended for the trade but others were produced on such a large scale that they were clearly for the general public. Gee, for instance, printed 11,000 copies of a prospectus for the *Gwyddoniadur* in 1871.[93] Both firms went to considerable lengths to secure favourable notices of new books; Gee favoured complimentary copies to leaders of Welsh opinion, soliciting comments which could be (selectively) quoted in his advertisements.

Following several decades of prosperity both firms encountered increasingly adverse conditions during the 1890s. Although several of Gee's later ventures were expensive failures, Hughes appeared to be more aware of the new climate. As early as 1887 Charles Tudor Hughes warned Owen Evans (1829-1920), author of religious best-sellers such as *Oriau gyda'r Iesu* (*Hours with Jesus*), that 'the sale of volumes of sermons (be they ever so good) is at a minimum' and complained of the losses the firm had incurred by publishing such books.[94] Both firms reacted negatively to changing conditions by becoming increasingly reluctant to broaden their lists. It was, for instance, Isaac Foulkes of Liverpool who responded to the challenge of cheap reprint series of English classics by launching his shilling series, 'Cyfres y Ceinion' (The series of fine works), and in 1898 a threepenny series of Welsh classics, 'Y Clasuron Cymreig', widely advertised as containing the cheapest books in Welsh. The most imaginative response of all came from outside the book trade from the late 1880s onwards as O. M. Edwards began to publish periodicals and books designed to appeal to his idealized vision of the *Welsh gwerin* (common people). Although Hughes was associated with several of his publications, it was responding to his initiative rather than breaking new ground of its own accord. There was thus considerable justification for J. E. Southall's condemnation of Hughes in 1893 for being 'willing to run scarcely any risk' despite its wealth.[95] Well before 1914 both firms were complaining that the sale of Welsh books was steadily diminishing. From the early 1890s Hughes attempted to revive flagging sales by promoting special offers and cut-price parcels of remainders.[96] In 1903 Gee held a clearance sale.[97] By the first decade of the twentieth century even the largest Welsh publishers had come to believe that they were too small to risk launching new products in an increasingly hostile and unpredictable marketplace as educational and demographic developments eroded their hitherto captive monoglot Welsh readership.

NOTES TO CHAPTER 14

1. G. J. Williams, *Y wasg Gymraeg ddoe a heddiw* (Y Bala, 1970) and his 'Cyhoeddi llyfrau Cymraeg yn y bedwaredd ganrif ar bymtheg', *JWBS*, 9 (1958-65), 152-61. But c.f. Philip Henry Jones, 'A golden age reappraised: Welsh-language publishing in the nineteenth century', in *Images & texts: their production and distribution in the 18th and 19th centuries*, ed. Peter Isaac and Barry McKay (Winchester, 1997), pp. 121-41.
2. *Report of the Committee appointed to inquire into the condition of Intermediate and Higher Education in Wales and Monmouthshire: Vol. II, Minutes of evidence and appendices*, Parliamentary Papers, 1881, XXXIII, C. 3047 [= *Aberdare Evidence*], Q. 6281.
3. For Anglesey see Bedwyr Lewis Jones, *Argraffu a chyhoeddi ym Môn* ([Llangefni], 1976) and for Cardiganshire, David Jenkins, 'Braslun o hanes argraffu yn Sir Aberteifi', *JWBS*, 7 (1950-3), 174-92 (with English summary).
4. P. H. Jones, 'Cylchrediad *Y Faner*, ffeithiau a chwedlau', *Y Casglwr*, 28 (March 1986), 10-11.
5. NLW, MS 15517C, p. 9.
6. *Caneuon*: NLW, MS 15517C, pp. 50, 132, MS 15518c, fol. 13^r; *Yr Ail Gynnyg*: NLW, MS 15517C, p. 9, MS 15518C, fol. 86^v; *Y Trydydd Cynyg*: NLW, MS 15517C, p. 88, MS 15518C, fol. 28^r.
7. NLW, MS 15517C, p. 59, MS 15518C, fol. 16^r.
8. For the publications of Thomas Jones and the founding of his press see Idwal Jones, 'Thomas Jones o Ddinbych — awdur a chyhoeddwr', *JWBS*, 5 (1937-42), 137-209. The account given in S. I. Wicklen, 'The two Thomas Gees — a celebration', *TDHS*, 42 (1993), 91-102 is unreliable. For the incident of the bribed compositor, see Jonathan Jones, *Cofiant y Parch. Thomas Jones o Ddinbych* (Denbigh, 1897), p. 182.
9. The biography in the second edition of *Y Gwyddoniadur Cymreig*, X, 614B-614D, remains the most detailed account of Gee senior's career. His printer's certificate, dated 16 October 1813, is in Rhuthun, Denbighshire (formerly Clwyd) Record Office, BD/A/191.
10. T. Bassett, *Braslun o hanes Hughes a'i Fab, cyhoeddwyr, Wrecsam* (Oswestry, 1946), draws heavily on the obituary of Richard Hughes published in the *Wrexham Advertiser*, 21 Jan. 1871. A fuller study is now available in P. H. Jones, '"We only publish what we think will pay for publishing": agweddau ar hanes Hughes a'i Fab, Wrecsam, 1820-1920', *THSC*, ns, 3 (1997), 118-35 (pp. 118-23).
11. Welsh title-pages are frequently ambiguous, but the expression 'argraffedig ac ar werth gan' ('printed and sold by') generally indicates that the printer also acted as the publisher.
12. Pughe's diary, NLW, MS 13248B (Mysevin MS 28) chronicles his growing (and sometimes convivial) friendship with Gee.
13. T. Gwynn Jones, *Cofiant Thomas Gee* (Denbigh, 1913), pp. 130-4.
14. See, for instance, Brynley F. Roberts, 'Printing at Aberdare, 1854-1974', *The Library*, 5th ser., 33 (1978), 125-42 (pp. 139-41).
15. NLW, MS 8310D (Gee MS 6) (473), Thomas Gee senior to Thomas Gee junior, 8 June 1837.
16. NLW, MS 8310D (Gee MS 6) (474, 476), Thomas Gee senior to Thomas Gee junior, 9 July and 24 July 1837.
17. NLW, Thomas Gee MSS, O 1, Articles of agreement between Thomas Gee senior and Thomas Gee junior, 1 Feb. 1845, and appended receipts.
18. P. H. Jones, 'A nineteenth-century Welsh publisher: some aspects of the career of Thomas Gee (1815-98)' (unpublished Library Association Fellowship thesis, 1977), pp. 30, 130-5.
19. Main narrative sources are the obituaries in the *Wrexham Advertiser*, 27 March 1886, and *Bye-gones*, 31 March 1886, pp. 33-4.
20. Thus a review of the first volume of the *Gwyddoniadur* in the *Herald Cymraeg*, 21 June 1856, maintains that Gee deserved the highest place in the list of those who had served Wales by means of the press.
21. *Aberdare Evidence*, QQ. 6248, 6324.
22. Clarke is not included in the *DWB*. A brief (but not wholly accurate) account of his career is provided by Huw Williams, 'Y cyhoeddwr a anghofiwyd', *Y Casglwr*, 6 (Christmas 1978), 7.

[23] Bangor, UCNW, MS 3590 (83), Morris T. Williams to Dr Thomas Richards, 11 Sept. 1940.
[24] His obituary, *Baner ac Amserau Cymru*, 9 Dec. 1903, states that he had suffered from Bright's disease for many years.
[25] Bassett, pp. 48-52.
[26] Paper: NLW, Hughes and Son Donation 1958, Hughes letter-book 1862-73 (86), R Hughes & Son to G. McCorquodale & Co., 15 Dec. 1868; printing: (108[b]), R. Hughes & Son to Ballantyne & Co., 29 July 1869; casing: (96[b]), R. Hughes & Son to Ballantyne & Co., 3 March 1869.
[27] The uncertainty arises because of the problem of recognizing unacknowledged borrowings.
[28] 'You are the best judge of what [*Livestock of the farm*] may be worth to you' (NLW, Thomas Gee MSS P 48, R. O. Pringle to Thomas Gee, 17 Dec. 1874).
[29] When granting Gee the Welsh translation rights to D. L. Moody's *Addresses*, its English publisher hoped 'that the circulation of them in Wales may be blessed of God to many souls' (NLW, Thomas Gee MSS P 63, James C. Hawkins to Thomas Gee, 12 Aug. 1875).
[30] 'What do you want for your *Aelwyd*, if you will sell it cheap we may do something with it' (NLW, Hughes and Son Donation 1958, Hughes letter-book 1862-73 (28[b]), R. Hughes & Son to Griffith Jones, 23 July 1863). Jones was made bankrupt 1 June 1866 (*Typographic Advertiser*, 1 July 1866).
[31] For Clarke see NLW, Hughes and Son Donation 1958, Hughes letter-book 1862-73 (143-44), Hughes & Son to Ll. Adams, Rhuthun, 2 Aug. 1872; for Foulkes (misdated to 1878) see Charles Ashton, 'Llyfryddiaeth Gymreig [1811-99]' (unpublished bibliography in NLW), 1862, fol. 37.
[32] P. H. Jones, 'Thomas Gee and his authors', in *Studies in the provincial book trade of England, Scotland, and Wales before 1900: papers presented to the British Book Trade Index, seventh annual seminar [...] 1989*, ed. David Stoker (Aberystwyth, 1990), pp. 33-44 (p. 39).
[33] Jones, 'Thomas Gee and his authors', pp. 38-9.
[34] There is a valuable contemporary discussion of the problem in the introduction to R. J. Derfel, *Traethodau ac areithiau* (Bangor, 1864), pp. v-vi.
[35] NLW, Hughes and Son Donation 1958, Hughes letter-book 1862-73 (8), R. Hughes & Son to W. T. Thomas, 20 Sept. 1862.
[36] NLW, Hughes and Son Donation 1958, Hughes letter-book 1862-73 (48), R. Hughes & Son to Lewis Edwards, 30 Jan. 1865.
[37] NLW, Christopher Davies Deposit 1978, Hughes & Son copyright records book.
[38] Jones, 'Thomas Gee and his authors', p. 41.
[39] *Ibid.*, p. 42.
[40] Thus, for example, Thomas Rees, *Miscellaneous papers on subjects relating to Wales* (London and Swansea, 1867), pp. 34, 49.
[41] P. H. Jones, 'Ymweliad Y Gohebydd â swyddfa argraffu Thomas Gee, Awst 1860', *TDHS*, 40 (1991), 9-28 (pp. 16-17).
[42] NLW, Hughes and Son Donation 1958, Hughes letter-book 1862-73 (11), R. Hughes & Son to [Clay, Son & Taylor?], 11 Dec. 1862.
[43] NLW, Thomas Gee MSS P 249, Sir D. S. Davies to T. Hargreaves, 23 March 1918.
[44] NLW, Hughes and Son Donation 1958, Hughes letter-book 1862-73 (38 & 37), Charles Hughes to John Roberts, 'Ieuan Gwyllt', 7 April 1864.
[45] Thus W. Gwenlyn Evans and three other compositors from Caernarfon were employed by Ballantyne to set a Welsh Bible in the early 1870s (*CROB*, 3 (1970), 14).
[46] Jones, 'Ymweliad', p. 17.
[47] NLW, MS 12029C (ii) (J. T. Evans 40 (ii)) (178), 'William' to [O?] Evans, Llanrwst, 1 Dec. 1860.
[48] NLW, Hughes and Son Donation 1958, Hughes letter-book 1862-73 (113[b]), R. Hughes & Son to Miller and Richard, 16 Sept. 1869.
[49] NLW, MS 964E (i) (65), D. Silvan Evans to Thomas Stephens, 13 Jan. 1859, and (68), D. Silvan Evans to Thomas Stephens, 21 March 1859.
[50] R. Ambrose Jones, *Camrau mewn grammadeg Cymreig* (Denbigh, 1881), p. 150.
[51] P. Gaskell, *A new introduction to bibliography* (Oxford, 1972), pp. 207-8.
[52] NLW, Thomas Charles Edwards Collection, 1495, Thomas Gee to Lewis Edwards, 12 Nov. 1846.

53. NLW, MS 965E (i) (252), R. I. Pryse, 'Gweirydd ap Rhys', to Thomas Stephens, 14 Dec. 1858.
54. *Baner ac Amserau Cymru*, 1 March 1871.
55. Jones, 'Ymweliad', pp. 23-4.
56. NLW, Hughes and Son Donation 1958, Hughes letter-book 1862-73 (49), R. Hughes & Son to Ballantyne & Co., 21 March 1865.
57. See, for example, NLW, Hughes and Son Donation 1958, Hughes letter-book 1862-73 (116), R. Hughes & Son to Wrigley Son & Co., 14 Dec. 1869.
58. NLW, Hughes and Son Donation 1958, Hughes letter-book 1862-73 (63[b]), R. Hughes & Son to Childs & Son, 7 Sept 1867.
59. Gaskell, pp. 139-40.
60. *Ibid.*, pp. 198-200.
61. On several pieces of jobbing printing produced from 1834 onwards Hughes called his office the 'Albion Press', and had a 'double crown Albion to sell cheap' in 1855 (*Yr Amserau*, 30 May 1855).
62. In 1869 the firm attempted to part-exchange a double demy Columbian made by Clymer & Dixon in 1852 (No. 1520) (NLW, Hughes and Son Donation 1958, Hughes letter-book 1862-73 (93), R. Hughes & Son to William Dawson & Sons, Otley, 16 Feb. 1869).
63. 'I have 2 strong men and a Boy working until between 10 and 11 [every?] night at them [...] I have had one man knocked up already with the press' (NLW, Thomas Charles Edwards Collection (1496), Thomas Gee to Lewis Edwards, 8 Dec. 1846).
64. Jones, 'Ymweliad', p. 19. *Y Cronicl*, March 1853, p. 74, stated that Gee now used steam-powered machinery.
65. Pierce Owen, 'Rhuddenfab', *Y Geninen*, Gwyl Dewi 1922, 11-15 (p. 13); NLW, MS 12029C (ii) (J. T. Evans 40 (ii)) (174), 'William' to [O?] Evans, Llanrwst, 24 June 1858.
66. Jones, 'Ymweliad', pp. 19, 21.
67. NLW, Hughes and Son Donation 1958, Hughes letter-book 1862-73 (23), R. Hughes & Son to an unknown recipient, 5 May 1863.
68. NLW, Hughes and Son Donation 1958, Hughes letter-book 1862-73 (93), R. Hughes & Son to William Dawson & Sons, Otley, 16 Feb. 1869.
69. Gaskell, p. 304.
70. NLW, Thomas Gee MSS D 1-3.
71. *Baner ac Amserau Cymru*, 16 Sept. 1903.
72. Based on machine-room books, NLW, MSS 15517C and 15518C.
73. NLW, Hughes and Son Donation 1958, Hughes letter-book 1912-22 (304), Hughes & Son to Ballantyne, Hanson & Co., 20 March 1916, apparently marks the end of the link.
74. Jones, 'Ymweliad', pp. 12-13.
75. NLW, Hughes and Son Donation 1958, Hughes letter-book 1887 (76), Hughes & Son to Straker & Son, 6 July 1887.
76. NLW, Hughes and Son Donation 1958, Hughes letter-book 1862-73 (35), R. Hughes & Son to [James Burn?], 9 Jan. 1864, is a typical example.
77. *Aberdare Evidence*, Q. 6299.
78. 'Hanging back': NLW, Hughes and Son Donation 1958, Hughes letter-book 1862-73 (13), Charles Hughes to an unidentified recipient, 5 Jan. 1863; 'getting the money': (46), R. Hughes & Son to John Roberts, 'Ieuan Gwyllt', 6 Dec. 1864.
79. NLW, Hughes and Son Donation 1958, Hughes letter-book 1862-73 (13), Charles Hughes to an unidentified recipient, 5 Jan. 1863.
80. NLW, Hughes and Son Donation 1958, Hughes letter-book 1912-22 (219), Hughes & Son to T. B. Evans, Brynaman, 3 Dec. 1914.
81. NLW, Hughes and Son Donation 1958, Hughes letter-book 1862-73 (69[a] and 70), R. Hughes & Son to John Curwen, Plaistow, 2 Dec. 1867.
82. NLW, Hughes and Son Donation 1958, Hughes letter-book 1862-73 (13), Charles Hughes to an unidentified recipient, 5 Jan. 1863.
83. *Baner ac Amserau Cymru*, 25 Aug. 1943.

[84] Bassett, p. 47.
[85] *Ibid.*, p. 55.
[86] NLW, Hughes and Son Donation 1958, Hughes letter-book 1862-73 (69[a] and 70), R. Hughes & Son to John Curwen, Plaistow, 2 Dec. 1867; *Aberdare Evidence*, Q. 6286.
[87] NLW, Hughes and Son Donation 1958, Hughes letter-book 1887 (18), Charles Tudor Hughes to Thomas Thomas, 28 March 1887.
[88] Bangor, UCNW, MS 8468B.
[89] One of the first to articulate this view was Dan Isaac Davies in 1886 in a series of letters to *Baner ac Amserau Cymru*, the second of which was so critical of Welsh publishers that Gee insisted it be toned down before he agreed to its appearance (J. Elwyn Hughes, *Arloeswr dwyieithedd: Dan Isaac Davies 1839 - 1887* (Cardiff, 1984), pp. 56, 127-8).
[90] Thus W. Eilir Evans, 'Welsh publishing and bookselling', *The Library*, 7 (1895), 391-7 (pp. 396-7) and O. M. Edwards, *Cymru*, 35 (1908), 247, and *Cymru*, 45 (1913), 141.
[91] For example, Hughes printed 5,000 copies of a catalogue of its books in June 1877 and 10,000 copies in July 1886 (NLW, MS 15517C, pp. 87, 147).
[92] NLW, XBV 465 U55 contains an eight-page prospectus for four Hughes titles ranging in price from a shilling to five shillings.
[93] NLW, Thomas Gee MSS J 1 (Machine-room and piece book, 1868-77).
[94] NLW, Hughes and Son Donation 1958, Hughes letter-book 1887 (32), Hughes & Son to Owen Evans, 20 April 1887.
[95] J. E. Southall, *Wales and her language* (Newport, 1892), p. 307.
[96] Several special offers of this kind were advertised on the wrappers of *Y Cerddor* in January 1892.
[97] *Baner ac Amserau Cymru*, 16 Sept. 1903.

CHAPTER 15

SPURRELL OF CARMARTHEN

Richard E. Huws

THE death in November 1985 of Lt.-Col. Hugh William Spurrell terminated the association which four generations of the Spurrell family had enjoyed with west Wales for over two centuries.[1] Two of its members, William Spurrell (1813-89) and his son Walter Spurrell (1858-1934), were associated with a notable printing and publishing house at Carmarthen chiefly remembered today for its popular Welsh dictionaries which were so valued by several generations of schoolchildren, teachers, and scholars.

The family's roots can be traced to the Norfolk village of Sporle, near Swaffham, William de Sporle being admitted a freeman of Norwich in 1349.[2] A branch of the family later migrated to the West Country, finally settling at Bath during the early seventeenth century; Robert Spurrell, a schoolmaster, was the author of the first book printed in the city in 1730.[3] The first member of this branch to move to Wales was Robert's grandson, John Spurrell (1748-1801), who settled at Carmarthen during the last quarter of the eighteenth century to work as an auctioneer and to assist Sir William Mansell of Is-coed in managing his estate.[4] Like many of his contemporaries, Spurrell was attracted by the thriving economy of a busy commercial and administrative centre. The presence in Carmarthen of several master printers, notably the Scottish-born John Ross and also John Daniel, who had worked as one of the King's Printers in London, reflected the town's status as the principal centre of the book trade in eighteenth-century Wales.[5]

Richard Spurrell (1782-1847) was the third of six children born to John and his wife Sarah.[6] A magistrate's clerk, he lived in Quay Street, a fashionable quarter of the town and, as his diary shows,[7] enjoyed the acquaintance of a large circle of influential friends whom he met at local biddings, dances, and field-sport gatherings. On 13 September 1809 he married Elizabeth Thomas, the daughter of a local farmer. Eight children were born to the couple during the following fifteen years, including William Spurrell, the founder of the firm, who was born at 13 Quay Street on 13 July 1813.[8]

Until he was sixteen William received a sound education at Carmarthen's Queen Elizabeth Grammar School for Boys. Despite an attempt to persuade him to continue his studies to university level he decided to enter the printing trade and was apprenticed to John Powell Davies of 58 Lammas Street, Carmarthen, on 1 November 1830.[9] After completing four and a half years of his seven-year apprenticeship he left for London on 27 July 1835 in order to gain additional experience. He was to spend four years there, mainly at the printing office of Bradbury & Evans of Whitefriars, a large establishment which employed more than a hundred printers. During his stay in London Spurrell kept a detailed diary[10] which includes interesting references to the regular visits made by Charles Dickens to the office to review progress on printing his early novels. After completing his apprenticeship on 1 November 1837 Spurrell remained in London to gain additional experience as a journeyman printer.

William finally returned to Carmarthen in 1839, possibly because of the death of his mother. By the end of the year, he noted in his diary that he was richer than he had ever been, thanks to a substantial legacy from a wealthy great-aunt in Newcastle-upon-Tyne whose family had extensive mining interests in that area. This enabled him to purchase the plant and machinery necessary to establish his own office. In April 1840, having sought the advice of a printer in Llandeilo,[11] he acquired an Albion press and commenced trading in Lower Market Street (now Hall Street). He remained there until 1843 when he transferred to more spacious premises at 37-38 King Street which became the home of the press for over a century. Spurrell appears initially to have concentrated solely on jobbing printing, his larger pamphlets being printed for one of his many local competitors, Hannah White & Sons. However, soon after his move to King Street Spurrell rapidly established himself as a printer and bookbinder in his own right, supplementing his growing income from 1847 with an agency for the Experience Life Assurance Society.[12] From 1847 onwards he also ventured into the far more risky field of publishing, and by 1851 was employing five printers and two bookbinders.[13] As early as 1854 the increase in his output led Spurrell to invest in a Columbian press, which accommodated a larger sheet size than the Albion,[14] and by 1872 a second Columbian had been acquired. As well as binding books for local dignitaries and institutions, the firm cased its own publications until the increase in its output made it more economical to have its edition binding executed in London from about 1880 onwards.[15]

William, like his father, was a deeply religious man and a faithful communicant at the parish church of St Peter's, Carmarthen. He was acquainted with many clergymen in the diocese of St Davids and regarded Bishop Connop Thirlwall, who resided nearby at the Bishop's Palace in Abergwili, not only as a valued customer but also as a good friend. Spurrell's ecclesiastical connections brought him a steady trade in printing church accounts, leaflets, sermons, and hymnals, and provided him with a virtual monopoly in printing Anglican publications throughout west Wales. He later undertook the printing and publishing of two Anglican monthlies, *Yr Haul* (*The Sun*) from 1857 onwards and *Y Cyfaill Eglwysig* (*The Church Friend*) from 1862. As well as providing a steady income these periodicals were also useful vehicles for advertising new publications.

Since Spurrell was an accomplished — if self-taught — linguist, grammarian, and historian, he was well equipped to take advantage of the growing demand for Welsh reading material following the 1847 Blue Books. In 1847 he commenced publication of *A Dictionary of the Welsh language with English synonyms and explanations* in twelve sixpenny parts. This, like his complementary English-Welsh dictionary published in 1850, was primarily intended to assist the Welsh to master the English language, the key to worldly success. The popularity of these dictionaries — seven editions were issued before his death in 1889 — encouraged Spurrell to publish a range of titles designed to meet the demand for useful knowledge and self-improvement. Many of these, including Welsh and English primers, medical and agricultural handbooks, works on local history, and an anthology of English poetry with accompanying Welsh translations, were written or translated by Spurrell himself.[16] He also sought to promote Welsh literary culture by publishing new editions of standard classics such as *Y Ffydd Ddi-ffuant* by Charles Edwards, *Drych y Prif Oesoedd* by Theophilus Evans, and Ellis

Wynne's *Gweledigaethau y Bardd Cwsg*.[17] The most ambitious of Spurrell's scholarly publishing ventures was Daniel Silvan Evans's huge (and regrettably unfinished) Welsh dictionary, of which the first 420-page part, 'A to AWYS', appeared in 1887.[18]

Spurrell's interest in improving the techniques of printing and his regular contributions on a host of subjects to the *Printers' Register*[19] made him a familiar figure in English printing circles. He had a particular interest in the improvement of composition techniques, and contributed several constructive ideas to the lengthy contemporary discussion of type-case layout. He took an active part in the lively debate on type body-sizes which engaged the attention of nineteenth-century printers on both sides of the Atlantic, devised a formula for calculating the weight of type required for a given job, and appears to have been the first printer to have given serious thought to the problems of setting Welsh texts.[20] His innovative use of a gas-engine as early as 1872-3 to power his newly acquired Bremner printing machine was well in advance of the general adoption of gas power by printers in England.[21]

Walter Spurrell, the eighth of William Spurrell's thirteen children, assumed control of the family business following the death of his father.[22] Born in 1858, Walter was educated at the local grammar school, then at the Cathedral School at St Davids, and at Liverpool College before joining the family firm in 1876, where he served his apprenticeship under the watchful eye of his father. In January 1889, four months before the death of William Spurrell, he became a partner in the business, its imprint being changed to 'W. Spurrell & Son'.

With great determination, Walter Spurrell set about enhancing the growing reputation which the firm had enjoyed since 1840. He placed a high priority on ensuring that his plant and machinery were up to date, and soon acquired a Golding Jobber platen machine which improved his colour printing because of its advanced inking system. He was also one of the first printers in Wales to adopt the Monotype composing machine, which he had installed before 1909.[23] The introduction of the latest, electrically driven[24] Wharfedale printing machines ensured that his office was well prepared to meet the challenges which the opening decades of the twentieth century would provide. By 1900 Spurrell employed thirteen hands, many of them long-serving and very experienced craftsmen.

Unlike the majority of contemporary Welsh printers, Spurrell came under the influence of the revival in the craftsmanship of book production which was largely inspired by William Morris and his Kelmscott Press. Spurrell's adoption of recently revived techniques, notably the frequent use of colour on his title pages, further enhanced his firm's reputation for fine work. He was particularly interested in the design of his title-pages and is known to have frequently sought advice on their layout from Sydney Morse Brown, Principal of the Carmarthen School of Arts and Crafts.[25]

Walter Spurrell remained true to the family tradition, serving as a sidesman in St Peter's Church, and later as an elected member of the Governing Body of the Church in Wales. His ecclesiastical connections ensured that the firm's hold on the Anglican market remained as strong as ever,[26] while the resolution of the disestablishment controversy made it possible for it to penetrate the lucrative Nonconformist market for the first time during the 1920s. Walter's wide range of public activities and interests brought him into contact with many potential customers. He was more of a public figure than his father, being elected a town councillor at a young age and later serving three terms as mayor of Carmarthen. Other public offices included serving as a Justice of the Peace and as the governor of more than one school. He was a Freemason, played a leading role in the affairs of the local Conservative and Unionist Association, served as Chairman of the Carmarthen National Eisteddfod Music Committee in 1911, was a founder-member and Treasurer of the Carmarthenshire Antiquarian Society, and was an active member of the RSPCA. His interest in the printing trade led to his election as President of the Carmarthenshire Association of the Federation of Master Printers of Great Britain, and he served as a committee member of the South Wales and Monmouthshire Master Printers' Alliance from its inception in 1919.

Just as William Spurrell had successfully judged the mood of his age and taken advantage of its thirst for useful knowledge, so Walter, too, was fully aware of the commercial potentialities of the emergence of a strong cultural nationalist movement at the turn of the century. By 1910 the University of Wales, a National Museum, and a National Library had been established, and local and national societies dedicated to the study of local history, bibliography, archaeology, and genealogy, were being founded.

Taken together, these factors — a willingness to invest in new plant, inherited good will, a general climate of learning and scholarship, excellent typographic standards, and a continuation of the monopoly of Anglican printing — led to the creation of one of the leading publishing and printing houses in Wales. The University of Wales Press, the National Library of Wales, the Carmarthenshire Antiquarian Society, the West Wales Historical Records Society, and — perhaps most significantly — the Welsh Bibliographical Society were amongst the new customers who required a steady stream of works printed to exacting standards. The Spurrell dictionaries, revised by the Revd J. Bodvan Anwyl, were particularly profitable, the seventeen editions produced between 1914 and 1937 selling over 50,000 copies.[27] A Church hymnal, *Hymnau yr Eglwys*, achieved even higher sales, over 100,000 copies being sold between 1891 and 1927.[28]

By 1930 the House of Spurrell had reached its zenith. It was generally acknowledged to be the leading printer and publisher in south Wales, and in terms of craftsmanship could claim to be the finest commercial press in Wales. However, when Walter Spurrell pondered its future he had to conclude that his family's association with the press could not be prolonged much further. Now in his seventy-second year, he was beginning to contemplate semi-retirement. He had moved from living above the printing office to Carmarthen's fashionable Parade, and had taken a lengthy holiday in the United States in 1929.[29] As a result of his marriage in 1893 to an Englishwoman and because of contemporary middle-class prejudices, his three sons had been raised in total ignorance of Welsh culture and were encouraged to pursue careers outside the printing trade. The eldest, Hugh William Spurrell, had reached the rank of Colonel in the Somerset Light Infantry, and both other sons, Walter Roworth Spurrell and Ivor Pritchard Spurrell, had followed their uncle Dr Charles Spurrell into the medical profession. Thus when Walter Spurrell died suddenly on his way home from a Borough Council meeting in April 1934 his widow had no alternative but to dispose of the business.[30] The firm was largely a victim of the family's financial success; of English origin, the family had within two generations become fluent Welsh speakers only to lose, within another two generations, virtually any semblance of Welshness.

The firm was purchased by a wealthy local man (and fellow-Freemason), Captain J. W. Nicholas of Llandeilo, who vowed to keep the imprint 'W. Spurrell & Son' on all its publications. Nicholas had gained some experience of publishing as a journalist on the staff of *Country Life* after being invalided out of the army in 1924, but possessed no practical knowledge of the techniques and economics of printing. When he sought to delegate the administrative work previously handled by Walter Spurrell to Ernest Waters, his overseer and finest craftsman, serious problems arose and staff morale declined. By 1938 the totally demoralized Waters had resigned and his departure persuaded others to retire or seek employment elsewhere.[31] Nicholas was fully aware of these difficulties, but did not appear unduly concerned about their consequences. He made some attempt to improve staff relations by introducing a profit-sharing scheme,[32] but as the firm was by now almost wholly dependent on jobbing work the scheme's impact on wages was insignificant. The truth of the matter was that Nicholas was far too busy pursuing his ambition to enter Parliament to have sufficient time to attend to the firm. His involvement in local affairs — even his purchase of the firm of Spurrell — was largely designed to smooth his path towards this goal. Shortly after his adoption in 1938 as Conservative candidate for the Pembroke constituency[33] he bought a house in Tenby in order to devote more time to his electors. This inevitably meant that he could devote even less attention to the work of the printing office.

The outbreak of war in September 1939 added to the firm's difficulties. The workforce was depleted by military service, and management was entrusted to a new overseer, John Harries, when Nicholas enrolled in the Royal Pioneer Corps. Perhaps the most promising (but ultimately abortive) venture during 1941-2 was printing Welsh paperbacks for the innovative publisher, Llyfrau'r Dryw. Fresh problems arose following Nicholas's untimely death in June 1943.[34] His executors entrusted Harries, as general manager, with full responsibility for the day-to-day running of the printing office, the nature and extent of its workload being left to his personal judgement. The firm consequently attempted to survive on what were known as 'standing jobs', most of which were inherited from Walter Spurrell's era. This cautious policy of deliberately avoiding any risk of outlay in publishing at least ensured that the firm realized an annual trading profit from 1943 to 1957.[35] Although sufficient to pay occasional bonuses to the employees, these profits were not consistently high enough to permit any large-scale investment in new plant. However, it did prove possible to purchase a new S. W. 2 Demy 'Standard' Wharfedale in 1953.[36] The early 1950s also witnessed a few substantial jobbing orders; in 1952 and 1953 two lengthy biblical plays were printed for the Revd I. D. E. Thomas, and *The Story of Llandefaelog Parish*, an eighty-seven page local history, was undertaken for Ethel M. Davies.

As competition intensified, the firm's turnover gradually declined. The retirement of the experienced John Harries in 1953, after fourteen years as general manager, added to its difficulties.[37] From 1954 to 1957 Nicholas's son, John, his brother, Commander T. C. Nicholas, and the new manager, Ronald Davies, spent a great deal of time assessing the potential of the business. Having decided that its future was at best uncertain, Commander Nicholas negotiated its private transfer in the summer of 1957 to his acquaintance, the Narberth newspaper proprietor H. G. Walters, for an undisclosed sum.[38]

In acquiring W. Spurrell & Son, Walters was primarily interested in extending the sphere of influence of his existing business. Since his company owned a more modern printing office at Narberth he decided to sell the outmoded plant at Carmarthen. In October 1957 a sale of plant and machinery was held on the premises, and ten employees were made redundant.[39] The new proprietors maintained an office at 37 King Street to receive printing orders which, although executed at Narberth, continued to carry the Spurrell imprint. In 1960 the office was moved, first to Nott's Square and then to rented accommodation at 46 Lammas Street. The closure of the Lammas Street office in 1963 finally ended Spurrell's long association with Carmarthen.[40] The imprint 'Carmarthen: Printed by W. Spurrell & Son' survived for a further six years on a few items printed at Narberth, but was finally abandoned after 129 years in 1969 when Walters moved to new premises at Tenby and adopted the 'Five Arches Press' imprint.[41]

Walters sold the copyright of the Spurrell dictionaries to William Collins of Glasgow in 1960 for the seemingly generous sum of £500.[42] Collins immediately engaged Professor Henry Lewis of University College, Swansea, to revise the work and prepare what is now familiarly known as the *Collins-Spurrell Welsh Dictionary*. Total sales since 1960 have exceeded 500,000 copies, and continuing average annual sales of around 25,000[43] have justified investment in a revised edition, prepared by Dr David Thorne of St David's University College, Lampeter, and issued by Harper Collins in 1991.[44] This has been followed by the publication of a companion pocket dictionary in the Gem Series in 1992.[45] The continuing healthy sales and high profile which these dictionaries enjoy throughout the British Isles and beyond have ensured that although its presses have long been silent, the name of Spurrell is not forgotten.

NOTES TO CHAPTER 15

This study is largely based on research undertaken for 'A history of the House of Spurrell, Carmarthen, 1840-1969' (Library Association Fellowship thesis, 1981). Copies may be consulted at the National Library of Wales, Carmarthen Record Office, and the Library Association. A facsimile was published by University Microfilms International, Ann Arbor, MI, in 1985. Footnotes have been restricted to a minimum; readers who require further information are advised to consult the thesis.

[1] Obituary notices of Lt.-Col. H. W. Spurrell appeared in the *Cardigan and Tivy-Side Advertiser*, 29 Nov. and 6 Dec. 1985.

[2] Walter Rye, *Norfolk families* (Norwich, 1913), pp. 337-9. The surname Spurrell is still largely localized in East Anglia, the 1994 Norwich area telephone directory listing eleven Spurrell entries in its residential section.

[3] Robert Spurrell, *The elements of chronology: or, the calendar explained* (Bath, 1730). Apart from East Anglia, the Bath area still shows the greatest concentration of the Spurrell surname, the 1993 Bath & Swindon telephone directory including twenty-one entries in its residential section.

[4] NLW, Spurrell Family Papers, 16-18; (these papers, originally in the possession of Lt.-Col. H. W. Spurrell, were presented after his death to the National Library of Wales by his niece, Mrs Joan Kovats, London); NLW, Griffith Owen Papers, 3352 and 7512; NLW, Derwydd Documents, 415.

[5] 'Carmarthen and the book trade, 1720-1820' (unpublished typescript of an address by Eiluned Rees, delivered at Carmarthen, March 1976, to celebrate the opening of the new public library).

[6] Richard Spurrell, born at Bath 27 September 1782, was baptized at the age of 26 years 11 months at the parish church of St Peter's, Carmarthen, 11 September 1809.

[7] Carmarthen Record Office, CRO Museum 302.

[8] William was baptized at the parish church of St Peter's, Carmarthen, 4 August 1813.

[9] *W. Spurrell & Son, 1840-1940, by the Spurrell family* (Carmarthen, 1940), p. 4.

[10] 'Journal of William Spurrell, 1835-39' (in the possession of Mr A. Spurrell, Oundle, Northants).

[11] William Spurrell's 'Commonplace Book also Journal, January 1st 1840 — October 3rd, 1841 (1st year of Carmarthen Business)' (in the possession of Mr A. Spurrell, Oundle, Northants); the entry for 19 March 1840 records his visit to Llandeilo.

[12] *Carmarthen Journal*, 24 Sept. 1847; *Scammell's Directory* (Bristol, 1852), p. 56.

[13] Census Returns, 1851. PRO HO/107/2473.

[14] Beneath an illustration of the Columbian press, Spurrell's *Arweinydd i addysg* (1854) notes: 'Above you see a printing press like that which was used to print the book that you are now reading'.

[15] NLW, MS 1887C, 88b, 90c.

[16] *Arweinydd i addysg* (1854); *The rail road to learning* (1858); *Llyfr i ddechrau dysgu darllen* (1858); *Y meddyg rhad, neu lawlyfr iechyd* (1851); *Y ffermwr, neu hyfforddiadau yn egwyddorion amaethyddiaeth* (1848); *Carmarthen and its neighbourhood*, (1860 and 1879), and *Gems of English verse / Tlysau barddoniaeth Saesneg* (1853).

[17] *Drych y Prif Oesoedd*, first published by Spurrell in 1851 with the support of local and Anglican subscribers, sold well enough to reach a fourth edition in 1899.

[18] It was not until 1906 that the fifth and last part to be published, E-ENNYD, appeared.

[19] His contributions to the journal are summarized in his obituary, *Printers' Register*, 6 June 1889.

[20] *Printers' Register*, 6 Nov. 1868.

[21] *W. Spurrell & Son*, p. 8.

[22] *Carmarthen Journal*, 24 April 1889.

[23] NLW, Correspondence Files, Walter Spurrell to John Ballinger, Librarian, 14 July 1909.

[24] *Catalogue of the valuable letterpress printing and Monotype composing plant and machinery at 37 King Street, Carmarthen to be sold by auction, 22 October 1957*. Lot 257, a 2 h.p. electric motor, had been used to drive a new Wharfedale machine.

[25] Oral evidence supplied by Mr Cliff Harries, Carmarthen, who served his apprenticeship under Walter Spurrell from 1926 to 1931.

[26] The firm was fortunate that the Welsh Church Press Co., established at Lampeter in 1897, was never very successful and had to suspend printing operations in 1918.
[27] Figure based on the extensive correspondence between Walter Spurrell and the Revd J. Bodvan Anwyl, preserved in the Bodfan Collection at the National Library of Wales. Detailed citations are given in my thesis, Vol. I, 205-18.
[28] Figure based on information published in *Yr Haul*, Jan. 1895, July 1897, March 1898, and March 1899; *Y Cyfaill Eglwysig*, Christmas 1900; and sales figures quoted in the published catalogues of W. Spurrell & Son.
[29] NLW, Bodfan Papers, 1/1185-6, Walter Spurrell to J. Bodvan Anwyl, 16 Sept. and 5 Dec. 1929.
[30] Walter Spurrell had some four years earlier invited Anwyl to use his 'fertile and active brain' to assist him to find a successor, and had even entertained hopes that David Davies (1880-1944), 1st Baron Davies of Llandinam, might purchase the firm. (Bodfan Papers, 1/1192 Walter Spurrell to J. Bodvan Anwyl, 10 Dec. 1930). For Walter Spurrell's obituary notice, see *Carmarthen Journal*, 27 April 1934.
[31] Oral evidence provided by Miss Irene Nicholls, Carmarthen, who was employed as a shop assistant by W. Spurrell & Son from 1916 to 1919, and as manageress of the bookshop from 1919 to 1939. Her sister, Miss Agnes Nicholls, was also employed by Spurrell from 1916 to 1939 as a bookbinder. This version of events was also confirmed in oral evidence provided by Mr Elwyn Thomas, Cardiff, who joined Spurrell & Son as an apprentice in 1930 and worked as a clerk and finance officer with the firm until 1946 (Alun Treharne, 'Elwyn Thomas: un o gymeriadau gwreiddiol y byd cyhoeddi', *Llais Llyfrau*, Winter 1980, pp. 12-13).
[32] Oral evidence: Mr Elwyn Thomas.
[33] *Western Telegraph*, 28 April, 5 May 1938.
[34] *Carmarthen Journal*, 25 June 1943.
[35] Information supplied by Mr Tom Jones, Thatcher & Paine (Accountants), Carmarthen. This firm of chartered accountants was granted a rent-free room at 36, King Street, from 1943 to 1957 in return for keeping the accounts of W. Spurrell & Son in order.
[36] *Catalogue*, Lot 260 which is described as 'new late 1953'.
[37] For additional information on the contribution made by the overseers who served W. Spurrell & Son, see now Richard E. Huws, 'Spurrell of Carmarthen: the contribution of the overseers of the printing office', *CA*, 33 (1998), pp. 115-21.
[38] Information supplied by Mr H. G. Walters in a letter to the author dated 9 Aug. 1977 (NLW, Minor Deposits, 1552).
[39] Oral evidence: Mr Tom Jones; *Catalogue*; *Printers World*, 30 Oct. 1957, p. 457; *Carmarthen Journal*, 20 Sept. 1957.
[40] The exact date of closure has been difficult to establish, but no evidence has been found to suggest that the office was maintained after December 1960.
[41] Probably the last major item to bear the Spurrell imprint was Volume 5 of *The Carmarthenshire Antiquary: the Transactions of the Carmarthenshire Antiquarian Society and Field Club*, printed at Narberth by H. G. Walters and published in July 1969.
[42] Information supplied by Mrs Freda Walters in a letter to the author, 9 Aug. 1977 (NLW, Minor Deposits, 1552).
[43] Information supplied in letters to the author from Collins Publishers, 18 Jan. 1980, 23 July and 29 Aug. 1990 (NLW, Minor Deposits, 1552).
[44] *The Collins Spurrell Welsh dictionary*, new edn revised in collaboration with David A. Thorne and the Department of Welsh Language and Literature, St David's University College, Lampeter (London, 1991).
[45] *Collins Gem Welsh dictionary* (Glasgow, 1991).

CHAPTER 16

THE PERIODICAL PRESS TO 1914

Huw Walters

ALTHOUGH the Welsh almanacs published by Thomas Jones and others from the later seventeenth century onwards contained some literary material and can thus be regarded as the precursors of the Welsh-language periodical press, the growth and development of that press was a slow and painful process. When Lewis Morris published the first Welsh periodical, *Tlysau yr Hen Oesoedd* (*Gems of Past Ages*), at Holyhead in 1735, the Welsh gentry had become increasingly Anglicized, the old bardic tradition was a fading memory, and the nation's literary heritage was in jeopardy. Morris had hoped that the *Tlysau*, a 'Collection of our British Antiquities, on the best Subjects handled by the Antients',[1] would arouse the interest of his fellow countrymen in their language by providing entertaining literature and selections of Welsh classical poetry. But his venture was premature: because of lack of support only one issue of the magazine appeared.

A period of thirty years elapsed before the next attempt was made to establish a Welsh periodical. This was *Trysorfa Gwybodaeth, neu Eurgrawn Cymraeg* (*A Treasury of Knowledge, or Welsh Magazine*), fifteen fortnightly issues of which were printed by John Ross at Carmarthen between March and September 1770. Its editor and publisher, Josiah Rees of Gelli-gron (1744-1804), a Unitarian minister, claimed that its purpose was '*to divert and edify the Welsh, hoping to revive the splendid old language [...] by reforming our morals, and increasing knowledge amongst us*'.[2] Each number comprised four separately paginated sections: eight pages of Welsh history (the text of Brut y Tywysogyon), eight pages of miscellaneous essays, eight pages of verse, and eight pages of home and foreign news. At the end of the year, purchasers were expected to bind up the magazine into four volumes. Although the contents were varied and interesting, the Welsh reading public was unready for such an ambitious project, and after incurring debts of over a hundred pounds Rees was compelled to bring the periodical to an end. The first attempt, in 1773, to publish an English-language magazine in Wales was even less successful. Daniel Thomas of Llandovery printed only two issues of a monthly, *The Cambrian Magazine*, for what described itself as a 'Society of British Gentlemen'.[3]

During the 1790s, three periodicals were published which were notable for their controversial content. In February 1793 its editor, the Baptist minister Morgan John Rhys (1760-1804), published the first number of *Y Cylch-grawn Cynmraeg* (*The Welsh Magazine*). Rhys was a fervent advocate of reform. As well as supporting the French Revolution, which he regarded as part of God's plan for the overthrow of the Papacy, he advocated the adoption of William Owen Pughe's scheme for a 'reformed' Welsh orthography. He would have used Pughe's new letter-forms for his periodical had the type been available in time; as it was, his adoption of the spelling 'Cynmraeg' for 'Cymraeg' in its title indicated his adherence to Pughe's doctrines. Although neither Rhys's political nor his linguistic views were calculated to increase the periodical's success, it would appear that it was his opposition to Calvinism that caused most offence. As well as this controversial material the periodical contained poetry, biographical accounts, and the first book-review to appear in Welsh. As its radical nature became increasingly explicit, the printing of *Y Cylch-grawn Cynmraeg* had to be moved from Trefeca to Machynlleth and then to Carmarthen because of its printers' fear of prosecution; it has been claimed that Titus Evans of Machynlleth was dismissed from his post as an excise officer for printing the issue for August 1793. The failure of the periodical following the appearance of the fifth number for January-February 1794 is only partly attributable to its radical content: problems of distribution (particularly in north Wales) and in collecting payment from distributors sealed its fate.

In the summer of 1795 the first issue of *The Miscellaneous Repository, neu y Drysorfa Gymmysgedig* appeared from the press of John Ross at Carmarthen. Its editor, the weaver and Unitarian minister Thomas Evans, 'Tomos Glyn Cothi' (1764-1833), included translations from the writings of Joseph Priestley and other English reformers, as well as his own trenchant articles denouncing the slave trade and extolling the principles of the French Revolution. Only three numbers of this quarterly were published, possibly because of financial problems. It is also possible that pressure from the authorities compelled the editor or printer to abandon the venture. Like many of the radicals of the 1790s Evans was a marked man and was eventually imprisoned for two years in 1801-2 for sedition, his crime being the singing of a pro-French song.

Y Drysorfa Gymmysgedig was followed by the first Welsh-language monthly, *Y Geirgrawn* (*The Magazine*). This was edited by David Davies (d. 1807), an Independent minister at Holywell, and handsomely printed by William Minshull of Chester. Although it claimed that it was intended to enlighten the Welsh and preserve the Welsh language, *Y Geirgrawn* was, if anything, more audacious than either of its predecessors, possibly because of its links with radical members of the London-Welsh community. As well as publishing favourable accounts of the writings of Tom Paine, Davies ventured to include a Welsh translation of the 'Marseillaise' preceded by an inflammatory reference to the 'invincible' forces of France. After nine numbers had appeared between February and October 1796 *Y Geirgrawn* came to an abrupt end. There is nothing to suggest that it suffered from any financial difficulties, and in 1798 it was alleged that Davies had been coerced into giving it up:

> Certain Knaves (Scoundrels) took great care to frighten the man, and prevent him from proceeding with his task, and threatened to send him out of the country (as I have heard) for publishing beneficial things, namely that which struck at the root of Oppression.[4]

A new era commenced in the history of the Welsh language periodical press with the publication of the first number of *Trysorfa Ysprydol* (*Spiritual Treasury*) in April 1799. This sixpenny magazine, founded and edited by two of the leading Calvinistic Methodists of north Wales, Thomas Charles of Y Bala (1755-1814) and Thomas Jones of Denbigh (1756-1820), was the product of the eighteenth-century religious revival. The stated intention to publish a part every quarter was soon frustrated by the ill-health of both editors and no more than six numbers could be issued between 1799 and 1801. Thomas Charles revived the periodical in 1809 under the title *Trysorfa* (*Treasury*) and four volumes in all were issued between 1799 and 1827. Though not particularly successful — probably no more than six hundred copies of the first volume were sold, and Thomas Jones had to cover its losses — it set a standard which many subsequent denominational periodicals aspired to attain but all too often failed to achieve.

The other religious denominations soon realised the need for periodicals to spread their message, reinforce their group identity, and meet the demand for reading material created by the rapid expansion of Welsh Nonconformity and, more particularly, the growth of Sunday schools. The Welsh Wesleyans were the first denomination to publish a monthly, *Yr Eurgrawn Wesleyaidd* (*The Wesleyan Magazine*), which was founded in 1809 and took full advantage of the Wesleyans' well-developed system for distributing literature. Largely as a result of what they considered to be the unfair aspersions made against them by prominent Calvinistic Methodists, the Independents of north Wales launched their monthly, *Y Dysgedydd Crefyddol* (*The Religious Instructor*) in January 1822 following the publication of a trial number the previous November. Under Cadwaladr Jones, its editor until 1852, *Y Dysgedydd* expressed with increasing confidence the liberal values of Old Dissent by supporting the peace movement, the abolition of the slave trade, and parliamentary reform.

In 1818, Joseph Harris, 'Gomer', revived his failed newspaper of 1814-15, *Seren Gomer* (*The Star of Gomer*), as a fortnightly magazine of a patriotic and generally reformist nature.[5] He had anticipated the main objections to his periodical and had taken steps to forestall them. In particular, at a time of intense and acrimonious theological debate he successfully avoided any appearance of denominational bias so that *Seren Gomer* became a forum for virtually all the leading Welsh writers and scholars of the day. A highly gifted editor, Harris was in touch with the views of his readers and managed to retain their interest and good will. As a businessman Harris drew up strict terms for subscribers and distributors which overcame those financial problems which had bedevilled earlier Welsh periodicals. He thus ensured that the popularity of *Seren Gomer* — within a year between 1,500 and 2,000 copies were sold of each number — was translated into commercial success. *Seren Gomer* became the model for its many rivals and successors and ensured a place for Harris as one of the most important figures in the history of the Welsh periodical press.[6] Following Harris's death in 1825 *Seren Gomer* gradually became a Baptist publication, though it had no official connection with the denomination until 1880.

The success of *Seren Gomer* prompted the Chester printer and Calvinistic Methodist minister, John Parry (1775-1846), to launch *Goleuad Cymru* (*The Illuminator of Wales*) in 1818 as its north Wales counterpart. This was also a successful venture, but following the demise of the *Drysorfa* in 1827, Parry came under considerable pressure to wind up the *Goleuad* (which had committed the unpardonable sin of publishing contributions by non-Methodists) in favour of a new periodical under direct denominational control. This he did at the end of 1830, launching a new monthly, *Y Drysorfa* (*The Treasury*), in January 1831 which survived as the Calvinistic Methodists' official monthly until 1968. In 1847 the Unitarians founded *Yr Ymofynydd* (*The Inquirer*) as a monthly. Although it suffered several breaks in publication during the nineteenth century, it is now the only denominational magazine established before 1850 which is still published today.

Religious denominations also published a number of short-lived periodicals. Some, such as the Wesleyan Reform titles *Blaguryn y Diwygiad* (*The Bud of the Revival*) (1842) and *Gedeon* (*Gideon*) (1853-6), were the product of denominational disputes and schisms. Others were published on behalf of the smaller sects; between 1852 and 1858 the Campbellite Baptists published three Welsh periodicals — *Yr Hyfforddwr* (*The Guide*), *Yr Hyfforddiadur* (*The Directory*), and *Y Llusern* (*The Lamp*). Many other short-lived periodicals were intended for a local readership, such as *Trysorfa Grefyddol Gwent a Morganwg* (*The Religious Treasury of Gwent and Glamorgan*) (1838-9), *Cyfrinach y Bedyddwyr* (*The Baptists' Association*) (1827), *Y Golygydd* (*The Editor*) (1846-7), and *Y Tyst Apostolaidd* (*The Apostolic Witness*) (1846-51).

Welsh Nonconformists invested a great deal of money and energy in overseas missions, an activity reflected in the number of missionary periodicals which were published throughout the period. One of the earliest, *Cronicl Cenadol* (1818-23), a non-denominational monthly printed by John Evans at Carmarthen, published extracts from *The Missionary Chronicle*. Joshua Morgan Thomas of Cardigan edited and published two short-lived periodicals, *Brud Cenadawl* (1832) and *Brud Cenadol* (*The Missionary Chronicle*) (1839), which contained news of foreign missions and the activities of the Baptist Missionary Society.

Most denominations also supported the temperance movement. Established in the United States, the movement spread across the Atlantic and many Welsh temperance societies were formed from the mid-1830s onwards, partly in response to the cholera epidemic of 1832. Publishers who believed that the movement would create a demand for temperance literature in Welsh launched several teetotal periodicals, notably *Y Cymedrolwr* (*The Moderationist*) (1835-6), *Y Cerbyd Dirwestol* (*The Temperance Chariot*) (1837-8), and the Liverpool-published *Y Dirwestydd* (*The Abstainer*) (1836-9).[7] Despite the numerical strength of the movement and the enthusiasm of its supporters, it proved impossible to keep a purely temperance periodical alive for longer than a few years. Perhaps significantly, the longest-lived, *Yr Athraw* (*The Teacher*) (1836-44), offered its readers much more variety than its competitors by adding material of general interest to its accounts of temperance meetings, pledge-signings, and the horrible deaths of drunkards. Despite its laudable aims, the temperance movement aroused considerable controversy and was savagely attacked by *Yr Adolygydd* (*The Reviewer*) (1838-9), ostensibly for making total abstinence a 'new religion', but also because its editor, William Williams, 'Caledfryn', had personal scores to settle with several prominent teetotallers.

The United States was the birthplace of another influential movement, Mormonism, which found a firm foothold in various parts of Wales in the mid-nineteenth century. Dan Jones (1811-61), a native of Abergele, was captain of the Mississippi steamboat *The Maid of Iowa*. On one of its journeys between New Orleans and St Louis he met the brothers Joseph and Hyrum Smith, founders of the Church of Jesus Christ of Latter Day Saints. Jones soon joined the Mormons and visited Wales on several occasions as their missionary. As well as publishing Welsh tracts and pamphlets to disseminate their beliefs, he established two periodicals, *Prophwyd y Jubili* (*The Prophet of the Jubilee*) (1846-8), and *Udgorn Seion* (*The Trumpet of Zion*) (1849-62), both of which are of considerable importance in the early history of the Mormon Church.[8]

In the absence of Welsh-language newspapers, Welsh denominational magazines usually included several pages of domestic and foreign news culled from English papers.

Most of them also engaged in forceful political comment. Nonconformity had acquired a political identity in its struggles for equal rights, and the rising generation of Dissenting preachers, particularly Independents such as William Rees, 'Gwilym Hiraethog', William Williams, 'Caledfryn', David Rees, Samuel Roberts, 'S. R.', and Hugh Pugh of Mostyn, expressed a far more radical line in their journalism than did *Y Dysgedydd*. From 1835 onwards a monthly battle was waged between *Yr Haul* (*The Sun*), a Church and Tory magazine edited by David Owen, 'Brutus' (1795-1866), a brilliant satirist and polemical journalist of genius, and *Y Diwygiwr* (*The Reformer*), edited, printed, and published by the Independent minister David Rees of Llanelli (1801-69). It has been claimed, with some justification, that the ferocious debates between *Yr Haul* and *Y Diwygiwr* provided the main political education of the monoglot Welshman between 1835 and 1860.[9] In north Wales, the sixpenny monthly *Y Seren Ogleddol* (*The Northern Star*), published in Caernarfon in 1835-6, expressed stridently anti-Tory and anti-Church views and joined in the sport of baiting Brutus. Attacks on the Established Church (particularly over church rate and tithes) were also the *raison d'être* of *Tarian Rhyddid a Dymchwelydd Gormes* (*The Shield of Freedom and Overthrower of Oppression*), a short-lived monthly edited by Gwilym Hiraethog and Hugh Pugh in 1839. The Caernarfon-published *Cylchgrawn Rhyddid* (*The Magazine of Freedom*) (1840-2), technically not a journal but a stamped newspaper, served the growing body of Anti-Corn Law League supporters in north-west Wales by printing discussions of the Corn Law question and Welsh translations of League publications and circulars. The predominantly radical and Nonconformist alignment of the Welsh-language periodical press — what a correspondent of the *Times* reporting on the Rebecca disturbances in south Wales described as 'the pernicious agitation of dissenting preachers'[10] — was sufficiently obvious to cause concern in high places.

Welsh writers frequently deplored the fondness of their compatriots for strident and often acrimonious theological debates on issues such as the atonement, predestination, and infant baptism:

> *It is not fitting that such a belligerent attitude should manifest itself in the writings of religious people. They reproach and taunt one another in such controversies, and to a large extent lower the standards of the publications. It is a pity that people who profess religion should trample on one another in such a way.*[11]

Readers, however, greatly relished such controversies. Indeed, useful-knowledge periodicals which attempted to avoid religious debates found it very difficult to survive. In the early 1830s the Society for the Diffusion of Useful Knowledge decided to publish a Welsh monthly similar to *The Penny Magazine* which had proved so popular in England. An Anglican cleric, John Blackwell, 'Alun' (1797-1840), was appointed editor, and the first issue of *Cylchgrawn y Gymdeithas er Taenu Gwybodaeth Fuddiol* (*The Magazine of the Society for the Diffusion of Useful Knowledge*) was published by D. R. and William Rees at Llandovery in January 1834. Its primary aim was to impart all kinds of 'useful' knowledge to the common man while avoiding the denominational bickering prevalent in other periodicals. Despite containing many striking illustrations and engravings given to the publishers by the SDUK, the periodical failed after eighteen numbers.

William Rees claimed in his evidence to the 1847 Education Commissioners that *Y Cylchgrawn's* non-religious stance and secular content were a major factor in its rapid demise:

> In 1834 I started a Welsh monthly magazine called *Cylchgrawn* [...] on the same plan as the *Penny Magazine*, but published monthly at 6d. I continued it for 12 months, at a loss of £200. When I gave it up, it was continued by Mr Evans of Carmarthen for another six months; who also lost by it, and then it was abandoned. It wanted religious information, and consequently excited but little interest [...] The people have not been accustomed to think much upon any but religious topics.[12]

Its refusal to indulge in invective also helps to explain the limited popularity enjoyed by *Y Gwyliedydd* (*The Sentinel*), a sixpenny monthly published by a group of learned clergymen between 1822 and 1837. It contained articles on Welsh literature and antiquities which reflected the cultural interests of the *'hen bersoniaid llengar'* (old literary-minded parsons) as well as the scientific material favoured by its editor, Rowland Williams (1779-1854), rector of Ysgeifiog. Despite the quality of its content *Y Gwyliedydd* was never commercially viable, its monthly sales declining steadily from some 950 in 1823 to below 600 by 1831.

Some potential readers of *Y Gwyliedydd* may have been lost to *Y Gwladgarwr* (*The Patriot*), a similar monthly. In 1830, Evan Evans, 'Ieuan Glan Geirionydd' (1795-1855), the curate of Christleton (near Chester) and a noted literary figure, sought the support of the Welsh bishops in publishing a useful knowledge monthly based on *The Saturday Magazine*, an Anglican rival of the *Penny Magazine*. *Y Gwladgarwr* was launched as an ostensibly undenominational general-knowledge periodical at the beginning of 1833, but despite the range and excellence of its content and its use of illustrations, it lost money, and after three years Evans had to relinquish the post of editor. Despite various vicissitudes the periodical survived until mid-1841.

Material of a scientific nature, albeit generally on a superficial level, and usually translated or adapted from popular English works, appeared in several denominational periodicals. The mathematician Griffith Davies (1788-1855) published articles on popular science in *Seren Gomer, Yr Ymofynydd*, and *Lleuad yr Oes* (*The Moon of the Age*); John Williams, 'Corvinius' (1801-59), submitted several articles on anatomy to *Y Gwyliedydd*, and Jesse Conway Davies, a medical practitioner, made a significant contribution to various aspects of popular science in the pages of *Y Tyst Apostolaidd*.[13]

Despite the predominance of denominational literature, valiant attempts were also made by individuals to establish independent journals. In 1828 for example, Joseph Davies, a Liverpool lawyer, published eight numbers of *Y Brud a'r Sylwydd* (*The Chronicle and the Observer*), a bilingual monthly which was unconnected with any religious denomination. Davies was particularly interested in science, philosophy, and economics and by coining a number of new Welsh words to meet contemporary needs in theses fields he added considerably to the vocabulary of the language. More specialist periodicals of the same period include two very short-lived Welsh medical journals, *Y Meddyg Teuluaidd: The Family Physician* (1827), and *Y Cynghorydd Meddygol Dwyieithawg:*

The Duoglot Medical Adviser (1829). *Yr Amaethydd* (*The Farmer*), edited by Caledfryn, was published as a supplement to *The Carnarvon and Denbigh Herald* between January 1845 and October 1846. *Y Wawr* (*The Dawn*), fifteen monthly numbers of which were published at Cardiff under the editorship of Robert Parry, 'Robyn Ddu Eryri', between July 1850 and September 1851 was probably the most ambitious magazine of the period which devoted itself to scientific subjects.

The promotion of self-help among the Welsh working classes led to the establishment of 'sick clubs' or benefit societies in the 1830s and 1840s. The most popular of these friendly societies, the Independent Order of Odd Fellows and the Philanthropic Order of True Ivorites, both published their own short-lived monthly magazines, *Y Gwron Odyddol* (*The Odd Fellow's Hero*) (1840) and *Yr Odydd Cymreig* (*The Welsh Odd Fellow*) (1842). The True Ivorite Society took a very active part in promoting the Welsh language and culture, and supported several periodicals such as *Yr Iforydd* (*The Ivorite*) (1841-2), *Y Gwir Iforydd* (*The True Ivorite*) (1841-2), *Ifor Hael* (*Ivor the Bountiful*) (1850-1), and *Y Gwladgarwr* (*The Patriot*) (1851).

Although contemporary English-language periodicals — *The Cambro-Briton* (1819-22), *The Cambrian Quarterly Journal and Celtic Repertory* (1829-33), and the more ambitious and scholarly *Archaeologia Cambrensis* (1846+) — placed great emphasis on Welsh and Celtic antiquities, the monoglot Welshman had few magazines of a similar nature. *Trysorfa Rhyfeddodau a Hynodrwydd yr Oesoedd* (*A Treasury of Wonders and Peculiarities of the Ages*), published by Richard Jones of Dolgellau in 1833, contained historical notes and news of a sensational nature, but ceased publication after ten numbers. The cooper and self-taught antiquarian Owen Williams, 'Owain Gwyrfai' (1790-1874), enjoyed little success with his *Y Drysorfa Hynafiaethol* (*The Antiquarian Treasury*), only four numbers of which were published between 1838 and 1842. Historical and antiquarian periodicals in the Welsh language did not become popular until the second half of the nineteenth century.

The Welsh periodical press came of age in 1845 with the commencement of *Y Traethodydd* (*The Essayist*), a literary quarterly printed by Thomas Gee for its chief editor, Lewis Edwards, Principal of the Calvinistic Methodist Theological College at Y Bala.[14] As a young man, Edwards accidentally came across some issues of *Blackwood's Magazine* and felt a new world open up before him as he was introduced for the first time to the literature of England and Germany. He became henceforth an avid reader of the great English reviews and magazines and decided, probably as early as the 1830s, that a similar Welsh publication would play a key part in his schemes to broaden the intellectual horizons of his fellow countrymen and create a learned ministry. Edwards modelled *Y Traethodydd* on periodicals such as *The Edinburgh Review, Blackwood's Magazine,* and the *North British Review.* Its contents, a mixture of lengthy original articles, reviews, shorter notices of books, and a little poetry, reflected his own broad interests. As a Christian but non-sectarian periodical it attempted to emphasize the common ground between the various denominations. While earlier Welsh periodicals had been ready to print virtually anything which came to hand, Edwards attempted to rely upon experienced writers who might be depended upon to produce 'articles full of life and spirit and at the same time without spleen or malice'.[15] To reinforce *Y Traethodydd's* claim to be considered 'the highest court in the realm of Welsh literature'[16] it sought to add authority to its pronouncements by a policy of authorial anonymity. Despite its high price of 1s 6d, the limited size of its potential readership, widespread suspicion of secular reading, and the novelty of the venture, *Y Traethodydd* was remarkably successful. By the end of its first decade sales had settled at some 1,400 to 1,500 copies of each issue. It has survived all its English models, and still plays an important cultural role today.

Reaction to the Blue Books of 1847 largely shaped the educational and literary ethos in Wales during the second half of the century. As the Welsh people sought to convince themselves that they were as civilized and cultured as any other nation, education and general knowledge came to be regarded as the keys which opened the door to economic and social advancement and as the means of curing every social ill. These attitudes are clearly reflected in the output of the periodical press. A number of titles were established in the 1850s with the twofold aim of promoting general knowledge amongst ordinary working people and improving their morals. Eighteen issues of *Y Gwerinwr* (*The Peasant*), appeared in 1855-6 under the editorship of John Thomas (1821-92), a Congregationalist minister in Liverpool. Its wordy sub-title, *Athraw Misol, er Dyrchafiad Cymdeithasol, Meddyliol a Moesol y Dosbarth Gweithiol* (*Monthly Teacher for the Social, Mental and Moral Elevation of the Working Class*), clearly reveals its aims and purpose. *Charles o'r Bala* (1859), significantly named after Thomas Charles, the founder of the Welsh Sunday schools movement, was followed in 1860 by *Yr Aelwyd* (*The Hearth*). Both were edifying magazines which claimed to have the moral welfare of their readers at heart.

Religious periodicals remained important during the second half of the century. In particular there was a proliferation of expository and theological journals such as *Y Bugail* (*The Shepherd*) (1859-60), and *Y Symbylydd* (*The Encourager*) (1864-5), which were designed to provide ministers, preachers, and Sunday-school teachers with material for sermons and lessons. Although most religious magazines included sermons, a few were entirely devoted to material of this kind. One of the first was *Y Pregethwr* (*The Preacher*) (1841-2), a monthly edited by Roger Edwards of Mold, which published sermons by leading Calvinistic Methodist ministers. Despite the Welsh liking for lengthy sermons, virtually all sermon periodicals were short lived, the main exception being the undenominational *Pulpud Cymru* (*The Pulpit of Wales*), 264 monthly issues of which appeared between 1887 and 1908.

As in England, publication of a literary quarterly was regarded as a sign that a denomination had attained intellectual maturity. Although *Y Traethodydd* was not formally under the auspices of the Calvinistic Methodists, it was generally regarded as belonging to that denomination. The Congregationalists consequently established their own quarterly, *Yr Adolygydd* (*The Reviewer*), in 1850. Following its termination after the thirteenth issue in June 1853, it was resurrected as *Y Beirniad* (*The Critic*) in 1859. *Yr Adolygydd* and *Y Beirniad* were similar in content to *Y Traethodydd*, containing substantial articles on mining, agriculture, and geology as well as on literature and theology. The second and third series of *Seren Gomer* in mid-century imitated *Y Traethodydd* and *Y Beirniad* by publishing weighty essays, articles, and reviews.

The second half of the century witnessed the development of Welsh periodicals for specific groups. Periodicals for women, commencing with *Y Gymraes* (*The Welshwoman*) (1850-1) are discussed in Chapter 27, those for children and young people, commencing with the *Addysgydd* (*The Educator*) (1823) in Chapter 23, and music periodicals in Chapter 19. By the later 1870s even such an esoteric group as the supporters of Welsh shorthand had its own publication, *Y Phonographwr* (*The Phonographer*) (1878-80).

From the later 1850s onwards magazines of a lighter and more popular nature also began to appear. *Y Brython* (*The Briton*) (1858-63), edited by the learned cleric and lexicographer, Daniel Silvan Evans, though chiefly literary and antiquarian in content also included articles on folk literature, material hitherto ignored (or derided as mere superstition) by the denominational periodicals. *Golud yr Oes* (*The Wealth of the Age*), a popular monthly published in Caernarfon between 1862 and 1864 by the adventurous and innovative printer Hugh Humphreys (1817-96), was one of the century's most ambitious Welsh periodicals in its use of illustrations. Over a decade later, the penny monthly, *Y Darlunydd* (*The Illustrator*) (1876-9), placed particular emphasis on the large picture and accompanying biography of a prominent Welshman which appeared on the front of each number. Engravings and cartoons were also a very important feature of *Y Punch Cymraeg* (*The Welsh Punch*) (1858-64). Broadly based on the English *Punch*, it satirized everyone and everything in Wales. Like the weekly Welsh-language newspapers, many of the popular magazines included serialized novels, often translations or adaptations of moralistic or propagandist English and American fiction. In 1861 William Aubrey of Llannerch-y-medd ventured to established a short-lived penny monthly, *Y Nofelydd a Chydymaith y Teulu* (*The Novelist and Family Companion*), wholly devoted to improving fiction.

From the late 1850s onwards the eisteddfod became an important feature of Welsh cultural life, and several periodicals were established to publish successful poems and essays together with the adjudications. *Taliesin* (1859-61), edited by John Williams, 'Ab Ithel', was founded soon after the controversial Llangollen Eisteddfod of 1858. Eight numbers of its successor, *Yr Eisteddfod*, edited by William Williams, 'Creuddynfab', and John Prydderch Williams, 'Rhydderch o Fôn', were issued by Hughes and Son of Wrexham on behalf of the council of the eisteddfod's governing body between 1864 and 1866. The periodical (particularly the number which contained a Welsh translation of *Hamlet*) incurred considerable losses which had to be borne by Hughes since the council failed to reimburse the firm.

The last quarter of the nineteenth century witnessed the founding of several influential magazines, notably *Y Geninen* (*The Leek*) (1882-1923), a quarterly journal edited by John Thomas, 'Eifionydd' (1848-1922), an eccentric character who had once been employed at the printing office of Eyre and Spottiswoode in London and was one of the most experienced Welsh editors of his generation. Like the English monthly reviews, *Y Geninen* attempted to provide a forum for the discussion of literary, political, social, and religious issues. An annual supplement, *Y Geninen Eisteddfodol*, which was solely devoted to the successful entries at numerous local eisteddfodau, became exceptionally popular with poets in north and south Wales alike. Beriah Gwynfe Evans (1848-1927), subsequently managing editor of the Welsh National Press Company at Caernarfon, was another versatile and enthusiastic editor who established *Cyfaill yr Aelwyd* (*The Friend of the Hearth*) (1881-94), a popular illustrated monthly which published poetry, literature, and articles on science and current affairs.

Though many of these periodicals, especially the denominational journals, carried a great deal of political comment, the role of the political reformer had gradually been assumed by the vernacular newspaper press from the mid-1850s onwards. Nevertheless, a few political journals were published towards the end of the century, notably *Cymru Fydd* (*Future Wales*) (1888-91), a bilingual monthly serving the Welsh Liberal party, which demanded disestablishment, education, temperance, and land reform, and openly advocated political separatism. An even more radical monthly, *Cwrs y Byd* (*The Course of the World*) (1891-1903), founded by Ebenezer Rees at Ystalyfera enjoyed a wide circulation in the mining and tinplate areas of east Carmarthenshire and west Glamorgan. Edited by the redoubtable Evan Pan Jones (1834-1922) it advocated land reform, supported trade unionism, and published articles on socialism by R. J. Derfel and T. E. Nicholas.

Cymru (*Wales*) (1891-1927), a non-denominational monthly founded by O. M. Edwards (1858-1920), was perhaps the most successful and influential of all Welsh periodicals. Edwards's intention to immerse the Welsh in their history and culture by placing particular emphasis on national heroes, events, and authors (and thus counteract the 'British' ideology propagated by the state educational system) can be seen in his prefatory remarks to the first volume:

> *I believe that nothing will invigorate the Welshman's character as much as the knowledge of his own country's history; I believe that there is nothing equal to the Welshman's education as the knowledge of his own literature [...] What my colleagues and I intend to accomplish with Cymru is to trace the history of Wales, relate her traditions, give voice once again to her poets and men of letters, give her heroes their rightful place. And we will accomplish these things because the present age is the age of Wales's education [...] by restoring Wales to her rightful place we will strengthen the Welshman's character, purify his soul, nourish his genius, and enrich his life.*[17]

Edwards wrote a great deal of *Cymru* himself but also drew upon a growing body of contributors. *Cymru* offered many young writers who later became prominent literary figures their first opportunity to venture into print. Its pages were lavishly illustrated with pictures and photographs, some of the latter taken by O. M. Edwards himself, and its attractive layout showed an awareness of the new fluidity of page-design associated with late-nineteenth-century illustrated magazines. Other magazines established by O. M. Edwards included *Cymru'r Plant* (*The Children's Wales*) (1892+), *Y Llenor* (*The Man of Letters*) (1895-8), and *Heddyw* (*Today*) (1897). Apart from *Cymru* itself and the enormously popular *Cymru'r Plant*, which achieved sales of 11,500 a month in 1900, none of these enjoyed any great success, possibly because O. M. Edwards overestimated Welsh readers' readiness to tackle solid literary fare.

O. M. Edwards's *Wales* (1894-7), a short-lived English-language title intended to make the non-Welsh-speaking Welsh aware of their cultural heritage was no more successful than the earlier *Red Dragon* (1882-7), a self-styled 'National magazine for Wales' which had offered a mixture of light fiction, gossip, and antiquarianism, or *Young Wales* (1895-1904), and *Wales* (1911-14), both of which attempted to grapple with the major Welsh issues of the day. Their failure raises the question whether the market that they attempted to address — the English-speaker who was interested in Welsh Wales — actually existed.[18]

Most Welsh periodicals were edited by ministers of religion who belonged to (or had emerged from) the same social background as their working-class readers: '*When we look at Welsh literature, we can regard it as the literature of the working classes*' said one observer in 1865, '*It is entirely in the hands of the workers and Ministers of the Gospel, and most of those ministers have at one time been workers with literary interests.*'[19] Some ministers edited several magazines. Caledfryn, an Independent minister, edited no fewer than eleven periodicals between 1831 and his death in 1869, and the Calvinistic Methodist minister Owen Jones, 'Meudwy Môn', edited five between 1834 and 1866. Other ministers established their own printing presses, such as the Independent Josiah Thomas Jones (1799-1873), who printed at Caernarfon, Merthyr Tudful, Cowbridge, Carmarthen, and Aberdâr.

As well as the national publications issued by these printers, many periodicals of a purely local nature were published to serve parishes, churches, chapels, and the multifarious societies which had become such prominent features of nineteenth-century Welsh life. By the end of the century the Welsh-language periodical press could thus offer its readers a far more attractive and diverse range of reading material than was available in contemporary Welsh books.

NOTES TO CHAPTER 16

For a general discussion of the Welsh periodical press see Huw Walters, *Y Wasg gyfnodol Gymreig, 1735-1900 = The Welsh periodical press* (Aberystwyth, 1987). Welsh periodicals published between 1735 and 1900 are listed in Dot Jones, *Statistical evidence relating to the Welsh language 1801-1911* (Cardiff, 1998), pp. 499-510.

1. *Tlysau yr Hen Oesoedd*, p. 2.
2. 'Fe amcanwyd y gwaith hwn yn gystal er difyrwch ag er adeiladaeth i'r Cymry, gan ewyllysio adfywio'r hen iaith ardderchog [...] trwy ddiwygio moesau, a chynnyddu gwybodaeth yn ein plith' (*Trysorfa Gwybodaeth*, 15 Sept. 1770, sig. *P1[r]).
3. Ifano Jones, *A history of printing and printers in Wales to 1810* (Cardiff, 1925), pp. 91-2.
4. 'Ond fe gymmerodd rhyw *Gnafiaid*, (Dihirwyr) fawr ofal i ddychrynu y dyn, a'i rwystro i fyned ymlaen yn ei orchwyl, a bwgwth ei yrru i ffwrdd o'r wlâd (mal y clywais sôn) am iddo gyhoeddi pethau buddiol, sef yr hyn ag oedd yn taro at wreiddyn Gorthrymder' (Thomas Roberts, *Cwyn yn erbyn gorthrymder* (London, 1798), p. v).
5. Following the Six Acts of 1819 *Seren Gomer* had to be transformed from a threepenny fortnightly to a sixpenny monthly, gaining in the process paper wrappers carrying advertisements for books and other commodities.
6. Glanmor Williams, 'Gomer: "sylfaenydd ein llenyddiaeth gyfnodol"', in his *Grym tafodau tân; ysgrifau hanesyddol ar grefydd a diwylliant* (Llandysul, 1984), pp. 237-67.
7. Huw Walters, 'Y wasg gyfnodol Gymraeg a'r mudiad dirwest, 1835-1850', *NLWJ*, 28 (1993-4), 153-95.
8. Ronald D. Dennis, *Welsh Mormon writings from 1844 to 1862: a historical bibliography* (Provo, Utah, 1988), pp. 27-32, 72-9.
9. R. T. Jenkins, *Hanes Cymru yn y bedwaredd ganrif ar bymtheg* (Cardiff, 1933), p. 99.
10. *Times*, 26 Sept. 1843.
11. 'Nid yw yn weddus i yspryd o'r fath i ymddangos mewn ysgrifau crefyddwyr. Y maent trwy ddadlau, sathru ar eu gilydd, a dal ar wendidau y naill y llall yn iselhau y cyhoeddiad i raddau. Trueni yw meddwl fod crefyddwyr yn sathru cymaint ar eu gilydd' ('Dadleuaeth y misolion', *Y Drysorfa Gynnulleidfaol*, 7 (1849), 14).
12. *Reports of the Commissioners of Inquiry into the State of Education in Wales*, (London, 1847), I, 235.
13. The treatment of scientific subjects in the Welsh periodical press is examined in R. Elwyn Hughes, *Nid am un harddwch iaith: rhyddiaith gwyddoniaeth y bedwaredd ganrif ar bymtheg* (Cardiff, 1990).
14. J. E. Caerwyn Williams, 'Hanes *Y Traethodydd*', *Y Traethodydd*, 136 (1981), 34-49; and his 'Hanes cychwyn *Y Traethodydd*', *LlC*, 14 (1981-2), 111-42; Philip Henry Jones, '*Y Traethodydd* 1845-1995: ychydig o hanes masnachol y degawd cyntaf', *Y Traethodydd*, 150 (1995), 133-47.
15. Lewis Edwards to Morris Davies, 27 Nov. 1844, quoted in Thomas Charles Edwards, *Bywyd a llythyrau [...] Lewis Edwards* (Liverpool, 1901), p. 236.
16. Lewis Edwards to Morris Davies, 24 April 1846, quoted in Thomas Charles Edwards, p. 288.
17. 'Yr wyf yn credu nad oes dim a gryfha gymaint ar gymeriad Cymro a gwybod hanes ei wlad ei hun; yr wyf yn credu nad oes gystal moddion addysg i Gymro a'i lenyddiaeth ei hun [...] Amcan *Cymru* ydyw gwneyd yr ychydig allaf fi a'm cydweithwyr [...] i adrodd hanes Cymru, i adrodd ei thraddodiadau, i roddi llafar eto i'w beirdd a'i llenorion, i godi arwyr ein hen wlad yn ei hol. A gwnawn hyn oherwydd mai cyfnod addysg Cymru ydyw'r cyfnod hwn [...] trwy 'godi'r hen wlad yn ei hol' y rhoddir cryfder i gymeriad Cymro, purdeb i'w enaid, dysg i'w athrylith, a dedwyddwch i'w fywyd' ('Rhagymadrodd', *Cymru*, 1 (1891), [i]).
18. Brynley F. Roberts, 'Welsh periodicals: a survey', in *Investigating Victorian journalism*, ed. Laurel Brake, Aled Jones, and Lionel Madden (London, 1990), pp. 71-84 (pp. 81-4).
19. 'Ond pan yr edrychom ar lenyddiaeth Gymraeg, gellir ei galw yn llenyddiaeth y gweithwyr. Y mae yn hollol yn nwylaw y gweithwyr, a gweinidogion yr Efengyl, a'r gweinidogion hyny gan mwyaf wedi bod unwaith yn weithwyr llengar' (J. H. E[vans], 'Llenyddiaeth y gweithiwr', *Yr Eurgrawn Wesleyaidd*, 57 (1865), 19).

CHAPTER 17

THE NEWSPAPER PRESS IN WALES 1804—1945

Aled Jones

A curious anomaly afflicts the history of the newspaper press in Wales. Whilst individual titles and journalists from the late-Victorian 'golden age' have been regarded with awe and ascribed powers that approach the mythic, the growth and transformation of the Welsh newspaper press as a whole has over the years eluded systematic analysis. One reason for this relative neglect is that newspapers have, for far too long, been regarded as the poor relations of the book and the periodical. Thus, although the growth in Wales of an indigenous newspaper press made a crucially important contribution to the transformation of the country's economy and culture, it is important to begin this brief account by making reference to the newspaper's place in relation to the numerous other products of the printing press. Its connections with the book and the periodical, particularly in the nineteenth century, were close but complex. Firstly, each required the acquisition of much the same labour skills and technology to impress ink on multiple sheets of paper; secondly, it may be seen that in some cases the economy of book production was in some part cross-subsidized by the advertising income attracted by newspapers; and, thirdly, writers of books, periodicals, and newspapers required a similar range of literary ability and were dependent on the same high levels of literacy among their target readerships. But newspapers occupied a very different niche within the market for printed goods and thus within print culture. Regarded by one mid-Victorian commentator as the 'elemental form of modern literature',[1] the newspaper was not only torrential in its periodicity, cheap, and popularly accessible, but it also encapsulated a dazzling range of content. Within the one format, it combined text and illustration, prose and poetry, editorial and advertisement, 'fact' and fiction, criticism and counsel, news and opinion, topicality and matters of more general interest. In addition, it was believed to exert a powerful though largely unspecified influence over its readers, and, through them, over the moral and political behaviour of society at large. Even a brief historical account of the newspaper press in Wales from its origins to the end of the Second World War must, therefore, be sensitive to the many levels at which the newspaper was perceived in relation to the book and the periodical, and the ways in which its particular properties were defined and its purposes understood.

By the beginning of the nineteenth century the accretion of printing capacity in Wales had reached the point at which the proliferation of small printing businesses could provide a springboard for launching a nation-wide network of independent weekly newspapers, all save one in the English language. The *Cambrian* appeared in Swansea in 1804, and in 1807 the Chester firm of Broster extended its operations into north Wales and began to publish the *North Wales Gazette* at Bangor in January of the following year. In 1810 the *Carmarthen Journal* appeared in the town that had served as the cradle of printing in Wales. The first Welsh-language weekly, *Seren Gomer*, was founded in 1814 by a group of Swansea businessmen. Although it soon sold over two thousand copies a week, the paper had to be wound up in 1815, largely because of a general reluctance to place advertisements in a Welsh-language paper. The costly failure of *Seren Gomer* —the publisher lost a thousand pounds, if not more — may have discouraged the appearance of Welsh-language papers for two decades. Meanwhile several English-language titles, including the *Monmouthshire Merlin*, the *Welshman*, and the *Glamorgan, Monmouth and Brecon Gazette and Merthyr Guardian* were launched in the late 1820s and early 1830s.[2]

The early development of newspapers was constrained both by the state of the economy and by the law. The former was being transformed by the growth of industry and commerce, urbanization, and population growth, developments which shaped a society in which the services of journalism were in ever greater demand. But the law, on the other hand, remained hostile to a popular commercial press. As well as the perils of libel actions, fiscal burdens — the heavy duties on paper and advertisements, and a purchase tax on individual copies of weekly newspapers — rendered newspapers prohibitively expensive. These deeply unpopular 'taxes on knowledge' priced legal newspapers out of the reach of most potential buyers: in 1832, for example, a newspaper that cost its publisher threepence a copy to produce was legally required to pass on to its buyers an additional duty of fourpence per issue. Following a protracted political struggle, known as 'the War of the Unstamped', during which journalists and printers confronted the State and won a partial victory, the newspaper stamp was reduced to one penny in 1836.[3] The subsequent reorganization of the newspaper press in Britain posed new difficulties as well as fresh marketing opportunities. In Wales, however, the difficulties tended to be more severe, and the opportunities less tempting. Hugh Hughes, publisher of *Y Papyr Newydd Cymraeg* (*The Welsh Newspaper*) apologised to his readers for an increase in the price of his paper in 1836, attributing the necessity to do so to his failure to compete economically with 'English newspapers', which, while paying the same duties, could 'sell, or expect to sell, as much as ten times as we can ever expect to sell in Wales'.[4] Nevertheless, a number of new titles were launched in the post-1836 period of relatively light taxation, such as the innovative monthly, *Cronicl yr Oes* (*The Chronicle of the Age*), in 1835 and *Yr Amserau* (*The Times*) in 1843. Attempts to avoid stamp and advertising duty took a number of forms, including offshore publication. *Cronicl Cymru* (*The Chronicle of Wales*) was published weekly in Jersey in 1847, and in July of the following year production of *Yr Amserau* was transferred from Liverpool to Douglas on the Isle of Man to facilitate its transformation into a weekly. The passing of the Postage on Newspapers (Channel Islands) Act in August 1848 eventually withdrew the privilege of free postage from these islands and compelled the mainland newspapers printed there to close or to return to their places of origin.[5]

As these attempts at tax avoidance suggest, the much-publicized growth in the number of titles and production units in the period leading up to the reforms of mid-century concealed private histories of human endeavour, high aspiration, and dashed hope. Although for much of this period the newspaper was a highly experimental form of mass communication, it was anything but glamorous. Editing and publishing newspapers were exhausting and poorly paid tasks, and Hugh Hughes of *Y Papyr Newydd Cymraeg* voiced in March 1837 a view widely held among his peers that the physical and financial strains were too great and the returns too small to justify the continuation of titles such as his.[6] Yet, despite the poor pay and prospects, editors were increasingly required to be highly proficient at a number of complicated tasks, including the writing of leading articles, collecting and writing news items, correcting proofs, and keeping accurate accounts of labour and capital costs and of sales and advertisement income. All too often, at the end of an exhausting week, the editor would also supervise or personally carry out the composition and the printing of the newspaper, and arrange for its distribution. In the second half of the nineteenth century, a division of labour gradually led to the construction of more complex systems of management. This may be seen most clearly in the ways in which news was gathered. The basis of the news service of the early provincial press was the shameless quarrying of the London daily newspapers, both by the English-language weeklies and by the Welsh-language denominational periodicals which, in the absence of vernacular newspapers, provided their readers with pages of general news. Thus it was that the new Church monthly, *Yr Haul* (*The Sun*), contained in 1836, in addition to literary reviews, six and a half pages of Parliamentary and British political news as well as reports of robberies, murders, suicides, accidental deaths, poisonings, attacks of rabies, shipwrecks, religious news, and items of commercial interest such as a calendar of fairs and markets and a list of wool prices. There were also articles chronicling events in Ireland, France, Spain, Portugal, Germany, Greece, Tunisia, the West Indies, Egypt, the East Indies, South America, and Mexico. In time, more or less formal news agencies began to offer a more streamlined access to news items, although they did not wholly displace informal scissors-and-paste journalism. As early as November 1841, Hugh Jones, 'Erfyl', was asked by the editor of *Yr Athraw* (*The Teacher*) to provide him with a regular two-page compendium of home and foreign news at a cost of between two and sixpence and three shillings per page. In addition, Erfyl was asked to contribute items on Parliamentary news, reports of the Corn Laws controversy, and accounts of 'amazing accidents', and was given strict instructions as to how to avoid political bias in his reports.[7]

Patterns of newspaper production and methods of news gathering were eventually to be transformed by the repeal of the duty on newspaper advertisements in 1853, the abolition of the Newspaper Stamp Duty in 1855, and of import and excise duties on paper in 1861. These reforms ended the legal and political instabilities imposed by the newspaper taxes and created a free market for newspapers. The repeal of the newspaper stamp in July 1855 occurred at the height of the Crimean War, which provided a much needed opportunity for the now cheaper newspapers to satisfy the news-hunger of a rapidly growing readership. The dual impetus of legislative reform and war gave an enormous early boost to such papers as *Yr Herald Cymraeg* (*The Welsh Herald*) that had emerged in 1855, and convinced others that new markets were opening up for newspapers in both Welsh and English languages. Thomas Gee was only one entrepreneur among many who optimistically entered the field in the years immediately following 1855, launching his *Baner Cymru* (*Banner of Wales*) in March 1857 and the penny weekly *Udgorn y Bobl* (*The People's Trumpet*) a year later. A host of other newspapers embodying Liberal Nonconformity followed Gee's example, many of them identifying their editorial policies closely with the interests of specific denominations. *Y Goleuad* (*The Illuminator*), for example, was established independently by John Davies in 1869, but effectively remained a mouthpiece of the Calvinistic Methodists until they formalized the relationship by buying the title in 1914. The Independents, likewise, had direct access to the editors of *Y Tyst Cymreig* (*The Welsh Witness*) and *Y Celt* (*The Celt*), established in 1867 and 1881 respectively, as did the Baptists to *Seren Cymru*. Many copies of such 'denominational' newspapers were distributed by ministers, some of whom deftly side-stepped their own Sabbatarianism by selling their newspapers at Sunday services.[8] There can be no doubt that Nonconformity and an important section of the Welsh press powerfully reinforced one another in this manner, but it also rendered the press vulnerable to changes in the social patterns of devotion. When Liberal Nonconformity began to weaken in the early twentieth century, the commercial fragility of those newspapers which in better times had committed themselves to sectarian groups was to be cruelly exposed.

In the new commercial environment inaugurated in 1855, religious newspapers in particular were to come under fresh and sometimes unexpected pressures. One which combined an admixture of both money and morals was advertising. Prior to the fiscal reforms of mid-century, newspapers in Wales were vulnerable precisely because of the difficulties in acquiring sufficient advertising revenue to sustain them. The failure of the *Merthyr and Cardiff Chronicle* in 1837 was ascribed by its editor, W. E. Jones, 'Cawrdaf', to the political nature of the allocation of advertisements in the 'two towns whose organ we profess to be [where] all patronage [is] in the hands of our opponents. [We] had little to hope from the usual source of profit — advertisements [and] therefore mainly depended on our circulation.'[9] Following the liberalization of press legislation, however, advertising though now more plentiful, continued to raise serious ethical issues. In August 1891 the directors of *Y Tyst a'r Dydd* (*The Witness and the Day*) agreed that their printer, Joseph Williams of Merthyr, could, without consulting them, refuse to print any advertisement which he judged to be contrary to 'the character of the paper'.[10] The first issue of curiously titled *Ye Brython Cymreig* in January of the following year informed its readers that it would be easy for it to fill its pages with items advertising medicines, the occult, money lenders, and so forth, but that it had taken an editorial decision 'to stand or fall by not doing so'.[11] Such conflicts of interest between moral and commercial imperatives among some publishers reveal disturbing signs of the emergence of a two-tier newspaper industry in Wales. Whilst the newspapers at the lower level remained poor, bereft of adequate advertising revenue, and bound to the interests of specific religious or political formations, others were better able to take advantage of the new commercial opportunities after 1855 and to expand their consumer base accordingly. The distinction became even more apparent from the late 1860s, with the success of English-language dailies, first morning, and in due course also evening papers, particularly the *Western Mail* (1869+) and the *South Wales Daily News* (1872-1928), both launched in the rapidly growing port and financial centre of Cardiff.

Daily newspapers were also rendered increasingly viable by further improvements in systems of news gathering, developments which also vastly expanded the news coverage of many of the Welsh weeklies. The establishment of the Press Association in 1870, William Saunders's Central News Agency in 1871, and the National Press Agency in 1873 enabled provincial newspapers possessing few staff reporters outside their local areas to print an impressive range of news items and features. *Central News* and *National*

Press Journal were daily newspapers printed on one side of the paper only, so that they could be cut up and pasted in the pages of subscribing titles. Material was also supplied in the form of stereotype plates for the 'split printing' of newspapers. These plates, on which columns of text, advertisements, and pictorials had been pre-typeset at the agencies' foundries, when combined with columns of locally produced material, enabled editors to produce a newspaper of far greater variety and popular appeal than could otherwise have been possible. Evidence suggests that English-language newspapers in Wales drew heavily on these and other agencies. In February 1878, for example, Central News supplied the *Glamorgan Gazette* with the text of the Queen's Speech,[12] and regular payments were made to the same agency by the *North Wales Chronicle* for a variety of syndicated editorial material.[13] Despite such specialization, news gathering in Wales remained for the most part an essentially informal process, and as late as 1897 it was acknowledged that 'Welsh periodical literature, generally speaking, is the work of amateurs and the production of voluntary effort'.[14]

The dailies also began to distinguish themselves from the older weeklies by means of their formats and news-values. The development of more sophisticated hot-metal composing machines (above all the Linotype, used in Wales from the early 1890s onwards) and highly productive web-fed rotary printing machines enabled dailies to begin to target a more undifferentiated readership by introducing such English and American-inspired innovations as interviews, bold headlines, by-lines, and competitions. One aspect of this change was the professionalization of journalism. Hitherto, training had, in the main, been confined to editorial advice and directives delivered in a relatively *ad hoc* fashion, and reporting had been a trade learnt on the job. But the growing emphasis on commercial competition required newspapers continuously to outdo their rivals with regard to 'exclusive' news stories and features. Speed and novelty became essential considerations in both news gathering and modes of address. For newspapers to be able to report and interpret the world in their own particular ways required specialist staff, but the development of political journalism, for example, was impeded as much by structural obstacles as by the constraints imposed by distance from London. The affairs of the Lords and the Commons had been reported by Welsh newspapers continuously since 1804, but attempts to formalize the relationship between the Welsh dailies and the Houses of Parliament in the early 1890s met with only limited success. The entry of reporters into the Lobby of the Commons had been restricted in 1871, and further tightened after a bomb scare in 1884. The ensuing Lobby System excluded many provincial newspapers, and in 1892 David Duncan, proprietor of the *South Wales Daily News*, began a long campaign to gain admission to the privileged Parliamentary sanctum.[15]

Professionalization, in turn, affected the ways in which journalists in Wales saw themselves and the status of their work. Places were reserved for reporters in law courts, Inquiries and Commissions, meetings of voluntary associations, and local councils, the last being enshrined as a right in the Admission of the Press Act of 1908 thanks largely to the campaigning of Frank Mason, editor of the *Tenby Observer*. Individual editors and reporters were also assiduously courted by local and national politicians. But the journalist's self-image remained deeply individualistic, which in part explains the resistance to unionization. The Institute of Journalists, founded in 1884 as the

National Association of Journalists, made little progress in Wales, and it was not until August 1907, when the National Union of Journalists (NUJ) was registered as a trade union, that reporters began to exert effective collective pressure on newspaper managements. By 1911 the *South Wales Daily News* office was solidly unionized, but wages remained low in comparison with other professions, even with the manual trades. T. A. Davies, a founding member of the NUJ in Cardiff, ruefully informed the National Arbitration Tribunal that when his wage first reached forty-five shillings a week he was living next door to a docker who was reputedly earning £8 a week.[16] But even this minimal degree of organization was to provide journalists with a very different sense of themselves and their social worth. It signalled a shift away from the idea of journalism being a kind of moral crusade, and confirmed the status of the newspaper press as a branch of commerce where the principal commodities were information and entertainment.

Although the distinction between the moral and the commercial was never wholly to be eradicated, the processes which for half a century had conspired to drive an ever larger wedge between those newspapers whose managements had embraced commercialization and those whose approach had been more circumspect reached their terminus during the First World War. The war caused a radical disjunction in the history of the Welsh newspaper in three ways. Firstly, increased demand for foreign news favoured the dailies, which were also able to meet that demand more flexibly in the face of paper rationing, gas shortages, the scarcity of type-metal, and a reduction in advertising space; secondly, the politics of the war left many of the Nonconformist weeklies confused, exhausted, and very vulnerable to changes in the pattern of demand in a new and uncongenial environment. This had a particularly damaging effect on the Welsh-language newspapers. Finally, by 1914 the technological innovations which had led to the expansion of the press in the 1880s and 1890s had reached their maturity. Consequently, competition at the level of cover prices and advertising capacity enabled the publishers of daily and, to a lesser extent, high-circulation weekly newspapers — in other words, those papers which had established themselves most securely in the market by 1914 — to survive the pressures brought about by the war. Others could not, and the failure rate during or as a result of the war was spectacular.

For the dailies, however, the war appeared to offer an opportunity to regain the regional dominance they had briefly enjoyed before competition from the London press had intensified in the 1890s. In September 1914, the *Western Mail* was confident it could publish and distribute official announcements and other news at much shorter notice than its London-based rivals. Provincial papers were, however, subjected to the same degree of government censorship. In 1914 a Press Bureau and a Foreign Office News Department were established to provide the government with a means of channelling and co-ordinating war news, and between August 1914 and March 1915 a series of Defence of the Realm Acts were passed which were to have serious consequences for the press, as did the Defence-notices that began to be issued from 1915. Nevertheless, in spite of these material and military restrictions, Fred Hodson of the *Western Mail* was, at the outbreak of the war, optimistic that the country could not 'live without daily papers, however long the war will last',[17] and that mass bankruptcies and closures among the weeklies, the principal victims of the war, would further clear the field for the resurgence of a strengthened daily press when the war was over. Hodson was right, and, with retrospect, it can be seen that the widespread social habit of reading daily newspapers in Wales dates from the First World War.

One of the most important consequences of the war for the newspaper press was the concentration of its pattern of ownership. Whereas for most of the nineteenth century ownership had been highly diversified and localized, by 1918 it had become possible for a single individual, the Welsh coal-owner, D. A. Thomas, Viscount Rhondda, to gain a controlling interest in papers as different in their styles and locations as the *Western Mail*, the *South Wales Journal of Commerce*, *Y Faner*, the *North Wales Times*, *Y Tyst*, *Y Darian* (*The Shield*), the *Cambrian News*, the *Merthyr Express* and the *Pontypridd Observer*. These recently independent titles formed the basis of one of the largest newspaper empires Britain had ever known when transferred to the Merthyr-born Henry Seymour Berry. Berry, created Baron Buckland of Bwlch in 1926, was the first Welsh press baron. By incorporating his newspapers into larger industrial and financial interests associated with the south Wales coalfield he created a powerful media-industrial complex. Following his death in a riding accident in 1928, ownership of these and other titles passed into the hands of his two younger brothers, William Berry, ennobled as Lord Camrose in 1929, and Gomer Berry, ennobled as Viscount Kemsley in 1936, whose business partnership lasted until 1937. William Berry started his journalistic career as a fourteen-year-old apprentice at the *Merthyr Tydfil Times*, leaving Wales for London in 1898, and, with Gomer Berry, established the immensely profitable *Advertising World* a few years later. In 1915, the brothers acquired the *Sunday Times*, in 1919 the *Financial Times*, in 1920 the *Daily Graphic* and the Cassell publishing business, and in 1924 bought from Lord Rothermere the *Daily Dispatch*, the *Sporting and Evening Chronicle, and the Empire News*, through their holding company, Allied Newspapers Ltd.[18] One direct response to the rapid expansion of the Berry empire into the provincial press was the establishment in 1928 of Rothermere's Northcliffe Newspapers Ltd.

Turning once more to the lucrative south Wales market in 1928, William and Gomer Berry bought the Liberal newspapers of the Duncan family, consisting of the *South Wales Daily News*, the *South Wales Echo* and the *Cardiff Times*, and incorporated them into the Conservative-oriented *Western Mail*. The following year, by way of retaliation, Rothermere acquired both Swansea dailies, the *Cambria Daily Leader* and the *South Wales Daily Post*. Following an agreement between the Berrys and Rothermere in 1932, Rothermere abandoned his plans to take over the Cardiff press in return for the Berrys' recognition of south-west Wales as a Rothermere monopoly. But the conflict continued in the form of a circulation war involving myriad attempts to expand the readership and to attract readers away from other newspapers with offers of free insurance, prize competitions, lotteries, 'guessing competitions', and a variety of publicity stunts. The agreement between the Northcliffe and Allied companies in 1932 consolidated the control of the two media empires in Wales and strengthened the links between the major Welsh dailies and other British publishing firms. Western Mail Ltd, formed in 1896, thus by 1930 was linked not only with the Berry Group through Lords Buckland and Riddell, both of whom were directors of the *News of the World*, but also, again through Riddell, with George Newnes Ltd, and C. Arthur Pearson Ltd. By 1936 the Berry Group owned four British national papers, and forty-nine provincial newspapers including the *Western Mail*, the *South Wales Evening Express*, the *Weekly Mail*, and the *Cardiff Times*,[19] while the *Daily Mail* and *Daily Mirror* Group owned the *South Wales Daily Post* and the *Cambria Daily Leader*. In January 1937, the Berry newspaper empire was divided, Camrose taking the Amalgamated Press, with a capital of £6.2 million, and fifty-eight weekly papers, twenty-one monthlies, and a controlling interest in the *Financial Times* and the *Daily Telegraph*, and Kemsley taking Allied Newspapers (renamed Kemsley Newspapers in 1943) and the *Sunday Times*.

Among the more unfortunate consequences of the concentration of ownership was a marked reduction in the number and diversity of titles. The number of titles on the market at any one time, which had shown a continuous increase since 1855, began for the first time to fall sharply in the 1920s. Numbers fell from 152 in 1920 to 126 in 1940,[20] eighteen disappearing in the 1920s alone, and a further twelve in the 1940s, both immediate post-war periods. The ratio of Welsh-language titles was halved from 17% in 1914 to 8% in 1960. *Y Genedl Gymreig* (*The Welsh Nation*), for example, having failed to turn itself into a national Welsh newspaper, was incorporated into the *Herald* company in 1932, and by 1937 it was estimated that nearly 20% of all newspapers were operating at a deficit.[21] Furthermore, the absence of a north Wales daily newspaper strengthened the position of the *Liverpool Daily Post* in all parts of the north, among Welsh- as well as English-speaking readers. Despite these major structural changes in the newspaper economy in both north and south Wales in the inter-war years, the overall picture for the weekly press was not one of unrelieved gloom. An alternative, opposition press, based on a production model that resembled more closely the nineteenth-century sectarian newspapers than the dominant commercial papers, not only made an appearance but, in some circumstances, thrived. For example, locally produced socialist papers, principally associated with the South Wales Miners' Federation (SWMF), made a considerable impact on political life in the 1930s. The SWMF's two official journals, the *Colliery Workers' Magazine* (1923-7) and the *Miners' Monthly* (1934-9), were supplemented by such unofficial organs as the *Bedwas Rebel* in the early 1920s and the *Cwmtillery Searchlight*, associated with the Minority Movement, in the mid-1930s. The *South Wales Miner* ran from 1933 to 1935, edited and produced by Arthur Horner and others in the miners' Rank and File Movement, and was followed by the Communist Party's *Rhondda Vanguard* in 1935. The Labour Party continued its presence in the post-war Welsh press with *Y Dinesydd Cymreig* (*The Welsh Citizen*), which remained extant until 1924, and, in south Wales, with such papers as the *Rhondda Clarion* in the mid-1930s.

The Second World War reintroduced many of the restrictions that newspapers had first encountered between 1914 and 1918. Censorship returned in the form of the Emergency Powers (Defence) Act of 1940, and a Regional Office of the Chief Press Censor was promptly set up in Cardiff. Reporters and printers were conscripted into the armed forces, and newspapers had once again to learn how to survive lean times. The greatest difficulties were replacing plant and acquiring an adequate supply of newsprint. The Control of Paper Orders of 1940 and 1941 rationed the amount of paper a newspaper could consume, and in consequence paper consumption fell to little more than 20% of pre-war levels.[22] Newspapers also faced the dangers of aerial bombardment of their offices and plant. In 1941, Luftwaffe bombing twice prevented the production of the *Western Mail* and the *South Wales Echo* in Cardiff and the *South Wales Evening Post* in Swansea, and as a result production of all three was transferred to the presses of the *South Wales Evening Argus* in Newport. In an extraordinary gesture of home-front solidarity, the entire daily press of south Wales was, for a period, printed in the same building.

Wartime rationing of paper and other supplies continued in the years of austerity that followed 1945. Even in 1948, Paper Control Regulations imposed severe limitations on the supply of paper for new titles which effectively held their circulations to a ceiling of only four thousand copies per month. Publishers were also squeezed by the continuing pressure on advertising space, since advertisements were prohibited from exceeding 20% of the total printing space of any single title.[23] Furthermore, the cost of newsprint trebled between 1939 and 1962. The consequences of the war for the Welsh newspaper industry had become clear by 1948, by which time the numbers of both morning and evening daily papers had been halved since 1921, morning papers from two to one, and evening papers from four to two. The number of weekly titles in Wales (excluding Monmouthshire) had also been reduced from 106 in 1921 to 95 in 1937 and to 88 in 1947.[24]

Despite the economic strains of the previous half-century, there remained in Wales after the Second World War a newspaper press which the Royal Commission on the Press could describe in 1949 as 'still very numerous and of great variety'.[25] Weekly newspapers continued to be published in fifty-five towns throughout Wales, and as late as 1955 R. T. Jenkins could still savour the 'smells of paper and ink' in the streets of Caernarfon.[26] Circulations had once again been expanded by war, but, as in 1914-18, the Welsh newspaper press was once more placed at a disadvantage in the face of Fleet Street competition. In 1947 it was estimated that one hundred thousand copies a day of British national dailies were being delivered to Cardiff for distribution in south Wales.[27] In consequence, the balance struck in the nineteenth century between the Welsh and English languages, between the regional weeklies and the dailies, and between the relative share of the market enjoyed by newspapers produced in Wales and those imported from England, had each been irrevocably altered.

The technological, economic, and political considerations briefly described above have each powerfully influenced the newspaper's relations to other modes of communication within print culture over the past two centuries. In fact, so elusive is the paradigmatic Welsh newspaper that it is easier to search for a definition by contrasting it to other print forms than it is to describe its characteristics as a discrete medium. The fundamental distinction is that newspapers were regarded as being more accessible and interactive than either books or periodicals. The prospect of the unsolicited item — a snippet of local news, the report of a meeting, a letter, a poem, or a review — tantalized both impecunious editors and readers ambitious to see their names in print. Such amateur writing for newspapers, even to some extent after the professionalization of their reporting staffs, required no formal route to authorship and no initiation into a network of facilitators such as agents, publishers, or printers. The mediation of the editor was all that was required, and the editor, unlike the publisher of a book or the printer of a pamphlet, could, within limits set by the libel laws, take a degree of risk. An unsolicited item's quality, relevance, or even accuracy might be questionable, but the editor might reasonably calculate that its impact on the reader would be nuanced or counter-balanced by the range of other material, composed by a variety of writers in different registers, with which it was juxtaposed within the overall format. With some justification, then, the newspaper was regarded as being more socially permeable than the book, providing a more democratic, or at least a more diversified, social distribution of the status that accompanied authorship. The consequences of that permeability may be seen in virtually any copy of any Welsh newspaper, in which the abundant fruits of the voluntary labours of ministers, teachers, and skilled workers, the organic intelligentsia of nineteenth and early twentieth-century Wales, may be read. No doubt a proportion of the readers' letters were printed simply as inexpensive fillers (often following extensive correcting and editing) but they did have the advantage for the editor of covering a wide range of subject matter. They also generated fresh writing through critiques and rejoinders, in letter, article, fictional, or poetic form, often extending over several issues and across a number of different newspapers. W. Williams of Liverpool contributed some three hundred such unsolicited letters and articles a year to Welsh newspapers in the late 1870s,[28] and the hill farmer Richard Griffith (1861-1947) wrote prolifically for *Y Genedl Gymreig* as 'Carn', for *Baner ac Amserau Cymru* as 'Syr Rhisiart', and for *Yr Herald Cymraeg* as 'Carneddog'.[29] Writers such as these, amateur but erudite, brought a flavour of the unschooled and predominantly oral intellectual life of Wales to the pages of the newspaper press, and by so doing stamped it with their own versions of cultural authenticity.

Posterity's anomalous disregard for the majority of newspapers produced in Wales since 1804 may thus be explained, partially at least, in terms of their fragility. As business ventures, they were acutely vulnerable to a variety of changing economic and political circumstances, notably technological innovation, legislative reform, and war. But they were fragile also in another sense. Formats, contents, modes of address, even titles, were repeatedly revised, and the history of both the economies and the styles of newspapers reveals as many instances of sudden disjunctures as it does periods of smooth continuity. The notion of an evolutionary progression, in which the newspaper press gradually refined its style, expanded its range of content, and firmly established itself within a secure media market, is distinctly unhelpful. What complicates the newspaper's relationship with the book is that, as a medium of communication, the newspaper was continuously in a state of flux, and, as a result, its place in the constellation of other forms of print was constantly under revision. The newspaper of 1836 was not that of 1896, and was emphatically not that of 1945. The tensions that defined social relations in nineteenth and early twentieth-century Wales — the two languages, religion, gender, class, and politics — were mediated and represented in newspapers in a variety of ways and in changing proportions at different times. It is precisely the indeterminacy of the newspaper as a form of communication that makes the discussion of its social influence so problematic, and, ultimately perhaps, so sterile. It is conceivable that all that may be said in relation to its impact is that the newspaper press operated in contradictory ways on the societies that consumed it. Whilst individual titles signalled many levels of social difference, the accumulated consequences of the medium as a whole may have been to project a far more inclusive cultural consensus that went beyond the underpinning of an important but temporary Liberal and

Nonconformist hegemony at the end of the nineteenth century to the construction of national identities in a much more complex but durable form. It is perhaps this which J. Evans Owen had in mind in 1907 when he claimed that Welsh newspapers were 'strengthening the ties of our nationality'.[30] The tragedy for Wales, however, was that this process was never completed. Despite the extraordinarily prolific growth of the local press throughout the country in the period that spanned the 1850s to the end of the 1880s, no truly national newspaper emerged in the years of capitalist consolidation that followed. By 1918 it was too late. By the 1930s, the role of national medium had been appropriated by radio, and by the end of the Second World War the newspaper was obliged once again to re-orient, even re-invent, itself in relation to external pressures, most notably the looming challenge posed by television to its century and a half's dominance as a news medium. In 1945, the newspaper press in Wales was about to experience yet another difficult period of transition in a history punctuated by such discontinuities.

NOTES TO CHAPTER 17

For an overview of the period covered see Aled Gruffydd Jones, *Press, politics and society: a history of journalism in Wales* (Cardiff, 1993).

1. 'Popular literature — the periodical press', *Blackwood's Edinburgh Magazine,* (February 1859), p. 181.
2. For a fuller list of newspapers and their dates, consult *Newsplan: report of the Newsplan project in Wales* (London and Aberystwyth, 1993).
3. For an account of this conflict, see Joel H. Wiener, *The War of the Unstamped* (Ithaca, 1969), and P. Hollis, *The pauper press: a study in working class radicalism of the 1830s* (Oxford, 1970).
4. *Y Papyr Newydd Cymraeg*, 5 Oct. 1836.
5. Philip Henry Jones, 'Yr Amserau: the first decade 1843-52', in *Investigating Victorian journalism,* ed. Laurel Brake, Aled Jones, and Lionel Madden (London, 1990), pp. 85-103 (pp. 91-3).
6. *Y Papyr Newydd Cymraeg,* 8 March 1837.
7. NLW, MS 9030E, H. Gwalchmai to Hugh Jones, 27 Nov. 1841.
8. Sian Rhiannon Williams, 'Rhai agweddau cymdeithasol ar hanes yr iaith Gymraeg yn ardal ddiwydiannol Sir Fynwy yn y bedwaredd ganrif ar bymtheg' (unpublished doctoral thesis, University of Wales, Aberystwyth, 1985), p. 282.
9. *Merthyr and Cardiff Chronicle*, 16 Dec. 1837.
10. NLW, MS 8842D, *Y Tyst a'r Dydd* papers.
11. *Ye Brython Cymreig,* 1 Jan. 1891.
12. Cardiff, Glamorgan Record Office, *Glamorgan Gazette* Letter Book, Hemming to Saunders, 12 Feb. 1878.
13. Caernarfon, Gwynedd Archive Service, NWC1, Cash Balances, *North Wales Chronicle*, 1886, 1887.
14. *Journalist and Newspaper Proprietor*, 6 Nov. 1897.
15. NLW, T. E. Ellis Collection, 378, David Duncan to Sir Edward Reed, 14 March 1892.
16. H. C. Strick, 'British newspaper journalism, 1900-1956: a study in industrial relations' (unpublished doctoral thesis, University of London, 1957), pp. 248-54.
17. Picton Davies, *Atgofion dyn papur newydd* (Liverpool, 1962), p. 132.
18. Brief biographies of the Berry brothers are provided in *Dictionary of business history,* ed. David J. Jeremy, (London, 1984-6), I, 299-309.
19. Jane Soames, *The English press: newspapers and news* (London, 1936), pp. 53-5.
20. Figures abstracted from Mitchell's and Benn's *Press directories* for the period 1914 to 1960.
21. UCNW, Bangor, MS 16009; Stephen A. Koss, *The rise and fall of the political press in Britain* (London, 1984), II, 559.
22. Leonard Fletcher, *They never failed: the story of the provincial press in wartime* (London, 1946), pp. 11-13.
23. The Labour Party, *Your own journal: a guide for Labour Parties* (London, 1948), p. 1.
24. *Report of the Royal Commission on the Press 1947-1949* (London, 1949), p. 89.
25. *Ibid.*, p. 9.
26. R. T. Jenkins, 'Edward Morgan Humphreys 1882-1955', *Y Traethodydd,* 3rd series, 23 (1955), 156-67 (160).
27. *Newsprint 1939-1949. The crisis of the British press,* supplement to *Report of the Royal Commission on the Press* (London, 1949), p. 18.
28. NLW, MS 4613A.
29. E. Namora Williams, *Carneddog a'i deulu* (Denbigh, 1985), pp. 60-1. The work of Bob Owen, Croesor, is discussed in Dyfed Evans, *Bywyd Bob Owen* (Caernarfon, 1977), p. 85.
30. J. Evans Owen, 'The Welsh newspaper', in *Wales today and tomorrow,* ed. T. Stephens (Cardiff, 1907), pp. 340-4 (p. 344).

1   Mid-sixth-century stone bearing Latin and ogam inscriptions commemorating Vortipor. (© *Crown copyright: RCAHMW (NMRW)*).

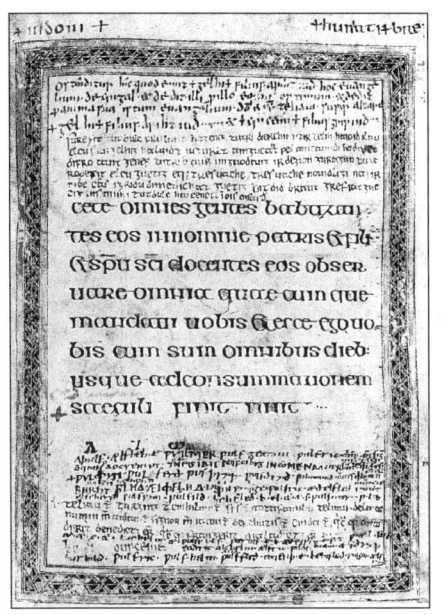

2   The page from the Lichfield Gospels containing the 'Surexit' memorandum. The earliest surviving example (other than isolated words) of Welsh written in a book, the memorandum was added about 800 AD.

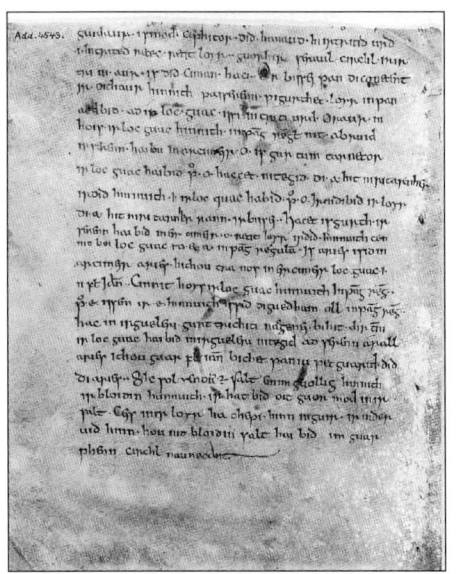

3   A page from the early-tenth-century Welsh Computus fragment, Cambridge University Library, Add. 4543.

4   An inscribed slate from Strata Florida bearing accounts in Welsh.

5   Gilt-bronze figure of Christ in Majesty from the lower cover of the Book of Llandaf (NLW MS 17110E). The oak board beneath the figure, once covered in metal, is probably one of the original boards.

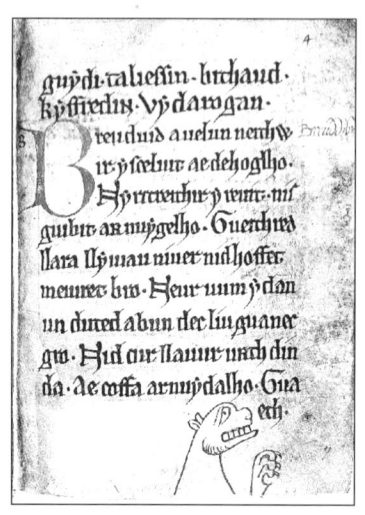

6   A page from the mid-thirteenth-century Black Book of Carmarthen (NLW, Peniarth MS 1, fol.4^r), the earliest collection of Welsh poetry.

7   Illustration of the court judge in his chair, a lawbook in his hand, from NLW, Peniarth MS 28, fol. 4ʳ.

8   Late-fourteenth-century full-page miniature of the Trinity, perhaps the work of a Caernarfon illuminator, from the Llanbeblig Hours, NLW MS 17520A, fol 4ᵛ.

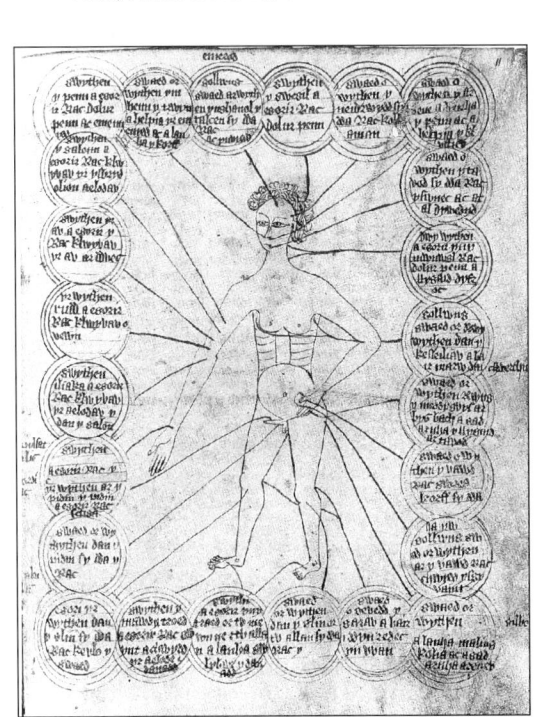

9   A medical drawing in the hand of Gutun Owain from NLW MS 3026C (Mostyn MS 88), p. 26.

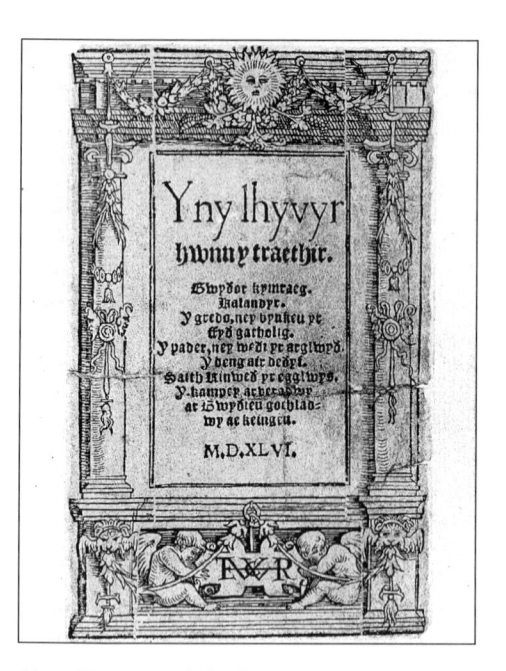

10   Title-page of *Yny lhyvyr hwnn* (1546), the first printed book in the Welsh language.

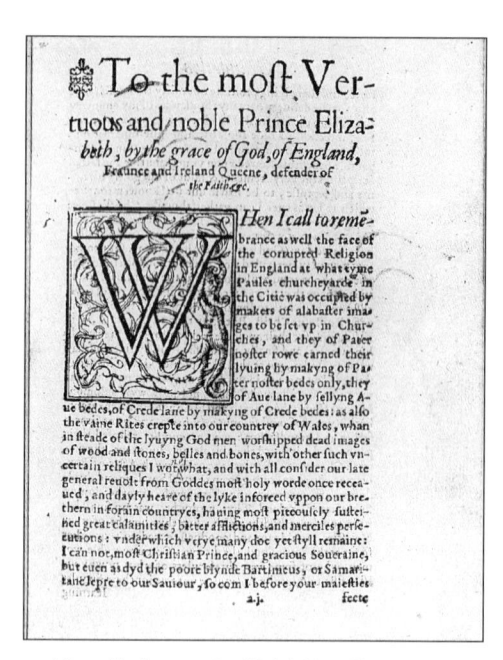

11   Preface to the Welsh New Testament of 1567.

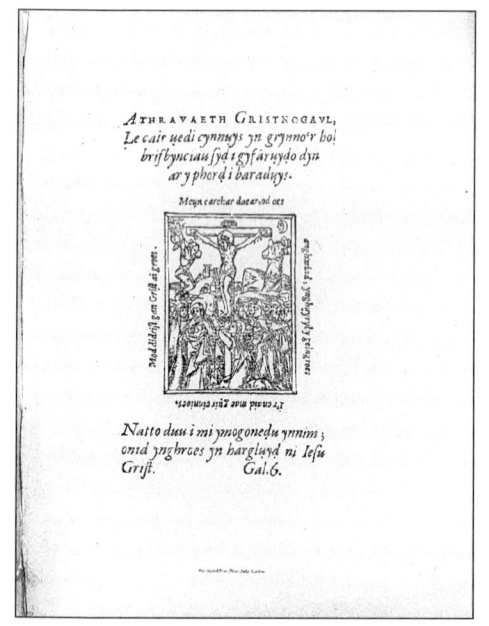

12   Facsimile of the title-page of *Athravaeth Gristnogavl* (Milan, 1568).

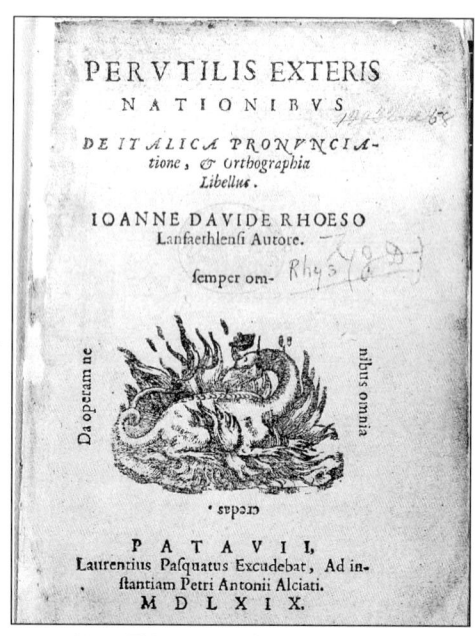

13   Title-page of Sion Dafydd Rhys, *Perutilis Exteris Nationibus De Italica Pronunciatione et Orthographia Libellus* (Padua, 1569). (BL shelfmark C117a54).

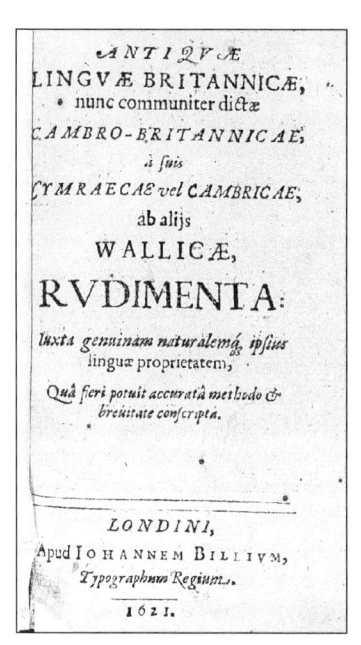

14   Title-page of John Davies, *Antiquae linguae Britannicae [...] Rudimenta* (London, 1621).

15   Portrait of Lewis Morris by an unknown painter.

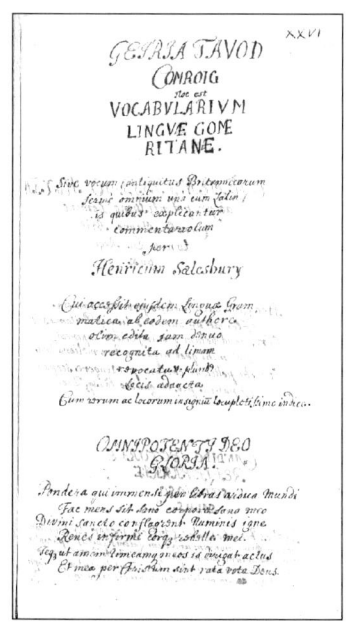

16   Title-page prepared by Henry Salesbury for his unpublished dictionary, 'Geiria Tavod Comroig', NLW MS 13215E, p. 315.

17 Printing in Wales before 1820.

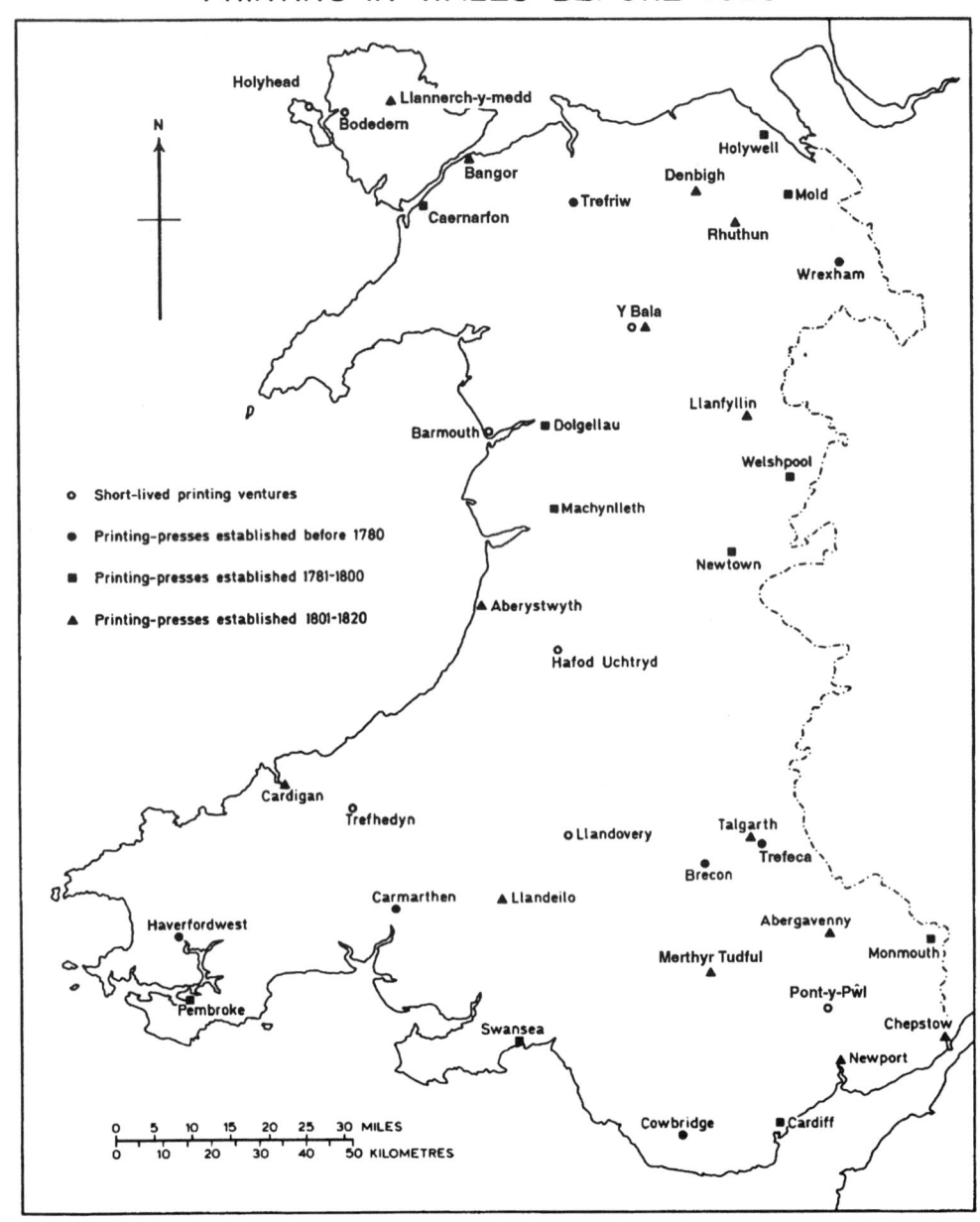

18 Pencil drawing by J. P. Neale of Charles Heath's premises, Monmouth, in 1819.

19 Oil painting by Hugh Hughes of the Carmarthen printer John Evans and his family at breakfast (c.1822-3).

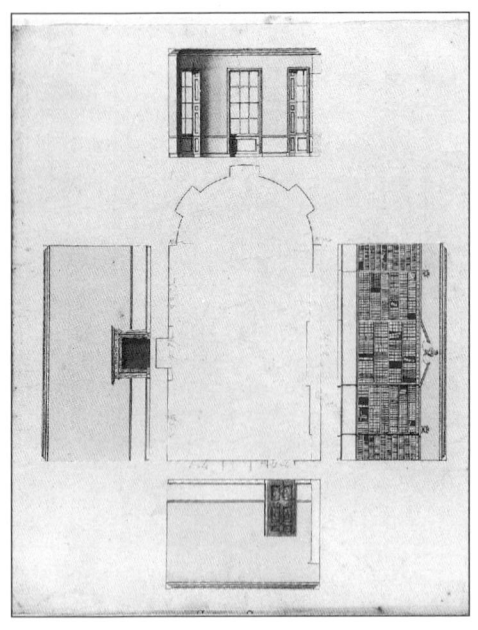

20 Plan of the library of Slebech Park (Pembrokeshire), probably by Anthony Keck.

21 Library of Treberfydd House (Breconshire). (© Crown copyright: RCAHMW (NMRW)).

23 Library of Dingestow Court (near Monmouth).

22 Library of Picton Castle (Pembrokeshire). (© Crown copyright: RCAHMW (NMRW)).

24 Bookplate of Sir Foster Cunliffe of Acton Park (Wrexham).

25 Binding bearing arms of Sir Thomas Stepney (d.1745).

26 Bookplate of Anna Maria Owen of Henllys (Pembrokeshire).

27 Bookplate of Jones-Parry family of Madryn (Caernarfonshire).

28 Bookplate of Richard Mostyn of Penbedw (Flintshire).

29 Etching by R. Woodman of Thomas George's portrait of William Owen Pughe.

30 Etching of Owain Jones 'Owain Myfyr' by Gauci (1828) based on an original portrait by John Vaughan.

31 Water-colour of Edward Williams 'Iolo Morganwg' by William Owen Pughe.

32 Title-page of the first volume of *The Cambrian Register*.

33   Front of Thomas Gee's printing office, Swan Lane, Denbigh. The press first occupied part of the site in the early 1830s and the buildings today are little changed from the late1850s.
(© Crown Copyright: RCAHMW (NMRW)).

34   Compositors at Gee's office.

35   Thomas Gee (fourth from left in the second row) and his workers.

36   Richard Hughes, founder of Hughes a'i Fab, Wrexham.

37   William Spurrell of Carmarthen.

38   Spurrell's bookshop, Carmarthen, in 1938.

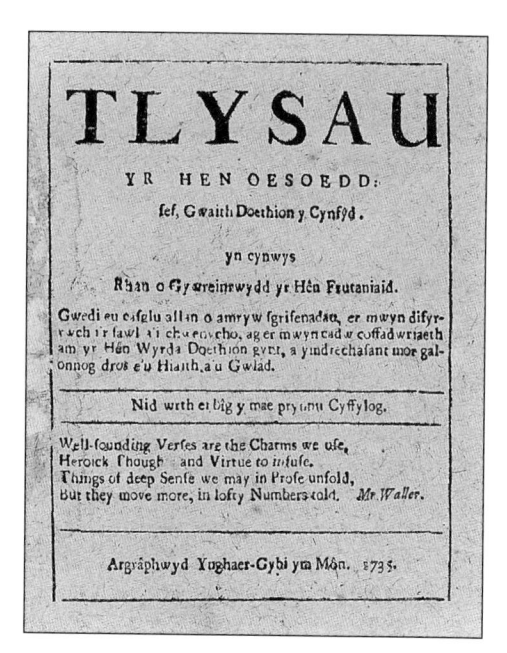

39 Title-page of *Tlysau yr Hen Oesoedd* (1735) the first Welsh periodical.

40 The front page of *Seren Gomer*, 19 February 1814. The two right-hand columns are mainly taken up by a list of Welsh books printed and sold by John Evans of Carmarthen.

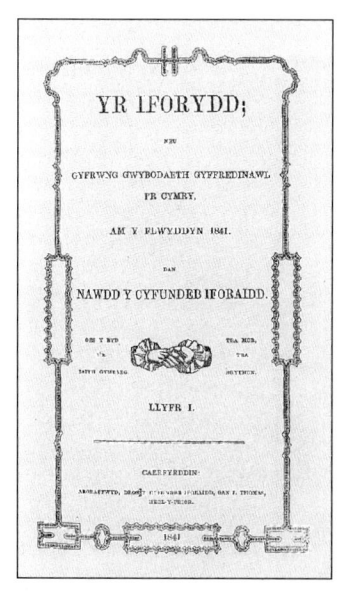

41 Title-page of volume 1 of an Ivorite monthly, *Yr Iforydd* (1841).

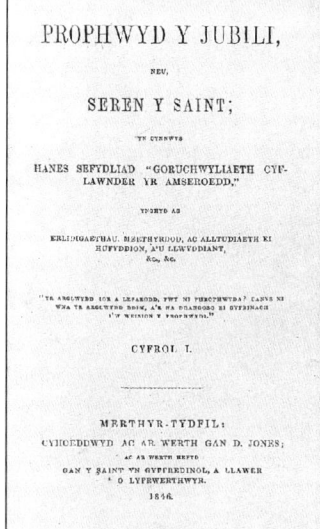

42 Title-page of volume 1 of *Prophwyd y Jubili* (1846), a Welsh-language Mormon monthly.

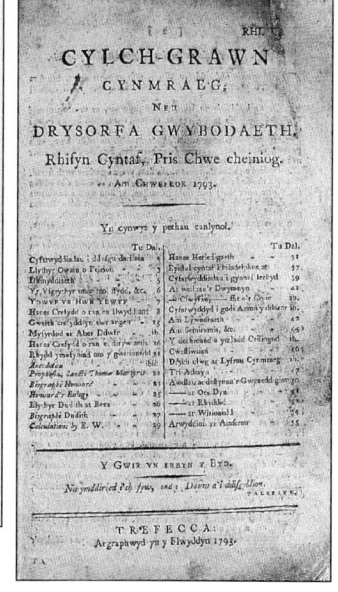

43 Cover of the first number of *Cylchgrawn Cynmraeg* (1793).

44 Photograph by John Thomas of John Griffith 'Y Gohebydd', Thomas Gee's 'London Reporter'. A copy of *Baner ac Amserau Cymru* is prominently displayed in Griffith's hat.

45 Photograph by John Thomas of 'Business Bob', Llanrwst, perusing *Yr Herald Cymraeg*.

46 Photograph by John Thomas of Abel Jones 'Bardd Crwst'.

47   Oil painting by Hugh Hughes of Walter Davies 'Gwallter Mechain', rector of Manafon and Welsh scholar (1825-6).

48   Title-page of J. Gwenogvryn Evans's edition of *The White Book Mabinogion.*

49   J. Gwenogvryn Evans.

50 Broadside by Owen Griffith 'Ywain Meirion' commemorating the Chartist attack on Newport in 1839. The turbaned figure in the centre of the illustration is the most obvious of many indications that a stock block has been used.

51 An eighteenth-century Shrewsbury-printed ballad, *Ymddiddan rhwng Hen wr Dall ar Angeu.* For once, the illustration relates to the text: Death holds forth to the blind old man. First published in *Cynghorion Tad i'w Fab* (London, 1683), this ballad retained its popularity well into the nineteenth century.

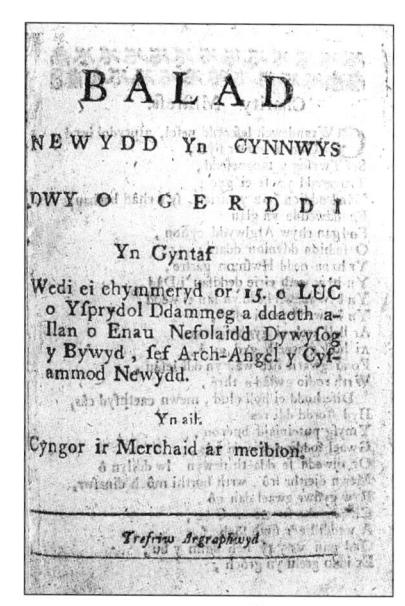

52 An eighteenth-century Trefriw-printed ballad pamphlet containing two ballads, one sacred, the other secular.

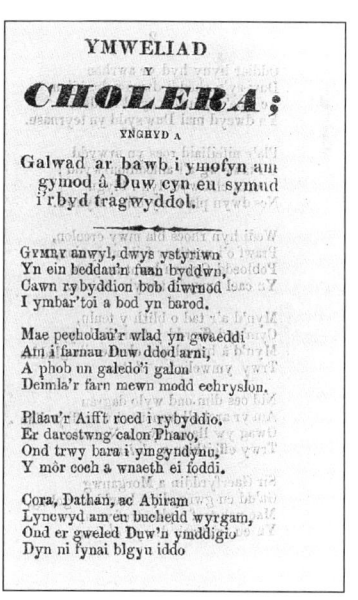

53 Mainstays of the ballad included murders, executions, and disasters.

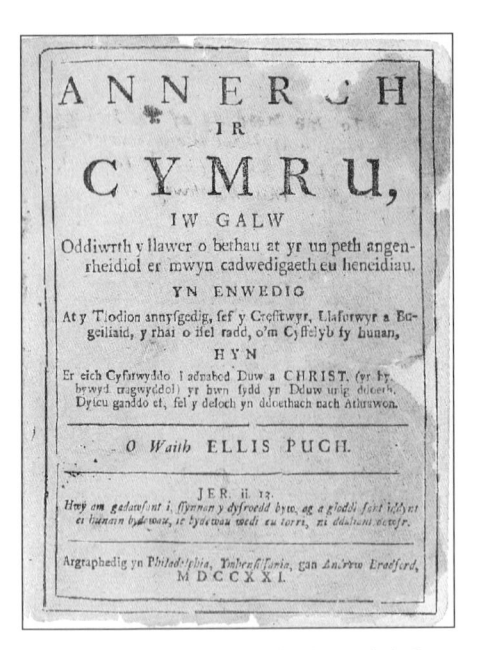

54 Title-page of Ellis Pugh, *Annerch ir Cymru* (Philadelphia, 1721), the first Welsh book to be printed in colonial America.

55 Lewis Jones, founder of *Y Wladfa*, the Welsh settlement in Patagonia.

56 Engraving by C. J. Smith of Saint David's College, Lampeter, in 1827.

57 The Drapers' Library (Welsh Library) Bangor.

58 Saunders Lewis.

59 Alun Edwards, Librarian of Cardiganshire Joint Library and a highly effective campaigner for promoting the publication of Welsh books.

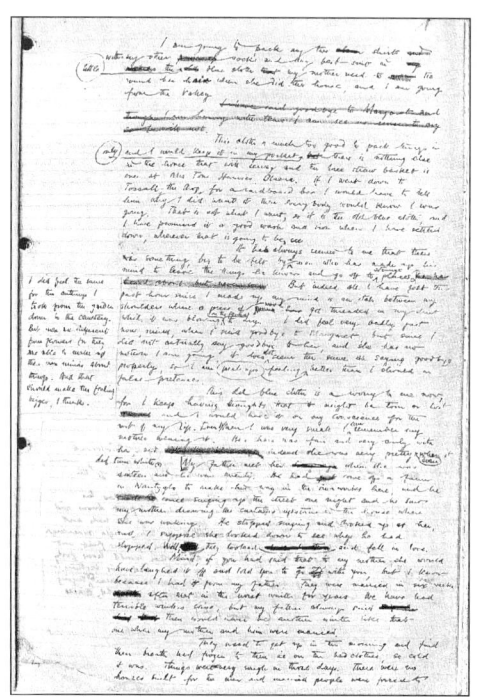

60 Portion of the manuscript of *How Green was my Valley*. (NLW 22669E).

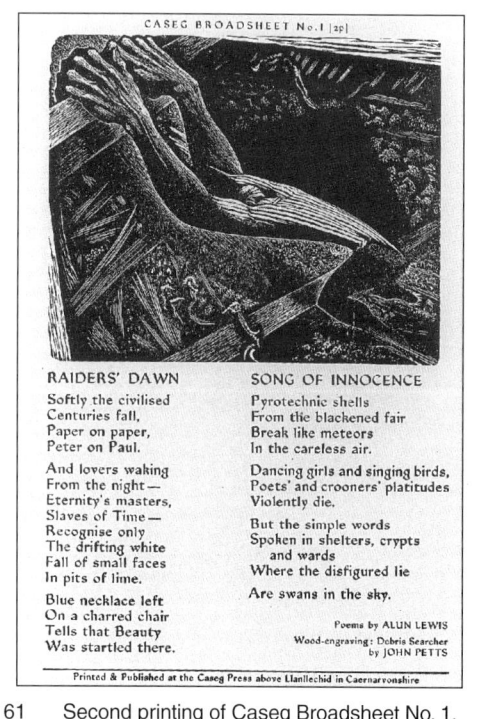

61 Second printing of Caseg Broadsheet No. 1.

CASEG BROADSHEET No. 1 [2p]

RAIDERS' DAWN

Softly the civilised
Centuries fall,
Paper on paper,
Peter on Paul.

And lovers waking
From the night —
Eternity's masters,
Slaves of Time —
Recognise only
The drifting white
Fall of small faces
In pits of lime.

Blue necklace left
On a charred chair
Tells that Beauty
Was startled there.

SONG OF INNOCENCE

Pyrotechnic shells
From the blackened fair
Break like meteors
In the careless air.

Dancing girls and singing birds,
Poets' and crooners' platitudes
Violently die.

But the simple words
Spoken in shelters, crypts
    and wards
Where the disfigured lie
Are swans in the sky.

Poems by ALUN LEWIS
Wood-engraving: Debris Searcher
by JOHN PETTS

Printed & Published at the Caseg Press above Llanllechid in Caernarvonshire

62   Advertisement for Penmark Press books published in *Welsh Review* 5.

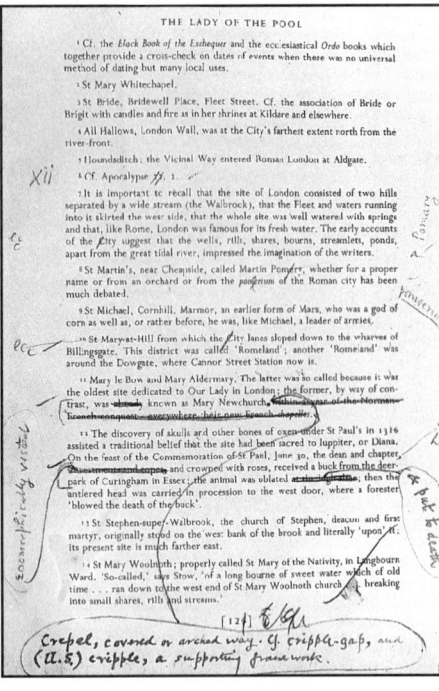

63   Proof of David Jones, *The Anathemata* with corrections in author's hand. (NLW David Jones Manuscripts and Papers).

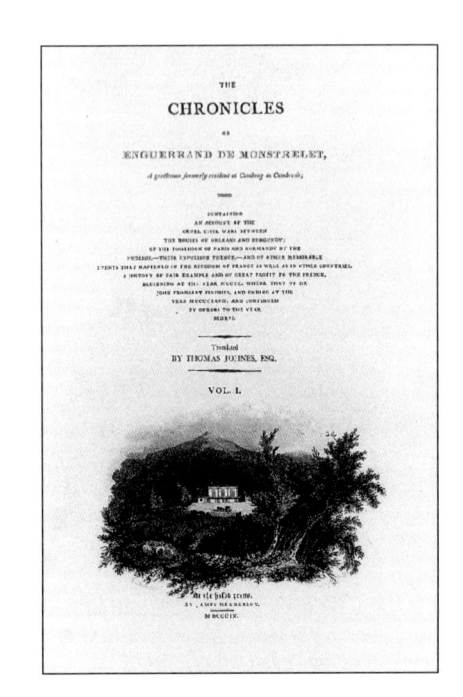

64   Title-page of *The Chronicles of Enguerrand de Monstrelet* (Hafod, 1809) bearing an engraving of Hafod.

65 Title-page of the Gregynog Press *Cyrupaedia* (1936).

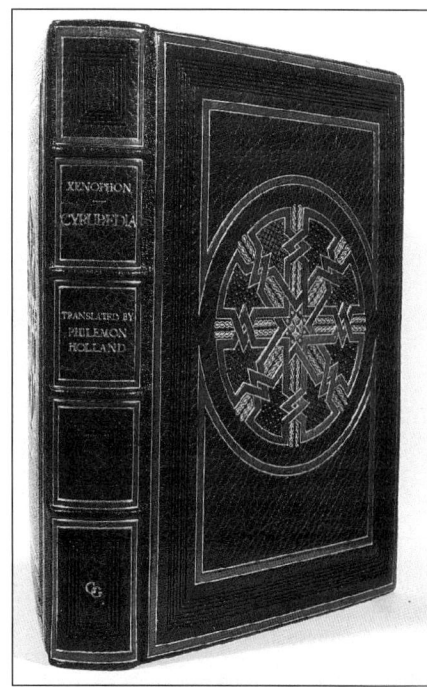

66 Binding by George Fisher for the Gregynog Press *Cyrupaedia*.

67 Title-page Kate Roberts, *Two Old Men and other stories* (Gwasg Gregynog, 1981).

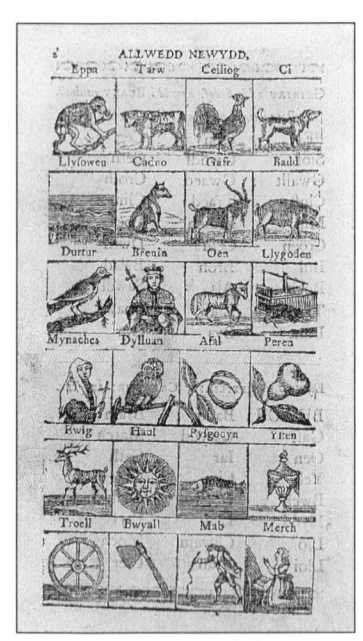

68　Owen Hughes, *Allwedd newydd, i bobl ieuaingc i ddysgu darllain Cymraeg,* contains this illustrated alphabet. Since it was designed for the English language the Welsh words are a poor fit.

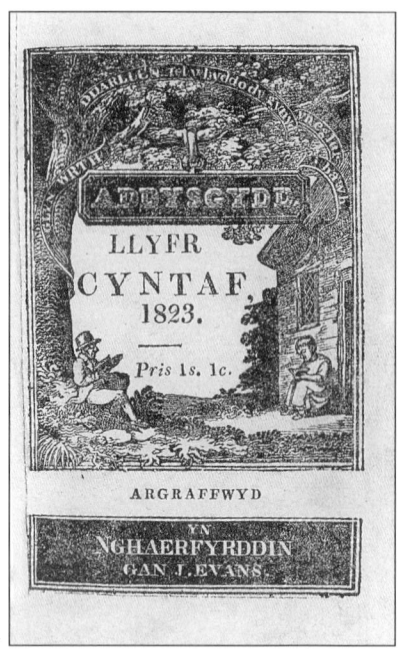

69　Wood-engraved title-page by Hugh Hughes for *Yr Addysgydd* (1823), the first Welsh-language periodical expressly intended for children.

70　O. M. Edwards.

71　Advertisement for *Cymru'r Plant* in *Cymru* 1.

72   Incunabula at the National Library of Wales: Terence, *Comoediae* (Lyons, 1493).

73   Sixteenth-century books at the National Library of Wales: *Meliadus de Leonnoys* (Paris, 1528).

74   A copy of the *Book of Common Prayer* bound by Edwards of Halifax.

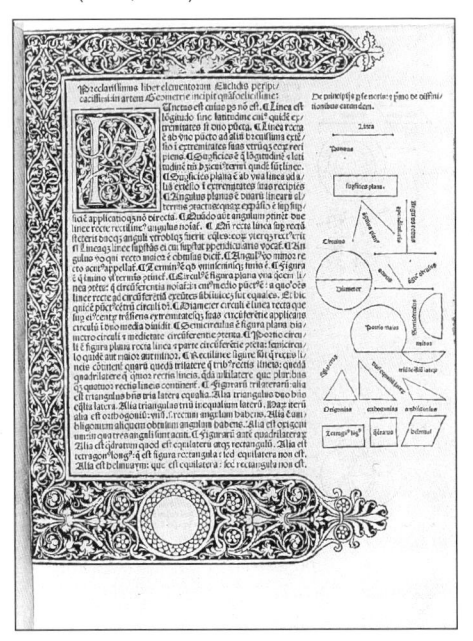

75   The Euclid collection at the National Library of Wales: a page from the first printed edition of Euclid's *Elements* (Venice, 1482).

76   The National Library of Wales.

77   The atrium at the National Library of Wales, a part of the extension opened in May 1996.

CHAPTER 18

SCHOLARLY PUBLISHING 1820—1922

B. F. Roberts

SCHOLARSHIP is by its nature a communal activity. It flourishes best in an environment where discoveries are shared, ideas exchanged, and theories tested: it is at its most effective when there is mutual criticism. Publishing is, therefore, an essential component of scholarship, the main means of contributing to the sum of knowledge and of ensuring that information is disseminated and that new insights and opinions are tested. Certainly, there have always been scholars who were not part of a visible or physical community, but it is difficult to imagine a scholar who is not part of that wider, unseen company for whom publishing is the medium of communication.

The nearest Welsh scholarship had approached the norm of modern scholarly life prior to the establishment of the Jesus Chair of Celtic at Oxford in 1877 was in the person of Edward Lhuyd between the late 1680s and 1709. His early death and the dispersal of his team of researchers foiled his ambitious yet practical plans, and the pupils who attempted to continue Lhuyd's work lacked not only his strength of character but also his university connections.

Although Lhuyd's ideals were not forgotten, without a university in Wales his work could be continued only in some other kind of society devoted to the cultivating of learning. The Constitutions of the first Cymmrodorion Society of 1751 made it clear that the encouragement of enquiry into the 'genuine History and Antiquities' of the Welsh was a primary aim, and that the achieving of means to that end was to be an important part of its activities.[1] Although the Society's high intentions were not to be realized, to a great extent it was its Constitutions which would provide both the motivation and the pattern of future Welsh scholarly publishing.

The achievements of the Gwyneddigion Society, of William Owen Pughe, and of Owen Jones, 'Owain Myfyr', have been discussed in Chapter 12. But although London-Welsh clubs continued to proliferate in the first half of the nineteenth century, the encouragement of scholarship was not their primary aim. The second Cymmrodorion Society, however, was in the older mould. Its re-establishment in 1820 was 'directly due' to the impetus given to the regeneration of Welsh culture in poetry and music, and the rekindling of informed interest in the Welsh literary inheritance by the remarkable group of Montgomeryshire clerics, *'yr hen bersoniaid llengar'* ('the old literary-minded parsons'), who gathered around John Jenkins, 'Ifor Ceri' (1770-1829), rector of Ceri, Walter Davies, 'Gwallter Mechain' (1761-1849), rector of Manafon, and W. J. Rees (1772-1855), rector of Casgob in Radnorshire.[2] Gwallter Mechain, the eldest, had been involved in the attempts of the Gwyneddigion to publish old Welsh literature and was a major influence in reawakening these aspirations among some of his fellow clergy. The Ceri group soon attracted other like-minded clerics and Ifor Ceri kept open house at his rectory for all who showed interest in traditional Welsh culture. In 1818, with the keen support of Thomas Burgess, bishop of St. David's, the Dyfed Cambrian Society was set up, not simply to nurture poetry and literature but also to undertake a farsighted programme of transcribing and publishing old Welsh manuscripts, preparing catalogues of the major collections, and collecting Welsh books for the Cymmrodorion library. All these activities continued the work of the earlier generation of London-Welsh societies.[3]

In 1819 the Dyfed Society held the first of a new order of provincial eisteddfodau, and by 1821 there were three similar Cambrian Societies in Gwynedd, Powys, Glamorgan and Gwent. Links with the London-Welsh were re-formed in 1820 when the Cymmrodorion Society was re-created as the Metropolitan Cambrian Society. As well as undertaking a similar programme of activities, the London society co-ordinated the activities of the four Welsh societies. Just as the Dyfed society had drawn up a scheme for cataloguing and publishing old Welsh manuscripts, so too did the Metropolitan Cambrian Society declare that its paramount aim would be to preserve and illustrate the ancient remains of Welsh literature and to promote its cultivation by collecting or copying Welsh manuscripts, by preparing catalogues, by collecting books printed in Welsh and those connected with Wales and its literature and 'that of its kindred tongues, the Armoric, the Cornish and the Irish', by encouraging the writing of original dissertations on Welsh history and literature, and by publishing these essays and ancient manuscripts.[4]

The Society had only a brief existence. When it was dissolved in 1843 it had achieved almost none of its high ideals, though some of the material published in its *Transactions* (two volumes, 1822, 1828-43) reflected the original intention of publishing historical essays and accounts and catalogues of manuscripts. Robert Williams's *Enwogion Cymru: a Biographical Dictionary of Eminent Welshmen* (1852) was the result of a Cymmrodorion eisteddfod competition in 1831, and A. J. Johnes's *On the Causes which have produced Dissent in Wales from the Established Church* (1831) was also a prize essay. Johnes also published *Translations into English verse from the Poems of Davyth ab Gwilym* (1834), a further link with the work of a previous generation, the Gwyneddigion, who had published *Barddoniaeth Dafydd ab Gwilym* in 1789.

Cymdeithas Cymreigyddion y Fenni, the Abergavenny Welsh Society, was the provincial society which adhered most faithfully to the ideal of using the eisteddfodau to encourage scholarly essays on Welsh history and literature, probably because it numbered among its leaders such dedicated students as Thomas Price, 'Carnhuanawc' (1787-1848), Lady Llanover and Sir Benjamin Hall, and Lady Charlotte Guest. The society's eisteddfodau attracted the support of gentry and of Welsh and foreign scholars, and over the years a number of substantial dissertations were awarded prizes.[5] The most significant essay produced by the Abergavenny eisteddfodau was *The literature of the Kymry* by the young Merthyr chemist Thomas Stephens (1821-75) which won a prize in 1848 and was published in the following year. This history of Welsh literature from 1080 to 1350 was the first attempt to employ a 'scientific' approach based on the texts, their dates, and interpretation, rather than a preconceived view of the bardic tradition, druids, and the like. Stephens's book gave Welsh literature credibility at home and abroad (a German translation appeared in 1864), became the established text-book, and set the standard for subsequent literary histories. His questioning attitudes in essays in scholarly journals — in particular his sceptical treatment of the Madog legend —

did not endear him to all his contemporaries, but there is no doubt that he was a seminal figure in the new approach to Welsh studies.

The library of the first Cymmrodorion Society, intended to be the foundation of a national library, represented another ideal which was not forgotten. The second Society purchased Owain Myfyr's collections from his widow for £50 and arranged for a catalogue to be prepared and published in the first number of its *Transactions*. William Owen Pughe, the cataloguer, was subsequently invited with Gwallter Mechain to draw on these newly available resources to prepare a fourth volume of the *Myvyrian Archaiology of Wales* which would contain hitherto unpublished poetry to 1500 and a selection of prose works.[6] Unfortunately, neither this nor the hoped-for cheaply priced collections of Welsh literature appeared, apparently because funds were short and the Cambrian societies in Wales were unwilling to devote the proceeds of their eisteddfodau to this purpose. Nevertheless, the objective of printing unpublished poetry was achieved in part, though not in the form originally envisaged.

In 1833, John Jones, 'Tegid' (1792-1852), precentor of Christ Church, Oxford, was invited to edit the works of the fifteenth-century poet Lewys Glyn Cothi as part of the *Myvyrian Archaiology* project. Later that year, Gwallter Mechain was appointed co-editor and henceforth the two clerics, one in Oxford, the other in Manafon, were to collaborate on the edition, Tegid being responsible for the text and the historical introduction, Gwallter Mechain for most of the notes. *Gwaith Lewis Glyn Cothi: the Poetical Works of Lewis Glyn Cothi*, printed by the Oxford University printer, was published by the Society in two parts in 1837 and 1839. Although Tegid's editorial methods suffered from serious weaknesses,[7] the publication marked the partial fulfilment of long-standing aims and, in retrospect, it can be seen to form an important link in the chain which leads from the first Cymmrodorion Society to the beginnings of modern scholarly publishing in the early twentieth century.

The appearance of *Gwaith Lewis Glyn Cothi* did not quell the fears of those who believed that the Cymmrodorion and the other Cambrian Societies were not devoting their energies wholeheartedly to the publication of Welsh literature and historical sources. C. W. W. Wynne, the dedicatee of the work, was sharply critical of the Cymmrodorion:

> If the Cymmrodorion apply themselves to the encouragement of Poetry and Music in preference to the other objects I should be glad that another Society exclusively literary, historical and antiquarian should be formed.[8]

The patience of the antiquaries and historians was finally exhausted and Wynne's hint (or threat) was taken up at a meeting of Cymdeithas Cymreigyddion y Fenni in November 1836.[9]

The Society for the Publication of Ancient Welsh Manuscripts (or the Welsh Manuscript Society) was founded the following year. The first committee, chaired by Sir Benjamin Hall of Llanover, represented well those groups which shared a concern for the fate of the Welsh manuscripts and who wished to see the materials for the study of Welsh history made available — the Abergavenny Cymreigyddion, the Montgomeryshire clerics, the Cymmrodorion Society, antiquarians and scholars among the gentry, and some of the leading Welsh scholars such as Carnhuanawc, Tegid, and Taliesin Williams, 'Ab Iolo'. There was a strong group of corresponding members from Wales and elsewhere, and no fewer than six Editors and Collators of Manuscripts were appointed. The Society set out its aims clearly:

> transcribing and printing the more important of the numerous unpublished Bardic and Historical Remains of Wales [...] that have hitherto been allowed to continue in a state of obscurity, without any effective measures being adopted to lay their contents before the public, and secure them from the various accidents to which they are liable.

The aim was to procure copies of the most important prose and verse manuscripts and to publish them with notes and an English translation.

By 1840 the Society was able to claim that it was working 'in conjunction' with the Cymmrodorion Society, but it was an uneasy alliance of competing priorities. The anxieties expressed by J. M. Trahearne in 1840 were probably shared by others:

> Here I may be allowed to express my regret, that while large sums are annually expended on Eisteddfodau, &c., &c. the Welsh MSS. Society should be cramped in its operations by the scantiness of its funds. The Cymmrodorion Society has distinguished itself of late by printing the Poems of Lewis Glyn Cothi, with Annotations in English. I venture to indulge the hope that the laudable efforts of these Societies now acting in conjunction with others, will be duly appreciated, and that the aid of additional subscriptions will enable them speedily to publish other productions of our ancient Poets, as they are valuable in throwing light on various points in the history and manners of Wales in the Middle Ages.[10]

W. J. Rees, Casgob, the moving spirit of the Society, was the editor of its first work, *Liber Landavensis*, published in 1840. This was followed by a number of titles of varying importance.[11] The quality of the editing was never of the highest, but after the death of Rees in 1855 the nature of the Society's publications deteriorated sharply under the editorship of John Williams, 'Ab Ithel' (1811-62), who was responsible for publishing uncritical selections of spurious texts from the papers of Iolo Morganwg and for some poor editing. All the Society's publications were printed by W. J. Rees's nephew, William Rees of Llandovery (1808-73), probably the finest Welsh printer of his day. Himself an antiquary, William Rees also printed Lady Charlotte Guest's *Mabinogion* (1838-49) and the prize essays of the Abergavenny eisteddfodau.

While Tegid and Gwallter Mechain were working on *Gwaith Lewis Glyn Cothi*, a young protégé of the clerical literati of Montgomeryshire was a student at Jesus College, Oxford. This was Robert Jones of Llanfyllin (1810-79) who matriculated in 1833 and graduated in 1837. It is not over-imaginative to hear the ageing Gwallter Mechain calling the young student's attention to the work being carried out in Oxford and at neighbouring Manafon, work which was for Gwallter the fulfilment of what he and William Owen Pughe had failed to achieve in the 1820s. Tegid entrusted Robert Jones with carrying some of his precious parcels from Christ Church to Manafon. Jones brought the final instalment to Oxford on 1 March 1836, and later in the same year returned the first printed sheets to Gwallter. By the time he was ordained, Robert Jones had surely been infected with the ideals of the local clerical literati and must have heard a great deal about the hopes of the second Cymmrodorion Society. After a few years in Wales, Jones was appointed vicar of All Saints church, Rotherhithe, in 1842 and remained there until his death. The moribund second Cymmrodorion Society was dissolved about 1843 but Robert Jones quickly made his vicarage the meeting-place of all who were interested in Welsh life and culture or who were concerned for the well-being of the Welsh people. Jones himself was to be involved in every movement and committee in the second half of the century which aimed to develop Welsh educational and cultural life. Showing perhaps more enthusiasm than discretion he became a member of the Cambrian Institute, established by Ab Ithel as a rival to the Cambrian Archaeological Association when his bizarre ideas and lack of critical judgement made it impossible for him to collaborate any longer with H. Longueville Jones.[12] Ab Ithel, unfortunately regarded by many influential people as a leading Welsh scholar, published his edition (text, translation, and notes) of *Y Gododdin* in 1852. This was followed by editions of *Annales Cambriae* and *Brut y Tywysogyon* in the Rolls Series in 1860, none of which met acceptable standards of scholarship. On paper, the ideals of the Cambrian Institute were high and honourable, echoing the well-established aims of the Cymmrodorion and other cultural societies but Ab Ithel soon inflicted his eccentric druidical views on its *Cambrian Journal* (1855-64). Nevertheless, Robert Jones remained a faithful member, serving as Secretary to the London branch of the Institute and enabling it, in a new age and changed ethos, to distance itself from the previous London-Welsh societies while retaining the aura of a London-based interest in Wales.

By the early 1870s Wales had experienced considerable educational developments, the eisteddfod was reforming itself as an influential national cultural festival, and the idea of a Welsh identity which might be expressed through national cultural and educational institutions was gaining ground. R. T. Jenkins has traced the ways in which 'some central organisation to direct their energies' was being sought by many Welsh people — a Welsh Antiquarian Society, Ceiriog's *Urdd y Vord Gron* (Round Table League), a revived Cymmrodorion Society.[13] Robert Jones was one of a group of London Welshmen promoting this third suggestion which was adopted at the 1873 Mold National Eisteddfod. The first meeting of the third Cymmrodorion society was held in London in November of that year, the fifteen men present constituting themselves the Council of the new society. Jones spoke warmly at the meeting, his brief account of the two previous societies providing the sense of continuity which was so important to the new body. The aim of the Society was to encourage literature, the arts, and science as they related to Wales. Although the Constitutions laid down that the Society would publish an annual volume of transactions, this did not prove possible until 1876. In that year the Council adopted a more wide-ranging scheme for its publishing activities drawn up by Robert Jones who succeeded in putting flesh on the bare bones of 'encouraging literature, the arts and science'. According to the new arrangements, the transactions would be a periodical,

> *Y Cymmrodor* to be delivered to members in half-yearly parts, and to form, with a supplement, an annual volume of not less than 400 pages. The parts to be

made up of three divisions, each having a separate pagination.
The first to embody the transactions of the Cymmrodorion with those of kindred societies, historical notices of Eisteddfodau, and of current matters bearing upon the literature, philology, and antiquities of the Cymry; notes on national music; and critiques on books and other Celtic publications.
The second to be devoted to the printing of valuable Welsh MSS.
The third to consist of reprints of rare and interesting works, chiefly in English, connected with the language, literature, or history of Wales.
The different divisions are thus to form independent works of value [...] each division consisting, as nearly as possible, of a third of the whole.[14]

The scheme was an adaptation of the first intentions of the Powys-Land Club, whose 'journal', *Collections Historical and Archaeological relating to Montgomeryshire*, was intended to be a collection of material preparatory to writing the county history which could be brought together to form independent publications.[15] Robert Jones became editor of the three sections of *Y Cymmrodor,* assisted by a literary committee. He was the proprietor of the periodical and bore the full cost of printing aided by a contribution by the Society according to the number of members.[16] The first volume, published in 1877, gives a good idea of how the scheme was to operate. It contained a history of the Cymmrodorion societies by Robert Jones (with its own title-page), articles, reviews and 'literary intelligence', letters, poems, translations, and reports of Council. During the year there appeared parts of a reprint of William Salesbury's 1547 Dictionary and also the first parts of Jones's new edition of the poetry of Iolo Goch (again with its own title-page).

Jones threw himself wholeheartedly into his editorial work but by his death in 1879 he had edited only two volumes of *Y Cymmrodor*. The editorship passed to Thomas Powel, who continued the tripartite pattern, and then to Egerton Phillimore, but difficulties arose with publishing the three parts on a half-yearly basis and especially with ensuring that lectures delivered during a given year appeared during the following one. It must be assumed, too, that the editorial work placed the editor under a particular strain since, unusually, it involved both copy editing and scholarly textual editing. The *Transactions* of the Society were published separately from 1892-3 onwards, *Y Cymmrodor,* containing articles and lectures (sometimes with a supplement) being continued until 1937. From 1938 to 1951 (volumes 45-50) it became a series of monographs, but rising costs forced its abandonment in the bicentenary year of the Society, the official history of the Cymmrodorion forming the final volume.

The aspirations of Robert Jones to publish editions of texts and documents and to reprint rare books was not forgotten after his death. His facsimile reprint of Salesbury's Dictionary (1877) was followed in 1880 by a facsimile of Morys Clynnog's *Athravaeth Gristnogavl* of 1568, a publication which he himself had instigated but which was taken up by Isambard Owen with the enthusiastic co-operation of the owner of the unique copy of the book, Prince Louis-Lucien Bonaparte, a friend of both Jones and Owen. This was followed by Thomas Powel's edition of *Ystorya de Carolo Magno* from the Red Book of Hergest (1883) and his edition of Thomas Stephens's *Gododdin of Aneurin Gwawdrydd* (1888). Powel's photographic facsimile of *Psalmau Dafydd O'r vn cyfieithiad a'r Beibl Cyffredin* (1588), published in 1896, was presumably inspired by the work of the Cymmrodorion.

One of the aims of *Y Cymmrodor* was to publish texts, especially the work of fourteenth and fifteenth-century poets, which would comprise the fourth volume of the *Myvyrian Archaiology* since the Society, though it had transferred its library to the British Museum, still held the Myvyrian manuscripts in high, proprietorial, regard. Editions and translations of individual poems appeared, but Robert Jones's ambitions were better formulated. In the first two volumes of his *Cymmrodor,* he began to publish *The Works of Iolo Goch, with a Sketch of his Life,* but died after only sixty-four pages of text, variant readings, and notes had been published. This publication had its origins in the aims of the second Society, and was heavily indebted to its only real fruits, *Gwaith Lewis Glyn Cothi.* Jones had studied the methods of that work's editors carefully — their editing, the English translations, the historical annotations — and also the layout of this information on the page; summary, text, two columns of notes. The same scheme and format (apart from the translation) was adopted, as E. D. Jones observed, by Robert Jones for his *Iolo Goch.*[17] *Gwaith Lewis Glyn Cothi* thus provided both an inspiration and a model.

Robert Jones's hopes of publishing manuscripts and other historical documents in the third part of his *Cymmrodor* were fulfilled (albeit in a different way) when the Cymmrodorion Record Series fund was set up in 1889 and an impressive programme was embarked upon. Thirteen well-produced works of a very high standard, some texts, others discussions, appeared between 1892 and 1936.[18]

The Cymmrodorion had hoped to continue Jones's edition of Iolo Goch but failed to discover a capable and willing editor. The problem was resolved when the Caernarfon National Eisteddfod of 1894 offered a prize for a 'Collection of the Poems of Iolo Goch with Historical and Critical Notes'. Charles Ashton's prize-winning edition was published in the now familiar format of introductory matter, text, and bicolumnar notes by the Cymmrodorion in 1896, no doubt as an act of piety to the memory of one to whom the Society owed so much.[19] The National Eisteddfod had now taken up the aims of the old Cambrian eisteddfodau, and by means of competitions was actively involved in the production and publication of literary and scholarly works. One major enterprise was a multi-volume history of Welsh literature, continuing Stephens's *Literature of the Kymry.* At the Cardiff Eisteddfod of 1883, R. J. Pryse, 'Gweirydd ap Rhys', won the prize for a history of Welsh literature from 1300 to 1650. His essay was published by the Association in 1885, a year after Charles Wilkins's *The History of the Literature of Wales from the year 1300 to the year 1650,* which was probably submitted for the same competition. In 1891 Ashton gained the prize for his *Hanes Llenyddiaeth Gymreig o 1651 hyd 1850,* published in 1893. This type of competition, a feature of National Eisteddfod activities until comparatively recently, produced a number of other important studies.[20]

The Works of Iolo Goch was not Robert Jones's first excursion into scholarly editing. In 1864 he had published a facsimile reprint of John Davies's *Flores poetarum Britannicorum* (Shrewsbury, 1710), together with Wiliam Midleton's *Llyfr Barddoniaeth.* Between 1876 and 1878 he also published *Poetical Works of the Rev. Goronwy Owen with his Life and Correspondence, edited with notes, critical and explanatory,* a book which shows how thoroughly he had understood the implications and demands of editing from his study of *Gwaith Lewis Glyn Cothi.* The edition of Goronwy Owen prepared Robert Jones for what he hoped would be the new beginnings of scholarly publishing so long desired and planned for by the London-Welsh societies. It was the practicality of his vision and the example which he set in his pursuit of the ideal which at last enabled scholarly publishing to become a 'collegiate' activity, for the third Society was seen by some of its founders as a learned society for Wales, fulfilling the role of the learned societies of London and the Continent.

Scholarly publishing, however, was not the exclusive preserve of learned societies and groups like the Cymmrodorion and the Welsh Manuscript Society; nor was it motivated only by eisteddfodic competitions. The cultural revival of the latter part of the nineteenth century prompted commercial publishers and individual editors to produce works for the general reader. The literary histories produced under the aegis of the National Eisteddfod were clearly intended for such a readership, as were collections of the works of eighteenth-century poets such as *Gwaith y Parchedig Evan Evans (Ieuan Brydydd Hir)* (1876), *Gwaith Prydyddawl Edward Richard, Ystradmeurig* (1866), *Gwaith Beirdd Môn* (1879), *Gwaith Thomas Edwards (Twm o'r Nant)* (1874), and new anthologies of Welsh literature — *Ceinion Llenyddiaeth Gymraeg*, edited by Owen Jones, 'Meudwy Môn' (1876), *Cymru Fu*, edited by Isaac Foulkes (1862-4). Of greater scholarly significance were the revised editions of eighteenth and nineteenth-century collections and studies of earlier Welsh literature. Between 1868 and 1870 Thomas Gee reprinted in a single volume an expanded edition of the *Myvyrian Archaiology of Wales*, presumably because he thought the high prices commanded by second-hand copies of the first edition indicated a profitable market for such a volume. The demand for an English edition of early Welsh poetry was met by W. F. Skene's *The Four Ancient Books of Wales* (Edinburgh, 1868).

A better selection of prose works than that offered by the *Myvyrian Archaiology, Selections from the Hengwrt manuscripts* was published under the editorship of Robert Williams in 1876, followed by a second volume, completed and translated by G. Hartwell Jones, in 1892. The poet, preacher, and antiquary, Robert Ellis, 'Cynddelw' (1812-75), had already produced an expanded edition in 1864 for Hugh Humphreys of Caernarfon of *Gorchestion Beirdd Cymru* (1773), which claimed in its Preface to be an attempt to provide and explain the compositions of the old poets in a cheap and popular form. By revising the text in the light of variant readings from the *Myvyrian* and *Barddoniaeth Dafydd ab Gwilym*, providing a glossary which explained unfamiliar words and references, placing the poets in their chronological order, and supplying a substantial historical introduction, Ellis transformed Rhys Jones's valuable collection of medieval poetry into an annotated edition designed to meet the needs of a new readership. Ellis seems to have been encouraged by the reception of his new *Gorchestion* as he published a similar re-edition of the 1789 *Barddoniaeth Dafydd ab Gwilym* in 1873. This had the same missionary purpose and was supplied with a new essay on the life and genius of the poet, notes, and a glossary. It was published by Isaac Foulkes (1836-1904), a Liverpool-based Welsh publisher and author who regarded the publication of Welsh classics as a particular responsibility of his press. As well as publishing several important literary biographies (such as his own of Daniel Owen and Ceiriog), he produced two series of Welsh classics, Cyfres y Clasuron Cymreig (including *Gweledigaethau'r Bardd Cwsg* and *Llyfr y Tri Aderyn*) and Cyfres y Ceinion, the works of 'Twm o'r Nant', Goronwy

Owen, *Beirdd Môn,* a modern Welsh translation of the Mabinogion (1880), a reprint of the Welsh Manuscript Society's *Iolo MSS* in 1888, and a photographic facsimile of *Tlysau yr Hen Oesoedd* in 1902. He showed his readiness to venture into the field of scholarly publishing in the modern sense by issuing in 1899 John Fisher's *The Cefn Coch MSS.*, a diplomatic edition of two manuscripts of *cywyddau.*

The work of D. Silvan Evans (1818-1903), 'the last of the literary-minded parsons' and later of John Fisher (1862-1930), is a sign that Welsh scholarship was, at last, freeing itself from the pseudo-learning of Ab Ithel and his kind. Though Thomas Stephens, Gweirydd ap Rhys and others had shown a critical attitude to Welsh literary history, they had worked without properly edited texts and without the benefits of a university education. The appointment of John Rhŷs to the new chair of Celtic at Oxford in 1877 was a turning-point in the development of Welsh scholarship. He not only gave Welsh a university presence for the first time but was also able to provide young scholars with formal instruction in Welsh language and medieval literature as well as in the broader Celtic and linguistic disciplines, thereby giving the new university departments at Aberystwyth, Bangor, and Cardiff a firm academic foundation.[21] The immediate need was for reliable texts of medieval and early-modern literature to supersede the laudable but less than adequate editions of Foulkes, the Welsh Manuscripts Society, and the Cymmrodorion. By a happy coincidence, John Gwenogvryn Evans (1852-1930), forced through ill-health to abandon his vocation as a Unitarian minister, arrived in Oxford in 1880 and began to attend Rhŷs's classes. Lectures on the Mabinogion led Evans to study and then to transcribe the texts from the Red Book of Hergest (a Jesus College manuscript housed in the Bodleian), an enterprise which became a plan to produce diplomatic editions of a large number of medieval Welsh manuscripts. The first volumes to appear bore the name of John Rhŷs as well as that of Gwenogvryn Evans on their title-pages, but there is no doubt that it was the latter who undertook the greater part, if not the whole, of the labour of transcribing and indexing the texts and of writing the introductions These introductions vary greatly in their value; Evans's palaeographic notes were authoritative, but his interpretations were often uncritical and perverse, leading him to produce texts and translations which were as ill-founded as those of the previous generation of eccentric scholars. Fortunately, his 'revised' texts were published separately from his remarkably accurate diplomatic editions. His service to Welsh scholarship in providing reliable texts was crucial. The Series of Old Welsh Texts[22] brought (and still bring) to the desks of scholars a typographical facsimile (and sometimes photographic reproduction) of the manuscripts. Evans's aim was to reproduce in print as closely as possible the appearance of the manuscript page — each line, the space between each word, the form of certain letters — while indicating uncertain readings. It was inevitable that he should be led to study the craft of printing (he set and apparently printed some texts himself) and his books, in their various editions, papers, and bindings are examples in their own right of innovative fine printing.

Evans became the Inspector of Welsh Manuscripts for the Historical Manuscripts Commission in 1894, and his descriptions of the main collections, almost all of which were then still in private hands (two volumes, 1898-1910) remain indispensable guides. However, his Series of Old Welsh Texts which allowed students to read manuscripts at first hand met an even more pressing need. His example was followed by others. John Rhŷs and John Morris Jones edited *The Elucidarium and other tracts in Welsh from Llyvyr Agkyr Llandewivrevi A D 1346* (Oxford, 1894). A. W. Wade-Evans's *Mediaeval Welsh Law* (Oxford, 1909), the first serious attempt to classify and edit the Welsh law-texts since Aneurin Owen's *Ancient Laws and Institutes of Wales* (1841), marked the beginning of a new era in the study of Welsh law. Evans himself also began a Series of Welsh Classics for the People in 1897.[23]

The establishment of the University of Wales in 1894 not only enabled degrees in Welsh to be set up but also allowed departments to embark upon postgraduate study for the first time. The new professors and others responded to the demand for essential books. Gwenogvryn Evans's Classics were intended for intermediate classes, Edward Anwyl reprinted *The Poetry of the Gogynfeirdd* (1909) from the *Myvyrian Archaiology*, W. J. Gruffydd prepared an anthology of *cywyddau*, *Y Flodeugerdd Newydd* (1909), John Morris Jones edited and analysed *Gweledigaethau y Bardd Cwsc* (1894), and Ifor Williams began his long career of editing with *Breuddwyd Maxen* in 1908. Non-academics also made a contribution: John Jones, 'Myrddin Fardd' (1836-1921), a blacksmith, produced the still useful *Cynfeirdd Lleyn* (*Early Llŷn Poets*) in 1905. Other authors published works on aspects of literary history such as J. C. Morrice, *Manual of Welsh Literature* (1909) and T. Gwynn Jones's *Llenyddiaeth y Cymry* (*The literature of the Welsh*) (1915). These were all ventures undertaken by commercial publishers, perhaps the most elegantly produced being those published by Jarvis and Foster of Bangor, and were written to met individual college needs. Three bodies, however, undertook a more planned and co-ordinated programme of publications.

The Guild of Graduates of the University was set up in 1894. At its inaugural meeting, the first Warden, O. M. Edwards, suggested that it could 'do much for the publication of Welsh manuscripts', a theme soon taken up more explicitly by other members of the Guild. In 1896, T. E. Ellis advocated the preparation and publication of a series of the poets of Wales, a collection of the statutes relating to Wales, and the history of the Courts of Great Sessions, and by 1897 had inspired the Guild to formulate plans for publishing Welsh classics for the use of college and extra-mural students and the general reader.[24] Ellis's own edition of *Gweithiau Morgan Llwyd*, Vol. 1, appeared in 1899 as the first of a series of Reprints of Welsh Prose Works.[25] The Guild subsequently undertook a Series of Welsh (Manuscript) Texts, and was responsible for publishing several notable higher-degree dissertations, such as E. A. Lewis's, *The Mediaeval Boroughs of Snowdonia* (1912), described as the first number of a Series of Literary and Historical Studies.

A rather different publishing venture began in 1900. Cymdeithas Llên Cymru was formed as a result of a conversation between John Ballinger, then Librarian of Cardiff Free Library, and J. H. Davies (1871-1926), a leading Welsh bibliophile and book-collector. Both men were anxious to promote fine printing and to encourage a higher standard of book production in Wales. With the support of other prominent scholars — Sir John Williams, Edward Anwyl, Gwenogvryn Evans, T. J. Evans — they agreed to establish a private society to produce books for their own pleasure. This esoteric aim was quickly lost sight of, and after the first publication the Society regularly printed more copies (some 125-200) than were subscribed for. Ballinger was responsible for the printing arrangements, Davies for the selection and editing of the texts. Six numbers (five titles) of collections of free-metre poetry in blue covers appeared between 1900 and 1905. These were followed from 1907 to 1915 by a series of three seventeenth-century Puritan pamphlets in red covers. A series of classic hymn writers bound in yellow covers was commenced in 1910 with the publication of *Gwaith Morgan Rhys* but was not continued. The booklets, printed by William Lewis of Cardiff, reflected the Society's concern for fine printing and have always been collectors' items.[26]

The choice of free-metre poetry was an imaginative attempt to introduce a new area of research to academics but the colleges continued to be more interested in medieval Welsh literature, doubtless viewing this as the classical period of Welsh. Yet the list of subscribers to the Society printed in the 1905 number indicates a cordial response by the academic community, a response which may well have encouraged the founding of the Bangor Manuscript Society in 1906. The prime mover was Thomas Shankland whose achievements at the library of the University College are discussed in Chapter 26. With John Morris Jones, J. E. Lloyd, and W. Lewis Jones, Shankland circularized prominent Welsh scholars and public figures in February 1907:

> It is proposed to form a Society in accordance with the requirements of modern scholarship for printing MSS. bearing on the literature and history of Wales which have not hitherto been given to the public, or have been inadequately edited. Without in any way trenching upon larger and more ambitious schemes of this kind, it is believed that valuable service can be rendered to Welsh studies by reproducing in this way some of the *shorter* pieces in prose and verse, in Latin and in Welsh, upon which students are dependent for their material.

The response was sufficiently favourable for the new society to be established on 20 February 1907. By 1910 there were about eighty members and a strong Council of ten experienced scholars. Shankland was the Secretary, Ifor Williams the Assistant Secretary. The object of the society was 'the transcribing and publishing of Original Documents relating to Wales' and it was intended to publish one number a year for members only. In practice, the Society failed to publish a volume annually, nor was distribution restricted to members: normally 200 copies were printed. Council meetings became less regular and less frequent and at the Annual General Meeting of 1927 — the first since 1914 — it was decided to dissolve the Society. But between 1908 and 1914 four editions of *cywyddwyr* by Bangor staff or research students were published, as well as a volume of two saints' lives in Welsh and Latin.[27] The Bangor Society, like Cymdeithas Llên Cymru, paid regard to the quality of its typography and printing, its publications being produced to a high standard by the Bangor firm of Jarvis and Foster. Although the Society had a well-formulated programme most of the prospective editors proved unable to fulfil their promises and the most active editorial members were extremely busy scholars who could not devote much time to this additional work The 1914-18 war dealt the death-blow by depriving the Society of young postgraduate scholars to transcribe and edit texts. The Bangor editions do not meet the requirements of today's scholarship, but the methodology of editing is one which modern scholars recognize and within the constraints of the time — unavailability of manuscripts, lack of dictionaries, incomplete understanding of the process of transmission of poetic texts and of the development of *cynghanedd* — these volumes were a significant step forward.

What all these efforts revealed was that the preparation of texts, primary research material, and teaching aids for college and extra-mural classes should be a responsibility of the University itself. When the Royal Commission on University Education in Wales was set up in 1916 under the chairmanship of Viscount Haldane, J. H. Davies, by now Registrar of the University College at Aberystwyth, seized the opportunity to submit a detailed and informative memorandum on the needs of Celtic studies, more especially those of Welsh language, literature, and history. In it he unequivocally claimed:

> One of the supreme needs of the University of Wales is to obtain funds for the organisation of a School of Celtic Studies. At the present time there is no such school in existence, though an increased amount of attention is being paid both in Wales and Ireland to the study of the Celtic Languages.

He described the current position, paying tribute to the work of national and provincial eisteddfodau, the university colleges and the Guild of Graduates, and the learned societies. As its founders had done, he appears to have regarded the Guild as a body organizing research activities within the University: it had made grants for the publication of important research work and it

> had in contemplation the publication of text-books, and of texts for study at the Schools and Colleges [...] Many of the graduates of the University have undertaken the writing of such books, but they have been published either at their own expense or by arrangement with some local publisher.

Davies concluded that the 'considerable sum of money' required for the purpose should be allocated 'for a few years at least' and that a University Board of Celtic Studies should be established to carry out the programme of work which he outlined — a survey of materials, copying of texts and records, compiling a Welsh dictionary, the printing and publishing of texts, records, and studies. 'Eventually', he suggested, the Board of Celtic Studies 'might develop a University Press'.

The Haldane Committee took particular note of the memorandum and in its Final Report (Cd 8991, 1918) it called for closer co-operation between the University and the National Library of Wales and National Museum of Wales 'as laboratories and centres of learning', recommending

> the establishment of a new element in Welsh University organization which would [...] serve as a strong link between the University and the Welsh people, and would also give new opportunities and much-needed encouragement to students and researchers, both within and without the University.

Since valuable work produced by members of the University was either not published at all or was scattered through various journals where it was difficult to trace and remained unknown, the Committee believed that the proposed University Press would not only give staff confidence that the University would support their research by undertaking its publication but would also encourage research and publication by school teachers and students of the extra-mural classes. It would also assist in the provision of educational books and other material for school use. The Committee recognized that for some time at least it will need substantial financial help, but we recommend that this should be afforded by the University as soon as provision has been made for the more immediately pressing needs.

The Board of Celtic Studies held its first meeting in January 1919 but the Press was not established until January 1922.[28] Commercial publishers — notably Hughes of Wrexham — continued to undertake scholarly publishing during the 1920s and beyond, but behind Haldane's watershed recommendation (and the proposal by J. H. Davies) lay the conviction that the organization or even the pursuit of research was not a matter of personal inclination; nor could the publication of scholarship be left solely to the economics of the market and to the enterprise of individual commercial publishers. Welsh learned societies and eisteddfod competitions had an important part to play in the writing and dissemination of research but the experience of the Cymmrodorion and later of groups like Cymdeithas Llên Cymru and the Bangor Manuscript Society showed that publication could no longer be undertaken by amateur or voluntary labour. Without the skills and expertise of a specialist publisher and a knowledgeable commissioning editor, and without the support of a parent organization in what must inevitably be a restricted market, Haldane realized that it was doubtful whether scholarly publishing in Welsh studies could flourish. The Commission would probably come to a similar conclusion today.

NOTES TO CHAPTER 18

1. Reproduced in R. T. Jenkins and Helen M. Ramage, *A history of the Honourable Society of Cymmrodorion and of the Gwyneddigion and Cymreigyddion Societies 1751-1951* (London, 1951), p. 236.
2. Jenkins and Ramage, pp. 138-9, and Bedwyr Lewis Jones, *'Yr hen bersoniaid llengar'* ([Penarth], 1963) are the best accounts.
3. B. L. Jones, pp. 19-20.
4. Robert Jones, 'Sketch of the history of The Cymmrodorion', *Y Cymmrodor*, 1 (1877), pp. xi-xii.
5. For the Gwent Society see Mair Elvet Thomas, *Afiaith yng Ngwent* (Cardiff, 1978).
6. Jenkins and Ramage, p. 167, and B. L. Jones, p. 36, which refers to the project for printing a new edition of the *Myvyrian* and three additional volumes.
7. E. D. Jones, *Gwaith Lewis Glyn Cothi, 1837-39* (Cardiff, 1973).
8. Jenkins and Ramage, p. 169.
9. Thomas, pp. 9, 139.
10. J. M. Trahearne, *Historical notices of Sir Matthew Cradock* (Llandovery, 1840), p. 13.
11. The other volumes comprised Lewis Dwnn, *Heraldic visitations of Wales*, ed. S. R. Meyrick (1846), *The Iolo manuscripts*, ed. Taliesin Williams (1848), *The lives of the Cambro-British saints*, ed. Rice Rees and W. J. Rees (1853), and the three volumes 'edited' by John Williams, 'Ab Ithel', *Dosbarth Edeyrn Davod Aur* (1856), *The physicians of Myddfai* (1861), *Barddas* (1861).
12. For the early history of the Cambrian Archaeological Association see Ben Bowen Thomas, 'The Cambrians and the nineteenth-century crisis in Welsh studies 1847-1870', *AC*, 127 (1978), 1-15.
13. Jenkins and Ramage, pp. 174-6.
14. *Y Cymmrodor*, 1 (1877), xxix.
15. *MC*, 1 (1868), i-vi.
16. Jenkins and Ramage, pp. 220-1.
17. E. D. Jones, pp. 49-50.
18. For an (incomplete) list of Cymmrodorion 'Supplemental Volumes' and Record Series titles see G. O. Williams, *Index to the publications of the Honourable Society of Cymmrodorion* (London, 1913), pp. 50-7.
19. See Jenkins and Ramage, p. 181, for the official minute of Council.
20. Notable examples are the studies of Welsh Puritans by Thomas Richards published in the 1920s, and G. J. Williams, *Iolo Morganwg a chywyddau'r ychwanegiad* (1926). For a list of National Eisteddfod Association publications see *Rhestr o lyfrau'r Gymdeithas ynghyd a'u cynnwys a'u prisiau* (1917) and *THSC*, 1933-34-35 (1936), pp. 153-4.
21. For the development of Welsh studies in the University of Wales see R. M. Jones, *Llenyddiaeth Gymraeg a Phrifysgol Cymru* ([s.l.], 1993).
22. The first of these was *The text of the Mabinogion [...] from the Red Book of Hergest* (1887), followed by texts of the Black Book of Carmarthen, the Bruts from the Red Book of Hergest, Book of Llandaf, Chirk Codex of Laws, White Book of Rhydderch Mabinogion, Book of Aneirin, Book of Taliesin, Poetry in the Red Book of Hergest, and *Kymdeithas Amlyn ac Amic*. Details of their complex publishing history are given by E. D. Jones in his *DWB* article on Evans.
23. The series included *Llyvyr Iob* (1897), *Pedeir Kainc y Mabinogi, Breuddwyd Maxen, Lludd a Llevelys* (1897, 1905).
24. T. I. Ellis, *The Guild of Graduates 1864-1969* ([s.l.], 1969), pp. 1-4, and see T. E. Ellis, *Speeches and addresses* (Wrexham, 1912), pp. 143-62.
25. The six reprints, 1899-1908, included *Drych y Prif Oesoedd, Yny lhyvyr hwnn,* and *Deffynniad Ffydd Eglwys Loegr*. Three transcripts of manuscripts appeared under the imprint of the Guild between 1916 and 1921, and the series was continued by the University Press.
26. See E. D. Jones, 'Hen geinder mewn coch, glas a melyn', *Y Casglwr*, 5 (Summer 1978), 16. The free-metre (blue cover) titles were *Carolau Richard Hughes* (1900), *Hen gerddi gwleidyddol, 1588-1660* (1901), *Casgliad o hen ganiadau serch* (1902), *Casgliad o hanes-gerddi Cymru* (1903), *Caniadau yn y mesurau rhyddion* (1905). The Puritan pamphlets (red covers) comprised *The Parliament explained to*

Wales by John Lewis (1907), *An Act for the Propagation of the Gospel in Wales* (1908), *Strena Vavasoriensis* (1915). The sole yellow-cover title was *Emynau I: Gwaith Morgan Rhys.*

[27] *Gwaith Barddonol Howel Swrdwal a'i fab Ieuan*, ed. J. C. Morrice (1908), *Vita Sancti Tathei and Buched Seint y Katrin*, ed. H. Idris Bell (1909), *Casgliad o waith Ieuan Deulwyn*, ed. Ifor Williams (1909), *Detholiad o waith Gruffudd ab Ieuan ab Llewelyn Vychan*, ed. J. C. Morrice (1910), *Gwaith Dafydd ab Edmwnd*, ed. Thomas Roberts (1914).The records of the Society are at the University of Wales, Bangor. I am grateful to the Archivist, Mr Tomos Roberts, for making them available to me and for his assistance. For the Society see Brynley F. Roberts, 'Ysgolheictod chwaethus', *Y Casglwr*, 56/57 (Summer 1996), 20.

[28] On the later history of the University of Wales Press see T. H. Parry-Williams, *Bwrdd Gwasg Prifysgol Cymru: rhai hen atgofion* (Cardiff, 1972) and J. Gwynn Williams, 'Gwasg Prifysgol Cymru', *Llais Llyfrau*, October 1990, pp. 3-4. There was considerable continuity; the Guild was responsible for initiating several important publications after the Press had been established and the Press took over many of the Guild's titles and continued some of its series.

CHAPTER 19

MUSIC PUBLISHING

Rhidian Griffiths

MUSIC printing is almost as old as the art of printing itself. A few examples can be dated to the fifteenth century, the most notable being the Konstanz Gradual, printed around 1473. Yet just as printing came late to Wales, so it was not until the seventeenth century that printed music appeared in a Welsh text. It is generally acknowledged that the first Welsh book to include printed music was the collection of metrical psalms issued in 1621 by Edmwnd Prys, archdeacon of Merioneth, under the title *Llyfr y Psalmav*. Prys included with his metrical versions of all 150 psalms twelve tunes, most of which are to be found in English and continental collections of psalms. No printer is named on the title-page of the work, but since it appeared in London with an edition of the Prayer Book printed by Bonham Norton and John Bill, who had been responsible for at least one English collection of psalms and hymns with music, it is not unreasonable to suppose that they were the printers of *Llyfr y Psalmav*. This publication did not, however, inaugurate a tradition of Welsh music printing. Though Prys's psalms were reprinted several times in the course of the seventeenth and eighteenth centuries, only two subsequent editions, those of 1630 and 1638, are known to have retained the tunes. It was not until 1770 that tunes again appeared with Prys's words, in an edition of the Prayer Book printed at Cambridge: this collection of twenty-four hymn melodies was compiled by Evan Williams (b. 1706), who retained some of Prys's tunes while adding later examples, including some of his own compositions.

Wales did not, therefore, profit directly from the development of music printing during the seventeenth century, when better, more readable types were perfected, and experiments made in printing from engraved plates. Specialist printing of this kind was out of the question in a poor country such as Wales, and it was again in London, under the patronage of the gentry and through the agency of learned societies such as the Cymmrodorion, that Welsh music printing continued in the eighteenth century, with the issuing of collections of harp-tunes and songs compiled by John Parry (?1710-82), the blind harper, and Edward Jones, 'Bardd y Brenin' (1752-1824). John Parry, whose patron was Sir Watkin Williams Wynn of Wynnstay, published his *Antient British Music* in 1742, and further collections containing Welsh melodies in 1761 and 1781. Three years later, in 1784, appeared the first edition of *Musical and Poetical Relicks of the Welsh Bards*, compiled by Edward Jones. Jones, who had in the Prince of Wales, later George IV, an even more distinguished patron, collected the melodies which he feared were disappearing from the repertoire of Welsh harpers, and was responsible for recording a number of famous tunes, such as 'Gorhoffedd Gwr Harlech'. In addition to the music he provided a fashionable, though totally erroneous, history of Welsh music, tracing its origins to the time of the druids. A second edition of *Relicks* appeared in 1794, followed in 1802 by a third collection, *The Bardic Museum*, and a posthumous volume, *Hen*

Ganiadau Cymru (*Old songs of Wales*), in 1825. Some of these were also published in Dublin.

Such collections, though milestones in musical antiquarianism, could not be deemed popular publications. They were produced in limited editions for the wealthy gentry who subscribed to them. Towards the end of the eighteenth century, however, some attempt was made to bring printed music to the mass market in Wales. Only one copy is known to survive of the harbinger of this movement, a musical grammar entitled *Cyfaill mewn Llogell* (*A friend in the pocket*), by John Williams, 'Siôn Singer' (c.1750-1807). Printed by John Daniel at Carmarthen in 1797, *Cyfaill mewn Llogell* can claim to be the first book printed in Wales to include music. Daniel does not appear, however, to have possessed any music type, for when music examples are required, they are entered in manuscript on a printed stave. The same technique was used in Joshua Watkins's *Difyrwch i'r Pererinion* (*The pilgrims' diversion*), a slightly modified reprint of *Cyfaill mewn Llogell*, printed at Carmarthen in 1810; in *The Rudiments of Thorough Bass* by 'an amateur of Pembroke', printed at Pembroke in the same year; and in *Agoriad byr ar y Gamut* (*A short introduction to the gamut*), printed at Aberystwyth by John James (1771-1848) and Samuel Williams (1782-1820) in 1811. These early attempts at music publishing are a reflection of the revival of interest in music and music education which Wales was experiencing. In 1816, five years after the appearance of *Agoriad byr ar y Gamut*, came the first known attempt to print music in Wales, with the publication of *Mawl yr Arglwydd* (*The Lord's praise*), a collection of hymn-tunes and anthems by John Ellis (1760-1839) of Llanrwst, issued at Trefriw by Ishmael Dafydd (1758-1817). Only part of the work was printed at Trefriw, and the remainder in London; but the appearance of *Mawl yr Arglwydd* was a milestone, inaugurating a tradition of music printing and publishing which was to have a substantial impact on the cultural life of Wales.

The publishing output of the following generation, from about 1820 to 1860, falls into three broad categories: first, works on the rudiments of music; second, collections of tunes and anthems for use by congregations in churches and chapels, which were often combined with treatises on rudiments; and third, collections of national airs. With a few notable exceptions, such as Maria Jane Williams's *Ancient National Airs of Gwent and Morganwg*, printed by William Rees (1808-73) of Llandovery in 1844, and *Y Caniedydd Cymreig* (*The Welsh singer*) by John Thomas, 'Ieuan Ddu', printed by David Jones of Merthyr Tudful in the following year, the works in the third category were 'foreign' publications, produced in London for wealthy subscribers, as the collections of John Parry and Edward Jones had been. Such, for instance, were the collections of John Parry, 'Bardd Alaw' (1776-1851), especially his *Welsh Harper* of 1839 and 1848, in which he reissued much material obtained from Edward Jones. This London tradition was to continue, and become somewhat less élitist, with the series of *Welsh Melodies* published between 1862 and 1874 by John Thomas, 'Pencerdd Gwalia' (1826-1913), harpist to Queen Victoria, and was to culminate in the publication in 1873 of Boosey's *Songs of Wales*, edited by Brinley Richards (1819-85), a volume which acquired a popularity in Wales said to be exceeded only by that of the Bible.[1]

Native music publishing developed markedly within the first two categories identified above. These publications, usually in the Welsh language, appear to have been aimed at a popular market within Wales: they were printed in Wales and their prices put them within the reach of Welsh purchasers. Many of them combined instruction in the rudiments of music with a collection of tunes for everyday use. In 1837 John Parry (1775-1846) of Chester produced his *Peroriaeth Hyfryd* (*Delightful music*), a book of one hundred tunes, priced at four shillings, and directed specifically, so the preface states, at Welsh church and chapel congregations. Such too were the collections of John Roberts (1807-76) of Henllan, *Caniadau y Cyssegr* (*Songs of the sanctuary*) (1839), and of the various members of the Mills family of Llanidloes, pioneers in music education: *Caniadau Seion* (*Songs of Zion*) (1840) and *Yr Arweinydd Cerddorol* (*The musical leader*) (1842-45) by Richard Mills (1809-44), and *Y Salmydd Eglwysig* (*The Church psalter*) (1847) by John Mills (1812-73). Llanidloes became a centre of music publishing owing to the work of the Mills family and of the printer John Mendus Jones (1814-99), who was also responsible for a number of collections compiled by Thomas Williams, 'Hafrenydd' (1807-94), and for one of the earliest attempts at a Welsh music periodical, *Yr Athraw Cerddorol* (*The Music Teacher*), four numbers of which appeared during 1854. In South Wales, Merthyr Tudful, a thriving industrial community and one of the early centres of choral singing, also became a centre for publishing, and it was there that Rosser Beynon (1811-76) published his collection of sacred music, *Telyn Seion* (*Zion's harp*), in 1848.

Such publications met the growing needs of church and chapel, but also of the musical societies which flourished from the 1820s onward, and which provided the main thrust of music education. It was for local societies that works of music theory were issued. *Egwyddor-ddysg Ragegorawl*, an adaptation by Owen Williams (1774-1839) of Charles Dibdin's *Music Epitomized*, appeared in London in 1817, but several later works were to be published in Wales, among them *Grisiau Cerdd Arwest* (*Steps in minstrelsy*) (Swansea, 1823), by John Ryland Harris (1802-23), and *Y Caniedydd Crefyddol* (*The religious song-book*) (Newtown, 1828) by William Owen (1788-1838). The culmination of this movement came in 1838 with the appearance of John Mills's *Gramadeg Cerddoriaeth* (*Musical grammar*), an extremely influential work, printed by John Mendus Jones, which ran to at least six editions of 10,000 copies.[2]

From about 1860, as Welsh music life developed and became more varied, so publishing was to diversify. Tune-books and musical grammars would be submerged in a flood of sheet music for concerts, eisteddfodau, and *cymanfaoedd canu* (singing festivals). With the spread of musical education a generation of native Welsh composers grew up, and as choral singing gained popularity in the 1860s and 1870s, more and more music for choirs was published. In the 1870s the concert solo became an established musical form, and so the pattern of music publishing was set, a pattern which was to continue for close on a hundred years. Improved communications made distribution easier. In 1861 also the last tax on paper had been removed, thus paving the way for the issuing of cheap sheet music. As music became 'not merely a distant delight to, but an activity for, the many',[3] so publishers sought to take advantage of a ready and growing market.

That market was in essence an internal one. Music publishers of the period between 1860 and 1960 were concerned with the publishing not of European, but of Welsh music. They took advantage of a lively popular culture to produce that which, though often not of a high musical standard, was acceptable in those eisteddfod- and chapel-centred circles where native music was heard. The growing prominence of choral competitions at eisteddfodau from the 1870s and the demand for anthems at the *cymanfaoedd canu* which flourished from the 1880s ensured a steady supply of compositions which were taken up by publishers. A few compositions became popular, and were sung almost to death; their success made good in financial terms the losses sustained on other publications. It was perhaps an introspective culture. Editors of music journals regularly complained that the Welsh were lovers of singing rather than lovers of music, and that they would not support the periodicals published for the enhancement of their musical education. Nevertheless, such journals did appear, albeit with varying degrees of success. The first successful periodical was *Y Cerddor Cymreig* (*The Welsh Musician*), which ran from March 1861 to December 1873 under the editorship of John Roberts, 'Ieuan Gwyllt' (1822-77). Its didactic tone and the quality of much of its content had a profound impact on a generation of musicians, and two of its devotees, D. Emlyn Evans (1843-1913) and David Jenkins (1848-1915), were to edit a distinguished sequel, *Y Cerddor* (*The Musician*), which was launched in January 1889 and continued, in successive series, until the outbreak of the Second World War. It is nevertheless true that these periodicals, and others like them, though long-lived, survived only through heavy subsidies by their publishers; and it is significant that, however lively and vigorous the musical culture, no publishing house could afford to be dependent for its income on music alone. The Welsh market was just too small.

Another feature which helped to distinguish the Welsh market from its English counterpart was the dominance of the tonic sol-fa notation. Like so many movements of the Victorian age, this had its moral purpose:

> The Tonic Sol-fa movement touched almost all efforts for the elevation of mankind. By simplifying musical notation, the art in its domestic and religious aspects entered thousands of homes which had before been without music. Thus the method was the indirect means of aiding worship, temperance and culture, of holding young men and women among good influences, of reforming character, of spreading Christianity.[4]

In rural Wales, where facilities for teaching music were scarce, sol-fa became the accepted method of teaching the people to sing and quickly became the standard notation for Welsh choristers. John Curwen's textbooks were translated into Welsh by Eleazer Roberts (1825-1912), in a series called *Llawlyfr Caniadaeth* (*The handbook of singing*), published between 1862 and 1875, and so common did sol-fa become that South Wales came to be recognized as one of the most profitable outlets for the publications of the Tonic Sol-fa Agency. But the ease with which it can be printed — it is a notation based on the letters of the alphabet, and sol-fa fonts could be bought relatively cheaply — led many Welsh printers to master the technique: hence the assertion of John Graham in 1923 that 'music, cheaper than ever, music which could be printed in almost any Welsh village, was available'.[5] From the musical point of view, that was not always an advantage: the ease with which they could find a publisher tempted less experienced composers to rush into print. Yet so great was the impact of sol-fa on the Welsh musical scene that in 1912 it was estimated that ninety per cent of younger musicians in Wales could read no other notation.[6] When works were issued in both notations, it was not uncommon to print fifty sol-fa copies for every one in staff notation.

Some Welsh printers are known to have used music type for letterpress printing, among them John Mendus Jones, David Jenkins (c.1810-72) of Aberystwyth, Griffith Jones of Y Bala, and Robert Jones (1811-77) of Bethesda. These four were active in the 1840s, 1850s, and 1860s, and their productions were suited to letterpress, being comparatively few, and on a small scale. When solo songs became popular, it became increasingly difficult to contemplate the use of music type, which was not suitable for more complex music. Increasingly, therefore, Welsh printers turned to specialist engravers outside Wales. Isaac Jones (1835-99), a successful printer-publisher of Treherbert, Rhondda, employed during the 1880s the experienced music compositor Benjamin Morris Williams (1832-1903) who had learned his craft from Robert Jones and who had also worked for Thomas Gee of Denbigh. It is known, however, that Isaac Jones came to rely almost exclusively on London engravers such as Lowe and Brydone for his later publications. Benjamin Parry (1835-1910) of Swansea likewise used the London engravers, notably Spottiswoode and C. G. Röder, and John Wright of Bristol. Even a large concern like Hughes a'i Fab of Wrexham, which employed its own music compositor, Richard Mills (1840-1903), made extensive use of the London firms.

Welsh music publishing never gave rise to a Welsh Novello or Boosey. Even for the house once called 'the Welsh Novello',[7] Hughes a'i Fab of Wrexham, music was only one part of its total publishing activity, and other, smaller firms were usually linked to general printing offices or music retail outlets. There seems to be no reason to believe that the business of publishing Welsh music in the century between 1860 and 1960 was a profitable one, though the dearth of archive material for publishing houses makes precise assessment impossible. Apart from some popular anthems and choral pieces, which, because of their use in *cymanfaoedd canu* and eisteddfodau over a number of years, would be reprinted in thousands, print runs of music titles appear to have been quite short. It appears that five hundred or a thousand was the standard run for a solo song. In 1893 Hughes a'i Fab printed five hundred copies of 'Hyd fedd hi gâr yn gywir' (She will love truly to the grave) by the popular songwriter D. Pughe Evans (1866-97); thirteen months later Benjamin Parry printed 1,050 copies of the same composer's 'Brad Dynrafon' (The treachery of Dunraven).[8] The Welsh-language market was, after all, limited; and since Welsh publishers confined themselves almost entirely to vocal music (though with English as well as Welsh words), their sales outside Wales would be comparatively few. In the same way, the sums paid to composers for their copyrights, which were almost invariably bought outright, were not enormous, in general ranging from half a guinea to five guineas. Sometimes extra payments were promised. In 1894 Hughes a'i Fab undertook to publish the song 'Gwlad y bryniau' (Land of the hills) by M. W. Griffith (1855-1925), for the sum of two guineas; but if 750 copies were sold within two years a further guinea would be forthcoming. No doubt that is some measure of the expected level of sales.[9]

Yet if the operations of music publishers were on a small scale compared with those of their English counterparts, there is no denying the vigour of their activity during the late nineteenth and early twentieth centuries. One of the first houses to respond to the call for Welsh music was Hughes a'i Fab. In 1861 it launched a series of octavo choral works called 'Y Gyfres Gerddorol Gymreig' (The Welsh Musical Series) which, along with the monthly musical supplements to *Y Cerddor Cymreig*, for which Hughes assumed responsibility in 1865, was to set a pattern for such publications. The supplements to the several journals which Hughes published between 1865 and 1939 became the mainstay of the firm's choral catalogue. From the 1870s on, following the example of Isaac Clarke (1824-75) of Rhuthun, it published large numbers of solo songs and duets, secular and sacred, so that by 1946 it was estimated that over two thousand music titles had appeared under the Hughes imprint over the previous eighty years.[10]

A number of smaller firms were also active. Between 1870 and 1914 there were music publishers in several Welsh towns: D. L. Jones, 'Cynalaw' (1841-1916), of Briton Ferry and J. R. Lewis (1857-1919) of Carmarthen were, like Isaac Jones of Treherbert and Benjamin Parry of Swansea, printers who did their share of jobbing and who also kept stationers' shops. The North Wales Music Company was associated with the music retail business of E. D. Williams (?1853-1916) at Bangor, and David Trehearn of Rhyl was likewise a shopkeeper rather than a printer. The Welsh Publishing Company of Caernarfon specialised in educational books, and had originated as a newspaper publishing company: by 1914 it had around a hundred music titles in its catalogue. The Jones family of Llannerch-y-medd in Anglesey had a long association with music. Before his death in 1877 Lewis Jones (b. 1841) had published a number of musical items, a tradition continued by his sisters Jane (1837-91) and Elisabeth (1848-1920), who ran the business until 1910. In addition, a large number of composers published their own works, one in particular, David Jenkins, professor of music at the University College of Wales, Aberystwyth, and co-editor of *Y Cerddor*, becoming an important publisher in his own right.

The situation was to change after the First World War. The number of composer-publishers declined as the depression of the twenties took hold, and many smaller firms sold out. Hughes and Son acquired the imprints of David Trehearn, and subsequently, those of John Jones of Bethesda. But the main beneficiary of the decline of the smaller publisher was D. J. Snell (1880-1957) of Swansea. A shopkeeper who began as a retailer of music, musical instruments, and gramophones, Snell acquired in 1910 the stock and copyrights of Benjamin Parry, and so began a career which was to make him one of Wales's foremost music publishers. Not a printer-publisher as so many of his predecessors had been, he retained and expanded his retail business while at the same time acquiring the stock and copyrights of defunct businesses and of composers who no longer wished to be burdened with selling their own compositions. It was he who bought up Isaac Jones, D. L. Jones, J. R. Lewis, the North Wales Music Company, David Jenkins, and the Welsh Publishing Company, along with many others, to amass a substantial catalogue of nearly 1,500 titles by 1939. He was also responsible for publishing new works by composers of a younger generation, such as Idris Lewis (1889-1952), W. Bradwen Jones (1892-1970) and Meirion Williams (1901-76).[11]

Greater diversity was brought to the Welsh publishing scene by the National Council of Music. In 1918 the Haldane Commission on the University of Wales recommended the establishment of a Council of Music, which came into being the following year, with the charismatic Walford Davies as its Director. One of the Council's many positive contributions to Welsh life was the publication of Welsh music in authoritative, well-edited editions, usually in conjunction with the Oxford University Press: many of these works, which were directed especially at the educational market, later reappeared under the imprint of the University of Wales Press. They included editions of European compositions with Welsh words and arrangements from the rich corpus of folk-songs collected by the Welsh Folk-Song Society from its inception in 1908. Similarly, the Gwynn Publishing Company, founded in 1937 by the composer W. S. Gwynn Williams (1896-1978), pioneered multilingual editions of European choral works and Welsh folk and dance music, many of which were to be popularised at the Llangollen International Musical Eisteddfod begun by Williams and others in 1947.

The Second World War was to bring further changes, and the demise of a number of long established houses. Snell and Sons ceased publishing in the early 1960s, and ceased trading altogether in 1971. Hughes and Son, Gwynn, and the University of Wales Press published less and less, being content to sell existing titles; and by 1980 this proverbially musical nation was almost devoid of active music publishing. In succeeding years, however, a slow improvement occurred. The Hughes imprint was acquired by Christopher Davies and subsequently by the Welsh television channel S4C, and a number of popular titles were reprinted. In the same way the Snell imprint was revived in 1982 for the reissue of its most successful titles. The firm of Gwynn was bought and removed to Pen-y-groes, Gwynedd; it acquired the music stocks of the University of Wales Press, and, more important, issued some new titles. Both the Guild for the Promotion of Welsh Music and the Welsh Music Information Centre have published contemporary Welsh works, and Y Lolfa and Cyhoeddiadau Curiad have emerged as publishers of Welsh-language items. The advent of computerized typesetting for music has opened up new possibilities for home-based publishers; and if economic considerations and the smallness of the potential market still make the publishing of Welsh music a slow and expensive business, the general buoyancy of musical life as the century draws to its close gives reason to hope that the tale has not been fully told.

NOTES TO CHAPTER 19

1. A. J. Heward Rees, '"Songs of Wales": a brief centenary note', *Welsh Music*, 4(5) (1973-4), 90-2.
2. Richard Mills and N. Cynhafal Jones, *Buchdraeth y Parch. John Mills* (Aberdâr, 1881), pp. 51-2.
3. Percy M. Young, *The choral tradition* (London, 1962), p. 191.
4. Quoted in Herbert Simon, *Song and words: a history of the Curwen press* (London, 1973), p. 15.
5. John Graham, *A century of Welsh music* (London, 1923), p. 38.
6. *Y Cerddor*, 24 (1912), 2.
7. *Y Gerddorfa*, 1 (1872-73), 28.
8. S4C, Hughes & Son Archive, 'Copyrights, Musical', 12 Oct. 1893; NLW, Snell & Sons Archive (Benjamin Parry), 1 Jan. 1895.
9. S4C, Hughes & Son Archive, 'Copyrights, Musical', 15 and 31 Dec. 1894.
10. Thomas Bassett, *Braslun o hanes Hughes a'i fab, cyhoeddwyr, Wrecsam* (Oswestry, 1946), p. 26.
11. Rhidian Griffiths, 'Swansea's "Mr. Music": the career of D. J. Snell, music publisher', *Y Llyfr yng Nghymru/Welsh Book Studies*, (1998), p. 59-90.

CHAPTER 20

WELSH BALLADS

Tegwyn Jones

A few Welsh ballads on such subjects as the Babington plot to assassinate Queen Elizabeth in 1586, the translation of the Bible into Welsh and the defeat of the Spanish Armada in 1588, and the Gunpowder plot of 1605 have been preserved in manuscripts but none appears to have been printed before 1700 apart from the enigmatic *Byd y Bigail* (*The shepherd's world*), preserved in the Pepys collection of ballads in Magdalen College, Cambridge, and printed probably in London between 1603 and 1640.[1] These manuscript ballads, recorded just as the old literary tradition based on the traditional strict metres began to give way to the free metres, probably represent the last generation of a long line of such orally transmitted poems. Although printed ballads in England can be traced to the early sixteenth century, problems discussed elsewhere — the sparse and scattered nature of the Welsh population, its general poverty and illiteracy, and the restrictions placed on printing to 1695 — delayed the advent of the printed ballad in Wales by almost two centuries.

A key event was the removal of Thomas Jones, the Corwen-born almanac-maker, from London to Shrewsbury in 1695 and his establishment of a press there. He was rapidly followed by other printers such as John Rogers, Thomas Durston, Siôn Rhydderch, and Stafford Prys who sensed that a considerable demand for exciting popular verse existed just over the border and who set about providing such material. The gradual growth in literacy, greatly stimulated by Griffith Jones's circulating schools from the early 1730s onwards, helped to provide such printers with an expanding market. In Wales itself, the first publications of Isaac Carter's pioneering press at Trefhedyn in 1718 were two ballads, one being a diatribe against tobacco and the other a consideration of conscience and its properties. Ballad-pamphlets were by far the most frequently printed Welsh items produced by the new presses established in Wales during the eighteenth century. Presses in Border towns such as Chester and Oswestry were also important, catering for the prolific ballad writers of Caernarfon and Denbighshire, of whose compositions well in excess of seven hundred have survived. Even so, it has been suggested that the number of lost ballads must be considerably higher:

> Of the 104 books of Welsh religious verse and sayings published between 1710 and 1730, some ninety per cent were ballads [...] It is probable, however, that those printed editions that are extant after 1710 are merely the tip of an iceberg, and that only a small proportion of ballads of the day has survived. The most popular editions were probably those that left fewest extant copies, and where no copies survive the consumption is likely to have been at its greatest.[2]

When one considers the richness of the material preserved in the surviving corpus of ballads, the loss must be deeply lamented by historians and students of folk music and folk poetry.

During the eighteenth century the term *baled* or *balad* could refer either to a pamphlet (normally of eight pages) containing as many as three or four separate poems, or to a single poem of this type. Individual ballads also appeared in Welsh almanacs and formed an important part of the *anterliwtiau* (interludes) that enjoyed such popularity during the eighteenth century. The pages of ballad pamphlets would be stitched together, and the title-page would usually indicate the title of each individual ballad and the air to which it was to be sung. It would also bear the printer's imprint, and the name of its publisher — possibly the author, but more usually the seller or distributor. There were naturally several variations; J. H. Davies lists almost a hundred eighteenth-century ballad pamphlets which lack an imprint of any kind, and others note only where they were printed.[3] The paper used for ballads was normally the cheapest to hand, and there were few adornments. J. H. Davies could describe as 'unique' a ballad pamphlet printed by Stafford Prys of Shrewsbury in 1758 which has both the word *Cerddi* (Songs) and the imprint on its title-page printed in red ink.[4] Decorative devices are the exception rather than the rule; fewer than fifty examples of illustrated eighteenth-century ballads have survived.[5] Although often crudely executed and frequently bearing little or no relevance to the ballad they seek to illustrate, devices can sometimes help to identify a printer. Few broadside ballads of the eighteenth or nineteenth centuries have survived, perhaps because their large size made binding impractical and thus rendered them more liable to destruction when carried about in the pocket. Perhaps, too, such broadsheets were pinned or stuck to the walls of houses and would be torn down or pasted over when a new favourite was acquired.

Publishers and printers took advantage of the ballad pamphlet as a vehicle for advertising a wide variety of wares at 'fair and reasonable' prices. Evan Ellis of Llanfihangel Glyn Myfyr, for example, described himself as a 'seller of books and British Oil',[6] while John Thomas of Bontnewydd near Caernarfon announced that he had for sale a dial which showed how far the sun travels in a minute and another which told the time at night by the moon and stars. William Jones of Wrexham listed the chapbooks which he had for sale in addition to his ballads, his imprint accordingly lengthening as his stock increased. (Welsh chapbooks appear to have been produced on a far less extensive scale than ballads for some reason.) Sometimes Jones added a rhyming couplet extolling the virtues of a medicine obtainable from him which was guaranteed to cure the breathlessness suffered by 'miners and colliers'. Space could be used for matter other than advertisements; Evan Ellis once used the space at the end of a ballad to deal with a charge of theft brought against him by claiming that he was drunk at the time and had subsequently suffered much scolding by his wife.

Although the ballads sold by individual sellers or hawkers will often provide a clue to their preferred material, sellers would have been unwise to restrict themselves to a particular subject or theme, and the evidence, though scanty, suggests that they would generally be sensitive to the history and traditions of the area in which they plied their trade. As a result, ballads could be a lucrative source of income to their hawkers and printers as well as being a source of delight to purchasers.

The subject matter of the ballads encompassed all the circumstances and experiences of life. The vast majority are concerned with religious topics, often urging readers or listeners to adopt a higher morality and decrying swearing, blaspheming, drunkenness,

Sabbath-breaking, and miserliness towards the poor. All aspects of love — both requited and unrequited — and of marriage are also exhaustively covered. Many ballad pamphlets consequently contain startling juxtapositions of the profane and religious; in one, printed for Evan Ellis, a lament for a lost maidenhead is immediately followed by an account of the Last Judgement. Current events, particularly disasters such as wars, plague (as at Marseilles in 1720), and earthquakes (notably the 1755 Lisbon catastrophe), are recorded in verse, as are sensational events like murders and loss of life in accidents or shipwrecks. Historical subjects were also popular, both actual incidents and fabulous tales, the latter often deriving from Geoffrey of Monmouth's legendary 'history' of Britain. Legends common to the folk traditions of many countries were also occasionally turned into ballads. In a word, this 'metrical journalism of the masses'[7] reflects the life and interests of the ordinary Welshman and Welsh woman in a period as yet innocent of vernacular newspapers and periodicals.

The first hawkers of printed ballads, one must assume, would have been the authors themselves. By having a product to sell they would no longer be wholly dependent on the few coins thrown at their feet as they sang in the market-place or fairground. Ballads were so avidly purchased that it was soon realized that a market for them existed whether or not they were sung, and the printed ballad accordingly became a part of the pedlar's pack, thus creating a secondary group of distributors. These balladmongers (several of whom were women) would either buy their ballads from a printer's existing stock at a wholesale price, such stocks being frequently advertised by the printer on his ballad pamphlets, or would have their own choice of ballads — some written at their request, others traditional favourites, yet others by poets long-dead — printed for an agreed fee. The printer would bestow a certain status on balladmongers by including their names in the imprint — 'Printed at Bala by John Rowland for William Davies' — thus preserving the names of many of those who trudged the countryside, selling their ephemeral wares from door to door or sometimes singing them in some public place. Sometimes, too, the name may be followed by a brief description of the occupation — 'smith', 'weaver', 'cooper', 'joiner' — to which balladmongers presumably returned during the winter months or when compelled for some other reason to give up their itinerant habits.

The pattern of ballad production and distribution remained essentially the same into the nineteenth century, although all aspects of the activity were on a larger scale and industrialized south Wales became an increasingly important market. During the century ballads were printed in no fewer than 96 towns and villages throughout Wales, many towns boasting several presses. A few ballads were also printed in England, at Bristol, Bath, Gloucester, Liverpool, and London as well as at the traditional Border centres of Welsh printing, Shrewsbury, Chester, and Oswestry. In Wales itself, the main centres of ballad production were Carmarthen, Merthyr, Swansea, Caernarfon, and Aberystwyth (in that order). Examples of well over 1,700 nineteenth-century Welsh ballads have been preserved in libraries, but as in the case of their eighteenth-century forerunners these may well represent the tip of an iceberg. At least 359 printers appended their imprint to ballads, and the hundreds of ballads which lack an imprint may conceal the identity of several more.

Nineteenth-century ballads (apart from a few exceptions in the early years of the century) were no longer eight-page pamphlets but rather a single small sheet folded once and containing one main ballad, any space left over being filled with a shorter poem or a few *englynion*. Decorative devices came to be used to a far greater degree, although the use by one printer of a block of a large black bear to illustrate the extremely popular '*Mochyn du*' (Lament upon the death of the black pig) suggests that the relevance of illustrations to the ballads they accompanied was still not a primary concern. The ballads themselves were for the most part devoid of the metrical intricacies so characteristic of their earlier counterparts. Any printer worth his salt would have a constant supply of the most popular ballads which travelling balladmongers would purchase to supplement the more journalistic ones of their own composition in order to add to the variety of material they would have on offer at their next stop. The salesbook of the Aberystwyth printer Samuel Williams casts some light on the scale of these transactions between 1816 and 1820. David Jones, 'Songster', bought 4,000 copies of '*Chwech o gablwyr meddw*' (Six drunken blasphemers) for two pounds in 1816, and a 'ballad songstress' purchased a thousand ballads for eighteen shillings in January 1818.[8] The profit to be made from the sale of ballads — one shilling per hundred copies — was scarcely generous. Even so, the leading ballad singers might hope to make a fair living; it has been suggested that Richard Williams, 'Dic Dywyll', (composer of a number of the most robust ballads) might have made as much as three pounds a week at the peak of his popularity.[9]

The basic subject-matter of nineteenth-century ballads remained much the same as those of the preceding century, but their numerous authors constantly embraced new subjects and topics which reflected contemporary society. Industrial developments and innovations gave rise to ballads which rejoice in the coming of the railway, while one of the darker sides of industrialization is represented by the large body of ballads which record the frequent and heavy loss of life in mining and industrial accidents. Ballads from the 1830s onwards on the new subject of temperance reflect the division between teetotallers and the advocates of moderation. Popular disturbances such as the Merthyr Riots of 1831, the Rebecca Riots of the early 1840s, and the 'Tithe War' of the later 1880s all attracted their share of ballads.

Piracy of ballads appears to have become a far more pressing issue during the nineteenth century, and dire warnings threatening transgressors with the full rigours of the law became a common addition to ballad sheets. Such warnings were sometimes versified, or offered a reward for any information which might prevent the practice. A few ballad writers preferred to appeal to the better nature of potential pirates; Robert Jones, 'Callestr Fardd', begged printers to reprint a ballad for no one other than John Lloyd, 'a poor blind man'.[10]

A considerable number of ballad singers were blind, some from birth like 'Dic Dywyll', others as a result of accidents. There are a few instances of women composing ballads. Jane Hughes, 'Deborah Maldwyn', concentrated on religious subjects but Rebecca Williams was prepared to relate a notorious murder and Mary Roberts praise the bravery of the Marquis of Anglesey at Waterloo.[11]

Although one of the most prolific balladmongers of his day, Owen Griffith, 'Ywain Meirion' (1803-1868), continued to carry with him a supply of 'beads, small-tooth combs, purses and spoons',[12] as the nineteenth century wore on the balladmonger-cum-pedlar gradually became a figure of the past. However, the public singing of ballads probably became more common as ballad-singers exploited to a greater degree the crowds that gathered at fairs and markets, horse sales, public auctions, eisteddfodau, and on the main streets of industrial centres on a Saturday pay-night. One of the best descriptions of a ballad singer at work is that of 'Dic Dywyll' at Merthyr:

> He would stand in the middle of the street on a Saturday night, ballads in hand, a penny a piece, and begin to talk, setting everybody in a roar with generally some allusion either to some comical person of the neighbourhood or some queer circumstance that was tickling the imagination of the people, or perhaps some political allusion. When he found he had got an audience, and all were in good-humour, he would begin his singing, and his ballads usually went off like wild-fire.[13]

Ballads reached their peak of popularity between the 1840s and the 1860s. The large number of well-thumbed copies preserved in public collections shows that they were bought in their thousands. Although ephemeral publications, ballads were clearly cherished by many of their purchasers; farmers, farm servants, and local craftsmen often had a dozen or more favourites crudely stitched together and bound between rough-and-ready boards. The alacrity with which they were purchased and the avidity with which they were perused suggests that these simple and colloquial ballads must have played a significant part in recruiting new Welsh readers.

Ballads also reflected the progress of Anglicization. An elegy to 'Dic Dywyll' (who probably died before 1860) notes that he could sing well in both languages.[14] In the industrialized areas of Gwent and east Glamorgan bilingual ballads describing disasters and murders became more common from the 1860s and uninspired translations of the most popular Welsh ballads also appeared.[15]

From about 1870 onwards the story of the street ballad in Wales is one of decline. By then, ballads and their sellers had earned the censure of the Nonconformist worthies and the contempt of the fashionable poets of the day who associated themselves with the increasingly popular and respectable eisteddfod.[16] New, more 'refined' forms of popular entertainment such as the public concert and penny readings (both of which had strong temperance overtones) gained ground, while the balladmongers' traditional outlet, the fair, was increasingly frowned upon — so much so that chapel elders often arranged other events to draw the young away from its dire influence. The Welsh-language newspaper press, which developed so rapidly from the mid-1850s onwards, dealt ballads a mortal blow, even though ballad writers — as they themselves frequently acknowledged — made full use of those papers they happened to chance upon:

> *The story can be seen in Yr Utgorn*
> *And in the Herald from Caernarfon*
> *In the Cambrian Daily Leader*
> *And the Gwladgarwr, and Y Faner.*[17]

Balladmongers might have their work on sale very soon after the events they related took place — a ballad describing an execution at Knutsford on 8 April 1890 was on sale in the remote village of Dinas Mawddwy by the 23rd of the month[18] — but could not hope to compete with the greater currency and reliability of the newspaper press.

Well before his death in Llanrwst workhouse in 1901, Abel Jones, 'Bardd Crwst', author of well over a hundred ballads, had come to be regarded as a relic of the past. Though Evan Williams of Bangor printed Welsh ballads telling of the execution of Dr Crippen in 1910, of the sinking of the *Titanic* in 1912 (over 24,000 copies of this were allegedly sold), of the 1916 Easter Rising in Dublin, and of Zeppelin raids on London,[19] these were probably for sale at his premises; there is nothing to suggest that they were ever sold following their singing in some public place. They represent the last vestiges of a tradition that had served Wales well for two centuries.

NOTES TO CHAPTER 20

1. J. H. Davies, 'An early printed Welsh ballad', *JWBS*, 2 (1916-23), 243-6.
2. Geraint H. Jenkins, *Literature, religion and society in Wales, 1660-1730* (Cardiff, 1978), p. 161.
3. J. H. Davies, *A bibliography of Welsh ballads printed in the 18th century* (London, 1908-11).
4. Davies, *Bibliography*, p. 27.
5. Peter Lord, *Words with pictures: Welsh images and images of Wales in the popular press, 1640-1860* (Aberystwyth, 1995), p. 88.
6. A. Cynfael Lake, 'Evan Ellis, "Gwerthwr llyfrau a British Oil"', *Y Traethodydd*, 144 (1989), 204-14 (p. 206).
7. Alan Bold, *The ballad* (London, 1979), p. 67.
8. Eiluned Rees, 'The sales-book of Samuel Williams, Aberystwyth printer', *Ceredigion*, 10 (1984-7), 255-67, 357-72 (p. 262).
9. Hefin Jones, *Dic Dywyll y baledwr* (Llanrwst, 1995), p. 6.
10. Tegwyn Jones, 'Baledi a baledwyr y bedwaredd ganrif ar bymtheg', in *Cof cenedl VI: ysgrifau ar hanes Cymru*, ed. Geraint H. Jenkins (Llandysul, 1991), pp. 101-34 (pp. 105-6).
11. Jones, 'Baledi a baledwyr', p. 104.
12. Tegwyn Jones, *Baledi Ywain Meirion* (Y Bala, 1980), p. xxvi.
13. Charles Herbert James, *What I remember about myself and old Merthyr* (Merthyr Tydfil, 1892), p. 20.
14. Ben Bowen Thomas, *Baledi Morgannwg* (Cardiff, 1951), p. 20.
15. Thomas, pp. 9-10.
16. E. G. Millward, 'Canu'r byd i'w le', *Y Traethodydd*, 136 (1981), 4-26.
17. Yr hanes welir yn *Yr Utgorn*,
    Ac yn yr *Herald o Gaernarfon*
    Yn y *Cambrian Daily Lider*
    A'r *Gwladgarwr*, gyda'r *Faner*.
18. Jones, 'Baledi a baledwyr', p. 125.
19. Dafydd Owen, *I fyd y faled* (Denbigh, 1986), p. 255.

CHAPTER 21

WELSH PUBLISHING IN THE UNITED STATES OF AMERICA

D. H. E. ROBERTS

IN delineating the various phases of Welsh emigration to the United States, the late Professor David Williams maintained that probably only a handful of Welshmen were involved in the initial colonization, and that very little is known about them.[1] More is certainly known about the next group of emigrants. To escape religious persecution in the seventeenth century, early Dissenters fled from Wales to North America. Williams notes in particular the large numbers of Baptists who fled from Swansea and Radnorshire and the flight of the Quakers from Meirionnydd and Montgomeryshire after 1690. These emigrants tended to settle in close-knit groups, adhering to their religious and cultural ideals and using the Welsh language as their medium of communication.

As in Wales, printing was viewed as the handmaiden of religion.[2] Ellis Pugh (1656-1718), a Quaker emigrant from the Dolgellau area, is the author of the work generally accepted as being the first Welsh book produced in North America, *Annerch ir Cymru, Iw galw oddiwrth y llawer o bethau at yr un peth angenrheidiol er mwyn cadwedigeth eu heneidiau* (*An Address to the Welsh, to call them away from the many things to the one essential thing to ensure the salvation of their souls*), printed in Philadelphia by Andrew Bradford in 1721. Abel Morgan, a Baptist minister from Ceredigion, was the author of the second book, *Cyd-gordiad Egwyddorawl o'r Scrythurau* (*A Concordance of the Scriptures*), posthumously printed in 1730 by Samuel Keimer and Dafydd Harry (or Henry) of Philadelphia. The third work, also published in 1730, is a substantial pamphlet entitled *Y Dull o Fedyddio a Dwfr* (*The Way to Baptise with Water*). The fourth, John Morgan's *Myfyrdodau Bucheddol ar y Pedwar Peth Diweddaf* (*Moral Meditations on the Four Last Things*), a pamphlet printed in 1735, can be attributed to the initiative of Griffith Hughes, a missionary for the Society for the Propagation of the Gospel in Pennsylvania during the 1730s.

Philadelphia was the main printing centre, Welsh authors initially turning to existing American presses. Two Philadelphia printers appear to have a Welsh connection: Dafydd Harry may have come from Wales and the name Hugh Meredith suggests Welsh descent. The latter has enjoyed some notoriety on account of his excessive liking for drink and his stormy relations with his famous partner, Benjamin Franklin.

The growth of religious tolerance meant that for much of the eighteenth century emigration from Wales to America was reduced to an intermittent trickle, but in the 1790s the floodgates were opened. As Hywel Davies suggests, the motivating forces were many and varied:

> Emigration from Wales to America during the 1790s was neither unified nor collective. It was a free movement of individuals and families who could not live comfortably in Wales for a variety of reasons, who had a connection with

the United States, and who were sufficiently motivated to brave the considerable perils of the transatlantic crossing to discover a new future for themselves in America.[3]

Davies further emphasizes the influence of press propaganda by Morgan John Rhys and others, the attraction of an 'ideal' place where free speech could flourish, and the preponderance of emigrants from the artisan class — the very people who were to form the foundation of a golden age for vernacular publishing in Wales during the nineteenth century.

Professor Glanmor Williams has suggested that one of the over-riding considerations for emigrants was to secure a future for their children,[4] a concern reflected in the Welsh press in the United States throughout the nineteenth century. As late as 1870 H. J. Hughes could state that his pictorial monthly, *Yr Ysgol* (*The School*), was intended *'for the use of the Sunday School and the Band of Hope: and especially for all the children and youth of Welsh Americans'*.[5]

The great majority of early-nineteenth-century emigrants from Wales were monoglot Welsh, thoroughly steeped in their country's religious, cultural, and literary traditions. Although they have often been described as semi-literate, the extensive correspondence between them and their families in Wales suggests that standards of literacy in Welsh were quite high. A letter from Thomas B. Morris providing guidance to Samuel Roberts, 'S.R.', regarding the amount of English material that should be included in his *Pregethau, Areithiau a Darlithiau* (*Sermons, Speeches and Lectures*) states that even in 1864:

> There are a number here who tend to think that the English ones are the ones that should be omitted, since it is likely that the Welsh speakers will constitute most of the subscribers, they can all make use of that which will be in Welsh whilst some hundreds of them would be unable to make anything of the English sermons, and they may feel that they have been made to pay for material that is of no value to them.[6]

Welsh emigrants tended to remain together, showing little inclination to venture into the vast American heartland. Alan Conway's analysis reveals that in 1850, 95% of all Welsh emigrants and their descendants lived in the northern and eastern states, and of that 95% a significant proportion resided in New York state. By 1890 about 80% had remained in the same states, 80% of that total remaining in New York state. Conway concludes that 'the majority of the Welsh were [...] neither frontiersmen nor trail blazers'.[7] It is possible that the propaganda of Morgan John Rhys encouraged this tendency. National, linguistic enclaves were part of his philosophy, and he was not alone in expounding his theories. Even within the United States the Welsh were subjected to further propaganda in favour of remaining together. A biographical note on John Mather Jones (one-time editor and owner of *Y Drych* (*The Mirror*), a particularly powerful organ of communication in Welsh America) notes that: *'he felt the need to encourage the Welsh to settle close together for the sake of moral and welfare benefits, rather than being scattered all over the continent'*.[8]

It was probably because the Welsh tended to remain in a few favoured localities, in particular around Scranton in Pennsylvania and New York, that Welsh printing and publishing could develop in the United States. A settled society gave birth to a range of institutions, developed a need to communicate, and demanded a medium of individual and collective expression. In his study of Scranton, William Jones emphasizes how its Welsh community, especially in its business ventures, 'maintained a remarkable degree of continuity'.[9] The Welsh-language press ensured that traditional Welsh institutions and their activities were chronicled in print while exploiting their administrative framework as a ready-made means of communication with its market and as a sales network.

As Professor Glanmor Williams points out, from over 600 Welsh chapels founded in America

> [...] sprang a spate of activities that linked the members of all ages and both sexes: the Sunday school, missionary work, the temperance cause, women's and young people's societies, philanthropic and literary meetings, the singing-school and the *gymanfa* (singing festival). Wider denominational and religious organization provided some of the main connecting-links between the far-flung settlements.[10]

The eisteddfod also gained its place as a significant institution. Virtually every Welsh settlement held its eisteddfod and even when most of the settlements had been totally anglicized (or Americanized) the eisteddfod often remained. The various other Welsh societies and institutions are too numerous to note here but the printing press was deployed to provide a service for each of them and to produce a permanent record and reflection of their activities.

The printers responsible for most of the output in Welsh during the first half of the nineteenth century were either Welsh settlers or their immediate descendants. Negligible use was made of American printers for several reasons: the language probably presented a major barrier to non-Welsh printers; the Welsh naturally wished to support their compatriots; and the relatively small-scale demand meant that profits (if they existed at all) were too small to attract significant outside interest. However, one Welshman, Isaiah Thomas (1749-1831), became a major American printer in the English language, employing 150 people at his seven presses, bindery, and paper mill.[11]

Henry Blackwell claims that an emigrant from Ceredigion, Evan E. Roberts (1806-88), was 'the father of Welsh printing in America'.[12] Roberts established a small printing shop and bindery in Utica. Although fairly successful for several years, he was forced to abandon printing in 1855 when he lost his printing press in an attempt to repay a friend's debt. He produced few books but was sufficiently bold to publish the first number of a successful Baptist monthly, *Y Seren Orllewinol* (*The Western Star*) in 1844, and to edit and publish the second Welsh-American newspaper, the short-lived *Haul Gomer* (*Gomer's Sun*) in 1848.[13]

William Williams (1787-1850),[14] printer of *Caniadau Sion* (*Songs of Zion*) (Utica, 1827), the second collection of hymns published in America, was born in the United States and Blackwell bestows upon him the title 'pioneer'. Probably out of necessity he combined printing and publishing with binding, wood-engraving, and bookselling. In 1840 he transferred his business to Robert W. Roberts,[15] a native of Llanuwchllyn. Roberts's brother, Ellis Henry Roberts (1827-1918),[16] showed some interest in printing but is better-known as a politician and educationalist.

A Congregationalist minister, Robert Everett (1791-1875),[17] was another who engaged intermittently in printing. What Blackwell called 'printer-divines' were not uncommon. Edward Davies (1827-1905)[18] who edited, printed, and published *Y Cenhadwr Americanaidd* (*The American Missionary*) in the 1880s was a Congregationalist minister, and Richard Edwards (1819-1902)[19] who printed and published *Y Seren Orllewinol* at Pottsville for much of the 1850s and 1860s was a Baptist preacher.

These early printers had to struggle against adversity. Many printed for a very short time, their output is often spasmodic, and usually technically poor. Most of their ventures into periodical publishing met with little success. A New York fortnightly, *Y Beread* (1842), survived for a year.[20] *Y Traethodydd yn America*, a selection from the heavyweight Welsh quarterly, *Y Traethodydd*, appeared between 1857 and 1861 when it ceased publication because its circulation was no more than 750 copies.[21] The faltering progress of the Welsh-American press in the first half of the nineteenth century can be attributed to many factors; economic fluctuations, social hardship, and very limited resources, but above all to poor transport and communications.

As the number of settlers from Wales increased and as economic conditions gradually became more favourable, the demand for Welsh-language publications increased. It would appear that the 1850s was the crucial decade in the history of printing and publishing in Welsh in the United States. The weekly newspaper, *Y Drych Americanaidd* (*The American Mirror*), subsequently known as *Y Drych*, was established in 1851 and, as the recognized organ of Welsh Americans, came to be the most successful Welsh publishing venture in the United States. Its success — at one time its circulation reputedly exceeded 12,000 — owed a great deal to the initiative and enterprise of T. J. Griffiths.

Thomas J. Griffiths was born in Deerfield, Oneida County, New York, the son of an emigrant from Y Bala. He was trained as a printer at the office of the *Utica Morning Herald*, eventually buying his way into the printing concern of D. C. Davies in 1860. The 1860s were clearly a difficult period for Griffiths; although he became sole owner of the firm in 1862, he appears to have taken one of his employees into partnership briefly in 1867 before resuming full ownership from 1868 onwards.

Letters between Griffiths and Samuel Roberts provide many insights into Welsh-American publishing. Some indicate that Griffiths's early years in business were rather insecure. In 1882, Roberts reminded Griffiths of his circumstances in the mid-1860s:

> Dear Sir. The first book — of Sermons Addresses and Poetry which you printed for me sold as you said like hot cakes and brought to your office a good sum of money at a time when it was of important service to you. Instead of paying me the amount due, you begged to have a loan of the money, and requested me to prepare a second volume for you to print for me — that you might pay me that loan in work and not in *cash*.[22]

Griffiths, now a successful business man, denied the existence of such an arrangement, 'now what an idea of my inducing you to publish a book for my benefit the idea is preposterous in the extreme.'[23] He may have chosen to forget that in 1865 he had requested an advance to help meet the cost of binding the volume:

It would relieve me greatly as I could pass these notes in payment for Binding which amounts to $675. Now if you will make your notes of $250 each I think I can get along otherwise I shall have to come to the wall. This way will in no way interfere with you and greatly assist me and perhaps save me from failure or something about as bad.[24]

Other letters help to explain why Griffiths had to struggle and why so many of his predecessors had failed. In 1864 he suggested that publishing Welsh books was influenced by economic fluctuations:

The books [Samuel Roberts's *Pregethau, Areithiau a Darlithiau*] have all been dispensed of and more could have been sold if we had them say 300 to 600. Mr Evan Owen wishes and wants you to publish your other book [...] he thinks they could be sold like 'Hot Cakes'. I think it is a good time to get out another book now if at all as money is plenty all over the country.[25]

Elsewhere, Griffiths maintained that seasonal influences were also important:

We are getting along very finely with the work having between 200 and 300 hundred pages up already [...] I think it would be well for parties acting as agents to urge forward the work of getting names before it gets to the busy time of farming. I shall have Morris mention it in the Drych as now is the time while money is plenty and everything prosperity. Push it forward now I should say.[26]

T. J. Griffiths could neither speak nor write Welsh. Indeed, Blackwell suggests that he could not even understand Welsh, allegedly saying 'for my sake it is better as it is, I don't read or speak Welsh and it saves people complaining to me'.[27] He therefore had to employ Welshmen as overseers to supervise his Welsh-language publications, advertising extensively for Welsh-speaking printers and offering continuous employment in his 'Welsh section'.[28] He employed some of the most able editors and correspondents for his newspapers and demanded a high standard of skill from his printers who were equipped with up-to-date machinery.[29] Welsh-language material constituted only a portion of the output of his presses; Griffiths was primarily a commercial printer and that is probably why he refers to the 'Welsh section' of his establishment in advertisements. His Welsh output is wholly in keeping with the tradition established by William Williams, Everett, and others during the first half of the century. Griffiths printed and published materials for chapels and Sunday schools, and for many Welsh organizations, institutions, and societies. He printed their reports and proceedings, and the output of literary societies and eisteddfodau. He also published biographies and verse elegies and eulogies of many prominent Welsh Americans. But many will argue that his most important contribution was as owner and publisher of *Y Drych*; as such he ensured that the Welsh in America maintained active links with one another, with their traditions, and with Wales.

Griffiths produced more Welsh material than all his contemporaries put together. The output of the smaller printers was no different in nature. An advertisement embodies all the primary functions of nineteenth-century Welsh presses in the United States and indicates virtually all the institutions they served:

> *Now ready a Sacred Play on Mordecai and Haman (based on a descriptive poem victorious in Providence Eisteddfod, March 1869) [...] for the use of Sunday Schools, Literary Meetings and Eisteddfodau.*[30]

Because of the small and scattered nature of many Welsh settlements outside Utica and perhaps Scranton, Welsh-American printers and publishers employed the subscription system which was so important in Wales itself during the eighteenth and much of the nineteenth centuries. They could depend on a network of local Welsh churches, businesses, and agents, and on the inestimable value of *Y Drych* and other newspapers as advertising media and as a means of attracting subscriptions. References in correspondence and in the press suggest that each Welsh settlement of any significance possessed an agent for Welsh-American publishers. Sales through bookshops appear to have been extremely limited, and the dearth of Welsh book-shops, even in Scranton and New York, is a complaint frequently expressed. The periodical press regularly contained enticing advertisements for booksellers and subscription agents:

> *Our terms for agents are especially beneficial to the Welsh who keep or serve in post offices and to Welsh postal servants, and our terms for itinerant agents are favourable.*

Although the advertisement seeks to attract 'Ministers, or any other persons of trust and honour who wish to reduce their travelling costs when they are called away from home',[31] as in Wales, selling publications on the Sabbath provoked strong feelings. The *Drych* begged its agents:

> *Do not place it in the Churches nor anywhere else where a reader might get hold of it on the Sabbath. Do not offer it to anyone nor take names nor payment for it on the Sabbath. There may not be any harm in having ministers doing it, and for agents to distribute denominational publications on a Sunday, but to see men peddling books in Chapels on God's day seems to us against the counsel of the Apostles to do everything in an orderly and appropriate fashion.*[32]

Just as the book trade in Wales suffered greatly because of the inherent inadequacies of the subscription system, particularly the difficulty of maintaining links with agents and representatives, Welsh-American publishers similarly found it to be inconvenient and often loss-making. Some publishers eventually abandoned it, John Mather Jones informing customers that *'the only way to get the books published by us is by sending an order containing the selling price'*.[33] E. E. Roberts sent his son to Welsh settlements to sell *Y Meddyg Teuluaidd* (*The Family Doctor*) directly, announcing that:

> *Mr G. E. Roberts, the son of Mr E. E. Roberts, printer Utica, was now on a journey with his book. He has visited this city and the areas about and has received a warm welcome from our compatriots. He left New York on Tuesday, the 26th of this month for Pennsylvania intending to stop at Carbondale first, and from there work his way through the various Welsh Settlements in this state, ending up in Pittsburgh then he intends visiting Welsh settlements in Ohio and Wisconsin.*[34]

Despite the drawbacks of the subscription method and of selling through agents the Welsh book trade in the United States was largely dependent on it. In an editorial in 1871 *Y Drych* refers to the various problems:

> Mr A. O. Jones, Columbus [...] now requires Agents who would be responsible in each Welsh settlement for receiving orders, who shall be paid a commission for their labours. Many of the Welsh in America have 'burnt their fingers' by sending money in advance to Booksellers; and from the other side it is not reasonable for a dealer to send goods some hundred of miles on credit, especially to strange customers. Mr Jones's plan would avoid the difficulties on all sides, since no one would be called upon to pay for books before receiving them from the local representative.[35]

There are many references to the problems of distributing books in the correspondence between T. J. Griffiths and Samuel Roberts. In 1864, Griffiths wrote:

> The books are being sent off as they can be bound. I have sent off about 1000 now shall send the balance next week. In some few of the packages where they were to remit to me I have urged upon them to do so immediately. I think it would have been a good plan to have sent all the books marked COD it would save you a good deal of trouble or have the money in advance. But I do hope you will not have any trouble in getting your pay.[36]

Since sending out copies in this way proved costly, Griffiths asked Roberts

> What shall I do [...] in regard to cases where parties send for one copy, if I send by mail it will cost too much as it has to be prepaid and if I send it by Express it will cost the person receiving it very high [...] I think we had better put a notice in 'Y Drych' stating that when they order the books they remit the money by mail for it will be a job to collect money from this one and that all through the country.[37]

Another letter referred to a long list of debtors; since many of them were friends or relatives, seeking settlement proved to be even more difficult, 'You may write to the above', Samuel Roberts told Griffiths ,'but I beg you not to press for they may not have sold the books'.[38]

The price of most publications was kept fairly low, most books costing a dollar and the annual subscription to most periodicals being a dollar or two. The maximum number of copies printed of major works was some 2,500 but considerable numbers of works in constant demand such as hymn books could be sold over a period of time.

Working in the Welsh language posed problems even for Welsh printers or printers of Welsh descent. Blackwell refers to *Cor-Drysor y Bedyddwyr* (*The Choral Treasure of the Baptists*) (Shenandoah: J. S. Kirkwood, 1887), a Baptist hymn-book that had to be completely reprinted because of the appalling number of typesetting errors it contained. Samuel Roberts insisted that the proofs of his volume be sent to Wales for correction, T. J. Griffiths reporting to him 'I got a letter from Mr Jones of Wales [probably a Dolgellau printer] the other day stating that he had got the proof sheets very regularly but that one sheet had got lost.'[39]

Such problems would undoubtedly have reduced profits considerably: indeed evidence tends to suggest that it was rare to profit from Welsh publishing. The owner of the *Drych* found it necessary to inform his readers in 1851 that '*we do not now, and we have never, expected to make money, nor even make a living out of it, we have other things to depend on*'.[40]

As in Wales, there is evidence of dissatisfaction with standards of workmanship. 'Veritas' complained to the editor of *Y Drych*:

> It is a well-known fact, and a general complaint that virtually all the Welsh books published in America [...] are cast out of the press in a most poverty-stricken and slovenly guise. We can hardly look at some of them without fear of affecting our eye-sight as they are so ugly [...] The excuse or reason given for this most unbecoming behaviour towards the old language of our homeland is that it does not pay the publisher to execute good, tidy, pleasing work since the number of subscribers will be insufficient to meet his investment [...] but if genuinely interesting and educational books of good appearance should be published, it is possible that a much larger imprint could be sold than is possible at present [...] Is it possible for us to see an improvement in the paper, the printing, the binding as well as in the correctness of the setting? We can only hope for the best, and if we should be disappointed then we can refuse to buy them.[41]

The technical and aesthetic shortcomings of American-Welsh printing may explain to a certain extent the continuing interest shown in books exported from Wales. One advertisement claimed that:

> The need for them is great so that we retain our language, and prepare ourselves for religious usefulness, because we cannot be fluent in the language which we love so much, nor flourishing in our religious circles, without the output of the Welsh press which is so rich nowadays.[42]

The Aberystwyth printer, John Cox, was probably amongst the first to recognise the potential of the American market, sending his brother there on a selling mission in 1834

> [...] with a quantity of Gurney's dictionary in the hope of meeting a sale for them amongst our countrymen settled in and about Utica who I hear are not only deficient of but desirous of obtaining Welsh books. The experience is of so novel a nature that its success can only be a matter of conjecture.[43]

The venture received the blessing of Samuel Roberts:

> Our friend, Mr Cox, a respectable printer and publisher at Aberystwyth, understanding that many of our countrymen who have settled in America are desirous of obtaining Welsh Books, has commissioned the bearer — who is his Brother — to visit some of the Welsh settlements in the United States this Spring.[44]

By 1870 many of the agents who sold books published in the United States also acted as agents for leading Welsh publishers. Athelstan O. Jones, for example, represented Hughes a'i Fab, Thomas Gee, Humphreys of Caernarfon, P. M. Evans of Holywell, and E. Griffiths of Swansea.[45] Welsh-American publishers such as H. J. Hughes often combined their own publishing ventures with agencies for the main publishers in Wales:

> Let it be known to all the Welsh in America that we have established in New York as a representative for Welsh Publishers, to sell their books in this country. Our relationship with them is such that we can obtain any book or parts of books on sale in Wales.[46]

In Racine, Wisconsin, a William Hughes represented Gee, Hughes a'i Fab, and others;[47] in Cambria, Wisconsin, a Mrs Perry Williams represented Gee and Hughes and Son, and also sold *Y Drych* and the tea of the American Tea Company.[48]

Interest in material published in Wales was fairly general and the growth of the practice of reprinting and republishing Welsh best-sellers in the United States was probably a natural development. Many problems and bitter episodes resulted. The 1854 Remsen translation of *Uncle Tom's Cabin* was possibly a piracy,[49] and H. J. Hughes poured considerable scorn on E. R. Roberts in a letter to *Y Drych* outlining their respective rights to the American edition of *Tonau Ieuan Gwyllt* (*Ieuan Gwyllt's Tunes*) and their merits as printers:

> *Let it be known to him, that it is I who have the honourable right from Ieuan Gwyllt to publish [...] in America and if Mr. R. argues that the author's permission is of no significance in the eyes of the law and that he has as much right as I to publish, I will tell him that there is a law which is of greater consequence than International Law, and that he should respect it [...] We have a new Music Type of the same size as the original British edition — remember they are not old and half worn out. Also, we have one of the best setters in New York working on it every day — remember that he is not a bungler of a typesetter.*[50]

Although Welsh publishing and the Welsh book trade in America was at its most productive and prosperous between 1860 and 1880, social processes were already at work which were to bring about a decline in the number of Welsh-speakers. Some historians claim that considerable indifference towards things Welsh can be detected among certain early-nineteenth-century immigrants, accentuated later when the number of non-Welsh-speaking immigrants from industrial south Wales increased. It is also claimed that Welsh loyalty was easily exchanged for social progress and that the Welsh showed greater commitment to integration than any other immigrant group.[51] William Jones argues also that those cohesive forces that had briefly created a stable Welsh society had largely been dissolved by the last decade of the nineteenth century. He attributes the decline primarily to a crisis in chapel life: 'a lethal mix of the failure to keep their younger members (either because of a lack of Welsh or a move away from religion altogether) with an inability to recruit new blood through immigration'.[52] Welshness could not survive in this new 'modern, secular, urban and industrial environment'.[53] Welsh immigration ceased, second-generation Welshmen were dispersed and increasingly integrated into American life, and the Welsh communities virtually disintegrated. These processes quickly undermined the brittle foundations on which the Welsh book trade in the United States was built. Writing in 1872 to the Welsh newspaper *Baner ac Amserau Cymru*, D. S. Davies maintained that the decline in the book trade was indicative of the way in which the ideals of the Welsh settlers had been eroded, and the way in which the new generation was slowly but surely becoming good Americans:

> *Everything here destroys our common heritage. Many of those who emigrate here from Wales join the English when they want their support and influence to uphold religion and Welsh ways. But as Welsh settlements in this strange land are weaker than the*

> *English they give their wealth, support and intelligence to further English causes [...] The result is that Welsh causes do not flourish in America. There is not and we shall never have a Welsh college here. Those who have acquired great wealth do not become more Welsh. There is not a Welsh bookstore in the country nor a Welsh public library. The circulation of Welsh newspapers is poor so that they cannot compete with the larger newspapers in price. [...] I estimate that there are no more than ten thousand who get the Drych, Baner America, and Dysgedydd (weeklies), the Cenhadwr, Cyfaill, Glorian and Blodau yr Oes (monthlies) between them. We have perhaps four hundred Welsh chapels in different states and the English pressing on them all and taking over many of them. It is true that the four Welsh denominations have twenty-two thousand members throughout the country after a hundred years of emigration but a great proportion of this number is unable to understand Welsh. The Welsh language has no prospect of success in this country and the worst thing of all is that that opinion is wholly true.*[54]

Similar sentiments were reiterated by other writers. The decline of the Welsh book trade was an inevitable corollary of Americanization. Yet we cannot but sympathize with the sadness that pervades the words of J. M. Hughes, Emporia, Kansas, in 1896 acknowledging receipt of a copy of a book written by a friend in Wales:

> *I will do what I can out of heartfelt love to urge others to buy it. But I will have the old people only to buy Welsh books since the young ones here are becoming — have become if it comes to that — Englishmen.*[55]

The Welsh-language book printing and publishing industry and the periodical press which had grown so naturally as part of Welsh society in America could not be expected to survive its almost total demise. But certain vestiges, in an English-language guise, survived well into the first half of the twentieth century.

NOTES TO CHAPTER 21

Italicized quotations are translations of material originally in Welsh.

[1] David Williams, 'The contribution of Wales to the development of the United States', NLWJ, 2 (1941-2), 97-108.
[2] William Williams, 'The first three books printed in America', NLWJ, 2 (1941-2), 109-19; 'More about the first three Welsh books printed in America', NLWJ, 3 (1943-4), 19-22.
[3] H. M. Davies, ' "Very different springs of uneasiness": emigration from Wales to the United States during the 1790s', WHR 15 (1990-1), 368-98 (pp. 397-8).
[4] Glanmor Williams, 'A prospect of Paradise? Wales and the United States of America, 1776-1914', in his *Religion, language, and nationality in Wales* (Cardiff, 1979), pp. 217-36 (pp. 221, 226).
[5] Y Drych, 20 Jan. 1870.
[6] NLW, MS 3265D, David Morris to Samuel Roberts, 12 March 1864.
[7] *The Welsh in America: letters from the immigrants*, ed. Alan Conway (Cardiff, 1961), p. 11.
[8] Y Drych, 24 Dec.1874.
[9] William D. Jones, *Wales in America: Scranton and the Welsh 1860-1920* (Cardiff and Scranton, 1993), p. 23.
[10] G. Williams, p. 229.
[11] J. H. Thomas, 'Cymry enwog yr Amerig', *Barn*, 302 (March 1988), pp. 15-16 (p. 16).
[12] NLW, MS 9272A.
[13] The first newspaper, *Cymro America*, published in New York by John A. Williams in 1832, survived for only a month.
[14] NLW, MS 9277A.
[15] NLW, MS 9272A.
[16] *Ibid*.
[17] NLW, MS 9257A.
[18] NLW, MS 9254A.
[19] NLW, MS 9256A.
[20] Henry Blackwell, *A bibliography of Welsh Americana*, 2nd edn (Aberystwyth, 1977), p. 63; Huw Walters, *A Bibliography of Welsh Periodicals 1735-1850* (Aberystwyth, 1993), pp. 8-9.
[21] Blackwell, p. 81.
[22] NLW, MS 3265D, Samuel Roberts to T. J. Griffiths, 21 Jan. 1882.
[23] NLW, MS 3265D, T. J. Griffiths to Samuel Roberts, 22 Feb. [1882?].
[24] NLW, MS 3265D, T. J. Griffiths to Samuel Roberts, [c.1865].
[25] NLW, MS 3265D, T. J. Griffiths to Samuel Roberts, 14 July 1864.
[26] NLW, MS 3265D, T. J. Griffiths to Samuel Roberts, 24 March 1865.
[27] NLW, MS 9258A.
[28] Advertisements in *Y Drych*, 25 April 1867 and 20 Jan. 1870 are but two of many.
[29] *Y Drych*, 25 April 1867.
[30] *Y Drych*, 10 March 1870.
[31] *Y Drych*, 26 Oct. 1851.
[32] *Y Drych*, 11 Nov. 1850.
[33] *Y Drych*, 29 Aug.1867.
[34] *Y Drych*, 4 May 1871.
[35] *Y Drych*, 30 Aug. 1871.
[36] NLW, MS 3265D, T. J. Griffiths to Samuel Roberts, 19 May 1864.
[37] NLW, MS 3265D, T. J. Griffiths to Samuel Roberts, 21 March [1864?].
[38] NLW, MS 3265D, Samuel Roberts to T. J. Griffiths, 19 July 1867.
[39] NLW, MS 3265D, T. J. Griffiths to Samuel Roberts, 11 March 1864.
[40] *Y Drych*, 15 Nov. 1851.
[41] *Y Drych*, 9 Jan. 1868.

[42] *Y Drych*, 20 April 1871.
[43] NLW, MS 14092C, C. Cox to Samuel Roberts, 6 March 1834.
[44] NLW, MS 14092C, Samuel Roberts [1834?].
[45] *Y Drych*, 4 April 1871.
[46] *Y Drych*, 7 March 1867.
[47] *Y Drych*, 13 April 1871.
[48] *Y Drych*, 8 June 1876.
[49] Blackwell, p. 122.
[50] *Y Drych*, 27 June 1867.
[51] David Maldwyn Ellis, 'The assimilation of the Welsh in Central New York', *WHR*, 6 (1972-3), 424-50 (pp. 445-6).
[52] Jones, pp. 109-10.
[53] Jones, p. 112.
[54] *Baner ac Amserau Cymru*, 23 Oct. 1872, translated in Conway, pp. 321-3 (p. 323).
[55] NLW, MS 19331E, J. M. Hughes to Henry Hughes, 22 May 1896.

CHAPTER 22

THE WELSH PRESS IN PATAGONIA

Gareth Alban Davies

ON 24 May 1865 over a hundred and fifty emigrants embarked on the tea-clipper *Mimosa* in Liverpool, bound for New Bay in Patagonia, their ultimate destination being the Chubut Valley some forty miles away. The intended settlement, *Y Wladfa*, lay some six hundred miles south-west of Buenos Aires, and was bounded by virtually uninhabited wilderness. The nearest point of settlement was on the Río Negro some two hundred miles to the north. Buoyed up with the hope of creating a Nova Cambria, the emigrants had been forced to settle for the status of a far-flung outpost of the Argentine, part of its territories and subject to its laws. A small advance party awaited the ship's arrival and disembarkation on an open beach on 28 July 1865, a day celebrated subsequently as *Gŵyl y Glaniad* (The Landing Anniversary).[1]

During the first winter the settlers almost starved or died of cold. Ill-prepared for the rigours of an arid climate, they knew nothing of irrigation, the basic requirement for their success. Although largely urbanized with little regular contact with agriculture, they possessed two great virtues vouchsafed by experience in mine or quarry or ironworks, or on the bleak uplands: an ability to adapt and a gift for survival. Despite its many crises, emigrants from Wales and elsewhere had increased the population of *Y Wladfa* to 3,050 by 1895.[2] Population growth was matched by the increase in wheat and livestock production[3] but progress was checked by the ruinous floods of 1899 and 1901, and after a brief recovery the economy suffered further decline as a consequence of the First World War.

Emigration from Wales now came to an end, thus exacerbating the threat to the Welshness of the community posed by considerable non-Welsh immigration,[4] outward migration, and mixed marriages. Further loss of social status came about with the collapse of the Co-operative Society (C.M.C.) in 1928 and the virtual nationalization of the Irrigation Society in 1943, two institutions in which the Welsh had played a leading role.[5] Education through the medium of Spanish relegated Welsh largely to the sphere of the Sunday school. Against that ultimate decline, however, must be set the fact that in 1895 87% of the population of the Lower Chubut Valley still spoke Welsh, many of them being monolingual.[6] During its first forty years *Y Wladfa* had lived its dream of a virtually independent and self-governing community whose dominant means of expression was the Welsh language — a great opportunity, indeed, for a Welsh press that had contributed so much to its foundation.

Although the press in Wales had created a millenarian vision of the New Cambria, it placed little emphasis on cultural matters. An interesting exception was an article in *Y Faner* by the philologist John Peter, 'Ioan Pedr', entitled 'Y Wladychfa a Llenyddiaeth' (The Settlement and Literature).[7] He foresaw a process of renewal in which the press would have its part: '*The Wladychfa will be a new beginning for us as a Nation,*'[8] and predicted that handbooks in the sciences and arts would be required to form the nucleus of an original literature: '*let all of it be original, and possessed of Welsh characteristics [...] A*

Welsh printing-press should be set up at once, and a literary sensibility and reverence for learning should be nurtured among the settlers from the start'.[9]

Some of the leaders certainly possessed the background and energy to put this vision into effect. Lewis Jones (1836-1904) was an experienced journalist, his colleague Hugh Hughes, 'Cadfan Gwynedd' (1824-98), a man of letters. A few other early settlers showed an awareness of a new place with a different history.[10] Yet it was to be a long while before literature and the press flourished.

It is not difficult to explain why no immediate attempt was made to set up a periodical. The first years were racked with crisis and failure. Only with the institution of irrigation did the settlers gradually and painfully extend their control over the environment. Even then, the settlement remained below the level at which a press might operate economically. Furthermore, energy that could have gone into a journalistic enterprise, however rudimentary, was dissipated in the controversy in 1866-7 over the wisdom of creating *Y Wladfa*.[11]

A beginning was made, nevertheless, when in January 1868 the first number of *Y Brut: Newyddur y Wladfa Gymreig* (*The Brut: newspaper of the Welsh Settlement*) appeared. The choice of title — redolent of the belief that the Welsh were descendants of Brutus the Trojan, and used in medieval times to denote a history of the British people — signified the arrival in a new land, where a new history was being made and recorded. A monthly, consisting of twenty-five hand-written pages, it was no ordinary periodical. The few copies produced were to be passed on to a neighbour two days after receipt, and payment was to take the form of twelve pages of writing-paper per year.[12] The place of publication was Trerawson (Rawson), the first township in the settlement, and the editor was R. J. Berwyn (1836-1917) who would subsequently play a central role in the affairs of *Y Wladfa*. The contents of the first number suggest that *Y Brut* attempted to bridge the gap between the leadership and the ordinary people, whilst offering news and an occasional topical column. *Y Brut* has received the accolade of being the earliest newspaper to appear in the Argentine south of Bahía Blanca,[13] but presumably because of production and distribution difficulties, it lasted only for that year.

The first printed newspaper did not appear until 1878, almost ten years later. Why did it take so long to satisfy an already felt need? The settlement remained small and the decade had been one of struggle, culminating in a backbreaking programme of canal construction.[14] An outside stimulus also proved necessary. Firstly, more than five hundred immigrants arrived in 1875-6, mostly from the mining valleys of South Wales.[15] New to agricultural work for the most part, they may well have been radicalized by the demand in Wales for a widening of the franchise. In consequence, the difficulty in allocating land to them was met with protest, rather than acquiescent apathy. Secondly, the children of the first settlers, now reaching adulthood, were impatient of the old ways and the old leadership. By this time too, there was tension between the Welsh and local officials of the Buenos Aires government.[16]

Ein Breiniad (*Our Enfranchisement*) was first published on 21 September 1878.[17] The title carried resonances of revolutionary and nationalist voices of the 1790s calling for reform, but the immediate impulse behind the newspaper, the council elections in late 1878, was more prosaic. The first editorial called on settlers to assume the responsibilities of citizenship, an appeal especially directed towards the newcomers who, it was claimed, had not shaken off the apathy induced by centuries of subservience. That appeal had a more immediate political context: the growing tension with central government. Democratic participation would strengthen the settlers' hand and ensure a measure of independence.

Although the paper included a range of views, it presented its own pragmatic standpoint in its second issue on 28 September 1878: since *Y Wladfa* could not manage without help from Buenos Aires, co-operation with central government and an acceptance of its administrative structures were necessary. The only alternative, falling into the hands of Great Britain, was wholly unacceptable. *Ein Breiniad*, a single printed sheet appearing weekly, went to seven issues, by which time its immediate task was at an end. The last number claimed that discussion of the position and needs of *Y Wladfa* had proved an excellent political discipline; furthermore, two readers called for the paper to continue — which it did, beginning a new series on 23 November 1878. The diet remained one of serious political discussion, relieved somewhat by a Bardic Column. *Ein Breiniad* appeared at monthly intervals until May 1879, after which its fate is unclear. At least two numbers appeared in late 1881.

The special Christmas issue of 1883, a copy of which was sent to each *gwladfawr* (settler), publicized a series of meetings reporting on discussions with the Provincial Governor, Lorenzo Winter. The visionary eloquence and metaphorical style bear the hallmark of Lewis Jones. There was no quarrel with the right of Buenos Aires to govern, but the prosperity and well-being of the community depended on the right to organize its life with little outside interference. At the heart of the discussion is the *breiniwr*, the citizen who enjoys the privilege of his enfranchised status. The ideal is *'that every citizen is intelligent, so that he can decide upon every political question that comes before him, and has the opportunity to be heard and felt as an equal within the body politic'*.[18] In contrast, an oppressive government creates servile citizens, given to corruption. The idealism of the *gwladfawyr* was finally appealed to: having escaped poverty at home, they might succumb to pursuing materialist ends, as had happened in Welsh settlements elsewhere. Unless the *gwladfawyr* bore this danger in mind, they would sink into the apathy that characterized individuals lost in a heterogeneous and unequal society. This moving document was an act of self-definition based on experience of a society that had established from the outset a democratic system, whose adult members (including women) were enfranchised.[19] But it was surely ironic that the *gwladfawyr*, having sought to escape from an alien regime, were again obliged to fight the same battle, wielding once more the arm of the press.

When Lewis Jones lost the support of his fellow-settlers in 1866 he found work in Buenos Aires with an English-language newspaper, *The Standard*.[20] That connection enabled him many years later to purchase an old press, and bring it to *Y Wladfa*. Sir T. H. Holdich saw it in use during his visit in 1902 as commissioner in the arbitration of the dispute between Chile and the Argentine. It was, he noted, 'an old hand-machine which is an interesting relic — for it is the identical machine with which the first "Standard" (the oldest newspaper in Buenos Aires) was printed 43 years ago.'[21]

For his publications, Lewis Jones used an orthography that nowadays looks very unusual. In its most striking feature it roughly conforms to medieval Welsh usage, the v-sound being represented by *v*, the *f* being reserved for the f-sound. Jones claimed that he was obliged to use an orthography more suited to the sorts available in Spanish or English founts.[22] His explanation is disingenuous; since he had used the same orthography in the original series of *Y Ddraig Goch* (*The Red Dragon*) published in Liverpool, his choice sprang from conviction not convenience. Like other authors and printers in Wales he adopted both William Owen Pughe's orthography, and the idiosyncratic language that Pughe had forged for his *Dictionary*.[23] Pughe had stood firmly on the path of social reform and of national renewal, and if Lewis Jones espoused his orthography and language it was partly because he believed that the settlement required a distinctive language for the conduct of its affairs. The minting of the word *Gwladfa* in 1863 confirms this interpretation, as does the invention, even before the arrival of the first settlers, of the name *Camwy* for the Chubut river:[24] the characteristic Pugheian word-formation *cam-(g)wy* (winding-water) also signified linguistically a new beginning. Sadly, if the orthography exemplified a new order, its clumsiness proved a hindrance to progress.

As leader of his community until his death in 1904, Lewis Jones naturally became the founder and editor of *Y Dravod: Newyddur y Wladva* (*The Discussion: Y Wladfa's Newspaper*), which first appeared on 17 January 1891 and has survived to the present day. Why was the life-span of *Ein Breiniad* so short and why did some eight years go by before a new periodical was launched? And this during a decade of prosperity, which also saw the establishment of sister colonies, particularly the Andean settlements in Esquel and Cwm Hyfryd after 1885.[25] The answer may be that once again an external stimulus was required. Although *Y Dravod* offered no specific reason for its appearance, its contents point to a general malaise. The political situation, both in the Argentine and internationally, is uncertain. More particularly, the young people, their lives lacking direction, are a growing problem. Their support, both as readers and contributors, is therefore specifically sought. *Y Dravod* would '*seek to reduce tensions*'[26] by providing a forum for discussion and the interchange of ideas and opinions. But there was a duty also to civilize and refine, as well as to spread the influence of reading and thinking throughout *Y Wladfa*. Local events and affairs would be given priority, but there must be a place for variety and for opinion expressed in a clear and level-headed fashion. The editor is aware too of a more general problem, the danger that the '*lack of stimulus and debate*' brought about by isolation might lead to an '*intellectual stupor*' and expose young people to '*corrupting influences*'.[27]

During its first two decades *Y Dravod* appeared weekly as a four-page broadsheet. Initially at least, distribution was effected by leaving packages of twenty to twenty-five copies at various points to be picked up by readers, who later paid their account to a visiting 'messenger'.[28] Not all the promises made — for instance, a woman's column and one devoted to science — could be fulfilled but from the beginning it offered an extremely varied content, often of high intellectual calibre. Much depended on the co-operation of the best informed *gwladfawyr*, hence the editor's occasional call for their support, particularly that of the young people. Correspondingly, the generation gap and an increasing sclerosis among the regular readership are themes that recur.

The paper provides a clear insight into the everyday round; chapel meetings, concerts, eisteddfodau, cultural lectures, the annual rituals of *Gŵyl y Glaniad* and the anniversary of the Argentine Republic, the arrival and departure of ships, the impending visit of an official from Buenos Aires or a dignitary from Wales. Obituary accounts of original settlers related a saga for the benefit of a new generation. Occasionally, advice was given on health, agriculture, or horticulture, whilst editorials, articles, and readers' letters debated the Settlement's problems. In addition there were advertisements, mostly in Welsh, but later increasingly in Spanish: well into the twentieth century the business community, whose names betray their Argentinian, Italian, or German origin, felt it worthwhile to advertise in the Welsh language.

Exciting contemporary events were duly reported and commented upon. The discovery of gold in the Andean foothills led to a minor gold-rush in the late eighties and early nineties. An editorial reflecting on these events in February 1891 expressed the fear that an inrush of people and an increasing materialism would affect the ideals of *Y Wladfa* but consoled readers with the reflection that the strike had been on such a modest scale that little could come of it.[29] Two expeditions attracted attention in the early 1890s. Some years passed before the Andean settlement in Cwm Hyfryd was properly settled, and a very entertaining account of that long epic journey appeared in February 1891.[30] In 1893 the prospect of gold and other precious metals took another expedition from *Y Wladfa* beyond Lake Colhué Huapi (first reached in 1877) and into the Andes, a round journey of eighteen hundred miles through largely unknown territory, which was related to the readers of *Y Dravod* in October of that year.[31] Lastly, during the winter of 1899 the swollen waters of the Chubut river flooded the whole Valley, an event that almost led to the abandonment of the Settlement. *Y Dravod*, printed at Trelew which providentially escaped inundation, could report the catastrophe under the arresting heading 'Anrhaith y Gorlifiad' (The Flood Devastation).[32]

Whereas the journalism of the emigration movement had been pursued at a high pitch of missionary intensity, *Y Dravod* preferred a lower key. Possibly the movement had lost some of its radical zeal. Certainly the act of settlement and the problems accompanying it had pushed ideology to one side, but it must also be recognized that certain aspirations — the removal of oppressive landlords, English capital, and English bosses, and the hope of being enfranchised — had been realized. Also, despite the constant problems and challenges, settlers felt free, and were in fair degree in charge of their destiny. *Y Dravod*, therefore, tended to concentrate on specific issues. None exercised the editor more than the Argentinian government's decision to drill male settlers on a Sunday. This crystallized both a deep concern over the keeping of the Sabbath and a hesitant loyalty to a government alien in language, demonized by distance, and represented at times by unwise local officials. It also touched the raw nerve of the extent to which *Y Wladfa* and its people really had the power to live their lives in their own way. *Y Dravod* responded sharply under the heading 'Yr Ormes' (The Oppression), but significantly did not challenge the Argentine government's right to rule.[33] In an earlier, important editorial, when local government had been perceived as listless, its function as the motive power of the Settlement's daily life was given prominence. Although the councils wore the trappings of Argentine authority, a sense of citizenship inhered in their ability to develop their own identity: *'In practice Y Wladfa at present has no government but a local one; and that is sufficient and appropriate.'*[34]

Y Dravod returned more than once to the theme of education. On one occasion, it eloquently denounced the Welsh settlers' lack of interest: *'They have never felt the value of knowledge, and they know next to nothing of the pleasure of reading, of thought, of understanding, and refinement.'*[35] In the next issue Lewis Jones returned to the topic, and argued for the need for education as a basis for making 'enlightened citizens'. He even envisaged setting up a centre of higher education.[36]

The turn of the century marked a change in *Y Dravod*'s fortunes. Maybe the editor's health was already beginning to fail, or his other duties imposed too great a strain; for one reason or another the paper faltered and its standards slipped. Indeed, in the issue dated 4 October 1907 a letter-writer could refer to it as 'a creature that has died three times'. After the death of Lewis Jones in 1904, the task of the new editor, R. J. Berwyn, was made more difficult by the changes around him. The influx of Spanish speakers and the effects of Spanish-medium schooling led to a local press in that language, *El Chubut* and *La Cruz del Sur* (*The Southern Cross*) both being founded in 1907.[37] So obsolete was the press on which *Y Dravod* was printed that it could not compete on price for advertising space. An unsuccessful attempt was made to get extra finance from the shareholders, but by early 1908 the paper had been taken over by the C.M.C., the dominant marketing company in the Settlement.

Under Berwyn's editorship *Y Dravod* became *Y Drafod*, its amended title reflecting the acceptance of a modern orthography and a form of Welsh which, though still literary, was closer to ordinary speech. Nevertheless, the occasional contribution in the Glamorgan or Gwentian dialect points to the continuing gap between the newspaper and much of its potential readership. From about 1910 onwards *Y Drafod* recovered its remarkable early level of attainment and entered upon a second Golden Age. Its attention to local issues enabled it to compete with the periodicals from Wales regularly available in *Y Wladfa*. A local competitor, *Y Gwerinwr*, did emerge in 1914; presumably in response, *Y Drafod* doubled its size to eight pages in July of that year.

The First World War brought a problem of identity to the surface. Despite the ambition to set up an independent Welsh homeland, the *gwladfawyr* found themselves citizens of a separate nation, whose future they were helping to shape. Their instinctive Britishness would occasion a further ambivalence: when the *Mimosa* weighed anchor in 1865 it had been to the strains of 'God Save the Queen'.[38] Even many years later, British loyalty still placed great emphasis on English and on instilling a knowledge of 'the three languages'. The competing claims of Argentine and British allegiances were put to the test in 1898 during the crisis over Sunday drilling, when a small minority committed the error of seeking the official help of the British government.[39] The persistence of British sentiment is reflected too in the sadness occasioned by Edward VII's death in 1910. Jubilation at the coronation of George V even occasioned a patriotic ode.[40]

During the war, issues of loyalty were often contested in the pages of *Y Drafod*. At the very outset the paper gave a calm and rational response — countries were displaying a 'mad enthusiasm', their people's readiness to sacrifice and to display bravery called forth admiration, yet everything would end only in loss of life. The same number, however, also reported the attempt to dismiss a local British vice-consul because of his part-German origins on the presumption that he must be a spy. Even the writer of a letter in his defence refers to the *gwladfawyr* as 'the Welsh Britishers of Chubut'.[41] We hear soon of attempts to raise money to support the widows and orphans of soldiers.

Now and again the voice of jingoism is heard, most noticeably in a letter signed 'Briton', calling for active support for Britain:

> Hasn't she always kept true to us ever since the British Colony started, and especially to the old settlers, who she helped at various times, and keeps doing even now?

He invokes the Chubut's 'loyalty to the British Empire', and expresses the hope that finally they will all join together in singing 'Britannia rules the Waves' and 'God Save the King'.[42]

Jingoism did not get it all its own way. One of the most persistent critics of war was Arthur Hughes (1878-1965),[43] who was savagely attacked by a local Anglican clergyman for his supposed lack of patriotism.[44] As war inexorably made its sacrificial demands even on the young volunteers from Y Wladfa, the intolerance increased. Paradoxically, despite regular reports from many fronts, war never dominated the news, testimony surely to distance from the conflict and to overriding local concerns.

Y Gwerinwr (El Demócrata): Newyddiadur Annibynnol Wythnosol Gwladfaol (The Man of the People [...] Y Wladfa's Independent Weekly) launched on 1 August 1914, claimed that it was not intended to challenge Y Drafod, but rather to defend, enlighten, and entertain, particularly its younger readers. Gradually, the paper did develop its own, slightly different, radical agenda. Its tone, and the contributions of certain authors (Arthur Hughes among them), were clearly anti-war. 'B' protested against the 'noise and almost savage enthusiasm' of those who supported a conflict caused not by the people, but by wealthy groups acting in their own financial interest. A later article praised the brave protests of the German anti-war veteran, Karl Liebknecht.[45] The paper had no avowedly antireligious stance, but certain contributors expressed sceptical views which provoked lively controversy. It was also critical of the Settlement's leadership for not accepting the logic of the failure to achieve political independence. For instance, a proper effort should be made to give the new generation a good knowledge of Spanish. Significantly, it carried articles in the 'three languages'. After two years of unbroken publication, the editor declared modestly that Y Gwerinwr was 'a fact in the life of the Settlement'. It certainly enlivened the scene until the end of 1916,[46] but eventually folded, presumably for lack of support.

Yn Y Drafod too the issue of identity and allegiance caused heart-searching. The Gŵyl y Glaniad issue in July 1917 acknowledged the failure of the first settlers' aims, and ruefully commented that their heirs, bereft of their own native characteristics, had assumed others that were no better. The hard quest for economic advancement had also impaired progress in education and religion.[47]

Post-war economic problems deepened the settlers' sense of crisis, which found an appropriate echo in Y Drafod. Meanwhile, the linguistic balance was shifting. Even before the end of the war the paper had included more advertisements in Spanish. By 1922 it was inviting articles in Spanish on topics of general interest to the Settlement.[48] Two contributions by 'Gwir Gymro' (A True Welshman) in 1923 offer a more specific analysis.[49] The hold of the Welsh language on the community has weakened, and people are apathetic towards the original settlers' ideals. Moreover, the Welsh now take pride in their ability to speak Spanish and to be Spanish in their ways, *'at the expense of showing contempt and lack of respect for their language and nation'*.[50]

As linguistic decline was intensified by further ethnic dilution, *Y Drafod* made brave and repeated attempts to maintain its function and position. In the early 1930s it remained the Welsh community's instrument of self-expression and identity, as well as its window on the world. By 1933 it had a new format, two large broadsheets, folded one inside the other; the first, *Y Drafod* as before; the second, its Spanish-language *alter ego, El Mentor*. Presumably as deliberate policy, very many of the advertisements were in Welsh. By 1936, however, there was a return to the old format, but on poor paper, and badly printed. Moreover, it could no longer function as a 'counter for the exchange of opinion',[51] but anticipated its purpose as a link between the descendants of the original settlers, and an occasional reminder of what they had stood for.[52] The remorseless reality is revealed in a 1945 issue: young people are now more Argentinian than Welsh.[53]

From the 1930s onwards *Y Drafod* had to contend with a series of military regimes and, from 1943, with *peronismo*'s more intrusive nationalistic policies. There are few signs that the paper danced to any political drum; indeed, occasionally it revealed its continuing allegiance to democratic principles. It had to adapt, however, to economic and demographic pressure. Gradually the weekly becomes a fortnightly, then seasonal, and in recent years it matches the double beat of *Y Wladfa*'s heart, *Gŵyl y Glaniad*, and the annual Eisteddfod, whose winning entries, both Spanish and Welsh, now form much of the content. A special expanded issue appeared in January 1991 to celebrate the paper's centenary.

The decline in readership should not be confused with a fall in quality, a fact that is more surprising given the changes in management and place of publication since 1953 — Elías Jarme in Gaiman gave way to Luis Feldman in the *Jornada*'s offices in Trelew; and then from 1973, to Donald Thomas, first in Gaiman, then Rawson, and finally Esquel in the Andes.[54] Paradoxically, standards could be better maintained once the pressures of finding adequate material and meeting printing deadlines were reduced. Occasional production also provided some relief from the ravages of inflation. But beyond these considerations lay the services of two very dedicated editors. Firstly there was Evan Thomas, editor from 1945 to his early death in 1952.[55] For a few years, Thomas also edited another periodical, *Yr Eisteddfodwr* (1947-50),[56] as well as the Spanish-language *El Regional*. Secondly there is the present editor of many years' standing, Irma Hughes de Jones. The daughter of Arthur Hughes and inheritor of his intellectual and lyrical talent, and a portion of his impressive range of learning, she became the natural successor to Evan Thomas.[57]

Few Welsh books have been published in *Y Wladfa*. A small and not always enthusiastic readership was from the first a problem. The gap between the purchase of a newspaper and of a book was another. In addition, Welsh-language publishers in Wales and Merseyside were already supplying the needs of Welsh readers whose interest in *Y Wladfa* guaranteed a far larger readership than the settlement itself could provide. In consequence, books about *Y Wladfa* and by those authors whose residence or roots were there, usually bear the imprint of a press in Great Britain.

Looked at in this way, Welsh Patagonia has produced an abundance of printed material, notably handbooks for prospective emigrants published in New York, Liverpool, or Treorci, and histories such as Abram Mathews, *Hanes y Wladfa Gymreig yn Patagonia* ([s.l.], 1894), Lewis Jones, *Hanes y Wladva Gymreig Tiriogaeth Chubut* (Caernarfon, 1898), W. M. Hughes, *Ar Lannau'r Gamwy ym Mhatagonia: Atgofion* (Liverpool, 1927), and the standard history by Bryn Williams, *Y Wladfa* (Cardiff, 1962). In the realm of fiction, the names of Eluned Morgan and Bryn Williams dominate. Travellers' accounts include those of Darwin, Musters, Holdich, Tschiffely, and Bruce Chatwin.

In the Chubut Valley itself, Ioan Pedr's call for appropriate school texts did not go entirely unheeded, the distinction of being the first Welsh book to be published in South America belonging to R. J. Berwyn and Thomas Pugh's *Gwerslyvr i Ddysgu Darllen Cymraeg. Wedi ei baratoi at wasanaeth Ysgolion dyddiol y Wladva* (Y Wladva, 1878).[58] R. J. Powel, a school-teacher appointed by the Argentinian government,[59] sought to use Welsh as an introduction to Spanish in his *Gwerslyvr Cymraeg-Hispaenaeg. Wedi ei barotoi* [sic] *at wasanaeth ysgolion y Wladva* (Y Wladva, 1881). Despite Powel's clear aims and methods, the book's appeal would have been considerably diminished by its cumbersome Welsh, very poor grasp of Spanish, and rather bizarre orthography. That Powel possessed a good notion of *Y Wladfa's* educational needs is shown by his introduction to the geography and history of South America, *Daearyddiaeth ac Hanesiaeth Amerig y De* (Buenos Aires, 1880).[60] In the 1890s a more ambitious project was begun. In August 1892 *Y Dravod* advertised Glan Caeron's *Hanes y Weriniaeth Arianin* (*A History of the Argentine Republic*) (1891), as part of a series of school texts, which also included E. Emment and Eluned Morgan, *Trefnusrwydd Teuluaidd* (*Family Orderliness*), and Mrs T. Williams, *Dylanwad Mam* (*Mother's Influence*). These were on sale at *Y Dravod*'s office at 50 dollars each.[61]

Among the items celebrating *Y Wladfa*'s centenary in 1965 was a Welsh-Spanish dictionary, *Proto diccionario gales-castellano: Rhag-eiriadur Cymraeg-Ysbanaeg* (Trelew, 1969), a volume of over 240 pages. The author, Albert Cecil Lloyd, intended his dictionary for future emigrants from Wales who, under the aegis of a Welsh State, would settle the broad expanses of South America in the footsteps of the mythical Prince Madoc. An obsession with esoteric 'Druidic' notions is reflected in the curious choice of headwords. The dictionary shows a poor grasp of both Spanish and Welsh (it is under the spell of Pughe's dictionary) and fails to include those words that had come into Welsh as a direct consequence of Welsh settlers' contact with a new country. The main impression is one of forlornness, of a task that should have been undertaken with more scholarly acumen in the Settlement's early days.

Y Wladfa continues to inspire anthologies and travel books published abroad, which will be read also in Patagonia. Thanks to *Y Drafod* the annual Eisteddfod competitions also command an audience. Periodicals from Wales are still to be found on the shelves of certain loyal families. Even so, it would be over-optimistic to believe that a book in Welsh of any size and pretension will again be published in El Chubut. Although the language has not been entirely abandoned, it usually appears as an adjunct to a work in Spanish, or as in the case of the memorable historical record, *Los galeses en Chubut: Fotografías* (*The Welsh in Chubut: Photographs*) (1987), Welsh is merely one of the 'three languages' in which the text appears. Some words from the English version are a just acknowledgement of the point finally reached by this brave but ill-fated transfer of a people and its culture:

> To bring this heritage to lonely Chubut, creating the institutions necessary for its conservation and at the same time adapting it to a different environment in a new country, was the solemn undertaking that gave Argentina a special and unexpected dimension to its national identity.[62]

The Press, more particularly the periodical press, had a noble role to play in that process.

NOTES TO CHAPTER 22

1. R. Bryn Williams, *Y Wladfa* (Cardiff, 1962), pp. 58-96; Glyn Williams, *The desert and the dream: a study of Welsh colonization in Chubut 1865-1915* (Cardiff, 1975), pp. 42-51. See also Gareth Alban Davies, 'Wales, Patagonia, and the printed word: the missionary role of the press', *Llafur*, 6(4) (1995), 44-59.
2. Glyn Williams, *The Welsh in Patagonia: the state and the ethnic community* (Cardiff, 1991), p. 95.
3. Williams, *Welsh in Patagonia*, pp. 82, 85.
4. Williams, *Desert*, p. 170, gives a total population of 23,000 by 1915.
5. Williams, *Welsh in Patagonia* provides an excellent analysis.
6. *Ibid.*, p. 240.
7. *Y Faner*, 8 March 1866. Significantly, discussion of a future university for Wales, in a periodical dedicated to establishing the Welsh colony, made no mention of any place in it for such an institution (*Y Ddraig Goch*, 2nd ser., 6 (14 Nov. 1863), 3.
8. 'Bydd y Wladychfa yn ddechreuad o newydd i ni fel Cenedl.'
9. 'Bydded y cwbl yn wreiddiol, ac yn meddu neillduolion Cymreig [...] Dylid gofalu am argraphwasg yn ddioed, a magu ysbryd llenyddol a pharch i ddysg yn mysg y gwladychwyr o'r dechreu.'
10. Gareth Alban Davies, *Tan tro nesaf: darlun o Wladfa Gymreig Patagonia* (Llandysul, 1976), p. 43. See also an account of the original landing by Edwyn Cynrig Roberts, in Aled Lloyd Davies, *The great adventure* ([s.l.], 1987), p. 42.
11. Williams, *Y Wladfa*, pp. 99-101, and the letters quoted by Lewis Jones, *Hanes y Wladva Gymreig Tiriogaeth Chubut, yn y Weriniaeth Ariannin, De Amerig* (Caernarfon, 1898), pp. 50-5.
12. Williams, *Y Wladfa*, pp. 123-4.
13. '97 años de periodisimo' in *Argentina Austral* (1975?), cited in NLW, Kenneth E. Skinner Research Papers; Luis Feldman, 'Centenario del Primer Periódico editado en la Patagonia', *Cuadernos de Historia del Chubut*, 2 (April 1968). For an outline history of the periodical press, see R. Bryn Williams, *Rhyddiaith y Wladfa* (Dinbych, 1949), pp. 17-24.
14. Williams, *Desert*, pp. 62-5.
15. Williams, *Desert*, p. 74; also his *Welsh in Patagonia*, pp. 40-1.
16. Williams, *Y Wladfa*, pp. 169-71.
17. UCNW, Newyddiaduron y Wladfa Collection: first series, 1 (21 Sept. 1878) — 7 (9 Nov. 1878); second series, 1 (23 Nov. 1878) — 7 (17 May 1879); unnumbered issues, 22 Oct. 1881, 26 Nov. 1881, and a special Christmas number 1883. For the original issue I correct the year given in Williams, *Y Wladfa*, p. 169.
18. '[...] vod pob breinwr yn ddeallus, vel ag i vod yn abl barnu pob mater gwleidyddol ddelo ger ei vron, a chanddo y cyvle i beri ei glywed a'i deimlo vel cydradd yn y corf gwladol.'
19. Williams, *Y Wladfa*, pp. 122-3 and Appendix VIII.
20. *Ibid.*, pp. 100-1.
21. Thomas Hungerford Holdich, *The countries of the King's award*, edition de luxe (London, 1904), p. 242.
22. Williams, *Y Wladfa*, p. 198. Cf. *Ein Breiniad*, 2nd series, 6 (3 May 1879): 'Ar y dechreu, gorvodaeth argrafyddol a barodd i ni ddev[n]yddio v' (Initially, typographical exigency compelled us to employ v).
23. Glenda Carr, *William Owen Pughe* (Cardiff, 1983), pp. 82-9.
24. Davies, *The great adventure*, pp. 40-5, quoting the diary of Edwyn Cynrig Roberts.
25. Williams, *Y Wladfa*, pp. 217-22.
26. '[...] lleddvu gerwinder sydd gymaint provedigaeth i'n sevyllva.'
27. 'O ddifyg cyvleusdra cymundeb â'r byd, teimlo yr ydys er's blynyddau vod perygl i ni geulo ar ein sorod, heb hogi ein gilydd, a gloywi wynebau ein cyveillion; ac yn enwedig vod ein pobl ieuaingc heb gyvleusdra gwybod na thravod, tra yn agored i lawer o ddylanwadau mall ac anghaeth.'
28. *Y Dravod.*, 17 Jan. 1891.

29 *Ibid.*, 7 Feb. 1891; Williams, *Y Wladfa*, pp. 234-7.
30 *Ibid.*, 28 Feb. 1891; Williams, *Y Wladfa*, pp. 230-1; Williams, *Desert*, pp. 130-1.
31 *Ibid.*, 12 Oct. 1893; Williams, *Y Wladfa*, pp. 238-9.
32 *Ibid.*, 4 Aug. 1899; Williams, *Welsh in Patagonia*, pp. 144-5.
33 *Ibid.*, 9 Sept. 1898; Williams, *Y Wladfa*, pp. 253-6.
34 'Yn ymarverol mae y Wladva heb lywodraethiad yn awr ond yr un leodrol; ac y mae hono yn ddigon ac yn briodol' (*Y Dravod*, 14 Sept. 1893).
35 'Ni theimlasant erioed werth gwybodaeth, ac ni wyddant nemawr ddim am swyn darllen, a meddwl, a deall, a choethder' (*Y Dravod*, 21 Feb. 1891).
36 *Y Dravod*, 28 Feb. 1891.
37 '97 años de periodismo' and the notes in NLW, Kenneth E. Skinner Research Papers, Archive 16: Biblioteca Popular Agustín Álvarez, Trelew, on the early numbers of *El Chubut* which first appeared on 27 Sept. 1907. The contents show clearly the extent to which they appealed for readers among the *gwladfawyr*.
38 Davies, p. 57.
39 Williams, *Y Wladfa*, pp. 257-62.
40 *Y Drafod*, 8 Sept. 1911.
41 *Ibid.*, 2 Oct. 1914.
42 *Ibid.*, 16 Oct. 1914.
43 Son of the novelist Gwyneth Vaughan, and compiler of *Cywyddau Cymru* (Bangor, 1908), his contribution to *Y Drafod* is discussed in Williams, *Rhyddiaith y Wladfa*, pp. 50-6.
44 *Y Drafod*, 7 July 1916.
45 *Y Gwerinwr*, 10 Oct. 1914; 1 May 1915.
46 The last issue in the comprehensive collection in the NLW is 110, dated 25 Nov. 1916.
47 *Y Drafod*, 20 July 1917.
48 *Ibid.*, 24 Feb. 1922.
49 *Ibid.*, 30 March 1923; 1 June 1923.
50 '[...] ar draul diystyru ac amharchu eu hiaith a'u cenedl' (*Y Drafod*, 1 June 1923).
51 Williams, *Y Wladfa*, p. 198.
52 For instance, Arthur Hughes in *Y Drafod*, 19 Jan. 1951, or summer 1981(reprinting an article of 1947). The paper's difficulties in continuing are also mentioned.
53 *Y Drafod*, 19 Oct. 1945.
54 For these changes see the centenary number, *Y Drafod*, 17 Jan. 1991
55 *Y Drafod*, 9 May 1959. Evan Thomas, 'Nodion o'r Wladfa', *Y Cymro*, 14 Sept. 1945.
56 A few issues are preserved in the NLW.
57 *Y Drafod*, 22 Nov. 1946. For her career see *Edau gyfrodedd: detholiad o waith Irma Hughes de Jones*, ed. Cathrin Williams (Denbigh, 1989), which gives 1953 as the year she assumed the editorship.
58 Cited in Williams, *Y Wladfa*, p. 323, as is a second revised and expanded edition dated 1881.
59 Williams, *Y Wladfa*, pp. 155-8.
60 *Ibid.*, p. 325.
61 *Y Dravod*, 11 Aug. 1892. For the background see Williams, *Y Wladfa*, pp. 197-8.
62 *Los galeses en Chubut: Fotografías* ([s.l.], 1987), p. 91.

CHAPTER 23

WELSH PUBLIC LIBRARIES TO 1914

Philip Henry Jones

FROM 1850 onwards, certain local authorities in England and Wales were empowered to establish rate-supported public libraries.[1] An incongruous parliamentary alliance of Tory reactionaries and doctrinaire supporters of *laissez-faire* had ensured that the legislation was adoptive: although the procedures were frequently modified, until April 1965 local authorities could chose whether or not to exercise library powers.[2] Those which did adopt the Acts were under no obligation to put them into operation: by 1914 nine or more authorities in Wales had taken this step but, perhaps wisely given their limited resources, had gone no further.[3]

Between 1855 and 1919 the maximum library rate which could be levied was limited to a penny in the pound. Although an improvement on the halfpenny originally stipulated in 1850, this restriction prevented smaller authorities from providing more than the most basic service. Financial problems were less obvious in larger authorities but here too the penny rate impeded development, particularly where, as at Cardiff, the 'nimble penny' had also to sustain a museum and schools of science and art.[4] Only the largest authorities such as Swansea in 1889 and Cardiff in 1898 could contemplate private legislation permitting a higher rate. To make things worse, from 1877 onwards local authorities were authorized to levy a lower rate should they so wish. Welshpool, which would have been hard-pressed even on the proceeds of the full rate, set a halfpenny rate when it adopted the Acts in 1887 and kept to this until 1926.[5]

There is little, if any, evidence that public libraries in Wales were set up because of demand from their intended working-class users. Local authorities generally adopted the Acts as the result of the persistence of a few library-minded individuals who were often pursuing broader philanthropic, educational, or moral objectives. Such men, aided by the local press, had to struggle against at best apathy and at worst virulent opposition from those who refused to countenance any further increase in the rates.

As in England, there were few adoptions before the later 1880s. Between 1850 and 1886 only six Welsh authorities assumed library powers. Four — Cardiff, Newport, Swansea, and Wrexham — were thriving commercial and industrial centres, while the small towns of Bangor and Aberystwyth had special reasons for adopting. The first adoption was at Cardiff. Following discussion in the local press in 1858, the proposal was defeated by one vote at a poorly attended meeting in October 1860. Supporters of adoption promptly set up a voluntary library and reading room which proved so successful that, according to the official account, opponents were won over, permitting the Acts to be adopted with only one dissenting vote in September 1862.[6] The persistent reluctance of Cardiff's council to finance the library adequately until the mid-1880s suggests a rather different interpretation: that opponents of the library, realizing that no further political advantage could be derived from open opposition, resorted to covert methods of limiting its cost.[7]

A meeting of Newport's ratepayers voted unanimously in favour of adoption in February 1870, doubtless believing that an offer of the assets of the financially troubled Newport Athenaeum and Mechanics' Institute was too good a bargain to miss.[8] Although successful mechanics' institutes initially tended to strengthen the case of local opponents of adoption, as at Neath in June 1870,[9] institutes eventually came to constitute the nucleus of several public libraries in Wales, most notably at Llanelli and at Neath itself in the later 1890s.

The offer of the library of Rowland Williams (1817-70), of *Essays and Reviews* notoriety, was probably a major factor in overcoming strong resistance to adoption at Swansea.[10] The town's long and rich tradition of library provision for the middle and upper ranks of society[11] may well have retarded the public library movement there but more powerful inhibiting factors were the borough's size, its high rate, and bitter local political disputes. A particular grievance was that ratepayers in outlying areas such as Morriston believed that they were to be taxed to provide a service which would benefit residents of the town centre only. This was a common problem which led to repeated rejections of adoption elsewhere, notably at Aberdâr and Merthyr. When adoption was first voted upon in 1868, feelings ran so high that a Morriston industrialist sent three canal-boats of workmen, liberally refreshed *en route* and entertained by a band, to vote against the proposal. The Acts were finally adopted in October 1870 at a tumultuous public meeting allegedly attended by two thousand or more townspeople. Although the show of hands appeared to be equal, the Mayor, a strong advocate of adoption, declared the proposal carried since opponents had held up both hands.[12] Retribution swiftly followed as he and other supporters of the library lost their seats at the next election. The triumphant opposition delayed setting up a library committee until 1874 and it was not until 1875 that Swansea began to provide a free library service.

Bangor and Aberystwyth also adopted the Acts in order to secure gifts. To enable it to take over and maintain an existing library and museum, Bangor's Local Board of Health obtained library powers through a local Act in 1870. The ratepayers still had to be consulted, but the proposal was unanimously accepted in November 1870.[13] Aberystwyth adopted the Acts in December 1871 in order to set up a gallery to house paintings offered to the town by G. E. J. Powell of Nanteos, a local landowner, aesthete, and intimate friend of Swinburne.[14] Before municipal faction-fights and ineptitude led to the withdrawal of Powell's offer, the vicar of Llanbadarn (President of the moribund and debt-ridden Aberystwyth Literary Institute), supported by the local press, had persuaded the council that a public library would improve the moral tone of the town. After further squabbles and delay which led Powell to withdraw his offer, Aberystwyth's library eventually opened in the autumn of 1874.

Wrexham in 1878 was the only Welsh authority to assume library powers during the next fifteen years.[15] Even though Pontypridd, Caernarfon, and Welshpool, the three authorities which celebrated Victoria's jubilee in 1887 by adopting the Acts, all stood to acquire the assets of earlier institutions, a substantial minority of ratepayers voted against adoption in each, and the proposal was rejected at Aberdâr, Mountain Ash, Carmarthen and, possibly, at Cardigan.[16] Two years later, Llandudno also refused to adopt the Acts despite being offered a library worth two thousand pounds.[17] Many of the Anglicized and comparatively wealthy coastal resorts of North Wales were reluctant to adopt, Colwyn Bay finally venturing to do so in 1901, followed by Rhyl in 1904, and Llandudno in 1907.[18] The less prosperous resorts of west Wales such as Tywyn and Aberdyfi generally did not adopt, some preferring to rely, as did Aberdyfi from 1882 onwards, on subscription-based institutes.[19]

Since the county councils set up in 1889 were not granted library powers until 1919, the parish councils established in 1894 were the only potential library authorities for much of rural Wales. In February 1895 Llanuwchllyn became the first Welsh parish to adopt, largely because of the enthusiasm of O. M. Edwards. The detailed account he published of its library probably encouraged other parish councils in North Wales to adopt.[20]

As elsewhere in Britain, local benefactors made generous gifts to many Welsh public libraries. Books (all too often of dubious value) and other materials were frequently given or bequeathed. Swansea, in particular, benefited from the donations of books and prints made by the artist John Deffet Francis (1815-1901). Several authorities were given sites for their libraries by local landowners, and public appeals for money often raised considerable sums.[21] These local philanthropists were eclipsed from 1897 onwards as Andrew Carnegie began to give library buildings 'wholesale' to authorities undertaking to adopt the Acts, provide a site, and levy a penny rate.[22] By 1914, twenty-six Welsh library authorities had received over £78,000 in building and furnishing grants, the majority being for some £1,500 to £3,000.[23] Carnegie's gifts were largely responsible for a spate of adoptions during the first decade of the twentieth century which more than doubled the number of library authorities in Wales from 26 to 57. Unfortunately, many of these new authorities were too small and impoverished to provide an adequate service. Authorities such as Cardiff and Newport which already possessed adequate buildings received Carnegie grants for constructing branch libraries.

In 1913 the ageing Carnegie established the Carnegie United Kingdom Trust (CUKT) to continue his philanthropic activities. In order to assess the effects of his benefactions the CUKT commissioned Professor W. G. S. Adams to prepare a report on library provision and policy in the United Kingdom. The Adams Report, published in abbreviated form in 1915, showed that, apart from Cardiff, the public library movement had achieved little in Wales during the past half-century.[24] Even in 1913 over half the population of Wales (54%) lived in areas which had not adopted the Acts. Most rural areas were still without public libraries, and many populous industrial areas had not adopted the Acts either. The mining valleys of South Wales generally relied on the libraries of the miners' institutes whose income fluctuated according to the fortunes of the coal industry and which normally levied a charge on users other than miners and their families.

The combination of small, poor authorities and the penny rate limit condemned the inhabitants of most library areas to receive a service which was inadequate even by the undemanding standards of the day. Almost half the Welsh libraries surveyed by Adams (21 out of 52) had an annual income of less than £100 in 1910-11, and a further 13 an income between £100 and £200.[25] Cardiff, spending £7,862, was responsible for almost a third of the total expenditure on libraries in 1913-14 of £21,402. Much of the money spent was on buildings and staffing rather than on books. Adams considered that an expenditure on books of £150 a year was 'a very small sum if a library is to be kept moderately efficient',[26] a modest target which was met by only six Welsh authorities. Although Cardiff spent no less than £1,295 in 1913-14, almost four times as much as the next heaviest spender, Swansea (£329), nineteen authorities spent less than £50, some (such as Llanuwchllyn) as little as a pound. The total expenditure on newspapers and periodicals of over £3,000, very little less than that on books and binding, underlined the heavy emphasis public libraries placed on providing these materials. The newsroom was often the first part of the library to open to the public, followed usually by the lending department. A few libraries were too impoverished to establish a lending department for many years: Wrexham, for instance, had to do without a lending library for a decade until it received £390 from the profits of the 1888 National Eisteddfod.[27] Even after this windfall, in order to build up its lending stock Wrexham had to resort until 1906 to running a book club which gave subscribers first access to new books, and was pleased to receive a further £250 from the 1912 Eisteddfod.[28] Reference services were generally neglected, Swansea providing the best service until overtaken by Cardiff in the early 1890s. Both lending and reference libraries were usually closed-access collections, although some of the poorer libraries such as Aberystwyth adopted open access (or what purported to be so) during the 1890s in order to save money.[29]

Even though staffing absorbed much of the total resources devoted to libraries, the number and quality of staff was unsatisfactory. Only at Cardiff (47) and Swansea (10) did the number of staff reach double figures in 1913-14. Twenty other authorities employed from two to eight members of staff, the remainder one only.[30] Outside the larger authorities, 'librarians' were usually caretaker-librarians, without any training or previous experience of library work. Welshpool's librarian in the late 1880s had been a sergeant in the Army Hospital Corps, and Corwen's in 1896 was a former engine-driver.[31] Several of the smaller authorities such as Aberystwyth began to employ women as chief (or sole) librarians during the 1890s because their wages were so much lower. The unqualified Librarian of Holyhead, for instance, was paid a superior domestic servant's wage of £30 a year for working over 46 hours a week, and her (female) assistant £7 10s.[32]

The Victorian belief in the value of statistics, and the availability of cheap clerical labour to compile them, have provided a wealth of information on the users of the larger services. Swansea's annual report for 1879-80 reveals rather more women borrowers than might have been expected — 589 compared with 1,016 men. As elsewhere in Britain, the heaviest users were adolescents aged 14 to 20 (400 youths, 213 girls). Clerks (175) were by far the largest male occupational group, followed by 104 'schoolboys and students'. The vast majority of women were listed as 'ladies — no occupations' (480), the largest group gainfully employed being thirty dressmakers and milliners. Two barmaids were listed as borrowers, a figure which showed a gratifying increase to five by 1886-7.[33]

Contemporary advocates of public libraries such as Thomas Greenwood praised the progress made in the face of great odds in 'gallant little Wales'[34] but appeared to be wholly unaware that these libraries made little or no provision for the million or so people who were bilingual or spoke Welsh only. Public libraries clearly did not consider the provision of current Welsh-language books to be part of their responsibilities. The larger authorities, admittedly, had acquired Welsh books and manuscripts from the

1870s onwards but regarded them as research materials to be segregated in special collections. Thus Swansea acquired the library of Rowland Williams, rich in Welsh antiquarian and literary material, in the early 1870s and purchased the notable collection of Robert Jones, vicar of Rotherhithe, in 1879 for £650.[35] However, these books were not properly organized for public use until after the turn of the century and, even when Swansea's Welsh Department was professionally developed from 1905 onwards by D. Rhys Phillips (1862-1952),[36] it remained essentially a research collection.

Although Cardiff had made a feeble attempt to collect Welsh books from 1870 onwards, the stained-glass windows placed in its new reference room in 1882 depicting Milton, Scott, Raleigh, and Gibbon[37] rather than Welsh writers epitomized the prevailing ethos. Indeed, the Cardiff Welsh Society made setting up its own Welsh reading room one of its first objectives in the mid-1880s.[38] Within a few years a dramatic change in emphasis became apparent as Cardiff rapidly developed its Welsh collection, largely as part of its campaign to gain city status and recognition as the capital of Wales. In 1891 it purchased the important collection of 7,000 printed books and a hundred manuscripts formed by the Rees family of Tonn, notable antiquaries and printers, £350 of the cost being raised by public subscription. The Welsh manuscripts from the Phillipps library (including the Book of Aneirin) were purchased in 1895, the Marquess of Bute contributing £1,000 towards the total cost of over £3,500.[39] Following the appointment of J. Ifano Jones (1865-1955)[40] to the Welsh Department in 1896, and the publication of his catalogue of it in 1898 (which remains of considerable value today given the lamentably undeveloped state of Welsh nineteenth-century bibliography), further important accessions flowed in.[41] Its rich holdings tended to reinforce the view that Cardiff's Welsh library was a specialized research collection.

The smaller municipal libraries did little or nothing to promote the reading of Welsh books. Aberdâr, a major centre of Welsh publishing during the second half of the nineteenth century,[42] adopted the Acts in 1900 following several unsuccessful attempts from 1873 onwards and began to operate a service (with a Birmingham man as librarian) in 1904. Total issues in 1904-5 were 21,925 volumes, of which Welsh books amounted to 697. About 1912, a few readers took the unusual step of complaining of 'the paucity of Welsh literature in the library' but even though Aberdâr was bequeathed a substantial private collection which included several 'rare' Welsh items in 1912, the number of Welsh books issued continued to decline so that by 1917-18 they comprised only 216 of a total issue of 33,770.[43] At Pontypridd, where about a third of the population was Welsh-speaking at the turn of the century, only two of the 1,999 volumes listed in the 1897 catalogue were in Welsh — and they were duplicate copies of an obsolete dictionary.[44] Neath, another library serving a substantial Welsh-speaking population, made virtually no provision for Welsh readers. Only 54 volumes of the 1,345 listed in its 1899 catalogue were in Welsh, and hardly any Welsh books were borrowed: 16 out of a total of 9,562 in 1900 and 23 out of a total of 10,336 in 1901.[45]

Public libraries operated by a few parishes in north Wales appear to have been a little more in touch with the linguistic abilities of their potential users. Over a quarter of the 400 volumes which Llanuwchllyn possessed in 1895 were in Welsh, and an eighth consisted of English works relating to Wales. Even so, over half the stock consisted of a complete set of Cassell's National Library, presented by two local well-wishers.[46] At another small parish, Halkyn, roughly a quarter of the library's live stock of about 370 volumes consisted of books in Welsh, though many of them had been lent to the library.[47] The wholly inadequate provision of Welsh-language books by public libraries gives considerable force to the argument that their restricted development, particularly in rural areas, limited the threat they posed to the survival of the Welsh language.[48]

There are several reasons why public libraries failed to stock Welsh-language books. The most important was the low status and widely perceived non-utility of the language. Supporters of public libraries were drawn from the upper ranks of society, the clergy (both Nonconformist and Anglican), the professions, and successful industrialists and businessmen, all of whom were to a greater or lesser extent Anglicized in language and values. Many understandably equated the English language with enlightenment and progress, and believed that its further diffusion would better equip their compatriots to take full advantage of the opportunities now open to them.[49] Welsh could make no contribution to worldly success but might perhaps survive as the language of religion, and as a field for study by scholars tracing the emotional 'Celtic' contribution to the British character.

The output of the Welsh-language press reinforced such prejudices since it consisted predominantly of religious works rather than the type of book which, in English, constituted the mainstay of public library bookstocks. Few Welsh books contained 'useful knowledge', and very few Welsh novels were published until the 1890s. Even during the so-called golden age of Welsh-language publishing, the number of new titles appearing each year could be counted in tens, and many of these were intended for a local readership. Virtually all were cheap (a 3s. 6d. book was considered expensive) or were published in parts so that they could be more easily purchased. Since Welsh readers tended to buy their own books, the close relationship between the book trade and libraries which was so important in nineteenth-century England did not develop in Wales until the 1950s.

Welsh books were rarely to be found in those libraries which were the predecessors and contemporaries of early public libraries. Nineteenth-century book clubs provided the gentry, clergy, professional men, and their wives with current works in English, as did the private subscription libraries which flourished in the larger towns.[50] Welsh books clearly had no place at all in the local commercial subscription libraries which proliferated in nineteenth-century Wales nor in the chain of libraries operated by W. H. Smith and Boots[51] which catered for those who wished to borrow clean copies of fashionable works and who tended to regard public libraries as repositories of grubby books for the lower orders.

Given their original emphasis on useful knowledge and subsequently on fiction, the libraries of the mechanics' institutes had little incentive to acquire Welsh books. Since these libraries greatly influenced later public libraries, their stock and loan figures are significant. Not one of the 612 volumes which Neath Mechanics' Institute possessed in 1847 was in Welsh, and only two related to Wales.[52] The 1851 catalogue of the Brecon Literary, Scientific and Mechanics' Institute lists some 620 titles, two of which were in Welsh and fewer than ten of which related to Wales.[53] Similarly, the 1868 catalogue of the Carmarthen Literary and Scientific Institute listed about 2,400 works, of which three were in Welsh and fewer than fifty related to Wales.[54] There is some evidence that the less Anglicized institutes may have provided a little more material in Welsh. Ebbw Vale Literary and Scientific Institute possessed 177 Welsh titles and 1,681 in English in 1870-71, its Welsh loans amounting to 231 of a total of 2,514. The fiction loans are particularly telling: six in Welsh and 1,302 in English.[55] Welsh loans at Llanelli in 1864 were slightly below 10% of the total: of the 5,269 volumes borrowed, 502 consisted of works of 'Welsh literature', but the 1870 catalogue lists only about 90 Welsh titles out of a total stock of 2,000 or more.[56] At Swansea, the Royal Institution of South Wales, established in 1835, built up an impressive Welsh library (regarded by some as the nucleus of a future national library) but, like the rich public library collections at Swansea and Cardiff, this was primarily for research.[57]

By the later nineteenth century many small towns which had not adopted the Acts had come to possess subscription reading rooms and libraries, often established with the assistance of English or Anglicized well-wishers.[58] Although most were in strongly Welsh localities, the provision of Welsh-language material once again failed to reflect this. The post-1894 catalogue of Llanrwst, for instance, listed about 540 titles (including, inevitably, a set of Cassell's National Library), fewer than 30 of which were in Welsh.[59]

Welsh books may have been acquired more enthusiastically by the *cymdeithasau darllen* (reading societies) which flourished fitfully in several parts of Wales from the later 1840s onwards.[60] Although the best-documented, that at Pentrefoelas, owed its inception to the local vicar, others appear to have come into existence as a result of initiative from below and would thus have been compelled to provide Welsh-language material for those members who could not read English. These societies require further investigation, as do Welsh Sunday-school libraries, where the most basic questions remain unanswered.[61]

NOTES TO CHAPTER 23

1. Thomas Kelly, *A history of public libraries in Great Britain 1845-1975*, 2nd edn (London, 1977) outlines the legislation and provides the framework for this study.
2. Mountain Ash UDC was the last authority in Great Britain to adopt the Acts as late as 1963.
3. Kelly, pp. 515-16, lists Broughton, Ogmore and Garw, and Higher Newcastle (1895); Ynyscynhaiarn (1900) (his 'Carmarthen' should be Caernarfon); Abersychan, Cyfoeth y Brenin, and Pencoed (1901); Gorseinon (1902); Llanfair-is-Gaer (1908).
4. J. Ballinger, *The Cardiff Free Libraries* (Cardiff, 1895), pp. 12, 16-17.
5. J. Roe, 'The public library in Wales; its history and development in the context of local government' (unpublished master's thesis, Queen's University of Belfast, 1970), p. 46.
6. The official version of events is presented in Ballinger, pp. 3-12, and in *Cardiff Public Libraries: 50th anniversary celebration of the opening of the Central Library. A brief survey of the library movement in Cardiff* (Cardiff, 1932), pp. 3-8.
7. 'There was still a certain amount of prejudice against the Institution existing in some minds [...] there was a niggardly spirit displayed in voting money' (Ballinger, p. 12).
8. Roe, p. 38.
9. Gareth Williams, 'Battling for books: an abortive attempt to adopt the public libraries acts at Neath in 1870', *TNAS*, (1980-1), pp. 155-9.
10. Gareth Williams, 'Adoption at Swansea', *Library History*, 4 (1976-8), 81-4.
11. Eiluned Rees and G. Walters, 'Swansea libraries in the nineteenth century', *JWBS*, 10 (1) (1966-71), 43-57; David Boorman, *The Brighton of Wales: Swansea as a fashionable seaside resort, c.1780-c.1830* (Swansea, 1986), pp. 56-66.
12. Gareth Williams, 'The longest and most stormy meeting that Swansea ever had', *Gower*, 30 (1979), 18-21.
13. Roe, p. 41.
14. N. Roberts, 'A town and its library: Aberystwyth: December 1871 — October 1874', *Ceredigion*, 3 (1956-9), 161-81, provides a sardonic account of events.
15. Thomas Greenwood, *Public libraries: a history of the movement and a manual for [...] rate supported libraries*, 4th edn (London, 1894), p. 279.
16. Greenwood, p. 269.
17. *Ibid.*, p. 279.
18. Roe, pp. 59, 65-6.
19. Henry K. Birch, *The pages of time: a brief history of the Aberdovey Literary Institute 1882-1982* ([Aberdyfi], 1982).
20. An account of the library and a catalogue was published in *Seren y Mynydd*, 1(2) (1895), 3-16, and a briefer account in *Heddyw*, 1 (1897), 37-8.
21. Pontypridd was given a site for its library and well over a third of the cost of the building was met by public subscription (Roe, p. 44); at Halkyn the Duke of Westminster provided a site and donated £200 (Roe, p. 51).
22. James G. Ollé, 'Andrew Carnegie: the unloved benefactor', *Library World*, 70 (1968-9), 255-62, provides a concise and balanced appraisal of Carnegie's gifts and their effects.
23. Roe, p. 214.
24. Much of the following draws upon the report, W. G. S. Adams, *A report on library provision & policy to the Carnegie United Kingdom Trustees* (Dunfermline, 1915).
25. These and subsequent figures are based on Adams, pp. 50-5.
26. Adams, p. 13.
27. Greenwood, p. 279.
28. *Library Association Record*, 9 (1907), 139-40; A. H. Dodd, *A history of Wrexham, Denbighshire* (Wrexham, 1957), p. 130.
29. Thomas Greenwood, *British library yearbook 1900-1901* (London, 1900), p. 267.
30. Adams, pp. 50-5.

[31] Welshpool: *The Library*, 1 (1889), 37; Corwen: Greenwood, *British library yearbook*, p. 111.
[32] Greenwood, *British library yearbook*, p. 141.
[33] Borough of Swansea, *Sixth annual report of the Public Library Committee. 1879-80* (Swansea, 1880), pp. 8-9; Borough of Swansea, *Thirteenth annual report of the Public Library [...] Committee. 1886-7* (Swansea, 1887), p.13.
[34] Greenwood, *Public libraries*, p. 269.
[35] Brynley F. Roberts, 'Llyfrgell Gymraeg Abertawe', *JWBS*, 12(1) (1983-4), 26-50 (with English summary).
[36] *Ibid.*, pp. 43-9, provides the best account of his career.
[37] Greenwood, *Public libraries*, p. 272. In his opinion these windows were the 'prettiest and most appropriate' to be found in any public library.
[38] J. Gwynfor Jones, *Y ganrif gyntaf: hanes Cymrodorion Caerdydd 1885-1985* ([Cardiff], 1987), pp. 7-8.
[39] *Cardiff Public Libraries*, p. 16; J. Brynmor Jones, 'Cefndir Llyfrgell Caerdydd', *Y Casglwr*, 9 (Nadolig 1979), 17-19.
[40] W. W. Price, 'James Ifano Jones, M.A. (1865-1855) [sic]', *JWBS*, 8 (1954-7), 53-7.
[41] Wyndham Morgan, 'The Welsh Library and special collections', in *Report of the proceedings of the 17th conference of library authorities in Wales and Monmouthshire [...] 1950* (Swansea, 1950), 22-7.
[42] Brynley F. Roberts, 'Printing at Aberdare, 1854-1974', *The Library*, 5th series, 33 (1978), 125-42, and his 'Argraffu yn Aberdâr', *JWBS*, 11 (1973-6), 1-53.
[43] The above is based on *Aberdare Central Public Library: golden jubilee 1904-54* (Aberdare, 1955).
[44] Patrick F. Tobin, 'Pontypridd public library 1890-1990', in *The bridge and the song: some chapters in the story of Pontypridd*, ed. P. F. Tobin and J. I. Davies (Bridgend, 1991), pp. 67-78 (p. 70).
[45] Stock: Neath Public Library, *Catalogue of books, 1899*, (Neath, 1899); issues: S. A. Parfitt, 'Neath public library' (unpublished typescript), p. 3.
[46] *Seren y Mynydd*, 1(2) (1895), 7-16.
[47] Halkyn Parish Council, *Catalogue of books in the Halkyn Parish Library*, (Holywell, 1900).
[48] This is the implicit conclusion of Norman Roberts, *Y llyfrgell mewn cymdeithas* (Llanbadarn Fawr, 1967), which further demonstrates the inadequacy in a bilingual community, where one language is subjected to crushing social and commercial pressures, of an ostensibly impartial professional ideology.
[49] E. G. Millward, 'Pob gwybodaeth fuddiol', in *Brad y Llyfrau Gleision; ysgrifau ar hanes Cymru*, ed. Prys Morgan (Llandysul, 1991), pp. 146-65, provides a balanced introduction.
[50] A comprehensive study of these libraries is badly needed. Apart from a few detailed local studies such as that of Swansea by Eiluned Rees and G. Walters noted above, a great deal of valuable information is hidden away in local histories such as Keith Kissack, *Victorian Monmouth* (Monmouth, [1986]), pp. 128-32.
[51] As early as 1908 *Kelly's directory of stationers, printers, booksellers, publishers* listed seven Boots libraries in Wales and Monmouthshire, all in towns which already possessed a public library.
[52] The *Fourth annual report of the Neath Mechanics' Institution* (Neath, 1847), pp. 12-29, includes a catalogue of its library.
[53] *Catalogue of books in the library of the Brecon Literary, Scientific, and Mechanics' Institution* (Brecon, 1851).
[54] Carmarthen Literary and Scientific Institution, *Catalogue of the library* (Carmarthen, 1869).
[55] Sian Rhiannon Williams, *Oes y byd i'r iaith Gymraeg: y Gymraeg yn ardal ddiwydiannol Sir Fynwy yn y bedwaredd ganrif ar bymtheg* (Cardiff, 1992), p. 100.
[56] Loans: Heather Ann Evans, 'The Llanelly Mechanics' Institute and its library' (unpublished student assignment, College of Librarianship Wales, 1980), p. 18; stock: Llanelly Mechanics' Institute, *Rules & catalogue* (Llanelly, 1870).
[57] Brynley F. Roberts, 'Llyfrgell Gymraeg Abertawe', pp. 27-30, includes a discussion of Welsh material listed in the 1848 and 1876 catalogues.
[58] Supporters of Llangollen library included Sir Theodore Martin, Robert Browning, and George Smith of Smith, Elder and Co. (*The Library*, 2 (1890), 466).

[59] Llanrwst Reading Room and Library, *Catalogue of books in the circulating library section* (Llanrwst, [189?]).
[60] Bob Owen, 'Cymdeithasau darllen gan mlynedd yn ôl', in *Report of the proceedings of the twenty-first conference of library authorities in Wales and Monmouthshire [...] (1954)* (Swansea, 1955), pp. 30-7. His notes for the lecture, NLW, MS 16283E, contain much information omitted from the published text.
[61] L. S. Jones, 'Church and chapel as sources and centres of education in Wales during the second half of the nineteenth century' (unpublished master's thesis, University of Liverpool, 1940), pp. 287-92, contains some tantalizing observations.

CHAPTER 24

WELSH PUBLIC LIBRARIES 1914 — 1994

G. I. Evans

THERE has been a long tradition in the United Kingdom of linking the growth and development of the public library system with evolution and change in the local government structures which underpin that system. In essence, reorganized, viable structures have been viewed as the precursors of reorganized, viable library systems. From 1915 to 1994 there was a constant quest to define such 'viability' by establishing criteria to indicate the optimum size of the local government unit which could provide a comprehensive and efficient library service. Whichever criteria were promulgated — population, rateable value, or expenditure — could all be (and were) countered by examples of small library authorities devoting a high level of resources to the provision of a library service. The quest for viability also foundered because it tended to set local authorities one against another.

By the end of 1913 fifty-nine authorities in Wales — thirteen boroughs, twenty-nine urban districts, and seventeen civil parishes — had adopted the Acts and were providing some kind of library service.[1] The quality of the service varied greatly since library legislation did not specify the standard of service to be provided, and the size and resource base of a library authority were apparently not considered to be important. Following the Adams Report[2] of 1915 which highlighted the lack of provision in rural areas, the Carnegie United Kingdom Trust (CUKT) decided to offer grants to certain authorities to enable them to commence what were described as experimental rural library schemes which would circulate boxes of books to villages, the village school usually serving as a distribution centre. This embryonic county library service was formalized with the passing of the Public Libraries Act of 1919 which repealed the penny rate limitation and empowered counties to adopt the Acts for any area within their boundaries not already served by an existing library authority. Counties could exclude areas within their boundaries when they adopted, a power regrettably used by Glamorgan to exclude two urban districts, the Rhondda and Mountain Ash, on the grounds that they were already well served by workmen's libraries and that the county could not afford to provide a service to such densely populated areas.

Caernarfonshire was the first CUKT rural scheme in Wales. Following lengthy discussions during 1916, it was awarded an annual grant of £400 for a five-year period in 1917. In October of that year the county education committee leased premises at Plas Llanwnda, Caernarfon, for use as a repository and appointed a librarian at an initial salary of £130 a year. The first librarian, who remained in post until his death in 1942, was T. O. Jones, 'Gwynfor', a noted Welsh dramatist, actor, and adjudicator. Although he possessed no professional qualifications or experience of library work, after a brief period of training by the Trust at Dunfermline he approached his task with enthusiasm. The service started in November 1918 and within its first year of operation over 2,000 books had been dispatched from the central repository. Gwynfor drew up a list of the most popular titles (mainly juvenile works); in this, Welsh books occupied nine of the top twenty places.

Although over 8,000 volumes were issued in the scheme's fourth year of operation, the CUKT continually pressed the county to expand the service and, in particular, to increase the proportion of books for adults. In April 1923, when the five years of support from the CUKT had come to an end, Caernarfonshire adopted the Acts, but on account of the education committee's lack of enthusiasm the library rate was set at a farthing in the pound. Since it remained at this low level for many years the bookfund for much of the 1920s and 1930s was no more than about £200 a year. Another problem which caused Gwynfor great concern was the library's inability to meet the increasing demand for Welsh-language material. In 1927 he requested a special grant from the CUKT for the publication of Welsh books. The Trust rejected his request since it would create a precedent for grants for books in Scottish Gaelic and Irish,[3] a surprising reaction by a philanthropic organisation based in Scotland.

On hearing of Caernarfonshire's negotiations with the CUKT, Cardiganshire approached the Trust in the spring of 1917 and in January 1918 was granted £4,500 over a five-year period in order to establish the second CUKT scheme in Wales. Cardiganshire's first librarian, William Williams, formerly Sub-librarian of the Liverpool Athenaeum, was appointed in July 1918 and had dispatched books to thirteen schools before moving to the National Library of Wales in the autumn of 1919. Under its second librarian, D. G. Griffiths, a journalist by training, Cardiganshire's service expanded rapidly: by September 1920 all the 109 elementary schools in the county were serving as distribution centres for boxes dispatched from the repository in a converted hotel in Aberystwyth.[4] A well-established scheme was taken over from the Cardiganshire Rural Libraries Committee in November 1922 when the county adopted the 1919 Act and placed the service on a formal rate-supported footing. As in Caernarfonshire, the library experienced great difficulty in providing an adequate supply of Welsh books. In 1927 the Chairman of the Libraries Committee, John Ballinger, Librarian of the National Library of Wales, stated that although 2,000 of the service's total stock of 10,000 volumes consisted of Welsh books, the paucity of new Welsh-language titles meant that stock had to be supplemented by purchases from second-hand booksellers. Even this source was becoming depleted as other Welsh counties established their libraries.[5]

Six Welsh counties — Caernarfonshire, Cardiganshire, Denbighshire, Brecon and Radnorshire (initially a joint service), and Montgomeryshire — commenced library services maintained by CUKT grants before adopting the 1919 Act and levying a library rate. The remaining counties adopted and gradually began to operate services, Carmarthenshire in 1932 enjoying the unenviable distinction of being the last to do so. These later county services received grants from the CUKT to cover their capital costs; in all (including book-purchase grants in the 1930s which kept some of the smaller systems such as Merioneth afloat) the Trust gave almost £51,000 to Welsh county libraries between 1917 and 1940.

Since county libraries were run on a shoe-string, a variety of premises had to be pressed into service as repositories: Breconshire rented rooms at the offices of the *Brecon and Radnor Express*; Montgomeryshire adapted a room in a flannel warehouse in Newtown; the Denbighshire scheme was launched in the White Bear, Rhuthun, and later moved to the old gaol in the same town; Carmarthen's repository was also in former prison cells; Anglesey took up the tenancy of the Old Billiard Room at the Llangefni Memorial Institute. Usually people with little if any training or experience in librarianship were appointed county librarians: Montgomeryshire selected a minister of religion; Pembrokeshire appointed its Assistant Director of Education as a 'temporary' measure which lasted for twenty-eight years. In Merioneth, a librarian was chosen from eighty-seven applicants including the noted Welsh bibliophile, Bob Owen, Croesor.[6] The most illustrious figure to be appointed was Saunders Lewis, later a leading writer and playwright of European standing. His career as librarian was relatively short; he took up his duties in Glamorgan in July 1921 and resigned fourteen months later in September 1922. Lewis complained that his activities had been restricted by the lack of trust placed in him by members of his committee.[7] He gave sharper focus to his dissatisfaction in a letter to the *Western Mail* in which he claimed that the dearth of Welsh-language material was retarding the progress of the library service both in Glamorgan and in Wales in general.[8]

The adoption of library legislation by a range of local authorities of very disparate size and resources led to the development of a number of discrete services rather than the co-ordinated evolution of a linked system. This realization led to the appointment of a departmental committee of the Board of Education in 1924 under the chairmanship of Sir Frederick Kenyon to enquire into the adequacy of library provision under the Public Libraries Acts and to investigate the means of extending such provision throughout England and Wales.[9] The Kenyon Report revealed that Cardiff had continued to build upon the tradition of excellence established by John Ballinger. For its size it was one of the best libraries in England and Wales, largely because of the city's generous funding. However, few other Welsh libraries could bear comparison with their English counterparts. Difficulties were particularly acute in the smaller authorities to which Kenyon paid special attention, the Report concluding that communities with a population below 20,000 would find it hard to deliver an efficient library service. Statistics presented at the end of the Report indicated that 84% of the urban and parish libraries of Wales served populations below 20,000. These Welsh authorities were on average spending less per head on their library services and had fewer volumes and fewer borrowers per hundred population served than comparable English authorities.

Kenyon's solution, a greater degree of co-operation, developed from the later 1920s on a local level; county systems began lending boxes of books on a subscription basis to the smaller parish and municipal libraries. Unfortunately, prolonging the existence of such hopelessly inadequate systems by providing them with a life-support system in this way tended to postpone amalgamations which would have produced more viable library authorities. Co-operation on a larger scale developed in the early 1930s as an interlending system was developed, largely as a result of pressure by the CUKT and with its financial aid. Local rivalries led to two regional library bureaux being established in Wales, one at the National Library of Wales and the other (to meet the allegedly peculiar needs of Glamorgan and Monmouthshire) at Cardiff Public Library. Development of the system was not entirely beneficial since it provided the weaker libraries with a plausible excuse for not buying standard middlebrow titles.[10]

The next attempt at rationalization was the McColvin Report of 1942.[11] Lionel McColvin, a much-respected public librarian, was invited by the Library Association in 1941 to undertake a survey of British libraries. His report, an uncompromising personal statement, presented conclusions which, though logical, were sometimes unrealistic. McColvin recommended the creation of library units which, with a population of between 300,000 and 800,000, would possess sufficient resources to deliver an effective library service. For Wales, his remedy was drastic. The sixty-seven library authorities then in existence — a mixture of counties, county boroughs, non-county boroughs, urban districts, and parishes — should be reduced to just five library units. The severe reduction necessary to meet McColvin's population targets created units based almost exclusively on population and paid minimal consideration to other criteria. This is best exemplified by the unit for Mid-Wales (the National Library serving as its headquarters); to attain a population of 540,000 it had to embrace more than 80% of the land area of Wales.

Though McColvin's remedy was too radical for the librarians of Wales, the accuracy of his diognosis was underlined in a survey of the municipal, urban district, and county libraries of Wales produced by the Wales and Monmouthshire Branch of the Library Association in 1948.[12] This claimed that over 15% of the population of Wales in areas controlled by county councils (approximately 400,000 people) were not receiving a library service of any sort, that six of the thirteen county systems had made scant progress since adoption, and that much the same could be said of many small urban authorities. In the municipal and urban libraries the picture remained one of a service concentrated on a few towns, two-thirds of the total lending stock being held by the three largest libraries, Cardiff, Swansea, and Newport. Of the total lending stock held by urban libraries, only 2.9% (just over 20,000 volumes) was in Welsh — a meagre level of provision even if set only against the 42,138 residents of Cardiff, Swansea, and Newport who declared themselves to be Welsh speakers at the 1951 Census.[13] At the same census, 29% of the inhabitants of Wales stated that they were Welsh speakers. Counties such as Caernarfonshire, Cardiganshire, Carmarthenshire, and Merioneth, which all recorded a level of over 75% Welsh speakers, could justly be described as strongholds of the language, yet the 1948 survey revealed that the percentage of Welsh-language bookstock in these counties was nowhere higher than 20%. This disparity was but one example of a wider malaise and the Report concluded that although the planning of a library system to meet the needs of all the residents of Wales appeared to be a comparatively simple undertaking, it had yet to be achieved.

In the late 1950s central government began to display a belated interest in the public library service, leading to the Roberts Report of 1959[14] which recommended that every public library authority in England and Wales should have a statutory duty to provide an efficient service. Such efficiency would be measured in terms of population (40,000 was given as a base-line) and a minimum annual expenditure on books (£5,000 or 2s. per capita, whichever was the greater). When the fifty-two library authorities providing a service in Wales in 1957-8 were set against these criteria, 66% were below the population target and not a single authority was able to match the dual requirement on book expenditure. Difficulties were compounded by a higher proportion in Wales of small, inadequately financed library authorities and by the obligation to deliver what Roberts called a 'comparable' service to both English and Welsh speakers. Although the Report recognized that this would place an extra pressure on the strained resources of public libraries in Wales, no special solution such as grant-in-aid from the Exchequer was proposed to ease the difficulties of providing a comparable service to bilingual communities.

The reaction to the Roberts Report in Wales was for the most part narrow and partisan as each stratum of local authority defended its own record and argued, with a certain degree of justification, that size alone was not an infallible guarantee of expenditure. Central government also realized that Roberts was not a practical basis for legislation and that a further investigation was required. The outcome was the Bourdillon Report of 1962,[15] which moved away from reliance on the simplistic criteria of population and expenditure on books towards what was described as a 'basic library unit' with detailed recommendations on purchase levels for different categories of materials within that unit. The key recommendation, the provision of 250 volumes per annum for every 1,000 population served, and the other stipulated purchase levels represented the standards which central government expected of an effective library service. The Bourdillon investigation had a Welsh representative, Alun Edwards, Chief Librarian of Cardiganshire Joint Library, who clearly influenced the comments of the Report concerning Wales. These dealt almost entirely with the provision of Welsh-language material and were the basis of a recommendation that for every 1,000 Welsh speakers served, 50 of the 250 volumes to be purchased should be in Welsh — the first official acknowledgement that public libraries in Wales had a specific responsibility to meet the needs of Welsh-language readers. Even this recommendation was not enough for Alun Edwards, who presented a minority report. Bourdillon had to face many of the criticisms earlier levelled at the Roberts Report; in particular, it was argued that such standards might say a great deal about the quantity but little or nothing about the quality of a library service which was striving to meet them.

Roberts and Bourdillon had both called for the public library service to be placed on a new statutory footing and a Public Library Bill was introduced during the 1963-4 Parliamentary Session. Although some ministers regarded the Bill as non-urgent or uncontroversial, Members of Parliament proved anxious to debate its underlying principles and pass comment on the efficacy of the library service in their own constituencies. Interest on the part of Welsh MPs was considerable (five of the twenty-six members who spoke during the second reading represented Welsh constituencies) and although much of this centred on support for individual library services, Goronwy Roberts, the Member for Caernarfon, raised the point that any new Act would place extra demands on the public library service in Wales:

> If a Welsh authority is to meet the requirements of this measure [...] it must provide reading matter in both languages. This is an additional duty which applies only to library authorities in Wales. Exactly as the Minister of Education is bound to ensure that Welsh local authorities are enabled to provide education in both languages in Welsh speaking counties, so he should ensure that Welsh library authorities are enabled financially [...] to provide a service in both languages.[16]

His cogent demand — repeating the call made by the Roberts Report for a comparable service to Welsh and English-speaking groups, and the Bourdillon requirement to purchase a certain number of Welsh-language titles each year — received no answer in the Parliamentary debate and, to all intents and purposes, remains unanswered today.

The Bill received the Royal Assent on the 31 July 1964, its provisions to come into effect on the 1 April 1965. The Public Libraries and Museums Act of 1964 placed a legal obligation on all local authorities to provide a 'comprehensive and efficient' library service and although the Act itself gave no definition of the two key words, 'comprehensive' and 'efficient', it was clear that additional resources would have to be devoted to library services. Indeed the ten years that followed the passing of the 1964 Act have been characterized as a decade of dramatic change.[17] The average annual increase in expenditure on public libraries in Wales between 1952 and 1957 was 9.5%, between 1961 and 1964 it was 10%, whereas for 1964 to 1968 the increase was 18.5%. The completely different character of the period before and after 1964 is obvious: expenditure in the earlier period was constant while the second exhibited real progress in monetary terms.

Library authorities responded to the 1964 Act according to local needs and circumstances. Flintshire, for instance, embarked on an extensive programme of building branch libraries which culminated in a new, purpose-built county headquarters at Mold. In the municipal areas, Newport opened a new central library in 1968, and Wrexham constructed a fine new central library and adjoining Arts Centre in 1972-3. In terms of meeting the needs of Welsh speakers and readers, one of the most significant developments was the introduction by Cardiganshire of small mobile libraries to reach individual houses and farms in isolated areas, a development which had been specifically recommended by Bourdillon. The first rural mobile was inaugurated in the Lampeter and Tregaron districts in 1963 and within five years the whole of the county was covered by this service. By 1971-2 some two thousand homes were borrowing over 96,000 titles a year from four rural mobiles and Cardiganshire could claim with some justification that this innovative service had reached a completely new category of users, the majority of whom were Welsh speakers.[18]

The 1964 Act was largely overtaken by events since it was followed by wide-ranging investigations into the structure of local government in England and Wales. In Wales, the establishment of the Welsh Office in 1964 meant that the issue of local government reform could be considered in a specifically Welsh context, and the Welsh Office initially formulated policies which could have given Wales a distinctive local government structure. For England, the Redcliffe-Maud Report of 1969[19] recommended a single tier of unitary authorities. When this proposal was abandoned because of political expediency rather than any rationale of reform, Wales was brought into line with England so that the Local Government Act of 1972 set up a two-tier structure of counties and districts. Within this structure, library powers were allocated to counties and metropolitan districts in England and to the eight new counties in Wales. There was, however, a proviso in Section 207 of the Act that powers could also be allocated to Welsh districts which led to near farce. On the 29 March 1974, the last working day before the great change-over, the Secretary of State for Education and Science laid an order before Parliament constituting the four district councils of Cynon Valley, Llanelli,

Merthyr Tydfil, and the Rhondda as library authorities. This last-minute, politically motivated decision was an ironic comment on the debate over viable public library authorities which had for so long preoccupied librarians in Wales.

The ideals and objectives of local government reorganization were swiftly modified by the harsh realities of economic stringency. Reorganization coincided with a sharp rise in costs of public and private services: Britain's inflation rate shot up to over 24% in 1974;[20] between 1973 and 1983 prices, as measured by the Retail Price Index, increased by 260%.[21] Against this spiral of rising costs, local authorities, as a result of successive expenditure plans and rate-support grant settlements, were forced to work within standstill or declining budgets. The eight new Welsh counties were, however, able to reap economies of scale as their size and financial base meant that they could begin to offer specialized and increasingly sophisticated library services. Clwyd, for instance, developed an European information service while South Glamorgan gave special attention to electronic databases and commercial on-line services from the new Cardiff City Library which was opened in 1986.

Three studies have examined the response of the new county and district library authorities to the needs of Welsh speakers. The first, The Book Trade in Wales,[22] was a market-research survey undertaken by the College of Librarianship, Wales (now the Department of Information and Library Studies, University of Wales, Aberystwyth) on behalf of the major organizations concerned with state patronage of publishing in Wales. Information for 1986-7 obtained from all Welsh public library authorities revealed that the proportion of library expenditure allocated to Welsh books was extremely small. The sum varied from authority to authority but even in those which were staunchest in their support of the Welsh language and culture, expenditure on Welsh books amounted to less than 10% of the bookfund. The survey also revealed that not one public library authority in Wales, even those areas with a high incidence of Welsh speakers such as Gwynedd and Dyfed, managed to attain Welsh issues which represented 10% of the total book issues.

The second study, The Teifi Library Project,[23] examined the library and information requirements of users of mobile library services in south Ceredigion. It revealed significant changes in the linguistic make-up of rural communities; for example, almost 70% of the users of the large village-type mobile stated that English was their first language; figures for the small mobile appeared more encouraging since 55% of users stated that Welsh was their first language. However, even on the small mobile the preponderance of Welsh speakers was not reflected in borrowing patterns since some two-thirds of the material borrowed was in English.

The third investigation was a baseline study of public library provision commissioned in 1995 by the Library and Information Services Council (Wales) and undertaken once again by the Department of Information and Library Studies, Aberystwyth.[24] Although some authorities could demonstrate compatibility between the percentage of Welsh speakers in their area and Welsh-language stock as a percentage of their total bookstock, the gap between the two values was most noticeable in areas with a relatively high incidence of Welsh speakers such as Dyfed, Gwynedd, and Llanelli. The study did, however, acknowledge that since the number of Welsh titles published annually (618 in 1993) was so much lower than new titles in English (83,322 in 1993) it would be unrealistic to expect library authorities in Wales to achieve a level of Welsh-language stock which represented a statistical match with the Welsh-speaking population. On the question of issues, the 1995 study confirmed earlier research in that not one library authority attained Welsh issues which represented 10% of the total. These three studies inevitably lead to the conclusion that Welsh speakers are not necessarily Welsh readers. Taking a broader view it would seem reasonable to claim that for the public library service the concept of a 'Welsh heartland' — an area with a high proportion of Welsh speakers and high use of Welsh material — is no longer valid.

Although the Local Government Act of 1972 put in place a reformed and seemingly stable structure of local authorities, in 1994 central government embarked on a further round of reorganization and in so doing moved full circle to implement the previously rejected Redcliffe-Maud philosophy of a single tier of unitary authorities. This move reversed the direction of reform: instead of the aggregation of units to create larger, more powerful local authorities, the 1994-5 process has brought about the separation of units and a consequent break-up of the pattern of service delivery. In Wales, reorganization has resulted in 22 library authorities, their population ranging from 60,000 (Merthyr Tydfil) to 295,400 (Cardiff). In one sense these figures are irrelevant, for this latest reorganization all but abandons size as the yardstick of effectiveness for a local authority. In its place, heavy emphasis is put on two related concepts, enabling (local authorities identifying requirements, setting priorities, but not directly delivering services) and joint working (local authorities specializing in certain services and purchasing such services from one another). It remains to be seen whether these concepts will provide a sufficiently firm foundation for the continued growth of a wide range of public library services in Wales and an enhanced level of provision for Welsh-language users and readers. In a broader context two developments are worthy of mention. The first is the heightened awareness of the role and function of Welsh arising from the Welsh Language Act 1993. This legislation (and the recommendations of the related Welsh Language Board) will place new demands on all aspects of the work of local authorities including the provision of a public library service. The second is the establishment of a Welsh Assembly. Initially it appeared that the Assembly would have few real powers but it is becoming evident that devolution has the potential to be far more radical than believed. Welsh Office ministers have already secured some small but significant departures from mainstream Whitehall policy in the field of education. These changes could herald even greater policy innovations and in particular deliver a public library srvice planned and designed for Wales rather then one which has constantly measured itself against the target — 'for Wales, see England'.

NOTES TO CHAPTER 24

1. John Roe, 'The public library in Wales; its history and development in the context of local government' (unpublished master's thesis, Queen's University of Belfast, 1970), p. 71.
2. W. G. S. Adams, *A report on library provision & policy to the Carnegie United Kingdom Trustees* (Dunfermline, 1915).
3. T. Elwyn Griffiths, 'Caernarvonshire and its libraries: development of the first county library in Wales', *CHST*, 33 (1972), 170-89 (p. 182).
4. Frank Keyse, 'CUKT rural library experiments 1915-1919' (unpublished Library Association fellowship thesis, 1968), p. 69.
5. Cardiganshire Education Committee, Carnegie Rural Libraries Scheme, *Supplemental list of books, 1927*, p. v.
6. Dyfed Evans, *Bywyd Bob Owen* (Caernarfon, 1977), p. 47.
7. Susan Scott, 'Public library development in Glamorgan 1920-1970: an area study with particular reference to Glamorganshire County Library' (unpublished Library Association Fellowship thesis, 1979), p. 70.
8. *Western Mail*, 21 Feb. 1922.
9. Board of Education, Public Libraries Committee, *Report on public libraries in England and Wales* (Cmd 2868, 1927).
10. For a scathing critique, see E. Luke, 'The future of library co-operation in Wales', in *Report of the proceedings of the 18th conference of library authorities in Wales and Monmouthshire [...] 1951* (Swansea, 1951), pp. 24-38.
11. L. R. McColvin, *The public library system of Great Britain: a report on its present condition, with proposals for post-war reorganisation* (London, 1942).
12. Library Association, Wales and Monmouthshire Branch, *Report on the municipal, urban district and county libraries of Wales and Monmouthshire, 1948* (Morriston, 1950).
13. John Williams, *Digest of Welsh historical statistics*, 2 vols ([Cardiff], 1985), I, 83-4.
14. Ministry of Education, *The structure of the public library service in England and Wales* (Cmnd 660, 1959).
15. Ministry of Education, *Standards of public library service in England and Wales*, (London, 1962).
16. HC Deb., 1963-4, 5 February 1964, Vol. 688, Col. 1200.
17. Thomas Kelly, *A history of public libraries in Great Britain 1845-1975*, 2nd edn (London, 1977), p. 426.
18. Alun Edwards, *Yr hedyn mwstard: atgofion* (Llandysul, 1980), pp. 126-34; Cardiganshire County Council, *Cardiganshire Joint Library 1947-1972* ([Aberystwyth, 1972]), p. 11.
19. Royal Commission on Local Government in England, 1966-1969, *Report* (Cmnd 4040, 1969).
20. John D. Hey, *Britain in context* (Oxford, 1979), p. 16.
21. Nick Gardner, *Decade of discontent: the changing British economy since 1973* (Oxford, 1987), p. 184.
22. Welsh Books Council, Market Research Working Party, *The book trade in Wales* (Llandysul, 1988).
23. Geraint I. Evans and Elaine Griffin, *The Teifi library project* (Aberystwyth, 1991); Geraint I. Evans and Elaine Griffin, 'Socio-linguistic changes in Wales: implications for public library providers in rural bi-lingual communities', *JLIS*, 24 (1992), 149-58.
24. Geraint I. Evans and Tim Hayward, *LISC (Wales) baseline study* (Aberystwyth, 1995).

CHAPTER 25

THE MINERS' INSTITUTE LIBRARIES OF SOUTH WALES 1875 — 1939

C. M. Baggs

FOR the general reader, there has traditionally been one openly accessible library — the public library. The south Wales coalfield during the late nineteenth and early twentieth centuries witnessed the growth of a network of alternative libraries and reading rooms, independent of the developing local authority services. Hailed as 'the brains of the coalfield',[1] these libraries, associated with Miners' Institutes and Welfare Halls, have gained fame as genuine working-class libraries, funded, controlled, and used by local miners.

Workers in South Wales were encouraged to 'read, read, read',[2] in order 'to obtain information which might be turned to a good account'.[3] The *Rhondda Socialist* urged workers to read books to enable them 'to fight against the flaunting evils of the time, the tyranny that fastens on men's lives'. Books which rendered workers 'content with their social conditions', or dealt 'with the selfish interests of the upper ten' were unacceptable.[4] Recreational reading was frowned upon, especially when this meant trying to 'spot the winner of the Grand National, [...] some rugby information',[5] or turning to detective stories and other sensational fiction. Positive reading could be an instrument in the class struggle, providing it comprised 'books that treat of the things that matter to us as workers';[6] it also meant self-discovery and self-improvement.

South Wales miners were renowned for their belief in self-education, and the received view is that in accordance with the above advice, their reading fare comprised the hard meat of social criticism. Marx and Dietzgen were second nature to men who discussed Einstein's theory of relativity at the double parting. The 'profound character' of the Welsh and English books bought by miners impressed a professional librarian,[7] and the London-based trade journal, *Book Monthly*, depicted

> the Welsh miner [as] a great reader, nay a student of serious books, including Carlyle and Emerson and the prophets of what might be called the social gospel.[8]

Miners' autobiographies confirm this impression. Their pages teem with the names of authors from an inter-disciplinary academic reading-list: Ruskin, Marx, J. S. Mill, Haeckel, Darwin, Comte, with Hardy, Dickens, and Meredith for dessert.[9] Much reading material was bought from market stalls,[10] bookshops, or at political meetings, and although these purchases meant considerable sacrifices,[11] books represented precious commodities to the initiated.

Since not every miner could afford even the cheap reading material increasingly available, many had to rely on libraries. For the two decades before 1914 these organizations were usually Miners' Institute libraries. Some older urban districts such as Merthyr and Aberdâr developed rate-supported public libraries between 1890 and

1910,[12] and although these services were inadequate,[13] their symbolic significance in fostering a 'sense of social solidarity' was noted by the Commissioners enquiring into industrial unrest during the First World War.[14] Public and Miners' libraries could overlap. Treharris was served both by the Workmen and Tradesmen's Library, and by a branch of Merthyr Public Libraries. The inter-relationship between Miners' and public libraries around Aberdâr was more complex, as the local authority extended funding to Workmen's Institute libraries. Most mining communities had no association with public libraries until county library services developed in the 1920s and 1930s.

Estimates of the number of Miners' Institute and Welfare Hall libraries differ. In 1934 Thomas Jones suggested that there existed '53 Workmen's and Miners' Institutes, [and] 56 Miners' Welfare Institutes',[15] a total broadly supported by the South Wales Coalfield History Project.[16] 253 libraries and reading rooms were reported in a more widely based official survey in 1946.[17] Whatever the exact figure, Institutes covered the entire coalfield, from Abersychan to Pontyberem, from Hirwaun to Caerffili. They were especially numerous in central Glamorgan and the western Monmouthshire valleys, where they provided a greater number of static outlets than public library services ever did. The Rhondda Fawr valley alone housed twenty libraries between Trehafod Welfare Hall and Glenrhondda Institute, Blaen-cwm.

Miners' Institute libraries generally date from the 1890s, although a few had their origins in the earlier Mechanics' Institute movement. But many mining communities had set up simple reading-rooms and libraries over a decade before any official Institute was established. Beginning with donated newspapers and magazines, stored upstairs in a pub or in the front room of a miner's cottage, the collection might evolve into a small lending and reference library. Pontlotyn opened such a reading-room in 1867 and there were similar forerunners at Abercynon and Nelson. So eager were residents to gain access to reading material that libraries were often the first community facilities to be established after the chapels and pubs. Purpose-built Institutes, incorporating libraries, meeting-rooms, theatres, and even gymnasia and swimming baths, began to appear in the 1890s, as at Blaenafon in 1895. These buildings visibly confirmed growing wealth, stability, and social maturity. Grand opening ceremonies were occasions for pomp and speechifying. Compared with their modest antecedents, these 'temples of culture' were not cheap: Blaenafon Institute cost nearly £10,000. The growth of Miners' Institutes before 1914 is impressive, 23 being opened or extended between 1890 and 1899 and no fewer than 61 between 1900 and 1914,[18] the busiest decade matching a general rise in manpower and output in the coal industry. Institute finances appeared healthy, their libraries flourished, and book stocks expanded: at Abertridwr, for example, stock trebled to 3,000 items between 1909 and 1914.

Institutes are commonly perceived as self-funding organizations, their finances based on poundage and special levies.[19] But money so raised was rarely sufficient to pay for the extravagant edifices being erected. In 1910, the new Ferndale complex incurred over £16,000 in liabilities. Accumulated funds provided building capital, and regular poundage, together with income from cinemas, theatre lettings, and billiards, contributed to covering the daily expenses of Institutes and their libraries. Even so, many Institutes owed their existence to the generosity of local coal-owners such as Clifford J. Cory at Ystrad, or of companies such as the Tredegar Iron and Coal Company.

Estate-owner Caroline Williams helped found Dinas Institute, Pen-y-graig, whilst Nant-y-glo received $1,000 from an American donor. Financial institutions also assisted: Llanbradach borrowed £3,000 from Lloyds Bank. As well as donating money for buildings or erecting Institutes at their own expense, coal-owners provided building sites or rent-free premises. Libraries similarly benefited from gifts of money and books.

Following the 1919 Sankey Commission, the main source of financial help changed. Poundage and income-generating activities continued, but capital funding to build new Welfare Halls and extend existing Institutes increasingly came from the Miners' Welfare Fund. Thirty-nine Welfare Halls were opened or extended between 1920 and 1929 and a further 25 between 1930 and 1939. The Fund's policy towards libraries is significant. Grants of up to £80 were made to new Welfare Hall libraries, like Trehafod in 1935, but existing Institutes were normally encouraged to contact county library systems for the assistance their libraries so desperately needed as the Depression intensified.

Large debts had been incurred before 1914 on the then reasonable assumption that the expanding coal industry and rising Institute income would clear them. The collapse in demand for coal, the permanent or temporary closure of numerous pits, mass unemployment, and the effects of the 1926 strike, combined to halt expansion; indeed, during the 1920s many Institute libraries experienced severe difficulties, as two reports dealing with libraries in the Aberdâr, Merthyr, and Rhondda areas vividly reveal.[20] Few of the older libraries were coping financially. Expenditure on new books fell dramatically or ceased altogether; gaps grew in subject coverage, and much existing stock was totally unfit for circulation. Keeping Maerdy open was 'a struggle'.

The 1930s brought some relief. Apart from the marginal economic improvement, Institute libraries were aided by various welfare organisations, notably the South Wales and Monmouthshire Council for Social Service. Such bodies recognized the value of reading facilities and directed funds towards these stumbling, but vital social amenities. Co-operation with the new county library systems offered another short-term lifeline. Since the latter needed to set up service points, but lacked the resources to do so a mutually beneficial solution emerged, whereby Institutes acted as distribution centres. With the county library providing regularly renewed up-to-date fiction, Institute libraries could devote their limited funds elsewhere.

There was some improvement during the 1930s, largely as a result of extensive assistance from external bodies. Even so, the majority of Institute libraries had suffered lasting damage. Funding would never reach the same level, and the county systems showed what a professionally run library could provide. When Rhondda UDC finally inaugurated a public library service in 1938, further pressure was put on Institute libraries in an area which was overprovided with them.

Thomas Jones reckoned that 109 Institute and Welfare Hall libraries contained 750,000 volumes.[21] His approximation, adopted by later writers, produces an average of just under 7,000 volumes per library, a considerable figure, given the small populations often served. In fact, this figure is an overestimate. By the early 1930s a few Institute libraries, such as Ebbw Vale, Tredegar, and Cwmaman, contained more than 7,000 volumes[22] but the vast majority were smaller. Fifteen libraries mentioned in the 1929 *Reports* averaged 1,700 volumes apiece,[23] and a further nineteen surveyed in

1925 averaged 2,157 volumes.[24] Since no major libraries possessing large stocks were omitted from these two sets of figures, and it is unrealistic to suppose that during the Depression stock could have been substantially expanded, Jones's estimate can be viewed as an inaccurate guess.

Autobiographical reminiscence often affords glimpses into the nature of Institute library stock. Will Paynter, an 'addicted reader', claimed he obtained 'a great deal of the available literature outlining the philosophy of socialism as presented by the Social Democrats and the Marxists',[25] from Cymer Library (his 'Cambridge') during the 1920s. Robert Morgan was particularly 'thrilled' by Russian novelists in Penrhiwceiber Miners' Library,[26] and Walter Haydn Davies describes books on spiritualism amongst others at Bedlinog.[27] But such recollections are very selective snapshots of a few Institute libraries which reveal something about the individual concerned, little about the library's stock, and even less about the generality of the reading experience in mining communities. Personal witness may itself be dubious. Another recollection of Cymer depicts a stock dominated by 'boy's books, [...] a range of outdated books in the sciences' and numerous novels 'called "cheaps" by the librarians'.[28] Stray examples cannot determine whether borrowing patterns were normal or idiosyncratic, or whether the books borrowed were typical or specialized parts of the stock.

Institute records describe the minutiae of stock selection; what was bought, from whom, for how much, when, and even by whom. Did the librarian choose the stock, or the Books Committee? Could individual miners suggest material for purchase? How instrumental was the local schoolmaster or minister in book selection? Did the Institute accept donations? Was any form of censorship exercised? Which newspapers and journals were held, and which added to or removed from the reading rooms, as funds dictated? What was stocked and why it was aquired varied from community to community, and from year to year.

Printed catalogues offer the fullest view of the books available, despite freezing a collection for an instant and thus hiding its dynamic nature. Comparative analysis of surviving Institute catalogues is problematic as they did not use standardized approaches, and cover a lengthy time-span. Nevertheless, by studying them in their entirety, rather than extracting selected tit-bits, generalized comments about Institute library bookstocks can be made.[29]

Fiction constituted the largest category, averaging around 38%. 'Light fiction' was explicitly excluded from Lewis Merthyr catalogue, although it was stocked at A. J. Cook's 'home' library. The actual proportion of fiction was higher, between 45% and 50%, if material in the Juvenile, Welsh-language, and Bound Periodical sections was added. Dickens and Scott supplied the greatest number of titles but other classic English authors were well represented.[30] Jack London, 'easily the most popular story teller of today',[31] was the second-best-represented foreign author, and at Gwauncaegurwen his novels outscored those by any other author. Contemporary best-sellers, including works by Rider Haggard and Hall Caine, were present, but what provides food for thought is the number of titles by female romantic and moralistic novelists. Mrs Henry Wood and Marie Corelli were well to the fore in Miners' Institute libraries. Does their presence imply an anticipated female readership, or did miners want something other than 'books on philosophy and social economy', described as 'good stuff for the earnest

1920s when the voters' dreams were muscled and ferocious',[32] something relaxing and less demanding?[33]

The proportion of Welsh-language books varied considerably. Lewis Merthyr had no Welsh material at all. Abercynon listed 450 items, or 15.3% of stock, whereas Welsh books constituted only 5.7% at Gwauncaegurwen at the west end of the coalfield where more Welsh-language material might have been expected. Successive editions of the same library catalogue often show a comparative decline in Welsh-language material. At Tredegar the percentage, already low in 1911 at 5%, fell further to 2.9% by 1923, although the number of Welsh-language books remained constant at around 250 volumes. The Welsh sections initially consisted largely of non-fiction, categories such as 'duwinyddiaeth' (theology) dominating. Thomas Jones detected a change 'from esboniadau [expositions] and cofiantau [religious biographies] to *Cartrefi Cymru*, *Gwr Pen-y-Bryn*, and *O Gors y Bryniau* [...] a movement from theology to history and fiction'.[34] In 1924 the Welsh section at Llwynypia Institute library was keeping members 'going well', with 'O. M. Edwards, Anthropos, Crwys, Wil Ifan and others'.[35]

After fiction, the combined categories of history and biography were the most popular, although numbers were inflated by including multi-volume series such as the Story of the Nations. Science was well represented, especially books on mining engineering, such as *The colliery manager's handbook*, but libraries also stocked the works of Darwin and T. H. Huxley. There were significant percentages of books on travel, geography, music, literature, and religion. Libraries also housed unique categories reflecting the peculiar tastes of the communities they served. Thus Tredegar had an Anglo-Jewish Section; Brynaman its 'War Books'; and Abertridwr listed one book under 'Vegetarianism'.

To what extent did Institute libraries become 'proletarian institutions in their contents' after 1918?[36] The evidence is patchy, as few surviving catalogues cover the most pertinent period, namely the 1920s and 1930s. Lewis Merthyr boasted titles by Marx, together with material by Lenin, Liebknecht, and Bukharin. Treharris possessed nothing by Marx, despite its quaintly named 'Reformers Bookshelves' section, and Tredegar had only *Capital* in 1923. Despite Aneurin Bevan's reference to Debs and de Leon,[37] their works do not feature in Tredegar catalogues up to 1923, although the section entitled 'Sociology and Political Economy' grew from 3.8% of stock in 1911 to 5.7% by 1923. Many of the later catalogues included similarly titled sections, whereas catalogues from the turn of the century did not. But just as Cymer purchased titles by Dietzgen and Lafargue between 1916 and 1919, it also bought the latest Zane Grey and Ethel M. Dell:[38] socialism plus westerns and romance.

Catalogues show book availability, but not what miners read. Issue statistics were dominated by fiction. At Senghennydd, 93.4% of books borrowed in 1925 were fiction titles;[39] at Penrhiw-ceibr the percentage was 98% in 1938.[40] These figures may be high, but they are not unrepresentative. During General Strike year, Bargoed loaned 83.5% fiction, whilst the number of borrowers increased by 25% and issues by 62%,[41] and in 1928 fiction comprised between 75% and 90% of loans at five Rhondda libraries.[42] Few issue statistics are fully broken down by subject, nor do they cover lengthy time periods. At Cwmaman, detailed statistics begin with lower fiction rates of around 65% in 1920. By the mid-1930s, fiction reaches 80%; when the predominantly fiction-based juvenile loans are added, this percentage rises to nearer 95%.[43]

Issue statistics and borrowing registers require close study if rather crude conclusions about what was being read are to be avoided. Since reconstructing reading habits by counting dates stamped inside surviving books 'involves certain inherent distortions',[44] thorough analysis of reading patterns should take account not only of what was borrowed but also of what was available but ignored. Institute libraries contained between 40% and 50% fiction; issue statistics show disproportionately greater percentages of fiction borrowed. This comes as no surprise to public library historians, nor indeed to Rhys Davies who found the novels of Corelli and Caine 'shabby' with use at Blaenclydach, whilst Marxist literature never left the shelves.[45]

Working miners became members of the Institute and library through poundage deductions from their wages. Membership levels were consequently high, although complaints abounded about non-members using the facilities, particularly reading-rooms. The poundage levy caused difficulties when miners became unemployed. During the 1930s, unemployed miners were denied access to certain Institutes, a tragic irony given their involuntary leisure. However, libraries were developed in some of the unemployed clubs set up to provide facilities for people not allowed into local Institutes.[46]

Library membership was not restricted to adult miners. With a lower age limit of around twelve years, libraries built up juvenile collections to encourage young readers, which at Cwmaman included 'boys and *girls*'.[47] The local postman or policeman might receive honorary membership and occasionally other groups of workers were admitted. Dinas Institute spent much time fruitlessly wooing local Co-op workers. Colliery management could be entitled to membership and representation on Institute Committees; indeed managers often occupied ceremonial positions such as Institute President. 'Outsiders' formed the most visible group of 'other' members: non-miners who paid regular, fixed subscriptions and were particularly welcome during periods of financial hardship. Local schoolmasters and ministers played crucial roles as members of Institute Book Committees, where their 'cultural' knowledge could be harnessed.

What was the female reader's experience in mining communities? Was it universally true that, 'effectively barred from Miners' Institutes', women 'couldn't even go along and borrow books themselves from Institute libraries', resulting in their 'not [being] part of a public collective autodidactic tradition'?[48] Women certainly took part in the WEA classes[49] held in some Institutes[50] and although Rhys Davies never saw women in Blaenclydach,[51] they were in fact both visible and invisible users of Institute libraries. Institute library rules frequently forbade 'lending on', a habit whereby members (male miners) borrowed books and allowed non-members (wives and sisters) to read them. These vain attempts to prevent 'lending on' suggest that the practice was widespread; this, in turn, helps explain why, although women did not borrow books themselves, authors favoured by female readers were so extensively stocked.

Borrowing records confirm that women openly used Welfare Hall libraries,[52] which may be a crucial distinction. The Welfare Associations, which ran these libraries, had a wider remit than the earlier Miners' Institutes, and women were involved as members, users, and committee representatives. Women — as staff or readers — were certainly not barred from all Institute libraries. Ferndale employed women as library assistants, and Bargoed had a ladies' reading-room. Crymlyn had an annual subscription for women of six shillings in 1923, and Llanbradach considered applications from girls and women on their merits. At Abergorci, a quarter of the 600 users registered between November 1918 and October 1920, were women.[53]

Despite its fame, Tredegar Institute library, which closed in 1964, does not represent the norm. As one of the oldest, largest, and most financially secure, it became, under the patronage of Aneurin Bevan and his Query Club associates, the zenith of the movement. Whilst Tredegar managed to maintain reasonable book funds during the Depression, Cwmaman obtained donations through *The Spectator*,[54] Ynys-hir received discards from Bethnal Green Public Library,[55] and Ynys-y-bŵl thanked Manchester City Libraries for their help.[56] Readers apparently demanded quantity not quality. Tredegar's very success, accentuated by subsequent writing on Institute libraries, has engendered a one-sided mythology about their usage, their stock, and their influence which the evidence does not sustain. It is the relative breadth, depth, and variety of the reading experience they offered which is the true monument to Institute libraries. They made large quantities of books available across a major part of south Wales, and had a profound effect on a mass reading public at a time when reading was an accepted and fostered form of self-education. To an active minority these libraries provided the opportunity to devour Charles Kerr and Left Book Club publications, the Thinker's Library, and the Home University Library. The more articulate and successful miners praised them accordingly. Less intellectual pursuits, from body-building through pigeon breeding to choral singing were also catered for, as Institute library catalogues confirm. The silent majority of users chose fiction; but was it George Meredith or Annie Swann?

NOTES TO CHAPTER 25

For a full discussion of this topic see Christopher M. Baggs, 'The miners' libraries of south Wales from the 1860s to 1939' (unpublished doctorol thesis, University of Wales, Aberystwyth, 1995).

[1] Dai Smith, *Wales! Wales?* (London, 1984), caption opposite p. 55.
[2] *The Pioneer*, 1 April 1911.
[3] *Glamorgan Free Press*, 15 Nov. 1909.
[4] *Rhondda Socialist*, 10 May 1913.
[5] *Glamorgan Free Press*, 5 March 1909.
[6] *Rhondda Socialist*, 10 May 1913.
[7] D. Rhys Phillips, 'Public library policy and provision in Wales', *Library World*, 19 (1916-17), 117-20, 147-52 (p. 119).
[8] *Book Monthly*, 12 (July-Sept. 1915), 655.
[9] Examples include D. R. Davies, *In search of myself* (London, 1961); Edmund Stonelake, *The autobiography of Edmund Stonelake*, ed. Anthony Mor-O'Brien (Bridgend, 1981); and W. J. Edwards, *From the valley I came* (London, 1956).
[10] Edwards, p. 123.
[11] B. L. Coombes, *These poor hands* (London, 1939), p. 221.
[12] John Roe, 'The public library in Wales: its history and development in the context of local government' (unpublished master's thesis, Queens University Belfast, 1970), Chapter 3.
[13] In 1942, a visit to Aberdare Public Library was described as 'a tragic experience' (L. R. McColvin, *The public library system of Great Britain* (London, 1942), p. 45).
[14] Great Britain. Commission of enquiry into industrial unrest. No. 7 Division. 1917, Cd 8668, p. 12.
[15] Thomas Jones, *Leeks and daffodils* (Newtown, 1942), p. 137.
[16] South Wales Coalfield History Project, *Final Report* (Swansea, 1974).
[17] Great Britain. Ministry of Fuel and Power. *South Wales coalfield (inc. Pembrokeshire)* (London, 1946), p. 151.
[18] The figures are based on verifiable opening dates for new Institutes, and the expansion of existing ones.
[19] Poundage was a system of regular weekly deductions made against a miner's pay on the basis of perhaps ½d. or 1d. per pound earned. These deductions were invariably made at the colliery office and covered health and welfare provision, including the local Institute. Special levies were one-off payments, again using a poundage formula, for specific purposes, such as raising capital for an Institute.
[20] Joint Committee for the Promotion of Educational Facilities in the South Wales and Monmouthshire Coalfield, *Report on the condition of workmen's libraries in the Rhondda Urban District*, prepared by Brinley Thomas (1929); and *Report on the condition of libraries in the Aberdare Urban District Council and County Borough of Merthyr Tydfil*, prepared by David E. Evans (1929).
[21] Jones, p. 137.
[22] Kelly's Directories for the period and Institute records.
[23] Joint Committee for the Promotion of Educational Facilities, *Reports*.
[24] Library Authorities in Wales and Monmouthshire, *Conference Proceedings* (Aberystwyth, 1925), pp. 39-41.
[25] Will Paynter, *My generation* (London, 1972), p. 33.
[26] Robert Morgan, *My lamp still burns* (Llandysul, 1981), p. 116.
[27] Walter Haydn Davies, *The right time — the right place* (Llandybïe, 1972), p. 237.
[28] Emrys Pride, *Rhondda, my valley brave* (Risca, 1975), p. 70.
[29] The following post-1900 catalogues have been used for the discussion on library stock: Aberaman (1914); Abercynon (1920); Abergwynfi (1909); Blaenclydach (1920); Brynaman (1928); Clydach Vale (1920); Cwmaman (1911); Cwm-parc (1924); Cymer (1913); Gwauncaegurwen (1925); Lewis Merthyr (1931); Maerdy (1903); New Tredegar (1909); Nixons (1923); Pentre/Tynybedw (1902); Tredegar

(1923); Treharris (1925); Tumble (1915); Windsor Collieries, Abertridwr (1909); Ynys-hir (1912). Some of the above dates are approximate.

[30] Based on a count of fiction titles from the catalogues listed above.
[31] Article by Emrys Hughes, Keir Hardie's son-in-law and later Labour MP for South Ayrshire, *The Pioneer*, 21 Aug. 1915; cf. also Aneurin Bevan, *In place of fear* (London, 1952), pp. 17-18.
[32] Gwyn Thomas, 'The Hoods', in his *The lust lobby* (London, 1971), p. 196.
[33] In John Ormond's 1961 television programme, *Once there was a time*, the miner using Maindy and Eastern Institute Library at Ton Pentre is shown borrowing a romance.
[34] Jones, p. 135.
[35] *Rhondda Fach Gazette*, 27 Dec. 1924.
[36] Hywel Francis, 'The origins of the South Wales Miners' Library', *History Workshop*, 2 (1976), 183-205 (p. 186).
[37] Bevan, p. 17. Bevan's own borrowing habits are discussed in Michael Foot, *Aneurin Bevan*, 2 vols (London, 1962-75), I, 56.
[38] Cymmer Colliery Workmen's Library, *Half yearly report and statement of accounts, 1915-19*. South Glamorgan Libraries, Cardiff Reference Library.
[39] *Caerphilly Journal*, 13 Feb. 1926.
[40] *Aberdare Leader*, 2 July 1938.
[41] *Merthyr Express*, 25 June 1927.
[42] Joint Committee for the Promotion of Educational Facilities, *Report on the condition of workmen's libraries in the Rhondda Urban District*.
[43] University College Swansea (UCS), Coalfield History Archive, Cwmaman Institute Records.
[44] Jonathan Rose, 'Marx, Jane Eyre, Tarzan: Miners' libraries in south Wales 1923-52', *Leipziger Jahrbuch zur Buchgeschichte*, 4 (1994), 187-207 (p. 187).
[45] Rhys Davies, *Print of a hare's foot* (London, 1969), p. 78.
[46] cf. the Unemployed Clubs Books Appeal, launched by the *South Wales Echo* and *Western Mail* in December 1935 and described in those newspapers until mid-January 1936.
[47] Cwmaman Workmen's Institute, *Catalogue* (Cwmaman, 1911), p. 7.
[48] Angela John, 'A miner struggle? Women's protests in Welsh mining history', *Llafur*, 4 (1984-7), 72-90 (p. 76).
[49] cf. Harold Watkins, *Unusual students* (Liverpool, 1947).
[50] NLW Archive, NLW, L5: Loans to WEA and University Tutorial Classes.
[51] R. Davies, p. 78.
[52] UCS, Coalfield History Archive. Dyffryn and Cynon Welfare Hall, and Markham and District Welfare Association records.
[53] UCS, Coalfield History Archive. Abergorky Institute records.
[54] *The Spectator*, 19 Jan. 1929, pp. 84-5; 2 Feb. 1929, p. 162; 16 Feb. 1929, p. 234.
[55] *Caerphilly Journal*, 16 March 1929, and personal correspondence with Tower Hamlets Library Department.
[56] *Aberdare Leader*, 5 March 1932.

CHAPTER 26

ACADEMIC LIBRARIES IN WALES TO 1914

Brian Ll. James

SINCE the history of academic libraries in Wales from the early 1920s onwards presents fewer distinctive features than do developments in the eighteenth and nineteenth centuries, this study concentrates upon the libraries of institutions of higher education to the First World War. A further advantage of this chronological limitation is that the history of Welsh collections at the college libraries casts considerable light on the circumstances surrounding the founding of the National Library of Wales.

The Dissenting Academies and Theological Colleges
Nonconformists, effectively excluded from Oxford and Cambridge by the Act of Uniformity (1662), developed their own institutions for training entrants to the ministry, many of the first being established by clergymen ejected in 1662. The academy set up at Brynllywarch in Glamorgan by Samuel Jones (1628-97), formerly a Fellow of Jesus College, Oxford, gained a considerable reputation and attracted the sons of local landowning families as well as those studying for the ministry. Brynllywarch is generally regarded as the precursor of the academy, founded in 1704 by William Evans (d. 1718), which was to be sited at Carmarthen for the greater part of the eighteenth century. The reputation of the Carmarthen Academy was enhanced by its broad curriculum and development of a tradition of free inquiry in theology which encouraged many tutors and students to abandon Calvinistic doctrines in favour of Arminianism.[1] The progression of some bolder spirits to Arianism led to a schism in 1757, when the adherents of Calvinism set up a rival academy at Abergavenny which imposed a religious test on entrants; after eighty years of moving between various Border towns, this settled at Brecon in 1839. The Carmarthen Academy, dominated by Unitarians and Independents, came to be known as the 'Presbyterian College' and that at Brecon as the 'Independent College' (later the *Coleg Coffa* or 'Memorial College' to commemorate the 'martyrs' of 1662).[2]

Early academies were small, with only one or two tutors and some ten to fifteen students. Since they were also migratory — even the Carmarthen Academy moved to five different locations as far apart as Abergavenny and Haverfordwest, and occupied several different premises in Carmarthen itself before finally settling in the Parade in 1840 — large collections of books were unlikely to be accumulated. Some material may have come from earlier collections: in 1900, Principal W. J. Evans claimed that 'the scribbles and inscriptions in some of the older books on the College shelves' supported the theory that they had come (perhaps in 1721) from the famous academy at Tewkesbury presided over by Samuel Jones (*c*.1682-1719).[3] Several references occur in the minutes of the Presbyterian Board, the London-based patrons of the Academy, to donations of books and to small book-purchase grants.[4] Private benefactors were also important. John Jones (1700-70), Cardiganshire-born vicar of Shephall, Hertfordshire, bequeathed his printed books and pamphlets to Dr Williams's Trustees:

to be by the said Trustees conveyed to the public Academy at Carmarthen [...] and placed in the same library there where several donations of his of the like were already deposited, to be preserved there [...] for the perpetual use and benefit of the students of the said Academy.

Jones also bequeathed £70 for the purchase of an orrery and other scientific instruments.[5] That this legacy was from an Anglican clergyman highlights the ecumenical nature of the Academy as a place where many Anglican clergy as well as Independent, Presbyterian, and even Baptist ministers received their education. The orrery and scientific instruments also indicate that what Jones had called the Academy's 'large and generous plan of Christian education' was far broader and more up-to-date than that provided by the English universities. The inclusion of Newtonian science and Lockean philosophy in the curriculum, reflecting the contemporary view that mathematics and science were essential elements in Christian apologetics,[6] ensured that the Academy played a critical role in the dissemination of Enlightenment ideas in Wales.[7]

The Academy's library reflected its pursuit of knowledge in all its contemporary forms. Most of the books known to have been studied there in the mid-eighteenth century were still listed in the nineteenth-century catalogues.[8] That the books were actually read — by some students at least — is shown by the common-place book of Thomas Beynon (1745-1833), a student in the 1760s and subsequently archdeacon of Cardigan and one of the chief promoters of St David's College, Lampeter.[9]

Repeated complaints about the indiscipline of the students so alarmed the Presbyterian Board that in 1779 a new principal was appointed and the Academy moved to Rhyd-y-gors, a mansion to the south of Carmarthen and its temptations.[10] As part of a general tightening of its grip upon the Academy, the Board promulgated a fearsome code of nine 'Rules for the Library' designed to ensure that books recommended in lectures should circulate fairly amongst all the students. Each week one of the students was to be named monitor to ensure that the rules were observed. Infringements were punished by fines, normally of a penny, though serious breaches such as when 'any student takes the pen and ink out of the library, or the Library Book, or the Catalogue of Books' would cost the delinquent sixpence.[11] A simplified version of these rules remained in force in 1820. Although the Academy had by then accumulated a library of some 2,500 volumes — probably the largest institutional collection in Wales[12] — a period of torpor ensued, and it was claimed in 1840 that no additions had been made for the last ten years.[13]

The other Welsh academies were of a rather different character. The Independent Academy (1757), the Countess of Huntingdon's College at Trefeca (1768), and the Baptist College at Abergavenny (1807) were all Calvinist institutions and owed much less to the spirit of the Enlightenment. Although the Independent Academy could number amongst its tutors eminent scholars such as Edward Williams (1750-1813) and the prolific Dr George Lewis (1763-1822), there are few references to its library other than comments on the difficulty and expense of transporting the collection from Abergavenny to Oswestry in 1782, and from Newtown to Brecon in 1839.[14] George Lewis, however, was a keen bookman who gave much attention to stocking and conserving the library.[15]

Little is known about the college library at Trefeca except that it was safely removed to the new college at Cheshunt in 1792.[16]

Following the failure of an academy established at Trosnant, Pont-y-Pŵl, in the 1730s,[17] Welsh Baptist ministerial students tended to study at the highly regarded Bristol Academy.[18] Micah Thomas (1778-1853), a former student there, finally opened an academy at Abergavenny in 1807. A shortage of books hindered his ambition to broaden the curriculum (indeed, the academy possessed no library at all for the first three years of its existence),[19] but in 1828 it received a gift of more than fifteen hundred volumes, valued at eight hundred pounds, from Hugh Williams (c.1770-1838), a Bristol-educated Welshman and pastor at Cheltenham for many years.[20]

Around 1840 the scene was transformed as four new institutions were founded. Both the North and South Wales Associations of the Calvinistic Methodists came to recognize the need for an educated ministry and began to support colleges at Y Bala (1837) and Trefeca (1842). The Baptists founded a college at Haverfordwest in 1838 (and a college for north Wales at Llangollen in 1862), and the Independents a college at Llanuwchllyn in 1841 which soon moved to Y Bala. These theological colleges were larger than the old academies, which themselves became colleges and attempted to strengthen their formal academic credentials. The Presbyterian College at Carmarthen became affiliated to the University of London in December 1841, thus becoming the first Welsh college to prepare its students for university degrees,[21] an example followed by Brecon in 1852. All the theological colleges were to play a major part in the intellectual life of Victorian Wales, and academics such as Lewis Edwards and Michael D. Jones became prominent national figures.[22] Stability, relative prosperity, and esteem favoured the development of large and important libraries.

The two Calvinistic Methodist college libraries at Trefeca and Y Bala were the most interesting and significant. Since the South Wales Association had acquired both the buildings at Trefeca and their contents from the last survivors of Howel Harris's 'Family',[23] when the College opened it possessed a considerable library of printed books and manuscripts, most of it the product of Harris's own voracious reading, voluminous correspondence, and diary-keeping.[24] A catalogue listing 674 books was printed at the Family's own press in 1793.[25] Further material relating to early Methodism was added when Daniel Davies of Ton (1840-1916) presented the remains of the library of William Williams, Pantycelyn.[26] Of more use to the students were the personal collections bequeathed to the college by former tutors such as John Harris Jones (1827-85)[27] and by well-wishers such as Edward Matthews, Ewenni (1813-92).[28]

Having raised £20,000 for an endowment fund for Trefeca in the 1860s and 1870s,[29] Matthews decided to provide it with a Welsh library. The idea of a national collection of books for Wales was in the air,[30] but Matthews acted where others were content to talk. In the spring of 1874 he flung himself with 'immoderate zeal' (his own phrase) into the task of collecting every book in Welsh or relating to Wales that might be obtained.[31] A circular was issued, begging books for the Llyfrfa Gymreig (Welsh Library), and leading Welsh publishers were requested to donate copies of their publications. So many books were given that only £165 needed to be spent on purchases. According to the sadly amateurish catalogue published in 1880 the collection consisted of some 1,350 volumes, including duplicates.[32] It was predictably rich in the works of leading

Methodists, and consisted mainly of nineteenth-century material, with a fair number of titles from the previous century and a sprinkling of seventeenth century imprints. Matthews himself was particularly proud to have secured two copies (one, regrettably, incomplete) of Bishop Morgan's 1588 Bible.

Unfortunately, the collection does not appear to have been heavily used, perhaps because of the relative remoteness of Trefeca. Worse still, as M. H. Jones and Gomer M. Roberts were later to complain, was the failure to take proper care of the valuable books and manuscripts. Students developed the reprehensible habit of taking a 'souvenir' from the library when they left the College, and a copy of Salesbury's *Testament Newydd* (1567) was 'begged' by a visitor though it subsequently found its way to the National Library.[33]

By the 1890s, ministerial students generally attended one of the university colleges for 'literary' and other courses before proceeding to a theological college for specifically theological studies. At the same time most of the theological colleges migrated to university towns: by 1895 two had moved to Bangor and one each to Aberystwyth and Cardiff. Trefeca (which became a purely theological college in 1897) also moved to Aberystwyth in 1906.[34] All were eventually recognized by the University of Wales as 'associated theological colleges' where Arts graduates might study for the BD.[35]

The Calvinistic Methodist College remained at Y Bala, becoming a purely theological college in 1891 and gaining 'associated theological college' status in 1902, when it had a teaching staff of five, three of whom were professors.[36] There was a substantial library, first formed following a successful appeal for books and money in 1837.[37] Subsequently books were donated or purchased from the collections of scholars such as John Parry (1812-74), tutor at the College and editor of the Welsh encyclopaedia, *Y Gwyddoniadur Cymreig*, and David Charles (1812-78), principal of Trefeca. In 1891 Bala College was given the private library of the scholarly minister Owen Thomas, Liverpool (1812-91). The Senate was so impressed by the size (7,500 volumes) and quality of this wide-ranging collection that a printed catalogue was issued and arrangements made for postal loans to ministers and preachers of the denomination.[38] The College also received the Welsh books and some of the English collection of Thomas Charles Edwards (1837-1900), its principal from 1891 onwards.

Several writers have noted the ease with which outsiders could gain access to the library. The historian R. T. Jenkins, a pupil at Bala grammar school in the 1890s, recollects that even as a schoolboy he was allowed to borrow books on obtaining the signature of one of the professors.[39] The quality of its collections was generally praised. Following a visitation in 1905, a committee of the Theological Board of the University of Wales reported: 'One of the finest features of the institution is the library, which is, in its own order, excellent, and must indeed be one of the best theological libraries in Wales'.[40] As well as benefiting from gifts, the library had received an annual grant of £100 since 1891, sufficient to purchase about a hundred books each year, many of which were scholarly works in German.

Bala library was an exception: book grants at the other theological colleges were much smaller and less regular. These colleges were therefore heavily dependent upon gifts and bequests: fortunately many benefactors were wealthy, scholarly ministers who were often bibliophiles. Even so, much dross and many duplicates were received and, as the Visitors of the Theological Board recognized, there was a shortage of the latest publications. Bala was also the only college with a librarian who was not also overburdened with teaching duties.

Although well beyond the time-span of this study, the sudden dispersal of the Bala Library in 1964, for a fraction of its true value under circumstances that still remain obscure, must be deplored as the major Welsh bibliographical catastrophe of the twentieth century.

St David's (University) College, Lampeter
A college to educate Anglican ordinands was an important element in the comprehensive scheme of reform conceived for the vast and impoverished diocese of St David's by Thomas Burgess (1756-1837), its bishop from 1803 onwards. The royal charters granted in 1829, 1852 (BD degree), and 1865 (BA degree) gave the College a privileged position which precludes it from being discussed with the Nonconformist colleges. The history and splendour of its library are also unmatched in Welsh academia.[41]

Although the location of the college was not settled until 1820, books were collected from 1809 onwards. By the time the building, a picturesque reinterpretation by C. R. Cockerell of the model provided by Oxford and Cambridge colleges, was completed in 1827, some 4,000 books had been received from clerical and lay donors. These formed the bulk of the miscellaneous and largely unremarkable collection listed in the catalogue compiled by the first Librarian, Rice Rees (1805-39), which was published in 1836. The most valuable portion of the library was scarcely noticed in the catalogue: a collection of 552 volumes of pamphlets, containing between nine and ten thousand separate pieces ranging in date from c.1520 to 1787 (but especially rich for the period 1680 to 1720), assembled by several generations of the Bowdler family, and presented to the College by Thomas Bowdler, expurgator of Shakespeare.[42]

After a few years of steady growth, the size and character of the library was transformed during the 1830s by two magnificent benefactions. In 1837 Thomas Burgess bequeathed his private library of some 8,000 volumes to the College. The working collection of a classical scholar, controversial theologian, and prolific author, many of the books were heavily annotated in Burgess's distinctive hand. Material of great bibliographical interest included four incunabula, a fine collection of early printed Bibles (from Jenson's Vulgate of 1476 onwards), and a thirteenth-century manuscript Vulgate.[43] The Bishop's widow fortunately donated £500 so that the library could be enlarged to accommodate his bequest.[44]

The second great benefactor of the 1830s was Thomas Phillips (1760-1851), a surgeon of Welsh descent, who employed the fortune he had made in the service of the East India Company to promote education in Wales, most notably by founding the 'Welsh Collegiate Institution' at Llandovery in 1847.[45] Between 1834 and 1852 he sent St David's College sixty consignments of books, amounting in all to some 22,500 volumes. Since Phillips purchased large quantities of books apparently quite at random at sales and from second-hand bookshops, the College acquired a significant cross-section of the printed literature of Western Europe. Phillips's gifts included fifty incunabula, many first editions, examples of the work of eminent Renaissance printers, atlases and dictionaries, books that had belonged to famous people such as Archbishop Cranmer and John Locke, and books from notable British and European libraries. There were even six medieval manuscripts.

By 1852, when the last consignment had been received, Lampeter possessed about 35,000 volumes. It was by far the largest library in Wales, and in England probably only the three copyright libraries were appreciably larger. In 1851, the antiquary Harry Longueville Jones (1806-70) informed the bibliomaniac Sir Thomas Phillipps (1792-1872), who was then toying with the idea of depositing his vast collection somewhere in Wales, that the College library was 'exceedingly rich and choice: — all the great books of reference: — all the fine editions'.[46] Perhaps more accurately, vice-principal Rowland Williams described it as a 'magnificent, though somewhat miscellaneous' collection, adding a rueful comment on 'the confusion which prevails to some extent' there. In truth, the College, with a teaching staff of four and thirty to forty undergraduates, had been overwhelmed by the avalanche of books. There were not sufficient shelves, the roof leaked, and there was no catalogue. The first two defects were made good in the 1850s, but it was not until 1902-5 that a complete catalogue was compiled. Lampeter had been presented with a library which was wholly disproportionate in its size and richness, and unrelated to its immediate concerns. As Longueville Jones told Phillipps, the students were 'admitted to it once a week: — for fear of reading too much?'.[47]

At the turn of the century, Lampeter was infected by the prevailing enthusiasm for Welsh studies. A new professor was appointed in February 1903 and the College's Welsh books were brought together to form a separate Welsh Library. The Welsh books of David Henry Davies (c.1840-1910), vicar of Cenarth, were bought for £110 in 1904, and a catalogue was printed. Lampeter did not possess a large Welsh collection, but it was varied and contained much material of scholarly importance.[48]

In recent decades the College has come to appreciate the value of its nineteenth-century inheritance, recognizing that in its Old Library it possesses what has been acclaimed as 'a museum of the art of the book'.[49]

The University Colleges

Religious influences, predominant in all the institutions discussed so far, were also strong in the training colleges for teachers established by the British and National Societies at Bangor, Brecon, Caernarfon, and Carmarthen in the 1840s and 1850s, and at Swansea (the first to admit women) in 1872.[50] With the exception of Swansea, which received the private library of its scholarly principal, David Salmon (1852-1944),[51] none of the training colleges built up a significant library until after the Second World War.

After a long struggle, the desire for 'unsectarian' higher education on the model of the Scottish universities or English civic universities resulted in the opening of the University College of Wales at Aberystwyth in 1872 (unchartered until 1889), and University Colleges at Cardiff (1883) and Bangor (1884). Since little grant aid was provided by the Treasury before 1909, the colleges all depended heavily on gifts to supplement the fees paid by students. Although desperately short of funds, each college began to build up a significant library and, despite an (at best) ambivalent attitude towards the Welsh language, each acquired collections of Welsh books that went far beyond the immediate requirements of undergraduate teaching.

University College of Wales Aberystwyth

The origins of the Welsh Library at Aberystwyth are inextricably intertwined with the movement to establish a national library for Wales and the prolonged dispute concerning where such a library should be located. At the Mold National Eisteddfod of 1873 a committee of prominent Welshmen was formed to consider the establishment of a national library. Although the newly founded college at Aberystwyth promised to provide accommodation for such a library, the committee never met and no such special collection was formed, perhaps fortunately in view of the disastrous fire at the College in 1885.[52] Those Welsh books which were incidentally acquired by the College over the next twenty-five years became part of its General Library: the printed catalogue of 1897 shows that the collection of Welsh material was small and undistinguished. It was not until Welsh became a degree subject after the University of Wales gained its charter in 1893 that the provision of Welsh books to support undergraduate and postgraduate studies became a necessity. But the main motive which lay behind the remarkable activity at Aberystwyth from October 1896 onwards was the intense rivalry which had developed between the various contenders for the national library. The pro-Aberystwyth party responded to the challenge of Cardiff by setting up a new Welsh Library Committee chaired by the leading Welsh Liberal politician, Tom Ellis, and with the great book-collector J. H. Davies as its Secretary. Principal T. F. Roberts launched a national appeal for books and J. Glyn Davies (later Professor of Celtic at Liverpool) was appointed Welsh Librarian in 1899 to oversee the creation of a separate Welsh Library. Important collections of Welsh material at last began to reach Aberystwyth.[53] When the Welsh Library was transferred to the National Library at the beginning of 1909, it contained some 13,400 printed volumes and several important groups of manuscripts.[54] Over half the printed books (some 7,500) came from the library of Owen Jones, Llansanffraid-ym-Mechain (1833-99),[55] and a further 1,300 (the 'Celynog Collection') from that of the Montgomeryshire antiquary, Richard Williams (1835-1906). The other major collection, purchased by the college for £60, was that of Walter Davies, 'Gwallter Mechain'.[56]

University College of South Wales and Monmouthshire, Cardiff

Although the physician-bibliophile Sir John Williams dismissed the inhabitants of Cardiff as 'mongrel and non-Welsh', recent writers have stressed the size and influence of the town's Welsh element and the Welshness of the College.[57] The first principal, John Viriamu Jones, and first registrar, Ivor James, were both Welshmen, and Thomas Powel, the College's Professor of Celtic, was appointed in 1884, a decade before John Morris Jones gained his chair in Welsh at Bangor. James and Powel secured for the College the great collection of Welsh books which had been formed by the lawyer and bibliophile, Enoch Robert Gibbon Salisbury (1819-90). Salisbury had begun to collect Welsh books as a boy, pursuing his interest so vigorously and systematically that by the end of the 1870s he possessed the largest collection relating to Wales and the Border Counties then in private hands, his only contemporary rival being perhaps Robert Jones, vicar of Rotherhithe.[58] In April 1886, when Salisbury's spectacular career had ended in bankruptcy, his collection, estimated to contain from thirteen to eighteen thousand volumes, was offered for sale. Neither Cardiff nor Bangor had money available to buy the books, and no one — least of all the creditors and the Official Receiver — had any notion of their market value. James and Powel, proceeding without official backing, but encouraged by promises of financial support from the Marquess of Bute, Lord Aberdare, and the leading Cardiff shopkeeper, James Howell, purchased the library for £1,100, a fraction of its true worth. The books were conveyed in triumph to Cardiff by a special train flying the Red Dragon.[59] Town and gown rejoiced over the coup, the editor of the *Western Mail* claiming that: 'The purchase [...] of such a library for Cardiff is second (if second) only in importance to the establishment of the College itself', and suggesting that it should become the nucleus of a national library.[60] Although Salisbury might hitherto have been considered a partisan of Aberystwyth, he took up the same theme in a letter to Ivor James in June 1886:

> I have but one hope left in relation to it, viz. — that the same public feeling which has enabled you to carry it away to Cardiff, may lead to its perfection, for although it is the most remarkable collection of Cambrian books known to me, there are very many works to be added to it, which a private person never could secure, but which will now be readily acquired, for the use of a National library.[61]

But for over thirty years nothing could be done even to arrange and catalogue the books since the College had no funds for this purpose.

From the early 1890s, the Welsh Department of Cardiff Free Libraries expanded rapidly and to many, including Powel himself, appeared to be a better basis for a national library. Indeed, in 1901 the College Council proposed that the Salisbury collection should be offered on loan to Cardiff Free Libraries for ten years, provided that it would be catalogued, insured, and suitably housed, conditions that the Free Libraries could not satisfy.[62]

As more generous aid was received from the Treasury following the recommendations of the Raleigh Committee (1909) and the Haldane Commission (1918), the College was able to appoint John Jenkins, 'Gwili' (1872-1936), to take charge of the Salisbury Library between 1920 and 1923. With some initial assistance from the Celtic scholar Henry Lewis (1889-1968), Gwili compiled a scholarly catalogue of the books.[63] At the same time strenuous efforts were made by the Professor of Celtic, W. J. Gruffydd, and others to enlarge the collection, especially by acquiring Welsh books published since 1862, the *terminus ad quem* of Salisbury's collection. Welsh and Celtic books which had accumulated in the Main Library since 1883 were incorporated into the Salisbury Library, and its scope was broadened to include all the Celtic languages and literatures, an objective facilitated by the acquisition of 700 duplicates from the library of E. C. Quiggin, Monro Lecturer in Celtic at Cambridge.[64] Thus it was only after 1920 that the Salisbury became a cornerstone of Welsh and Celtic studies at Cardiff.

University College of North Wales, Bangor

Although for most of its history Bangor has had fewer students than either Aberystwyth or Cardiff, by 1907 it possessed more books than either college and as recently as the mid-1970s it still maintained a handsome lead in the number of books per student.[65] It also possesses by far the most important manuscript and archival collections, largely assembled by Thomas Richards (1878-1962), College Librarian from 1926 to 1946.[66]

Three factors contributed to the success of Bangor's library. Firstly, the College was supported from the start by a long succession of bookmen who were eager to create a major academic and reference library for North Wales. Thus the 'quarryman's champion', W. J. Parry of Bethesda (1842-1927), who had already shown an interest in village libraries and reading rooms, issued a circular letter in September 1883 announcing that he wished to assemble as many books as possible for the College, and engaging to give 350 volumes himself. The circular set out ambitious objectives for the College Library which:

> ought to contain copies of all valuable old Welsh Publications, Manuscripts and Books bearing on the History of Wales, besides Works of Modern Literature. All Writers on Welsh subjects, have for years felt the want of a Library, containing all works bearing on the History of Wales, and the History of its Literature. It is my purpose to commence such a Collection, that must become more precious and valuable from generation to generation.[67]

The Library Committee, of which Parry was Secretary, re-emphasized these sentiments in June 1884 by unanimously affirming that 'the Library of the University College of North Wales ought to become specially distinguished for its Welsh literature, its books in the Welsh tongue, or relating to Wales, and for its Welsh manuscripts' and that no effort should be spared to achieve these objectives.[68] Despite its failure to secure the Salisbury collection, Bangor achieved much during the 1880s.

The second favourable factor was a bequest of £47,000 to the College by a Manchester Welshman, Evan Thomas (d. 1890), a former surgeon and eccentric purveyor of a popular patent medicine.[69] A thousand pounds was immediately spent in 1891 in purchasing the ten-thousand-volume library of Thomas's friend, Edward Watkin. As well as being rich in English literature and early material relating to Manchester, this included many rare and valuable items in Welsh and relating to Wales.

In 1904, the College registrar, J. E. Lloyd (1861-1947), and Professor John Morris Jones brought about the establishment of a Welsh Library Committee with a guaranteed grant for five years from the Evan Thomas bequest. Half the grant was used to employ Thomas Shankland (1858-1927), Baptist minister and critical historian of Welsh Nonconformity, as Assistant Librarian in charge of the Welsh Library from October 1904 onwards. The post was made full-time in 1909, and Shankland continued to occupy it until his resignation because of ill health in 1925.[70] Shankland was a systematic and indefatigable collector of Welsh material who deserves particular praise for his zeal in amassing Welsh periodicals.[71] He cultivated owners of Welsh books, such as Richard Hughes of Llannerch-y-medd, visited country houses, and frequented sales and second-hand bookshops both in Wales and farther afield. When funds were exhausted, he appealed for money to secure important collections: as he told the Haldane Commission in 1916, 'I have special friends who will support me if anything turns up. I may say that

I have not failed to get financial aid'. In this way, Henry Rees Davies of Treborth paid for D. G. Goodwin's magnificent collection of ballads.[72] The Welsh Library Committee was also exploited by Shankland in his quest for books:

> I endeavoured to get all the men interested in collecting Welsh books on this committee: it is really my way of getting at the material. These men are my agents, and they help me, they inform me continually, if they find any rare book, where it is to be had.[73]

Despite his lack of enthusiasm — or perhaps lack of time — for cataloguing his acquisitions,[74] possibly the most crucial factor of all in building up the Welsh Library was the appointing of Shankland to take charge of it, and the excellent choice of Thomas Richards as his successor.[75]

The success of collection-building at the Welsh departments of academic libraries was in stark contrast to other aspects of academic librarianship in Wales before the First World War, other than the provision of splendid library rooms, both given by the Drapers' Company of London, at Cardiff in 1909 and Bangor in 1911.[76] Wholly inadequate funding, professional librarians with low status and poor salaries, too few clerical assistants, and restricted opening hours were problems common to all three colleges. The findings of the Raleigh Committee and Haldane Commission led to more generous grants to the colleges, some of which trickled down to improve bookfunds and salaries. But despite the stress placed by the newly-formed (1919) University Grants Committee on adequate expenditure on the library as 'the central organ' of a university, the economic problems of the inter-war years severely limited progress in Wales as elsewhere.

NOTES TO CHAPTER 26

1. Geraint H. Jenkins, *Literature, religion and society in Wales, 1660-1730* (Cardiff, 1978), pp. 187-9.
2. Dewi Eirug Davies, *Hoff ddysgedig nyth* (Swansea, 1976); Geraint Dyfnallt Owen, *Ysgolion a cholegau yr Annibynwyr* (Swansea, 1939); H. McLachlan, *English education under the Test Acts* (Manchester, 1931), pp. 52-62.
3. Walter J. Evans, 'Carmarthen college', *Yr Ymofynydd*, n.s., 24 (1900), 226n.
4. Owen, pp. 31, 55.
5. W. D. Jeremy, *The Presbyterian Fund and Dr. Daniel Williams's Trust* (London, 1885), p. 19. The 'philosophical apparatus' and the greater portion of the library were transferred from Carmarthen to the library of the University College of South Wales and Monmouthshire Cardiff in 1963; see R. Elwyn Hughes, 'Gwaddol gwyddonol Coleg Caerfyrddin', *Y Gwyddonydd*, 31 (1994), 4-8.
6. R. T. Jenkins, 'Academïau yr Annibynwyr yng Nghymru', *Y Llenor*, 18 (1939), 162-71 (pp. 167-8).
7. Geraint H. Jenkins, *The foundations of modern Wales* (Oxford, 1987), pp. 314-15.
8. Davies, pp. 127-35.
9. R. George Thomas, 'The complete reading list of a Carmarthenshire student, 1763-7', *NLWJ*, 9 (1955-6), 354-64; D. T. W. Price, *A history of Saint David's University College, Lampeter,* 2 vols (Cardiff, 1977-90), I, 3-4; Mari Ellis, 'Thomas Beynon, archddiacon Ceredigion, 1745-1833', *Ceredigion*, 13(1) (1997), 44-66.
10. Francis Jones, *Historic Carmarthenshire homes* (Carmarthen, 1987), p. 173.
11. Eiluned Rees, 'An introductory survey of 18th century Welsh libraries', *JWBS*, 10 (1966-71), 197-258 (pp. 249-50).
12. An author/title catalogue and shelf list in the unscheduled T. George Davies Papers in NLW. See *NLW Annual Report* for 1963-4, pp. 49-50.
13. H. P. Roberts, 'Nonconformist academies in Wales (1662-1862)', *THSC*, (1928-9), pp. 1-98 (p. 29).
14. Owen, pp. 103-4, 122.
15. Owen, pp 112-13.
16. Roberts, p. 70; Edwin Welch, *Spiritual pilgrim: a reassessment of the life of the Countess of Huntingdon* (Cardiff, 1995), pp. 128-9.
17. T. M. Bassett, *The Welsh Baptists* (Swansea, 1977), pp. 68-9.
18. G. F. Nuttall, 'Welsh students at Bristol Baptist College, 1720-1797', *THSC*, (1978), pp. 171-99.
19. Roberts, p. 85.
20. D. M. Himbury, *The South Wales Baptist College* (Llandysul, 1957), pp. 28-9; J. Spinther James, *Hanes y Bedyddwyr yn Nghymru*, 4 vols (Carmarthen, 1893-1903), III, 333-4.
21. Davies, p. 144.
22. R. Tudur Jones, 'Diwylliant colegau ymneilltuol y bedwaredd ganrif ar bymtheg', *YB*, 5 (1970), 112-49.
23. K. Monica Davies, 'Teulu Trefeca', in *Y deffroad mawr: hanes Methodistiaeth Galfinaidd Cymru 1*, ed. Gomer Morgan Roberts (Caernarfon, 1973), pp. 356-77.
24. M. H. Jones, 'The Trevecka MSS. and library', *JWBS*, 1 (1910-15), 1-16; 'Catalogue of the Welsh books in the Trevecca library', *CCHMC*, 17 (1932), 113-15.
25. Rees, p. 250.
26. Gomer M. Roberts, *Y Perganiedydd*, 2 vols (Aberystwyth,1949-58), I, 230-1.
27. Edward Matthews and J. Cynddylan Jones, *Cofiant y Parchedig J. Harris Jones* (Llanelli, 1886), p. 258.
28. M. H. Jones, p. 2.
29. J. J. Morgan, *Cofiant Edward Matthews Ewenni* (Mold, 1922), pp. 119-59.
30. David Jenkins, 'A National Library for Wales: prologue', *THSC*, (1982), pp. 139-52 (pp. 141-2).
31. Morgan, p. 159; *Athrofa Trefecca. Cyfraniadau [...] o'r flwyddyn 1867 hyd 1880* (Newport, 1882), p. xiv.

[32] *Cyfres (catalogue) o'r llyfrau sydd yn bresenol (1880) yn y Llyfrfa Gymreig, yn Athrofa Trefecca* (Llanelli, 1880), which fails to list the contents of some 40 *amryw* (miscellaneous) volumes.
[33] M. H. Jones, 'The Trevecka and Pantycelyn books at the National Library of Wales', *CCHMC*, 5 (1920), 47-8; Roberts, *Perganiedydd*, I, 230-1.
[34] W. P. Jones, *Coleg Trefeca 1842-1942* (Llandysul, [1942]), pp. 74-5.
[35] J. Gwynn Williams, *The university movement in Wales* (Cardiff, 1993), pp. 129, 155-6.
[36] *The calendar of the University of Wales [...] 1903-1904* (Oswestry,1903), p. 171.
[37] G. A. Edwards, *Athrofa'r Bala 1837-1937* (Bala, 1937), p. 26; *Y Drysorfa*, 7 (1837), 365.
[38] *The calendar of the Calvinistic Methodist [...] Theological College, Bala [...] 1893-94* (Wrexham, [1893?]), pp. 50-2; *Catalogue of Dr. Owen Thomas's library* (Dolgellau, 1893).
[39] R. T. Jenkins, *Ymyl y ddalen* (Wrexham, 1957), pp. 56-7.
[40] Committee on the University of Wales and the Welsh University Colleges, *Minutes of evidence and appendices*, p. 110, Parliamentary Papers, 1909, XIX, Cd 4572, p. 810.
[41] Price, I, 175-87; Ll. J. Harris and B. Ll. James, 'The library of St David's University College, Lampeter', *The Book Collector*, 26 (1977), 195-227; *The Founder's Library, University of Wales, Lampeter* (Lampeter, 1994). See now also *The Founders' Library, University of Wales, Lampeter: bibliographical and contextual studies. Essays in memory of Robin Rider,* ed. William Marx. Published as *Trivium*, 29/30 (1997).
[42] Ll. J. Harris and B. Ll. James, 'The tract collection at Saint David's University College, Lampeter', *Trivium*, 9 (1974), 100-9; *A catalogue of the tract collection of Saint David's University College, Lampeter* (London, 1975), pp. xiii-xviii.
[43] *The library of Bishop Burgess at St David's University College, Lampeter* (Lampeter, 1987); Gwyn Walters, 'The bishop, the Bowdlers, the Botany Bay Surgeon', *NWR*, 1(1) (1988), 82-7, and his 'The library of Thomas Burgess (1756-1837)', *The Book Collector*, 43 (1994), 351-75.
[44] Price, I, 181.
[45] D. R. Davies, 'Thomas Phillips, founder of Llandovery College', *Province*, 3 (1952), 116-19; A. J. Sambrook, 'Thomas Phillips, 1760-1851', *Province*, 11 (1960), 127-31.
[46] A. N. L. Munby, *The dispersal of the Phillipps Library* (Cambridge, 1960), p. 5.
[47] Munby, p. 47.
[48] Price, II, 14.
[49] Walters, p. 87.
[50] D. G. Lewis, *The University and the colleges of education in Wales 1925-78* (Cardiff, 1980), chapter 1.
[51] B. C. Bloomfield (ed.), *A directory of rare book and special collections* (London, 1997), p. 688.
[52] W. Ll. Davies, *The National Library of Wales* (Aberystwyth, 1937), pp. 1-4; T. G. Lloyd, *The Old College Library: an historical account* (Aberystwyth, 1992), pp. 5-6; Hettie Glyn Davies, *Hanes bywyd John Glyn Davies (1870-1953)* (Liverpool, 1965), pp. 74-7; T. I. Ellis, *John Humphreys Davies (1871-1926)* (Liverpool, 1963), p. 166.
[53] The *UCW Calendar* for 1900-1 contains a six-page list of donors to the Welsh Library from October 1896 to July 1900.
[54] Moelwyn I. Williams (ed.), pp. 582-3; W. Ll. Davies, pp. 78-9.
[55] J. H. Davies, 'Welsh book collectors. 1. Rev. Owen Jones, B.A.', *JWBS*, 1 (1910-15), 17-20.
[56] Ellis, p. 167.
[57] G. O. Pierce, 'The Welsh connection', in *Fountains of praise,* ed. Gwyn Jones and Michael Quinn (Cardiff, 1983), pp. 25-40; J. Gwynfor Jones, *Y ganrif gyntaf: hanes Cymrodorion Caerdydd 1885-1985* (Cardiff, [1987]).
[58] For the fate of this collection see Chapter 23.
[59] J. Hubert Morgan, 'Y Salesbury', *Y Llenor*, 16 (1937), 39-51; B. Ll. James, 'The Salisbury collection', *NWR*, 1(2) (1988), 71-3; S. B. Chrimes (ed.), 'University College, Cardiff: a centenary history, 1883-1983' (unpublished typescript, 1983), pp. 413-15.
[60] *Western Mail*, 15 June 1886, p. 2.
[61] J. Hubert Morgan, 'A letter from a book collector; E. R. G. Salisbury', *JWBS*, 5 (1937-42), 33-40 (p. 37).

[62] John Ballinger, 'Obituary. Professor Thomas Powel, M.A., D.Litt.', *AC*, 77 (1922), 173-6; Brynmor Jones, 'Cefndir llyfrgell y brifddinas', *Y Casglwr*, 6 (Christmas 1978), 3; Chrimes, p. 414.
[63] E. Cefni Jones, *Gwili: cofiant a phregethau* (Llandysul, 1937), pp. 185-6.
[64] M. I. Williams, p. 581.
[65] Committee on the University of Wales and the Welsh University Colleges, *Report,* Parliamentary Papers, 1909, XIX, Cd 4571, and *Minutes of evidence*, Cd 4572; Harrison Bryan, *University libraries in Britain* (London, 1976), pp. 32-3, 160-3.
[66] Thomas Richards, *Rhwng y silffoedd* (Denbigh, 1978), pp. 152-66.
[67] Quoted in J. Gwynn Williams, *The University College of North Wales: foundations 1884-1927* (Cardiff, 1985), p. 99.
[68] Williams, *University College*, p.100.
[69] *Ibid.*, pp. 98, 101-2.
[70] T. M. Bassett, *Thomas Shankland, hanesydd* (Llandysul, 1966), pp. 30-4.
[71] Richards, pp. 139-40.
[72] Williams, *University College*, p. 179.
[73] Royal Commission on University Education in Wales, *Appendix to the second report [...] minutes of evidence [...]*, p. 48, Parliamentary papers, 1917-18, XII, Cd 8699, p. 392.
[74] Bassett, *Thomas Shankland*, p. 34.
[75] Strictly speaking Richards did not succeed Shankland since the latter was technically assistant librarian responsible to a librarian who was one of the professors, as explained in Williams, *University College*, pp. 456-7.
[76] Aberystwyth had received a new library, furnished through the generosity of North American benefactors in 1892 to replace that destroyed in 1885 (T. G. Lloyd, pp. 4-5).

CHAPTER 27

WOMEN'S WRITING IN NINETEENTH-CENTURY WALES

Kathryn Hughes

THE masculine bias of the Welsh literary tradition — only one woman poet, Ann Griffiths, is included in the canonical (if highly conservative) *Oxford Book of Welsh Verse* — makes it very difficult to establish the exact nature of the literary tradition of the women of Wales. Information regarding women who wrote before the nineteenth century is all too often minimal, is frequently unreliable, and may well understate the extent of a tradition which possibly depended more upon oral transmission than the written word.[1]

In the fifteenth century Gwerful Mechain (*c*.1462-1500) composed strong, hard-hitting poetry in the traditional strict metres comparable in its range and quality to that of the best male poets of the period. Although best known for her erotic poetry, she also wrote on traditional and religious themes. Capable of writing with humour, she could also address a powerful *englyn* to her husband in response to his physical violence.[2] In the sixteenth and seventeenth centuries poems by a few women such as Alis (*fl*.1550), daughter of Gruffudd ab Ieuan ap Llywelyn Fychan, appear in Welsh manuscripts but little is known about their lives. Angharad James (1677-1749) is the first known example of a woman poet who also copied literary manuscripts. Slightly later, another poet, Margaret Davies (*c*.1700-85), collected and copied the works of a number of women whose lives and motivations for writing remain unknown.[3]

The works of Ann Griffiths (1776-1805) are a major landmark in the history of Welsh women's writing.[4] Calvinistic Methodism encouraged each and every individual, male and female alike, to develop a personal relationship with God which could be publicly explored and discussed in the *seiat* (fellowship). In this way, women were encouraged to learn to express their emotions and to discuss their lives in a public context. The experience of speaking in public encouraged some women to speak and write for a wider audience. In her letters and hymns Ann Griffiths combined the influences of folk poetry with the language of the *seiat* to create an intense style of writing to convey her mystical experiences which has made her the most famous Welsh woman author.

Women's literature, as a significant body of writing, did not exist in Wales before the second half of the nineteenth century. The printed word of the first half of the century marginalized women or, particularly in popular literature such as sensational journalism and ballads, presented them as weak creatures who, despite their frailty, were responsible for the downfall of many an honest man. The change came towards the middle of the century. For women, the most important consequence of industrialization was the new emphasis on the separation of the workplace from home and hearth. Interlinked developments such as the rise of nationalism, the reaction to the 1847 Blue Books, and the spread of Nonconformity combined to stress the political correctness of the new ideology, the separateness of the two spheres, the public and the private, work and home. English literature of this period portrayed the ideal woman as a ministering angel high on her lofty pedestal and content with her position as unpaid housekeeper, nursemaid, and guardian of the family's moral and spiritual values. The role of the husband and father as the head of the household was unchallenged. Man, the hunter, ventured forth daily into the world of work and returned with bread for the family.

Although contemporary sources — statistics, diaries, letters, newspapers, and other factual accounts — indicate that the lives of ordinary women and men in Wales did not follow the patterns set out in both the didactic and the creative literature of the Victorian era picture, the idealization of this mythical social structure coloured the values, outlooks, and lives of every social class. Men, on the whole, were the moneyed class, empowered by their control of the economy. Women were not permitted significant access to personal or public finances. Economic, political, and social pressures all conspired to recast the acceptable definition of the female and the feminine in society. Many women accepted, and some positively welcomed, their redefined role. Even those who objected to certain elements accepted that woman's most important task, her chief duty, was to nurture the sick, the young, and the male. By remaining within the confines of the domestic sphere and acknowledging male supremacy, woman gained a new and somewhat ambiguous role as ruler of her own 'empire', her home and her children. Paradoxically, despite her weighty responsibilities as spiritual guide and moral mentor to her family she was still perceived as a member of the weaker sex. Supreme at home, she was incapable of meeting the demands of real life in the public sphere without male guidance.

Nineteenth-century Welsh literature certainly reflected the terminology of much English literature of the same period in its descriptions of women as 'angels' or 'household fairies'. The ideal, angelic woman was weak, her delicate constitution and frequent periods of undefined ill-health serving to prove her gentility and her femininity. Her manners were proper, even refined, reflecting urban civility but retaining a charming rustic *naïveté* as proof of her sweet and simple nature. Her character was virtuous, her household well-ordered, her children godly and, above all, she gladly submitted to the will of the head of her family. Although these characteristics of the English 'angel' abounded in Welsh literature of the time, the stereotype was alien in many ways to the experience of Welsh reading public. Most of those who were literate in Welsh came from a social group which has often been referred to as the cultured or educated peasantry or working class. Their daily lives, political and religious affiliations, and ambitions differed significantly from those of the English middle class and these differences expressed themselves in subtle shifts of emphasis in the character of the Welsh 'angel'. An amalgam of Welsh culture and English influences, she was more earthy than her Anglo-Saxon counterpart. The perfect Welsh girl was religious and obedient. Her purity unbesmirched, she met and married a suitable young man who was god-fearing, of the same sect, teetotal, and financially secure. Untainted by romance or sexuality, the angel produced virtuous children and dedicated herself to caring for the physical and spiritual well-being of her family. Despite her required subservience, she was to assume responsibility for the moral guardianship and spiritual conscience of her family. The Welsh angel is, in fact, the Madonna (minus the theological connotations) of many peasant cultures: the Welsh 'Mam', who emerged in the literature of the nineteenth century to become the butt of twentieth-century comedians, is a Nonconformist adaptation of the matriarch of an even earlier culture.

Angel, Madonna, or matriarch, nineteenth-century Welsh woman was culturally constrained to spend her days confined to the domestic sphere. The public sphere, the world of commerce, work, and politics, was a male preserve. During the first half of the century, the published literature of Wales was associated with the public sphere. It was written by men, and aimed primarily at a male audience. Women were not formally prevented from writing and publishing their writings and, indeed, the anonymity of eisteddfodic competition encouraged a few female authors. The cultural climate acted as a powerful deterrent to women writers, but fortunately was not powerful enough to silence them.

Two separate groups of women succeeded in publishing their literary endeavours during the nineteenth century. The wealthier, more leisured, and educationally privileged group naturally wrote in English. Indeed, apart from their sympathy with the language and culture of Wales there is little to distinguish them from contemporary middle- and upper-class women writers in England. The second group, women who wrote in Welsh — such as Sarah Jane Rees, 'Cranogwen' (1839-1916), Ellin Evans, 'Elen Egryn' (1807-76), Ellen Hughes, 'Elen Engan', and Alice Gray Jones, 'Ceridwen Peris' (1852-1943) — came from comparatively humble origins but had taken full advantage of whatever educational facilities were available to them. Despite being drawn from very different social and educational backgrounds, women in both groups shared an unshakeable faith in education as the panacea for all social ills, a belief in the importance of self-improvement, and an intelligent interest in the role of women in society.

Lady Charlotte Guest (1812-95), renowned for her three-volume translation of *The Mabinogion* (1838-49), came from an aristocratic background. Her marriage to the Dowlais ironmaster Sir John Guest brought her in touch with a different social class and she became involved with the schooling of the children of her husband's workers. Her diaries depict a woman who enjoyed her contact with her family but refused to allow womanly duties to interfere with her own work and her punishing daily schedule. If her words are to be believed, the birthing of a child was of little physical account to her and she would be back at her desk by the end of the day.

Charlotte Guest shared an aunt with Augusta Hall, Lady Llanover (1802-96). Both women were amongst the founder members of Cymdeithas Cymreigyddion y Fenni in 1833. Jane Williams, Ysgafell (1806-85), another member of the society, pursued a successful literary and scholastic career. Her published works included *The Autobiography of Elizabeth Davis* (1857), an important early example of oral history, *The Literary Women of England* (1861), *Celtic Fables, Fairy Tales and Legends* (1862), *A History of Wales derived from Authentic Sources* (1869), and *The Origin, Rise and Progress of the Paper People* (1856) which was illustrated by Augusta Hall. Jane Williams edited *The Literary Remains of the Rev. Thomas Price, Carnhuanawc [...] with a Memoir of his Life by Jane Williams* which was published in two volumes (1854-5) and Augusta Hall was responsible in part for the illustrations in this work.

Jane Williams and Augusta Hall were both incensed by the Blue Books of 1847. The former composed a scholarly defence of Wales, the Welsh language, and the morality of the women of Wales, *Artegall, or Remarks on the Reports of the Commissioners of Inquiry into the State of Education in Wales* (1848). Augusta Hall's response was to act as patron of *Y Gymraes* (*The Welshwoman*), the first Welsh-language magazine for women. Its editor, Evan Jones, 'Ieuan Gwynedd' (1820-52), had already responded forcefully in print to the 'Treachery of the Blue Books'; editing *Y Gymraes* constituted a further stage in his campaign to defend Welsh society and more particularly Welsh women against the accusations of the Commissioners. In the first issue, published in January 1850, Ieuan Gwynedd stressed that the periodical was intended to be a nondenominational publication designed to educate working-class women and inculcate in them a taste for reading.[5] Despite his hopes that women would contribute regularly and on an increasing scale to the pages of *Y Gymraes*, their contributions proved to be few. The periodical's over-didactic stance and unremitting emphasis on improving the conduct and elevating the moral standards of the women of Wales failed to appeal to working-class women.[6] The modern reader is struck by the similarities between *Y Gymraes* and other contemporary Welsh periodicals, rather than by its efforts to break new ground. Because of serious problems with distribution and finance, and its editor's failing health (Ieuan Gwynedd had to depend heavily on his wife for help with its production), *Y Gymraes* had to be terminated after two years.

In the July 1850 issue of *Y Gymraes* Ieuan Gwynedd warmly welcomed the publication of Elen Egryn's *Telyn Egryn* (*Egryn's Harp*), a 'slim volume of verse' dedicated to Augusta Hall.[7] During the earlier years of the century, several women had produced Welsh-language titles intended for a limited circulation, typically small collections of hymns for use in personal devotions or memorial verses dedicated to family and close friends.[8] *Telyn Egryn* was acclaimed as the first volume by a woman intended for wider circulation. Elen Egryn's poetry is competent but rarely outstanding, and on a first reading the sentimental religiosity expressed in some of her verses can hold little appeal for the modern reader.

Although several writers in the Welsh press expressed the hope that the appearance of *Y Gymraes* and *Telyn Egryn* marked the beginning of a new era, a long period of silence followed. This was broken in the later 1860s with the appearance of two significant publications. Margaret Jones of Rhosllannerchrugog went into service in Birmingham with the Revd E. B. Frankel, a converted Polish Jew. She travelled with this missionary and his family to Paris and then in 1866 to Jerusalem. Her letters to her parents, containing a wealth of information regarding the manners and customs of the places that she visited, first appeared in *Y Tyst Cymreig* (*The Welsh Witness*), before being published in book form as *Llythyrau Cymraes o Wlad Canaan* (*Letters of a Welshwoman from the land of Canaan*) in 1869. This enjoyed considerable success, reaching its fifth edition by 1872. A journey to Morocco led to the appearance in 1883 of her second book, *Morocco a'r hyn a welais yno* (*Morocco and what I saw there*). She later emigrated to Australia where she died in 1902.

Caniadau Cranogwen (*The poems of Cranogwen*) appeared in 1867. Cranogwen's poetry was popular and she was successful in numerous competitions and eisteddfodau in the early years of her career, notably at the 1865 National Eisteddfod where she triumphed over established poets such as Ceiriog and Islwyn. Poems with titles such as 'Ar farwolaeth baban' (On the death of a baby), 'Y fodrwy briodasol' (The wedding ring), 'Myfyrdod nosawl' (Nocturnal meditation), and the biblical 'Pedr yn nhy

Cornelius' (Peter in the house of Cornelius) indicate that the subject matter of *Caniadau Cranogwen* is generally typical of its period. Like *Telyn Egryn*, the volume does not immediately attract the modern reader but Cranogwen's confident style and her command of the Welsh language are worthy of attention.

Cranogwen was a woman of great ability and determination. As well as running a school which specialized in navigation and mathematics, she was a popular public speaker and fund raiser, a preacher, a prominent supporter of the Tonic Sol-fa movement, and a founder and first President of the South Wales Women's Temperance Union. She also established and edited *Y Frythones* (1879-91), the first successful periodical for women in Welsh. Her most important contributions to Welsh literature were certainly the part she played as a role-model to women of her time and the efforts that she made, particularly as editor of *Y Frythones*, to persuade women that their viewpoints were valid and that their literary efforts merited publication. Within a few years of its termination, *Y Frythones* was succeeded by new women's periodical, *Y Gymraes* (1896-1934), edited by Ceridwen Peris. Although a handful of women had submitted occasional verses and articles to the flourishing Welsh-language periodical press of the nineteenth century (two poems by Elen Egryn, for instance, had appeared in the denominational monthly *Y Cronicl* in 1849), it was the women's periodicals which gave many more the confidence to venture into print. Ieuan Gwynedd's *Gymraes* had failed to convince women that it was their magazine and the small number of female contributors decreased during its last months. The tone of both Cranogwen's *Frythones* and the new *Gymraes* edited by Ceridwen Peris was very different and neither seems to have suffered from any lack of female contributors. Both were written mainly by women, for women. Like modern women's magazines, they contained fiction, poetry, household hints, discussions of morals and matters of etiquette, readers' letters, and advice columns. Unlike the first *Gymraes* both contained illustrations.

Towards the end of the century, the names of several new authors began to become familiar to the readers of Welsh women's magazines. Women like Annie Catherine Prichard (who sometimes used the pseudonym 'Ruth'), Elen Engan, Mrs J. M. Saunders, Mrs. Oliver Jones (1858-93), and Mrs Ann Parry Ellis, 'Brythonferch' (d. 1935), all felt that they had something of value to say and to contribute to the public sphere. They shared interests such as writing, the temperance movement, teaching Sunday-school classes, good works, and employment involving domestic or nurturing skills. Many of them were skilled public speakers who turned their talents towards their faith and began to preach regularly. The advent of such a significant number of women into the public arena of writing for and speaking in front of an audience delivered an important cultural message: women realised that they could contribute to society in a variety of new ways. For the first time they could envisage themselves not only as teachers and nurses but as members of the boards of governors of schools and hospitals and, eventually, as voters and even as Members of Parliament.

These women's periodicals and their contributors paved the way for a host of female authors in the first half of the twentieth century. Writers such as Elizabeth Mary Jones, 'Moelona' (1878-1953), Winnie Parry (1870-1953), Annie Harriet Hughes, 'Gwyneth Vaughan' (1852-1910), Fanny Edwards (1876-1959), Eluned Morgan (1870-1938), and Elena Puw Morgan (1900-73) were not restricted by the same cultural restraints as their predecessors. Domestic duties may have left them short of time but it was no longer unusual for women to write and to see their work in print.

Kate Roberts (1891-1985), the acknowledged queen of twentieth-century Welsh literature, has paid tribute to these women. In an article entitled 'Merched tro'r ganrif' (Women of the turn of the century)[9] she refers to the work of Cranogwen and Ceridwen Peris and to the sudden flourish of women writers who appeared in their wake at the turn of the century. According to Kate Roberts, the dark years of the First World War drew the curtains on these exiting developments in the field of women's literature, but Kate Roberts herself read and enjoyed the works of these women. In the last decade of the twentieth century we look back at the period following that war and see Kate Roberts, a new star moving towards the centre of the stage.

NOTES TO CHAPTER 27

1. Ceridwen Lloyd-Morgan, 'Ar glawr neu ar lafar: llenyddiaeth a llyfrau merched Cymru o'r bymthegfed ganrif i'r ddeunawfed', *LlC*, 19 (1996), 70-8. See also her 'More written about than writing? Welsh women and the written word', in *Literacy in medieval Celtic societies*, ed. Huw Pryce (Cowbridge, 1998), pp. 149-65.
2. Ceridwen Lloyd-Morgan, '"Gwerful, ferch ragorol fain": golwg newydd ar Gwerful Mechain', *YB*, 16 (1990), 84-96.
3. A discussion of these early women poets with some examples of their work can be found in 'Beirdd benywaidd yng Nghymru cyn 1800', *Y Traethodydd*, 141 (1986), 12-27.
4. A. M. Allchin, *Ann Griffiths* (Cardiff, 1976) provides a brief introduction in English.
5. *Y Gymraes*, 1 (1850), 6-7.
6. For a valuable analysis see Sian Rhiannon Williams, 'Y Frythones: portread cyfnodolion merched y bedwaredd ganrif ar bymtheg o Gymraes yr oes', *Llafur*, 4(1) (1984), 43-56.
7. *Y Gymraes*, 1 (1850), 223-4.
8. Hymn-writers such as Jane Hughes, 'Deborah Maldwyn', Mary Owen, and Jane Edward are discussed in Jane Aaron, '"Anadnabyddus neu weddol anadnabyddus": cyd-awduresau Ann Griffiths yn hanner cyntaf y bedwaredd ganrif ar bymtheg', in *Cof Cenedl XII: ysgrifau ar hanes Cymru*, ed. Geraint H. Jenkins (Llandysul, 1997), pp. 103-36.
9. *Baner ac Amserau Cymru*, 9 Sept. 1965.

CHAPTER 28

THE MASS MEDIA IN TWENTIETH-CENTURY WALES

Jamie Medhurst

DR JOHN DAVIES, historian of the BBC in Wales, has maintained that in Wales 'to a greater extent than perhaps in any other country in Europe, broadcasting has played a central role, both positive and negative, in the development of the concept of a national community'.[1] Indeed, in his view

> the entire national debate in Wales, for fifty years and more after 1927, revolved around broadcasting [...] the other concessions to Welsh nationality won in those years were consequent upon the victories in the field of broadcasting.[2]

Economic, social, and political trends in Wales during the inter-war years and post-war decades were largely inimical to the survival of the Welsh language and an allegedly 'Welsh' way of life. The Second World War rid Wales of unemployment which at its peak in 1932 had reached forty per cent and had led to a massive outflow of population as some 440,000 left in search of work. In a new climate of optimism the 1945 Labour government nationalized basic industries, notably coal (in 1947) and steel (in 1951) as well as the railway network, road haulage, ports, and the electricity and gas industries. The post-war demand for energy meant that the coal industry remained relatively prosperous, 28 million tonnes being produced in 1947,[3] and growing emphasis on steel production led to heavy investment in plant along the South Wales coast from Llanwern near Newport (which opened in 1962) to Llanelli. Alternatives to heavy industry were also promoted during the post-war period as industrial estates housing small to medium-sized factories were established, and new towns such as Cwmbrân were developed.

The traditional heavy industries, generally characterized by high costs and low productivity, went into rapid decline from the mid-1970s onwards as high inflation was followed by the introduction of policies which focused on the ideals of a free market and the application of market forces, privatization, and severe restrictions on public spending. The result was disastrous for industrial Wales which experienced its worst crisis since the 1930s.[4] Nowhere was this crisis more apparent than in the coal industry where the number of miners fell from 34,000 in 1973 to 25,000 in 1983.[5] Worse was to come after the suicidal dispute of 1984-5, the last deep pit in Wales, Tower Colliery, closing in 1994.[6] New, high-technology industries have to some extent replaced heavy industry, a development aided by government investment in the infrastructure and by generous grants. Under the auspices of the Welsh Development Agency and the Development Board for Rural Wales, a strategy of attracting investment into the country has been successfully pursued. From the early 1970s Japanese companies have shown considerable interest in locating plant in Wales, and in the summer of 1996 the South Korean electronics giant *LG* decided to locate a £1.7 billion investment in the Newport area.

Rural Wales was characterized by economic decline and continuing depopulation during the post-war period. Rural industries such as slate quarrying in north Wales and the woollen industry of south-west Wales went into terminal decline. The closure of many railway lines following the Beeching Report of 1963 discouraged industrial development in rural areas. Despite grants, subsidies, and guaranteed prices, the number of farms in Wales halved between 1951 and 1971.[7] Mechanization led to a marked drop in the need for farm labour, the number employed declining from 8.2 per cent of the population employed in 1945 to 4.5 per cent in 1971. Dairy farming was hard hit in the 1980s following the imposition of EEC quotas on producers of milk, the greatest impact being felt by the farmers of south-west Wales where creameries were forced to close. Farming suffered further damage in the 1990s as a result of the mishandled BSE epidemic. Although tourism and the provision of leisure activities have provided many struggling farmers with a degree of relief in recent years, such part-time, casual, and seasonal employment does little to check the steady outflow from rural areas of the young and better qualified. At the same time, the linguistic effects of in-migration from England have been most apparent in rural areas. While permanent settlers are often sympathetic to the Welsh language, fears about the social and linguistic consequences of widespread holiday-home ownership led to the activities of Meibion Glyndŵr (Sons of Glyndŵr), a shadowy body which conducted a prolonged and extensive arson campaign directed against so-called second homes.

The post-war political scene in Wales was largely dominated by the Labour Party. Labour's emphasis on national planning (national, as Kenneth O. Morgan stresses, in the 'British' sense)[8] meant that Wales was not treated as a separate entity. The new controlling bodies for nationalized industries (other than gas) made little or no recognition of Wales as an administrative unit. Proposals for a Secretary of State for Wales were dismissed in 1948, and the Council for Wales and Monmouthshire, an advisory body established in that year, proved to be 'a somewhat shadowy body', so devoid of power that its demise in 1966 passed virtually unnoticed.[9]

By then, a sense of national identity had begun to take shape. In 1949, a Parliament for Wales Campaign had been launched by Undeb Cymru Fydd, an influential Welsh-language pressure-group, and in 1956 a 250,000-name petition calling for a Welsh Parliament was submitted to parliament. The appointment of Sir David Maxwell-Fyfe to the new post of Minister for Welsh Affairs in 1951 indicated that the incoming Conservative government was prepared to make at least a token recognition of Wales as a distinct region, and in 1955 Cardiff was pronounced the capital city of Wales. The late 1950s also saw a growth in Welsh nationalism, the Welsh nationalist party, Plaid Cymru, contesting twenty seats in the 1959 General Election. In its 1959 manifesto the Labour Party promised to establish a Welsh Office with a Secretary of State for Wales. Following the Labour victory in 1964 the Welsh Office was set up and has gradually come to assume extensive economic and social powers and responsibilities within Wales.

Throughout the late 1960s and early 1970s nationalism grew in strength. Plaid Cymru established itself as a credible political party following the Carmarthen by-election in 1966 in which Gwynfor Evans was returned as the first Plaid Cymru MP and a series of by-elections in south Wales constituencies where the party came a close second to Labour. Parallel developments in Scotland compelled Westminster to pay attention to the question of devolution. In 1973 the Kilbrandon Commission on the Constitution recommended that an elected assembly for Wales should be established. In the 1974 general election, Plaid Cymru won its second seat, Caernarfon, and in October regained the Carmarthen seat. The minority Labour government was compelled to make numerous concessions to retain nationalist support but in the referendum on devolution held on St David's Day 1979 the proposal was overwhelmingly defeated, eighty per cent of votes cast being against devolution. At the general election of 1979, the Conservative party won thirty-one per cent of the vote in Wales and in 1983 won no fewer than fourteen seats. Since then, the tide has turned. The Conservatives failed to hold a single one of their six remaining Welsh seats in the 1997 general election, and the subsequent referendum on a Welsh Assembly reversed, albeit by the narrowest of margins, the 1979 defeat.

During the half century between 1931 and 1981 the number of Welsh speakers declined from 909,261 to 508,207, a decline which caused great concern. The Second World War itself changed the social and linguistic make-up of many parts of Wales since Wales became home to 200,000 evacuees between 1939 and 1941. In strong Welsh-speaking areas many were assimilated into the community but in those areas where Welsh was weaker the evacuees often tipped the balance in favour of English, thereby changing the linguistic nature of many communities almost overnight.[10] The influx of incomers from England has continued so that by today about a fifth of the country's population consists of people born outside Wales.

It was in the key sphere of education that the effective action against linguistic decline first took place. During the nineteenth century the Welsh language was commonly considered to constitute a barrier to material progress and to personal advancement but from 1907 onwards the Welsh Department of the Board of Education took a more positive view and attempted to promote the language. The 1927 Board of Education report, *Y Gymraeg mewn Addysg a Bywyd* (*Welsh in Education and Life*), was a major step forward in encouraging the use of Welsh in schools. Described by Colin Baker as 'a document of great breadth, vision and erudition',[11] its immediate impact was in the primary schools of Wales as many began to teach a range of subjects through the medium of the Welsh language. In 1939, the first designated Welsh-medium primary school was opened in Aberystwyth as an independent school sponsored by Urdd Gobaith Cymru, the Welsh League of Youth. The school, as Jac L. Williams noted, was 'geared to the preservation and development of the pupil's Welsh heritage, not merely to educating Welsh-speaking pupils through the medium of their mother tongue.'[12] Indeed, as Baker points out, the aim of nurturing an awareness of, and respect for, the heritage of Wales has always been at the heart of Welsh-medium education:

> The development of bilingual education in Wales is not a purely educationally derived phenomenon. It does not derive from simple arguments about the educational virtues of bilingual education. Rather, such growth is both an action and reaction in the general growth of consciousness about the virtues of preserving the indigenous language and culture.[13]

The first Welsh-medium primary school to be run by a local education authority, Ysgol Dewi Sant in Llanelli, was opened on St David's Day 1947. This prompted

Flintshire Education Committee to establish Welsh-medium primary schools within travelling distance of every home in the county. As these schools increased in number it became clear that Welsh-medium secondary education would also have to be provided. Thanks to the vision of Dr Haydn Williams, Flintshire's Director of Education, Ysgol Glan Clwyd was opened in 1956 as the first officially designated Welsh-medium secondary school. This was followed in 1961 by Ysgol Maes Garmon in Mold, and in 1963 by Ysgol Morgan Llwyd in Wrexham. Meanwhile, the county of Glamorgan broke new ground by establishing in 1962 a Welsh-medium secondary school, Ysgol Rhydfelen, in the heart of Anglicized south Wales. The school proved very successful, the number of pupils increasing from 80 in September 1962 to 800 by 1972. Other Welsh-medium comprehensives followed.

The growth of Welsh-medium primary education also created a demand during the 1960s, particularly in the more Anglicized areas of Wales, for 'feeder' Welsh-medium nurseries. In 1971 Mudiad Ysgolion Meithrin (the Welsh Nursery Movement) was formed in Aberystwyth. A voluntary body at first, it was placed on a firmer footing in 1973 by a Welsh Office grant of £5,500 and is now a vital component of the Welsh-medium education system.[14]

By 1994, over twelve per cent of pupils in Welsh schools (20,962) were being taught Welsh as a first language and over sixty-six per cent (114,883) were learning it as a second language. A decrease of just over five per cent in the number of those studying Welsh as a first language between 1980/81 and 1993/94 was more than offset by an increase of thirty per cent in those taking Welsh as a second language.[15] A marked change in attitude to the use of the Welsh language in education has taken place as many non-Welsh-speaking parents have come to appreciate the benefits of a Welsh-medium education in terms of career enhancement. Even so, the growth of Welsh-medium and bilingual education has given rise to considerable and continuing controversy. Paradoxically, resistance to Welsh-medium secondary schools was strongest in those areas (such as Aberystwyth and north Pembrokeshire) where the Welsh language had remained comparatively strong. Opponents of Welsh-medium provision have argued that it is a divisive system which segregates pupils and squanders scarce resources on a dying language and culture. Its supporters point to the benefits of being able to use the language in a wide range of social and occupational domains.[16]

Higher education was also affected by the language issue. The colleges of the University of Wales recruited the majority of their students locally for many decades; as recently as 1951 eighty-four per cent of the University's students came from Wales. The rapid expansion of University education from the early 1960s onwards transformed recruitment so that by 1971 no more than thirty-seven per cent of students were from Wales. Fears that the minority within this minority who were Welsh-speaking would be swamped led to protests over the Anglicization of the University of Wales and to demands for the establishment of a separate Welsh-language college. The problem was alleviated to some extent by colleges adopting bilingual policies, by establishing Welsh halls of residence, and by the creation of designated posts for staff appointed to teach through the medium of Welsh.[17] In this way it has become possible for Welsh-speakers to be educated from pre-school to doctoral level in their own language.

On 13 February 1962 Saunders Lewis delivered his now famous broadcast *Tynged yr Iaith* (*The Fate of the Language*), a broadcast which led to the formation of Cymdeithas yr Iaith Gymraeg (the Welsh Language Society). From early 1963 onwards members of Cymdeithas yr Iaith employed a wide range of non-violent protest actions to demand that the language be given an equal footing with English. In 1967 a Welsh Language Act allowed the language to be used in legal proceedings and on official forms. 'Equal validity' was a vague concept which did not place the Welsh language on an equal footing with English, and further protests followed in the early 1970s; thus after a prolonged non-violent campaign the Bowen Report of 1972 approved the use of bilingual road signs. An important step was the establishment of Bwrdd yr Iaith (the Welsh Language Board) in 1988, initially as an advisory body. Following the Welsh Language Act of 1993 (itself regarded by Welsh activists as a weak measure), Bwrdd yr Iaith became a statutory body responsible for promoting and facilitating the use of the Welsh language and ensuring that public bodies treat the Welsh and English languages equally.

Concern about the fate of the language and the decline of a 'Welsh' way of life underlay the reaction of Welsh-speaking intellectuals to the new mass media of the twentieth century. The first of these, cinema, rapidly developed from being a travelling side-show attraction or music-hall act. Despite religious objections, cinema had become a firmly established form of cheap entertainment before the First World War.[18] Its popularity increased markedly during the inter-war years, notably following the advent of talking pictures in the later 1920s[19] and the construction of luxurious, purpose-built cinemas. For many people, particularly the young and members of the working class, cinema became their most important leisure activity, many viewing more than one film each week.[20] The Second World War reinforced habits of cinema-going; by 1946 there were no fewer than 315 cinemas in Wales,[21] and the number of venues peaked at some 350 in 1950.[22] As elsewhere in Britain, the advent of television led to a rapid reduction in the number of cinemas from the mid-1950s onwards, many becoming bingo halls and others, including buildings of considerable architectural interest, being demolished. By today, despite an increasing appreciation of film as a serious art form and the construction of a few modern multi-screen cinemas in major centres of population, there are no more than some fifty to sixty venues where films are regularly shown.[23]

Despite recent (if belated) interest amongst historians in the topic, the full effect of the cinema on Wales and on the Welsh language has yet to be assessed. Cinema was a purely commercial enterprise, largely dependent on Hollywood for its films which were distributed predominantly by national agencies. It could not therefore be expected to cater for minorities such as the Welsh, let alone for Welsh-speakers. Film portrayals of Wales were generally escapist or backward-looking and, as Peter Stead points out, the few films such as *Today we live* (1937) which challenged this stereotype were ironically 'seen more frequently in London's art cinemas than they were in south Wales itself'.[24] It was left to Ifan ab Owen Edwards, founder of Urdd Gobaith Cymru, to make the first Welsh-language talking picture, *Y Chwarelwr* (*The Quarryman*), in 1935.[25] This enjoyed some success when shown in north Wales but was not commercially distributed. The valiant attempts of the Welsh Film Board to produce Welsh-language films from 1971 onwards were handicapped by a lack of money, the British Film Institute proving particularly niggardly in its support for what it considered to be a 'language activity rather than a film activity'.[26] It was only with the advent of the Welsh television channel, S4C, that the funding for extensive Welsh-language film-making ventures became available.[27]

Radio broadcasting in Wales began at 5 p.m. on 13 February 1923 in a small room above a cinema in Castle Street, Cardiff.[28] Three months had passed since the British Broadcasting Company had been established by six wireless-set makers who wished to expand the market for their products.[29] During the early days of radio broadcasting in Wales, very little Welsh was to be heard on the air. Gwynfor Evans notes that the only substantial Welsh broadcasts were those made by Radio Éireann from Dublin.[30] The Company's programmes followed the pattern set by its London headquarters as there was no commitment to 'regional' or 'national' provision; indeed, a feeling prevailed that since the 'best' programmes were broadcast from London every effort should be made to imitate their style and content.[31] In order to ensure that the British Broadcasting Company was made aware of the language and culture of Wales, Cylch Dewi (David's Circle — a group of cultural nationalists) arranged the first broadcast of a Welsh-language religious service and in 1925, following consultations with E. R. Appleton, the Cardiff Station Director, produced a few programmes.[32]

The recommendation of the Crawford committee, set up in 1925 to consider the future of broadcasting, that a British Broadcasting Commission be established to oversee broadcasting developments, was rejected in favour of establishing a Corporation, funded by a licence fee and incorporated by Royal Charter. From the outset, fears were expressed in Wales at the centralization of power in London. As Aneurin Talfan Davies says, 'a radio system was forced upon the nation, without taking into consideration the differences between two nations.'[33] In 1927 *Welsh in Education and Life* included a scathing attack on the BBC: 'We regard the present policy of the British Broadcasting Corporation as one of the most serious menaces to the life of the Welsh language [...] nothing short of the full utilisation of the Welsh language in broadcasting will meet the case.'[34] The lack of understanding and of sympathy in the higher echelons of the Corporation is exemplified by Appleton's response to *Welsh in Education and Life*:

> Wales, of her own choice is part of the commonwealth of nations in which the official language is English [...] If the extremists who desire to force the language upon listeners in the area [...] were to have their way, the official language would lose its grip.[35]

During the 1930s representations from many quarters, notably the University of Wales and local authorities, urged the BBC to recognize Wales as a nation with its own cultural and linguistic needs. The BBC's insistence that technical problems arising from the mountainous nature of the country, its scattered population, and the scarcity of wavelengths made establishing a separate Welsh region difficult were viewed with some scepticism. In 1932 the BBC chose to ignore a plan which would have overcome the alleged technical problems[36] in favour of a scheme which brought together Wales and the south-west of England in one 'West Region'. Its reluctance to recognize the national identity of Wales, while making Scotland a region caused considerable indignation. Contemporary Welsh-language journals expressed widespread anger at the BBC's ignorance of, and lack of support for, all things Welsh. Their comments revealed a deep mistrust of the medium and a fear of the damage that broadcasting was inflicting upon the Welsh language and culture. Plaid Cymru's *Y Ddraig Goch* (*The Red Dragon*) claimed in 1932 that 'Most of the material broadcast is alien to our traditions, damaging to our culture, and constitutes a grave danger to everything special in our civilization.'[37] Such fears intensified as the number of households possessing radios increased.[38]

In 1935 Wales was granted a measure of independence in broadcasting terms. A number of Welsh-speakers such as T. Rowland Hughes, Tom Pickering, and Arwel Hughes were appointed to key positions in the Corporation, and Sam Jones was appointed to head the team at the newly opened Bangor studio, laying firm foundations for broadcasting from north Wales.[39] The slow process of separating Wales from the south-west of England had begun, and the Liberal politician Rhys Hopkin Morris was appointed as Director of the Welsh Region in June 1936. Although the transmitter in Penmon in Anglesey was opened in February 1937, it was not until 3 July 1937, when Sir John Reith, the Director-General of the BBC visited Cardiff for the opening ceremony, that the Corporation fully acknowledged Wales as a separate region with its own wavelength.

For the duration of the Second World War the BBC instituted a single unified service. As a result of considerable pressure (and an unfounded fear of German propaganda broadcasts in Welsh)[40] some Welsh-language broadcasting was permitted but transmissions were limited to three hours a week at the most. As prospects for an Allied victory improved, a lively discussion developed concerning post-war broadcasting. One consequence of the abandonment of a monolithic Reithian approach signalled by the introduction of the Light Programme (and subsequently the Third Programme) was the establishment of the Welsh Home Service at the end of July 1945.[41]

The post-war period was one of growth and development for the BBC throughout the United Kingdom. In Wales, the BBC built upon foundations laid before the war and, as Rowland Lucas notes, it was during this period that 'broadcasting in Wales began to spread its wings'.[42] Gwynfor Evans had called for an independent Broadcasting Corporation for Wales in 1944, claiming that 'the only system that will remove that possibility of a clash between the needs of Wales and the BBC's policy is an independent Welsh Corporation.'[43] By the end of the 1940s this proposal appeared attractive to others. In 1949 a cross-party group of Welsh MPs declared that an independent body should be formed by 1951 when the BBC's charter was next due for renewal. Since broadcasting was becoming an increasingly influential force in the lives of the people of Wales, they argued, should not the control of this be in the hands of those who were aware of the issues affecting the Welsh? Similar sentiments were expressed by Scottish MPs. In 1951 the Beveridge Committee, set up in 1949 to examine the finance and management of broadcasting in Britain, called for the establishment of National Broadcasting Councils for Scotland, Wales, and Northern Ireland. The proposal was accepted and on 6 January 1953 the Broadcasting Council for Wales met for the first time in Cardiff under the chairmanship of Lord MacDonald of Gwaenysgor.[44]

Although the 1930s also saw the advent of a new broadcasting medium, television, the service was confined to the London area, and was suspended at the outbreak of war. Programmes from English transmitters could be received in certain parts of Wales from 1949 onwards but television officially came to Wales on 15 August 1952 when the Wenvoe transmitter, near Cardiff, was opened. By 1954 over thirty-four hours per week were being broadcast in Wales, and by 1959 half the households in Wales possessed television licences.[45] Unfortunately, television broadcasting repeated the errors of radio in the 1920s and 1930s since Wenvoe served both south Wales and the south-west of England. The early 1950s saw the advent of the opt-out system whereby a 'national region' such as Wales would, at certain times, opt out of the national (British) network to broadcast programmes of a 'regional' interest. The system proved to be extremely unpopular. English-speaking viewers complained that by broadcasting Welsh-language programmes the BBC was depriving the English-language majority of programmes they wished to receive. In order to minimize such complaints, programmes in Welsh were broadcast at off-peak (and often extremely unsocial) hours. Welsh-speakers were consequently outraged by the lack of understanding (as they saw it) amongst BBC management of the needs of the Welsh people.

Following the Second World War, when the government had effectively controlled the radio service, concern was widely expressed over the ease with which monopoly powers facilitated control and manipulation of such a influential medium. Powerful commercial interests exploited these libertarian sentiments, claiming that the solution lay in creating a rival service to the BBC in the form of commercial television. Although the Beveridge Committee had rejected the idea in 1951, the debate over commercial television began in earnest following the Conservative election victory in that year. The newly elected government was in favour of commercial television and had the support of the advertising industry and television manufacturers. The opposition parties, rejected the idea in principle and could call on the support of the newspaper industry which feared a substantial loss of advertising revenue to a commercially based television service. The government view prevailed and on 30 July 1954, the Television Act reached the statute book.

Commercial television was based on a federal structure, regional companies being given franchises for different areas of the country. As with radio in the 1930s, Wales was linked to south-west England, this time for commercial reasons as Wales was not considered to constitute a viable commercial entity.[46] Television West and Wales (TWW), a company whose board included eminent Welshmen such as Huw T. Edwards and Sir Ifan ab Owen Edwards, was awarded the franchise for south Wales and the west of England on 24 October 1956. Technical difficulties delayed the start of broadcasting, but on 14 January 1958 TWW was officially opened. By 1960, the Independent Television Authority (ITA), the body responsible for the commercial television network, was eager to complete the network of regional companies. The remaining area which lacked any service was west and north Wales. In August 1960 the chairman of the ITA announced that a commercial company would be established in the near future to serve this area, and on 7 June 1961 the contract was awarded to Television Wales (West and North) / Teledu Cymru (TWWN). Broadcasting commenced in mid-September 1962 but from the outset TWWN was beset by financial problems and by the end of its first year had incurred losses of £159,339.[47] In September 1963 it was taken over by TWW, and programme output was merged from January 1964.[48]

It was during this period that BBC Wales as a separate region was formed. This was a major step forward in broadcasting in Wales and one which gave semi-autonomous powers to the BBC in Cardiff. By 1967 the Corporation had moved to new studios in Llandaf, a move which reflected the growing output of the BBC in Wales. Other developments, such as the take-over of the regional commercial franchise by Harlech Television (HTV) in 1968, gave a further impetus to television broadcasting in Wales, so that ownership of television sets grew during the 1960s from sixty per cent of Welsh households to ninety-two per cent.[49]

Predictably, the language issue dominated discussions of broadcasting in the 1970s. Opinion was sharply polarized between those who complained of being deprived of national network programmes because of Welsh-language broadcasts and those (such as Cymdeithas yr Iaith Gymraeg) who argued that scant regard was paid to the need for Welsh-language broadcasting. Emyr Humphreys, a proponent of the latter view, claimed in 1970 that broadcasting as a medium had simply failed to reflect the language and culture of Wales.[50] Once again protest in the form of symbolic actions such as the refusal to pay for television licences concentrated the official mind. In terms of Welsh-language broadcasting, the Crawford Committee's Report of 1974 could be seen as a milestone, as the fifth chapter of the report dealt exclusively with Welsh-language television. Perhaps paragraphs 72 and 75 are the most important in the history of broadcasting in Wales since they led to the eventual establishment of a predominantly Welsh-language fourth channel:

> Our conclusion is that the only way of providing a separate Welsh language service quickly enough to meet the urgency of the Welsh need would be to use the fourth channel [...] whatever decision may be reached in the rest of the United Kingdom, it should in Wales be allotted as soon as possible to a separate service in which Welsh language programmes should be given priority [...] it should be introduced on the Fourth Channel in Wales as soon as possible, without waiting for a decision on the use of the Fourth Channel in the rest of the United Kingdom.[51]

The report also advocated the separation of the Welsh-language Radio Cymru (on VHF) and Radio Wales (on medium wave), an arrangement which began in 1977.

Although the Conservative manifesto in 1979 was in favour of establishing a separate Welsh channel, the party's refusal once in office to honour this commitment led to widespread protests, including a threat by Gwynfor Evans to fast to death. A swift reversal of policy brought into being the Welsh fourth channel, S4C (Sianel 4 Cymru), which began broadcasting on 1 November 1982.[52] S4C has been at the forefront of Welsh-language developments since its inception and now transmits over thirty hours of Welsh-language programmes each week. Over the years its efforts to preserve and promote the language and culture of Wales have been widely praised. Certainly, the channel has done much to promote the cause of Welsh broadcasting by commissioning animated series (such as the internationally successful *SuperTed*, bought by Disney's Movie Channel) and hard-hitting, award-winning current affairs series such as the BBC's *Taro Naw* (*Striking Nine*). That certain programmes have been viewed by a high proportion (as much as thirty per cent) of the possible audience would appear to substantiate the claim that S4C has reached many Welsh speakers who would be reluctant to read (let alone purchase) material in the Welsh language.

The relationship between television and print culture has everywhere been an uneasy one. On a British level it has been alleged, for instance, that television threatens reading skills. In Wales, where the indigenous culture and language is so much weaker, such problems are even more acute and current developments are even more menacing. The advent of digital satellite television, a purely commercial enterprise offering hundreds of channels and run by international companies which are not amenable to national attempts at regulation, may well threaten the position of Welsh-language broadcasting. The example provided by an earlier, purely commercial medium, cinema is not encouraging. The Internet and other electronic communications methods may pose an even graver challenge by consolidating the global hegemony of American-English: indeed, writers such as Kevin Williams maintain that the so-called information revolution will finally 'kick away the chair of national identity'.[53]

NOTES TO CHAPTER 28

1. John Davies, *Broadcasting and the BBC in Wales* (Cardiff, 1994), p. ix.
2. Davies, *Broadcasting*, p. 50.
3. J. Graham Jones, *Hanes Cymru* (Cardiff, 1994), p. 161.
4. Dennis Thomas, 'Economi Cymru 1945-1995', in *Cof cenedl XI*, ed. Geraint H. Jenkins (Llandysul, 1996), pp. 147-79 (p. 168).
5. Thomas, p. 168.
6. The colliery was re-opened in 1995 following its purchase by the miners who had previously worked there under British Coal.
7. Thomas, p. 163.
8. Kenneth O. Morgan, 'Wales since 1945: political society', in *Post-war Wales*, ed. Trevor Herbert and Gareth Elwyn Jones (Cardiff, 1995), pp. 10-54 (p. 11).
9. Morgan, 'Wales since 1945', p. 12.
10. John Davies, *A history of Wales* (London, 1993), p. 602.
11. Colin Baker, 'The growth of bilingual education in the secondary schools of Wales', in *Perspectives on a century of secondary education in Wales 1889-1989*, ed. W. Gareth Evans (Aberystwyth, 1990), pp. 77-96 (p. 80).
12. Jac L. Williams, 'The Welsh language in education', in *The Welsh language today*, ed. Meic Stephens (Llandysul, 1973), pp. 92-109 (p. 100).
13. Baker, p. 79.
14. Catrin Stevens, *Meithrin: hanes Mudiad Ysgolion Meithrin 1971-1996* (Llandysul, 1996).
15. *Digest of Welsh statistics = Crynhoad o ystadegau Cymru. No. 41 1995.* (London, 1995), p. 49.
16. Colin H. Williams, 'Bilingual education as an agent in cultural reproduction: spatial variations in Wales', *Cambria*, 13 (1986), 111-29 (p. 113).
17. Geraint H. Jenkins, '"Prif faen clo cenedl y Cymry": Prifysgol Cymru 1893-1993', in *Cof cenedl X*, ed. Geraint H. Jenkins (Llandysul, 1995), pp. 121-52 (p. 150).
18. David Berry, *Wales and cinema: the first hundred years* (Cardiff, 1994), pp. 18-63.
19. *The Jazz Singer* (1927) was shown in Cardiff in 1928 (Berry, p. 122).
20. Berry, p. 126, quoting a Carnegie UK Trust study of 1936/7.
21. *Ibid.*, p. 8.
22. Davies, *History*, p. 635.
23. Berry, p. 12.
24. Peter Stead, 'Wales and film', in *Wales between the wars*, ed. Trevor Herbert and Gareth Elwyn Jones (Cardiff, 1988), pp. 161-85 (p. 166).
25. Berry, pp. 313-14.
26. *Ibid.*, p. 314.
27. *Ibid.*, pp. 321-41.
28. Rowland Lucas, *The voice of a nation* (Llandysul, 1981), p. 15.
29. Davies, *Broadcasting*, p. 2.
30. Gwynfor Evans, 'Hanes twf Plaid Cymru 1925-1995', in *Cof cenedl X*, ed. Geraint H. Jenkins (Llandysul, 1995), pp. 153-84 (p. 157).
31. Aneurin Talfan Davies, *Darlledu a'r genedl* (London, 1972), pp. 6-8.
32. Davies, *Broadcasting*, p. 32.
33. 'Gwthiwyd cyfundrefn radio ar y genedl, heb ystyried o gwbl y gwahaniaethau rhwng dwy genedl' (A. T. Davies, p. 11).
34. *Welsh in Education and Life* (London, 1927), p. 164.
35. *Western Mail*, 30 Aug. 1927, quoted in Davies, *Broadcasting*, p. 49.
36. Davies, *Broadcasting*, p. 52.
37. 'Y mae'r rhelyw o'r mater a ddarlledir yn estronol i'n traddodiad, yn niweidiol i'n diwylliant, ac yn berygl byw i bopeth sy'n arbennig yn ein gwareiddiad' ('Gorchfygwn y BBC', *Y Ddraig Goch*, Feb. 1932).

[38] The number of Welsh households holding radio licences increased from 136,320 in 1930 to 405,954 by 1939 (Davies, *Broadcasting*, p. 82).
[39] For a detailed account of the contribution of the Bangor studios to broadcasting in Wales, see *Babi Sam: yn dathlu hanner can mlynedd o ddarlledu o Fangor*, ed. Dyfnallt Morgan (Denbigh, 1985).
[40] Davies, *Broadcasting*, p. 127.
[41] *Ibid.*, p. 147.
[42] Lucas, p. 153.
[43] 'Yr unig drefn a allai symud yn foddhaol y posibilrwydd o wrthdrawiad rhwng anghenion Cymru a pholisi'r BBC fyddai Corfforaeth Gymreig annibynnol' (Gwynfor Evans, *Y Radio yng Nghymru* (Liverpool, 1944), p. 7).
[44] Lucas, p. 170.
[45] Davies, *Broadcasting*, p. 199.
[46] For further details see Bernard Sendall, *Independent Television in Britain Vol. 1* (London, 1984).
[47] *Wales West and North/Teledu Cymru Annual Report 1962* ([s.l.], 1962).
[48] Davies, *Broadcasting*, p. 229.
[49] Davies, *History*, p. 635.
[50] *Broadcasting in Wales in the seventies: an open conference held at the University College of North Wales, Bangor, 7th February 1970* (Bangor, 1970), p. 3.
[51] *Report of the Committee on Broadcasting Coverage*, Cmnd. 5774 (London, 1974), pp. 41-2.
[52] Angharad Tomos, 'Realizing a dream', in *What's this channel fo(u)r?: an alternative report*, ed. Simon Blanchard and David Morley (London, 1982), pp. 37-53.
[53] Kevin Williams, 'All wired up and nowhere to go', *Planet*, 115 (Jan./Feb. 1996), 26-9 (p. 29).

CHAPTER 29

WELSH-LANGUAGE PUBLISHING 1919 TO 1995

Gwilym Huws

IN 1951 the Home Office appointed a committee to examine 'the present arrangements for the publication of books, magazines and periodicals in the Welsh language'.[1] The subsequent report explained that the committee had been set up following a memorandum from the Union of Welsh Publishers and Booksellers which drew attention to the crisis facing commercial publishing in Welsh as a result of escalating production costs and an acute paper shortage in the aftermath of the Second World War. The eventual terms of reference, however, were broadened to include a wide-ranging discussion of Welsh-language publishing as it came to be recognized that it was facing a far more fundamental crisis than these immediate difficulties.[2]

Some of the weaknesses of the book trade in the early 1950s are linked to the socio-cultural, political, and economic changes which took place earlier in the century, most notably the decline in the number of Welsh-speakers from 977,366 (43.5% of the population) in 1911 to 714,686 (28.9%) in 1951.[3] The growing secularization of Welsh life progressively weakened the chapel and church culture which had sustained Welsh publishing for most of the nineteenth century by creating a ready market for works such as biblical commentaries, hymn-books, and religious periodicals.[4] Printer-publishers, whose secular output had often been subsidized by successful religious works, were not the only victims of this change as it was also responsible for the demise of two long-standing retail outlets for Welsh books — the peripatetic Dissenting preacher-cum-travelling-bookseller and the *dosbarthwr* (local distributor).[5] Although publishing religious and theological material still remained a fairly lucrative business, much of this trade was now undertaken by denominational publishing houses which printed, published, and distributed most of the profitable titles themselves. The disappearance of the *dosbarthwr* and the emergence of denominational bookrooms were cited as two of the reasons behind the difficulties faced by the Welsh book industry during the 1920s.[6]

Even so commercial publishers aggravated their problems by their reluctance to respond to changes in Welsh society. For example, the advent of new, Anglicized (or American) forms of mass entertainment such as the cinema and radio offered young people far more excitement than did the *Gymanfa Ganu*, the local choir, or the Sunday-school trip.[7] In the early 1930s Arthur ap Gwynn maintained that Welsh authors and publishers catered:

> for the taste of a century which is dead and gone [...] They do not seem to have realised that sixty years of education cannot pass without leaving some effect [...] it will have produced men and women of wide tastes and varied experiences, who have an interest in science as well as literature, in art as well as theology.[8]

Analysis of new titles published between 1923 and 1933 supports his claim since religion, theology, and creative literature continued to dominate most publishers' lists, whilst there was a dearth of titles discussing subjects such as the fine arts, sociology, science, and technology.[9] The virtual absence of Welsh books in fields such as science, technology, economics, and politics was a fair reflection of the low status of the language in many spheres of public life.

Although an intensifying malaise in Welsh publishing could be discerned from the 1890s onwards, problems came to a head during the First World War when the number of new titles dropped suddenly from 155 in 1909 to eighty-three in 1914, forty-six in 1916, and a mere twenty-four in 1918.[10] Although this catastrophic collapse in output to early-eighteenth-century levels could be attributed to wartime disruption, post-war recovery was painfully slow. Output rose to 127 in 1922 before slipping back to below a hundred titles a year for the following decade with the exception of 1927 (113) and 1931 (109). By the 1930s the economic depression had become a further threat to the viability of the industry since few families could afford to buy the latest volume of poetry or collection of short stories. The potential market for Welsh books was further eroded by the exodus of Welsh-speakers who left the industrial valleys in search of employment in the south-east England and the Midlands.[11]

Not all the changes were negative. Welsh literature experienced a revival in its fortunes inspired by poets such as T. Gwynn Jones, T. H. Parry-Williams, R. Williams Parry, and D. Gwenallt Jones, the short stories of Kate Roberts and D. J. Williams, as well as the literary and textual criticism of scholars such as Ifor Williams, Saunders Lewis, and W. J. Gruffydd. The departments of Welsh language and literature at the constituent colleges of the University of Wales played an important role in this literary revival and, with other recently established national institutions such as the National Library of Wales and the National Museum of Wales, helped create a new professional class of Welsh-speakers. The growing confidence of this younger generation gave rise to two exciting publishing initiatives. The first was the establishment of *Y Clwb Llyfrau Cymreig* (The Welsh Book Club) in 1937 by Edward Prosser Rhys (1901-45), the owner of Gwasg Aberystwyth. Prosser Rhys (1901-45) announced his intention to launch a book club if it could attract a thousand members prepared to purchase four titles a year.[12] Within eighteen months the membership exceeded 3,000.[13] Equally impressive was the range of titles and the stature of the authors on its list. Prosser Rhys did not attempt to disguise the fact that the inspiration came from the success of Gollancz's Left Book Club.[14] He was not the only one to imitate an English publishing initiative. 'Llyfrau'r Dryw', a paperback imprint established in 1940 by three brothers, Aneirin Talfan, Alun Talfan, and Elfyn Talfan Davies, was similarly inspired by the success of Penguin Books. Unlike Allen Lane, whose motives were strictly commercial, 'Llyfrau'r Dryw' (Wren Books) was established in order to safeguard the Welsh language and culture in a time of crisis. Because it could not hope to achieve Penguin's mass sales, 'Llyfrau'r Dryw' was far less ambitious than its English counterpart. Nevertheless, twenty-two original titles were published in the first three years. This early success was based on a shrewd selection of authors and topics, the low selling price of a shilling, and an extremely astute marketing strategy.[15]

Despite the relative success of these initiatives, the overall viability of the industry remained precarious. One indicator of this was the paucity of retail outlets. This was not a new problem. *Welsh in Education and Life*, an official report on the Welsh language published in 1927, had claimed that there were as few as ten bookshops selling Welsh books in Wales,[16] and had recommended that 'organised Welsh societies should endeavour to re-establish, if possible, the *dosbarthwr*, or to find some substitute'.[17] Ten years later, *Urdd Gobaith Cymru* (The Welsh League of Youth) — a voluntary cultural organisation for young people — took up this challenge by introducing the St David's Day Welsh Books Campaign, a scheme to sell Welsh books directly to the public through its membership. Following the success of a pilot scheme, this activity became an integral part of the Urdd's programme for two generations. Initially sales were quite modest but during the mid-1940s they rose sharply, reaching a peak of 54,043 volumes in 1944.[18] Although those who established the campaign deserve recognition for their efforts, its success merely underlines the parlous condition of the retail trade at this time.

During the Second World War the Welsh book trade enjoyed a brief but deceptive Indian summer. As in England, the curtailment of normal social and cultural activities, the rationing of many basic goods, and the long hours of enforced tedium experienced by so many of those engaged in wartime duties led to a marked increase in reading. In Wales, this development was reinforced by a campaign to protect its language and culture from Anglicizing forces which were much easier to identify during wartime. But the war provided no more than a temporary postponement of the crisis which came to a head when the industry's long-standing problems were exacerbated by a sharp increase in production costs and a shortage of paper. It was these circumstances which led to the first official investigation into the industry noted at the beginning of this study.[19]

Although the recommendations of the Ready report of 1952 were rejected by the government of the day, the report marked a watershed in Welsh publishing because the refusal to act led to increasing pressure on the government to accept its responsibility. Those who argued in favour of state assistance to Welsh publishing could now point to the claim in the report that:

> Books are an indispensable means to the preservation, continuity, and development of a national culture. A bookless people is a rootless people, doomed to lose its identity and its power to contribute to the common fund of civilisation [...] If the published language goes, the language itself as a cultural medium will soon follow: and if Welsh goes, a bastardised vernacular will take its place, lacking both pride of ancestry and hope of posterity.[20]

Eventually the government yielded to the pressure for a grant to support Welsh books. This radical solution to the industry's ailments had formed part of the original memorandum that led to the appointment of the committee in the first instance but had been dismissed because it allegedly involved 'a dangerous and impracticable principle'.[21] The annual grant of £1,000 was originally offered for five years only, but in 1960/61 it was increased to £3,000 and by a further £500 annually until 1964/65, when it was proposed that the grant should cease 'in the expectation that publishers of Welsh books will be in a strong enough position to carry on without assistance'.[22] However, a Council for Wales and Monmouthshire report published in 1963 claimed that Welsh books would once again be in jeopardy should the government withdraw this financial support and urged 'that this subsidy should be continued for so long as it is shown by the publishers to be necessary to ensure the production of an adequate selection of these books.'[23] Successive governments have duly honoured this recommendation, and, following a recommendation in a Council for the Welsh Language report published in 1978, have extended the grant, initially limited to adult books, to include 'Welsh publishing as a whole, including periodical and leisure reading [...] for children and young people'.[24] By 1994/95 the grant was worth £641,000 a year although £53,827 of this sum was spent on administering the scheme.[25] Since its inception in 1956 the grant has undoubtedly had a major impact on the state of the Welsh book industry. Initially its impact was modest, only twelve titles receiving a grant in 1957, but by 1960 the number of grant-supported titles had increased to forty-one.[26] Since then the curve has risen steadily so that by 1994/95 a total of 229 titles (including reprints and new editions) enjoyed support from this source.[27]

Despite its importance, this grant is only one of a number of developments which have contributed to the resurgence of the industry since the 1950s. Firstly, Wales, like the rest of the United Kingdom, enjoyed a period of relative prosperity following the austerity of the immediate post-war years. Secondly, there was a change in the climate of opinion towards the Welsh language and culture and, thirdly, political and administrative developments such as the establishment of the Welsh Office in 1964 strengthened the claim for separate treatment for Wales in fields such as the arts and culture.

One service to benefit from the improved economic conditions was the public library service, which experienced an unparalleled expansion during the 1950s and 1960s. Alun R. Edwards, Chief Librarian of Cardiganshire Joint Library, realized that the shortage of Welsh books prevented Welsh readers from sharing fully the benefits of this expansion. He was to dedicate much of his professional life not only to resolving the problems of providing a worthwhile library service to the Welsh-speaking community in his own authority and elsewhere, but also to bringing about a significant improvement in the supply and sale of Welsh books.[28] Although the Roberts report of 1959 had finally acknowledged that public libraries had a responsibility to provide a 'comparable service' to the two language communities in Wales,[29] Edwards appreciated that this statement was of little value unless the Welsh book trade could guarantee a regular supply of new titles, particularly of popular fiction. When a working party was set up to consider in detail the technical implications of the Roberts report, Edwards, the only Welsh representative, fought hard to persuade its other members to accept his proposal to establish a 'Public Libraries Welsh Books Fund' to secure a guaranteed pre-publication sale of 500 copies of 'every book considered suitable for schools and/or public libraries', each library's contribution to the fund depending on the number of Welsh-speakers residing in that authority.[30] Unfortunately Edwards failed to gain the support of the Working Party and his recommendations had to appear as a reservation to the main report.

Fortunately, Edwards's campaign to create an official organization dedicated to producing and promoting Welsh books was fought on several fronts and his dream was eventually realized with the establishment of the Welsh Books Council in 1962. The first step in the process had been the establishment of a number of voluntary book societies to encourage the public 'to buy more Welsh books, to provide a more viable market and to increase the interest in reading in a language which was in danger of being swamped by popular English-language publications'.[31] The proliferation of local book societies, and the award by one of them of author grants from public funds under Section 136 of the 1948 Local Government Act, provided a model on which a national organization could be built. Many bureaucratic obstacles remained to be overcome before the principle of a national body was acceptable to civil servants and Welsh local authorities, and without Edwards's vision and dogged stubbornness during these difficult negotiations it is doubtful whether the Welsh Books Council would ever have been established.

The Council's original aims were 'to secure the provision of popular literature in Welsh for the adult reader of every type and age' and 'to promote the sales of Welsh books by co-operation with the Welsh book trade and by such other means as may be deemed necessary'.[32] Its main activity during its formative years was to administer the work of its Publications Panel which judged manuscripts, awarded grants to authors, and recommended titles for the Libraries Purchasing Scheme which provided a guaranteed sale to libraries of up to 500 copies of new novels for adults. Other early activities included promoting the sale of Welsh books through sale-or-return arrangements with village shops, co-ordinating the St David's Day Bookselling Campaign, providing exhibition stands at the National Eisteddfod and the Royal Welsh Agricultural Show, and encouraging young children to read Welsh by organizing book quizzes for school pupils.[33] Lack of funding prevented the Welsh Books Council from extending its sphere of influence during the 1960s, but its activities expanded rapidly as soon as a new source of income, the Welsh Arts Council, was able to support its work.

The decline in the number of new books in the early 1950s had threatened to limit the effectiveness of Welsh-language education. School inspectors in the Welsh Department of the Ministry of Education submitted a memorandum to the Ready committee which described the difficulties experienced by Welsh schools in providing an education along 'modern lines' without an adequate provision of suitable reading books in the language.[34] This problem had arisen during a period of rapid expansion in Welsh-medium education. The first *Ysgol Gymraeg* was established in Llanelli in 1947[35] and by 1962 the number of Welsh-medium schools in predominantly English-speaking areas of Wales had grown to forty-three.[36] Their pupils, numbering over 5,300, represented a significant addition to the number of those attending 'natural' Welsh schools in predominantly Welsh-speaking areas. In 1956 the Welsh Joint Education Committee (WJEC), whose only previous involvement in the book world had been to note its approval of those Welsh books it considered suitable for classroom use, began to co-ordinate a central pool of money made available by local authorities for the purchase of Welsh books for schools. The advance announcement of the total sum available in the pool enabled publishers to plan a publishing programme of school books with greater confidence than ever before. Since the total expenditure on Welsh books by local education authorities was only £7,653 in the early 1950s,[37] an announcement that £16,000 would initially be made available in 1956/57 and that the sum would be increased to £30,000 per annum over the next few years represented an important step forward.[38] Meanwhile Cardiganshire set up a scheme to encourage new writers and promote the production of more books for schools through writing competitions and guaranteed sales. This was subsequently extended to cover seven counties before being adopted as a national scheme administered by the Welsh Joint Education Committee in 1966. Between that date and 1976 the scheme sponsored a total of 579 titles, over 90% of all children's and school books published during this period.[39]

As a result of these schemes there has been a marked increase in the number of Welsh books published each year. By 1976 the total was in excess of 300, in 1981 it exceeded 400, by 1991 the 500 mark was passed, and in 1993 no fewer than 618 Welsh books were published.[40] An attempt to bring about a comparable improvement in the quality and nature of Welsh books was made following the publication of a report in 1978 which led to the responsibility for administering the Government grant being transferred from the University of Wales Press to the Welsh Books Council.[41] The Council was granted additional powers including the right to commission titles and to reject applications from publishers in order to safeguard standards of production. The statement that the Council had no intention of interfering with the rights of publishers 'within reason' caused considerable controversy,[42] since some critics who believed that this was effectively a form of censorship, given the near-total dependence of publishers on such grants, claimed that it represented the final step towards nationalizing the industry.[43] In the event, despite minor skirmishes with one or two publishers, the new grant system has been generally welcomed for improving the quality of Welsh books. In particular, the range of material for children and young people has been significantly expanded through the efforts of the Council's Commissions Panel (Children's Books).

The great improvement in the number of books published is but one of the developments during the second half of this century. Another is the increased professionalism of the industry. The chief architect of this particular change was Meic Stephens, formerly Assistant Director of the Welsh Arts Council with responsibility for Literature. Soon after his appointment in 1967 Stephens maintained that the structure of the industry was a major obstacle to developments in Welsh and Anglo-Welsh literature, and in 1970 he submitted a report to the Council's Literature Committee which claimed that only the two leading publishing houses made any effort to establish professional standards. To improve matters he suggested the formation of a national publishing house with specialist departments covering the main activities of the publishing process. Although his vision met with great opposition at the time his proposals have come to form an integral part of the infrastructure which now supports various elements of the book industry.

An early step towards professionalizing the industry was taken in 1971/2 when the Welsh Arts Council offered funding to the Welsh Books Council to enable it to establish the proposed specialist departments. Most Welsh publishers now regularly use one or more of these services. For example, during the financial year 1994/95 the Welsh Books Council's Editorial Department handled 261 new manuscripts in Welsh and twenty-eight in English from eighteen different publishers. In 1976 the Welsh Arts Council offered funding to some publishing houses to enable them to appoint professional staff,[44] a scheme which was later administered by the Welsh Books Council.[45] Today the majority of Welsh publishers (including educational publishing agencies) employ their own in-house professional staff in addition to taking advantage of the Welsh Books Council's specialist services.

One feature of the book industry which has improved beyond recognition during the past twenty-five years is the design and quality of Welsh books. This has been possible partly because of the availability of production grants, but also because of the Welsh Arts Council's leadership in attempting to improve standards by organizing book design competitions in the late 1960s and 1970s as well as the financial support it has provided to the Welsh Books Council to enable it to establish a Design Department. The Department offers publishers a centralized service for producing illustrations and covers, as well as safeguarding standards in the design and production of books. Thus in 1994/95 the Design Department assisted 148 titles.[46] Although some publishers (notably Gomer, with its reputation for fine craftsmanship, and Y Lolfa, which projects a lively image) have always been conscious of the importance of design, this awareness now extends to most publishing houses.

Authors have also benefited from increased professionalism in terms of financial rewards and of improved rights. An early initiative of the Welsh Books Council was to introduce a scheme of author grants to supplement the (at best) meagre royalties earned by most Welsh authors. Although these grants were restricted to the authors of popular books, since 1967 the Literature Committee of the Welsh Arts Council has offered effective support to creative writers in both Welsh and English. The most important scheme was the provision of bursaries which enabled authors to be released from their normal employment so that they could write on a full-time basis and enjoy a taste of full-time authorship.[47] During the first seven years of the scheme fifty-one bursaries were awarded to Welsh and Anglo-Welsh writers.[48]

In addition to offering direct financial support to established authors, the Welsh Arts Council has improved conditions for all authors of creative literature by insisting that the publishers of literary magazines and books who receive production grants from the Council provide adequate remuneration to contributors.[49] The Welsh Books Council has also stipulated certain conditions relating to the author's royalties as one of the conditions for the award of a government grant to publishers. Chiefly through the influence of central agencies such as the Welsh Arts Council, the Welsh Books Council, and the Welsh Joint Education Committee, a much more business-like relationship between authors and publishers has been achieved during the past three decades.[50] Despite these improvements, a survey undertaken in 1987 revealed why the vast majority of Welsh authors remain part-time writers; over a three-year period, 55% earned less than £1,000, 35% less than £10,000, and only 10% earned more than £10,000. The report concluded that the annual salary of the Welsh professional writer (no more than seven or eight thousand pounds) was 'a totally inadequate sum according to any professional standards'.[51] Authorship therefore remains one area of the Welsh book world where full-time employment is the exception rather than the rule.

A major market-research exercise conducted during the second half of the 1980s claimed that marketing and publicity were 'the greatest weakness in the publishing process in Wales'.[52] This was largely because most publishing houses were also commercial printers and thus, apart from one or two notable exceptions, did not have to concern themselves greatly about the fate of their products once they had been published. For example, most publishers never visited booksellers even though establishing personal contacts with those who sold their products might well lead to additional sales. Welsh Arts Council funding has enabled the Welsh Books Council to establish a Publicity Department to provide a centralized service to publishers.[53] This Department (now amalgamated with the Council's Marketing Department) ensures that both the book trade and the general public receive regular information about new books and titles in print. The trade relies on the monthly list of new stock at the Distribution Centre as well as regular visits to booksellers from the Council's representatives,[54] whilst the public is kept informed through the Council's quarterly magazine, *Llais Llyfrau / Books in Wales*. The Publicity Department also administers the Sbondonics Book Club, established in the early 1980s to promote the reading and sale of Welsh books amongst children aged between seven and eleven. The club has proved to be extremely effective; during 1994/95, 23,518 items worth £61,545 were sold through 424 schools.[55] Another major marketing scheme administered by the Welsh Books Council is that to primary schools, which combines personal visits to advise teachers and termly mailings of appropriate posters and leaflets. During the two years 1994-95 a total of 1,596 school visits were conducted and orders worth £256,081 were received.[56]

One aspect of marketing, distribution, witnessed the first attempt to bring an element of professionalism into the book industry when the Welsh Books Centre was established in 1966 with the aim of centralizing book ordering and book distribution for the mutual benefit of publishers and booksellers. Today, the Distribution Centre (as it is now called) is housed in a substantial industrial unit near Aberystwyth and boasts annual sales of over £3 million.[57]

The final link in bringing the author and book buyer together is the retail bookseller. My childhood recollections of the late 1940s and early 1950s illustrates the very low ebb Welsh bookselling had reached at that time: I never once saw a new Welsh book displayed in any shop in Mold, the birthplace of the best-known Welsh novelist, Daniel Owen. This experience would have been shared by children of my generation in most towns in Wales. From the late 1960s onwards the marked improvement in the number and quality of Welsh books published and the ease with which books could be ordered following the establishment of the Welsh Books Centre encouraged language enthusiasts to set up shops in several Welsh towns. Although these shops generally call themselves 'Welsh bookshops', on average only some 36% of their takings come from selling Welsh books, an almost equal share being derived from the sale of records, cards, and various craft items.[58] This comparatively low proportion of book-derived income has prompted bodies such as the Welsh Arts Council and the Welsh Books Council to introduce a range of initiatives designed to encourage these 'Welsh bookshops' to improve their stock of books.[59] Whatever their shortcomings, these shops are now responsible for selling 64% of all Welsh books purchased, as well as offering a wide range of promotional services such as displays, book launches, and book sales.[60]

An analysis of the categories of books published in recent years shows that much of the output is determined by the official subsidy available. The best example of this has been the improvement in children's and school books. In 1972, when only the WJEC schemes supported this area, no more than seventy-three titles were produced (37% of the total for that year),[61] and these reflected 'the standards and objectives of the educationalists who play so essential a part in producing them'.[62] Later in the decade there was a move to improve their quantity and quality. Roger Boore, founder in 1970 of Gwasg y Dref Wen, an imprint which specialized in adapting some of the finest picture books published in other languages, went so far as to claim that the chief responsibility of minority-language publishers was to provide books for children and young people of a quality equal to the best available in the corresponding majority language: 'We want our Welshness to be a privilege for our children not a burden. Therefore they must be free to decide which books they wish to read — and select Welsh books from choice.'[63] Despite his efforts, there remained an urgent need to improve both the range and quality of books for children and young people since only the more enterprising publishers were willing to take a risk while there was no subsidy available. The Welsh Arts Council decision to include children's literature in its remit and the extension of the government grant to include children's leisure books had brought about a marked change by the end of the 1970s. The Welsh Arts Council, for example, financed a number of expensive illustrated volumes such as *Y Mabinogi, Culwch ac Olwen*, and also several standard anthologies which would not have been feasible under the WJEC schemes. The government grant was used to support a large number of popular books for children and teenagers, including a number of highly successful series such as 'Cyfres Corryn' and 'Cyfres yr Arddegau'.[64] Also by the early 1980s the WJEC's Textbook Scheme was proving to be inadequate to meet the growing demand from schools. The Welsh Office agreed to provide substantial funding towards the development and production of textbooks to meet this need and has been responsible for a very large number of titles produced to support the teaching of subjects such as geography, history, mathematics, and religious studies in the Welsh language. By 1995 the responsibility for commissioning Welsh learning materials had been transferred to the newly formed Curriculum and Assessment Authority for Wales which subsequently announced that it was investing £2,000,000 over two years in order to extend 'the range of educational opportunity through the medium of Welsh, and develop Welsh-specific aspects of the curriculum, the curriculum Cymreig'.[65] As a result of all these schemes, as well as the increased output there has been a huge improvement in the visual impact of most of these books. Admittedly, many benefited from international co-production. The improved conditions also helped produce a renaissance of children's and young people's writing thanks to the contribution of authors such as T. Llew Jones, J. Selwyn Lloyd, Irma Chilton, Angharad Tomos, Gwenneth Lilly and Gwenno Hywyn, and Penri Jones.

The provision of popular books for adults still remains unsatisfactory despite various schemes designed to increase the number of titles published. By the late 1970s, over fifteen years after the Welsh Books Council had been established primarily to promote popular books, the need for category fiction such as detective stories, thrillers, romantic novels, and westerns remained as urgent as ever.[66] A survey carried out in 1978 showed that readers generally preferred such undemanding fiction to 'modern' or psychological novels and stories,[67] but despite this finding there has been only a modest improvement during the past decade. On average, fewer than twenty new fiction titles for adults a year were published between mid-1984 and mid-1993. Although Kate Roberts, the most distinguished of all twentieth-century Welsh fiction writers, continued to produce novels and short stories throughout the 1960s and 1970s, the two most popular novelists — T. Rowland Hughes and Islwyn Ffowc Elis — had published their best novels during the 1950s. Few outstanding authors for adults emerged to take their place, the most notable being Marion Eames, Eigra Lewis Roberts, and Alun Jones. In recent years many Welsh writers have turned their attention to psychological novels. Caradog Prichard's semi-autobiographical *Un Nos ola' Leuad* (available in English translation as *One moonlight night*) is generally acknowledged to be the Welsh fiction masterpiece of the century, and younger writers such as Robin Llywelyn are establishing new dimensions to Welsh fiction. Since works such as these present a considerable challenge to the general reader, the Welsh Books Council has set up a number of schemes in co-operation with several publishers to address the problem of an insufficient supply of less-demanding category fiction by organizing author workshops, supporting adaptations of popular fiction from other languages, and by commissioning a series of romances, Cyfres Y Fodrwy (The Ring Series) and of detective stories and thrillers, Cyfres Datrys a Dirgelwch (Detection and Mystery Series).

The traditional subject areas for Welsh books, such as poetry, Welsh history and traditions, and linguistic and literary studies, have prospered. The range of literary criticism and literary history books published in recent years has been dependent on the generous production grants offered by the Welsh Arts Council as well as the popularity of Welsh literature as a school and university subject. As a result of the continued decline in chapel and church membership during the second half of the century and the inexorable secularization of the traditional Welsh Sunday, the religious books which had dominated Welsh-language publishing for four centuries lost ground from the 1960s onwards. Unfortunately the supply of books in those subject areas poorly represented during the first half of the century — science and technology, sociology, politics, and economics — has shown little, if any, improvement. Despite notable exceptions such as *Y Bywgraffiadur Cymreig* (*The Dictionary of Welsh Biography*), *Cydymaith i Lenyddiaeth Cymru* (*The Companion to the Literature of Wales*), *Geiriadur Prifysgol Cymru* (The University of Wales Dictionary of Welsh), and *Geiriadur yr Academi* (*The Welsh Academy English-Welsh Dictionary*), there is also a marked shortage of standard reference works in the Welsh language.

Today, despite the precarious state of the language, more Welsh books are being written and published than ever before. In recent years children's and school books have become the dominant feature of the Welsh book market; in 1993 no fewer than 369 titles (67% of all new titles produced) were aimed at this sector.[68] To have overcome the mid-century crisis and achieve such a high level of production is a very considerable accomplishment. But the main factor in this success has been the structure of state support which has evolved since the mid-1950s. As David Fanning has pointed out, this is not without its dangers:

> While mostly welcome — and frequently the deciding factor in whether or not a particular book is published — state subvention is an unreliable resource, subject to the whims of government and to the literary preferences of grant-making committees and referees. Too great a dependence on public sector assistance is an unwise strategy; without it several firms would not survive.[69]

Although Fanning's fears — which echo those of the Ready report — are far from groundless, the reality is that the industry's only hope of survival is through continued state subsidy. The greatest threat to the future of the Welsh book is no longer the economics of publishing but the continued decline of the language itself and the relentless competition provided by new global media.

NOTES TO CHAPTER 29

1. Home Office, *Report of the committee on Welsh language publishing* (London, 1952), p. ii.
2. *Report of the committee on Welsh language publishing*, p. 1.
3. Council for Wales and Monmouthshire, *Report on the Welsh language today* (London, 1963), pp. 131-2.
4. John Davies, *Hanes Cymru* (Harmondsworth, 1990), p. 482.
5. Board of Education, *Welsh in education and life* (London, 1927), p. 178.
6. William Williams, 'Welsh books', *Welsh Outlook*, 20 (1933), 129-31 (p. 129); *Welsh in education and life*, p. 179.
7. Kenneth O. Morgan, *Rebirth of a nation: Wales 1880-1980* (Oxford, 1981), pp. 198-201.
8. Arthur ap Gwynn, 'Modern Welsh books from the point of view of the reader and librarian', *Report of the proceedings of the eighth conference of library authorities in Wales and Monmouthshire* (Aberystwyth, 1933), p. 46.
9. Williams, pp. 129-31.
10. Figures here and below from Williams, pp. 129-31.
11. Morgan, pp. 230-1.
12. E. Prosser Rhys, 'Ledled Cymru', *Baner ac Amserau Cymru*, 23 Feb. 1937.
13. Rhisiart Hincks, *E. Prosser Rhys 1901-1945* (Llandysul, 1980), p. 178.
14. E. Prosser Rhys, 'Ledled Cymru', *Baner ac Amserau Cymru*, 9 March 1937.
15. For further details see Gwilym Huws, 'Llyfrau'r Dryw', *Llais Llyfrau / Book News from Wales*, Winter 1990, pp. 4-5.
16. *Welsh in education and life*, p. 179.
17. Ibid., p. 313.
18. Gwennant Davies, *The story of the Urdd (The Welsh League of Youth) 1922-1972* (Aberystwyth, 1973), pp. 112-13.
19. *Report of the committee on Welsh language publishing*, p. 1.
20. Ibid., pp. 2-3.
21. Ibid., p. 5.
22. *Report on the Welsh language today*, p. 67.
23. Ibid., p. 147.
24. Council for the Welsh Language, *Publishing in the Welsh language* (Cardiff, 1978), p. 80.
25. Welsh Books Council, *Annual report 1994/1995* (Aberystwyth, 1995), p. 36.
26. *Report on the Welsh language today*, p. 67.
27. Welsh Books Council, *Annual report 1994/1995*, p. 24.
28. Alun R. Edwards, *Yr hedyn mwstard: atgofion* (Llandysul, 1980), pp. 48-50.
29. Ministry of Education, *The structure of public library services in England and Wales* (London, 1959), p. 24.
30. Ministry of Education, *Standards of public library services in England and Wales* (London, 1961), pp. 61-2.
31. Alun Creunant Davies, 'Alun R. Edwards: the pioneer,' *Llais Llyfrau / Book News from Wales*, Autumn 1986, pp. 3-4 (p. 3).
32. Welsh Books Council, *Constitution* ([Aberystwyth], [1962]), p. 1.
33. See for example Welsh Books Council, *Annual report 1968-69* (Aberystwyth, 1969), p. 6.
34. *Report of the committee on Welsh language publishing*, p. 3.
35. Jac L. Williams, 'The Welsh language in education,' in *The Welsh language today*, ed. Meic Stephens, (Llandysul, 1973), pp. 92-109 (p. 101).
36. *Report on the Welsh language today*, p.101.
37. *Report of the committee on Welsh language publishing*, p. 5.
38. *Report on the Welsh language today*, p. 67.
39. *Publishing in the Welsh language*, p. 68.
40. Welsh Books Council, *Analysis of Welsh language books 1972-93* (Aberystwyth, 1994).

[41] *Publishing in the Welsh language*, p. 80.
[42] Welsh Books Council, *Grant Cyhoeddi 1981/82* ([Aberystwyth], 1981), pp. 2-3.
[43] Roger Boore, 'Y Cyngor Llyfrau Cymraeg a grant y llywodraeth: sensoriaeth, unffurfiaeth a gwladoli'r diwydiant cyhoeddi,' *Barn*, 219 (April 1981), 162.
[44] Welsh Arts Council, *Annual report 1976/77* (Cardiff, 1976), p. 30.
[45] Welsh Books Council, *Annual report 1988/89* (Aberystwyth, 1989), p. 12.
[46] Welsh Books Council, *Annual report 1994/1995* (Aberystwyth, 1995), p. 8.
[47] R. Gerallt Jones, 'The Welsh writer and his books,' in *The Welsh language today*, pp. 127-47 (p. 135).
[48] Welsh Arts Council, *The first seven years: a review of the work of the Literature Committee* (Cardiff, 1974), Appendix ii.
[49] *The first seven years*, p. 16.
[50] Jones, p. 136.
[51] Welsh Books Council, Market Research Working Party, *The book trade in Wales* ([Aberystwyth], 1988), p. 139.
[52] *Book trade in Wales*, p. 276.
[53] Welsh Arts Council, *Annual report 1970/71* (Cardiff, 1971),
[54] Welsh Books Council, *Annual report 1992/1993* (Aberystwyth, 1993), p. 14.
[55] Welsh Books Council, *Annual report 1994/1995* (Aberystwyth, 1995), p. 15.
[56] *Ibid.*, p. 18.
[57] Welsh Books Council, *Annual report 1996/1997* (Aberystwyth, 1998), p. 3.
[58] *Book trade in Wales*, p. 196.
[59] Welsh Arts Council, *Annual report 1977/78* (Cardiff, 1978), p. 35.
[60] *Book trade in Wales*, p. 200.
[61] Welsh Books Council, *Analysis of Welsh language books 1972-1993* (Aberystwyth, 1994).
[62] *Publishing in the Welsh language*, p. 61.
[63] Roger Boore, *Llyfrau plant mewn ieithoedd lleiafrifol* ([Cardiff], 1978), pp. 6-7.
[64] For a fuller account of improvements to children's and school books during the 1970s and early 1980s see D. Geraint Lewis, 'The quiet revolution', *Dragon's Tale*, 1 (1984), 8-11.
[65] Curriculum and Assessment Authority for Wales, *Newsletter*, 3 (June 1995), 1.
[66] *Publishing in the Welsh language*, p. 75.
[67] Full details of the survey can be found in Appendix 5 (pp. 88-97) of *Publishing in the Welsh language*.
[68] *Analysis of Welsh language books 1972-1993*.
[69] David Fanning, 'Publishing in Wales: challenging tradition and language', *British Book News*, Nov. 1991, pp. 728-33 (p. 728).

CHAPTER 30

ANGLO-WELSH LITERATURE

John Harris

FOR the historian of the book trade, Anglo-Welsh literature begins with Allen Raine (1836-1908): the first Welsh author to sell a million, to employ an agent, to have her work filmed, to live comfortably by her fiction. At sixty years of age she ventured into Hutchinson's with *Myfanwy*, a novel of Cardiganshire life. Her reception was lukewarm — 'the firm had received no stories about this part of the country before' — but they promised to read the manuscript for a fee and within forty-eight hours had telegrammed acceptance.[1] Adaliza Puddicombe became Allen Raine and *A Welsh Singer* (the retitled novel) appeared in September 1897. The house of Hutchinson, riding the nineties fiction boom, was equipped to exploit her appeal: a Welsh kailyard perhaps; wholesome romantic fiction with a new Celtic flavour. They pushed Raine forward in a variety of editions, most of all the sixpenny paperback with brightly illustrated covers. One such copy, fished up from a servant's trunk, transported the young Emlyn Williams ('I never dreamt of connecting [it] with the Welsh world around me').[2] Many others were captivated, as tabulated sales against her title-pages confirm: over two million copies by 1911, with individual titles exceeding 250,000. Hers was the bestseller's path: a regular output of novels commanding subsidiary rights — overseas editions, the occasional translation (into Welsh in 1983), magazine serialization, film rights.

Things are different for poets, though W. H. Davies's response to his rejection slips is the stuff of myth. Desperately poor, he raised £30 to print privately *The Soul's Destroyer, and Other Poems* (1905); 'Of the Author, Farmhouse, Marshalsea Road, S.E. 2/6d' as the imprint puts it, naming the London doss-house where Davies then lived. 'Old bloke', said Caradoc Evans, 'you've got wood for a leg and wonder in your eyes, but you're no simp'.[3] True enough. Davies posted copies to well-known literary people with an invitation to purchase. The book was duly noticed and Davies, a gift to publicists, found fame as the 'tramp-poet'. Thereafter he lived modestly by his writing, from 1921 under the wing of Jonathan Cape who had bought the Fifield list, with the bulk of Davies's poetry and the coveted *Autobiography of a Super-tramp* (still a heavy seller). Cape served Davies well, reassembling the corpus in numerous collected editions. His Welshness was never trumpeted, though like his compatriots he set great store by the sound of poetry. And some at least thought the description 'nature poet' unwarranted: 'The emotion is a kind of nostalgia, a harking back to the morning of life, of time, the lost realm of innocence, where everything is wonder, and nothing is knowledge.' The words of Richard Church,[4] Dylan Thomas's editor, touch an Anglo-Welsh emotion.

Davies was contracted to Andrew Melrose for a prose book on Wales when he met Caradoc Evans (1878-1945) and might well have suggested Melrose to him as a suitable publisher for *My People* (1915). Evans's own beginnings as author are more typically Anglo-Welsh. Publication in the *English Review* put him in the camp of literary fiction and he also dealt in short stories, an Anglo-Welsh speciality though a blight in publishing terms. Melrose had worked with George Douglas Brown, whose counterblast to kailyard imaginings gave the publisher a line on *My People*.[5] Melrose accepted the collection but with safeguards. A jacket must be prepared explaining that *My People* though 'not meat for babes', was justified by its realism and reforming intention. In the uproar that followed, Melrose stuck by Evans, alerting the Society of Authors to police harassment of Cardiff booksellers and stressing the warning he had given. 'Such were the conditions under which I published *My People*, and I can only say that if the decision were to be taken again it would not be altered.'[6] His loyalty was overstretched by *My Neighbours* (1920), two stories from which upset him. Evans withdrew them, knowing where responsibility in these matters rested;

> Listen to the counsel of editors, remembering always that they are the distributors and you only the lowly manufacturers [...] It is better to discover the secret of the things the magazines print than to stand forlornly in the by-ways of poverty shouting: 'My art is not for sale'.[7]

Evans avoided the by ways himself through work as Fleet Street journalist; it gave him the means to write short stories and to place them where their impact would be greatest, in predominantly non-literary journals.

Combining writing with a full-time job was a favoured Anglo-Welsh position, though residence in London was not deemed necessary for success. By temperament and persuasion the Anglo-Welsh are natives rather than exiles. Even so, the visibility of Caradoc Evans owed much to his Fleet Street contacts, and for Rhys Davies (1903-78), determined to live by his writing, London was the place to be. He knew the precarious edge of publishing, a world of little magazines, limited editions, and shaky enterprises like Holden's, publishers of *The Withered Root* (1927). There were dangers for a man with a living to earn — 'I shall have to make my next [novel] more popular in theme. I mustn't get the reputation of being unsaleable' — and one solid publisher would help ('I don't want my books to be here, there and everywhere').[8] Rejection from mainstream publishers he softened with Lawrence's talk of their irremediably timidity — 'too bloody English for me', as Davies said of Chatto. By 1932 Putnam's had taken him on as a writer able to disclose 'lonely lost valleys among the Welsh hills' with (they used C. Day Lewis's words) a 'Welsh turbulence of spirit, the exaggeration, the darts into fantasy, the slyness and obliqueness [...] all [helping] to create a personal style not to be imitated by the mass-fiction factories'. A flow of much-praised fiction proved insufficient to secure Rhys Davies financially. 'Thank God for America for a struggling writer then', he reflected, remembering how a generous Harcourt, Brace advance on his second novel had helped him move to France. Crucially he lacked his 'badge book', a popular novel by which he could be identified (only with *The Black Venus* did he go into paperback). Davies probed reasons for this: a prejudice against Welsh novels; his loyalty to the despised short story, the inappropriateness of high-paying society magazines for his own particular work. 'I can't see my Welsh stories among the glossy "kept" girls & elegant young men & stout stockbrokers handing out strings of pearls.'[9]

Other authors sensed a prejudice against Welsh fiction, though more in the minds of publishers than those of readers. Davies overheard the comment 'I can't bear novels about Wales' in a London bookshop,[10] and a bookshop report on *How Green Was My*

Valley confirmed a bias against Welsh books that Llewellyn's novel had to overcome. It is true that regional writing of any kind sets up resistance in some quarters (especially if dialect is prominent), though clearly not in all. For Davies in 1936 'the *gloom* associated with Welsh mining life' had become a liability; perhaps 'a novel of Welsh middle-class life written in a low-pitched Trollopian key' would stand more chance.[11] Wales could be fictionally worked in other ways, most naturally through pastoral romance (with varying degrees of bitterness): the abiding rural Wales with its centuries-old traditions and imagination. For the beginner Geraint Goodwin (1903-41) it seemed to demand pouring one's material into pre-existing fictional moulds. English readers demanded distortion — diverting bits and pieces, never the complex whole. How rigid were publishers' requirements, and how readily authors complied with them, are unanswerable questions but the image persists of Anglo-Welsh authors dancing to alien tunes. So R. S. Thomas, publishing in Carmarthen, could deplore those who sold 'stagey presentations of their countrymen to English capitalist publishers'.[12]

Goodwin (like Thomas) found his English publisher in Jonathan Cape. With his eye for regional writers, Cape's editor, Edward Garnett saw enough in Goodwin to warrant a three-book contract. *Call Back Yesterday* (1935) seemed to confirm his judgement: 'the kind of book', wrote Cyril Connolly, 'almost always rejected by publishers on the grounds of brevity and lack of general interest. Such refusals to conform to type widen exhilaratingly the scope of fiction.'[13] The challenge now became to coax a full-fledged novel out of Goodwin, and Garnett, adept at turning literary fiction into marketable products, made clear what was wanted:

> the chief characters in the chosen environment [...] should then possess your mind & work in your imagination till you want to put pen to paper. Better a few strongly or deeply drawn characters, clashing, than too many figures. And the environment should be ancestral, to give the feeling of roots deep in the Welsh soil [...] *Your course is perfectly clear now* [...] What you have got to do is to *be the* Welsh novelist-recorder & -narrator of the *popular* Welsh life — *as you know it*.[14]

The outcome was *The Heyday in the Blood* (1936), dedicated to Garnett who had suggested the novel's ending. Goodwin had here experienced creative editing; more painfully, he came to learn that, whatever an author's intention, it is readers who make meaning, and that for an influential body of readers in Wales any English-language novel less than adulatory of Welsh rural life was unsupportable. To the *Western Mail*, *The Heyday in the Blood* was 'sport for the Philistine' in the vein of Caradoc Evans. An injured Goodwin rallied with talk of the 'living talents in Wales [...] slaughtered by neglect and embittered by abuse, this jeering from the sidelines'.[15] Young writers needed encouragement and this Edward Garnett had given him ('you have no idea what your help means to a young man not yet sure of himself').

Other novelists were annexing their portions of rural Wales. 'I know this life more intimately than any other', said Hilda Vaughan (1892-1985) of the Brecon and Radnor farming communities, 'and I am anxious to record the old ways and types which are fast vanishing before the levelling influences of universal education, easy transportation, and wireless.'[16] It was a role much espoused by Anglo-Welsh novelists, ascribing their imaginative leaps to solid springboards of fact. Vaughan leapt higher than most, and for three major publishers. Her first Gollancz book, *The Soldier and the Gentlewoman* (1932), caught a larger public. Quickly Bernhard Tauchnitz re-issued it — not the first Anglo-Welsh novel to make his Leipzig list (Richard Hughes's *A High Wind in Jamaica* had already done so) — and three Tauchnitz titles gave Vaughan an international reputation.

The flowering of Anglo-Welsh literature has been many times described: first books by Dylan Thomas (1934), Jack Jones (1934), Gwyn Jones (1935), Glyn, David, and Lewis Jones (all in 1937), Idris Davies (1938), and Richard Llewellyn (1939), to join Caradoc Evans, Rhys Davies, Hilda Vaughan, Richard Hughes, Geraint Goodwin and others. It was part of a growth in fiction which helped the publishing industry withstand the slump and to which regional fiction most certainly contributed: whatever the specifics of Wales, a distinctiveness of setting caught the attention of fiction editors. Jack Jones (1884-1970) understood the requirement and his own particular role: the mining communities of South Wales needed someone to reveal their worth to the world. A miner himself for thirty years, Jones came to prominence with *Rhondda Roundabout* (1934), a well-received Faber novel. *Unfinished Journey* (1937) — 'a blazingly honest and vivid picture of a period, a class and a man', wrote J. B. Priestley — signalled a move to Hamish Hamilton, the publisher who became a close friend and adviser. He urged that Jones curb his plots and his prose: the 'generations novel' might vivify history but it encouraged a sprawling, inflated narrative. Even after pruning, Jones's novels remain epics, freely inventive and with arresting titles: *River out of Eden* (1951) gave the *Herald of Wales* a thirty-nine-part serial and as a two-volume Corgi reprint (1970) sold 60,000 copies in eight years. The requirement for shorter novels led a string of books whose failure struck Jones as the consequence of a too drastically curbed afflatus: 'Yes, I should have let it rip, let it *all* come out in the washing, as it did in my first half-dozen novels'.[17] To a London-Welsh bookseller the appeal of Jack the ripper was obvious:[18]

> With all its atrocious Welsh, its anachronisms, its irritating Jackesque talk in the mouths of all and sundry, its repetitious & dogmatic ramblings, *Off to Philadelphia* is a pulsating stirring human story.

The man was a genre in himself — which one might say of every genuine writer. And 'every genuine writer finds his own Wales', as Rhys Davies put it, addressing the perennial question of the writer's relationship to his material.[19]

> What *is* the real Wales? Every genuine writer finds his own Wales. I don't ask people to accept my picture of Wales as the real one; it is inevitable that as people differ in temperament, in views, in beliefs, many should reject my picture of their country, should find certain elements exaggerated, others omitted. A piece of writing is mainly a sort of flowering, a fulfilment of oneself.

If the life of the book is between its covers, publishers believed that the industrial novel was best vitalized through autobiography and family history. 'You are apt to philosophise a bit too much, and to make an essay of what should be a vivid and passionate "self-story" to be most effective' explained Hamish Hamilton when rejecting Idris Davies's 'Collier Boy'.[20] What might he have made of Lewis Jones's *We Live*? — about which the *New Statesman* commented; 'Were his book dealing with a London suburb or an American slum it would deserve no more than an honourable mention. As it is, the subject lends a vitality the treatment lacks'.[21] But here the choice of publisher could never have been in doubt: Lawrence & Wishart were the publishing arm of the British Communist Party and their Lewis Jones editions project not a novelist or miner-turned-novelist but a worker whose writings were intrinsic to the revolutionary struggle, 'written during odd moments stolen from mass meetings, committees, demonstrations, marches, and other activities'.[22] At forty-two Jones lay dead in a Cardiff bedsit following a January day in the Rhondda appealing for food for Spain (some thirty meetings addressed from a motor-van). As the dust-jacket of *We Live* proclaimed, 'if proletarian literature has any meaning, here is the real thing'.

Six months later, in October 1939, came Richard Llewellyn's *How Green Was My Valley*. Why the world should take possession of a novel set in a Welsh mining valley in the years before 1910 is something of a mystery. It is about other elemental things of course, this 'vivid and passionate self-story': childhood as Eden and the lost Golden Age; the bonding with family, with community and nation. Author and publisher de-localized the setting so as to draw out an age-old pastoral dimension. 'It covers a period', Michael Joseph's publicity explained, 'when South Wales prospered, and coal dust had not blackened the greenness of the valley. It is not an industrial or "proletarian" novel.' Joseph suggested the sudden cut-off ending and seemingly chose the title for its 'nostalgic and biblical connotation'. The first printing he set at a staggering 25,000 — first novels did well to sell 2,000 copies — and though launched three weeks after the outbreak of war, Llewellyn's novel sold a thousand copies a week to the end of 1941, and went through twenty-eight impressions in five years.[23] Its sales pattern confirms an archetypal best-seller, initially a fast-seller which moderates into a continuous appreciable demand. Subsidiary rights are always important in a publisher's reckoning and here the £6,600 won from Macmillan's of New York helped establish Michael Joseph Ltd after the break from Gollancz. As national boundaries are transcended (translations into more than twenty languages), so is the printed page. Besides the film of 1941, *How Green* became a radio play, a musical, and later a television mini-series. All this made Llewellyn a wealthy man: for his second novel he got an advance of £1,250, with an option on his next four books at not less than £1,000 each, at a time when one might live comfortably on £5 a week. Henceforth his circuit would be metropolitan and international, the sights set immediately on Hollywood.

It was a far cry from the modest commercial prospects of Anglo-Welsh letters. The worlds overlap in Dylan Thomas, a writer who still enjoys two readerships, one popular, one specialist, and whose *Under Milk Wood* (1954) gave Dent its most prolific title and the world another icon of 'Welshness'. Publication in the *Sunday Referee* led directly to Thomas's first book, *Eighteen Poems* (1934), largely financed by David Archer. He, as Richard Church makes clear, 'has the distinction of being the discoverer of Dylan Thomas. That should be universally recorded.'[24] It was to Church that Thomas next went, though the editor at Dent's could barely conceal the strangeness of Thomas's writing to his own traditionalist taste — 'It smelled of despair and the perverseness of nerves and senses that go with despair. But to be disturbed by a poet's work means that there must be something in it.' He urged that Thomas become more accessible, purging needless obscurity. Thomas could not be moved, so that the success of *Twenty-five Poems*, (3,000 copies sold, following publication in 1936), both surprised and embarrassed the editor.

The Map of Love (1939), a mixed poetry-and-prose collection, shows give-and-take on both sides, Church famously vetoing 'A Prospect of the Sea' and setting an order for the stories which Thomas wisely resisted. Church found a title for the book and lavished extra care on its design. The choice of frontispiece was inspired. The Augustus John portrait caught Dylan as Church first saw him, 'ripe, mulberry lips, large eloquent brown eyes [...] and a hyacinthine cluster of warm brown curls'.[25] It became a defining image and the dust-jacket twice announces it, alongside tactful talk of the poet's 'considerable advance out of his past obscurity — an obscurity quite necessary to his development — into a new clarity of vision and expression'. For wrapper quotes, Thomas had advocated an American opinion ('his poetry is verbal sculpture') and, most revealingly, Desmond Hawkins: 'He is neither English nor American, he is not in the ordinary sense a political poet, and he has avoided the universities.' Hawkins was edged out by Edith Sitwell, whose *Sunday Times* notice of *Twenty-five Poems* Church reckoned had done much to promote that book, and which he now blazoned across the cover of the second Dent collection. This time the magic failed. The real breakthrough came with *Deaths and Entrances* (1946), irresistible in its mini-format; as Robert Herring remarked, 'It has replaced the Temple Shakespeare as a book to go round with in one's pocket, and I can't say more than that!'[26] Inside, the diamonds and triangles of 'Vision and Prayer' command attention, a poem sent to the publishers as it had appeared in the *Sewanee Review* ('I do hope, & beg, that the poem will be printed in the book just as it is in the magazine').[27] Setting *Deaths and Entrances* caused difficulties, Thomas drastically reshaping the collection in proof. It appeared belatedly in February 1946 in a run of 3,000; a month later a similar reprint was called for. To his publishers, nevertheless, Thomas remained an artist who rarely capitalized upon his talents, particularly as a prose writer. That his earnings were high his biographers agree, but how high, at what times, and from what sources (publishing, broadcasting, film scripts), remain matters of dispute.

Coterminously with Thomas at Swansea, Glyn Jones (1905-95) was beginning in Cardiff. He has described the 'vast cultural moonscape of nothing and nobody' that was Wales for English-language writers at this period — no publishers, no magazines, no other writers to talk to.[28] The *Dublin Magazine* gave a focus of sorts, publishing Glyn Jones, R. S. Thomas (b. 1913), and Alun Lewis (1915-44). Lewis had first appeared in the *Western Mail*, a newspaper regularly passed over in surveys of Anglo-Welsh literature (largely, one suspects, on account of its Tory politics and hostility to particular writers). Conceived as the 'national daily' of Wales, the importance of the *Western Mail* lies less in the creative writing it published than in its hospitality to literary debate, its features and correspondence columns serving as a cultural forum open to every viewpoint. In 1933 the combative young journalist Glyn Roberts began a series of articles on the Anglo-Welsh (their first extended exposure), then proceeded to spread the message in English literary periodicals.

By the end of the 1930s Wales possessed two literary periodicals of its own. *Wales*, 'the militant journal of the Welsh literary renaissance', was launched in 1937, brainchild of the young Keidrych Rhys(1915-87). He set about the enterprise with confidence (and a little private money), suggesting to Vernon Watkins that 'behind my bovine mask and tender years I might know more things about Poetry than most'.[29] Rhys had a wider social mission, no less than to raise the national consciousness of a new generation of writers: 'Though we write in English, we are rooted in Wales', as his machine-gun manifesto puts it. 'A really grand idea' thought Dylan Thomas — of a literary magazine, that is; like other writers canvassed he had doubts as to the politics.[30] The presence of Thomas and his followers guaranteed an impact, though it struck some as at odds with the populist avowals. 'Can we speak of ourselves as rooted in Wales when so much of the *idiom* in which *Wales* is written is that of contemporary English letters of the most fashionable and Bloomsbury kind?' asked Goronwy Rees at the *Spectator* (conceding an admiration for the enterprise). Controversy clung to Rhys, seeking a unity of writers around literary modernism and nationalist politics. He needed his establishment enemies and found them readily enough in Welsh-language circles. But Rhys had more pressing problems. The financial risks he had understood, telling Dylan Thomas that a half-dozen issues made a realistic initial target, but after just three numbers — the magazine was designed as a quarterly — it seemed that *Wales* might close. By June 1939 matters had worsened. 'Certainly I can't afford to make a sacrifice — financial or otherwise', Rhys wrote to Vernon Watkins, 'now that there's an alternative publication, especially when I get so many kicks in the pants.'[31]

If *Wales* was the archetypal little magazine ('slim, fresh, provocative and very attractive' thought Idris Davies),[32] the 'alternative publication' belonged to a different tradition. The monthly *Welsh Review*, begun in February 1939 by Gwyn Jones (b. 1907), Gollancz novelist and university lecturer, was a broadly based cultural journal promising substance and stability — subscribers could even convert loose issues into bound volumes. Its format breathed amplitude and taste, a large quarto with woodcuts which, if they now seem backward-looking, were widely admired. Jones's challenges were those of every literary editor: balancing the creative and the critical, working up new features (he drew on broadcast talks), and establishing a distinctive editorial voice ('shrewd and wise and nicely bitter', thought one reader). Above all was the need to survive. As Keidrych Rhys saw it, the *Welsh Review* would tap a different market from *Wales* ('I hope so, for your sake' concludes his note to Gwyn Jones).[33]

For all the talk of a renaissance, Jones (like Keidrych Rhys) had doubts from the start about the readership for a magazine of Wales. A monthly, too, required tremendous financial resources but with promises from Creighton Griffiths, a magnanimous Cardiff businessman, he embarked upon the venture. Bulk orders from W. H. Smith (780 copies) encouraged a print run of 1,050, but when shop sales failed to materialize the journal ran into difficulties. By November 1939 the decision had been taken to close, 'owing to the state of the Company's finances'. The point has been obscured in discussions of *Wales* and the *Welsh Review*, that whatever the eventual impact of war (and both were revived in wartime), the magazines ran into immediate money problems and lacked sufficient readers. Yet in their first manifestations (nine issues of *Wales*, ten of the *Welsh Review*), they became productive rallying points. Glyn Jones testifies to the impact:

One could now believe in the existence of other writers, and even correspond with them, and if one was fortified sufficiently against disillusion, one could actually meet and get to know them personally. One could also read their work and compare it with one's own and come to some opinion about it.[34]

For Harri Webb (1920-94), Keidrych Rhys (briefly his employer) had created 'almost single-handed, a sense of community among English-language writers in Wales'.[35] Others would acknowledge Gwyn Jones. Editor, anthologist, lecturer, journalist, broadcaster, he promoted fellow Welsh writers with a selflessness uncommon in literary practitioners: but it is noticeable how many figures of this period combine creative writing with critical support for their contemporaries and an extraordinary commitment to the idea of the Anglo-Welsh.

The war affected the book trade in unexpected ways. You could sell anything which could be called a book, remembers Leonard Woolf of Hogarth Press. Yet the reading boom could not be fully exploited because a shortage of materials and labour restricted edition sizes and the growth in new titles. Periodicals too were affected. Although paper restrictions meant slimmed-down magazines and a crowding out of fiction, new outlets appeared in the form of anthologies and book-magazines. 'The best way [...] was to fill them with short stories', said Aled Vaughan, editing his own Celtic collection, 'pieces which in length at least suited the restless mood of a mobile population.'[36] More than most, the Anglo-Welsh benefited from this situation, being continuously represented in the titles edited from Llansanffraid by Reginald Moore (*Modern Reading*, *Stories of the Forties*), in the *English Story* annuals of Woodrow Wyatt, and in compilations by Denys Val Baker and Edward J. O'Brien. Exposure could be widespread, *Modern Reading* as a ninepenny Big Ben paperback selling nearly 150,000 copies. Meanwhile *Life and Letters Today* sailed on, always receptive under Robert Herring to Anglo-Welsh poetry and prose (Robert Herring Williams was himself of Welsh descent). In 1929 it had printed *A High Wind in Jamaica* and throughout the 1940s published special Welsh numbers.

This kind of exposure naturally attracted publishers, a Cape representative calling before the war on Glyn Jones at Cardiff. *The Blue Bed* (1937) was the outcome, a much-praised short-story collection which happened to carry the first commissioned Hans Aufseeser dust-jacket. In gouache on black paper, using colour and calligraphic lettering, Aufseeser's designs came to typify Cape's high standards of production. It was Glyn Jones's opinion, on the evidence of *Welsh Short Stories* (Faber, 1937) and *Welsh Short Stories* (Penguin, 1941), that publishers were more likely to risk short-story anthologies than collections by individual writers. Warnings against short stories are indeed legion, though to Rhys Davies this was 'sheer obstinate publishers' tradition & prejudice [...] they just *won't* fight for them. Don't abandon short stories, however disheartening it is about publication — I've been, & am still, in that struggle.'[37]

Gwyn Jones, recipient of this advice, enjoyed the non-professional's freedom to move between genres at will; and 'it is undoubtedly much easier for a man with a job to write short stories than novels'.[38] As novelist too he moved swiftly from an acclaimed epic on the life of Richard Savage to *Times Like These* (1936), his restrained personal testament to the 'dreadful heroic struggle I saw all around me [...] in the valleys. It was reportage, not invention [...] the exact opposite of the historical novel.' Jones published four short-story collections, and whatever the publishing wisdom, he was decidedly not alone. Idris Davies's opinion, 'The pearls of the "Anglo-Welsh" movement are its short stories'[39] was widely shared, H. E. Bates claiming that Welsh writers of the forties were in a position radically to influence the direction of the English short story.

For poets, as for short-story writers, commercial prospects were bleak. At Faber's it was accepted that certain categories of literature were published outside the ordinary economic rules: even David Jones's *In Parenthesis*, 'dripping with critical praise', sold just 1,500 copies on its publication in 1937 (with a reprint of 1,000). Vernon Watkins similarly was viewed as a long-term investment, Faber confirming how 'extremely anxious' they were to go on publishing him. Anxiety of a different kind surrounded Watkins's choice of title for his first collection, *The Ballad of the Mari Lwyd* (1942) — 'It's dollars to dimes that outside Wales everyone will call it *The Ballad of the Marie Lloyd*', said T. S. Eliot.[40] The author offered 'Gratitude of a Leper', which pleased few ('perhaps the volume should be surgically bound', wrote Dylan), and Eliot relented — 'I hope it will not grieve you to return to your first love' ran his last-minute note. Watkins's certainty as to poetic mission contrasts with Idris Davies (1905-53), whose insecurity the Faber imprint did little to remove. He essayed a range of styles before Dent (on Eliot's recommendation) published *Gwalia Deserta* (1938), his lyrical sequence on the Welsh industrial depression. Davies's work came to impress Eliot ('the best poetic document I know about a particular epoch in a particular place'),[41] and as a Faber poet he enjoyed his advice on the contents of three published collections, including *Selected Poems* (1953).

Faber, Dent, and Hogarth were the firms most attractive to poets. Far below (in a basement in Buckingham Palace Road) lurked R. A. Caton, whose Fortune Press published — along with its curious line in smut — Glyn Jones, Dylan Thomas, and others who became celebrated. 'Shabby, furtive, touchy and difficult to get away from', is how Glyn Jones remembers Reginald Caton,[42] yet he had a nose for winners and might have landed Alun Lewis but for a dire letter of acceptance. 'You give no sign of criticism or suggestion regarding the selection and order of the poems', Lewis responded.[43] Within a short time Philip Unwin was approaching him on behalf of Allen & Unwin, soon to be publishers of *Raiders' Dawn and Other Poems* (1942). Lewis raised the possibility of a portrait of himself, engraved by John Petts, as cover illustration for this, his first collection: 'I feel it makes the whole thing rather Rupert Brooke-ish, which may not be a good thing from the commercial point of view.' Unwin sensed possibilities. 'Rupert Brookeish it may be but I wouldn't at all mind you becoming in your own particular way the Rupert Brooke of this war.'[44] And it was this ideal of English soldier that the blurb chose to emphasize:

> And while this volume comprises a selection of his whole work, ranging from Chinese lyrics to a passionate and realist statement of life in his native mining valleys of South Wales, we believe the true importance of the book is that it speaks in the recognisable voice of England's poetry, the sensitive integrity of an English soldier.

For Lewis's biographer, the Petts engraving is 'the most important contemporary record we have and allows us to gauge his [Lewis's] state of mind perfectly'.[45] It was, the artist explains, 'cut straight on the wood, from life, a hazardous procedure, but time was short'.[46] In other respects the volume disappointed Lewis. 'I suppose 3/6 implied a cheap edition; I only hope it doesn't kill the book from the start. Reviewers will turn their noses up at a paper cover, won't they?'[47] On the contrary, within a month of publication *Raiders' Dawn* was reprinting, selling 2,500 copies by the end of 1942. The reading public had found its young soldier-poet.

A little earlier Lewis made his mark on Welsh publishing by issuing two poems in broadsheet form. His Caseg project, romantically designed 'to reach *the people* — with beauty, and love',[48] was modelled on chapbook literature ('ballads topped by a woodcut') and for illustrators he turned to Petts and Brenda Chamberlain, then living at Llanllechid. Lewis raised the capital and when on leave travelled through Wales drumming up support. Keidrych Rhys was sceptical, his own broadsheet venture having flopped disastrously. At first things went well, Lewis reporting (November 1941) how the first two sheets, in editions of 500 at fourpence each, were 'going like hot cakes'.[49] Although the printers, Gomerian Press, were soon warning of financial losses, Lewis persisted, issuing six broadsheets in all, including a Dylan Thomas text illustrated by Brenda Chamberlain. In retrospect the whole Caseg enterprise seems misguided, an uncomfortable mix of populism and preciosity. As artefacts the broadsheets disappoint, largely on account of the typography and printing. Hints of what might have been, had the artists kept control of production, can be seen in the fine second printing of Broadsheet 1, set by Petts himself at Llanllechid using Eric Gill's far more sympathetic 14-point Jubilee type.[50]

The mid-1940s saw two substantial attempts at literary publishing in Wales, both offshoots of revived periodicals. Keidrych Rhys and Gwyn Jones shadowed each other closely in re-launching their respective journals and in related publishing schemes. As early as 1942 a revived *Welsh Review* was mooted;[51] the periodical would receive 20 to 25% of its paper consumption for 1939 (when it had been a monthly), sufficient for a fair-sized quarterly. Not until March 1944 did the title recommence (again supported by Creighton Griffiths) by which time *Wales* had reappeared. Gwyn Jones detected 'a positive mushroom field of contributors' for both magazines;[52] readers were in shorter supply. A quarterly, he believed, might be viable with 500 subscribers and similar bookshop sales. He found his subscribers (about 400) but little over-the-counter buying. The remedy, thought Creighton Griffiths, was to move beyond a bookish circle into the professional and business communities; the *Review* was considered too highbrow, 'a national party organ with a distinct leaning to the left'. But no new markets were captured and with advertising revenue declining, a halt once again had to be called in 1948. The halt also terminated a publishing programme that in less that two years had produced five literary titles. From the outset Gwyn Jones advocated book publishing, encouraged by William Lewis, accomplished Cardiff printers with access to paper and cloth. He thought to lead off his Penmark imprint with Kate Roberts but *A Summer Day* came second (1946), behind his own short-story collection, *The Buttercup Field* (1945), each in a printing of 3,000 (it gave Kate Roberts her first-ever royalties cheque). Alun Lewis's *Letters from India* (1946) followed, Penmark here breaking new ground with the first published collection of modern Anglo-Welsh letters (Lewis had died in 1944 at the Burma front). The edition of 500 was heavily subscribed for, and seemed to confirm

Penmark's impressive start. But by 1947 the market had toughened appreciably: as Creighton Griffiths reported, 'sales of all books have dropped sharply away; most people have to think very hard indeed these days before spending 7/6d on any book.'[53] Strange then that the Press now played its weakest card, some Wyn Griffith poetry that proved impossible to sell. In late 1947, against a worsening economic background, Penmark gave up publishing books.

As with the *Welsh Review*, so with *Wales*: money problems dominated, with losses of £50 and £65 on the first two issues. Anxiously Rhys sought a winning format, trying to persuade John Ormond (then a staff writer on *Picture Post*) help make *Wales* the big national illustrated monthly.[54] With printing costs near £500 an issue, it needed to be selling at 3s. 6d. a copy; at 2s. 6d. subscribers were forthcoming, over 1,500 in all, though no more than half that number at any given moment. It simply was not enough and by Christmas 1949, after eighteen issues (two fewer than its rival) *Wales* also had folded.

'Did I tell you Keidrych has started a publishing firm, he has found someone who is willing to put up £200 — a young farmer in Cardiff. The firm is registered "The Druid Press"': so Lynette Roberts reporting to Robert Graves early in 1944.[55] The venture was close to Keidrych's heart, he having consistently taken an enlightened interest in Welsh book trade matters.[56]

> Authors must be paid for their work. There must be more concern for typography. Publishing must be segregated from printing. There must be more pride in the business — the *End* isn't merely having a job for your printer to do. There must be more bookshops. There should be 'Book Pages' in the Welsh newspapers. And there should be one central wholesaler. The doyens of the Welsh book-trade still visualize an old man with a sack of books and periodicals on his back crossing the hills to remote white farm-steads on the sky line.

In his Druid Press editions, solidly produced with eye-catching covers, Rhys was as good as his word. With R. S. Thomas, John Cowper Powys, and an offer from Robert Graves, there seemed no shortage of strong manuscripts. Yet sales needed to be fought for. In February 1948 he asked whether Vernon Watkins had any influence with the *Listener*, which had failed to notice a single Druid Press title. Richard Hughes was published in 1948, and a few non-literary offerings, but with 'most terrible debts' accumulating, Druid Press went down with *Wales*.

The press is best remembered for R. S. Thomas's first collection, *The Stones of the Field* (1946), an expressive artefact and not simply on account of the cover illustration by M. E. Eldridge, the poet's first wife ('it has a grace all its own', said one reviewer). Rhys acknowledged the Irish printing, going so far as to incorporate Dublin into the Druid Press imprint. R. S. Thomas, we know, admired Austin Clarke's creation in English of the atmosphere of older Irish verse, and himself drew on Welsh habits of internal rhyme, alliteration, and assonance in pursuit of an Anglo-Welsh idiom. The blurb accentuates this un-Englishness, and the accordant love of country, a far-back pastoral Wales:

> The *Stones of the Field* is a collection of verse which seeks to reaffirm man's affinity with the age-old realities of stone, field, and tree. These are essentially nature

poems, but they are not written in the English tradition. Their imagery is more akin to that of those early Welsh writers, whose clarity of vision was born out of an almost mystical attachment to their environment.

A generally favourable review in *Life and Letters Today* detected a hint of cliché: 'those endless fictions of feuds, lusts, soils and souls [...] foisted on us as works of Welsh genius in the nineteen thirties'.[57] For his next book, and at his own expense, Thomas turned to the Montgomery Printing Company. Its Newtown imprint intrigued Alan Pryce-Jones, editor of the *TLS* and a native of the town, who made *An Acre of Land* (1952) his book of the week on the influential BBC programme 'The Critics' — 'thus bringing an admirable poet to the notice of London publishers'.[58] James Hanley also helped: 'Finding that I had not yet been published in London, he undertook to correct this and introduced my work to Rupert Hart-Davis.'[59] 'This lovely chap' (as Glyn Jones remembers him) now sought a market for a poet who had yet to capture widespread attention. Cannily he chose John Betjeman as the 'name' to introduce *Song at the Year's Turning: Poems, 1942-1954* (1955), a collection — its title taken from Dylan Thomas — which within a year had run to three impressions. Thomas remained close to Hart-Davis, later taking his advice about a move to Macmillan. From then onwards R. S. Thomas has ridden something of a publishing switchback, employing a dozen companies including five in Wales.

All the while, however, Macmillan published the bulk of his new writing, and this requirement of an established publishing house for heightened literary visibility goes without saying. Gwyn Thomas (1913-81) was delighted at finally being taken up by Victor Gollancz, 'so large and exalted' a publisher of the Left:

> this will cause the stocks of my literary standing to shoot like a rocket among my valley comrades because Victor Gollancz is one of the few publishers to have carved his name deep into the consciousness of these folk here.[60]

Gollancz had refused his first novel on grounds of its 'unrelieved "sordidness"'. Then came a flurry of Thomas fiction from three minor publishers, one having advertised his willingness to consider books of non-standard length — a disposition not shared by Michael Joseph who demanded extensive cuts in *All Things Betray Thee* (1948). Gollancz took the next four novels, promoting them strenuously but failing to win for the author any large popular following (the paperback reprint eluded him). On his own admission, Gwyn Thomas possessed little sense of a contemporary audience, writing out of memories for 'those groups I loved as a boy, a circle of fruity, excitable characters sitting around me on the hillside at dusk'.[61] For Thomas, it was style more than subject matter that identifies the writer and had told against success. 'Cool' and 'quiet' are English words of praise; detachment their preferred position. 'Hope, social evangelism and the rich, unbuttoned humour of our common folk which is its most decent vehicle, must be shoved into a back lane of decent silence.'[62]

While Gwyn Thomas was becoming established, Emyr Humphreys (b. 1919) seemed to be answering Rhys Davies's call for Welsh middle-class novels in a low-pitched Trollopian key. His career (like Davies's) well illustrates the condition of authorship for a productive, much-praised novelist with no large-scale readership. Humphreys wished for popularity, abandoning other occupations so as to sharpen the primary incentive ('economic necessity is a very, very good spur').[63] As his middle-class settings are removed from the industrial south, so his economical, under-emphasized style contrasts with much Valleys writing — 'a large jelly of sentiment, made from wind, water, and words' was his verdict on *Off to Philadelphia in the Morning*.[64] Little surprise then that brevity not bulk should have caused his first publishing problem, Eyre and Spottiswoode deeming *A Toy Epic* too short at 25,000 words. An expanded version failed on grounds of quality though this second rejection, delivered by Graham Greene (then a director of the firm), came to convince Humphreys that here were publishers to stay with. His indebtedness to Greene as publisher and adviser is freely acknowledged and for twenty years — from *The Little Kingdom* (1946) to *Outside the House of Baal* (1965) — Eyre and Spottiswoode published eight of his novels, consolidating their reputation for fiction treating life outside London. Popularity escaped Emyr Humphreys, as it did Gwyn Thomas, though Thomas's sense of failure was not to be assuaged by the acclaim that undoubtedly came his way. This recognition Gollancz had exploited distinctively, weaving critical praise around the borders of his striking yellow book jackets. The publisher went further, incorporating reviewers' comments within the book's preliminaries, opposite the title-page even (a phenomenon which can also be seen in Gwyn Jones). Reception is thus integrated with text.

The power to elicit reviews, to generate talk about writers, to effect a showing in the bookshops, are what Richard Church had in mind when he spoke of 'the machinery of a great publishing house' that had helped Dylan Thomas find the widest possible audience. But the machinery is active long before a book appears, as publishers and authors collaboratively seek an artefact that might find sufficient readers to justify the cost of producing it. Even poets are made mindful of length: 'the more we approximate to 64 pp. the more interested the public is', Church told Dylan Thomas.[65] Anglo-Welsh novelists have responded as variously as others to editorial badgering over text length, angles of approach, style, and content. Short-story collections, like volumes of poetry, need to be structured: Rhys Davies believed that Glyn Jones's *The Water Music* (1944) suffered by having the difficult stories placed first ('one still has to use bait [...] with the general public'),[66] while Edward Garnett advised that an explicit division of stories on geographical lines would assist Geraint Goodwin's *The White House*.

In suggesting that volume's title Garnett performed another editorial service, and his concern for design and marketing reflects a basic publishing approach. The physical book, at once commercial product and embodiment of an author's text, is never a neutral object. Increasingly we have come to recognise the expressive dimensions of format, typography, illustration, and binding (with its dust-jacket fusion of the textual and visual). Design flows out from the text page, poets in particular having long used the resources of typography to help carry meaning. David Jones (1895-1974) was one for whom the appearance of the printed page was important. *In Parenthesis* (1937) he had imagined as a noble crown folio (long double columns in Joanna type) but was persuaded that demy octavo would suffice.[67] With Jones the typographical challenge was to distinguish the blocks of so-called 'prose' from those of so-called 'poetry'. (Reviewers garbled their quotations by ignoring Fabers' careful setting.) John Ormond's books likewise reflect his firm views on layout, more especially *Cathedral Builders* (Gregynog, 1991), for which he provided drawings. Interpretative illustration always conditions response and in Dylan Thomas Wales possesses probably the most widely illustrated author in modern literature. And one is talking not of limited editions but of commercial printings of his popular prose pieces like *A Child's Christmas in Wales*, universalized by Ardizzone's drawings.

A sense that resourceful entrepreneurial publishing is the cornerstone of literary life prompted in the sixties some dramatic moves by the Welsh Arts Council. It was an intervention that for Roland Mathias banished the 'Dolorous Time' of Anglo-Welsh literature (1948-65) — he had in mind the absence of magazines.[68] Subsidy rescued the *Anglo-Welsh Review*, as it now underpins *Poetry Wales, Planet,* and the *New Welsh Review*. But the Arts Council went further in an effort to stimulate a book trade professionalism in Wales. Specific titles were sponsored through individual production grants, publishers given assistance towards editorial departments (a process which continues), and one English-language publisher — Poetry Wales Press (later Seren Books) — was awarded an annual block grant towards its total operation. The case of Seren is instructive: publishing many of the talented younger Welsh writers and with an impressive backlist, it has required additional Arts Council subvention in order to remain in business. The emphasis has now shifted to marketing ('the *End* isn't merely having a job for your printer to do'), but marketing involves huge efforts on any publisher's part: a progressive publishing programme, a strong imprint image (embracing the *outside* of a book as well), and the promotion of individual titles. Such commercial vigour and inventiveness are not encouraged by the climate of subsidy.

State subsidy takes the dynamism out of publishing, denying what Philip Larkin calls the fundamental nexus between writer and audience — 'the reader has been bullied into giving up the consumer's power to say "I don't like this, bring me something different".'[69] The hope remains that dependence on grants will diminish; that Welsh publishers of English-language books, aware of markets outside Wales, will develop well-balanced publishing programmes that in part are commercially profitable. Meanwhile Anglo-Welsh authors place their typescripts where they can, locally or with an English (now multi-national) publisher. It is a matter of some importance, for if authors make books so do publishers, with crucial consequences for visibility and reputation. As Geraint Goodwin put it, a novel without a publisher is like a rocket without a stick: 'The stick in comparison with the rocket may be unimportant but the stick in *relation* to the rocket is a very different affair.'[70]

NOTES TO CHAPTER 30

1. John Harris, 'Queen of the rushes: Allen Raine and her public', *Planet*, 97 (1993), 64-72.
2. Foreword to T. Rowland Hughes, *From hand to hand* (London, 1950).
3. 'W. H. Davies', in *Fury never leaves us: a miscellany of Caradoc Evans*, ed. John Harris (Bridgend, 1985), pp. 126-30 (p. 127).
4. *Eight for immortality* (London, 1941), p. 9.
5. John Harris, 'From his Presbyterian pulpit: Caradoc Evans and Andrew Melrose', *Planet*, 90 (1991-2), 31-7.
6. Andrew Melrose, quoted in *Western Mail*, 22 Nov. 1915.
7. 'A Talk on short-story writing', in *Fury never leaves us*, pp. 131-6 (p. 135).
8. Quotations here are from Rhys Davies's letters to Charles Lahr (undated), University of London Library (Sterling Collection).
9. Letter to R. B. Marriott, 25 May 1936, NLW, Rhys Davies MSS.
10. Rhys Davies, 'Incident in a bookshop', in *Wales on the wireless: A broadcasting anthology*, ed. Patrick Hannan (Llandysul and Cardiff, 1988), pp. 1-2.
11. Letter to R. B. Marriott, 14 Sept. 1936, NLW, Rhys Davies MSS; 'How I write' [broadcast interview], 17 Jan.1950, NLW, BBC (Wales) Archive, Scripts.
12. 'Wales in literature' [letter], *Western Mail*, 12 March 1946.
13. Quoted in Sam Adams, *Geraint Goodwin* (Cardiff, 1975), p. 38.
14. Rhoda Goodwin, 'The Geraint Goodwin-Edward Garnett letters', *Anglo-Welsh Review*, 22(49) (1973), 10-23 (p. 16); 'The Geraint Goodwin-Edward Garnett letters II, *Anglo-Welsh Review*, 22(50) (1973), 119-52 (pp. 129-30).
15. *Western Mail*, 5 Nov. 1936, responding to *Western Mail*, 31 Oct. 1936.
16. Quoted in *Twentieth century authors: a biographical dictionary of modern literature*, ed. Stanley J. Kunitz and Howard Haycraft (New York, 1942), p. 1451.
17. Quoted in Keri Edwards, *Jack Jones* (Cardiff, 1974), p. 79.
18. William Griffiths to Gwyn Jones, 15 Oct. 1947, NLW, Gwyn Jones Papers.
19. 'How I write' [broadcast interview], 17 Jan. 1950, NLW, BBC (Wales) Archive, Scripts.
20. Letter, 9 Sept. 1936, NLW, Idris Davies Papers.
21. John Mair, Review of Lewis Jones, *We live, New Statesman*, 22 April 1939, p. 614.
22. Lewis Jones, Foreword to *Cwmardy: the story of a Welsh mining valley* (London, 1939).
23. John Harris, 'Not only a place in Wales: *How green was my valley* as bestseller', *Planet*, 73 (1989), 10-15.
24. The Richard Church quotations in this paragraph are from his review of *Dylan Thomas: letters to Vernon Watkins, Truth*, 15 Nov. 1957, p. 1295.
25. Richard Church, *Speaking aloud* (London, 1968), pp. 210-11.
26. Letter to Gwyn Jones, 2 May 1946, NLW, Gwyn Jones Papers.
27. *The collected letters of Dylan Thomas*, ed. Paul Ferris (London, 1985), p. 569.
28. *Setting out: a memoir of literary life in Wales* (Cardiff, 1982), p. 19.
29. Letter, 22 Oct. 1937, NLW, Vernon Watkins Papers.
30. The responses of Dylan Thomas and other Anglo-Welsh figures are to be found in the Keidrych Rhys/*Wales* archive, NLW, summarized in John Harris, 'Not a *Trysorfa Fach*: Keidrych Rhys and the launching of *Wales*', *NWR*, 3(11) (1990-1), 28-33.
31. Letter, 22 Oct. 1937, NLW, Vernon Watkins Papers.
32. Letter to Gwyn Jones, 3 Sept. 1947, NLW, Gwyn Jones Papers.
33. Letter, 3 Jan. 1939, NLW, Gwyn Jones Papers.
34. *Setting out*, p. 14.
35. 'Harri Webb' [autobiographical essay], in *Artists in Wales 3*, ed. Meic Stephens (Llandysul, 1977), pp. 87-96 (p. 92).
36. Introduction to *Celtic Story: Number One*, ed. Aled Vaughan (London, 1946).
37. Letter to Gwyn Jones, 18 May 1949, NLW, Gwyn Jones Papers.

[38] The Gwyn Jones quotations here are from 'How I write' [broadcast interview], 12 April 1950, NLW, BBC (Wales) Archive, Scripts.
[39] Letter to Gwyn Jones, 22 Nov. 1949, NLW, Gwyn Jones Papers.
[40] The circumstances are recorded in Gwen Watkins, *Portrait of a friend* (Llandysul, 1983), p. 95.
[41] T. S. Eliot to Islwyn Jenkins, 22 April 1955, quoted in Islwyn Jenkins, *Idris Davies of Rhymney: a personal memoir* (Llandysul, 1986) p. 224.
[42] *Setting out*, p. 1.
[43] Quoted in John Pikoulis, *Alun Lewis: a life* (Bridgend, 1984), p. 121.
[44] *Ibid.*, p. 150.
[45] John Pikoulis, Review of *Alun Lewis: letters to my wife*, ed. Gweno Lewis, *NWR*, 4, 1 (13) (1991) 18-23 (p. 20).
[46] 'John Petts' [autobiographical essay], in *Artists in Wales 3*, ed. Meic Stephens (Llandysul, 1977), pp. 171-84 (p. 179).
[47] Letter to Brenda Chamberlain (Jan. 1942), quoted in Brenda Chamberlain, *Alun Lewis and the making of the Caseg broadsheets* (London, 1970), p. 29.
[48] *Ibid.*, p. 7.
[49] *Ibid.*, p. 24.
[50] I am grateful to Jeff Towns for bringing this rare second printing to my notice.
[51] NLW, Gwyn Jones Papers. Further detail comes from the recently deposited archive relating to the *Welsh Review*.
[52] Letter, *Wales*, 2nd ser., 3 (1944), 104.
[53] Letter to Gwyn Jones, NLW, Gwyn Jones Papers.
[54] John Ormond, Letter to Gwyn Jones, 9 July 1947, NLW, Gwyn Jones Papers.
[55] 'The Correspondence between Lynette Roberts and Robert Graves', ed. Joanna Lloyd, *Poetry Wales*, 19(2) (1983), 51-124 (pp. 69-70).
[56] Keidrych Rhys, 'Welsh commentary', *Books: News Sheet of the National Book League*, 191 (Aug. 1945), 57-8.
[57] Denis Bottrall, *Life and letters Today*, 58(133) (1948), 258.
[58] Alan Pryce-Jones, *The bonus of laughter* (London, 1987), p. 152.
[59] 'R. S. Thomas, 1913-' [autobiographical essay], in *Contemporary authors: Autobiography series*, vol. 4, ed. Adele Sarkissian (Detroit, 1986), pp. 301-13 (p. 309).
[60] Quoted in Ruth Dudley Edwards, *Victor Gollancz: a biography* (London, 1987), p. 579.
[61] 'How I write' [broadcast interview], 16 March 1950, NLW, BBC (Wales) Archive, Scripts.
[62] 'Gwyn Thomas' [autobiographical essay], in *Artists in Wales*, ed. Meic Stephens (Llandysul, 1977), pp. 67-80 (p. 79).
[63] 'The dissident condition: Emyr Humphreys interviewed by Marray Watts', *Planet*, 71 (1988), 22-9 (p. 28).
[64] *New English Review*, Oct. 1947, 373-4.
[65] Letter, 25 March 1936, J. M. Dent Archive.
[66] Letter to Gwyn Jones, 1 Jan. 1945, NLW, Gwyn Jones Papers.
[67] *Dai greatcoat: a self-portrait of David Jones in his letters*, ed. Rene Hague (London, 1980), pp. 54, 81, 195.
[68] Roland Mathias, *The lonely editor: a glance at Anglo-Welsh magazines* (Cardiff, 1984), p. 14.
[69] *Required writing: miscellaneous pieces 1955-1982* (London, 1983), p. 81.
[70] 'Thoughts on the Welsh novel', *Welsh Outlook*, March 1930, 72-4 (p. 72).

CHAPTER 31

PRIVATE PRESSES

Dorothy A. Harrop

THE term 'private press' conjures up images of luxury and literary indulgence rarely affordable in a country where the resources for acquiring even the basic equipment necessary to the reportage of its life, events, and literature was very often lacking. The number of Welsh private presses is thus small, but a lack in quantity is compensated for by their quality in terms of interest.

The first private press was that of Lewis Morris who acquired a press and a fount of full pica type in 1732 with the aim of setting up in business at Llannerch-y-medd an indigent printer, Siôn Rhydderch (1673-1735), who had formerly printed in Shrewsbury. Morris solicited subscriptions to support this venture in March 1732 but was unsuccessful and eventually set up the press in his own house at Holyhead. A single, sixteen-page issue of the first Welsh periodical, *Tlysau yr Hen Oesoedd*, was printed there in 1735. Morris is reputed to have borrowed a man from J. Powell, a Dublin printer, to teach him the art of printing, but the typography and presswork are so poor that he himself probably printed it unaided. Proposals for printing another work in April 1736 failed to gain sufficient support, and when Morris left Anglesey for Cardiganshire the press was left behind at Holyhead. It was eventually sold to Dafydd Jones of Trefriw in or around 1776.

Paul Panton, Jnr (1758-1822), barrister, antiquary, and keen traveller, spent much of his time at the family seat, Plas Gwyn, Pentraeth, Anglesey where he set up a small press in 1794. Although he did not speak the language, Panton took great interest in Welsh studies but sadly no examples of his printing are now extant. The sole record of the press lies in two letters to Panton from the London printer, Luke Hansard, replying to queries regarding the technicalities of printing.

In 1801, the Breconshire antiquary Theophilus Jones sent George Murray, Bishop of St David's, a prospectus for Edward Davies's *Celtic Researches* bearing a note that William Turton (1762-1835), a Swansea medical practitioner who possessed a printing press, had undertaken to produce the book. This did not happen, but the second edition of one of Turton's own medical works, *A Treatise on Cold and Hot Baths* appeared with the imprint 'Swansea: Printed at the Author's Private Press, 1803'. The standard of printing suggests that the presswork was probably that of a professional printer. Although Turton wrote numerous works on medicine and natural history, no other work from his press has been identified.

The Hafod Press is the first truly significant Welsh private press. It was established by Colonel Thomas Johnes (1748-1816) at his Hafod estate in one of the remotest parts of Cardiganshire. Johnes was a translator of French medieval chronicles, a collector of fine books and *objets d'art*, a lover of the picturesque, and an enthusiastic reforming agriculturist. His grand house, designed by Thomas Baldwin and altered and extended by John Nash, was damaged by fire in 1807 but rebuilt. Many titled, literary, and artistic visitors came to admire its art treasures and magnificent library.

Johnes initially entrusted the production of his work to commercial concerns. *A Cardiganshire Landlord's Advice to his Tenants* was printed by Biggs and Cottle of Bristol in 1800 and a Welsh translation by William Owen Pughe was produced by the London printer S. Rousseau in the same year. After his translation, *Memoirs of the Life of Froissart*, had been printed by Nichols and Son of London in 1801, Johnes decided that dealing with distant printers was too slow and by October 1802 had established his own press at Pwllpeiran, a farmhouse about a mile and a half from Hafod mansion. The first printer was dismissed after six months and replaced by the Scottish printer, James Henderson, who brought with him his assistant, William Lhind. The sole purpose of the press was printing Johnes's own works. The earliest was *Sir John Froissart's Chronicles of England, France and the Adjoining Countries*, a four-volume work dated 1803-5. Three hundred sets in quarto, with copper engravings (produced elsewhere), were issued and twenty-five in folio on Whatman paper, six of which had a duplicate set of hand-coloured plates. The type used was Caslon's English No. 1. The type of the quarto version also was re-imposed from the folio setting. The quartos sold so well that cheap octavo editions, printed in London, appeared in 1806 and 1808. After printing Froissart, the press was removed to Pendre which was much nearer to the mansion.

The printing of Froissart was possibly preceded by an undated edition of *A Cardiganshire Landlord's Advice* which, since it bears Henderson's usual imprint and colophon, could not be earlier than April 1803. The type is the same as that of the larger Hafod books, but the presswork is less careful. In 1804 and 1807 Henderson printed editions of *The Rules and Premiums of the Society for the Encouragement of Agriculture and Industry, in the County of Cardigan*, earlier versions of which had been printed for Johnes since 1787 in Carmarthen.

An octavo, *A Catalogue of the Late Pesaro Library at Venice, now Forming Part of the Hafod Library* (1806), has been ascribed to the Hafod press because of the types, but the work bears no imprint, device, or colophon and the long ſ used by Henderson does not appear. To fill gaps in the Pesaro collection, Johnes purchased in 1806 a small collection of early printing amassed by Stanesby Alchorne, Master of the Mint in the 1790s. The National Library of Wales possesses a printed catalogue of this collection, *Bibliotheca Alchorniana*. The printer is not identified, but it is set in Caslon's English No. 1 type and, at the beginning, in what appears to be a contemporary hand, someone has noted 'Catalogue of the Library at Hafod saved from the fire & printed at the Hafod Press'. To this work is appended *Bibliotheca Rudingiana Topographica* (1807) and *Bibliotheca Pesaroniana* (1807), the latter being a revision of the 1806 catalogue.

The dedication of a two-volume quarto translation by Johnes, *Memoirs of John, Lord de Joinville [...] Containing [...] Part of the Life of Louis IX*, is dated 9 February 1807. 230 copies were printed, and ten more on large paper. Some sets contain a unique wood-engraved press device. Also printed in 1807, with a dedication to his deceased sister dated 22 March, was Johnes's translation of *The Travels of Bertrandon de la Brocquière [...] during [...] 1432 & 1433*. This is an octavo, still set in the Caslon type, on a roughish, unpressed paper, but with indifferent presswork. The penultimate piece of printing was Johnes's translation of *The Chronicles of [...] Monstrelet [...] Beginning [...] where that of [...] Froissart Finishes* (1809), a five-volume work in folio and quarto sets to match the Froissart. Some copies of both the folio and quarto sets contain hand-coloured etchings.

The notes to volumes 3 and 4 were printed by H. Bryer of London. Since the three hundred quarto sets sold rapidly it was reissued in twelve volumes octavo, with quarto plates, in 1810 and 1840. The first three volumes of the 1810 edition were the last works to be printed at Hafod, the remainder being printed by Bryer. In 1810, between producing the 1809 Monstrelet and the 1810 octavo reprint, the press printed *Memoirs of the Life of [...] Froissart* which included a revision of the 1801 *Memoirs*. As Johnes's financial difficulties intensified and his health deteriorated, the press was abandoned and its equipment dispersed. Johnes himself died in Dawlish on 23 April 1816. Although the Hafod Press books were typographically unadventurous they were carefully printed. Johnes's true achievement was his lively translations of works hitherto largely unknown.

Two pieces from minor nineteenth-century presses are to be found in the National Library of Wales. NLW, Cwrtmawr 971 is a broadside printed by the Revd John Evan Williams with a manuscript note, 'Printed at the Llanwenllwyfo Rectory, Anglesey by the then rector, c.1880.' The other piece is an election ballad, *Can i Etholwyr Rhan-barth Llanybyther*, printed in 1892 by two brothers, Alan Gerwyn Davies Evans and Delme William Campbell Davies Evans, who ran a small press as a hobby at their home, Highmead, Llanwenog, Cardiganshire.

Jonathan Ceredig Davies (1859-1932) was born in Llangynllo, Cardiganshire. In 1875 he visited Patagonia, returning to Wales in 1891 to become editor of *Yr Athrofa*, a collection of sermons published in parts. Between 1898 and 1902 he travelled in Western Australia where he studied the native peoples and worked to further spiritual and cultural movements among Welsh and English immigrants. Thereafter, apart from brief visits abroad, he remained in Wales where he devoted himself to the study of Welsh history, genealogy, and folklore. Six of his works were published between 1891 and 1911, and then, during the last five years of his life, he printed two books himself at his home, 'Myfyrgell' (The Study), Llanddewibrefi. The first, *Welsh and Oriental Languages*, was reprinted in his second remarkable book entitled *Life, Travels and Reminiscences of Jonathan Ceredig Davies*. Despite his failing eyesight and deteriorating health he managed to print seventy copies, setting and printing one page at a time, using a platen press. This was no mean feat since the book consisted of 438 quarto pages. The printing was amateurish, but the work was intended for private circulation only.

William Gilbert Williams (1874-1966), for many years headmaster of Rhostryfan school in Caernarfonshire, acquired a small quantity of type with the intention of teaching the older boys to print. When local unions objected to this, Williams demonstrated the craft to his pupils by printing three small books on Welsh history which he himself had written. These were: *Rhostryfan: Hanes a Chynnydd y Pentre*, of which he printed sixteen copies in 1926, *Braslinelliad o Hanes Cymru rhwng 1282 a 1485*, of which he printed twenty-two copies in 1927, and *Rhwng Gwyll a Gwawr: Briwsion Hanes o 1688 hyd 1720*, of which he printed forty-four copies in 1928. He also printed a series of school examination papers.

The latest of the small private presses is that of Huw Ceiriog Jones, a Senior Assistant Librarian in the Department of Printed Books at the National Library of Wales. He started printing in 1969 on an Adana horizontal quarto flatbed press at Llety Gwyn, Llanbadarn Fawr. Under the imprint 'Gwasg Llety Gwyn' he produced five pamphlets containing Welsh poems and also a few greetings cards. Two years later he moved to

Aber-ffrwd in the Rheidol valley where he renamed his cottage and his press 'Yr Arad Goch' (The Red Plough). In 1973 he purchased a crown folio Arab treadle platen press and a foolscap Jardine treadle platen press from the widow of John Ellis, a Llanidloes printer. Fifteen pamphlets, mainly poetry, were produced before he married in 1977 and moved to Y Wern, Bow Street. The press was renamed once again, becoming 'Gwasg y Wern'. In 1980 it produced its only book to date, *Y Gwir Degwch*, poems by Iolo Morganwg with illustrations by Tegwyn Jones. Printer and artist have since co-operated in producing Christmas greetings cards each year.

The most important private presses in Wales are the Gregynog Press and its successor, Gwasg Gregynog. The former was founded in 1922 at Gregynog Hall, near Newtown, Montgomeryshire, by Gwendoline and Margaret Davies, cultured grand-daughters of the self-made millionaire industrialist, David Davies. The Davies sisters had intended to establish an arts and crafts centre but the press was the only part of their original plan to survive. Their aim was to stimulate an interest in fine books and thereby encourage better book printing. They also hoped to foster Welsh literature and, of the forty-two books published, seven are in Welsh, one is bilingual, and a dozen of the remainder have Welsh associations. The stables and coach houses at Gregynog were converted into a print shop and bindery, and Robert Ashwin Maynard, a promising young artist forced to earn his living as a theatrical painter, was appointed Controller in July 1922. The first book, *Poems by George Herbert*, published in December 1923 was well received.

Horace Walter Bray was appointed resident artist in February 1924 and, up to 1930, he and Maynard were responsible for the design and illustration of seventeen more books which are characterized by sound typography, pleasing wood engravings, and well-designed and well-executed wood-engraved initials. The first four books were set in Kennerley type, later books being set in a variety of types produced on a Monotype caster. The first book, and one other, were printed on an Albion hand-press, after which all books were printed on a Victoria platen press using hand-made paper from various mills. Presswork from 1927 to 1936 was by Herbert John Hodgson, a printer of incomparable skill.

After the press became a limited company in 1928, its affairs were managed by a board of directors which consisted of the Davies sisters, their friend, Dr Thomas Jones, Deputy Secretary to the Cabinet, and their financial adviser, W. J. Burdon Evans. Jones acted as chairman and was instrumental in finding suitable authors, editors, and translators, largely from his wide literary acquaintance. The most notable works from the Maynard and Bray era are: *The Life of Saint David* (1927), *The Autobiography of Edward, Lord Herbert of Cherbury* (1928), *Psalmau Dafydd* (1929), *The Stealing of the Mare* (1930), *Elia and the Last Essays of Elia* (1931) and the two-volume folio edition of *The Plays of Euripides*, translated by Gilbert Murray (1931). Early in 1930, Maynard and Bray left Gregynog to found the Raven Press. In their place, William McCance, an artist, was appointed Controller and Blair Hughes-Stanton, a noted wood-engraver, was appointed resident artist. Their wives, Agnes Miller Parker and Gertrude Hermes, both of them notable artists in their own right, were appointed engravers. Typographic standards declined, but the books became artistically more interesting, chiefly because of Hughes-Stanton's wood engravings which display great skill and fineness of detail. The most striking books from this period are: *Comus* (1931), *The Fables of Esope* (1932), which has lively wood engravings by Agnes Miller Parker, who also illustrated *Twenty-one Welsh Gypsy Folk-tales* (1933), and Hughes-Stanton's two masterpieces, *The Revelation of Saint John the Divine* (1933) and *The Lamentations of Jeremiah* (1934). Following considerable personal and artistic tensions, Hughes-Stanton and McCance left the press in September 1933.

Loyd Haberly, an American who had been running his own private press, was appointed non-resident Controller in January 1934. Of the five books he designed, the most outstanding is Xenophon's *Cyrupaedia* (1936). For Robert Bridges's *Eros and Psyche* (1935) a new typeface was devised from a redrawing of a fifteenth-century type used at Foligno in Italy. This, initially known as 'Gwendoline' and subsequently as 'Gregynog', was not considered a success and was not used again for a Gregynog book. James Wardrop of the Victoria and Albert Museum was appointed to succeed Haberly in June 1936. His typographical taste was more formal and traditional, his greatest achievement being Joinville's *The History of Saint Louis* (1937), a superlatively rich folio with initials designed by Alfred Fairbank and armorial shields by Reynolds Stone.

George Fisher, who had been apprenticed to Rivière and Son, the fashionable London bindery, presided over the Gregynog bindery for almost twenty years from 1925 to 1945. The special bindings of between fifteen and twenty-five copies of each edition were the work of Fisher himself except for one or two in the later years when he was assisted by his apprentice, John Ewart Bowen. These bindings are superbly executed in every detail. Artistically, the most satisfying bindings are those designed by the various press artists, especially those of Hughes-Stanton who devised mainly abstract designs incorporating gold and blind tooling and coloured onlays. McCance also designed interesting bindings for *The Fables of Esope* and Robert Vansittart's *The Singing Caravan* (1932).

In addition to the forty-two published volumes, the press printed three books for private circulation. A considerable amount of ephemeral printing was also undertaken, including book prospectuses, programmes for the Gregynog festivals of music and poetry held each year between 1933 and 1938, special services, Christmas cards, and concert and conference programmes for the many events which took place at the Hall. With the onset of war, the younger staff were drafted into the armed forces and the press closed in 1940.

In 1974, the University of Wales, to which Margaret Davies had bequeathed Gregynog Hall, established a new press there under the imprint 'Gwasg Gregynog'. Michael Hutchins, a lecturer in typography, was appointed Printing Fellow and in 1976 produced R. S. Thomas's *Laboratories of the Spirit*. Eric Gee, retired Head of the Birmingham School of Printing, was appointed to direct the press in 1978 and set high standards. When he retired in 1985 he was succeeded by David Esslemont, a former pupil of Blair Hughes-Stanton who had run his own press in Newcastle-upon-Tyne. Gwasg Gregynog books have been printed in a variety of Monotype faces on the original Gregynog Victoria platen press, a Soldans proofing press and, more recently, a Heidelberg cylinder press. The press has published more than twenty major works, thirty smaller books, three commissioned works, and over a hundred pieces of ephemera. The standard of production has remained high.

Following the Gregynog pattern, the majority of the books are illustrated and include wood engravings by Sarah van Niekerk and Colin Paynton, line drawings by Peter Reddick, linocuts by Kyffin Williams, and water-colours by John Piper. Outstanding titles are: Kate Roberts's *Two Old Men and Other Stories* (1981), *The Curate of Clyro* (1983), Dylan Thomas's *Deaths and Entrances* (1984), *Wood Engravings by Gertrude Hermes, being Illustrations to Selborne, with Extracts from Gilbert White* (1988), *Giraldus Cambrensis, Itinerary through Wales* (1989), and Wolfram von Eschenbach's *The Romance of Parzival and the Holy Grail* (1990). Two of these, *Selbourne* and *Parzival,* made use of illustrations originally prepared for the Gregynog Press and this exploitation of past riches has continued during the 1990s with the republication of works such as Agnes Miller Parker's illustrations to *Esope*. A certain number of copies of each edition have been bound to a special design and executed by various binders, notably Sally Lou Smith, Sydney Cockerell, James Brockman, and Julian Thomas. In 1990, Alan Wood was appointed as resident bookbinder to the press. It is greatly to be regretted that financial constraints have recently led to a drastic curtailing of all activities of the press

The Old Stile Press, was founded in 1978 in Blackheath by Nicholas McDowall, formerly an educational publisher, and his wife, Frances. In 1986 the press moved to Catchmays Court, Llandogo, near Monmouth. The chief inspiration at Old Stile is the work of artists and poets who work very closely with the printer. A formative influence was the Wiltshire pastoral etcher Robin Tanner, who was responsible for the name of the press and for the design of its device. Tanner also provided the illustrations for the first significant work, an edition of Gray's *Elegy,* published in 1981. The same year, Robert Buchanan's *The Ballad of Judas Iscariot* appeared with striking linocuts by J. Martin Pitts. The originality of the works produced and the freshness of vision which inspires them has ensured a solid core of collectors. Two of the most important artists' works were published in 1992. *Kippers and Sawdust* is a book of biographical reminiscence by the artist, Rigby Graham, illustrated with large expressionistic woodcuts printed in up to four colours. The other work is a portfolio of fifteen separate woodcuts by Bert Isaac entitled *The Landscape Within*. Presses used at Old Stile have included a small Victorian amateur Caxton press, a foolscap folio Albion, a double crown Albion, an 1854 Columbian, and a Vandercook SP15 repro press. Frances McDowall is an inspired creator of hand-made papers which have been used in bindings and in the production of some of the smaller items to come from the press. Ordinary bindings have been provided by the Fine Bindery of Wellingborough, but in 1991 Old Stile launched a series of limited edition bindings. The first of these, created by Andrew Cotton, appeared on Robin Tanner's *The More Angels Shall I Paint*. Cotton was also responsible for the binding of McDowall's own book, *A Wall in Wales*. Habib Dingle produced an unusual and striking largely wooden binding for Kevin Crossley-Holland's translation of the Anglo-Saxon poem, *The Seafarer*. Anton Henley devised a binding for George Mackay Brown's *In the Margins of Shakespeare*, and Julian Thomas, binder at the National Library of Wales, was commissioned to create a binding for *Houses of Leaves*, translations of poems by Dafydd ap Gwilym.

The most recent press is the Red Hen Press, established in South Croydon in 1983 by Shirley Jones who was born and brought up in the Rhondda and who moved in 1994 to Llanhamlach near Brecon. This is a unique press where the owner produces, almost single-handed, artist's books in which the texts consist of her own poems, prose pieces, and translations from Old English or Welsh. These are illustrated with etchings, aquatints, and mezzotints of considerable power and haunting beauty which demonstrate the artist's skill in these very taxing autographic mediums, and which are printed using carefully chosen handmade papers of the highest quality. The works are hand bound or boxed by some of Britain's most distinguished bookbinders, and each is conceived as a total artistic concept. One work is produced annually and each consists of an edition not exceeding forty copies. Titles produced at the time of writing are: *Scop Hwilum Sang* (1983), with six colour etchings; *Impressions* (1984), with eight aquatints; *A Dark Side of the Sun* (1985), poems by the artist illustrated with six mezzotints; *Ellorgast* (1986), poems from Old English exploring the theme of Beowulf, illustrated with eight mezzotints; *Nocturne for Wales* (1987), poems about the Rhondda with five aquatints; *For Gladstone* (1988), ten mezzotints celebrating a favourite cat; *Soft Ground Hard Ground* (1989), twelve personal pieces illustrated with mezzotints; *Five Flowers For My Father* (1990), with floral mezzotints; *Two Moons* (1991), nine poems and mezzotints; *Ordinary Cats* (1992), selected texts and a poem with five large mezzotints; *Llym Awel* (1993), with seven colour mezzotints and a relief etching of landscapes; *Falls the Shadow* (1995), short essays accompanied by six mezzotints and seven blind-printed etched plates cut out in the shape of shells.

Whatever the eventual fate of Gwasg Gregynog, these smaller presses should ensure that the tradition of the private press continues in Wales.

SELECT BIBLIOGRAPHY TO CHAPTER 31

Dearden, James A., 'Thomas Johnes and the Hafod Press, 1803-10', *The Book Collector*, 22 (1973), 315-36

Esselmont, David and Glyn Tegai Hughes, *Gwasg Gregynog: a descriptive catalogue of printing at Gregynog 1970-1990* (Gregynog, 1990)

Harrop, Dorothy A., *A history of the Gregynog Press* (Pinner, 1980)

Jones, Bedwyr Lewis, *Argraffu a chyhoeddi ym Môn* ([Llangefni], 1976)

Moore-Colyer, R. J., 'Thomas Johnes of Hafod (1748-1816): translator and bibliophile', *WHR*, 15 (1990-1), 399-415

'The Old Stile Press: the printing of Nicholas McDowall, the art-work of J. Martin Pitts', *The Private Library*, 5 (1982), 167-83

Rees, Eiluned, *The Welsh book-trade before 1820* (Aberystwyth, 1988)

CHAPTER 32

CHILDREN'S LITERATURE IN WELSH TO 1950

Menna Phillips

AS a result of the developments discussed in Chapter 29, the majority of the new Welsh-language titles published today consist of books for children or for schools; in 1996, for example, over 67% of new titles (385 of 572) fell into this category. The number of titles currently available and the wide range of topics they cover is in sharp contrast to earlier centuries. Indeed, before the reign of Queen Victoria there are very few examples in the Welsh language of any kind of literature written especially for children. All too often it is difficult to distinguish books that were intended for children from those that were intended for adults. The presence of the words 'plant', 'plentyn', or 'ieuenctid' in titles does not guarantee that the book's content would today be considered suitable for a child. Children were not considered to be different from adults in any way except in age and lack of experience. Once the years of infancy were past, the child was dressed as a little adult; toys and childish pastimes were put aside as most children prepared for the world of work.

The frequent deaths of children in infancy and childhood, often from what today would be easily curable ailments, was a common part of life's experience, touching both their parents and their surviving siblings. The uncertain nature of life makes the urgency with which religious works stressed the need for salvation all the more understandable; the work of saving young souls could not begin too soon. In 1671 James Janeway published *A Token for Children being an exact Account of the Conversion, holy and exemplary Lives and joyful Deaths of several Young Children*, a work centred on the assertion that 'children are not too little to go either to Hell or Heaven'. In 1816 a Welsh adaptation by the prominent Calvinistic Methodist, Thomas Jones of Denbigh, *Anrheg i Blentyn, sef Hanes Cywir am Ddychweliad Grasol, Bucheddau duwiol, a Marwolaethau Dedwyddol, amryw Blant Ieuaingc* was published by Thomas Gee, senior. Although the Welsh title is a literal translation of that of Janeway's book, typically no mention is made anywhere in the text of *Anrheg* to the English work on which it was based.

Although *Anrheg i Blentyn* has been considered to be the earliest book in Welsh written specifically for children, this is not wholly correct. The 1633 edition of the Welsh ABC and Catechism (*LW* 4), for instance, states that it is to be learnt 'gan bob plentyn' (by every child). In 1715, *Llwybr Hyffordd y Plentyn Bach i Fywyd Tragwyddol*, a translation by Theophilus Evans (1693-1767) of *The Heavenly Messenger, or, the Child's Plain Pathway to Eternal Life*, was published at Shrewsbury and was twice reprinted there in the 1750s. Another early example in the same vein was *Gwagedd Mebyd ac Jeungctid yn yr hwn y dangosir natur lygredig pobl jeuainc, ac y cynhygir moddion er eu diwygiad*, first published in London in 1728 and reprinted there in 1739 and 1759. This was a translation by Thomas Baddy of a sermon by Daniel Williams (?1643-1716), *The Vanity of Childhood and Youth where is shown the corrupt nature of young people, and means are proposed for their reform*. Peter Williams (1723-96) provided his *Blodau i Blant* (*Flowers for children*) (Carmarthen 1758) with a far more attractive title than any earlier Welsh book for children but its contents comprised biblical verses, prayers, and hymns, some of the latter being translations of pieces by Isaac Watts.

The circulating schools established by Griffith Jones and the later Sunday-school movement both placed great importance on learning to read in order to understand the Bible and thereby save one's soul. Many early Welsh books for children are consequently primers or simple spelling-books designed to inculcate elementary reading skills. As such they have no claims (or indeed pretensions) to literary merit, nor do they make any concessions to the tender years of the pupils in format, type-face, or the provision of illustrations.[1] The title of a typical primer reveals their method: *Darlleniadur, sef Hyfforddiadur hawdd ac eglur i ddysgu darllain Cymraeg wedi eu hamcanu megis silliadur cyntaf i blant, ac yn cynnwys amrywiaeth helaeth o wersi, wedi eu gosod mewn trefn gymmwys i arwain yr ieuangc ym mlaen o râdd i râdd, o hawdd i anhawdd* (*A reader, that is a simple and clear instructor to teach the reading of Welsh, intended as a first spelling-book for children, containing a wide selection of lessons, set out in a suitable order to lead the young from step to step from the easy to the difficult*), published in Dolgellau in 1820. Similar works, progressing from the alphabet through ever-lengthening words to verses from the Bible, were amongst the first titles to be published by Richard Hughes of Wrexham in the later 1820s.

Small tracts and pamphlets intended for children published in the early years of the nineteenth century show no lessening in the sobriety of their content. A sermon by the enormously popular Calvinistic Methodist preacher, John Elias (1774-1841), *Buddioldeb yr Iau i Bobl Ieuangc: neu Bregeth ar Galar. 3: 27* (Trefriw, 1818) was reprinted by several other publishers during the next four or five decades. There was even an English translation published in Liverpool by Nevett in 1820 as *The Advantage of the Yoke to Young People, considered in a Sermon on Lam. 3. 27*. The closely packed print and dull wrappers of early editions made no attempt to attract the readership for whom the work was presumably intended, possibly because both author and publishers believed that the subject-matter was too important for such external frivolities. A very attractive edition of the sermon was, however, published by Hugh Humphreys of Caernarfon in mid-century, probably as a Sunday-school reward or prize book. The title was slightly changed to the less off-putting *Buddioldeb Crefydd i'r Ieuenctyd* (*The advantage of religion to young people*), it was given an attractively patterned paper cover and a frontispiece, and was set in a more readable type-face, better suited to younger readers.

Other authors were quicker to appreciate the need for appealing titles. In 1818 the Aberystwyth printer Samuel Williams published on behalf of its author, Thomas Phillips of Neuadd-lwyd, *Ychydig Fasgedeidiau o Swpiau Grawnwin, wedi eu casglu ar Faes yr Ysgrythyrau, er difyrwch a budd i blant yr ysgolion Sabbothol* (*A few basketfuls of bunches of grapes collected from the field of the scriptures for the amusement and benefit of Sunday-school children*). Although the promising title concealed a dreary catechism, so great was the dearth of suitable works for children that it was seized upon by other publishers and at least nine editions had appeared by 1840.

By mid-century a gradual change can be seen in the attitude of Welsh authors towards children and the sort of books considered suitable for them. Social, economic, educational, and religious changes all combined to emphasize that the world of childhood was completely different and set apart from the world of adults. Even so there remained an acute shortage of Welsh books specifically written for children and much of what was available consisted of translations of English works published by bodies such as the Religious Tract Society and the SPCK.

Small-format books, often based on English or American originals and embellished with attractive covers, a frontispiece, and perhaps a few illustrations, began to be produced by publishers such as Hugh Humphreys of Caernarfon and Hughes a'i Fab of Wrexham. Publishers large and small often advertised extensive lists of such books in ornate bindings for use as Sunday-school rewards and prizes. Hughes a'i Fab, for instance, listed in their catalogues prize books (some with coloured pictures) and offered bundles of assorted titles at a range of prices. The eccentric printer John Jones of Llanrwst took the trend for small-format books to extremes between 1835 and 1845 by publishing a series of five little hymn-books as Sunday-school prizes for children which remain the smallest Welsh books ever published.

For most of the nineteenth century Welsh periodicals for children reached a far more extensive readership than did books. The first Welsh periodical expressly intended for children, *Yr Addysgydd* (*The Educator*), was published in Carmarthen at the beginning of 1823. A tiny and unattractive penny monthly, whose moralizing and highly edifying contents could hardly have interested an adult, let alone a child, it survived for only a year. Even so, it proved to be the forerunner of many children's periodicals. Production difficulties, high costs, problems with distribution, and a lack of knowledge of what would appeal to a child meant that there were many casualties: the penny monthly published by John Jones, Llanrwst, *Cydymaith yr Ieuengctid* (*The Young People's Companion*), ran from June 1826 to May 1827; *Yr Oenig* (*The Little Lamb*) from 1854 to 1856; *Telyn y Plant* (*The Children's Harp*) from 1859 to 1861; *Y Ffenestr* (*The Window*) from 1873 to 1875. Even such an attractively designed periodical such as *Y Medelwr Ieuanc* (*The Young Gleaner*), designed to promote the temperance movement in Wales and to take advantage of the popularity of the Band of Hope, failed to attract sufficient subscribers and ran only from 1871 to 1873.

The periodicals which survived despite all these difficulties were those which enjoyed denominational support. Each denomination provided a loyal body of purchasers and an efficient means for distributing monthly periodicals through its Sunday schools. Titles supported in this way could enjoy continued success and achieve impressive longevity: *Y Winllan* (*The Vineyard*), the successor to the Wesleyans' first periodical for children, *Trysor i Blentyn (A Child's Treasure)* (1825-42), ran from 1848 to 1965; and the Independents' *Dysgedydd y Plant* (*The Children's Instructor*) from 1871 to 1933. The most successful of all nineteenth-century children's magazines was the Calvinistic Methodists' penny monthly, *Trysorfa y Plant* (*The Children's Treasury*) which ran from 1862 to 1965. Towards the end of the century this was sufficiently profitable to subsidize both *Y Drysorfa*, the denomination's monthly magazine for adults, and its quarterly review, *Y Traethodydd*. The success of *Trysorfa y Plant* can be attributed to the exceptional skills of Thomas Levi (1825-1916), its editor from 1862 to 1911. As editor of two short-lived periodicals, *Yr Oenig* and *Telyn y Plant*, Levi had already gained considerable experience of what was required in order to interest, amuse, instruct, and entertain children. He ensured that *Trysorfa y Plant* was engagingly written in simple and direct language rather than the inflated style of earlier periodicals for children. The scope and variety of items in each month's issue is surprisingly wide; stories (including the first Welsh Western), poems, homilies, biographies, and even a few jokes (Levi was famous for his ready wit). On the other hand, descriptions of edifying infant death-beds remained a regular feature. By the later 1870s Levi — who appreciated the promotional value of such figures — could claim monthly sales of 40,000 copies, many to members of other denominations.

As well as editing *Trysorfa y Plant*, Levi wrote about thirty books and translated sixty or so from English into Welsh. Most of these translations were of works for children, and many of them first appeared in *Trysorfa y Plant* before being published as books. An enthusiastic supporter of the Religious Tract Society, Levi prepared Welsh translations of many of its most popular publications following the founding of its Welsh branch in 1875. Hesba Stretton's *Jessica's First Prayer* became *Gweddi Gyntaf Jessica* (1876) and *Little Meg's Children* became *Plant Meg Fach* (1886); *Christie's Old Organ* and *Angel's Christmas* by Mrs Walton became *Hen Organ Christie* (1880) and *Nadolig Angel* (1884). Levi was an excellent translator, who almost invariably avoided any tell-tale stiffness of idiom or style. His translations read so naturally that the English or American names provide the only clue to their provenance. Levi was also an enthusiastic supporter of the sol-fa movement and supplied the words for the most popular of many extended Welsh compositions for children, Joseph Parry's *Cantata y Plant* (*The Children's Cantata*), first published in 1873 by Hughes a'i Fab and frequently reprinted up to the late 1930s.

Nowhere is the change in attitude towards children and their reading needs better or more clearly shown than in the monthly *Cymru'r Plant* (*The Children's Wales*). Launched by O. M. Edwards in January 1892, *Cymru'r Plant* was the first successful non-denominational children's magazine. It was very different in content and style from any of its contemporaries. Its contents reflected O. M. Edwards's concern to inculcate an awareness of Welsh history and traditions and included folk-tales, nursery rhymes, tales from Welsh history, stories, and poems. Everything was written in simple and direct Welsh far removed from the inflated (and often English-influenced) language of its contemporaries. Care was taken to ensure that the type was clear and easy to read. And at long last a Welsh magazine for children provided plenty of illustrations, carefully chosen to complement the text.

O. M. Edwards also succeeded in attracting many capable authors to contribute to *Cymru'r Plant*, not least by offering them payment for their work. Writers such as Winnie Parry (1870-1953), Hugh Brython Hughes (1848-1913), Fanny Edwards (1876-1959), and the Welsh-Patagonian Eluned Morgan (1870-1938) could all express themselves in a lively manner and produced a range of stories that entertained and interested their readers. By 1900 monthly sales of *Cymru'r Plant* had reached 11,500. As well as editing *Cymru'r Plant* and its adult counterpart, *Cymru* (*Wales*), O. M. Edwards wrote many attractive books for children including collections of nursery rhymes, *Plant y Beirdd* (*The poets' children*) (1892), *Cartrefi Cymru* (*The homes of Wales*) (1896), *Llyfr Del* (1906), *Llyfr Nest* (1913), and the posthumous *Llyfr Haf* (1926). Following the untimely death of O. M. Edwards in May 1920, his son Ifan ab Owen Edwards edited *Cymru'r Plant*, rebuilding its circulation (which had declined from the early years of the century) to 15,000 copies a month by 1929. In order to cater for teenagers Ifan ab Owen Edwards created *Y Capten* (*The Captain*) in 1931, a periodical for twelve to eighteen year olds. Unfortunately it was short-lived because of a shortage of suitable material.

The inter-war years were an interesting and innovative period in the history of Welsh books for children. The number of new titles for children increased markedly during the 1920s and 1930s, partly because publishers such as Hughes a'i Fab believed that the prospect of sales to schools made this a safer and more lucrative venture than publishing Welsh books for adults. By the 1920s, teachers had largely replaced preachers as authors of books for children. New genres such as the historical novel, the mystery novel, and the adventure story all proved popular, but it is worth noting that no Welsh-language writer for children ventured to address contemporary life in industrial Wales.

A taste for fantasy and for the rural past is clearly visible in the work of the Wesleyan minister E. Tegla Davies (1880-1967). Between 1920 and 1928 he edited that denomination's monthly for children, *Y Winllan*. As well as including work by writers as eminent as Kate Roberts, he followed up the success of his own *Hunangofiant Tomi* (*Tomi's Autobiography*) (1912) by publishing several humorous (if sometimes moralizing) books, most notably *Nedw* (1922). Following serialization in *Y Winllan*, this portrayal of a mischievous boy appeared in book form in 1922 embellished with illustrations by the cartoonist Illingworth. Davies's other works for children included a pioneering fantasy of lunar travel, *Rhys Llwyd y Lleuad* (1925). Tegla Davies was a born story-teller whose lively tales of the mischievous doings of children set in a rural background proved to be firm favourites for several decades.

Another author who had first established herself as a writer for children shortly before the First World War was Elizabeth Mary Jones, 'Moelona' (1877-1953), whose *Teulu bach Nantoer* (*The little family of Nantoer*) gained the prize for a novel for children in the 1912 National Eisteddfod. First published in 1913, it was reprinted several times and, despite its technical weaknesses, eventually achieved sales of over thirty thousand copies.

R. Lloyd Jones (1878-1959) specialized in adventure stories. The son of a merchant-navy captain, in books such as *Ynys y Trysor* (*Treasure island*) (1925) and *Mêt y Mona* (*The Mona's Mate*) (1929), he set gripping adventures against a detailed background of faraway places and seafaring life and offered readers a view of the world that was very different from that provided by earlier Welsh authors.

1931 saw the publication of the first volume of a very special book for children which remained a great favourite for many years. This was *Llyfr Mawr y Plant* (*The big book for the children*), one of the first attempts in Welsh to imitate the popular English annuals. It was edited by Jennie Thomas and J. O. Williams, with illustrations (some in colour) by the English artist Peter Fraser. Many of the animal characters it featured such as the fox, Sion Blewyn Coch (John Redfox), and the loveable little duck, Wil Cwac Cwac, remained firm favourites for many years; indeed the adventures of the latter were subsequently immortalized in a Welsh video. *Llyfr Mawr y Plant* itself was sufficiently popular to be reprinted and was followed by three further volumes.

The end of 1938 saw the launch of *Gwybod* (*Knowing*), an encyclopaedia for children which was planned to be published in monthly parts over four years. As well as including articles on music, Welsh history, and famous people it broke new ground in its treatment of science and industry. Ably edited by E. Curig Davies and Thomas Parry, it was visually attractive, well-designed, and adequately illustrated. Unfortunately it had to be terminated after twelve numbers because of the outbreak of the Second World War and consequent rationing of paper.

A bleak period ensued as very little was published in Welsh for children during the 1940s and early 1950s, at a time when English writing for children went from strength to strength. Notable exceptions were the historical novels of Elizabeth Watkin Jones (1887-1966), several of which were successful in National Eisteddfod competitions. Stories such as *Luned Bengoch* (*Red-headed Luned*) (1946), *Y Dryslwyn* (1947), *Esyllt* (1951), and *Lois* (1955), generally set in Civil War and Commonwealth times, proved very popular. As a result of economy measures introduced during the war and the post-war problems of Welsh publishers, the few Welsh books that appeared during the later 1940s had a grey and dreary appearance. A welcome contrast was provided by the Welsh comic *Hwyl* (*Fun*) launched in July 1949 by D. J. Williams (1886-1950). This broke new ground by providing colourful cartoons, serials, and puzzles, and proved to be a refreshing addition to the restricted range of material for children available at that time. From the 1950s onwards, as described in Chapter 29, the production of Welsh books for children was transformed so that by today, Welsh children's books are more varied, colourful, and abundant than they ever have been.

NOTES TO CHAPTER 32

A comprehensive study of writing for children in Welsh during this period to which the above is indebted is provided by Mairwen and Gwynn Jones, *Dewiniaid difyr: llenorion plant Cymru hyd tua 1950* (Llandysul, 1983). A full checklist of children's books in the Welsh language published between 1900 and 1991 can be found in *Llyfrau plant = Children's books in Welsh, 1900-1991* (Aberystwyth, 1997). Victorian periodicals for children are discussed in detail in R. Tudur Jones, 'Darganfod plant bach: sylwadau ar lenyddiaeth plant yn oes Victoria', *YB*, 8 (1974), 160-204. A full listing of pre-1850 periodical titles can be found in Huw Walters, *Llyfryddiaeth cylchgronau Cymreig / A bibliography of Welsh periodicals 1735-1850* (Aberystwyth, 1993). Children's fiction between 1915 and 1950 is examined in Siân Teifi, 'Llenyddiaeth storïol i blant yn y Gymraeg, 1919-1950' (unpublished masters thesis University of Wales, Aberystwyth, 1987). A key figure, Thomas Levi, is the subject of a recent study (based on a doctoral dissertation) by Dafydd Arthur Jones, *Thomas Levi* (Caernarfon, 1996).

[1] An interesting exception to the general reluctance to provide illustrations is Owen Hughes, *Allwedd newydd i ddysgu darllain Cymraeg* (*LW* 2533-8). This contains a picture alphabet designed for the English language, with incongruous results.

CHAPTER 33

THE NATIONAL LIBRARY OF WALES, THE ART OF THE BOOK, AND WELSH BIBLIOGRAPHY

Gwyn Walters

RECENT years have witnessed an intensive application of advanced conservation techniques in national libraries and certain major academic libraries. At the same time there has been an associated movement towards promoting these libraries as 'Centres' or 'Museums of the Book', and towards publishing volumes portraying what it is now fashionable to call the 'History of the Book' or the 'Art of the Book'.[1] To understand the position of the National Library of Wales as a centre for studying the history and art of the book it is necessary to trace briefly its establishment. Although the ambitious plans of the Morris brothers in the mid-eighteenth century included aspirations to create a collection of Welsh and Celtic material, it was not until the mid-nineteenth century that a Welsh national library began to be considered as a feasible objective. Of the various early schemes, that of Sir Thomas Phillipps (1792-1872), the legendary collector of manuscripts and printed books, is rich in tragi-comic elements.[2] Sir Thomas, having reached an advanced age, began to focus his attention on finding a permanent home for his collections in a suitable Welsh location — for he proudly claimed descent from the Philipps family of Picton Castle. In 1864 it was the Old Palace of the Bishops of St David's which seized his imagination, but a proviso that the shell of the building should be refurbished at Welsh cost led to dithering which made him impatient. Soon, however, the ancient castle of Manorbier appeared to him to have greater historical relevance; the birthplace of Giraldus Cambrensis, it also stood on land owned by the Picton Castle Philippses. Legal delays prompted him to abandon this scheme, apparently the only one which contemplated the relinquishing of his incomparable manuscripts as well as his printed books. A third plan foundered when a galvanized iron structure erected by Sir Thomas at Llandovery was damaged in a 'hurricane' and haggling arose over payment for an envisaged librarian's house. His final attempt was to re-erect the iron structure on Phillipps land, only to find the building too damp when a consignment of books was sent there from Thirlestaine House, Cheltenham. Phillipps balked at the cost of a suggested brick building, and the books — probably duplicate copies, representing a scaling-down of the original grand design — were soon returned to Cheltenham.

The history of the National Library thus begins with the committee formed at the Mold National Eisteddfod in 1873, but, as explained in Chapter 26, little was achieved until a new Welsh Library Committee was set up in 1896 to ensure that the proposed library would be located in Aberystwyth.[3] Meanwhile, from 1893 onwards, Sir J. Herbert Lewis, the Liberal MP for Flint Boroughs, campaigned for a share of the annual museum grants which supported national museums and libraries in England, Scotland, and Ireland.[4] In June 1905 a committee of the Privy Council decided that the library would be sited in Aberystwyth and the national museum in Cardiff. In justifying its decision the committee pointed out that Aberystwyth was a more convenient centre for Welsh-speaking Wales, that a considerable quantity of material had been collected there as the 'Welsh Library' of the University College of Wales, and that a site on Penglais hill had been given by Lord Rendel. However, the decisive consideration was that the owners of the two most important Welsh private libraries, Sir John Williams and J. H. Davies, had promised to give their collections to the library if (and only if) it was established at Aberystwyth. The Library's Royal Charter of incorporation, granted on 19 March 1907, placed a particular emphasis on its acquiring and preserving Welsh and Celtic materials, but it was also charged with the broader responsibility of 'the furtherance' of higher education and research.

Several months before the Library opened in temporary premises in the Old Assembly Rooms in Aberystwyth at the beginning of 1909, six architects had been invited to submit plans for the permanent building.[5] In June 1909 the successful candidate, Sidney K. Greenslade, was appointed architect. The foundation stone of the first stage of the building was laid in 1911, and before the end of 1916 the collections had been moved there. Apart from cost-cutting modifications to the central hall in the early 1950s, Greenslade's scheme was adhered to until the completion of the first stack in 1965. Pressure on space, acute during 1980s, was relieved by a five-floor 'temporary' stack in 1990-1, and the latest addition, the Third Building, opened at the end of May 1996, should provide storage for the next twenty-five years. The burden of building costs (up to the mid-1960s the Treasury had borne less than half the costs of construction) has imposed severe limitations on the Library's ability to purchase material.

Sir J. Herbert Lewis played a most important part in ensuring that the National Library gained its invaluable legal deposit privileges under the 1911 Copyright Act.[6] While this allowed it to acquire the major proportion of printed material (including maps, atlases, and music) published in the United Kingdom and Ireland from 1 July 1912 onwards, fierce resistance by the publishers imposed limitations on the Library's right to claim expensive books and those published or imported in limited editions,[7] precisely those works which might be considered to be of greatest significance for the art of the book. As well as material acquired by deposit, purchase, and an international exchange scheme, the Library has benefited from a flow of donations and bequests.

This chapter concentrates upon those collections in the Library's Department of Printed Books which are a historic testimony to the book as an art form. The three foundation collections contribute only modestly to the concept of the 'Art of the Book'. The 'Welsh Library' is primarily of literary, historical, and general Welsh cultural significance. But the other two have wider artistic connotations. The Shirburn Castle collection — originally the books of Moses Williams (1685-1742) — which forms the nucleus of the Sir John Williams collection, is visually imbued, in mellow bindings, with a compelling antiquarian aura which excites the most fastidious bibliophile. Sir John's collecting had other elegant diversions: a set of Kelmscott Press books, and sixteenth-century illuminated volumes of French, Dutch, and Flemish imprint. In like manner the third foundation collection, the Tŷ Coch library of the antiquary and bibliophile Edward Humphrey Owen (1850-1904), contains more than select Welsh treasures. Owen shared Sir John Williams's delight in fine copies and echoed his Kelmscott interest with notable volumes from the Baskerville and Strawberry Hill presses.

The National Library has gradually assembled from various sources four collections which are particularly apposite to the art of the book: incunabula, sixteenth-century European imprints, private-press books, and bindings.

Incunabula, inheriting the design and artistry of the Renaissance manuscripts which they so frequently imitate, are, in many instances, the high-water mark of typographic elegance and woodcut illustration. Because they were often illuminated by the artists whose workshops had long been devoted to decorating manuscripts, they embody the confrontation between a new technology, printing, and an old art, painting in books.[8] Moreover, this illumination in printed books has supplied dated evidence (in imprints) of great utility to the art historian. The National Library incunables are not over-endowed in illumination, but the *Astronomica* of Manilius (Bologna, 1474) serves as an admirable example of illuminated capital and border. More commonly the Library's incunables are fine reservoirs of early woodcuts, instanced by the first illustrated Terence (Lyons, 1493), of fundamental importance as a source for stage design; and notably by Schedel's *Liber Chronicarum* (Nuremberg, 1493), one of the first sources of late-medieval cityscapes. The Library now owns some 250 incunables, predominantly German, Italian, and French imprints.[9] Strasburg and Basle printers account for most of the Library's Germanic group, and Venice dominates as a centre of Italian printing. Seven different editions of the *Roman de la Rose* add lustre to the Parisian imprints. They came to the Library by way of the notable collector F. W. Bourdillon, who will be discussed below.

The sixteenth-century European imprints in the Library (some 2,500) have been specially catalogued with full bibliographical details and references including provenance. This attention reflects their peculiar importance in the art of the book as printing spread throughout Europe. The Dutch bibliographer Wouter Nijhoff first assigned the name 'post-incunable' to the period from 1500 to 1540, flamboyantly calling that phase the 'metamorphosis of printing from the swaddling-clothes of the incunabula period to an adult typography'.[10] His picturesque turn of phrase was perhaps a somewhat harsh verdict if taken literally, for the incunable page was, more often than not, scarcely less than elegant. What the printers of the early sixteenth century did was to lighten the heavy shadow cast by the gothic manuscript book by using new Roman and italic types and by introducing new ornament and illustration in imaginative page designs. By virtue of their editorial and linguistic powers and their care in the preparation of texts, these printers have justifiably been called 'scholar-printers', a fair reflection of their role in Renaissance scholarship. Leading scholar-printers were Johann Froben of Basle, Jodocus Badius of Lyons and Paris, Robert Estienne of Paris, and Aldus Manutius of Venice. Works from all these printing houses are well represented in the Library's collection. Some of the more famed German presses represented are those of Johann Grüninger of Strasburg, Erhard Ratdolt of Augsburg, Anton Koberger of Nuremberg, and Johann Amerbach of Basle. The last was the master of Froben, who modelled his type and styling on Aldus, whom he befriended. Froben also cultivated close personal and professional ties with Erasmus, and employed Hans Holbein as illustrator.

French printers represented are no less important. Antoine Vérard of Paris was strictly a publisher, engaging printers and illustrators. He often veered towards exotic illustration, even hand-coloured, for wealthy patrons. Jodocus Badius used a woodcut device of a press in action which, in the opinion of some art historians, was designed by Dürer. Geoffroy Tory of Paris was the epitome of a Renaissance figure, scholar, linguist, illuminator, and wood-engraver, who designed both type and ornament. The Estiennes founded a veritable printing dynasty, Robert Estienne, son of the founder, Henri, providing his scholarly age with formidable Greek, Latin, and Hebrew dictionaries, and reputedly conducted business at his press in Latin.

Aldus Manutius of Venice stands apart from his Italian contemporaries by his dedication to printing newly discovered Greek and Latin texts. His editorial team of illustrious scholars included Theodore Gaza, Pietro Bembo, Marcus Masurus, and Erasmus. Aldus made his own ink, used the finest Fabriano paper, and commissioned new roman, Greek, and italic types. In 1501 he revolutionized the publishing scene by producing an edition of Virgil in small octavo format, a Renaissance prototype of the twentieth-century Everyman series, and in 1502 introduced his famed (and widely imitated) dolphin and anchor device. Aldines have always engaged the affections of collectors. There have been two notable Welsh examples of Aldine bibliophily. One large group was acquired by the second Earl of Powis (1785-1848) in 1841 at the disposal of the virtually perfect set formed by Samuel Butler, bishop of Lichfield.[11] Butler's collection was itself largely based on that of Antoine Augustin Renouard, bibliographer and historian of the Aldine dynasty, which was sold in London in 1828. The Earl's Aldines were eventually bought by Quaritch in the 1923 sale of Powis books.[12] The other notable Welsh collection was that of Thomas Johnes of Hafod who acquired 550 Aldines from the Pesaro family of Venice. These he arranged in chronological order (from 1494 to 1594) in his privately printed catalogue of the Pesaro library.[13] Aldines were one of Johnes's passions; three days before he died he shared a bottle of champagne with the Harrovian classical editor Henry Drury and fell to discussing the Hafod Aldines.[14] The National Library's collection includes about a hundred examples of Aldines from the library of J. Burleigh James.

The listing of sixteenth-century highlights is not complete without referring to the Library's Low Countries holdings, notably from the Antwerp press of Christophe Plantin, who introduced copper-plate illustrations, an embellishment which found fruition when his son-in-law, Balthasar Moretus, forged a working partnership with the incomparable Rubens as designer of frontispieces and title-pages in the Baroque manner.

In 1890 William Morris set up his Kelmscott Press at Hammersmith and began printing in the following year. It was the beginning of what we now term the Private Press Movement, the outstanding presses being Kelmscott (1890-1898), Doves (1900-1917), and Ashendene (1894-1935), 'the great trilogy of English Private Presses' as Ruari McLean has called them.[15] In its seven years existence the Kelmscott Press produced fifty-three books, in all some 18,000 copies. Its supreme moment was, of course, the *Chaucer*, with its elaborate ornament by Morris and woodcuts by Burne-Jones. The Doves Press shared Morris's insistence on good composition, margins, and paper. A real difference was the choice of type, based on Jenson's roman, and the eschewing of illustration other than coloured initials, seen at their compelling best in the Doves *Bible*. The Ashendene Press books were illustrated, but its creator, the versatile C. H. St. John Hornby, commissioned a special hybrid gothic-roman type, based on the Subiaco type used by early German printers in Italy, to replace the Caslon and Fell types used initially. In this he followed in Morris's footsteps by creating inevitable (if decorative) barriers to ease of reading. The care, time, and craftsmanship inherent in making these frequently hand-printed volumes has prompted some to say, almost as if in criticism, that they are to be viewed as works of art as distinct from products of the printing press. But given the low level of printing design at the end of the nineteenth century they should rather be thought of as restating fundamentals, known to the printers of the Renaissance but gradually eroded by catering for a mass market.

The National Library has gradually assembled a collection of some 1,200 private-press volumes, a great reservoir of art, design, and inspiration. The core of this collection was that formed at Gregynog during the first phase of the history of that illustrious press, providing, one can imagine, a context of reference in which the emerging Gregynog Press could function. Moreover, within the collection passed on to Aberystwyth were both ordinary and special bindings of the Gregynog books themselves. Other donations, notably Sir John Williams's Kelmscott volumes, contributed to the Library's private-press holdings, and increasingly there have been purchases by the Library, for many of these volumes fell outside the legal deposit provision. In this way the Library has come to include a fair cross-section of the notable revival of smaller private presses throughout Europe and America in the 1970s and 1980s.

Fine bindings were clearly one of the elements in book design which necessitated the establishment at the Library of a special collection. As with the products of private presses there are, almost certainly, exceptional examples of the craft lying undetected in the larger holdings. The present collection was brought together by the Library's first Conservation Co-ordinator, Eiluned Rees, and is best approached through her series of bookbinding descriptions in the 'Biographica et Bibliographica' section of the *National Library of Wales Journal* between 1984 and 1990 which analyse and illustrate a remarkable range of bindings. The technique of under-painted vellum (paintings visible under translucent vellum) is found in a Welsh *Book of Common Prayer* (Cambridge, 1770) bound by Edwards of Halifax, whose characteristic borders of Greek key-board design are also a feature of this example.[16] A volume of Shakespeare's *Sonnets* (Chiswick Press, 1928) features a modern corollary to Edwards's under-painting, a hand-painted miniature of Shakespeare inset under glass on the upper cover.[17] Two exotic bindings of the Victorian age are a carved wood design (in imitation of medieval carved bindings) executed on a chromolithographic volume by Owen Jones, son of 'Owain Myfyr'; and moulded *papier-mâché* covers on a work by Henry Noel Humphreys.[18] The brilliant French traditions of bookbinding are sampled in descriptions of the work of Charles Meunier[19] and Petrus Ruban,[20] the latter illustrating the art nouveau style, which also features in descriptions of volumes bound at the Hampstead Bindery,[21] by the Guild of Women-Binders,[22] and by Morley of Oxford.[23] A binding of shimmering gold and black rules by Bernard C. Middleton is representative of the best of modern binders,[24] while the art of the fine Gregynog Press binder, George Fisher, is analysed in relation to that press's issue of Xenophon's *Cyrupaedia* (1936).[25] The traditions of fine craftsmanship at the Library's own bindery are continued in John Ewart Bowen's binding for the first volume of the *History of Merioneth* (1967)[26] and in Julian Thomas's coloured inlays forming an 'all-over' landscape to a Vermont edition of *Reynolds Stone Engravings* (1977).[27] The bindery extended its obligation to fine bindings by securing, in the late 1970s, an archive of albums recording the work of the notable Birdsall bindery of Northampton.[28]

We have, up to this point, considered those Library collections assembled to illustrate the book crafts of the fifteenth and sixteenth centuries and the modern period, and also the wider chronological span of the holdings of fine bindings. We can now turn to collections which, with one exception, centre on individual collectors.

The purchase in 1922 of the library of Francis William Bourdillon (1852-1921) of Midhurst, Sussex, poet, literary scholar and bibliographer, must rank as that which primarily allowed Aberystwyth to be a major centre for the study of the art of the book of the early and high Renaissance. The purchase included sixty-six incunables and 320 sixteenth-century books. While early illustrated books and fine bindings are present in profusion, the great specialities are French medieval romance, and, more strikingly, no fewer than twenty-three editions printed before 1550 of the *Roman de la Rose* with their famed woodcuts.[29]

In 1981 the National Library acquired 211 works either designed by or relating to the American book designer Bruce Rogers (1870-1957), a major purchase which complemented its existing holdings of fine printing. Most of Rogers's corpus is now available at the Library for viewing as a separate collection. From 1900 to 1912 Rogers was consultant to the fine book department of the Riverside Press, Boston, where he was allowed to indulge his liking for translations of classical and Renaissance texts. Critics have singled out for special praise his *Essays of Montaigne* in a new type based on Jenson, the *Song of Roland* with hand-coloured roundels, and Auguste Bernard's *Geoffroy Tory* in Riverside Caslon.[30] Rogers's second period in England between 1916 and 1919 has been described as 'part of the folklore of the history of British 20th-century book typography'.[31] In September 1917 he was appointed typographical adviser to the Cambridge University Press. The closely argued and uncompromising report which he delivered to the Syndics at the end of 1917[32] urged that their books should have an 'unmistakable stamp', and this he helped initiate before his departure in the summer of 1919.

Between 1919 and 1928 Rogers worked with William Edwin Rudge at Mount Vernon while acting as a consultant to the Harvard University Press and the Monotype Company. During his third period in England, from 1928 to 1932, he designed and oversaw the printing of two of his finest achievements. The first, a translation by T. E. Lawrence of Homer's *Odyssey* (1932) which was printed slowly and intermittently on Emery Walker's small jobbing press,[33] was acclaimed as reaching the finest style of the Doves Press.[34] Rogers's final triumph in England was the printing of the majestic *Oxford Lectern Bible* (1935) at the University Press, Oxford.[35] Here, as with the *Odyssey*, there was meticulous preparation and constant adaptation to accommodate the idiosyncrasies of the text which most printings simply ignored. As well as these major works, Rogers designed several books for the Limited Editions Club of New York. Printers and book designers are rarely honoured by national institutions, but a fresco on the ceiling of Enoch Pratt Free Library, Baltimore, and a stained-glass window at the American Type Founders Company, Jersey City, depict his colophonic device. More impressively, it also appears on one of the six bronze panels on the doors of the Rare Book Room of the Library of Congress, alongside those of Fust and Schoefer, and of the Kelmscott Press.

Of the many personal collections of scholars and literary figures acquired by the Library, two are of particular artistic interest. The purchase in 1978 of the large library of David Jones provides intimate access to his workshop. Replete with his annotations (and sometimes drawings), they illuminate the sources in religion, mythology, legend, history, literature, and art, which lie behind his paintings, inscriptions, and poetry.[36] The library of Professor Gwyn Jones, Norse scholar and doyen of the Anglo-Welsh literary movement, was given to the Library in 1987 and is also kept as a discrete collection. Comprising over six hundred volumes, it is a collector's library of fine and rare volumes, mainly from the eighteenth century.[37] A further collection of material relating to Icelandic saga (the Borg Collection) was donated by Professor Jones in 1993 and both donations have been subsequently augmented by him.

A group of scientific collections does not immediately suggest artistic relevance, but such is not the case. The Euclid collection of Sir Charles Thomas-Stanford (1858-1932) was presented to the Library in 1927 and has become one of the key reference points of Euclidean bibliographical scholarship. Of Welsh stock, Sir Charles was a collector on a major scale, 750 of his incunables eventually being sold to the American antiquarian bookseller Rosenberg. Sir Charles himself explained the artistic motivation behind his purchases of Euclid:

> I was led to collect and to study the early editions of Euclid's *Elements* by the beauty of some of the books, and by the interest attaching to the ingenuity of printers in associating a continuous series of diagrams with the text.[38]

The edition printed by Ratdolt in Venice in 1482, with its famed woodcut border on the first page, has become a prized collector's item.

The library of the Swansea naturalist Lewis Weston Dillwyn (1778-1855) was purchased in 1928. About a thousand volumes illustrate the history of botany from the sixteenth century to the nineteenth century. The herbals and flower books include the highly prized early-nineteenth-century issues of Redouté's *Les Roses* and Thornton's *Temple of Flora*. Redouté's plates have enormous artistic, botanical, and documentary value, and the Parisian production is perhaps the most celebrated of all flower books. Thornton's work is certainly the most impressive English botanical plate book. Intended as a pictorial celebration of the sexual system of Linnaeus, the plates are the greatest achievement of nineteenth-century graphic art, employing artists for hand-colouring and leading contemporary engravers for the mezzotint and aquatint content of these complex creations. Notable are the romantic, atmospheric, and exotic settings in which each flower is illustrated.

Bibliography
Under the terms of its Charter, the National Library is required to 'keep and make up annually' a register of all books printed in Welsh or other Celtic languages or relating to Wales and the other Celtic countries. From 1909 to 1984 the Library met this obligation by the publication of *Bibliotheca Celtica*, supplemented from 1978 onwards by the *Subject Index to Welsh Periodicals*.[39] From 1985 onwards these publications were merged to form

Llyfryddiaeth Cymru / A Bibliography of Wales which is available on-line as well as in printed form. As its title indicates, the scope of the new bibliography is narrower than that of its predecessor; rather than covering the entire Celtic field it restricts itself to books and articles that relate to Wales or are in the Welsh language.

Retrospective bibliography has been well-served in recent years with the publication in 1987 of *Libri Walliae: a Catalogue of Welsh books and books printed in Wales 1546-1820*, a work happily subjected to the design oversight of John Ryder of Bodley Head. The first volume of *Llyfryddiaeth Cylchgronau Cymreig / A Bibliography of Welsh Periodicals* covering the period from 1735 to 1850 appeared in 1993, and work on the second volume is well advanced.

The Welsh Bibliographical Society

The founding of the National Library was not the only indication of a growing Welsh interest in bibliographical study. D. Rhys Phillips, after brief periods in a Neath printing office and at the reading and editorial department of the Oxford University Press, became responsible in 1905 for the Welsh collections at Swansea Public Library. Mulling over the existence of a bibliographical society in Glasgow fathered the thought 'if Glasgow, why not Wales?'.[40] Since the 1873 National Eisteddfod had been the setting for the creation of the 'Welsh Library' committee, the Caernarfon National Eisteddfod of 1906 seemed the obvious place to promote the new venture. Thomas Shankland, Assistant Librarian in charge of the Welsh Library at the University College in Bangor, secured the Caernarfon Guild Hall as meeting-place. An appeal in the *Welsh Leader* was followed up by postcards circulated to Welsh 'bookmen' bearing the names of Ifano Jones, Thomas Shankland, J. Glyn Davies and, as convenor, D. Rhys Phillips. Among those present at the Guild Hall meeting were J. H. Davies, Ernest Rhys, W. J. Gruffydd, E. Vincent Evans, and J. D. Lewis. Although the meeting scarcely rivalled in dramatic appeal the nearby performance of Elgar's *Caractacus* by a three-hundred-voice choir — as Phillips put it, it was 'a day of small things and dreams in the dark' — a committee was appointed and a constitution subsequently drafted. Symbolically, the society's foundation preceded by some eight months the official setting up of the National Library.

The following year, at the first annual meeting of the new society in Swansea, J. H. Davies, its first Chairman, read a paper on 'Welsh bibliography and its aims', a classic statement of the nature and possibilities of bibliographical studies in a Welsh context.[41] Davies highlighted the essential difference between a catalogue and a bibliography, maintaining that the latter was pre-eminently the preserve of the collector possessing the bibliophilic instincts of viewing books in their complex environment of typography, paper, binding, provenance, and library and publishing history. Welsh printed books presented the collector and scholar with considerable difficulties. Early books were scarce in a land of few booksellers, and the miscellaneous *Amryw* volumes, economically bound in crude local styles, concealed an idiosyncratic range of works. Davies surmised, correctly, that the most fruitful bibliographical approach was for a collector to concentrate on a single title (such as *Canwyll y Cymry*), the works of one author, the output of one press (or the presses of one town), or a single genre such as hymnals, ballads, *marwnadau* (elegies), almanacs, or tracts.

In 1910 the Society issued the first number of its periodical, the *Journal of the Welsh Bibliographical Society*, under the editorship of J. H. Davies. Rather curiously, an editorial note stated that the decision to start a journal was 'not arrived at until every other form of interchange of knowledge between the members had been found impracticable'.[42] Despite the euphoria which initially may have seized some of the members, Davies had his feet firmly on the ground, for he ruefully acknowledged that 'the matter of such a Journal must of necessity be dry and uninteresting to all who are not concerned with the collection of Books, even though they may be lovers of literature.'

The pattern of the first volume (1910-15) generally abided by the precepts set out by J. H. Davies in his Swansea paper. Thus there was an account of a leading almanac publisher, a bibliography of Welsh Quaker literature, notes on local printers, and a bibliography of the Celtic scholar Heinrich Zimmer. There was also an account of the printed books formerly in the Hengwrt library, the beginning of a series on Welsh book collectors, and, perhaps more technical than Davies had envisaged, the analysis of a cancel in *Welch Piety*. Later volumes contained lists of Welsh titles entered in the registers of the Stationers' Company, a short-title list of Welsh books to 1700, and a series of bibliographies of translations into Welsh from languages other than English. During the early years imposing supplementary publications appeared including J. H. Davies's bibliography of eighteenth-century Welsh ballads (published in conjunction with the Honourable Society of Cymmrodorion between 1908 and 1911), a reprint of Moses Williams's pioneering 1717 bibliography of Welsh printed books (1912), a bibliography of works printed by John Ross of Carmarthen (1916), and a list of works by William Williams, Pantycelyn published between 1744 and 1800 (1918).

From the 1940s onwards articles by professional scholars, research students, and librarians tended to replace the contributions of enthusiastic bibliophiles. Since many of these writers were members of university departments of Welsh language and literature, Welsh became the predominant language of the *Journal*, thus reversing an earlier committee decision to prefer 'to err in the direction of giving greater consideration to the English language'.[43] For some reason the *Journal* was very slow to provide English-language synopses of its Welsh articles. Despite an editorial statement in 1966 that 'in future' synopses would be added 'for the sake of the very large number of members who are unable to read Welsh',[44] none were to appear until 1984. The natural (and historically apposite) practice of holding meetings annually at the National Eisteddfod (which itself finally adopted an 'all-Welsh rule' in 1950) constituted a further psychological barrier to the recruitment of non-Welsh-speaking members. At the same time, Welsh-speaking members had to decide whether to attend the Society's meetings in preference to rival Eisteddfod attractions.

Despite the high quality of contributions to the *Journal*, during the 1960s and 1970s the number of members remained well below that of the 1920s and 1930s.[45] Its restricted membership and persistent reluctance to raise its subscription to a realistic level[46] meant that the Society could no longer finance the publication of the *Journal* on a regular basis. Attempts were made by some members to revitalize the society during the 1970s, notably a resolution at the 1974 meeting to convene the Council 'to consider the whole pattern of the Society's work', but the end was near. Perhaps symbolically, the last issue of the *Journal* noted that an article on Swansea Borough Library's Welsh collection appeared by permission of Cymdeithas Bob Owen.

Although journals such as the *National Library of Wales Journal* and the *Transactions of the Honourable Society of Cymmrodorion* have frequently contained material of interest to historians of the book, as have county historical journals, the mantle of the Welsh Bibliographical Society fell, many would say, on Cymdeithas Bob Owen. From 1977 onwards this society, named after a renowned book-hunter and collector, has issued a thrice-yearly Welsh-language publication *Y Casglwr* (*The Collector*). Intended for the intelligent layman, it contains lively articles on a range of book-related topics. Since many of its articles include the fruits of primary research scholars cannot afford to overlook it.

In 1970, well before the demise of the Welsh Bibliographical Society, a new bibliographical organization came into existence with the founding of the Aberystwyth Bibliographical Group. Set up to 'foster a scholarly interest in printed books, manuscripts, and maps' it has, for over quarter of a century, regularly attracted as speakers the leading authorities in their fields from the United Kingdom and Ireland. In addition to its regular meetings the group has organized a number of residential bibliographical symposia, such as that at Gregynog in 1992 on the theme of 'The European Book' and at Tan-y-bwlch in 1995 on 'The Book in Wales'. Unlike the Welsh Bibliographical Society, the group has not ventured to publish a journal or other serial.

In 1997 three institutions located in Aberystwyth, the National Library of Wales, the Welsh Books Council, and the Department of Information and Library Studies at University of Wales Aberystwyth co-operated to launch Canolfan y Llyfr Aberystwyth / The Aberystwyth Centre for the Book. The Centre's aim is to study and promote the book in all its aspects, and one of its first ventures has been to launch an annual journal *Y Llyfr yng Nghymru / Welsh Book Studies*. As well as publishing bibliographical studies this bilingual publication is intended to provide an ongoing record of current research in the field of Welsh books, and should fill the gap created by the demise of the *Journal of the Welsh Bibliographical Society*. The Centre itself may well provide the central directing force to realize what D. Rhys Phillips saw as 'dreams in the dark' at the Guild Hall, Caernarfon, in 1906.

NOTES TO CHAPTER 33

1. A seminal conference was that organized by the Rare Books Group of the Library Association at Harrogate in 1986 under the title 'Exhibiting the word: book exhibitions and museums of the book'.
2. A. N. L. Munby, *Portrait of an obsession; the life of Sir Thomas Phillipps, the world's greatest book collector: adapted by Nicolas Barker from the five volumes of 'Phillipps Studies'* (London, 1967), pp. 256-7.
3. The fullest modern discussion is David Jenkins, 'A National Library for Wales: prologue', *THSC*, (1982), pp. 139-52.
4. Thomas Parry, 'Herbert Lewis a'r Llyfrgell Genedlaethol', in *Syr Herbert Lewis 1858-1933*, ed. K. Idwal Jones (Cardiff, 1958), pp. 56-78 (pp. 65-75).
5. Daniel Huws, *The National Library of Wales: a history of the building* (Aberystwyth, 1994) is the definitive study of this topic.
6. Parry, p. 76.
7. Initially the Library was restricted to claiming books published in editions of more than 300 copies. Over 400 copies of books costing more than £5 had to published and 600 of books costing over £10 for the Library to be allowed to claim them. Material of Welsh and Celtic interest was exempt from these restrictions (W. Ll. Davies, *The National Library of Wales: a survey of its history, its contents, and its activities* (Aberystwyth, 1937), pp. 172-5).
8. Lilian Armstrong, *Renaissance miniature paintings and classical imagery: the Master of the Putti and his Venetian workshop* (London, 1981), pp. 1-6.
9. Victor Scholderer, *Handlist of incunabula in the National Library of Wales* (Aberystwyth, 1940) supplemented by *Addenda & corrigenda, I* (Aberystwyth, 1941).
10. H. D. L. Vervliet (ed.), *Post-incunabula and their publishers in the Low Countries: a selection based on Wouter Nijhoff's L'art typographique* (The Hague, 1979), p. 2.
11. Gwyn Walters, 'The Herbert libraries of Montgomery and Powis', *NWR*, 3(4) (1990-1), 10-13 (p. 13).
12. Seymour De Ricci, *English collectors of books & manuscripts (1530-1930) and their marks of ownership* (Cambridge, 1930), p. 115.
13. The copy at the Old Library, St David's College, Lampeter, is one of the three known extant examples.
14. Elisabeth Inglis-Jones, *Peacocks in paradise* (London, 1950), p. 238.
15. Ruari McLean, *Modern book design from William Morris to the present day* (London, 1958), p. 28.
16. *NLWJ*, 23 (1983-4), 431-2.
17. *NLWJ*, 24 (1985-6), 277-8.
18. *Ibid.*, 389-92.
19. *NLWJ*, 26 (1989-90), 223-4.
20. *Ibid.*, 225-6.
21. *NLWJ*, 25 (1987-8), 467-8.
22. *Ibid.*, 468-9.
23. *NLWJ*, 26 (1989-90), 108-9.
24. *NLWJ*, 25 (1987-8), 122-4.
25. *Ibid.*, 121-2.
26. *Ibid.*, 241-2.
27. *Ibid.*, 351-2.
28. *NLWJ*, 26 (1989-90), 466-8.
29. F. W. Bourdillon, *Early editions of the Roman de la Rose* (London, 1906).
30. Frederic Warde, 'On the work of Bruce Rogers', *The Fleuron*, 4 (1925), 99-150. Reprinted in Francis Meynell and Herbert Simon, *Fleuron Anthology* (London, 1973), 138-59.
31. David McKitterick, 'Bruce Rogers at Cambridge, 1917-19', *Book Collector*, 29 (1980), 208-38 (p. 208).
32. *Report on the typography of the Cambridge University Press* (Cambridge, 1917), reprinted as a Cambridge Christmas Book in 1950 and by the Wynkyn de Worde Society in 1968.
33. Bruce Rogers, *Paragraphs on printing* (New York, 1943), pp. 148-60.

[34] Douglas Cleverdon, 'England', *The Dolphin*, 1 (1933), 342-56 (p. 356).
[35] Bruce Rogers, *An account of the making of the Oxford Lectern Bible* (Philadelphia, 1936).
[36] Paul Bennett Morgan, 'David Jones: an artist's library', *NLWJ*, 26 (1989-90), 337-42. The contents are listed in Huw Ceiriog Jones, *The library of David Jones (1895-1974): a catalogue* (Aberystwyth, 1995).
[37] Paul Bennett Morgan, 'Casgliad Castell Gwyn: the Gwyn Jones gift to the National Library of Wales', *NLWJ*, 26 (1989-90), 102-6.
[38] Quoted in Stephen Gaselee, 'The Euclid collection in the National Library', *NLWJ*, 1 (1939-40), 3-8 (pp. 3-5).
[39] The Library's formal responsibility for the *Subject Index to Welsh Periodicals*, originally produced by the Wales and Monmouthshire Branch of the Library Association, commenced with the volume for 1968-70.
[40] D. Rhys Phillips, 'The Welsh Bibliographical Society: some notes on its history', *JWBS*, 6 (1943-9), 242-8 (p. 242).
[41] Included in the Society's *Annual Report* for 1907.
[42] *JWBS*, 1 (1910-15), 32.
[43] *Ibid.*, 238.
[44] *JWBS*, 10(1) (1966-71), 1.
[45] The number of members exceeded 200 in the mid-1920s (*JWBS*, 3 (1925-31), 118) and stood at 54 institutional and 105 individual members in 1970 (*JWBS*, 10 (1966-71), 278).
[46] Personal subscriptions, initially 5/-, were not raised to 7/6 until 1949 and remained at that level until increased to 50 pence in 1971 and to £1 in the mid-1970s.

CHAPTER 34

THE NATIONAL LIBRARY OF WALES AND THE FUTURE OF THE BOOK

Lionel Madden

ANY discussion of the present and future role of the National Library of Wales as collector and preserver of the book must start with the Royal Charter granted to the Library on its foundation in 1907 and subsequently updated. The Charter makes two points very clearly: first, the Library's remit is not confined to printed materials or even to 'the book' in its printed and manuscript forms; and second, the Library's collections are not limited to Welsh and Celtic materials. The following passage from the Supplemental Charter granted in 1988 indicates the guidelines which underlie the Library's collecting policies:

> The objects of the Library shall be the collection, preservation and maintenance of manuscripts, printed books, periodical publications, newspapers, maps, photographs, paintings, pictures, engravings, drawings and prints, musical publications and works of all kinds whatsoever especially manuscripts, records, printed books and other works which have been or shall be composed in Welsh or any other Celtic language or which relate or shall relate to the antiquities, language, literature, philology, history, religion, arts, crafts and industries of the Welsh and other Celtic peoples as well as all works including audio-visual material whether connected or not with Welsh subjects composed, written or printed, filmed or recorded, in whatsoever language on whatsoever subject and wheresoever published which may help to attain the purposes for which the educational institutions existing in Wales were created and founded especially the furtherance of higher education and of literary and scientific research.[1]

It has been understood from its foundation that the Library has a primary responsibility to acquire and preserve items of Welsh interest. To this end each of the Library's curatorial departments — Printed Books, Manuscripts and Records, and Pictures and Maps — has attempted to build up Welsh collections which are as nearly comprehensive as is possible. A natural adjunct to this has been the acquisition of a wide range of materials in the Celtic languages and relating to the Celtic peoples. It is inconceivable that the acquisition and preservation of Welsh and Celtic materials should ever be other than the first priority of the Library. Inevitably, a great deal of staff effort is devoted to ensuring that all new publications of Welsh interest are acquired and that gaps in the stock of older Welsh books are systematically filled.

However, the Library's intention to be more than a Welsh and Celtic library was early signalled by its application for the legal deposit privilege. In 1911, only four years after the granting of the Charter, a revised Copyright Act named the new institution as one of the legal deposit libraries. Although certain limitations were placed on the Library's right to claim — and, indeed, were not lifted until 1987 — the Act effectively placed the National Library of Wales on a par with the National Library of Scotland, the Bodleian Library, Cambridge University Library, and Trinity College Dublin. All these libraries have the right to claim without charge any printed item newly published in Britain and Ireland. In this they differ from the British Library which has a statutory duty to receive **all** printed items published in the United Kingdom.

The exercise of the legal deposit privilege has meant that although collecting printed items relating to Wales and the Celtic peoples has always been central to the Library's activities, in terms of shelf space occupied they are far outstripped by other materials. The increasing output of British and Irish publications made it expedient for the Library to join the other legal deposit libraries in 1983 in using the services of the Copyright Libraries' Agent in London to identify, claim, and acknowledge relevant books and periodicals. Although the Library itself makes strenuous efforts to track down and claim everything published in Wales it relies heavily on the Agent for other materials.

One of the most striking developments of the last half century has been the enormous increase in printed material published in the United Kingdom. In 1947 the output of new books (including new editions) in the UK was 13,046. By 1968 that had increased to 31,470, and by 1988 to 62,063. The figure has continued to rise in the 1990s. In 1996 output for the first time exceeded 100,000. The figure fell slightly in 1997 but still reached 100,029, of which 23,693 were new editions.[2]

Since many factors were responsible for this increase in output it would be wrong to take the figures as necessarily indicating an equivalent increase in the book-buying public. For example, changes in marketing strategies and the growth of niche publishers have both been contributory factors to the increase in the number of titles.

So great an output of printed materials makes a selection policy essential and the current collection development policy of the Department of Printed Books clearly defines the criteria for claiming publications under legal deposit. Unfortunately, the legal deposit privilege does not extend to such print surrogates as microform and CD-ROM. These have to be bought from the Library's purchase grant and are becoming an increasing drain on it. Microform and CD-ROM sets are often expensive and their purchase inevitably restricts the number of non-UK and Irish printed publications that can be afforded. However, this may change quite soon. In 1997 the government issued a discussion paper on legal deposit.[3] It is hoped that legislation will subsequently be introduced to extend legal deposit to non-print publications.

Although the bulk of the Library's intake of printed works is acquired by legal deposit, it is vital that this is supplemented by purchases of non-UK and Irish books and periodicals if the Library is to fulfil the Charter requirement to serve the needs of higher education and research. The first priority is to create a comprehensive collection of materials of Welsh interest and a strong collection of Celtic interest. The second priority is to create international research collections in a range of specific humanities and social science topics. For other subjects of academic study, especially in the fields of science and technology, the Library aims at a comprehensive collection of UK and Irish materials but is not able to purchase significantly beyond these.

In addition to legal deposit and purchase, the Library has always benefited greatly from donations and bequests, both of money and of materials. Many great printed collections, as well as small groups of materials and single items, have come and continue to come to the Library as gifts. The Library welcomes offers of gifts, though, because of pressure of space, it usually cannot accept those that duplicate existing holdings.

The Charter makes it clear that the Library is charged not only with the collection of printed materials but also with their preservation. With a stock of nearly four million printed volumes, not to mention vast collections of other materials, the task of preservation is both time-consuming and expensive. The Library has a full-time Conservation Officer who is responsible, with the Keepers of the curatorial departments, for planning priorities for the work of conservation. A team of trained conservators repair and protect items to ensure their survival for future generations. The Library also has an extensive programme of preservation microfilming. Many items, such as twentieth-century newspapers, have, in reality, virtually no chance of long-term survival in their original form. In these cases, the policy is to microfilm them so that at least the content, if not the physical format, can be preserved. Preservation microfilming is also carried out on items which are subject to heavy use, so that wear and tear on the originals can be reduced. Although the Library seeks to preserve all its materials as well as possible, the cost of conservation means that it cannot avoid prioritization in this as in other areas of its work. As would be expected, Welsh materials have a very high priority. Since many books in Welsh and relating to Wales are heavily used, the Library acquires, where appropriate, a second copy as a conservation copy. This policy is applied systematically to new publications and is also pursued retrospectively for antiquarian and out-of-print books.

Once the legal issues of copyright are clarified it seems certain that digitization will offer the opportunity to copy and disseminate widely both printed and manuscript texts. It is likely, too, that digitization will in due course replace microform as a long-term preservation medium. Even then the Library would not lightly choose to destroy or discard original printed volumes simply because they were copied and stored in digitized form. So drastic a step could be contemplated only for selected materials within the context of a well-formulated co-operative policy which would ensure the survival within the United Kingdom legal deposit libraries of a minimum of two copies of every original, or where the originals were too fragile for preservation in their published form. And, of course, whatever may happen to other printed materials the Library has a clear duty to preserve indefinitely the originals of Welsh and Celtic books and finely printed and illustrated items.

Few would doubt the continuing need of the Library to acquire and preserve printed books, periodicals, and newspapers. Many, though, would ask how long the Library can expect the flow of printed materials to continue. Will print on paper remain a major medium for the dissemination of knowledge and entertainment or will it give way to other media? This is a question which, while it occupies the thoughts of all who are concerned with books, does not admit of an easy answer.

The question is not, in fact, a new one. Even before the impact of computers on information storage and dissemination became widely recognized, the use of microform prompted some commentators to predict the death of the book in its printed form. I recall, as a postgraduate student in librarianship in the early 1960s, hearing a lecturer predict that in the near future printed items would all be available on microform at low cost. Users requiring copies would purchase them from central stores to use on their personal microform readers. Because the cost would be so low there would no longer be a need for libraries. Certainly such a development was technically possible then and has remained so ever since. That it has not occurred is due to a combination of factors, not least the economic interests of producers of information and the enduring popularity of the printed book.[4]

The development of computerized methods of information storage and dissemination has, however, given a much stronger impetus to predictions of the death of the book. The 1970s saw a spate of predictions that the printed book would be replaced or at least have its influence greatly curtailed by the computer. In the late 1970s the advent of the Post Office's Prestel system (originally under the name of Viewdata) prompted many writers to predict a new revolution. In 1978 Peter Large wrote a piece in the *Guardian* under the eye-catching heading 'Throw away the books — Viewdata's coming', which prophesied the demise of works of reference in printed form.[5] In April of the same year Peter Fletcher announced in *The Times*:

> By this time next year the British will be able to do something that no other nation can. They will have available — in their homes and offices — as a public utility a service which will be capable of meeting almost all their needs for information.[6]

Prestel did not, of course, fulfil the dreams of its proponents but the debate did serve to clarify a growing feeling that computers may replace the printed word, at least for the storage and transmission of certain kinds of data.

The drawbacks of printed volumes were well set out over thirty years ago by the American information scientist J. C. R. Licklider who argued that, although the printed page is a superb medium for the display of information, bound books and journals are far less satisfactory except for use in consecutive reading.[7] As a means of storing information they are only fair; for retrievability they are poor; and they make no active contribution to the organization of a body of information. If this is true of individual books it is, argued Licklider, even more true of libraries of books. The same point was made a decade later by F. W. Lancaster who argued that a natural evolutionary process would ensure that by the end of the century communication in science and technology would necessarily operate through an almost exclusively electronic system.[8]

Both Licklider and Lancaster were attempting to predict the likely impact of computers on the printed book by the year 2000. Now that we are approaching that date we can see that, if their predictions have not come true as quickly or as completely as they expected, at least there is still a reasonable possibility that they will be ultimately realized. Bibliographic documentation early proved its suitability to dissemination on-line and through CD-ROM technology, and both methods are widely and increasingly used by the academic community. The National Library of Wales, like other research libraries, has a large and growing collection of CD-ROMs and makes extensive use of on-line bibliographical services. Rapidly increasing amounts of textual material are now available on the Internet. There is considerable and increasing pressure to promote the electronic journal as the answer to the undoubted problems of print communication, particularly in the fields of science, technology, and medicine. It seems very likely that the next few years will see a considerable development in the electronic dissemination of scientific, technical, and medical material which is currently published in hard-copy journals. At the same time, though, it is apparent that the advent of desk-top publishing has made it increasingly easy for individuals and groups to produce their own journals and newsletters without recourse to outside printers and it is not impossible that such publications will proliferate alongside the electronic journals.

Of course, the computer is not the only medium threatening the book. The rapid growth of the video industry, for example, has reinforced the competitive threat posed by television to the book as a medium of instruction and entertainment. Interactive multi-media formats pose a clear challenge to illustrated reference books. As the National Library of Wales will wish to access works in electronic form so it will also continue to acquire works produced in video and multi-media formats.

In his editorial to the issue of the Welsh Books Council's *Book News from Wales* celebrating the centenary of Gwasg Gomer in 1992 John Rhys speculated on the effects of audio-visual forms of communication and computerized information systems on the printed book. He recognized that sales of children's comics have been greatly reduced by competition from television and video and that they may eventually be entirely supplanted by them. Similarly, he predicted that computer technology would rapidly replace traditional reference books. Yet, despite these challenges, he saw reason to believe that the book will survive:

> It is still one of the seminal human inventions and still a viable technology in its own right. We have found nothing to beat it for convenience of carrying around, turning back and fore to other pages, marking passages and making marginal notes.[9]

It may still be true, as Jenny Rowley argued as long ago as 1981, that the continuing appeal of the book will lie in its extreme portability, the fact that it needs no intermediate equipment other than possibly a pair of spectacles, and the ease with which it can be scanned and compared with other texts. It is also true, as Rowley notes, that the book can be 'a work of art, with both a tactile and visual appeal'.[10]

All the authors quoted so far were writing before the impact of the Internet had begun to make itself felt. Whatever else it has done, the Internet has made everyone conscious of its potential as a world-wide medium for the exchange of information and ideas. Faced with the awesome possibilities of such a vast system of electronic communication, and the changing habits and expectations it may induce, it would be a brave person who would state categorically that the book could not ultimately be marginalized. Even so, despite the undoubted potential of the Internet, it has to be said that we appear at present to be a very long way from such a situation. A recent assessment by Philip Altbach seems to offer a reasonable statement of the outlook for the book:

> Book publishing is a small but complex industry. It faces significant challenges from changing patterns of ownership, from changing markets and from the implications of new technologies. It is unlikely, as some have argued, that the book will become obsolete in an era dominated by computers and the Internet.

Books are simply too convenient and too affordable. Books permit easy access to information. And in many parts of the world, there is little or no access to the new means of communication. The book as a cultural icon and as a knowledge product is here to stay.[11]

We can confidently predict a continuing move in the UK during the next few years towards the electronic publishing of academic and technical information. We can see an increasing threat to reading by children and teenagers because of the alternative attractions of productions in other media, particularly for entertainment but also possibly for information and study. Whether these trends will be exactly mirrored in Wales and whether there will be a more general move away from the book is more difficult to predict and will depend on a complex interaction of several different forces. Certainly there is nothing at present to suggest that Welsh-language publishing is in decline. The number of titles published annually in the Welsh language has increased enormously during the last seventy years. In 1925 a mere 74 new books (including reprints) were published in Welsh; fifty years later in 1975 the figure was 308.[12] Today, with the support of government grants administered through the Welsh Books Council, the Arts Council of Wales, and ACCAC (the Qualifications, Curriculum and Assessment Authority for Wales), and through the work of the Welsh Joint Education Committee and others, the figure is over 600. During 1997 a total of 641 Welsh-language titles were published of which 66% were aimed at the children's market. The number of English-language titles of Welsh interest received at the Welsh Books Council's distribution centre during 1997 was 425.[13]

It must be recognized that the provision of government funding to underpin publishing in the Welsh language makes the situation in Wales different from that in other parts of the UK. Since almost all Welsh-language publishing would be destroyed at a stroke were that financial support withdrawn, one must hope that, as long as the book survives as a vehicle for entertainment and the communication of knowledge, government funding for Welsh-language publishing will be maintained.

As the quotation from the Charter at the beginning of this chapter makes clear, the wide variety of formats which the National Library of Wales is committed to collect means that even so extreme a contingency as the death of the book would still leave the Library with plenty of work to do. Happily, the signs are that, at least for the foreseeable future, books will continue to form a major part of the Library's acquisitions. What we shall most probably see is an increasing proliferation of other formats which will find a place in the Library alongside its printed volumes. Just as earlier predictions — such as that photography would kill off painting, or the cinema would kill off the theatre, or television would kill off the cinema — have not been realized, so we may exercise a reasonable scepticism towards predictions that the book will be killed off by the newer technologies.[14] It has to be recognized, of course, that we may be deceiving ourselves and that a more apt historical comparison would be the impact on the horse of the internal combustion engine. Nevertheless, the Library's wholehearted participation in the foundation of the Aberystwyth Centre for the Book indicates its strong belief in the past and future significance of the book as a medium for human communication.

NOTES TO CHAPTER 34

1. Supplemental Charter and Statutes, 1988 Amendments. With the exception of some necessary additions for newer formats the wording follows closely the 1907 Charter.
2. *Bookseller*, 20 Feb. 1998, p. 18.
3. *Legal deposit of publications: a consultation paper* (Feb. 1997). The paper was issued by the Department of National Heritage, the Scottish Office, the Welsh Office, and the Department of Education Northern Ireland.
4. The idea was, in fact, a development of an argument advanced much earlier by an American librarian, Freemont Rider, in *The scholar and the future of the research library: a problem and its solution* (New York, 1944).
5. *Guardian*, 10 Jan. 1978.
6. *The Times*, 4 April 1978.
7. *Libraries of the future* (Cambridge, MA, 1965).
8. *Towards paperless information systems* (New York, 1978).
9. *Book News from Wales*, Autumn 1992, p. 3.
10. 'In defence of the book', *Library Association Record*, 83 (1981), 576-7.
11. 'Book publishing' in *World information report 1997/98*, ed. Yves Courrier and Andrew Large (Paris, 1997), p.326.
12. *Llais Llyfrau*, Winter 1977, pp. 24-5.
13. Figures supplied by the Welsh Books Council Jan. 1998.
14. These and other examples of inaccurate forecasting are cited by contributors to the thought-provoking, (but, irritatingly, unindexed) *The future of the book,* ed. Geoffrey Nunberg (Turnhout, 1996).

INDEX

Yr A.B.C. neu'r llyfr cyntaf i ddechreu dysgu darllain Cymraeg wrtho, Thomas Jones 102
ab Owen Edwards, Ifan 333, 336, 382–3
Abadam, Edward, Middleton Hall 140
Abercamlais, near Brecon, library 138, 143
Aberconwy Abbey, library 14, 45
Abercynon reading room 298, 301
Aberdâr public library 278, 281, 297, 298
Aberdare, Lord 314
Aberdyfi Institute 279
Abergavenny Academy 307
Abergavenny Baptist College 308, 309
Abergavenny Welsh Society *see* Cymreigyddion y Fenni
Abergorci Institute 303
Abertridwr Institute 298, 301
Aberystwyth 247
   Old Assembly Rooms 388
   public library 277, 278, 280
   Theological College 310
   Welsh-medium primary school 331
Aberystwyth Bibliographical Group 396
Aberystwyth Centre for the Book 396, 404
Aberystwyth Literary Institute 278
An Acre of Land, R. S. Thomas (1952) 366
Act for the Better Propagation and Preaching of the Gospel in Wales (1650) 99
Acts of Union, 1536–43 44, 83
Adagia, Erasmus 71
Adam, bishop of St Asaph 11
Adams Report (1915) 279–80, 287
Yr Addysgydd 205, 381
Yr Adolygydd (1838–9) 200
Yr Adolygydd (1850) 204
Advertising World 215
Yr Aelwyd 204
Agoriad byr ar y Gamut 238
Agoriad byrr ar Weddi'r Arglwydd, trans. by Robert Holland 59
Alchorne, Stanesby, Master of the Mint, 372
Alis (*fl.* 1550) 321
All Things Betray Thee, Gwyn Thomas (1948) 366
Allen & Unwin 363
Allen family, Cresselly, library 137–8
Allen, Mrs, Freestone Hall 141
Allen, Revd Joshua 138
Allied Newspapers Ltd 215, 216
Yr Allor Deuluaidd (1892) 176
Allwydd neu Agoriad Paradwys i'r Cymru, trans. by John Hughes (1670) 94, 98
Almanac y Miloedd 173, 179, 182
Yr Amaethydd 203
Amalgamated Press 216
Amerbach, Johann, Basle 389

American Type Founders Company, 392–3
Yr Amserau 168, 210
Analectica Glamorganica or *Analectica Morganica Archaeographia, Fragments of ye Antiquities of Glamorganshire* 88
Ancient Laws and Institutes of Wales, Aneurin Owen (1841) 230
Ancient National Airs of Gwent and Morganwg, Maria Jane Williams (1844) 238
Andria, Terence (1588) 72, 389
Aneirin 6
Angel's Christmas, Mrs Walton 382
Anglesey CUKT scheme 289
Anglica Historia, Vergil 69
Anglican works, seventeenth century 95–7
Anglo-Welsh publishing 355–70
Anglo-Welsh Review 368
Annales Cambriae 5, 29, 225
annals 5, 7–8
Annerch ir Cymru..., Ellis Pugh (1721) 253
Anrheg i Blentyn..., Thomas Jones (1816) 379
anterliwtiau 246
Antient British Music, John Parry (1742) 237
Antiquae Linguae Britannicae [...] Dictionarium Duplex, John Davies (1632) 71, 77–8, 79, 86, 96, 101
Antiquae Linguae Britannicae [...] Rudimenta, John Davies (1621) 70–1, 96
Anwyl, Edward 230
Anwyl, Revd J. Bodvan and Spurrell dictionary 192
Apologia, John Jewel, trans. by Maurice Kyffin 50, 59
Apperley, C. J., 'Nimrod', Plas Gronow, Wrexham 143
Appleton, E. R. 334
Ar Lannau'r Gamwy ym Mhatagonia: Atgofion, W. M. Hughes (1927) 273
Archaeologia Britannica, Edward Lhuyd 79, 88
Archaeologia Cambrensis 203
Archer, David 359
Ardizzone, Edward 368
Armageddon, Pae (1853) 176
Armes Prydein 6
Arwydd i Annerch y Cymru 99
Ars amatoria, Ovid , 6, 26
The art or crafte of rhetoryke, Leonard Cox (1532) 67
Artegall, or Remarks on the Reports of the Commissioners of Inquiry into the State of education in Wales (1848), Jane Williams 323–4
Articulau neu Byngciau, (The Thirty-nine Articles) 95–6
Yr Arweinydd Cerddorol, Richard Mills 239
Ashendene Press 390

Asser 6, 26
Astronomica, Manilius (1474) 389
Athravaeth Gristnogavl, Morus Clynnog (1568) 50, 59, 61
Athravaeth Gristnogavl, Morus Clynnog (facs. 1880) 226
Yr Athraw 200, 211
Yr Athraw Cerddorol 239
Yr Athrofa 373
Aubrey, Sir John, Llantrithyd 139
Aubrey, William, Llannerch-y-medd, printer 205
Aufseeser, Hans 362
Autobiography of a Super-tramp, W. H. Davies 355
Autobiography of Edward, Lord Herbert of Cherbury (1928) 374
The Autobiography of Elizabeth Davis, Jane Williams (1857) 323
Babington, Gervase 58
Badius, Jodocus, Lyons 389, 390
Bala College library 309, 310–11
Bale, John 46
The Ballad of Judas Iscariot, Robert Buchanan (1981) 376
The Ballad of the Mari Lwyd, Vernon Watkins (1942) 363
ballads 245–51
 production and distribution 247–8
 subject content 246–7, 248
Ballantyne, Hanson, Edinburgh, printers 181
Ballinger, John 230–1, 288, 289
Ban wedy i dynny air yngair allan o hen gyfreith Howel dda / A certaine case extracte out of the ancient Law of Hoel da, William Salesbury (1550) 57
Baner ac Amserau Cymru 173, 182, 211, 218
Bangor
 public library 277, 278
 Theological Colleges 310
 Training College 312
Bangor Manuscript Society 231, 233
Bangor Religious Tract Society 1254
Barddoniaeth Dafydd ab Gwilym, Owen Jones and William Owen (1789) 36, 149, 150, 152, 222
Barddoniaeth Dafydd ab Gwilym, Owen Jones and William Owen (1873) 228
Bardhoniaeth neu brydydhiaeth, y llyfr kyntaf, Wiliam Midleton 57
The Bardic Museum, Edward Jones (1802) 237
Bargoed Institute 301, 302
Barker, Christopher 60, 61
Barker, Robert, printer 60, 61
Barlow, William, bishop of St David's 26
Barnes, Albert
 commentary on the New Testament 177

Barnes, Joseph, Oxford, printer 61, 68
Basilikon Doron 57, 61, 85
Basingwerk abbey school 14
Baterie of the Popes Botereulx, William Salesbury (1550) 57
Bates, John, Holyhead, circulating library 131
Beaumaris Home Reading Society 130
'Be da fai y byd a fu', Siôn ap Robert ap Rhys ap Hywel 58
Beauties of British Antiquity, John Collinson (1779) 58
Bedlinog Institute 300
Bedwas Rebel 216
Y Beirniad 204
Bembo, Pietro 390
Y Beread 256
Bernard, bishop of St David's 10
Berry, Gomer, Viscount Kemsley 215
Berry, Henry Seymour, Baron Buckland of Bwlch 215
Berry, William, Lord Camrose 215
Berwyn, R. J. (1836–1917) 266, 270
Bevan, Aneurin 301, 303
Bevan, Madam Bridget, 112, 114
Beveridge Committee (1951) 336
Beynon, Thomas (1745–1833) 308
Bible 1588 50, 58, 60, 62, 310
Bible 1620 95
Bible 1630 98
A Bibliography of Welsh Periodicals / Llyfryddiaeth Cylchgronau Cymreig / 1735–1850 (1993) 394
A Bibliography of Wales / Llyfryddiaeth Cymru 394
Bibliotheca Alchorniana 372
Bibliotheca Celtica 393
Bibliotheca Pesaroniana (1807) 372
Bibliotheca Rudingiana Topographica (1807) 372
Biggs and Cottle, Bristol, printers 372
Bill, John 237
Bird, John, Cardiff, printer 127
Bishop, George 60
BL, Cotton Cleopatra B.V, pt. ii 33
BL, Cotton Faustina C.I, fols 66–93 28
Black Book of Carmarthen 8, 29, 34
Black Book of St David's (1326) 13
The Black Venus, Rhys Davies 356
Blackwell, John, 'Alun' 201
Blaenafon Institute 298
Blaenclydach Institute 302
Blaenpant, near Cardigan, library 138
Blaguryn y Diwygiad 199–200
Blodau i Blant, Peter Williams (1758) 379
The Blue Bed, Glyn Jones (1937) 362
Blue Books, 1847
 see Education Commission Reports 1847

Board of Celtic Studies 233
Bodfel, Peter, London and Chester, stationer 94
Bodrhyddan (Flint.), library 143
Bodwrda, Wiliam, Aberdaron (1593–1660) 85
Bodysgallen library 143
Bollifant, Edmund 61
Bonaparte, Prince Louis-Lucien 226
Book Clubs 130
  Welsh books in 282
Book of Aneirin 8, 29, 34, 75
Book of Common Prayer 50, 57, 58, 60, 61, 101, 391
  see also *Llyfr Gweddi Gyffredin*
Book of Commoneus 26
Book of Durrow 26
Book of Homilies 96
Book of Hours 35
Book of Kells 26
Book of Llandaf 3, 4, 26, 28
  see also Liber Landavensis (1840)
Book of Llywelyn the Priest 88
Book of Taliesin 6, 29, 31, 34
Book of the Anchorite 13
  see also 'Llyfr yr Ancr' *Llyvyr Agkyr Llandewivrevi*
book trade
  1718–1820 123–33
  nineteenth century 162–3
Book Trade in Wales 293
bookbinders 129
bookplates 139
Books in Wales / Llais Llyfrau 348
booksellers 348
Boore, Roger 349
Boots subscription libraries 282
Bosanquet family, Dingestow Court, near Monmouth, library 138
Botryddan family 85
Boultibrook, near Presteigne, library 138, 142–3
Bourdillon Report (1962) 291
Bourdillon, Francis William (1852–1921) 389, 392
Bowdler, Thomas 311
Bowen Report (1972) 333
Bowen, Revd John, Bath 141
Bowen, John Ewart, bookbinder 375, 391
'Brad Dynrafon', D. Pughe Evans 241
Bradbury & Evans 189
Bradford, Andrew, Philadelphia, printer 253
Braslinelliad o Hanes Cymru rhwng 1281 a 1485, William Gilbert Williams (1927) 373
Bray, Horace Walter, artist 374
Breckonshire CUKT scheme 288
Brecon
  Academy (Coleg Coffa) 307, 309

  Mechanics' Institute 282
  Training College 312
Brecon Gazette 210
Breuddwyd Macsen 154
Breuddwyd Maxen ed. by Ifor Williams (1908) 230
Breuddwyd Rhonabwy 15
The Breuiary of Britayne, Humphrey Lhuyd trans. by Thomas Twyne (1573) 60, 69
Bridges, Sir Harford Jones 143
A briefe and a playne introduction... , William Salesbury (1550) 55, 56
Brigstocke, Frances, Blaenpant 139
Bristol 127
  Academy 309
British Antiquities Revived, Robert Vaughan (1662) 87
Broadcasting Council for Wales 335
Brockman, James, bookbinder 376
Broster family, Chester and Bangor, printers 125, 128, 129, 143, 209
Broster, John, Bangor, printer 125, 126–7
Broughton, Hugh 72
Brown, Sydney Morse, principal of Carmarthen School of Arts and Crafts 191
Yr Brud a'r Sylwydd 202
Brud Cenadawl 200
Brud Cenadol 200
Brut: Newyddur y Wladfa Gymreig 266
'Brut Tysilio' 36
Brut y Brenhinedd 9, 29, 31, 36
Brut y Saesson 88
Brut y Tywysogyon 13, 29, 69, 86, 87, 88, 197, 225
Bryer, H., London, printer 373
Brynaman Institute 301
Brynbella (Flint.) 143
Bryngwyn (Mont.), library 140
Brynllywarch Academy 307
Y Brython 205
Bulkeley, Lady, Baron Hill 139
Buddioldeb Crefydd i'r Ieuenctyd 380
Buddioldeb yr Iau i Bobl Ieuangc..., John Elias (1818) 380
Y Bugail 204
Burgess, Thomas, bishop of St David's 221, 311
Burn, James, London, bookbinders, 181
Burne-Jones, Edward 390
Bute, third Marquess of 281, 314
Butler, Samuel, bishop of Lichfield 390
The Buttercup Field, Gwyn Jones (1945) 364
Byd y Bigail, ballad 245
Bynneman, Henry 61, 69
Bywgraffiadur Cymreig 350
C. Arthur Pearson Ltd 215

Cadell and Davies 127
Cadfan Stone 27
Caernarfon
  ballad production 247
  grammar school 14
  public library 278
  Training College 312
Caernarfonshire CUKT scheme 287, 288
Call Back Yesterday, Geraint Goodwin (1935) 357
Cambrensium Caroleia, William Vaughan (1625) 68
Cambria Daily Leader 215, 216, 249
The Cambrian 127, 180, 209
Cambrian Archaeological Society 225
Cambrian Institute 225
Cambrian Journal 225
The Cambrian Magazine 197
Cambrian News 215
The Cambrian Quarterly Journal and Celtic Repertory 203
Cambrian Quarterly Magazine 154, 155
Cambrian Register 151, 154
Cambrian Societies 222
Cambrian Tract Society 125
Cambridge University Press 392
The Cambro-Briton 154, 203
Cambrobytannicae Cymraecaeve Lingua Institutiones, Siôn Dafydd Rhys (1592) 57, 60, 70
Campbell, John, Stackpole Court 140
  library 142
Can i Etholwyr Rhan-barth Llanybyther (1892) 373
Caniadau Cranogwen, Sarah Jane Rees (1867) 324–5
Caniadau Seion, Richard Mills (1840) 239
Caniadau Sion (1827) 255
Caniadau y Cyssegr, John Roberts (1839) 239
Y Caniedydd Crefyddol, William Owen (1828) 239
Y Caniedydd Cymreig, John Thomas (1845) 238
Canolfan y Llyfr Aberystwyth / Aberystwyth Centre for the Book 396, 404
Cantata y Plant, Joseph Parry (1873) 382
Canwyll y Cymru, Rhys Prichard (1681) 97
Y Capten 383
Cardiff
  City Library, 1986 293
  public library 277, 279, 280, 281, 289, 290, 294, 314
  regional library bureau 289
  Theological College 310
  Welsh Society 281
Cardiff Book Society 130
Cardiff Times 215, 216
Cardigan 278
Cardigan Book Society 135
Cardiganshire

CUKT scheme 288, 290
  mobile libraries 292
A Cardiganshire Landlord's Advice to his Tenants Thomas Johnes (1800) 372
Carmarthen 44, 247
  Academy (Presbyterian) 307–8, 309
  circulating libraries 130
  printing, 123, 124, 125, 189–96
  public library 278
  Training College 312
Carmarthen Antiquarian Society 192
Carmarthen Book Society 130
Carmarthen Journal 132, 209
Carmarthen Literary and Scientific Institute 282
Carmarthen Priory, library 14
Carmarthenshire Association of the Federation of Master Printers of Great Britain 192
Carmarthenshire CUKT scheme 288, 289, 290
Carn
  see Griffith, Richard (1861–1947)
Carnarvon and Denbigh Herald, The 203
Carneddog
  see Griffith, Richard (1861–1947)
Carnegie United Kingdom Trust 279, 287–9
Carnegie, Andrew 279
'Carolau' St Richard Gwyn, 59, 62
Carolau, a Dyriau Duwiol, Thomas Jones 102
Carter, Isaac, printer 123, 132, 245
Cartrefi Cymru, O. M. Edwards (1896) 382
Car-wr y Cymru, yn anfon ychydig gymorth i bôb Tad..., Oliver Thomas (1630) 98, 100
Car-wr y Cymru, yn annog ei genedl anwyl..., Oliver Thomas (1631) 98
Caseg broadsheets 364
Y Casglwr 396
Cassell, publishers 215
Catalogue of Books belonging to the Pembroke Society (1791) 126
Catalogue of the Late Pesaro Library at Venice, now Forming Part of the Hafod Library (1806) 372
Catechism 50
Catechismus parvus, Alexander Nowell (1578) 58
Cathedral Builders (Gregynog, 1991) 368
Caton, R. A. 363
Caxton, William 42
Cefn Coch MSS 229
Cefn Treflaeth family, Llŷn 85
Ceinion Llenyddiaeth Gymraeg, ed. by Owen Jones 'Meudwy Môn' (1876) 228
Y Celt 212
Celtic Fables, Fairy Tales and Legends, Jane Williams (1862) 323

Celtic Remains, Lewis Morris (1878) 148
Celtic Researches, Edward Davies, 371
Celynog Collection 313
Cenhadwr Americanaidd 256
Central News 212
Central News Agency 212
Y Cerbyd Dirwestol 200
Y Cerddor 240, 242
Y Cerddor Cymreig 240, 242
Ceredigion 294
  see Cardiganshire
Cesail Gyfarch, near Tremadoc 140
Chamberlain, Brenda 364
The Character of a Quack-doctor, Thomas Jones (1676) 101
Chard, Thomas 60, 61
Charles o'r Bala (1859) 204
Charles, David (1812–78), principal of Trefeca 310
Charles, Thomas, Y Bala 125, 198
charters 2, 3, 10–12
Chatto 356
Cheshunt College 309
Chester 123, 125, 127, 245, 247
A Child's Christmas in Wales, Dylan Thomas 368
children's literature, to 1950 379–85
  periodicals 381–3
  religious works 379–81
Childs, Bungay, printers 180, 181
Chilton, Irma 349
Chirk Castle library 135, 136, 140, 142
Choice collections, collected out of large and valuable volumes... (1726) 123
Chronicles of [...] Monstrelet [...] trans. by Thomas Johnes (1809) 372
Christie's Old Organ, Mrs Walton 382
Church Defence Institution 169
Church Institution 169
Y Chwarelwr, film (1935) 333
Chwech o gablwyr meddw 248
Chwedleu Seith Doethon Rufein 87
cinema 333
Clarke, Isaac, Rhuthun, printer 176, 177, 242
'Y Clasuron Cymreig' 183
clera 34
Clerke, Bartholomew 72
Clerkenwell school 147
Y Clwb Llyfrau Cymreig 34
Clwyd library authority
  European information service 293
'Clwydian Press' 174
Clynnog, Morus (1525–81) 48
Cockerell, C. R. 311
Cockerell, Sydney, bookbinder 376

codex 25
Coedmor, near Cardigan, library 143
Coedrhiglan, near Cardiff, library 135
Cofrestr o lyfrau Cymraeg 128
Cofrestr o'r holl Lyfrau Printjedig [...] yn y Iaith Gymraeg hyd y flwyddyn 1717, Moses Williams 123
Collections Historical and Archaeological relating to Montgomeryshire 226
College of Librarianship Wales 293
'Collier Boy', Idris Davies 359
Colliery Workers' Magazine 216
Collins, William, Glasgow, publishers 194
Collins-Spurrell Welsh Dictionary 194
Colwyn Bay public library 279
Commentarioli Britannicae Descriptionis Fragmentum, Humphrey Lhwyd 69
computers, impact of 402
Comus (1931) 375
Constantine, George (c. 1500–?60) 46
Cook, A. J., home library 300
Coppi o lythyr crefydhvvr a merthyr dedhfol discedig at i dad, trans. by Roger Smyth (1612) 97
Cor-Drysor y Bedyddwyr 259–60
Corbet family, Ynysmaengwyn 85
Corgi Books 358
Corwen public library 280
Cory, Clifford J., Ystrad 298
Cotton, Andrew, bookbinder 376
Cotton, Sir Robert 86
Countess of Huntingdon's College, Trefeca 308, 309
Court Colman, near Bridgend, library 135, 138
Cowbridge Book Society 130
Cowbridge Diocesan Society 130
Cox, John, Aberystwyth, printer 260–1
Cox, William, Aberystwyth
  circulating library 131
  subscription reading room 131
Crawford committee (1925) 334
Crawford Committee Report (1974) 337
Crawshay, Richard 119
Crinnodeb o adysc Cristnogaul, trans. by Roger Smyth (1609) 97
Y Cronicl 325
Cronicl Cenadol 200
Cronicl yr Oes 210
Crowley, Richard 60, 61
Crymlyn Institute 302–3
'Crynodab or Diarebion sathredig', William Salesbury 56
Culhwch ac Olwen 6, 8, 349
Cunliffe, Sir Foster, Acton Park 139
The Curate of Clyro (1983) 376

Curriculum and Assessment Authority for Wales 349
Cwm Hyfryd, Patagonia 268, 269
Cwmaman Institute 299, 301, 302, 303
Cwmtillery Searchlight 216
Cwrs y Byd 206
Cyd-gordiad Egwyddorawl o'r Scrythurau, Abel Morgan (1730) 253
cydfodau 15
Cydymaith i Lenyddiaeth Cymru 350
Cydymaith yr Ieuengctid 381
Y Cyfaill Eglwysig 190
Cyfaill mewn Llogell, John Williams 238
Cyfaill yr Aelwyd 205
cyfarwyddiaid 8
Cyfreithieu Hywel Dda ac eraill, seu Leges Wallica, Wotton, William and Moses Williams (1730) 36
Cyfres Corryn 349
Cyfres Datrys a Dirgelwch 350
Cyfres y Ceinion 183, 228
Cyfres y Clasuron Cymreig 228–9
Cyfres y Fodrwy 350
Cyfres yr Arddegau 349
Cyfrinach y Bedyddwyr 200
Cyhoeddiadau Curiad 243
Cylch Dewi 334
Y Cylch-grawn Cynmraeg 197–8
Cylchgrawn Rhyddid 201
Cylchgrawn y Gymdeithas er Taenu Gwybodaeth Fuddiol 201–02
Cymdeithas Bob Owen 395, 396
Cymdeithas Llên Cymru 230, 233
Cymdeithas yr Iaith Gymraeg 333, 337
Y Cymedrolwr 200
Cymer Library 300, 301
Y Cymmrodor 225–6
Cymmrodorion Record Series 227
Cymmrodorion Society 116, 117, 147, 148, 149, 151, 155, 221, 225-7
  library 223
Cymreigyddion 153–4
Cymreigyddion y Fenni 222, 223, 323
Cymru 206, 382
Cymru Fu, ed. by Isaac Foulkes 177, 228
Cymru'r Plant 206, 382
Cymry Fydd 206
Cynddelw (fl. c.1155–95) 8
Cynfeirdd Lleyn, John Jones, 'Myrddin Fardd' (1905) 230
Cyngen, king of Powys 3
cynghanedd 49
Y Cynghorydd Meddygol Dwyieithawg 202–03
Cynon Valley library authority 292

Cynwal, Wiliam 83, 86
Cynwrig Sais 14
Cyrupaedia, Xenophon (1936) 375, 391
cywyddwyr 34
d'Ewes, Sir Simonds 87
Daearyddiaeth ac Hanesiaeth Amerig y De, R. J. Powel (1880) 273
Dafydd ap Gwilym 34, 87, 118, 149
  see also Barddoniaeth Dafydd ab Gwilym, Houses of Leaves
Dafydd ap Llywelyn 12
Dafydd Benwyn 86
Dafydd Epynt 34
Dafydd Nanmor 34
Dafydd, Edward (1600–78) 84
Dafydd, Ishmael, Trefriw, printer 238
Daily Dispatch 215
Daily Graphic 215
Daily Mail 216
Daily Mirror 216
Daly Telegraph 216
Daniel, John, Carmarthen, printer 128, 130, 132, 189, 238
Y Darian 215
A Dark Side of the Sun, Shirley Jones (1985) 377
Darlleniadur, sef Hyfforddiadur hawdd ac eglur i ddysgu darllain Cymraeg... (1820) 380
Y Darlunydd 205
Darmerth neu arlwy i weddi, trans. by Robert Holland 59, 61
datgeiniaid 34
Davies, Alun Talfan 342
Davies, Aneirin Talfan 342
Davies, Catherine, Llanforda 139
Davies, Christopher 243
Davies, D. C., USA, printer 256
Davies, D. S. 262
Davies, Daniel, Ton 309
Davies, David (d. 1807) 198
Davies, David (1818-90), industrialist 374
Davies, David Henry, vicar of Cenarth 312
Davies, E. Curig 383
Davies, Edward, USA, printer 256
Davies, Elfyn Talfan 342
Davies, Griffith, mathematician 202
Davies, Gwendoline and Margaret, Gregynog 374
Davies, Henry Rees, Treborth 316
Davies, Idris 358, 361, 363
Davies, Ishmael *see* Dafydd, Ishmael
Davies, J. Glyn 313, 394
Davies, J. H. (1871–1926) 230–1, 232, 233, 313, 388, 394, 395
Davies, Jesse Conway, medical practitioner 202
Davies, John, Brecon

see Rhys, Siôn Dafydd
Davies, John, *Y Goleuad* 211
Davies, John, Llandeilo, printer 132
Davies, John, Llanfihangel Ystrad, cobbler and bookbinder 129
Davies, Dr John, Mallwyd 70–1, 76–8, 87, 94, 95–6
Davies, John Powell, Carmarthen, printer 189
Davies, Joseph, lawyer 202
Davies, Margaret (*c.* 1700–85) 321
Davies, Margaret and Gwendoline, Gregynog 374
Davies, Rhys 302, 358, 362, 366
Davies, Richard, bishop of St David's 58
Davies, Richard, 'Mynyddog' 173
Davies, Robert (*c.*1658-1710), Gwysaney and Llannerch, naturalist and antiquarian 87, 136, 139
Davies, Ronald 193
Davies, T. A. 214
Davies, W. H., 300
Davies, Walford 242
Davies, Walter 'Gwallter Mechain' (1761–1849) 127, 221, 223, 224–5
library 313
Davies, William, partner in Cadell and Davies 127
Y Ddraig Goch (Lewis Jones) 268
Y Ddraig Goch (Plaid Cymru) 335
'De Bardis Dissertatio', Evan Evans 72
De Britannica Historia Recte Intelligenda, et cum Romanis Scriptoribus Reconcilianda (David Powel)
De Imitatione Christi, Thomas à Kempis 98
De Invectionibus (1216) 10
De Mona, Humphrey Lhwyd 69
De Senectute, Cicero 70
De Trinitate, St Augustine 6, 28
Deaths and Entrances, Dylan Thomas (1946) 360
Deaths and Entrances, Dylan Thomas (Gregynog ed., 1984) 376
Dee, Dr John 67
deeds 16
Defensio, John Prise (1573) 60, 61
Della costruttione latina (Siôn Dafydd Rhys) 70
Denbighshire CUKT scheme 288–9
Denham, Henry 61
Dent 359, 360, 363
Department of Information and Library Studies, University of Wales Aberystwyth 293, 396
Derfel, R. J. 206
Derwydd library 140
Descriptio Kambriae, Gerald of Wales (1194) 8, 69
A Design of a British Dictionary, Historical and Geographical, Edward Lhuyd 88
Devereux, Walter, earl of Essex 72
Dickinson, John, papermaker 180
dictionaries 75–81
A Dictionary in Englyshe and Welshe, William Salesbury 56, 60, 61, 75
A Dictionary in Englyshe and Welshe, William Salesbury (facs. 1877) 226
A Dictionary of the Welsh language, William Spurrell 190
Difyrwch i'r Pererinion, Joshua Watkin, 238
digitization 401, 404
Dillwyn family, Swansea, library 138
Dillwyn, Lewis Llewelyn 141
Dillwyn, Lewis Weston 127, 141
library donated to the National Library of Wales 393
Dilyniad Christ, trans. by Hugh Owen (1684) 98
Dinas Institute, Pen-y-graig 299, 302
Y Dinesydd Cymreig 216
Dingestow Court, library 138, 143
Dingle, Habib, bookbinder 376
Y Dirwestydd 200
Dissenting Academies, libraries 307–11
distribution agents 128–8
Y Diwygiwr 201
Diwygwyr, Merthyron a Chyffeswyr Eglwys Loegr, Thomas Jones (1813) 173
Dolau Gwyn family 85
Dolaucothi library 135
Dolgellau reading club 167
Dosparth byrr ar y rhan gyntaf i ramadeg Cymraeg, Gruffydd Robert 56, 60, 61, 62
Dottrina Christiana, Bellarmino 98
Doves press 390, 392
Y Drafod 270–2
Y Dravod: Newyddur y Wladva 268–70
Drexelius's Considerations on Eternity (1661) 96
Druid Press 365
Drury, Henry 390
Y Drych 254, 256, 257, 258, 259, 261
Y Drych Americanaidd 256
Drych Cristianogawl (1585) 47, 51, 59, 62, 87
Drych Cydwybod... (1661) 98
Drych y Prif Oesoedd, Theophilus Evans 190
Y Dryslwyn, Elizabeth Watkin-Jones (1947) 384
Y Drysorfa 158, 199, 381
Drysorfa Hynafiaethol 203
Dublin 127
first Welsh book printed in 99
Dubthach 5
Dull o Fedyddio a Dwfr (1730) 253
Duncan, David, proprietor of the *South Wales Daily News* 213

Durston, Thomas, Shrewsbury, printer 124, 125, 245
Dwnn, Lewys (c.1550–c.1616) 86, 88
Dwnn, Siams (c.1570–c.1660) 85
Dyfed Cambrian Society 221–2
Dyfed library authority 293
Dylanwad Mam, Mrs T. Williams 273
Dysgedydd Crefyddol 199, 201
Dysgedydd y Plant 381
Eames, Marion 350
Ebbw Vale Literary and Scientific Institute 283
Ebbw Vale Miners' Institute 299
economy, post-war 329–30
Eddowes family, Shrewsbury, printers and booksellers 127
education 99, 163, 331–2
Education Commission Reports 1847 158, 166, 202, 204, 321, 323–4
Edwards, Alun R., Librarian, Cardiganshire Joint Library 291, 344
Edwards, Charles 94, 100, 101
Edwards, Fanny (1876–1959) 325, 382
Edwards, Halifax, bookbinder 391
Edwards, Howell Holland, Pennant 140
Edwards, Huw T. 336
Edwards, John, Chirk 14, 36
Edwards, John III of Chirk 76
Edwards, Lewis 177, 203, 309
Edwards, O. M., 183, 301
  and Guild of Graduates of the University of Wales 230
  libraries 279
  periodicals 206, 382
Edwards, Richard, USA, printer 256
Edwards, Roger, Mold 204
Edwards, Thomas Charles (1837–1900) 310
Eglvrhad helaeth-lawn o'r Athrawaeth Gristnogavvl, trans. by Richard Vaughan 98
Eglvryn Phraethineb, Henri Perry (1595) 57, 60, 68, 71, 72
Eighteen Poems, Dylan Thomas (1934) 359
Ein Breiniad 266–7
Ein Kleinot von Trost und Hilfe in allerlei Trübsale, Otto Werdmüller (1595) 59
eisteddfod 167
  Caernarfon, 1906 394
  Mold National, 1873 387
  provincial 222
Yr Eisteddfod 205
Yr Eisteddfodwr 272
El Chubut 270
El Mentor 272
El Regional 272
Eldridge, M. E. 365

Elegy, Thomas Gray (1981 edn) 376
Elements, Euclid 393
Elfoddw, archbishop of Gwynedd (d. 809) 5
Elia and the Last Essays of Elia (1931) 374
Elias, John (1774–1841) 164
Eliot's Court Press 61
Elis, Islwyn Ffowc 350
Ellis, Mrs Ann Parry 'Brythonferch' 325
Ellis, Evan, Llanfihangel Glyn Myfyr, bookseller 246, 247
Ellis, Gwenni, intinerant bookseller 129
Ellis, John, Llanidloes, printer 374
Ellis, Tom MP 313
Ellorgast, Shirley Jones (1986) 377
The Elucidarium and other tracts in Welsh from Llyvyr Agkyr Llandewivrevi (1894) 230
Emmanuel, William Rees 178
Empire News 215
Emynau y Cyssegr 176
Engan, Elen 325
Enoch Pratt Free Library, Baltimore 392
Enwogion Cymru, Robert Williams (1852) 222
Epigrammatum Libri Quatuor, John Stradling (1607) 68
An epistle of a religious priest to his father, Robert Southwell (1612) 97
Erasmus 42–3, 46, 390
Erddig, near Wrexham, library 138
Eros and Psyche, Robert Bridges (1935) 375
Esquel 268
Essays of Montaigne 392
Esslemont, David, Gregynog, printer 375
Estienne, Henri 390
Estienne, Robert, Paris 389, 390
Esyllt, Elizabeth Watkin Jones (1951) 384
Etmic Dinbych 6
Yr Eurgrawn Wesleyaidd 199
Evans, Alan Gerwyn Davies 373
Evans, Beriah Gwynfe 205
Evans, Christmas 164
Evans, D. Emlyn (1843–1913) 240
Evans, Daniel Silvan (1818–1903) 205, 229
  dictionary 191
Evans, Delme William Campbell Davies 373
Evans, E. Vincent 394
Evans, Ellin 'Elen Egryn' (1807–76) 323
Evans, Evan 'Ieuan Fardd' (1731–88) 110, 115, 117, 118, 149
Evans, Evan 'Ieuan Glan Geirionydd' (1795–1855) 202
Evans, Gwynfor 330, 335, 337
Evans, John, Carmarthen, printer 125, 128, 130, 132, 200, 202
Evans, John Gwenogvryn (1852–1930) 229, 230

Evans, P. M., Holywell, printer and USA, 260
Evans, Samuel, Derby, papermaker 180
Evans, T. J. 230
Evans, Thomas 'Tomos Glyn Cothi' (1764–1833) 119, 198
Evans, Titus, Machynlleth, printer 125, 132, 198
Evans, W. J., principal, Carmarthen Academy 307
Evans, W. J. Burdon 374
Evans, William (d. 1718) 307
Everett, Robert, USA, printer 256, 257
Exposition of the Lord's Prayer, William Perkins 59
Eyre and Spottiswoode 174, 181, 205, 367
Faber 363
The fables of Esope (1932) 375, 376
Fagg, Filmer, Swansea circulating library 131
Fairbank, Alfred 375
Fairy Legends and Traditions of the South of Ireland, T. Crofton Croker (1828) 155
Falls the Shadow, Shirley Jones (1995) 377
Y Faner 215, 249
Farley, Samuel and Felix, Bristol and Pont-y-Pŵl, printers 124
Feldman, Luis 272
Fenton, Richard 140
Ferndale Institute 298, 302
Ffarwel Weledig, William Williams (1766) 114
Y Ffenestr 381
Y Ffydd Ddi-ffuant, Charles Edwards (1667) 99, 190
Financial Times 215, 216
The first book of the Christian exercise, appertayning to resolution, Robert Parsons 96
Fisher, George, bookbinder 375, 391
Fisher, John (1862–1930) 229
Fitzalan, Henry, twelfth Earl of Arundel 69
Five Arches Press, Tenby 194
Five Flowers For My Father, Shirley Jones (1990) 377
Flintshire public library 292
Y Flodeugerdd Newydd, W. J. Gruffydd (1909) 230
Flores Poetarum Britannicorum, John Davies (facs. repr. 1864) 227
Fonmon Castle library 136, 142
For Gladstone, Shirley Jones (1988) 377
Fortune Press 363
Foulkes, Revd Humphrey 79
Foulkes, Isaac, Liverpool, printer 177, 183, 228
The Four Ancient Books of Wales, W. F. Skene (1868) 228
Four Branches of the Mabinogi 2, 8
Francis, John Deffet (1815–1901) 279

Frankel, Revd E. B. 324
Fraser, Peter, artist 383
friendly societies 166
Froben, Johann, Basle 389
Y Frythones 325
Fuchs, Leonhard 56
Funerall sermon, Richard Davies (1577) 58, 61
Gambold, William (1672–1728) 79
Gardening Dictionary, Miller (1763) 137
Garnett, Edward 357, 367
Garthewin library (Denb.) 140
Gaza, Theodore 390
Gedeon 200
Gee, Eric, printer 375
Gee, J. Howel (1854-1903), Denbigh, printer 176
Gee, Thomas (1780-1845), Denbigh, printer 125, 151, 173, 174
Gee, Thomas (1815-98), Denbigh, printer 151, 173-83, 203, 211, 228, 241, 261
Y Geiniogwerth 175, 180
Y Geirgrawn 198
Geiriadur Cymraeg a Saesoneg: A Welsh and English Dictionary, W. O. Pughe 151
Geiriadur Prifysgol Cymru 75, 79, 350
Geiriadur yr Academi 350
Gems of Welsh Melody 177
Genealogy of the High and Mighty Monarch James, George Owen Harry (1604) 57, 61
Y Genedl Gymreig 216, 218
Y Geninen 205
Y Geninen Eisteddfodol 205
Geoffroy Tory, Auguste Bernard 392
 see also Tory, Geoffroy
George Newnes Ltd 215
Gerald of Wales 8, 9, 10, 11, 29
Gesta Romanorum 88
Gethin, 'Sir' Lewis 55
Gildas 3, 4
Gill, Eric 364
Giradoni, Vincenzo 61
Gladstone, William Ewart, as book collector 139
Glamorgan Gazette 210, 213
Glamorgan Library 127, 130, 141
Glamorgan, Monmouth and Brecon Gazette 210
Glenrhondda Institute, Blaen-cwm 298
Gloddaith library 143
glosses 6, 27
Glossography, Edward Lhuyd (1707) 79, 88
Glynllifon family, 85
Gododdin 8
Y Gododdin (1852) 225
Gododdin of Aneurin Gwawdrydd, ed. by Thomas Stephens (1888) 226

Godynogh, Isabella 33
Gogerddan family 85
Gogynfeirdd 9, 13
Y Goleuad 211
Goleuad Cymru 199
Gollancz 361, 366
Golud yr Oes 205
Y Golygydd 200
Gomer Press 347, 403
Gomerian Press 364
Goodwin, D. G. 316
Goodwin, Geraint 368
Gorchestion Beirdd Cymru, Robert Ellis (1864) 228
  Gorchestion Beirdd Cymru neu Flodau Godidowgrwydd Awen, Rhys Jones (1773) 36, 152
'Gorhoffedd Gwr Harlech' 237
Gorsedd Beirdd Ynys Prydein 150
gospel books 1, 7, 26, 27
Gouge, Thomas (?1605–81) 100–01
Gower, Henry (d. 1374) 14
Grafton, Richard 60, 61
Gramadeg Cerddoriaeth, John Mills (1838) 239
A Grammar of the Welsh Language, W. O. Pughe 151
Grammatica, William Salesbury (1593) 61
Grammatica Britannica, Henry Salesbury (1593) 57, 70, 78
grant 343–4
Grant, Edward 72
Graves, Robert 365
Y Greal 153, 154
Greenslade, Sydney K., architect 388
Gregynog library 136, 141
Gregynog Press 374–5, 391
  see also Gwasg Gregynog
Griffith, Hugh 58, 60
Griffith, John, Llanddyfnan 85
Griffith, Owain, 'Ywain Meirion', ballad singer 248
Griffith, Richard (1861–1947) 218
Griffith, William, stationer 60
Griffith, Wyn 357, 365
Griffiths family, Brynodol 139
Griffiths, Mr, Tenby circulating library 131
Griffiths, Ann (1776–1805) 321
Griffiths, Creighton 361, 364, 365
Griffiths, D. G., Cardiganshire, librarian 288
Griffiths, E., Swansea, and USA 260
Griffiths, Thomas J., New York, printer 256–7, 259, 260
Grisiau Cerdd Arwest, John Ryland Harris (1823) 239
Gruffudd Hafren (*c*.1590–?1630) 84

Gruffudd Hiraethog (d. 1564) 33, 36, 56, 84, 86
Gruffydd, Owen, Llanystumdwy (1643–1730) 87
Gruffydd, W. J. 314, 342, 394
Gruninger, Johann, Strasburg 389
Gryffyth, Jaspar, Cegidfa (d. 1614) 86
Guest, Lady Charlotte, 139, 155, 222, 323
Guest, Sir John 323
Guild for the Promotion of Welsh Music 243
Guild of Graduates of the University 230, 232
Guild of Women-Binders 391
Gulston, Eliza, Derwydd, 139
Gutenberg, Johann (*c*. 1316–1468) 41
Gutun Owain (fl. 1455–1500) 15, 32, 33, 36, 75, 86
Gwaedd Ynghymru yn Wyneb pob Cydwybod, Morgan Llwyd (1653) 99
Gwagedd Mebyd ac Jeungctid..., trans. by Thomas Baddy 379
Gwaith Beirdd Môn (1879) 228
Gwaith Lewis Glyn Cothi 223, 224, 227
Gwaith Morgan Rhys 231
Gwaith Prydyddawl Edward Richard, Ystradmeurig (1866) 228
  see also Richard, Edward
Gwaith Thomas Edwards (Twm o'r Nant) (1874) 228
Gwaith y Parchedig Evan Evans (Ieuan Brydydd Hir) (1876) 228
  see also Evans, Evan
Gwalia Deserta, Idris Davies (1938) 363
Gwasg Aberystwyth 342
Gwasg Gregynog 374, 375–7
  see also Gregynog Press
Gwasg Llety Gwyn 373
Gwasg y Dref Wen 349
Gwasg y Wern 374
Gwasg yr Arad Goch 374
Gwassanaeth Meir 35, 87
Gwauncaegurwen Institute 300, 301
Gweddi Gyntaf Jessica, trans. by Thomas Levi (1876) 382
Gweithiau Morgan Llwyd, ed. T. E. Ellis 230
Gweledigaethau y Bardd Cwsg, Ellis Wynne 190–1, 229
Gweledigaethau y Bardd Cwsc, Ellis Wynne ed. John Morris Jones, (1894) 230
Gwerful Mechain (*c*. 1462–1500) 15, 321
Y Gwerinwr (1855–6) 204
Y Gwerinwr (Y Wladfa) 270, 271
Gwerslyvr Cymraeg-Hispaeneg, R. J. Powel (1881) 273
Gwerslyvr i Ddysgu Darllen Cymraeg..., R. J. Berwyn and Thomas Pugh (1878) 273

Gwilym ap John ap Gwilym 32
Gwilym Tew 34, 75
Gwilym Wasta 31
Gwinnett, Emilia, Penllyn Castle 139
Y Gwir Degwch 374
Gwir Iforiaid 166
Y Gwir Iforydd 203
Gwlad y bryniau, M. W. Griffith 241
Gwladgarwr 202, 203, 249
Gwron Odyddol 203
Gwybod 383–4
Gwyddoniadur Cymreig (1854–79) 175, 183, 310
Gwyddorion y Grefydd Gristianogol, trans. by Charles Edwards (1679) 100
Gŵyl y Glaniad 265, 268, 271
Y Gwyliedydd 202
Gwyn, Francis, Llansannor 139
Gwyn, Richard (*fl.* 1557–84) 51
Gwynedd library authority 293
Gwynedd, John (?1490–?1562) 46
Gwyneddigion Society 118, 147, 149–55, 221
Gwynn Publishing Company 243
Gwynne, Marmaduke 114
'Y Gyfres Cerddorol Gymreig' 242
Y Gymraeg mewn Addysg a Bywyd (1927) 331, 334, 343
Y Gymraeg yn ei Disgleirdeb [...] The British Language in its Lustre, Thomas Jones, 79, 101
Y Gymraes 204, 324, 325
Haberly, Loyd 375
Hafod library 142
Hafod Press 371–3
Haldane Commission 242, 314-16
Halkyn public library 282
Hall, Lady Augusta, Llanover 323
Hall, Sir Benjamin, Llanover 222, 223
Hamner, William 62
Hampstead bindery 391
Hanes Llenyddiaeth Gymreig o 1651 hyd 1850, Charles Ashton 227
Hanes y Werinaeth Arianin, Glan Caeron (1891) 273
Hanes y Wladva Gymreig Tiriogaeth Chubut, Lewis Jones (1898) 273
Hanes y Wladfa Gymreig yn Patagonia, Abram Mathews (1894) 273
Hanesiaeth a Gwyddoniaeth y Beibl yn Wir a Chywir 179
Hanley, James 366
Hanmer, Sir Thomas, MP 139
Hannah White & Sons, Carmarthen, printers 190
Harleian Genealogies 5
Harries, John, printer 193
Harris, Howel 114, 115, 117, 124–5, 309
Harris, John 128

Harris, Jonathan, Carmarthen, printer 125, 128
Harris, Joseph, 'Gomer' 199
Harris, Joseph, scientist 114
Harris, Thomas 114
Harry (Henry), Dafydd, Philadelphia, printer 253
Harry, George Owen, rector of Dinas and Whitchurch 57, 61, 86
Hartsheath, near Mold, library 140
Harvard University Press 392
Yr Haul 158, 190, 201, 211
Haul Gomer 255
Haverfordwest Baptist College 309
Heath, Charles, Monmouth, printer 126
Heddyw 206
Hen Ganiadau Cymru, Edward Jones (1825) 237–8
Yr Hên Lyfr Plygain (1683) 101
Hen Organ Christie, trans. by Thomas Levi (1880) 382
Henderson, James, printer 372
Hendrefoilan, Swansea, library 141
Hendregadredd manuscript 13, 29, 30, 31, 32, 34
Henley, Anton, binder 376
Yr Herald 249
Herald Company 216
Yr Herald Cymraeg 211, 218
Herald of Wales 358
Herbert, Edward, first Baron Herbert of Cherbury 136
Herbert, William, first earl of Pembroke 49, 60, 69, 71
Hereford Cathedral MS P.l. ii 26
Hermes, Gertrude 374
The Heroic Elegies and Other Pieces of Llywarç Hen, W. O. Pughe 150, 151, 152
The Heyday in the Blood, Geraint Goodwin (1936) 357
Heylyn, Rowland (?1562–1631) 49, 95, 98
A High Wind in Jamaica, Richard Hughes (1929) 358, 362
Highmead private press 373
Hill, Nicholas 61
Historia Brittonum 5, 8
Historia Gruffud vab Kenan 9
Historia Regum Britanniae, Geoffrey of Monmouth 9, 29, 68, 69, 71, 247
Historiae Brytannicae Defensio, John Prise (1573) 56, 60, 61, 69, 71–2
Historical Manuscripts Commission 229
Historie of Cambria now called Wales, David Powel (1583) 56, 61, 69
History of Brecknockshire, Theophilus Jones 131
History of Merioneth (1967) 392
The History of Saint Louis, Joinville (1937) 375

The history of the Literature of Wales from the year 1300 to the year 1650, Charles Wilkins 227
A History of Wales derived from Authentic Sources, Jane Williams (1869) 323
Hodgson, Herbert John, Gregynog, printer 374
Hodson, Fred, *Western Mail* 214–15
Hogarth 363
Holdich, Sir T. H. 267
Holford, J. J., Cilgwyn (Carms.) library 137
Holl Ddled-swydd Dyn, trans. by John Langford 96
Holyhead public library 280
Holyland, Pembroke, library 138
Honourable and Loyal Society of Antient Britons 147
Honourable Society of Cymmrodorion *see* Cymmrodorion Society
Hopcyn ab Einion 86
Hopcyn ap Hywel, Pen-y-fai 88
Hopcyn ap Tomas 14, 31, 36
Horner, Arthur 216
Houses of Leaves, Dafydd ap Gwilym 376
How Green Was My Valley, Richard Llewellyn (1939) 356-7, 359
Howell, James, Cardiff, shopkeeper 314
HTV 337
Huet, Thomas, precentor of St David's Cathedral 58
Hughes a'i Fab, Wrexham, printers 205, 233
  and USA 261
  children's publishing 381, 383
  music publishing 241–2, 243
  see also individual members of the family
Hughes de Jones, Irma 272
Hughes, Albert Llewelyn (1864–1944) 176
Hughes, Annie Harriet 'Gwyneth Vaughan' (1852–1910) 325
Hughes, Arthur (1878–1965) 271, 272
Hughes, Arwel 335
Hughes, Charles, Wrexham, printer 173, 175–83
Hughes, Charles Tudor, Wrexham, printer 176, 182, 183
Hughes, Ellen 'Elen Engan' 323
Hughes, Griffith, missionary 253
Hughes, H. J., America, publisher 254, 260
Hughes, Hugh, artist and publisher of *Y Papyr Newydd Cymraeg* 132, 210, 211
Hughes, Hugh 'Cadfan Gwynedd' (1824–98) 266
Hughes, Hugh Brython (1848–1913) 382
Hughes, J. M., Kansas 262
Hughes, Jane 'Deborah Maldwyn' 248
Hughes, John, Wrexham, printer, circulating library 131

Hughes, John Ceiriog 225
Hughes, Richard 365
Hughes, Richard, Llannerch-y-medd 315
Hughes, Richard, Wrexham, printer 173, 380
Hughes, Robert 'Robin Ddu yr Ail o Fôn' (1744–85) 147, 149
Hughes, Stephen (c.1622–88) 78, 94, 97, 99, 100
Hughes, T. Rowland 335, 350
Hughes, William, agent USA 261
Hughes-Stanton, Blair 374, 375
Humphreys, Emyr 337, 366–7
Humphreys, Henry Noel 391
Humphreys, Hugh, Caernarfon (1817–96) 205, 380, 381
  and USA 260
Humphreys, Humphrey, bishop of Bangor (1648–1712) 87, 140
Hunangofiant Tomi, E. Tegla Davies (1912) 383
Huntingdon, Lady 114
Hutchins, Michael, Gregynog, printer 375
Hutchinson 355
Huw Cae Llwyd 34
Huw Machno (c.1560–1637) 84, 85
Huxley, Thomas, Chester, printer 125
Hwyl 384
'Hyd fedd hi gâr yn gywir', D. Pughe Evans 241
Yr Hyfforddiadur 200
Yr Hyfforddwr 200
Hymnau yr Eglwys 192
Hywel Dafi 34
Hywel Dda 9
Hywel Fychan ap Hywel Goch of Buellt 31
Hywel Swrdwal 34
Hywyn, Gwenno 349
Ieuan ap Sulien, Llanbadarn Fawr 5–6, 27, 28
Ieuan Llwyd ab Ieuan 34
Ieuan Ysgolhaig 30
Ifan Llwyd ap Dafydd 46
Ifor Hael 203
Yr Iforydd 203
illumination 33
Impressions, Shirley Jones (1984) 377
In Parenthesis, David Jones (1937) 363, 367
In somnium Scipionis 28
In the Margins of Shakespeare, George Mackay Brown 376
Independent Academy 308
industrialization, nineteenth-century 159–62
inscribed stones 3–4
Institute of Journalists 213
internet 338, 403
Iolo MSS 229
Iscoyd Park, library 142
Itinerarium Kambriae, Gerald of Wales (1191) 8,

INDEX

69
Itinerary through Wales, Gerald of Wales (1989, Gregynog ed.) 376
Jackson, William 139
James, Angharad (1677–1749) 321
James, Ivor, college registrar 313, 314
James, J. Burleigh, book collector 390
James, John, Aberystwyth, printer 238
Jarme, Elias 272
Jarvis and Foster, Bangor, printers 230, 231
Jenkin, David, Swansea, subscription reading room 131
Jenkins, David, Aberystwyth, printer 241
Jenkins, David, professor of music (1848–1915) 240, 242
Jenkins, John 'Gwili' (1872–1936) 314
Jenkins, John 'Ifor Ceri' (1770–1829) 221
Jenkins, R. T. 217, 225, 310
Jernegan, William, Swansea, architect 142
Jessica's First Prayer, Hesba Stretton 382
John of Monmouth (d. 1323) 14
Johnes, Thomas, Hafod 111, 151, 371–2, 390
  library 138–9, 140
Jonathan Cape 355, 357, 362
Jones W. Bradwen (1892–1970) 242
Jones, Abel 'Bardd Crwst' 250
Jones, Alice Gray 'Ceridwen Peris' (1852–1943) 323, 325, 326
Jones, Alun, novelist 350
Jones, Athelstan O., agent 260
Jones, Cadwaladr 199
Jones, Crispianus, Carmarthen, bookbinder and bookseller 124
Jones, D. Gwenallt 342
Jones, D. L. 'Cynalaw', Briton Ferry (1841–1916), printer 242
Jones, Dafydd, Trefriw, author, bookseller, and printer 125, 371
Jones, Dan (1811–61) 200
Jones, Daniel, Wrexham 131
Jones, David, author 358
  library purchased by the National Library of Wales 393
Jones, David, Carmarthen, runaway apprentice 132
Jones, David, Merthyr Tudful, printer 238
Jones, David, 'Songster' 248
Jones, Elisabeth, Llannerch-y-medd, printer 242
Jones, Elizabeth Mary 'Moelona' (1877–1953) 325
Jones, Elizabeth Watkin (1887-1966) 384
Jones, Evan, 'Ieuan Gwynedd' (1820–52) 324
Jones, Evan Pan 206
Jones, Glyn 358, 360, 362, 363

Jones, Griffith, Llanddowror 112–13, 117
  The Welch Piety 117
  see also schools, circulating
Jones, Griffith, Y Bala, printer 177, 241
Jones, Gwyn 358, 361, 362, 364
  library donated to the National Library of Wales 393
Jones, Harry Longueville (1806–70) 225, 312
Jones, Hugh, Erfyl 211
Jones, Huw Ceiriog, private press 373–4
Jones, Isaac, Treherbert, printer 241, 242
Jones, J. Ifano 281, 394
Jones, Jack 358
Jones, Jane, Llannerch-y-medd, printer 242
Jones, John (1700–70), vicar of Shephall 307–08
Jones, John, Aberystwyth, bookbinder 129
Jones, John, Bethesda 242
Jones, John 'Jac Glan-y-gors' (1766–1821) 118, 153
Jones, John 'Tegid' (1792–1852) 223, 224
Jones, John, Gellilyfdy (*c.* 1578–1658) 84, 86, 87, 88
Jones, John, Llanrwst, printer, 125, 381
Jones, John, Talsarn 177
Jones, John Harris (1827–85) 309
Jones, John Mather 254, 258
Jones, John Mendus, Llanidloes, printer 239, 241
Jones, John Morris 231, 313, 315
Jones, John Viriamu 313
Jones, Josiah Thomas, printer (1799–1873) 207
Jones, Lewis (1836–1904) 266, 267–8, 270, 358
Jones, Lewis, Llannerch-y-medd, printer 242
Jones, Michael D. 309
Jones, Mrs Oliver (1858–93) 325
Jones, Owen, Llansanffraid-ym-Mechain, book collector 313
Jones, Owen 'Meudwy Môn' 207
Jones, Owen 'Owain Myfyr' (1741–1814) 149–50, 152–4, 155
Jones, Owen, son of Owain Myfyr 391
Jones, Penri 349
Jones R. Lloyd (1878-1959) 383
Jones, Richard 60
Jones, Richard, Dolgellau, printer and bookseller 128, 131, 203
Jones, Robert, 'Callestr Fardd' 248
Jones, Robert, Bethesda, printer 241
Jones, Robert, Fonmon Castle 142
Jones, Robert, Llanfyllin, subsequently vicar of Rotherhithe (1810–79) 224–6, 227, 228, 281, 313
Jones, Robert Ambrose 'Emrys ap Iwan' 179
Jones, Sam, BBC 335
Jones, Samuel (1628–97) 307
Jones, Samuel (*c.* 1682–1719) 307

Jones, Shirley, private press 376–7
Jones, T. Gwynn 342
Jones, T. Llew 349
Jones, T. O., 'Gwynfor', dramatist and librarian 287–8
Jones, Tegwyn 374
Jones, Theophilus, historian 141, 371
Jones, Thomas (1756–1820) 94–5, 123–4, 173, 197, 198–9
Jones, Dr Thomas, deputy secretary to the cabinet 374
Jones, Thomas, London and Shrewsbury, printer and bookseller
  almanacks 102, 245
Jones, Thomas 'Y Bardd Cloff' (1768–1828) 153
Jones, W. E. 'Cawrdaf', printer 212
Jones, W. Lewis 231
Jones, William, Llangadfan 110, 118
Jones, William, Wrexham 246
Jones, William Collister, Chester, printer 125, 131
Jones-Parry, Madryn 139–40
Journal of the Welsh Bibliographical Society 395, 396
Juvencus 5, 6, 27
Keimer, Samuel, Philadelphia, printer 253
Kelmscott Press 388, 390, 391, 393
Kemeys-Tynte, Charles, Cefn Mabli 135
Kemsley Newspapers 216
Kenyon Report (1927) 289
Kippers and Sawdust, Rigby Graham (1992) 376
Koberger, Anton, Nuremberg 389
Konstanz Gradual 237
Kyffin, Edward 59
Kynniver llith a ban or yscrythur lan ac a ddarlleir yr Eccleis..., William Salesbury 57, 61, 71, 75
La Cruz del Sur 270
Laboratories of the Spirit, R. S. Thomas 375
Lackington, Allen & Co. 127, 141
Lamentations of Jeremiah (1934) 375
Lancych, near Newcastle Emlyn, library 136, 143
landed classes 109–11
The Landscape Within, Bert Isaac (1992) 376
Latin literature 67–74
Law of Hywel Dda 29, 88
lawbooks 1, 2, 9–10, 31
Lawrence & Wishart 359
Le Miroir de l'âme pecheresse, Margaret of Angoulême (1597) 59, 61
Le Roman de la Rose 14
Lebor na hUidre 29
Leeswood and Tower, near Mold, libraries 139
Leland, John 46
Les Roses, Redouté 393
Lesclarcissment de la langue Francoyse, John Palsgrave (1530) 75
Letters from India, Alun Lewis (1946) 364
Levi, Thomas (1825–1916) 381–2
Lewis Merthyr Institute 300, 301
Lewis, Alun 360, 364
Lewis, Dr. George (1763–1822) 308
Lewis, Henry, (1889–1968) 194, 314
Lewis, Idris, composer (1889–1952) 242
Lewis, J. D. 394
Lewis, Sir J. Herbert, MP 387, 388
Lewis, J. R., Carmarthen (1857–1919) 242
Lewis, John of Llynwene 67–8
Lewis, Saunders 289, 333, 342
Lewis, William, Cardiff, printer 231, 364
Lewys Glyn Cothi (fl. 1447–86) 15, 32, 34, 75
  see also *Gwaith Lewis Glyn Cothi*
Lhind, William, Hafod, printer 372
Lhuyd, Edward 87, 116, 117, 123, 221
Lhwyd, Humphrey (1527–68) 56, 69
Libellus de Erudienda Iuventute, Leonard Cox 67
Liber Antiquus 13
Liber Chronicarum, Schedel (1493) 389
Liber Commonei (817) 5, 26
Liber Landavensis (1840) 10, 224
  see also Book of Llandaf
Liberation Society 168
Liberator 168
libraries
  academic 307–19
  cathedral 25
  circulating 130–1
  country-house 135–46
  ecclesiastical 14, 29, 35
  mechanics' institute 297–305
  miners' institute 297-305
  mobile 292
  monastic 25
  parish 34
  private 14
  proprietary 130
  public libraries 167
    to 1914 277–86
    1914–94 287–95
  subscription 282
  Welsh books in 280–2
  Sunday-school 283
  theological college 307-11
  welfare hall 302
Library and Information Services Council (Wales) 293
Libri Walliae: a Catalogue of Welsh books and books printed in Wales 1546–1820, Eiluned Rees (1987) 394
Lichfield Gospels 1, 6

Life, Travels and Reminiscences, Jonathan Ceredig Davies 373
Life of St Cadog, Lifris of Llancarfan (*c*.1100) 8, 10
Life of St David (1927) 374
Life of St Germanus of Powys 5
Life of St Samson 4
Lilly, Gweneth 349
Limited Editions Club, New York 392
Lindisfarne Gospels 26
literacy
  mediaeval 1–17
  fifteenth century 41
  sixteenth century 48
  seventeenth century 93
  eighteenth century 112
  nineteenth century 165–6
The Literary Remains of the Rev. Thomas Price, Carnhuanawc ..., Jane Williams (1854–5) 323
The Literary Women of England, Jane Williams (1861) 323
The Literature of the Kymry, Thomas Stephens (1849) 222
The Little Kingdom, Emyr Humphreys (1946) 367
Liverpool 127
Liverpool Daily Post 216
Llais Llyfrau / Books in Wales 348
Llanbadarn Fawr, scriptorium 27–8
Llanbeblig Hours 33, 35
Llanbradach Institute 299, 303
Llandeilo Fawr 26
Llandudno public library 278, 279
Llanelli library authority 292–3
Llanelli Mechanics' Institute 283
Llanerchaeron (Cards.), library 138
Llangoedmor, near Cardigan, library 138
Llangollen Baptist College 309
Llangollen International Music Eisteddfod 243
Llannerch library 136
Llanover, Lady 138, 139, 222
Llanrwst Reading Room and Library 283
Llantarnam Abbey library 14
Llanthony Prima 14, 25
Llanthony Secunda 25
Llanuwchllyn
  Independent College 309
  public library 279, 280, 281
Llanwenllwyfo Rectory private press 373
Llawlyfr Caniadaeth, Eleazer Roberts 240
Y Llenor 206
Llenyddiaeth y Cymry, T. Gwynn Jones (1915) 230
Lleuad yr Oes 202
Lliver Gweddi Gyffredin, trans. William Salesbury (1567) 58

Lloyd, Sir Evan, Bodidris 58
Lloyd, Evan, Corwen, smith 182
Lloyd, Sir J. E. (1861–1947) 231, 315
Lloyd, Revd J. R., Troedyraur 135
Lloyd, J. Selwyn 349
Lloyd, John, 'poor blind man' 248
Lloyd, John, Wigfair, library 138
Lloyd, Lady, Garth, Welshpool (d. 1734) 139
Lloyd, Meredydd, Welshpool (*c*.1620–95) 87
Lloyd, Thomas, Plas Power 79
Lloyd, William, bishop of St Asaph (1627–1717) 87
Llusern 200
Llwybr Hyffordd y Plentyn Bach I Fywyd Tragwyddol..., trans. by Theophilus Evans (1715) 379
Llwybr Hyffordd yn cyfarwyddo yr anghyfarwydd i'r Nefoedd, trans. by Robert Llwyd (1630) 96, 98, 100
Llwyd, Angharad 139
Llwyd, Huw, Cynfal (?1568–1630) 84
Llwyd, Siôn, Ceiswyn (d. 1634) 85
Llwynypia Institute library 301
Llyfr Baglan 88
Llyfr Barddoniaeth, Wiliam Middleton (1864 facs. repr.) 227
Llyfr Coch Asaph 13
Llyfr Del, O. M. Edwards (1906) 382
Llyfr Emynau, E. Stephen and J. D. Jones (1869) 176
Llyfr Gweddi Gyffredin, John Davies (1621) 95, 97
  see also Book of Common Prayer
Llyfr Gwyn Hergest 87
Llyfr Haf, O. M. Edwards (1926) 382
Llyfr Hir Amwythig 88
Llyfr Hir Llanharan 88
Llyfr Hir Llywarch Reynolds 88
Llyfr Mawr y Plant (1931) 383
Llyfr Nest, O. M. Edwards (1913) 382
Llyfr Pawb ar Bob-peth (1874) 175
Llyfr Plygain, John Davies (1633) 95
'Llyfr Rhetoreg', William Salesbury 45
Llyfr y Psalmau, Edmwnd Prys (1621) 237
Llyfr y Resolusion, John Davies (1632) 96, 100
Llyfr y Tri Aderyn, Morgan Llwyd 99
Llyfr yng Nghymru, Y / Welsh Book Studies 396
'Llyfr yr Ancr' 30, 31
  see also Book of the Anchorite
    Llyvyr Agkyr Llandewivrevi
Llyfrau'r Dryw 193, 342
Llyfrfa Gymreig 309
Llyfryddiaeth Cylchgronau Cymreig / A Bibliography of Welsh Periodicals 1735–1850 (1993) 394
Llyfryddiaeth Cymru / A Bibliography of Wales 394

Llym Awel, Shirley Jones (1993) 377
'Llysieulyfr Meddyginiaethol', William Salesbury 45, 75
Llythur ir Cymru Cariadus, Morgan Llwyd 99
Llythyrau Cymraes o Wlad Canaan, Margaret Jones (1869) 324
Llyvyr Agkyr Llandewivrevi 88
Llywarch Hen 6
Llywelyn ap Gruffudd 11, 12
Llywelyn ap Iorwerth 11, 12
Llywelyn Bren of Glamorgan (d. 1317) 14
Llywelyn, Robin 350
Local Government Act (1972) 292, 294
Lois, Elizabeth Watkin Jones (1955) 384
Y Lolfa 243, 347
London 116, 123
  book trade, 93–4, 127–8
London-Welsh 147–56
Longman 127, 154
Los galeses en Chubut: Fotografías (1987) 273
Lowe and Brydone, music engravers 241
Luned Bengoch, Elizabeth Watkin-Jones (1946) 384
Luther, Martin 43
Y Mabinogi 349
The Mabinogi 153, 154
Mabinogion 29, 31
Mabinogion (1838–49), Charlotte Guest 155, 224, 323
MacDonald, Lord, Gwaenysgor 335
Mackworth, Sir Humphrey, Gnoll 139
Macmillan 359, 366
Madocks, William, Tremadoc 140
Madog legend 222
Madog ap Gruffudd 12
Madruddyn y Difinyddiaeth Diweddaraf, trans. by John Edwards 96
Maelgwn Gwynedd (d. 547) 3
Maelor, Edward (*fl.* 1586–1620) 85
Maesmynan, Caerwys 136
Mansel, Sir Lewis 87
Mansel, Sir Thomas 140
Mansell, William, Is-coed 189
Manual of Welsh Literature, J. C. Morrice (1909) 230
manuscript collecting 86–8
Manutius, Aldus, Venice 389, 390
The Map of Love, Dylan Thomas (1939) 360
Margam Abbey library 25, 28
Margam castle library 136, 140, 142
The Marrow of Modern Divinity (1651) 96
Marsh, Richard, Wrexham, bookseller and printer 125
Mason, Frank, editor of the *Tenby Observer* 213
Mason, Samuel, bookseller 124
mass media 329–40

Masurus, Marcus 390
Mathau, Dafydd Llwyd (*fl.* 1601–29) 84
Mathewes, Augustine, London, stationer 94
Matthews, Edward, Ewenni (1813–92) 309
Maurice, William, Cefn-y-braich, Llansilin, library 87, 142
Maurice, Sir William, Clenennau (1542–1622) 85
Mawl yr Arglwydd, John Ellis (1816) 238
Maynard, Robert Ashwin 374
McCance, William, artist 374, 375
McColvin Report (1942) 290
McDowall, Nicholas 376
Mechanics' Institutes 167, 282–3
  Welsh books in 282–3
Y Meddyg Teuluaidd 258
Y Meddyg Teuluaidd: The Family Physician, 202
Medelwr Ieuanc, Y 381
The Mediaeval Boroughs of Snowdonia, E. A. Lewis (1912) 230
Mediaeval Welsh Law, A. W. Wade-Evans (1909) 230
Melai family 85
Memoirs of John, Lord de Joinville, trans. Thomas Johnes (1807) 372
Memoirs of the Life of Froissart, trans. Thomas Johnes 372-3
Meredith, Hugh, Philadelphia, printer 253
Meredith, Luke, London, stationer 94
Merfyn Frych (d. 844) 3, 5
Merioneth CUKT scheme 289, 290
Merlin Silvester 9
Merthyr 247
Merthyr and Cardiff Chronicle 212
Merthyr Express 215
Merthyr Guardian 210
Merthyr Tudful public library 278, 297, 298
Merthyr Tydfil library authority 293, 294
Merthyr Tydfil Times 215
Mêt y Mona, R. Lloyd Jones (1929) 383
Methodist revival 113–16
Metropolitan Cambrian Society 222
Meunier, Charles 391
Michael Joseph 359, 366
microform 400, 401, 402, 404
Middleton, Bernard C. 391
Midleton, Wiliam 57, 59, 227
Milford, Lord (d. 1823) 137
Mills, Richard (1840–1903), music compositor 241
Miners' Institute Libraries 297–305
Miners' Monthly 216
Miners' Welfare Fund 299
Minority Movement 216
Minshull, William, Chester, printer 198
Miscellaneous Repository, neu y Drysorfa Gymmysgedig 198

INDEX

Miscellanies in Prose and Verse, Mary Jones (1750) 140
missals 34
The Missionary Chronicle 200
'Mochyn du', ballad 248
Monmouth Gazette 210
Monmouth Reading Society 167
Monmouthshire Merlin 210
Montgomery Castle, library 136
Montgomery Printing Company 366
Montgomeryshire CUKT scheme 288, 289
Moore, Reginald 362
The More Angels Shall I Paint, Robin Tanner 376
More, Thomas 46
Moretus, Balthasar 390
Morgan, Elena Puw 325
Morgan, Eluned 273, 325, 382
Morgan, Robert 300
Morgan, Thomas, Carmarthen 130
Morgan, William, bishop (1545–1604) 49, 58, 72
Morley, Oxford, bookbinder 391
Morocco a'r hyn a welais yno, Margaret Jones (1883) 324
Morris, David, Carmarthen, bookbinder 129
Morris, Lewis (1701–65) 116–17, 124, 147–8, 149, 151, 197
  private press 371
Morris, Rhys Hopkin 335
Morris, Richard (1702/3–79) 147–8, 149
Morris, Thomas B. 254
Morris, William (1705–63) 147–8, 149
Morris, William, Kelmscott Press 390, 391
Morris, Zechariah Bevan, Swansea, printer, 127
Morys, Huw 'Eos Ceiriog' (1622–1709) 85
Mosellanus, Petrus 56
Mostyn Hall library 135, 136, 143
Mostyn, Sir Thomas (1651–92) 87
Mountain Ash 287
  public library 278
Mudiad Ysgolion Meithrin 332
multi-media formats 403
Murray, George, bishop of St David's 371
Murray, John, publisher, 154
Music Epitomized, Charles Dibdin 239
music publishing 237–44
Musical and Poetical Relicks of the Welsh Bards, Edward Jones (1784) 237
My Neighbours, Caradoc Evans (1920) 356
My People, Caradoc Evans (1915) 355–6
Myddelton, Sir Thomas 95, 98
Myddelton, John, Gwaenynog 136
Myfanwy, Allen Raine 355
Myfyrdodau Bucheddol ar y Pedwar Peth Diweddaf, John Morgan (1735) 253

Myvyrian Archaiology of Wales (1801–7) 36, 118, 152, 154, 175, 223
  proposed 4th volume 227
Nadolig Angel, trans. by Thomas Levi (1884) 382
Namynun-deugain Erthyglau Crefydd Eglwys Loegr, trans. by Thomas Jones (1688) 101
Nanhoron, Pwllheli, library 137, 138, 140
Nant-y-glo Institute 299
Nanteos, near Aberystwyth, library 138
The National Church 169
National Council of Music 242
National Library of Wales 192, 232, 342, 387–405
  bibliography 393–4
  book, art of 387–93
  book, future of 399–405
  CD-Rom purchases 400, 402
  charter, original 399
  charter, supplemental 1988 399
  conservation 401
  Copyright Act 1911 399–400
  microfilming at 401
  microform purchases 400
  regional library bureau 289
National Library of Wales Journal 396
National Museum of Wales 232, 342
National Press Agency 212
National Press Journal 212
National Union of Journalists 214
Neath Abbey 13, 29, 45
Neath Mechanics' Institute 282
Neath public library 281
Nedw, E. Tegla Davies (1922) 383
Nelson reading room 298
Nennius 5
Nero: Tragaedia Nova, Matthew Gwinne 68
Nerquis Hall, near Mold, library 138
New Testament 1567 50
New Welsh Review 368
Newbery, Ralph 60, 61
Newport Athenaeum and Mechanics' Institute 167, 278
Newport central library 292
Newport public library 277, 278, 279, 290
News of the World 215
newspapers 209–20
  daily 212–15
  religious 211–12
  influence of World War 1 214–15
  influence of World War 2 216
Nicholas, Capt. J. W., Llandeilo 193
Nicholas, John 193
Nicholas, Commander T. C. 193
Nicholas, T. E. 206
Nicholl, John Cole, Merthyr Mawr, library 138

Nichols and Son, London, printers 372
NLW, Peniarth MS 540 (Bede, *De natura rerum*) 28
Nocturne for Wales, Shirley Jones (1987) 377
Y Nofelydd a Chydymaith y Teulu 205
The Nonconformist 168
North Wales Chronicle 213
North Wales Gazette 209
North Wales Music Company 242
North Wales Times 215
North, George, Brecon 128
Norton, Bonham 237
O'Brien, Edward J. 362
Yr Odydd Cymreig 203
Odyssey, trans. by T. E. Lawrence (1932) 392
Yr Oenig 381
Off to Philadelphia in the Morning, Jack Jones 358, 367
Officium Parvum Beatae Mariae Virginis 87
Ofyddion 150
ogam alphabet 2, 3–4
Okes, Nicholas 68
Old Stile Press 376
Oll Synnwyr pen Kembero ygyd, William Salesbury 56, 61
On the Causes which have produced Dissent in Wales from the Established Church, A. J. Johnes 222
Opus Catechisticum, trans. by Roger Smyth (1611) 97
oral culture 7, 8–9, 15, 33
Ordinary Cats, Shirley Jones (1992) 377
Orgraph yr Iaith Gymraeg (1859) 179
Oriau gyda'r Iesu, Owen Evans 183
The Origin, Rise and Progress of the Paper People, Jane Williams (1856) 323
Ormond, John 365, 367–8
Orwin, Thomas 70
Oswen, John, printer 60, 61
Oswestry 127, 245, 247
  grammar school 14
Outside the House of Baal, Emyr Humphreys (1965) 367
Owain Glyndŵr 14, 26, 32
Owen family, Henllys 45
Owen, Anna Maria, Henllys 139
Owen, Bob, Croesor, bibliomaniac 289
Owen, Daniel (1836–95) 176, 178, 181
Owen, David, 'Brutus' (1795–1866) 201
Owen, Edward Humphrey, book collector (1850–1904) 388
Owen, George, Henllys (*c.* 1552–1613) 86
Owen, Goronwy (1723–69) 72, 117, 149
Owen, Dr Henry, Poyston Hall 139
Owen, Isambard 226
Owen, J. Evans 219

Owen, John of Plas Du (*c.*1564–*c.*1628) 68
Owen, Robert, printer 130
Owen, Sir Robert, MP, Clenennau and Brogyntyn (d. 1698) 140
Owen, William, Haverfordwest, cabinet maker 143
Oxford Lectern Bible (1935) 392
Painter, John, Wrexham, printer 126, 127, 130, 131, 132
Panton, Paul, Plas Gwyn (1727-97) 140, 151
Panton, Paul, Jnr., Plas Gwyn, (1758–1822) private press 371
Y Papyr Newydd Cymraeg 210
Parker, Agnes Miller 374, 375, 376
Parry, Benjamin, Swansea, printer 241, 242
Parry, John (1775–1846) 199
Parry, John (1812–74) 310
Parry, John, Bardd Alaw, 'Welsh Harper' (1776–1851) 238
Parry, John Humphreys (1786–1825) 153, 154
Parry, R. Williams 342
Parry, Bishop Richard 95
Parry, Robert 'Robin Ddu Eryri' 203
Parry, Thomas 383
Parry, W. J., Bethesda (1842–1927) 315
Parry, Winnie (1870–1953) 325, 382
Parry-Williams, T. H. 342
Patagonia 265–76
  books 272–4
  Co-operative Society 265, 270
  Irrigation Society 265
  newspapers 266–72
patronage, seventeenth century 83–91
Paynter, Wil 300
Paynton, Colin 376
Pearson, J., Caernarfon, circulating library 131
Pearson, J. L., Treberfydd, Brecon 143
Pedwar math o faledau Cymraeg, Thomas Jones 102
Pelagius's Commentary on the Pauline Epistles 4
Pembroke Society 130
Pembrokeshire CUKT scheme 289
Penmark Press 364–5
Pennant, David, Downing 143
Pennant, Hugh (*fl.* 1565–1619) 36
Pennant, Huw 85
Pennant, Thomas, Downing 110, 140, 141
Pennant, Thomas, late abbot of Basingwerk 36
Penpont, near Brecon, library 135
Penpont Antiphonal 34
Penrhiwceiber Miners' Library 300, 301
Penrhyn family 85
Penrhyn Castle, library 142
Penson, Thomas 143
Pentrefoelas Reading Society 283

periodicals 197–207
Perl Mewn Adfyd (Huw Lewys, trans. of a text by Miles Coverdale) 50, 59, 60, 61, 72
Peroriaeth Hyfryd, John Parry 239
Perri, Henri 57, 60, 68, 71, 72, 78
Perutilis Exteris Nationibus De Italica Pronunciatione et Orthographia Libellus, Siôn Dafydd Rhys (1569) 70
Peterwell, Lampeter, library 141
Petts, John 363–4
Philipps library 281
Philipps, Sir Erasmus, Picton Castle (d. 1743) 137
Philipps, Sir John, Picton Castle (d. 1764) 111, 137
Phillimore, Egerton 226
Phillipps, Sir Thomas (1792–1872) bibliomaniac 312, 387
Phillips, D. Rhys (1862–1952) librarian 281, 394, 396
Phillips, Thomas (1760–1851) 311–12
Y Phonographwr 205
Phrases elegantiores ex Caesaris Commentariis, Cicerone…, Hugh Lloyd (1654) 68
Phylip family, Ardudwy 84
Pickering, Tom 335
Picton Castle, library 137, 142
Pilgrim's Progress, John Bunyan (1688) 100
Piozzi, Hester 143
Piper, John 376
Pitts, J. Martin 376
The Plaine man's Pathway to Heaven, Arthur Dent 96
Planet 368
Plans of Harbours, Bars, Bays and Roads in St. George's Channel, Lewis Morris (1748) 116
Plant Meg Fach, trans. by Thomas Levi (1886) 382
Plant y Beirdd, O. M. Edwards (1892) 382
Plantin, Christophe 390
Plas Gwyn (Anglesey) library 142
Plas Iolyn family 85
Plas Nantglyn (Denb.) 140
Plas Power (Denb.) library 140
A playne and a familiar Introduction, William Salesbury (1567) 56, 60
Plays of Euripides, trans. by George Murray (1931) 374
Poematum Libellus, William Vaughan (1598) 68
Poems by George Herbert (1923) 374
Poetical Works of the Rev Goronwy Owen… 227–8 *see also* Owen, Goronwy
poetry 6, 9, 15, 33–4, 49, 83–5
  Anglo-Welsh 363–4, 365
The Poetry of the Gogynfeirdd (1909) 230
Poetry Wales 368
Poetry Wales Press 368

politics, post-war 330
Pontlottyn reading room 298
Pontypridd Observer 215
Pontypridd public library 278, 281
population, nineteenth century 158–60, 161
Posterior Analytics, Griffith Powell (1594) 68
Potter, Joseph, Haverfordwest, circulating library 131
Powel, Antoni, Llwydarth (*c*.1560–1618/19) 88
Powel, Thomas, professor of Celtic, Cardiff 226–7, 313, 314
Powell, Edward (?1478–1540) 46
Powell, G. E. J., Nanteos 278
Powell, Griffith of Llansawel (1561–1620) 68
Powell, J., Dublin, printer 371
Powis Castle library 135, 136
Powis, Earl of (1785–1848) 136, 390
Powys, John Cowper 365
Powys-Land Club 226
Poynter, Ambrose 143
Poyston, library 143
A Practical Discourse concerning Death, William Sherlock 96
The Practice of Piety, Lewis Bayly (1629) 96
Praefatio, Humphrey Prichard 71
Pregeth Dduwiol, trans. by Robert Llwyd (1629/30) 96
Pregethau, Areithiau a Darlithiau, Samuel Roberts 254, 257
Pregethau a osodwyd allan trwy awdurdod…, trans. by Edward James (1606) 96
Y Pregethwr 204
press, private 371–8
Press Association 212
Prestel 402
Price, Robert, Giler 139
Price, Thomas 'Carnhuanawc' (1787–1848) 222, 224
Prichard, Annie Catherine 'Ruth' 325
Prichard, Caradog 350
Prichard, James, Trefeca, printer 125
Prichard, Rhys 95
Prif Achau Holl Gymru Benbaladr, Thomas Wiliems 86
Primer 50, 95
The Primitive History, William Williams, Ivy Tower (1789) 137
The Principles of Christian Religion, Thomas Gouge 100
printing
  sixteenth century 41–2, 45
  seventeenth century 93–107
  nineteenth century 161
Prise family, Brecon 45

Prise, John, Brecon (?1502–55) 36, 47, 50, 55, 68, 69
Prise, Richard 69, 71
Profiad yr Ysprydion, Rondl Davies (1675) 96
Propaedeumata Aphoristica, John Dee (1558) 68
Prophwyd y Jubili 200
proprietary libraries 130
prose 6–7, 9, 15, 94–7
Proto diccionario gales-castellano: Rhag-eiriadur Cymraeg-Ysbanaeg, Albert Cecil Lloyd (1969) 273
Pryce-Jones, Alan 366
Prys, Edmwnd (1544–1623) 49, 71, 72, 83, 84
Prys, Stafford, Shrewsbury, printer 245, 246
Pryse, Robert John 'Gweirydd ap Rhys' 151, 178, 227
Psalmae (Wiliam Midleton) 61
Psalmau Dafydd 58
Psalmau Dafydd (1929) 374
Psalmau Dafydd o'r vn cyfieithiad a'r Beibl Cyffredin (1896, photo facs.) 226–7
Public Libraries Act 1919 287
Public Libraries and Museums Act 1964 292
Pugh, Edward 141
Pugh, Hugh, Mostyn 201
Pughe, John 147
Pughe, William Owen (1759–1835) 79, 147, 150, 152–4, 155, 174, 197, 223, 268, 273
  dictionary 137
Puleston, Philip, Esclusham 139
Pulpud Cymru 204
Y Punch Cymraeg 205
Puritan works 98–101
Pwyll Pendefig Dyfed 154
Quiggin, E. C., Monro lecturer in Celtic, Cambridge 314
Radcliffe-Maud Report (1969) 292
radio 334–5
Radio Cymru 337
Radio Wales 337
Radnorshire CUKT scheme 288
Raiders' Dawn and Other Poems, Alun Lewis (1942) 363–4
Raleigh Committee (1909) 314, 316
Rasbrook, John, Bangor, printer 126–7
Ratdolt, Erhard, Augsburg, printer 389
Raven Press 374
reading rooms, nineteenth century 166–7
Ready Report (1952) 341, 342, 343
Record of Caernarvon 16
Recusant printing 48, 49, 50-1, 59, 61-2
Red Book of Hergest 14, 31, 34, 36, 87, 88, 229
Red Dragon 206
Red Hen Press 376–7

Reddick, Peter 376
Rees family, Tonn, Llandovery, printers and antiquarians 281
Rees, D. R. and William, Tonn, Llandovery, printers 201–02
Rees, David, Llanelli, printer 201
Rees, Ebenezer, Ystalyfera, printer 206
Rees, Eiluned 391
Rees, Goronwy 361
Rees, Josiah, Gelli-gron (1744–1804) 197
Rees, Owen, partner in Longman 127
Rees, Rice, librarian 311
Rees, Sarah Jane 'Cranogwen' (1839–1916) 323, 326
Rees, W. J., Casgob (1772–1855) 221, 224
Rees, William 'Gwilym Hiraethog' 168, 201
Rees, William, Llandovery, printer 224, 238
Reformation 43–5, 49
regional library bureaux 289
Reith, Sir John, 335
relics 1, 26
Religious Tract Society 125, 381, 382
Renaissance 42–51
Rendel, Lord 388
Renouard, Antoine Augustin 390
Revelation of Saint John the Divine (1933) 375
Reynolds Stone Engravings (1977) 392
Rhan o waith Mr. Rees Prichard [...] 97, 99
Rhann o Psalmae, Edward Kyffin 61
Rhetorica ad Herennium 85
Rhigyfarch ap Sulien (d. 1099) 6, 8, 27
Rhisiart Cynwal (d. 1634) 84
Rhiwedog family 85
Rhiwlas, Y Bala, library 138
Rhiwledin 51, 62
Rhondda 287
  library authority 293
  public library 299
Rhondda Clarion 216
Rhondda Roundabout, Jack Jones (1934) 358
Rhondda Socialist 297
Rhondda Vanguard 216
Rhostryfan, Hanes a Chynnydd y Pentre, William Gilbert Williams (1926) 373
Rhwng Gwyll a Gwawr: Briwsion hanes o 1688 hyd 1720, William Gilbert Williams (1928) 373
Rhyd-y-gors Academy 308
Rhydderch ab Ieuan, Parcrhydderch 36
Rhydderch, Siôn, Shrewsbury and Llannerch-y-medd, printer 79, 245, 371
Rhyl public library 279
Rhys ap Thomas, Sir (1449–1525) 32
Rhys Cain 86
Rhys Fardd 34

Rhys Llwyd y Lleuad, E. Tegla Davies (1925) 383
Rhys, Edward Prosser 342
Rhys, Ernest 394
Rhys, John 403
Rhŷs, John, professor of Celtic, Oxford 229
Rhys, Keidrich 361, 362, 364, 365
Rhys, Morgan John, 118, 197–8, 254
Rhys, Siôn Dafydd 49, 58, 59, 67, 70
'Ricemarch Psalter' 27
Richard ap John, Ysgorlegan (*fl.* 1578–1611) 86
Richard's Welsh-English Dictionary (1815) 137
Richard, Edward 117
  see also *Gwaith Prydyddawl Edward Richard Ystradmeurig...*
Richards, Thomas (1878–1962) College Librarian 315, 316
Ridd, Thomas, Cardiff, library 131
River out of Eden, Jack Jones (1951) 358
Riverside Press, Boston 392
Rivière and Son, London, bindery 375
Robert of Gloucester 12
Robert, Gruffydd 48, 49, 70
Roberts Report (1959) 290–1, 344
Roberts, E. R. 261
Roberts, Eigra Lewis 350
Roberts, Ellis Henry, USA, politician and printer 255
Roberts, Evan E., USA, printer 255, 258
Roberts, Evan, printer 125
Roberts, G. E. 258–9
Roberts, Glyn, journalist 360
Roberts, Goronwy, Caernarfon, MP 291–2
Roberts, John, 'Ieuan Gwyllt' (1822–77) 240
Roberts, Joseph, publisher's traveller 182
Roberts, Kate (1891–1985) 326, 342, 349
Roberts, Lynette 365
Roberts, Mary, ballad singer 248
Roberts, Mary, Caernarfon, printer 125
Roberts, Robert W., USA, printer 255–6
Roberts, Samuel 201, 254, 256–7, 259, 260–1
Roberts, T. F., principal, UCW, Aberystwyth 313
Roberts, Thomas, Caernarfon, printer 125
Robin Achwr 86
Robinson, P. F. 143
Robinson, Sir Thomas 138
Roden, Thomas, Denbigh, bookbinder 129
Röder, C. G., music engravers 241
Rogers, Bruce (1870–1957) 392
Rogers, John, Shrewsbury, printer 245
Roland cycle 29, 30
  see also *Song of Roland*
Roman Catholic authors 48, 50–1, 56, 59, 61–2, 97–8
Roman de la Rose 389

The Romance of Parzival and the Holy Grail, Wolfram von Eschenbach (1990) 376
Romanticism 117–18
Ross, John, Carmarthen, printer 125, 128, 130, 132, 141, 189, 197, 198, 395
Rousseau, S., printer 372
Rowland, Daniel, Llangeitho 114, 115
Rowland, John, Y Bala, printer 124
Royal Commission on University Education in Wales (Haldane) 232, 242
Royal Institution of South Wales 283
The Royal Tribes of Wales, Philip Yorke (1799) 126
Ruban, Petrus 391
Rudge, William Edwin 392
Rudiments of Thorough Bass (1810) 238
The Rules and Premiums of the Society for the Encouragement of Agriculture and Industry, in the County of Cardigan 372
runes 2
Ryder, John, Bodley Head 394
S4C 243, 334, 337
Salesbury, Henry 61, 70, 78
Salesbury, William (?1520–?99) 33, 42, 45, 46, 47, 49, 50, 55, 56, 61
  Dictionary (1877) 226
Salisbury, Enoch Robert Gibbon (1819–90), book collector 313–14
Salisbury, John, Gwyddelwern 59, 94
Salisbury, Thomas, London-Welsh stationer 58, 59, 60–1
Salmau Cân, Edmwnd Prys 97
Y Salmydd Eglwysig, John Mills (1847) 239
Salusbury family, Lleweni 45
Salusbury, John of Lleweni 71
Sanderson, Robert, Y Bala, printer 125
Sankey Commission (1919) 299
Saunders, Mrs J. M. 325
Saunders, William 212
Sbondonics Book Club 348
schools
  circulating schools 113, 165, 245, 380
  designated Welsh schools 332, 345
  see also under Ysgol
Scop Hwilum Sang, Shirley Jones (1983) 377
Scott, Ann, Carmarthen, printer 130
scripts 26–7, 28, 29, 30, 32–3
scriptoria 30
The Seafarer, trans. Kevin Crossley-Holland 376
Select Committee on Public Libraries 1849 167
Selected Poems, Idris Davies (1953) 363
Selections from the Hengwrt manuscripts, ed. Robert Williams (1876) 228
Selections from the Hengwrt manuscripts, ed. G. Hartwell Jones (1892) 228

Senghennydd Institute 301
Seren Cymru 212
Seren Gomer 199, 202, 204, 209–10
Y Seren Ogleddol 201
Y Seren Orllewinol 255, 256
Seren Press 368
Sermon [...] at the death of Sir Ieuan Lloyd, William Morgan (1588) 60
A Sermon of Repentance, Arthur Dent 96
Shankland, Thomas, librarian 231, 315–16, 394
Shirburn Castle collection 388
Shrewsbury 102, 123, 124, 127, 130, 245, 247
Sick Man's Salve, Thomas Becon (1594) 58, 61
Sieffre, Ieuan Llwyd 87
Simpkin Marshall 175
Simwnt Fychan (d. 1606) 56, 84
The Singing Caravan, Robert Vansittart (1932) 375
Siôn ap Hywel ab Owain, Cefn Treflaeth 85
Siôn Cain 85
Siôn Dafydd La(e)s, Penllyn (*c.*1660–95) 85, 87
Siôn Dafydd Rhys
  see Davies, John
Siôn Mawddwy (d. 1613) 84
Siôn Phylip (*c.*1543–1620) 84
Siôn Tudur (d. 1602) 83, 84
Siôn, Llywelyn, Llangewydd (1540–?1615) 87–8
Sir John Froissart's Chronicles of England, France and the Adjoining Countries trans. by Thomas Johnes (1803–5) 372
Sirleto, Cardinal 49
Slebech Park, library 142
Smith, Sally Lou, Gregynog, bookbinder 376
Smith, W. H., 361
  subscription libraries 282
Smyth, Dr. Roger (1541–1625) 97
Snell, D. J., Swansea (1880–1957) 242, 243
Society for Promoting Christian Knowledge 103, 113, 123, 125, 381
Society for the Diffusion of Useful Knowledge in Wales 167, 201
Society for the Propagation of the Gospel 253
Society for the Publication of Ancient Welsh Manuscripts 223–4
Soft Ground Hard Ground, Shirley Jones (1989) 377
The Soldier and the Gentlewoman, Hilda Vaughan (1932) 358
Some Specimens of the Poetry of the Antient Welsh Bards, Evan Evans (1764) 117, 152
Song at the Year's Turning: Poems, 1942–1954, R. S. Thomas (1955) 366
Song of Roland 39
  see also Roland cycle
Songs of Wales, ed. Brinley Richards 238

Sophistici Elenchi, Griffith Powell (1598) 68
The Soul's Destroyer and Other Poems, W. H. Davies (1905) 355
South Glamorgan library authority electronic databases 293
South Wales and Monmouthshire Council for Social Service 299
South Wales and Monmouthshire Master Printers' Alliance 192
South Wales Daily News 212, 213, 214, 215
South Wales Daily Post 215, 216
South Wales Echo 215, 217
South Wales Evening Argus 217
South Wales Evening Express 216
South Wales Evening Post 217
South Wales Journal of Commerce 215
South Wales Miner 216
South Wales Miners' Federation 216
Southall, J. E. 183
Southcott, Joanna 154
Sporle, William de 189
Sporting and Evening Chronicle 215
Spottiswoode, music engravers 241
Spurrell, Dr. Charles 192
Spurrell, Elizabeth 189, 190
Spurrell, Lt.-Col. Hugh William 189, 192
Spurrell, Ivor Pritchard 192
Spurrell, John (1748–1801) 189
Spurrell, Richard (1782–1847) 189
Spurrell, Robert, schoolmaster 189
Spurrell, Sarah 189
Spurrell, Walter, Carmarthen, printer 189, 191–2, 193
Spurrell, Walter Roworth 192
Spurrell, William, Carmarthen, printer 189–91
St Asaph gospel book 26
St Chad Gospels 26, 27, 33
St David's Day Welsh Books campaign 343, 345
St David's University College, Lampeter, library 311–12
St Deiniol, library 139
St Donat's, library 136
St Illtud 4
St Omer English college 98
St. John Hornby, C. H. 390–1
Stackpole Court library 135, 143
Stafford, Simon 61
The Standard 267
Stationers' Company 48, 93–4
Statute of Wales (1284) 15, 31
The Stealing of the Mare (1930) 374
Stephens, Meic 346
Stepney, Sir Thomas (d. 1745) 140
Stodart, Hugh, St Asaph, bookbinder 129

Stone, Reynolds 375
The Stones of the Field, R. S. Thomas (1946) 365–6
The Story of Llandefaelog Parish, Ethel M. Davies, 193
Stouthall, Gower, library 138, 142
Stradey Castle, Llanelli, library 137
Stradling family, St Donat's 45
Stradling, Sir Edward 49, 60, 68, 70, 71, 136
Stradling, Sir John of St Donat's 72, 15, 68
Stradling, Sir John (1563–1637) 136
Straker and Son, London, bookbinders 181
Strata Florida, 13, 30, 45
Strata Marcella 55
Subject Index to Welsh Periodicals 393
subscription lists 140
subscription publishing 124, 128–9, 259
Subscription reading rooms 131
Sulien 6, 27
Summa Casuum conscientiae, Fransisco Toledo 98
Summa Doctrinae Christianae, Petrus Canisius 97
A Summer Day, Kate Roberts (1946) 364
Sunday Referee 359
Sunday schools 165, 166, 380
  libraries 283
Sunday Times 215, 216
SuperTed 337
Surexit memorandum 27
Swansea 247
  public library 277, 278, 279, 280, 281, 290
  Royal Institution 167
Swansea Training College 312
Y Symbylydd 204
Symmons, Rev. Charles, Narberth 138
Syr Rhisiart
  see Griffith, Richard (1861–1947)
Taith, neu Siwrnai y Pererin, trans. by Stephen Hughes and others 100, 101
Talbot family, library 111
Taliesin 6
Taliesin 205
Tarian Rhyddid a Dymchwelydd Gormes 201
Taro Naw 337
Teifi Library Project 293
television 336–8
Telyn Egryn, Ellin Evans 324, 325
Telyn Seion, Rosser Beynon (1848) 239
Telyn y Plant 381
temperance literature 200
Temple of Flora, Thornton 393
Templum Experientiae apertum, Neu Ddrws y Society Profiad, William Williams (1777) 115
'the x commandements in Welshe' 60
Terence (1493) 389
Testament Newydd 1567 75, 310
Testament Newydd ein Arglwydd Jesv Christ, 1567 58*
Teulu Bach Nantoer, Elizabeth Mary Jones (1913) 383
Théâtre du monde, Pierre Boaistuau, 97
Theater du mond sef ivv Gorsedd y byd trans. by Roger Smyth (1615?) 97
Theatrum Orbis Terrarum, Abraham Ortelius 69
Thelwall, Simon 56
Theological Colleges, libraries 307-11
Thesaurus Linguae Latinae et Cambro-brytannicae, Thomas Wiliems 86
Thirlwall, Connop, bishop of St David's 190
Thomas family, Cefndyrys 140
Thomas ab Ifan, Hendreforfudd (fl. 1596–1633) 84
Thomas ap Ieuan ap Deicws (fl. 1500–23) 36
Thomas, D. A., Viscount Rhondda 215
Thomas, D. E., Haverfordwest 143
Thomas, Daniel, Llandovery, printer 197
Thomas, David 'Dafydd Ddu Eryri' 150, 153
Thomas, Donald 272
Thomas, Dylan 358, 361, 363, 367, 368
Thomas, Evan, editor of *Y Drafod* 272
Thomas, Evan, surgeon (d. 1890) 315
Thomas, Gwyn 366, 367
Thomas, Revd I. D. E. 193
Thomas, Isaiah, USA, printer 255
Thomas, Jennie 383
Thomas, John, Bontnewydd 246
Thomas, John, Congregational minister, Liverpool (1821–92) 204
Thomas, John, 'Eifionydd' (1848–1922) 205
Thomas, John, 'Pencerdd Gwalia'
Thomas, Joshua Morgan, Cardigan, publisher 200
Thomas, Julian, bookbinder 376, 391-2
Thomas, Lewis 94
Thomas, Micah (1778–1853) 309
Thomas, Nicholas, Carmarthen, printer 123, 124
Thomas, Oliver
Thomas, Owen (1812–91) Liverpool 310
Thomas, R. S. 357, 360, 365
Thomas, Rhys, Carmarthen printer 125
Thomas, Sarah, itinerant bookseller 129
Thomas, Thomas, Latin-English dictionary 76
Thomas, Thomas, Pont-y-Pŵl Baptist Academy 157–8
Thomas, W. T. 177
Thomas, William (d. 1554) 42
Thomas-Stanford, Sir Charles (1858–1932) 393
Thorne, David, SDUC, Lampeter 194
Times Like These, Gwyn Jones (1936) 362
Tlysau yr Hen Oesoedd (1735) 124, 148, 152, 197, 229, 371
Today we live, film (1937) 333

A Token for Children..., James Janeway (1671) 379
Tomos, Angharad 349
Tonic Sol-fa movement 240
Tory, Geoffroy, Paris 390
A Toy Epic, Emyr Humphreys 367
Toy, Humphrey 49, 60, 61, 69
Y Traethodydd 174, 179, 203–04, 256, 381
Y Traethodydd yn America 256
Trahearne, J. M. 224
Transactions of the Honourable Society of Cymmrodorion 396
Translations into English verse from the Poems of Davyth ab Gwilym, A. J. Johnes 222
Travels of Bertrandon de la Brocquiere... trans.Thomas Johnes (1807) 372
Trawsgoed, library 141, 142
The treasure of the Latin language and Welsh, or the richest and most extensive dictionary of the true pure British, Thomas Wiliems (1607) 76
A Treatise on Cold and Hot Baths, William Turton (1803) 371
Treberfydd (Brec.) library 138, 143
Tredegar Institute 299, 301, 303
Tredegar Iron and Coal Company 298
Trefeca College 309–10
Trefeca Press 124–5
Trefhedyn 124
Trefnusrwydd Teuluaidd, E. Emment and Eluned Morgan 273
Trehafod Welfare Hall 298, 299
Treharris Institute 301
Treharris Tradesmen's Library 298
Treharris Workmen's Library 298
Trehearn, David, Rhyl, seller of music 242
Trevor, John, bishop of St Asaph 35
Trevor, Sir Thomas, Trefalun 139
triads 8, 9
Trosnant, Pont-y-Pŵl, academy 309
Trysor i Blentyn 381
Trysorfa 198
Trysorfa Grefyddol Gwent a Morganwg 200
Trysorfa Gwybodaeth, neu Eurgrawn Cymraeg 197
Trysorfa Rhyfeddodau a Hynodrwydd yr Oesoedd 203
Trysorfa y Plant 381–2
Trysorfa Ysprydol 198
Turner, Sharon 152, 154
Turner, William 56
Turton, William, Swansea 127
Twenty-five Poems, Dylan Thomas (1936) 360
Twenty-one Welsh Gypsy Folk-tales (1933) 375
Two Moons, Shirley Jones (1991) 377
Two Old Men and other stories, Kate Roberts (1981) 376
TWW 336–7

TWWN (Television Wales (West and North)) 336
Tŷ Coch library 388
Tyndale, William 45
Tynged yr Iaith 333
Y Tyst 215
Tyst a'r Dydd 212
Y Tyst Apostolaidd 200, 202
Y Tyst Cymreig 212
Udgorn Seion 200
Udgorn y Bobl 211
Un Nos ola' Leuad, Caradog Prichard 350
Under Milk Wood, Dylan Thomas (1954) 359
Unfinished Journey, Jack Jones (1937) 358
United States of America
  Welsh publishing 253–64
University Colleges 312–16
  University College of North Wales, Bangor, library 312, 314–16
  University College of South Wales and Monmouthshire, Cardiff, library 312, 313–14
  University College of Wales, Aberystwyth, library 312, 313
University of Wales 230–3
University of Wales Board of Celtic Studies 232
University of Wales Press 192, 232-3, 243, 346
Urban, bishop of Llandaf 10, 12
urbanization 19th C 160–1
Urdd Gobaith Cymru 331, 343
Urdd y Vord Gron 225
Urien, Edwart (d. 1614) 85
Ussher, James 87
Yr Utgorn 249
Utica Morning Herald 256
Val Baker, Denys 362
Valle Crucis Abbey 36
van Niekerk, Sarah, wood-engraver 376
The Vanity of Childhood and Youth... (Daniel Williams) 379
Vaughan family, Corsygedol 85
Vaughan, Aled 362
Vaughan, Edward, bishop of St David's (1509–22) 13
Vaughan, Henry, 'The Silurist' 72
Vaughan, Hilda 357–8
Vaughan, Sir John, Trawsgoed (d. 1674) 141
Vaughan, Richard, bishop of Bangor, Chester, and London 60
Vaughan, Richard, Golden Grove 142
Vaughan, Robert, Hengwrt (*c.*1592–1667) 85, 86–7, 136
Vaughan, Sir Robert Howell, Hengwrt and Nannau 139
Vaughan, Rowland, Cae'r-gai 85
Vaughan, Thomas 72

Vaughan, William, Corsygedol 140
Vaughan, William, Golden Grove (1577–1641) 68
Vaynor Park (Montg.), library 143
Verard, Antoine, Paris 389–90
video 403
Viewdata 402
A Vindication of the Genuiness of the Antient British Poems, Sharon Turner (1803) 152
vitae of the saints 8, 26, 29
Voss, John, Swansea, printer, 127
Vulliamy, Lewis 143
Wales (1894–7) 206
Wales (1911–14) 206
Wales (Keidrich Rhys) 361, 364, 365
Waleys, Thomas (d. ?1350) 14
A Wall in Wales, Frances McDowall, 376
Walley, John 60, 61
Walter de Henley 15
Walters, H. G., Narberth, printers 193–4
Walters, Henry, Cowbridge 127
Walters, Revd. John, Cowbridge (1721–97) 79
Wardrop, James 375
Watcyn Clywedog (*fl.* 1630–50) 84
The Water Music, Glyn Jones (1944) 367
Waters, Ernest 193
Waterson, Simon 68
Watkin, Edward 315
Watkins, Vernon 361, 363, 365
Y Wawr 203
We Live, Lewis Jones 359
Webb, Harri 362
Weekly Mail 216
Welfare Hall libraries 302
Welsh and Oriental Languages, Jonathan Ceredig Davies 373
Welsh Archaiology 152
Welsh Arts Council 345, 346, 347, 348, 349, 350, 368, 404
Welsh Bibliographical Society 192, 396
Welsh Books Centre 348
Welsh Books Council 344–5, 346–7, 348, 350, 396, 404
Welsh Classics for the People 230
Welsh Collegiate Institution, Llandovery 311
Welsh Folk-Song Society 243
Welsh Girls' School, Ashford, Middlesex 147
Welsh Joint Education Committee 345–6, 348, 349, 404
Welsh Language Act 1967 333
Welsh Language Act 1993 333
Welsh Language Board 1988 333
Welsh-language publishing, 1919-95 341–53
Welsh Leader 394
Welsh Melodies, John Thomas 238
Welsh Music Information Centre 243

Welsh National Press Company 205
Welsh Publishing Company, Caernarfon 242
Welsh Review 361, 364, 365
Welsh Short Stories, Glyn Jones (Faber, 1937) 362
Welsh Short Stories, Glyn Jones (Penguin, 1941) 362
A Welsh Singer, Allen Raine (1897) 355
Welsh Trust 94, 100–1, 103, 123
Welshman 210
Welshpool
  public library 277, 278, 280
  Reading Society 130
West Wales Historical Records Society 192
Western Mail 212, 214, 215, 216, 217, 360
Whitchurch, Edward 60, 61
White Book of Rhydderch 13, 14, 29, 30, 31, 36
The White House, Geraint Goodwin 367
White, Hannah, Carmarthen, printer 132, 190
Whitford, Richard (*c.*1470–1541) 46
Whitgift, Archbishop 49
Whitland monastery 29, 30
The Whole Duty of Man, 96
Wicksteed, Edward, Wrexham, bookseller 129
Wiliam Llŷn 76, 84, 86
Wiliems, Thomas, Trefriw (*c.* 1545/6–1622) 67, 70, 76, 86
Wilkins, Thomas (1625/6–99) 88
Willett, Mark, Chepstow, bookseller 130
Williams, Miss, Penpont 139
Williams, Benjamin Morris, music compositor (1832–1903) 241
Williams, Caroline, estate–owner 299
Williams, Sir Charles Hanbury, Coldbrook Park 140
Williams, D. J. (1886–1950) 384
Williams, D. J. 342
Williams, Daniel (?1643–1716)
Williams, David, Swansea, printer, 127
Williams, E. D., Bangor (?1853–1916) 242
Williams, Edward 'Iolo Morganwg' (1750–1813) 118, 119, 126, 127, 130, 149, 150, 152–3, 154, 308
Williams, Emlyn 355
Williams, Esther, Aberystwyth, printer 125
Williams, Evan (b. 1706) 237
Williams, Evan, Bangor, printer 250
Williams, Evan, London, bookseller 127–8, 151
Williams, G. J. 153
Williams, Dr. Haydn, Director of Education 332
Williams, Hugh (*c.* 1770–1838) 309
Williams, Ifor 231, 342
Williams, J. O. 383
Williams, Jane, Ysgafell
Williams, John 'Ab Ithel' (1811–62) 205, 224, 225
Williams, John 'Corvinius' (1801–59) 202
Williams, Sir John, book collector 230, 388, 391

Williams, Revd John Evan, private press 373
Williams, John Prydderch 'Rhydderch o Fôn' 205
Williams, Joseph, Merthyr 212
Williams, Kyffin 376
Williams, Meirion (1901–76) 242
Williams, Moses (1685–1742) 388
Williams, Owen adapt. *Egwyddor-ddysg Ragegorawl* 239
Williams, Owen 'Owain Gwyrfai' (1790–1874) 203
Williams, Perry, Mrs, agent, USA 261
Williams, Rebecca, ballad singer 248
Williams, Richard (1835–1906), Montgomeryshire antiquary 313
Williams, Richard 'Dic Dywyll', ballad singer 248, 249
Williams, Robert Herring 362
Williams, Robert, clerk and publisher's traveller 182
Williams, Rowland (1817–70) 278, 281, 312
Williams, Rowland, rector of Ysgeifiog (1779–1854) 202
Williams, Samuel, Aberystwyth, printer 125, 129, 132, 238, 248, 380
Williams, Samuel, Llandyfriog (c. 1660–1722) 87
Williams, Taliesin 'Ab Iolo' 126, 224
Williams, Thomas, Dolgellau, printer 128
Williams, Thomas, 'Hafrenydd' (1807–94) 239
Williams, Thomas, London, bookseller 127
Williams, W., Liverpool 218
Williams, W. S. Gwynn (1896–1978) 243
Williams, William, USA, printer 255, 257
Williams, William, Brecon 131
Williams, William, Cardiganshire's first librarian 288
Williams, William 'Caledfryn' 200, 201, 203, 207
Williams, William 'Creuddynfab' 205
Williams, William, Llandygai 109, 110
Williams, William, Pantycelyn 113, 117, 309, 395
Williams, Sir William, Llanforda (d. 1740) 139
Williams, William, Y Wern 164
Wilmot, William, Pembroke, printer 126
Windet, John 61, 68
Y Winllan 381, 383
Winter, Lorenzo 267
The Withered Root, Rhys Davies 356
Y Wladfa 265–76
Y Wladfa, Bryn Williams (1962) 273
'Y Wladychfa a Llenyddiaeth', John Peter 265
women bibliophiles 139
women's writing, nineteenth century 321–7
Wood Engravings by Gertrude Hermes, being Illustrations to Selborne, with Extracts from Gilbert White (1988) 376
Wood, Alan, bookbinder, 376

Woodall, Minshall, Thomas & Co., Oswestry, publishers 176
The Works of Iolo Goch, with a Sketch of his Life 227
Wrexham
 central library 292
 fair 124
 public library 277, 278, 280
Wrexham Book Society 130
Wright, John, Bristol, music engraver 241
Wrigley, James, Bury, papermaker 180
Wyatt, Woodrow 362
Wyn, Robert, Maesyneuadd 85
Wynn family, Gwedir 45, 136
Wynn, John of Gwedir (1553–1627) 76, 77, 83, 86
Wynn, Owen 77, 78
Wynn, Sir Richard 77
Wynn, Sir Watkin Williams, Wynnstay 237
Wynne, C. W. W. 223
Wynne, Ellis (1671–1734), Y Lasynys 87
Wynnstay fire 1858 87, 135
Wynnstay library 136
Ximenes, Cardinal 43
Ychydig Fasgedeidiau o Swpiau Grawnwin..., Thomas Phillips (1818) 380
Ye Brython Cymreig 212
Ymadroddion Bucheddol ynghylch Marwolaeth, trans. by Thomas Williams 96
Yr Ymarfer o Dduwioldeb, trans. by Rowland Vaughan (1629) 96, 98, 100
'Ymddiddan Tudur a Gronw', Robert Holland (1595) 59, 61
Yr Ymofynydd 199, 202
Ynglynion, Gruffudd Robert 59, 62
Yny lhyvyr hwnn, John Prise 44, 47, 50, 55, 57, 60, 61
Ynys y Trysor, R. Lloyd Jones (1925) 383
Ynys-hir Institute 303
Ynys-y-bŵl Institute 303
Ynysfor, Merioneth, library 138
Young Wales 206
Yr Ysgol 254
Ysgol Dewi Sant, Llanelli 331, 345
Ysgol Glan Clwyd, St Asaph 332
Ysgol Gymraeg 345
Ysgol Maes Garmon, Mold 332
Ysgol Morgan Llwyd, Wrexham 332
Ysgol Rhydfelen 332
Ystorya de Carolo Magno, ed. Thomas Powel (1883) 226
Ystyriaethau Drexelius ar Dragwyddoldeb, trans. by Elis Lewis 96
Zimmer, Heinrich, Celtic scholar 395
Zwingli, Ulrich 43